S0-ADS-809

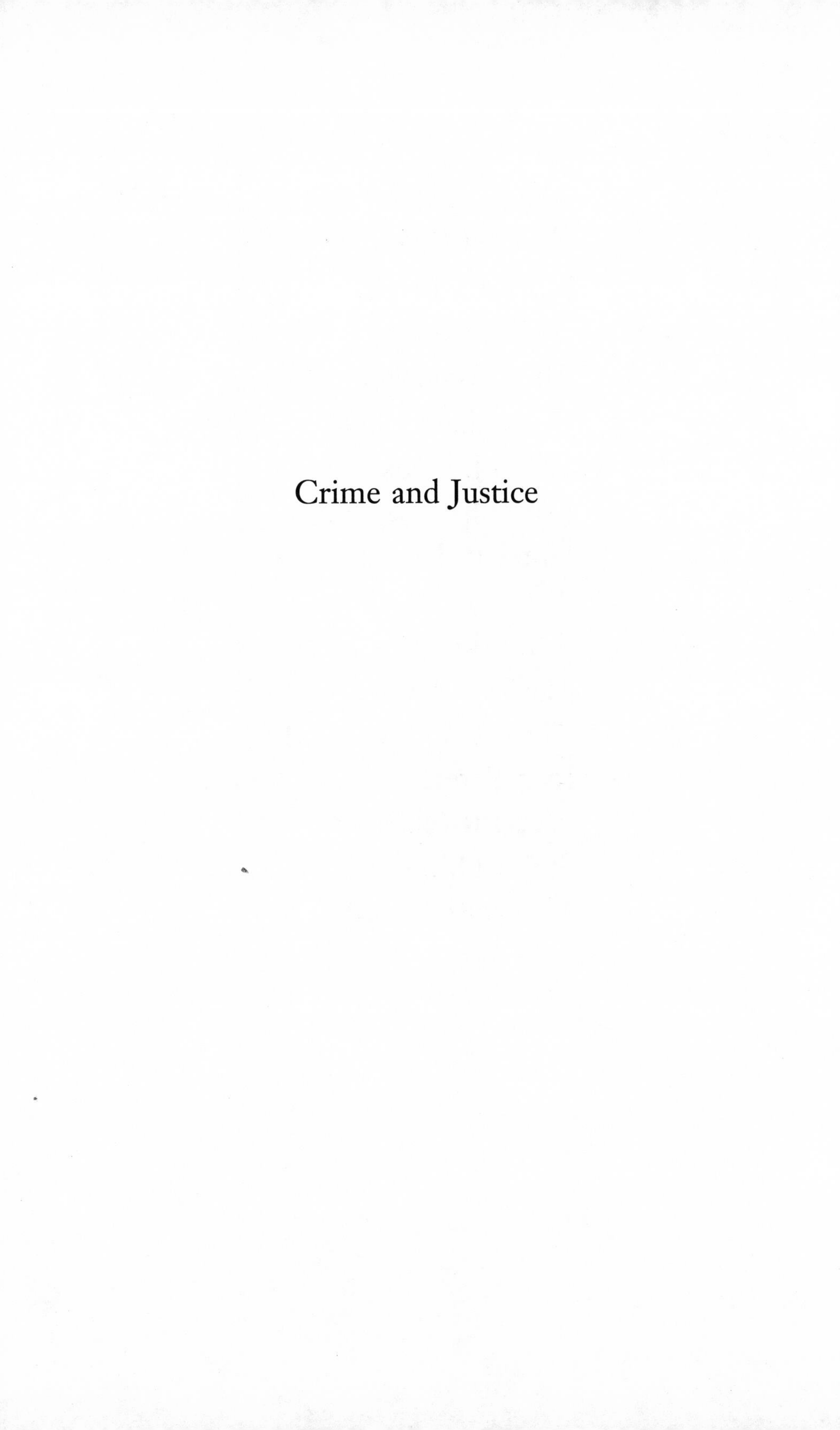

Crime and Justice

Crime and Justice

A Review of Research

Edited by Michael Tonry

VOLUME 22

The University of Chicago Press, Chicago and London

This volume was prepared under Grant Number 92-IJ-CX-K044 awarded to the Castine Research Corporation by the National Institute of Justice, U.S. Department of Justice, under the Omnibus Crime Control and Safe Streets Act of 1968 as amended. Points of view or opinions expressed in this volume are those of the editors or authors and do not necessarily represent the official position or policies of the U.S. Department of Justice.

The University of Chicago Press, Chicago 60637
The University of Chicago Press, Ltd., London

Printed in the United States of America

ISSN: 0192-3234

ISBN: 0-226-80820-3

LCN: 80-642217

The paper used in this publication meets the minimum requirements of American National Standard for Information Sciences—Permanence of Paper for Printed Library Materials, ANSI Z39.48-1984. ♾

Contents

Dedication

To
Paul Cascarano
and
Virginia Baldau,
The *Crime and Justice* series'
progenitor
and
protectors

Preface

Prefaces to *Crime and Justice* volumes usually comment on recent crime policy or research developments, offer thanks to the National Institute of Justice (NIJ), or occasionally other sponsors, for their support, and describe the volume's contents. This one is different because its primary aim is to disclose the longtime but little heralded roles of Paul Cascarano and Virginia Baldau in creating and sustaining the series. Paul retired from his position as NIJ's assistant director for The Office of Development and Dissemination at the end of 1995 and Virginia from the the same position at the end of 1996. Both are notorious for their enthusiasm, their energy, and their commitment to NIJ. Both are admired and loved by generations of NIJ staff members and by countless researchers and practitioners with whom they worked.

We worked with and for Paul and Virginia for twenty-five years and take second place to no one in our affection for them and our admiration for their work. In addition, however, to the relationships with them that we share with many others, we have had continuous contact with them in connection with this series of books. Our work on *Crime and Justice* has been among the joys of both our careers. Our names and those of various coeditors of thematic volumes appear on the books' spines, and support from a long line of NIJ directors and acting directors kept the series going. Few people realize, however, that the series' creation and survival owe as much to Paul and Virginia as to the editors and the NIJ directors.

Sometime in 1976, Paul proposed that NIJ launch an annual review to distill and disperse knowledge from the best of the accumulating body of criminal justice research. The aims were abstract—to advance understanding of the causes of crime and the operations of the justice system—and concrete—to make widely available the fruits of the public investment in NIJ and its work. Paul and Virginia developed the idea and persuaded Blair Ewing, then NIJ's director, of its merits. We were invited to serve as the series' editors, an editorial board was constituted, a planning meeting was held, and in 1977 the series was launched.

More than twenty years have passed, and this is the twenty-second volume—which may, in retrospect, give the series' longevity a tinge of inevitability. Without Paul and Virginia, however, it would not have survived. During the 1980s, NIJ's own survival was in doubt, and its budgets were cut deeply. Several of NIJ's directors were, at least initially, unsure whether they wanted to allocate scarce resources to the series' support, especially when *Crime and Justice* was conceived as and has always remained editorially independent of NIJ; the possibility of political embarrassment always existed. There were several multiyear hiatuses while new directors decided what they wanted to do. It is not that NIJ directors were hostile but that there are always more worthwhile projects under consideration than can be funded. The series would have died had Paul and Virginia not continued in house to urge that it be supported.

During Paul and Virginia's final years at NIJ, the series has been reenergized. A new editorial board was appointed in 1995. Several "annual" volumes are in development, as are "thematic" volumes on youth violence and prisons. We are most grateful to Jeremy Travis, NIJ's director, for giving the series his vote of confidence, and to Mary Graham, our monitor, for giving the series her unfailingly kind and efficient attention. Mary has worked with the series as loyally and almost as long as Paul and Virginia did. This volume, however, we dedicate to Paul Cascarano and Virginia Baldau. They have been good friends, and we shall miss them.

Michael Tonry
Norval Morris

James B. Jacobs and Kimberly A. Potter

Hate Crimes: A Critical Perspective

ABSTRACT

During the past decade, spurred by claims that the country is experiencing a hate crime epidemic, Congress and the majority of states have enacted laws increasing the punishment for crimes motivated by officially disfavored prejudices. Congress has also mandated a reporting system that aims to provide data on the incidence of hate crime. Some police departments have formed bias crime units. The upshot is the emergence of a new crime category and a new way to think about crime. The definition of hate crime, however, is fraught with problems, the federal data gathering effort has been completely unsuccessful, and enforcement of the hate crime laws has been minimal. Creation of a hate crime category fills political and symbolic functions but is unlikely to provide a useful indication of the state of various prejudices or to reduce crime generated by prejudice. Indeed, deconstructing criminal law according to the dictates of "identity politics" might exacerbate social divisions and conflict.

The terms "hate crime" or "bias crime" have established their places in the crime and justice lexicon and appear routinely in the media, scholarly journals, legislation, and judicial opinions. Many advocacy groups, politicians, scholars, and journalists claim that the country is experiencing a hate crime epidemic. A majority of states have enacted substantive hate crime laws or sentence enhancements for crimes motivated by officially disfavored prejudices. A few large police departments have formed bias crime units for investigative and data compilation purposes. In 1990, Congress directed the Department of Justice to provide a nationwide accounting of hate crimes.

James B. Jacobs is professor of law at New York University School of Law and director of its Center for Research in Crime and Justice. Kimberly A. Potter is a senior research fellow at the Center. The authors thank David Garland for his comments.

0192-3234/97/0022-0003$02.00

The goals of this essay are to assess the definition of "hate crime," to present what is known about its incidence, and to analyze how the criminal justice system is adapting to this new offense. Because hate crime is a legal construct, and one that varies from jurisdiction to jurisdiction, it is necessary to spend a good deal of time with definitions. Only after that groundwork is laid, does it make sense to ask empirical questions. Section I examines the concept of hate crime. Section II surveys different types of hate crime laws. Section III examines First Amendment objections to hate crime laws. Section IV presents what is known about the incidence of hate crime offending, emphasizing the difficulties involved in reliable data collection. Section V focuses on a number of different species of offending, offenders, and victims. Section VI examines the practical problems faced by police and prosecutors in investigating and prosecuting hate crime cases. Section VII speculates on the sociopolitical significance of this new category of crime. Section VIII offers a summary and conclusions.

I. What Is Hate Crime?

The term "hate crime" is a misnomer. The term actually refers to criminal behavior motivated, not by hate, but by *prejudice*, although there is undoubtedly some overlap. Generically, "hate crime" is meant to distinguish criminal conduct motivated by prejudices from criminal conduct motivated by lust, jealousy, greed, politics, and so forth. Unlike theft, burglary, or assault, hate crime emphasizes the offender's attitudes, values, and character. Lobbyists for special hate crime laws believe that prejudice is worse than all other criminal motivations (Crocker 1992/93, pp. 491–94).

Whereas the classical and the neoclassical models of criminal justice focus on the crime rather than the criminal, the movement to recognize and label hate crimes strives to make criminals' motivations salient and determinative. Hate crime laws condemn discrimination by criminals in the same way that Title VII of the Federal Equal Employment Opportunity Act condemns discrimination by public and private employers.

For some people, the importance of a hate crime offense category is that it condemns in the moralistic language of the criminal law values and attitudes already condemned via employment, voting rights, and constitutional laws. For others, hate crime laws are important because they punish prejudiced offenders more severely than other offenders who have less abhorrent motivations. Finally, in the context of the identity politics that characterize contemporary American society (Bernstein 1994; Gitlin 1995), minority groups perceive it to be in their interest to emphasize and even exaggerate their victimization (Epstein 1989, p. 20; Jacobs 1992/93, pp. 542–43; Sykes 1992; Sleeper 1993).

At some level of abstraction all crime, or at least a great deal of it, could be said to be motivated by manifest or latent prejudice—against victims because they are tall, short, rich, poor, good-looking, bad-looking, cocky, vulnerable, smart, dumb, members of one gang or another, and so forth. In contemporary American society, however, certain prejudices are officially disfavored—especially those based on race and religion. All hate crime laws include prejudice based on race, color, religion, and national origin (Wang 1995, app. B). However, only eighteen states and the District of Columbia include gender or sexual orientation bias as a hate crime trigger. Prejudice against Native Americans, immigrants, the physically and mentally handicapped, union members, nonunion members, right-to-lifers, and those advocating the right to choose are hardly ever included in hate crime laws (Wang 1995, app. B). Some states punish criminal conduct based on uncommon prejudices such as against service in the armed forces (Vermont Stat. Ann. tit. 13, § 1455) or "involvement in civil rights or human rights activities" (Mont. Code Ann. §§ 45-5-221). The District of Columbia has the most all encompassing hate crime statute; it covers religion, national origin, gender and sexual orientation, "personal appearance," "family responsibility," "marital status," and "matriculation." Clearly, the boundaries of hate crime legislation are fixed by political decision rather than by any logical or legal rationale.

A. The Nature of Prejudice

What does it mean to say that criminal conduct is *motivated* by *prejudice?* Prejudice is an extremely complicated concept which has generated substantial social psychological, philosophical, and other scholarly literatures (Allport 1954; Van Til 1959; Gioseffi 1993).[1] A simple definition of prejudice is "a negative attitude or opinion about a partic-

[1] "Prejudice is not a unitary phenomenon . . . it will take varying forms in different individuals. Socially and psychologically, attitudes differ depending upon whether they are the result of deep-seated personality characteristics, sometimes of the pathological nature, of a traumatic experience, or whether they simply represent conformity to an established norm" (*International Encyclopedia of the Social Sciences* 1968, s.v. "Prejudice," p. 444).

ular group or class of people" (*International Encyclopedia of the Social Sciences* 1968, pp. 439–40). Some commentators would include "irrational" as well. It can result from experience or from fantasies and myths (Ehrlich 1973, p. 15). It can be based partly on fact, or it can be completely fictional. Some people admit to their prejudices, and even espouse them as ideologies. Others deny their prejudices, sometimes because they do not recognize them and sometimes because they are ashamed of them. Prejudice can be "subconscious" as well as "conscious."[2] Not infrequently, whether a particular belief or attitude should be labeled as prejudice is a matter on which reasonable people can differ (e.g., Is Z prejudiced if he believes that blacks are more likely to have out-of-wedlock children than whites and Asians and therefore to raise their children less satisfactorily?).

There seems to be no agreement on whether "prejudice" includes a negative attitude toward a people which is based in fact (e.g., X does not like or wish to associate with Libyans, because of their government's sponsorship of international terrorism). Would it be a hate crime if X decided to rob only elderly Asian women because he believed they were likely to resist less than other elderly women? If the definition of prejudice is broad enough, practically everyone could be called prejudiced, or to put the matter differently, practically everyone could be said to hold some prejudiced beliefs and opinions. If so, then every crime in which the perpetrator and victim are members of different groups could potentially be labeled a hate crime.

B. Causality

For criminal conduct to constitute a hate crime it must be motivated by prejudice; that is, the criminal conduct must be causally related to the prejudice. How strong must that causal relationship be? Must the criminal conduct have been wholly, primarily, or slightly motivated by the disfavored prejudice? The answer determines how much hate crime there is. If a hate crime must have been *wholly* motivated by prejudice, there will be only a very small number of hate crimes—those

[2] "Americans share a common historical and cultural heritage in which racism played and still plays a dominant role. Because of this shared experience, we also inevitably share many attitudes and beliefs that attach significance to an individual's race and induce negative feelings and opinions about non-whites. To the extent that this cultural belief system has influenced all of us, we are all racists. At the same time, most of us are unaware of our racism. . . . In other words, a large part of the behavior that produces racial discrimination is influenced by unconscious racial motivation" (Lawrence 1987, p. 322).

perpetrated by individuals whose prejudice amounts to an ideology or perhaps an obsession. By contrast, if a hate crime must have been only *in part* motivated by prejudice, a significant percentage (possibly nearly all) of intergroup crimes is potentially classifiable as hate crime.

What percentage of robberies by black perpetrators against white victims might be classified as hate crime if the key question is whether the robbery or choice of robbery victim was *in part* attributable to anti-white prejudice? What percentage of violence by males against females ought to be investigated as possible hate crime if the critical question is whether the perpetrator was *in part* motivated by prejudice against women?

II. Types of Hate Crime Laws

As of spring 1996, the federal government, thirty-six states, and the District of Columbia have passed hate crime laws that fall into three categories: substantive crimes, sentence enhancements, and reporting statutes. (We exclude antimask and religious vandalism statutes.)

A. Substantive Hate Crimes

The majority of *substantive* hate crime statutes are based on the Anti-Defamation League's (ADL) Model Hate Crime Law, which establishes a separate "intimidation" offense:

> A person commits the crime of intimidation, if, by reason of actual or perceived race, color, religion, national origin or sexual orientation of another individual or group of individuals, he violates Section ______ of the Penal code (insert code provision for criminal trespass, criminal mischief, harassment, menacing, assault and/or other appropriate statutorily proscribed criminal conduct). Intimidation is a ______ misdemeanor/felony (the degree of the criminal liability should be at least one degree more serious than that imposed for commission of the offense). (Anti-Defamation League 1992, p. 4)

"Intimidation" is the only prosecutable hate crime under the ADL model law. Thus, in the "ADL states," hate crimes are low-level offenses, not the savage violence of organized terror groups but the shoves, pushes, and insults that result from frictions between ordinary, albeit prejudiced people, in a multiethnic, multiracial, multireligious, sexually diverse, and gendered society.

States' hate crime laws differ, not only with respect to which prejudices transform "ordinary" crime into hate crime, but according to which predicate crimes, when motivated by prejudice, qualify as hate crimes. In Pennsylvania and Vermont, for example, *any* offense is a hate crime if motivated by race, religion, national origin, and so forth (Pa. Cons. Stat. § 2710[a]; Vt. Stat. Ann. tit. 13, § 1455). Other states limit hate crimes to certain predicate offenses when motivated by a disfavored prejudice. For example, in New Jersey only simple assault and harassment, when motivated by prejudice, are classified as hate crimes (N.J. Stat. Ann. § 2C:12-1). Illinois designates nine predicate offenses: assault, battery, aggravated assault, misdemeanor theft, criminal trespass to residence, misdemeanor criminal damage to property, criminal trespass to vehicle, criminal trespass to real property, and mob action (Ill. Juris. Crim. Law & Proc. § 61:02).

Oregon provides that a person commits intimidation in the second degree, a misdemeanor, when the offender tampers or interferes with property or subjects an individual to alarm by threatening harm to the individual or his or her property or to a member of the individual's family by reason of race, color, religion, national origin, or sexual orientation. Where the offender causes physical injury to an individual or his or her property or places an individual in fear of imminent serious physical injury by reason of these characteristics, intimidation becomes a felony (Ore. Rev. Stat. Ann. § 166.155[1][c]).

Most hate crime laws (and sentencing enhancement provisions) do not employ the word "motivation." Instead, they speak of a person who commits an offense "because of" or "by reason of" one of the disfavored prejudices. The Washington, D.C., and Florida laws require that the offense "demonstrate prejudice" (D.C. Code Ann. § 22-4001; Fla. Stat. Ann. § 775.085[1]). Some jurisdictions make it an offense (or an aggravating sentencing factor) for a perpetrator to *select* a victim by reason of race, religion, and so forth (Ore. Rev. Stat. Ann. § 166.155 [1][c]; Cal. Penal Code §§ 422.6, 422.7), or to "intentionally select" the victim based on race (Wisc. Stat. Ann. § 939.645[1][b]). Read literally, this type of statute does not even require a showing of prejudice. Consider a defendant who selected his victim, say, an Asian man, because someone who had just seen the defendant's car broken into told him that the thief was an Asian man, so the defendant attacked the only Asian person in sight. The defendant, although not necessarily prejudiced against Asians, would be guilty of a hate crime because he selected the victim "by reason of" race. If the statute is not meant to cover this situation (which seems likely), then it is no different than a statute that explicitly requires a bias motivation. Professor Lu-in Wang, author of the only legal treatise on hate crime, explains that state courts have uniformly interpreted hate crime statutes to require proof of a prejudiced motive (Wang 1995, chap. 10, pp. 16, 34–35).

B. Hate Crime Sentence Enhancement

A second genre of hate crime law is comprised of statutes that provide sentence enhancements for prejudice-motivated crimes (Wang 1995, chap. 10, p. 22). These statutes either upgrade an existing offense (e.g., Fla. Stat. Ann. § 775.085[1]; Wang 1995, chap. 10, p. 11) or increase the maximum penalty for offenses motivated by prejudice (Wang 1995, chap. 10, p. 11; N.J. Stat. Ann. §§ 2C:43-7, 2C:44-3). The enhancement may apply to all or just to some predicate crimes. Under the Pennsylvania statute, for example, the bias offender is charged with a crime one degree higher than the predicate offense (Pa. Cons. Stat. § 2710[a]). Vermont's statute *doubles* the maximum prison term for bias-motivated crimes; if the maximum term is five years or more, the defendant's bias motivation becomes a factor for consideration by the judge at sentencing (Vt. Stat. Ann. tit. 13, § 1455). In Minnesota, the only bias-motivated crimes subject to enhanced punishment are harassment and stalking (Minn. Stat. Ann. § 609.749). In contrast, Nevada makes twenty crimes subject to enhanced sentences (Nev. Rev. Stat. Ann § 207.185). Florida subjects *any bias-motivated felony or misdemeanor* to enhanced punishment (Fla. Stat. Ann. 775.085[1]).

State laws vary with respect to the magnitude of the enhancement for bias motivation. The aggravated battery statute before the Supreme Court in *Wisconsin v. Mitchell*, 113 S. Ct. 2194 (1993), provided for a two-year maximum prison term, but if the perpetrator was motivated by one of the enumerated prejudices, the maximum punishment soared to seven years.

The federal Violent Crime Control and Law Enforcement Act of 1994 (Pub. L. No. 102-322) mandated a revision of the U.S. sentencing guidelines to provide an enhancement for hate crimes of three offense levels above the base level for the underlying offense. The guideline provides: "If the finder of fact at trial or, in the case of a guilty plea, . . . the court at sentencing determines beyond a reasonable doubt that the defendant intentionally selected any victim or any property as the object of the offense because of the actual or perceived race, color, religion, national origin, ethnicity, gender [not applicable for sex crimes], disability, or sexual orientation of any person, *an additional 3-level enhancement from [the base level offense] will apply*" (60 Fed. Reg., May 10, 1995, p. 25,082; emphasis added). In the case of aggravated assault, for example, the ordinary base level offense of 15 is elevated to 18 and the sentencing range is consequently elevated from eighteen–twenty-four months to twenty-seven–thirty-three months imprisonment.

C. *Hate Crime Reporting Statutes*

Many states, as well as the federal government, have enacted hate crime data collection and reporting statutes to generate statistics on the incidence of hate crime (Wang 1995, app. B). Ultimately, these reporting statutes may have more importance than the substantive laws and sentence enhancement statutes. The old sociological adage "what's counted, counts" suggests that the hate crime reporting statutes will reshape the way that Americans think about crime.

The federal Hate Crime Statistics Act of 1990 (HCSA), 28 U.S.C. § 534 (Supp. IV 1992), mandates the collection of nationwide hate crime data in order to help communities, legislatures, and law enforcement personnel appropriately respond to the problem by gathering information on the frequency, location, extent, and patterns of hate crime; increase law enforcement's awareness of and sensitivity to hate crimes in order to improve its response; raise public awareness of the existence of hate crimes; and send a message that the federal government is concerned about hate crime (U.S. Senate 1989, p. 3).

The Act directs the U.S. Department of Justice to collect and report data on hate crimes involving the predicate offenses of murder, nonnegligent manslaughter, forcible rape,[3] aggravated assault, simple assault, intimidation, arson, and destruction, damage, or vandalism of property (28 U.S.C. § 534 [Supp. IV 1992]). The attorney general, given discretion by the Act to add to or delete from the list of predicate crimes, added robbery, burglary, and motor vehicle theft (Federal Bureau of Investigation 1990, p. 4).

The HCSA defines a hate crime as "a criminal offense committed against a person or property, which is motivated, in whole or in part, by the offender's bias against a race, religion, ethnic/national origin group, or sexual orientation group." The FBI guidelines implementing

[3] The hate crime sentencing guideline is explicitly inapplicable to sex crimes.

the act define "bias" as "a *preformed negative opinion or attitude toward a group of persons based on their race, religion, ethnicity/national origin, or sexual orientation*" (emphasis added). According to this broad definition, most interracial and other intergroup crimes could be classified as (or certainly be investigated as possible) hate crimes.

The guidelines, although quite thorough, leave much ambiguity. For example, what is meant by "ethnic group or national origin"? Are "Hispanics" or "Latinos" counted as one group for purposes of the HCSA? Would an assault by a Cuban against a Colombian count as a hate crime if the assailant was motivated by a belief that Colombians are importing drugs into the community? Are "Asians" (e.g., Syrians, Indians, Vietnamese, Filipinos, Chinese, and Japanese) an ethnic group? Could conflicts between Chinese-Americans and Vietnamese-Americans or between Palestinians and Kuwaitis qualify as hate crimes?

III. Hate Speech, Hate Crime, and the First Amendment

Defining hate crimes and punishing hate criminals is akin to, but distinct from, the move to criminalize hate speech (Walker 1994; Schweitzer 1995). The anti–hate speech movement asserts that certain kinds of racist, sexist, anti-Semitic, misogynistic, and homophobic expressions and epithets impose emotional damage on persons to whom they are addressed and to other members of the groups to which these persons belong. Therefore, proponents of hate speech restrictions urge that such expressions and epithets be prohibited and that those who utter them be punished (Matsuda 1989; Lawrence 1990). However, hate speech laws have not fared well in the courts, which have declared them unconstitutional on First Amendment grounds (*Doe v. University of Michigan*, 721 F. Supp. 852 [1989] [declaring unconstitutional campus hate speech code]; *UWM Post v. Board of Regents of the University of Wisconsin*, 774 F. Supp. 1163 [1991] [declaring unconstitutional campus hate speech code]).

There is a lively debate among constitutional lawyers and civil libertarians over whether *hate crime* laws, like hate speech laws, should flunk a First Amendment test (Fleischauer 1990; Gellman 1991, 1992/93; Redish 1992; Gaumer 1994). Those who believe hate crime laws to be constitutional emphasize the familiar speech/conduct distinction in First Amendment law; people are entitled to speak their minds but not to impose physical harm on others in acting out their opinions (Crocker 1992/93, pp. 495–500). They argue that while an individual has a right to his bigoted thoughts, he has no right to act on them. According to this view, hate crime laws punish antisocial conduct just as Title VII provides a remedy against employment discrimination.

Those who believe hate crime laws to be unconstitutional argue that generic criminal law already punishes injurious conduct and that recriminalization or sentence enhancement for the same offense when it is motivated by prejudice amounts to extra punishment for values, thoughts, and opinions which the government deems abhorrent (Freeman 1992/93; Gellman 1992/93; Goldberger 1992/93). These critics ask: if the purpose of hate crimes is to punish more severely offenders who are motivated by disfavored prejudices, is that not equivalent to punishment for "improper thinking?" For example, suppose there are two defendants: A is a white supremacist who only robs black men; B is a communist who only robs rich people. Under the typical hate crime statute, B would be convicted of robbery, while A would be convicted of a hate crime or be subject to a sentence enhancement.

A few scholars have sought to distinguish between different formulations of hate crime offenses (Crocker 1992/93, pp. 495–500; Freeman 1992/93, pp. 582–83). They argue that a hate crime statute that does not use the word "motivation," but that prohibits *selection* of a victim *because of* or *by reason of* the victim's race, religion, or sexual orientation and so forth, has nothing to do with punishing ideas or speech, but punishes conduct. While there may be something to this subtle analytical distinction, most commentators and courts have treated such statutes as requiring proof of prejudiced motivation.

The U.S. Supreme Court so far has struck down one hate crime statute and approved one. In *R.A.V. v. City of St. Paul,* 112 S. Ct. 2538 (1992), the Supreme Court was faced with a constitutional challenge to a local ordinance which provided that "whoever places on public or private property a symbol, object, appellation, characterization or graffiti, including, but not limited to, a burning cross or Nazi swastika, which one knows or has reasonable grounds to know arouses anger, alarm or resentment in others on the basis of race, color, creed, religion or gender commits disorderly conduct and shall be guilty of a misdemeanor" (112 S. Ct. at 2541). R.A.V., a white juvenile, was convicted under the ordinance for burning a cross on a black family's lawn. The justices unanimously agreed that the ordinance violated the First Amendment, but there were at least two different rationales.[4] Justice

[4] The majority opinion was joined by Justices Scalia, Kennedy, Souter, Thomas, and Chief Justice Rehnquist. Justices Blackmun and Stevens filed concurring opinions, in

Scalia's majority opinion pointed out that while the government could criminalize constitutionally unprotected "fighting words" (the ordinance applied only to fighting words), it could not criminalize only those fighting words of which the government disapproved. Thus, "the reason why fighting words are categorically excluded from the protection of the First Amendment is not that their content communicates any particular idea, but that their content embodies a particularly intolerable . . . mode of expressing whatever idea the speaker wishes to convey. St. Paul has not singled out an especially offensive mode of expression. . . . Rather, it has proscribed fighting words of whatever manner that communicate messages of racial, gender or religious intolerance. Selectivity of this sort creates the possibility that the city is seeking to handicap the expression of particular ideas" (112 S. Ct. at 2549).

Justice White's concurrence stated that the ordinance could have been struck down simply by holding "that the St. Paul ordinance is fatally overbroad because it criminalizes not only unprotected expression but expression protected by the First Amendment" (i.e., both fighting and nonfighting words [Justice White concurring at 2550]). Therefore, according to Justice White, the majority need not have addressed whether the ordinance affected content-based discrimination.

In another concurring opinion, Justice Stevens stated that the ordinance did not, as the majority asserted, regulate speech based on the subject matter or viewpoint but distinguished different verbal conduct "on the basis of the *harm* the speech causes" (Justice Stevens concurring at 2570; emphasis in original). According to Justice Stevens, the ordinance did not prevent just one side from "hurling fighting words at the other on the basis of conflicting ideas, but it does bar *both* sides from hurling such words on the basis of the target's 'race, color, creed, religion or gender' " (at 2571 [emphasis in original]). Nevertheless, he concurred on the ground that the ordinance was unconstitutionally overbroad; in other words, the ordinance prohibits both constitutionally unprotected *and* protected speech.

The second hate crime statute to reach the Supreme Court was the sentence enhancement statute challenged in *Wisconsin v. Mitchell*, 113 S. Ct. 2194 (1993). It provided for an enhanced sentence when a person "intentionally selects the person against whom the crime . . . is

which Justices O'Connor and White joined. For a journalist's account of the facts surrounding the case, see Cleary (1994).

committed or selects the property which is damaged or otherwise affected . . . because of race, religion, color, disability, sexual orientation, national origin or ancestry of that person or the owner or occupant of that property" (113 S. Ct. at 2197 n.1). Mitchell, a black juvenile, was convicted of aggravated battery and subject to a sentence enhancement for selection of the white victim based on race. Prior to the attack, Mitchell and other black youths were discussing a scene from the movie "Mississippi Burning" which depicted a white man beating a black boy. Mitchell asked the group, "Do you all feel hyped up to move on some white people?" When the victim, a white juvenile, walked by, Mitchell said, "You all want to fuck somebody up? There goes a white boy; go get him." Mitchell and the group beat the boy unconscious (at 2196–97).

The Wisconsin Supreme Court, following the reasoning set forth in *R.A.V.*, struck down the statute for creating a "thought crime" which assigned more severe punishment to offenses motivated by disfavored viewpoints. In a unanimous decision, the U.S. Supreme Court, in an opinion written by Chief Justice Rehnquist, reversed and upheld the statute. The chief justice denied that the First Amendment was implicated by the Wisconsin statute. He distinguished Wisconsin's sentence enhancement law from the *R.A.V.* ordinance on the ground that the St. Paul ordinance was directed at politically incorrect viewpoints, whereas the Wisconsin statute was directed at unprotected criminal conduct that may properly be singled out by the legislature for increased punishment due to the greater harm such crimes are perceived to inflict on victims and society. Rehnquist explained that motive has traditionally been used by sentencing judges in determining sentences. " 'Motives are most relevant when the trial judge sets the defendant's sentence, and it is not uncommon for a defendant to receive a minimum sentence because he was acting with good motives, or a rather higher sentence because of his bad motives' " (Mitchell, at 2199 [quoting LaFave and Scott 1986]). (The Supreme Court did not adopt the subtle argument of some legal scholars that hate crime statutes worded in terms of target *selection* are different from *motivation* statutes.)

The *Mitchell* decision lifted the constitutional cloud from hate crime sentence enhancement statutes. Nevertheless, academic debate among constitutional scholars and civil libertarians continues. The critics insist that there is only a semantic difference between what is constitutionally impermissible under *R.A.V.* and what is constitutionally permissible under *Mitchell. R.A.V.*'s cross-burning ordinance could easily be redrafted as a vandalism statute with a penalty enhancement for offenders who select their targets because of race, religion, or sexual orientation.

IV. The Incidence of Hate Crime

There is a consensus among journalists, politicians, and academics that the United States is experiencing an unprecedented "hate crime epidemic" (see Levin and McDevitt 1993; but see Jacobs and Henry 1996). Incredibly, there are no reliable empirical data to support this conclusion. Indeed, until 1990, the only available data were those provided by advocacy groups like the Anti-Defamation League, the Southern Poverty Law Center, and the Gay and Lesbian Anti-Violence Project, all of which lobby for more government attention to hate crimes. In 1990, at the behest of these and other advocacy groups, Congress passed the Hate Crime Statistics Act (Jacobs and Eisler 1993). Because of the conceptual and definitional problems discussed earlier, and implementation problems, the data collected pursuant to HCSA are inadequate and disappointing.

A. The Hate Crime Epidemic Hypothesis

The "epidemic hypothesis" asserts that *all forms* of prejudice-motivated crime are rising alarmingly. Dozens of newspaper and magazine articles in the last few years have referred to "a hate crime epidemic" (Jacobs and Henry 1996). Many of the academics who have written on the subject begin with the assumption that hate crimes are on the rise and characterize the problem as a crisis or epidemic (*Harvard Law Review* 1988, 1993; Crocker 1992/93; *Santa Clara Law Review* 1994; Lawrence 1994; Smith 1994). Fordham Law School Professor Abraham Abramovsky has even asserted that "no one seriously questions the severity of the [hate crime] problem" (Abramovsky 1992).

We believe that there is reason to be skeptical about this epidemic thesis. First, criminologists are (or should be) professionally inured to claims about crime waves (Chaiken and Chaiken 1983, p. 11; Wright 1985). Second, the claim that the incidence of crime between members of different groups stands at an all-time high completely ignores history. A near-genocide against Native Americans, massive violence against blacks, attacks on ethnic and religious groups, and unceasing violence against women and homosexuals are themes that run throughout American history; they are certainly not new. Indeed, it is almost certainly true that there is far less prejudice and intergroup violence now than at most previous points in our history. For example, does anyone really believe that black Americans are now in as much danger from attack by white racists as they were during the Jim Crow era when hundreds of lynchings took place (Ames 1942; Ginzburg 1962)? Is it plausible that there is more virulent anti-Semitism (not to mention anti-Catholicism) now than in the heyday of Father Coughlin (Desmond 1912)? And could it likely be shown that there is more xenophobic violence against immigrants today than during the Sacco and Vanzetti era (Miller 1969; Alfredo 1987)? The rediscovery of hate crime is probably best explained not by an epidemic of prejudice-motivated violence but by our society's far greater sensitivity to prejudice.

B. The Advocacy Groups' Hate Crime Data Collection

Advocacy groups that collect and report hate crime statistics use those statistics to further their claims that the racial/religious/sexual orientation group they represent is experiencing unprecedented victimization at the hands of prejudiced criminals. Such claims are used to raise funds and to obtain government support on a whole range of issues.

No advocacy group has made as substantial a commitment to data gathering or has shown as much sophistication as the Anti-Defamation League, nor has any other group been gathering and reporting data for nearly as long. Since 1979, the ADL has published an "annual audit" of "overt acts or *expressions*" of anti-Semitic hostility, which includes criminal offenses, verbal harassment, and distribution of anti-Semitic literature. Many such incidents would not qualify as hate *crimes* under any federal or state statute. The inclusion of noncriminal acts, such as the distribution of anti-Semitic literature, and of acts for which the anti-Semitic motivation is questionable, are primary problems with the ADL's statistics from the standpoint of counting hate crimes.

The ADL's methods of data collection also leave much to be desired. The ADL's audit is based on data provided by its twenty-eight regional offices. The regional offices, in turn, rely on information from individuals and community groups who contact the ADL, newspaper reports, and local law enforcement agencies (Jacobs and Henry 1996). There are a number of obvious problems with such data collection. The sensitivity to perceived anti-Semitic acts or expressions necessarily varies from state to state, and from city to city, as does the willingness of individuals to come forward and report incidents. Further, reliance on newspaper reports also poses problems since newspaper coverage of anti-Semitic incidents varies depending on the size of the newspaper, the readership's concern with anti-Semitism (New Yorkers are more likely to be concerned with anti-Semitism than readers in Fargo, North Dakota), and competition from other high profile news events. Despite such shortcomings, these statistics, as well as others, are constantly used to support the claim that an epidemic of religious, racial, or other bias-motivated violence is plaguing the nation.

C. *The Federal Data Gathering Effort*

The 1990 federal Hate Crime Statistics Act mandated that the U.S. Department of Justice collect national hate crime data and publish an annual statistical report. The Act defines hate crime as any one of eight (later increased to eleven) predicate offenses (murder, nonnegligent manslaughter, forcible rape, aggravated assault, simple assault, intimidation, arson, destruction, damage or vandalism of property, robbery, burglary, and motor vehicle theft) "where there is *manifest evidence* of *prejudice* based on race, religion, sexual orientation, or ethnicity." No other predicate offense, even if motivated by one of the officially disfavored prejudices, will be counted as a hate crime. Prejudice is "manifest," according to the FBI guidelines, if "sufficient objective facts [are] present to lead a reasonable and prudent person to conclude that the offender's actions were motivated, in whole or in part, by bias" (Federal Bureau of Investigation 1990, p. 2). Prejudice which is palpable, even virulent, but not *manifest* on the face of the crime does not transform an ordinary crime into a hate crime.

This data collection system has been fleshed out by FBI *Hate Crime Data Collection Guidelines* and the *Training Guide for Hate Crime Data Collection*, prepared to aid state and local police in implementing the Act. In deciding whether a particular crime should be labeled a hate crime, the Training Guide instructs local police to consider the questions printed below. However, the exercise bristles with ambiguity and subjectivity. The Training Guide does not specify how much weight should be given to each question or how many questions need to be answered affirmatively to qualify criminal conduct as a "hate crime." Moreover, questions 10 and 15 seem to allow for a hate crime label even if the offender's prejudice is not "manifest" under the ordinary definition of the word. We have inserted in brackets possible difficulties in interpreting and answering these questions.

1. Is the victim a member of a target racial, religious, ethnic/national origin, or sexual orientation group? [*Are all ethnic groups "target"*

groups? Do "whites" count as a "target racial group"? Do all religious groups?]

2. Were the offender and victim of different racial, religious, ethnic/national origin, or sexual orientation groups? For example, the victim was black and the offenders were white. [*What if one of the offenders is from the same group as the victim?*]

3. Would the incident have taken place if the victim and offender were of the same race, religion, ethnic group, or sexual orientation?

4. Were biased oral comments, written statements, or gestures made by the offender which indicate his/her bias? For example, the offender shouted a racial epithet at the victim. [*What if the epithet was in response to bias statements or gestures by the victim?*]

5. Were bias-related drawings, markings, symbols, or graffiti left at the crime scene? For example, a swastika painted on the door of a synagogue.

6. Were certain items, objects, or things which indicate bias used (e.g., the offenders wore white sheets with hoods covering their faces) or left behind by the offender(s) (e.g., a burning cross was left in front of the victim's residence)?

7. Is the victim a member of a racial, religious, ethnic/national origin, or sexual orientation group which is overwhelmingly outnumbered by members of another group in the neighborhood where the victim lives and the incident took place? This factor loses significance with the passage of time, that is, it is most significant when the victim first moved into a neighborhood and becomes less significant as time passes without incident.

8. Was the victim visiting a neighborhood where previous hate crimes had been committed against members of his/her racial, religious, ethnic/national origin, or sexual orientation group and where tensions remain high against his/her group? [*This seems to call for historical data and sociological assessments that would be very difficult to make reliably.*]

9. Have several incidents occurred in the same locality at or about the same time, and are the victims all of the same racial, religious, ethnic/national origin, or sexual orientation group?

10. Does a substantial portion of the community where the crime occurred perceive that the incident was motivated by bias? [*How could the police make such a determination?*]

11. Was the victim engaged in activities promoting his/her racial,

religious, ethnic/national origin, or sexual orientation group? For example, the victim is a member of the NAACP, participates in gay rights demonstrations, etc.

12. Did the incident coincide with a holiday relating to, or a date of particular significance to a, racial, religious, or ethnic/national origin group (e.g., Martin Luther King Day, Rosh Hashanah, etc.)?

13. Was the offender previously involved in a similar hate crime or is he/she a member of a hate group? [*Searching out the defendant's organizational memberships and magazine subscriptions will set off First Amendment alarms.*]

14. Were there indications that a hate group was involved? For example, a hate group claimed responsibility for the crime or was active in the neighborhood.

15. Does a historically established animosity exist between the victim's group and the offender's group? [*How shall we answer such questions as whether there is historic animosity between blacks and whites, blacks and Latinos, whites and Latinos, Jews and gentiles, and so forth? Does historical animosity exist between all racial, ethnic, and religious groups or is it more complicated than that?*]

16. Is this incident similar to other known and documented cases of bias, particularly in this area? Does it fit a similar modus operandi to these other incidents?

17. Has this victim been previously involved in similar situations?

18. Are there other explanations for the incident, such as a childish prank, unrelated vandalism, etc? [*Won't many young hate crime offenders wish to characterize their conduct as pranks?*]

19. Did the offender have some understanding of the impact that his/her actions would have on the victim? [*Won't this be difficult to determine? What if the offender is not apprehended or does not make a statement?*] (Federal Bureau of Investigation 1991).

In December 1992, prior to the release of its first official hate crimes report, the FBI issued a preliminary report, entitled *Hate Crime Statistics, 1990: A Resource Book* (Federal Bureau of Investigation 1992*a*), compiling data based on statistics from states that had their own individual reporting systems. The most salient feature of the *Resource Book* was its complete inadequacy. Only eleven states submitted any data. The FBI commented: "Each state responded to its own needs and statutory requirements; therefore, a data collection instrument in one state is not necessarily comparable to that of another state. The groups covered by hate crime statutes often differed. In 1990, crimes motivated by hatred for an individual's sexual orientation were not covered by statute in Florida, Maryland, Pennsylvania, Rhode Island, and Virginia but were covered in Connecticut, Massachusetts, Minnesota, New Jersey, New York, and Oregon. Moreover, Oregon's hate crime statute covered crimes committed against individuals based on marital status, political affiliation, and membership in a labor union. . . . Varied reporting procedures also restrict data comparability" (Federal Bureau of Investigation 1992*b*, p. 3).

In January 1993, the FBI released its first official report, containing nationwide hate crime statistics for 1991 (Federal Bureau of Investigation 1993). It contained data from only thirty-two states; only 2,771 law enforcement agencies (of the 12,805 agencies nationwide reporting to the FBI) participated in the data collection effort, and of these, 73 percent reported no hate crime incidents. Once again, the FBI accompanied the report with a disclaimer.[5] A number of states reported fewer hate crimes than for the previous year.[6]

Even though the report found only 4,558 hate crimes nationwide (compared with over 14 million reported crimes), many newspapers cited it as confirming the existence of a hate crime epidemic. A *Houston Chronicle* editorial stated: "The specter of hate is unfortunately alive and well in the United States. . . . The national report reveals a grim picture" (*Houston Chronicle* 1993).

The FBI's second report, covering 1992 hate crimes, contained information from forty-one states and the District of Columbia and found 6,623 hate crimes (Federal Bureau of Investigation 1994). The statistics for 1993 were based on forty-six reporting states and the District of Columbia and reported 7,587 hate crimes (Federal Bureau of Investigation 1995). One newspaper opined that the 1990s may be remembered as "the decade of hate crime" and solemnly reported that "since the federal government began counting hate crimes in January 1991, hate crime has increased" (Rovella 1994, p. A1). The so-called increase could more accurately be attributed to an increase in the number of states submitting data rather than an increased *rate* of hate crimes. Indeed, some states that contributed data in 1990 and 1991 reported decreases for 1993.

[5] FBI Director William Sessions stated, "While these initial data are limited, they give us our first assessment of the nature of crimes motivated by bias in our society" (Federal Bureau of Investigation 1992*b*, p. 1).

[6] For example, in 1990, New York reported 1,130 hate crimes, while in 1991 it reported 943 hate crimes. Maryland reported 792 hate crimes for 1990 and 431 for 1991.

V. Portrait of Hate Crimes, Hate Criminals, and Hate Crime Victims

The macropicture of the incidence of hate crime in the United States is very sketchy. To say the least, even minimally reliable statistics on hate crimes are lacking. Moreover, the problem is not likely to improve because of the ambiguities in defining and the subjectivity in labeling hate crime.

A. The Typical Hate Crime[7]

During the lobbying that led to passage of the federal Hate Crime Statistics Act, not surprisingly, advocacy groups cited examples of hard-core ideologically based violence by individuals and groups (e.g., the 1982 beating death of Vincent Chin, an Asian American, by two unemployed auto workers in Detroit, Michigan, who blamed the Japanese for their job losses). In contrast, the data gathering effort has mostly picked up vandalism and low-level offenses by juveniles and "Archie Bunkers," not neo-Nazi violence by "Tom Metzgers."

The vast majority of reported hate crimes are not committed by organized hate groups and their members, but by teenagers, primarily white males, acting alone or in a group (Goleman 1990, p. C1; McKinley 1990, p. A1; Herek and Berrill 1992, pp. 29–30; Levin and McDevitt 1993, pp. 244–46; New York Police Department 1995). The New York Police Department (NYPD) Bias Unit found that 63.84 percent of hate crime offenders were under the age of nineteen. The San Francisco Community United Against Violence, a gay victim assistance organization, says that the typical "gay basher" is a white male under the age of twenty-one (although there are more black and Latino perpetrators than whites).[8] The FBI statistics do not provide any sociodemographic data on hate crime offenders. The federal data do indicate that the typical hate crime consists of low-level criminal conduct. For 1993, the FBI reported that the most common hate crimes were intimidation

[7] Jack Levin and Jack McDevitt (1993) identify and classify three types of hate crimes: thrill-seeking hate crimes, in which the individual acts with a group to achieve acceptance; reactive hate crimes, in which the individual acts to protect himself from perceived threats from outsiders; and mission hate crimes, in which an individual or group targets members of a particular group which is seen as the cause of personal or societal problems. However, these authors do not have data on the relative frequencies of these three types.

[8] Fifty-four percent of offenders were identified as twenty-one or under. Ninety-two percent of offenders were male. The racial break-down of offenders was: 40 percent white, 30 percent black, and 23 percent Latino (Herek and Berrill 1992, pp. 29–30).

(2,239 incidents),[9] destruction/damage/vandalism to property (1,949 incidents), and simple assault (1,249 incidents). There were only fifteen bias-motivated murders and thirteen bias-motivated rapes (Federal Bureau of Investigation 1995). The FBI's data provide information on the rate of apprehension and on the offenders' and victims' race and gender but not on religion, sexual orientation, or other sociodemographic characteristics. A large percentage of hate crime offenders go unapprehended—at least 42 percent. Of apprehended offenders, 51 percent were white and 35 percent were black. According to the FBI's 1993 statistics, vandalism, one of the most common hate crimes, has the lowest rate of apprehension—of 2,294 cases, 1,830 went unsolved. This low rate of apprehension, typical for vandalism offenses, is a significant obstacle to research.

Typical hate crimes in New York City show a similar pattern. In 1990, the New York City Police Department's Bias Unit recorded 530 hate crimes, including 87 incidents of vandalism/property damage, 171 incidents of aggravated harassment, and 172 bias-motivated assaults (New York Police Department 1991).

Between 1983 and 1987, the Boston Police Department classified 534 incidents as bias motivated. In marked contrast to the New York City and federal statistics, the most common hate crime in Boston was assault and battery with a dangerous weapon—136 incidents. Vandalism and simple assault were the second and third most common bias-motivated offenses, 98 and 77 incidents, respectively. Unfortunately, there is no explanation why the most common hate crime in Boston is more serious than the most common hate crime in New York City and nationwide, but undoubtedly the answer is rooted in the different coding practices of the Boston and New York police departments. The Boston police may ignore or undercount the less serious crimes.

B. Hate Crime Offenders

There are substantial scholarly literatures on prejudice in general and on specific prejudices, like homophobia, anti-Semitism, misogyny, and racism. Some of this literature focuses on the psychology or social psychology of various prejudices and some (a smaller genre) on the sociological character of groups, both loosely and more tightly orga-

[9] Intimidation is defined as "to unlawfully place another person in reasonable fear of bodily harm through the use of threatening words and/or other conduct, but without displaying a weapon or subjecting the victim to actual physical attack" (Federal Bureau of Investigation 1991).

nized, for whom prejudice is a key, or even *the* key, organizing principle. Much of this literature has been produced by advocacy groups, like the ADL (Anti-Defamation League 1987, 1988, 1995), but in recent years the U.S. government has also published a number of studies on hard-core hate groups (Schweitzer 1986; National Academy of Sciences 1996). Summarizing all this writing on the nature of general and specific prejudice and on the character of hard-core hate groups is far beyond the scope of this essay. However, in this section we attempt to draw some connections between the new hate crime literature and these other bodies of research.

For almost every prejudice condemned by hate crime laws, there is a separate, sometimes vast, academic and popular literature. We need to emphasize that only a small minority of offenders are hard-core ideologically committed haters. The typical hate crime offender is an individual, usually a juvenile, who, like the offenders in *Wisconsin v. Mitchell,* holds vague underlying prejudices which on occasion spill over into criminal conduct.

Moreover, not all bigoted ideologues act out their beliefs through crimes. Many groups that are labeled hate groups claim to be affirmative identity movements, not "anti" other groups. For example, some separatist militia groups might characterize themselves as survivalist and perhaps pro-Christian, but not antiblack. The Jewish Defense League might characterize itself as pro-Jewish, not anti-Arab. To complicate matters still further, some hard-core hate groups, like neo-Nazis, are virulently prejudiced against a number of groups: Jews, blacks, homosexuals, immigrants (Coates 1987; Hamm 1993; Kelly 1993).

1. *Antiblack Offending.* There is an enormous literature on racism against blacks (Ames 1942; Ginzburg 1962; Grimshaw 1970; Burk 1972, p. 309; Boskin 1976; O'Brien 1989; Toy 1989; Newton and Newton 1991). Most of it focuses on "white" racism against blacks, but there is also a small amount of literature on Asian conflict with blacks (Rieder 1990, p. 16; Gooding-Williams 1993; Madhubuti 1993; Alan-Williams 1994). Some literature focuses on prejudice, some on discrimination, and some on violence, including lynchings (Shay 1938; Ferrell 1986; Howard 1995).

At certain times and places in American history and society, groups like the Ku Klux Klan have perpetrated systematic and organized violence and terror against blacks. In the post-Civil War era until well into the twentieth century, lynchings reached a pinnacle (Ferrell 1986, p. 92). From 1882 to 1968, 4,743 people were lynched; the vast majority were black. During the peak lynching years, 1889-1918, the five most active lynching states were Georgia (360), Mississippi (350), Louisiana (264), Texas (263), and Alabama (244) (Ferrell 1986, p. 91; Howard 1995, p. 18). In 1892, 200 lynchings occurred in a single year. These numbers include only the recorded lynchings; historians can only speculate on the number of blacks whose deaths at the hands of lynch mobs went unreported (Ferrell 1986, p. 91). Even today certain skinhead groups on occasion engage in such conduct. The Southern Poverty Law Center's Klanwatch Project releases periodic reports on extremist racist groups and on vicious individual hate crimes (Klanwatch 1987, 1989, 1991). They do not necessarily engage in organized violence but their rhetoric, written and oral, is frightening. More common than the violence of ideologically driven racists is unorganized bullying and situational violence. And a good deal of reported antiblack hate crime could be attributed to repressed prejudice that erupts in the course of encounters based on nonracial issues. For example, the New York City Bias Investigation Unit investigated as a bias crime a dispute over a parking space between a black female and a white male. Initially, they argued over who was entitled to the parking space. As the argument became more heated, the white male told the black woman, "You blacks think you own it all—why don't you move—you don't belong here" (New York Police Department 1991, p. 18).

2. *Anti-Asian Offending.* Crime based on prejudice against Asians has generated far less research and writing than crime against blacks. Nevertheless, prejudice and violence against Chinese immigrants early in the century and against Japanese Americans during World War II have been documented (Miller 1969; Saxton 1971; Daniels 1978; Takaki 1989; McWilliams 1944).

In the Congressional hearings leading to passage of the 1990 HCSA, Asian-American advocacy groups appeared before Congress and testified to "the rising tide of violence" against Asian Americans. In a letter to the Senate, the National Democratic Council of Asian and Pacific Americans stated, "Our members in California, Texas, Massachusetts and New York are aware of an increase in violent crimes against Asian and Pacific Americans, most frequently new arrivals from southeast Asia and Korea, often elderly" (letter to Senator Paul Simon from Susan Lee, U.S. Senate 1988).

Anecdotal evidence documents outrageously humiliating and violent anti-Asian attacks. For example, in 1987, a Jersey City gang called "Dot Busters," beat to death Navroze Mody, an Asian Indian American (U.S. Congress 1987, pp. 34–37); in 1989, a Chinese American was murdered following a pool room fight in which he was called "gook," "chink," and blamed for American casualties in Vietnam (U.S. Commission on Civil Rights 1992, pp. 26–31). The 1992 Los Angeles riots revealed virulent anti-Asian, especially anti-Korean prejudice, by blacks. Mobs of blacks burned and looted Korean-owned stores; one looter stated, "Ask them will they hire blacks now" (Griego 1992, p. A2). Similar prejudice, although resulting in less violence, erupted in New York City, Chicago, and Dallas, in the context of black boycotts of Korean stores in the late 1980s and early 1990s (Rieder 1990, p. 16; Papajohn 1993, p. 1). Boycotters in Brooklyn stood in front of Korean stores chanting, "Koreans must go. They should not be here in the first place." The racial tensions caused by the boycotts spilled over into violence when a black youth brutally assaulted an Asian man while yelling, "Koreans go home" (Rieder 1990, p. 16).

3. *Ethnic Offending.* Prejudice and conflict, including the whole panoply of crime and violence, is a major theme in late nineteenth and early twentieth century American society. Italians, Irish, Jews, and Germans all had their ethnic conclaves. During the early part of the century, when such groups were immigrating in large numbers to the United States, they experienced a great deal of xenophobic and prejudice-specific violence and what would now be called hate crime, some of which is well documented (Desmond 1912; Lowenstein 1989; Isolan and Martinelli 1993; Markowitz 1993; Maffi 1995). Similarly, the history of anti-Hispanic, especially anti-Mexican, violence against legal and illegal immigrants has been documented over the last two decades (Prago 1973; Mazon 1984; Alfredo 1987; Pachon 1994).

In recent years, advocacy groups have called attention to anti-Arab violence. Representative Joe Rahall testified that "we are now confronted . . . with a wave of anti-Arab hysteria which is fueled daily by the media in this country . . . and worst of all, this hysteria has manifested itself in terrorist acts on Americans of Arab heritage" (U.S. Congress 1986, p. 2). The American-Arab Anti-Discrimination Committee (ADC) presented examples of anti-Arab hate crimes consisting primarily of vandalism and harassing and threatening phones calls, as well as instances of violence against individuals, such as the pipe bombing murder of Alex Odeh, director of the ADC (pp. 62–64).

4. *Anti–Native American Offending.* Perhaps indicative of how marginal their position is, even among minority groups, there is very little scholarship on anti–Native American hate crimes, although undoubt-

edly such violence occurs, especially in those states with large Native American populations. Native American historical literature portrays U.S. government policy toward Native Americans as one of ignorance, exploitation, and frequently extermination (Andrist 1964; Brown 1973; Debo 1983; Ehle 1988).

5. *Anti-Semitic Offending.* Anti-Semitic prejudice, violence, and vandalism is the subject of a large literature (Hendrick 1923; Simmel 1946; Adorno et al. 1950; Yinger 1964; *International Encyclopedia of the Social Sciences* 1968, 1:345; Higham 1985; Dinnerstein 1987; Toy 1989; Rubin 1990). The Anti-Defamation League has produced a tremendous amount of literature (Anti-Defamation League 1989, 1990*b*, 1990*c*, 1991). The ADL audits reveal that a significant amount of current anti-Semitism (not necessarily hate crimes) is expressed and perpetrated by black hate mongers, who seem to have a great deal of support in the black community (Anti-Defamation League 1990*a*, 1994). Khalid Abdul Muhammad, spokesman for Nation of Islam leader Louis Farrakhan, claimed that victims of the Holocaust brought it on themselves: "They went in there to Germany the way they do everywhere they go, and they supplanted, they usurped, they turned around, and a German in his own country would almost have to go to a Jew to get money" (Anti-Defamation League 1994). The most dramatic recent black anti-Semitic hate crime was committed in the course of four days of rioting in 1991 in the Crown Heights section of Brooklyn. Chanting "kill the Jews," mobs set fires, destroyed property, and looted stores, and assaulted and harassed citizens, and murdered rabbinical student Yankel Rosenbaum. Over the course of four days there were 259 calls to 911 regarding property offenses, 192 calls regarding offenses against persons, and 233 calls regarding roving groups of disorderly persons (more than double the number of calls logged during an average four-day period) (Girgenti 1993, p. 126). Nevertheless, the NYPD Bias Investigation Unit identified only twenty-seven bias-motivated incidents (Girgenti 1993, p. 129).

6. *Antiwhite Offending.* In recent years, there has been much more attention to antiwhite prejudice among blacks (Box 1993; Welch 1994). According to a recent Klanwatch report, more whites than blacks were the victims of racially motivated murders (nine white and six black hate murder victims) (Box 1993). Further, it is reported that when Louis Farrakhan mentioned Colin Ferguson, the black man who opened fire on a crowded commuter train killing six white passengers, at a rally in New York City the audience broke into a prolonged ova-

tion (Mills 1994, p. 13). In a speech before an audience of 2,000 at Howard University, Nation of Islam spokesman Khalid Muhammad drew similar applause when he stated, "I love Colin Ferguson, who killed all those white folks on the Long Island train" (Melillo and Harris 1994, p. B1). Moreover, literature about the virulently antiwhite, anti-Semitic black radio and press in the New York City area illustrates the climate of antiwhite hate (Sleeper 1990).

There is a dispute about what percentage of black-on-white crime is motivated by prejudice. Some writers seem to bend over backward to explain such crime as economically motivated or the result of repressed rage, but it is hard to see how a good deal of black-on-white street crime is not based, *in part*, on prejudice. Certainly crimes like Colin Ferguson's murder of six white Long Island Rail Road commuters in December 1993 could be considered antiwhite hate crime; Ferguson was carrying notes expressing hatred for whites, Asians, and conservative blacks. However, commentators disagreed over whether his killing spree should be characterized as hate crime (Wilson 1993, p. A14). Bob Purvis, legal director for the Center for Applied Study of Ethnoviolence, stated that while technically the offense could be classified as a hate crime, "mass murder is mass murder, it's not a hate crime." Criminologist Jack Levin disagreed, stating that "the hate crime issue should be brought out because this is a very rare form of hate crime and a very rare form of mass murder." Sociologist Ronald Holmes, while conceding that Ferguson selected his victims on the basis of race, declined to classify the incident as a hate crime: "He picked his victims and they were deserving in his mind. This person was disgruntled with the way things [were] going in society" (Wilson 1993, p. A14).

While most black rioting since the 1960s has involved black neighborhoods and black victims, some rioting has been targeted at whites and Asians. For example, the April 1992 Los Angeles riots, in which crowds of blacks erupted in response to the not-guilty verdicts in the trial of police officers accused of beating Rodney King, included numerous antiwhite hate crimes, including the near fatal attack on Reginald Denny and the murders of Howard Epstein and Matthew Haines.[10] There was also extensive violence directed against Koreans (Gooding-Williams 1993; Madhubuti 1993; Praeger 1993, p. 11; Chavez 1994, p. 22).

[10] "After Howard Epstein was shot in the head, onlookers, who gathered around his car, broke into applause when someone pointed out that the victim was white" (Lacey and Feldman 1992, p. A1).

7. *Anti-Gay Offending.* Crimes motivated by sexual-orientation bias have generated a body of research on offenders. Unlike other hate crime offenders, anti-gay offenders are more likely actively to seek out victims by traveling to neighborhoods or locations where gays live or congregate (Levin and McDevitt 1993). Reports and informal surveys indicate that the overwhelming majority of anti-gay offenders are males in their late teens to early twenties (Berk, Boyd, and Hamner 1992, p. 131; Berrill 1992, pp. 29–30; Harry 1992, p. 113). Other common characteristics of anti-gay attacks are that offenders typically act as a group; the offenders and victim are strangers; and offenders appear to have no underlying criminal motive, such as obtaining money or property from the victim (Berk, Boyd, and Hamner 1992, p. 131; Berrill 1993, pp. 156–57).

Sociologist Joseph Harry categorizes anti-gay hate crime offenders into two classes: the "activists" who seek out homosexual victims by traveling to gay neighborhoods, and the "opportunists" who engage in gay bashing only when the opportunity arises. Harry suggests that four elements must be present in order for gay bashing to occur: "(a) the *institution of gender*, which defines departure from a gender role, and especially sexual departure, as an abomination; (b) *groups of immature males* who feel the need to validate their status as males; (c) *disengagement* by those males from the conventional moral order; and (d) *opportunities for gay-bashing—gay neighborhoods for activists, visibly homosexual persons for opportunists*" (Harry 1992, p. 121).

Sociologists Richard Berk, Elizabeth Boyd, and Karl Hamner offer a conceptual foundation for hate crimes by categorizing anti-gay hate crimes into three types, with the premise that all hate crimes are "symbolic crimes" (Berk, Boyd, and Hamner 1992, pp. 127–28). A symbolic crime is defined as one in which the key ingredient in choosing the victim is that individual's membership in a particular social category. The first type of hate crime is the "actuarial crime." A good example involves a group of youths who decide to rob a gay man "not because of what his sexual orientation represents to them but because they apply a stereotype to him implying an upper-middle class income and a disinclination to fight back" (p. 128). "Expressive" anti-gay hate crimes, in effect, are a way of conveying the offenders' opinion or worldview. An expressive hate crime may be a way "to teach 'those people' a lesson," or it may simply be a homophobic reaction (p. 129). "Instrumental" hate crimes may be expressive, as well as acting as a means to an end, such as keeping homosexuals from moving into a neighborhood or closing down a gay bar or gathering place (p. 129).

Berk, Boyd, and Hamner suggest a list of empirical attributes of anti-gay hate crimes which may be useful in identifying, labeling, and researching this species of hate crime. Although based on scanty empirical evidence, they came up with the following set of attributes: more than one perpetrator, ranging in age from late teens to early twenties, ratio of perpetrators to victims (two to one), victim is stranger or "distant acquaintance," "location (outside of residences for person crimes)," occurring in the evening and during weekends, perpetrators are male, and no other underlying crime (e.g., robbery). Berk, Boyd, and Hamner acknowledge that this list of attributes may be unreliable given the slim database on anti-gay hate crimes. Further, they state that attributes applicable to anti-gay hate crimes may be irrelevant to anti-Semitic or racial hate crimes (1992, p. 132).

Social psychologist Gregory Herek applied the "functional approach" theory to examine gay bashing and the motivations of anti-gay offenders. The functional approach assumes that people hold and express certain attitudes because they derive some type of psychological benefit from doing so (Herek 1992, p. 151). As applied to gay bashing, the functional approach, in essence, asks whether participation in anti-gay violence serves a psychological function for the offender. Herek identifies five possible psychological functions of gay bashing. First, some anti-gay hate crimes may serve an "experiential function" in which the offender uses the victim as a proxy for another homosexual with whom he had a past negative experience (p. 159). Second, anti-gay violence may serve an "anticipatory function," which is essentially the same as Berk, Boyd, and Hamner's actuarial hate crime. Third, gay bashing may serve a "value-expressive" function by providing the offender with a way to express deeply held personal values that condemn homosexuality (pp. 159–60). "Social-expressive" functions may be affirmed and strengthened through gay bashing. For example, young males may bond and reaffirm their group solidarity by attacking homosexuals. According to Herek, "By clearly differentiating and then attacking an out-group [homosexuals], anti-gay violence can help in-group members [heterosexual males] to feel more positive about their group, and consequently about themselves as well" (p. 160). Similarly, ego-defensive violence provides a means for young males to reaffirm their masculinity, which they perceive to be associated with heterosexuality, by targeting "someone who symbolizes an unacceptable aspect of their own personalities" (p. 161). Statements by the Blue Boys, a gang of loosely organized young men, explaining why they use blue baseball bats to attack gays illustrates the ego-defensive and social-expressive functions: "We chose the blue baseball bats because it's the color of the boy. The man is one gender. He is not female. It is male. There is no confusion. Blue is the color of men, and that's the color that men use to defeat the anti-male, which is the queer" (Collins 1992, p. 195).

Herek's social-expressive and ego-defensive functions are nearly identical to the social identity theory, which sociologist Karl Hamner uses to explain gay bashing. In essence, the social identity theory posits that an individual's self-concept and self-esteem are based on identification with a particular "in-group," which is defined as "any group with which the individuals identifies and feels a sense of membership" (Herek 1992, p. 180; see also Hamner 1992, pp. 179–81). In order to evaluate and make judgments about themselves, individuals compare their own in-group to an "out-group." An out-group can be any group with which the individual does not identify or finds abhorrent. As applied to anti-gay violence, heterosexual males use their negative perception of homosexuals to increase their individual and group self-esteem (p. 182).

8. *Antifemale Offending.* Aggression, including violent crime, by men against women is very common (Rothschild 1993; Pendo 1994). Violence against women and girls is so common that to recognize it as a hate crime category would likely make it the most prevalent type of hate crime. If all rapes were counted as hate crimes, rape would be by far the most common violent hate crime (in 1993, there were 104,806 reported rapes: Federal Bureau of Investigation 1995, p. 23). Additionally, other criminal offenses for which women are the primary victims would also count as hate crimes. For example, the victims of serial murderers are almost always female, while the killers are male (Holmes and DeBurger 1988; Egger 1990, p. 7; Kiger 1990). It is highly plausible that these serial killers are motivated at least in part by antifemale bias.

Women's groups actively campaigned to have crime based on gender prejudice included in hate crime statutes, and in some states (although not in the federal HCSA) they have been successful (Wang 1995, app. B; Cal. Penal Code §§ 422.6-75, 1170.75; Mich. Comp. Laws. Ann. § 750.147b; Conn. Gen. Stat. Ann. §46a-58). Misogyny has generated a massive literature (Brownmiller 1976; Straus, Gelles, and Steinmetz 1980; Baron and Straus 1989; Jukes 1993). Certainly, a large percentage of male perpetrators of violence against women are motivated at least in part by antifemale prejudice.

In 1994, Congress passed the Violence Against Women Act of 1994 (Pub. L. No. 103-322), which creates a civil cause of action for victims of gender motivated crimes (although paradoxically, "gender-motivated crime" is not hate crime).[11] Under the statute, a victim may sue the offender for compensatory and punitive damages and injunctive and declaratory relief in federal court.

9. *Organized Hate Groups.* The labeling of various organized groups as hate groups is as fraught with definitional problems and social and political subjectivity as the labeling of individual acts of crime. Consider whether the Nation of Islam, the Jewish Defense League, Act-Up, and the Hell's Angels should be categorized as hate groups? Many commentators loosely label all the militia groups in the West and Midwest as hate groups although some of these groups at least resist the label (Coates 1987; Bennett 1988; Sargent 1995).

Some groups are uncontroversially and avowedly ideologically committed to prejudice—for example, the Ku Klux Klan, the Order, White Aryan Resistance, and small gangs of skinheads. Mark S. Hamm's *American Skinheads: The Criminology and Control of Hate Crimes* focuses on the history and evolution of American skinheads. He conducted empirical research through interviews and questionnaires of white supremacist skinheads and their organizations. Hamm differentiates between hate crimes and terrorist acts; hate crimes are motivated by prejudice with no underlying social or political objective, whereas terrorist acts are based on a social or political objective. According to Hamm, "not all acts of terrorism can be considered hate crimes, and hate crimes are not necessarily terrorism unless such prejudicial violence has a political or social underpinning" (Hamm 1993, p. 107). Fifty-eight percent of the 120 self-reported acts of violence by the skinheads Hamm interviewed were not directed at nonwhite individuals (Hamm 1993, p. 109).

Hamm's research presents a picture of two types of skinheads: terrorists (those who have regularly engaged in acts of violence based on prejudice) and nonterrorists (those who have not engaged in acts of

[11] The act defines a "crime of violence motivated by gender" as a felony "committed because of gender or on the basis of gender, and due, at least in part, to an animus based on the victim's gender" (Section 40302 [d][1]).

violence). As his sample, Hamm interviewed thirty-six skinheads; he identified twenty-two terrorists and fourteen nonterrorists. Hamm compared the backgrounds and ideologies of the terrorists and nonterrorists. He found that terrorists come from predominantly lower-class backgrounds and that the vast majority of terrorists and nonterrorists came from stable families with whom they got along. Hamm also found that terrorists scored significantly higher than nonterrorists on the Fascism Scale, or F-Scale, which was developed by Theodor Adorno and his colleagues at the University of California, Berkeley to measure authoritarian and fascist personality traits (Adorno et al. 1950).

10. *Hate Crime Victims.* Proponents of the new hate crime laws frequently contend that hate crimes are "different" because they inflict more injury to the individual victim and to third persons and community stability than crimes in the same offense category that are attributable to other motivations (Greenawalt 1992/93, pp. 617–28; Garofalo and Martin 1993, pp. 65–66; Marovitz 1993, pp. 49–50).[12] In 1986, the National Institute Against Prejudice and Violence (NIAPV) conducted a "pilot study" of seventy-two hate crime victims in seven states. The pilot study did not compare hate crime victims with ordinary crime victims. It simply examined the victims in order to create "a profile of an average hate crime victim and their [*sic*] reactions" (Weiss 1991, p. 97). Although this pilot study did not attempt to conduct empirical research supporting the claim that hate crime victims suffer greater emotional harm than ordinary crime victims, the NIAPV used the study to support such assertions. According to Joan Weiss, former director of NIAPV: "One of the most striking findings was the impact of these incidents of ethnoviolence [e.g., hate crimes] on victims compared to personal crimes [e.g., ordinary crimes]. How does one know, for example, whether being the victim of an act . . . motivated by racial or religious prejudice, was any worse than being the victim of a random act? . . . From working with the victims, it is apparent that they were not comparable, but there is no proof in terms of data" (Weiss 1991, p. 100). Despite the lack of data supporting the claim that emotional harm to hate crime victims is greater than emotional harm suffered by ordinary crime victims, Weiss concluded that "the comparison of symptoms of the victims of personal violence with victims of

[12] Chief Justice Rehnquist, writing for the majority in *Wisconsin v. Mitchell* (113 S. Ct. 2194, 2201 [1993]), accepted this "greater harm" rationale.

ethnoviolence was very graphic in this study. There were more symptoms, a greater effect on the individual, when the motivation was prejudice" (Weiss 1991, p. 100).

The NIAPV pilot study, in fact, did not compare the emotional damage to hate crime victims with those sustained by nonhate crime victims. There was no comparison research on victims of ordinary crimes. It comes as no surprise that hate crime victims report psychological and emotional effects of their victimization. The literature and research on criminal victimization, documenting the short- and long-term adverse effects of victimization, is vast (Burgess and Holstrom 1974; Notman and Nadelson 1976; Bard and Sangrey 1979; Forman 1980; Skogan and Maxfield 1981; American Psychological Association 1984; Elias 1986; Sank and Caplan 1991). The American Psychological Association Task Force on the Victims of Crime and Violence found that the victims of such different crimes as assault, rape, burglary, and robbery exhibit surprisingly similar reactions. The reactions include anger, shock, disbelief, fear, anxiety, and helplessness. These feelings may be accompanied by sleep disturbances, nightmares, and "an increase in psychosomatic symptoms and aggravation of previous medical problems" (American Psychological Association 1984, p. 25). Emotional reactions to crime may last for years, with victims experiencing depression, loss of self-esteem, and a deterioration of personal relationships. Frequently, victims change their behavior to cope with fear of future crimes, such as moving, changing phone numbers, leaving home less often, installing security devices, or purchasing firearms (American Psychological Association 1984, pp. 25–27).

A 1994 study of hate crime victims by social work professors Arnold Barnes and Paul H. Ephross found of fifty-nine hate crime victims of various racial, religious, and ethnic backgrounds that "the predominant emotional responses of hate violence victims appear similar to those of nonhate-crime victims of similar crimes. The behavioral coping responses of hate violence victims are also similar to those used by other victims of crime" (Barnes and Ephross 1994, p. 250) No direct comparison was made of ordinary crime victims; Barnes and Ephross examined the emotional responses of hate crime victims and compared them to common emotional reactions of ordinary crime victims based on existing victimization research and literature. Barnes and Ephross found only one significant difference in hate crime victims' emotional reactions, and this difference pointed to less severe emotional injury: "A major difference in the emotional response of hate violence victims appears to be the *absence of lowered self-esteem.* The ability of some hate violence victims to maintain their self-esteem may be associated with their attribution of responsibility for the attacks to the prejudice and racism of others" (Barnes and Ephross 1994, p. 250, emphasis added).

To date, there is no empirical research comparing the emotional reactions of hate crime victims and ordinary crime victims. Indeed, very little research exists which focuses exclusively on hate crime victims as a separate victim group.

It is frequently asserted that hate crime, or intergroup crime per se, is more traumatic to some or all members of the group of which the victim is a member. But the assertion that hate crime has greater adverse impacts on the victim's community has not been systematically documented. Obviously, a *campaign* of hate crime against a group ("Krystallnacht") will be more traumatic than an individual crime that can be rationalized as aberrational, if the community even finds out about it. Thus, the beating of Rodney King by a group of Los Angeles police officers angered Los Angeles's black community and, after the police were acquitted, touched off rioting in south central Los Angeles. The explosive black violence against Korean stores during the 1992 Los Angeles riots was said to be traumatic for the whole Korean community (Chavez 1994).

It is sometimes asserted, without supporting empirical evidence, that hate crime leads to reprisals and intergroup warfare (Coldren 1993; Greenawalt 1992/93, p. 627). If this is true at all, it only holds for interracial and interethnic violence and not for homophobic, anti-Semitic, and misogynistic crimes.

It is sometimes said that hate crime is more socially destabilizing than ordinary crime (Crocker 1992/93, p. 489; Greenawalt 1992/93, p. 627; Coldren 1993). That proposition is not obviously true. "Ordinary" street crime has devastated America's urban environment over the last several decades; among other things it has been a chief contributor to mass flight to the suburbs. Likewise, drug-related crime and black-on-black violence have been enormously destabilizing for the inner city. All kinds of horrifying crimes—carjackings, arson, drive-by shootings, serial murder—send shock waves through the community.

VI. Hate Crimes and the Criminal Justice System

How have the police adapted to the emergence of the new hate crime category? Have they shifted resources into hate crime investigations and away from other kinds of investigations? Has the recognition of hate crimes as a separate genre of crime meant a reordering of police priorities?

A. Police and Hate Crime Investigation

In 1988, Abt Associates and the National Organization of Black Law Enforcement Executives (NOBLE) released a joint study, referred to as the Abt Report, examining law enforcement and prosecutorial responses to hate crimes (Finn and McNeil 1988). Based on interviews with criminal justice personnel and representatives of community organizations, the study reached conflicting conclusions regarding the criminal justice system's response to hate crimes. Fifty-five percent of the respondents interviewed by NOBLE rated the law enforcement response as "good to exceptional," while all respondents believed that "the criminal justice system has not recognized the seriousness of hate violence, or that many criminal justice personnel do not want to believe that hate violence exists in the community" (Finn and McNeil 1988, p. 4).

The New York City Police Department, as well as a few other large police departments, have formed "bias units" to investigate bias crimes.[13] Typically, these units are staffed with officers whose sole responsibilities involve the investigation and labeling of hate crimes (Marx 1986). A police bias unit's responsibility for deciding whether particular crimes are bias motivated is fraught with sensitive, and potentially explosive, social and political ramifications. In New York City, racial groups have been known to mobilize and polarize over labeling or failing to label a crime as a hate crime (Sleeper 1990; Jacobs 1992*a*, 1992*b*, 1993*a*, 1993*b*). During the investigation and trial of the blacks youths who raped and nearly beat to death a female jogger in Central Park, journalists and some citizens charged that a double standard exists, whereby white-on-black crimes are quickly labeled hate crimes, while black-on-white crimes are explained in different terms (Benedict 1992, pp. 189–251). At the same time, some black observers branded the prosecution of the youths as itself racist (O'Sullivan 1989, p. 13; Anderson 1990, p. 52). So politically sensitive is the hate crime labeling decision that, in 1987, the NYPD created a Bias Review Panel to review the classification of bias-motivated crimes.

[13] The Abt Report identified twenty-seven police departments that made investigation of bias crimes a priority, either through the creation of specialized "bias units" or through new departmental policies for identifying and investigating bias crimes (Finn and McNeil 1988).

Another obstacle to identifying a bias-motivated offense is failure to apprehend the offender. No arrest is made in the majority of hate crimes; arrests are most rare in low-level offenses like bias-motivated vandalism. In 1990, only 127 of 530 bias offenses in New York City were cleared; of 167 anti-Semitic offenses, there were only sixteen arrests (New York Police Department 1991, p. 44).

Some incidents that initially appear to be hate crimes may turn out not to be hate crimes. For example, a Hispanic woman claimed that her white neighbor harassed her with anti-Hispanic epithets. On determining that the complainant and the neighbor had been involved in an ongoing dispute over building code violations, the NYC Bias Unit reclassified the incident as "a non-bias motivated personal dispute" (New York Police Department 1991, p. 25).

In some situations, the victim may misconstrue the offender's motivation or simply be unreliable. The NYPD Bias Unit investigated one case, in which six Hasidic men riding the subway were confronted by a group of black youths. One of the Hasidic men was sprayed with mace and robbed. After investigation, the Bias Unit discovered that fifteen minutes after the Hasidic men were attacked, the same group of black youths attacked and robbed a white man and then a Hispanic man. The Bias Unit concluded that "the groups' actions should not be considered anti-white or anti-religious but totally criminal in nature with robbery as their sole objective" (New York Police Department 1991, p. 24). That conclusion itself seems debatable since the offenders might well have been prejudiced against Jews, whites generally, and Hispanics (if indeed they perceived the Hispanic victim to be Hispanic rather than white).

B. *Prosecuting Hate Crimes*

Defendants have been prosecuted for crimes motivated by prejudice long before the emergence of the new hate crime laws. They were prosecuted under "generic" criminal laws, although on conviction prosecutors may have persuaded sentencing judges to treat the defendant's bias motive as an aggravating factor justifying a severe punishment. In a very small number of cases, hate crimes were prosecuted under the federal criminal civil rights act (18 U.S.C. § 241), which criminalizes conspiracies to interfere with constitutional or federal statutory rights.[14]

[14] Lu-in Wang provides an excellent summary of the federal civil rights laws and their use to prosecute hate crimes (Wang 1995, chap. 3, pp. 1, 35). For example, 18 U.S.C.

1. *The Decision to Charge.* Charging a defendant with a hate crime "ups the ante." The prosecutor, in addition to having to prove the underlying offense, shoulders the burden of proving that the defendant is a racist, anti-Semite, or homophobe. Consider the consequences for the prosecution if it had to prove the racism of the defendants in the Rodney King, Reginald Denny, or Yankel Rosenbaum cases (Lorch 1992, p. B3; Praeger 1993, p. 11; Schmich 1993, p. 1). In interracial cases like those, the prosecution usually tries to keep jurors focused on the essential elements of the offense, especially when the defense is intent on "playing the race card" (Jacobs 1992/93, p. 549). If the criminal conduct had been charged as a hate crime, it would have signalled the jurors that this is a "race case" and possibly polarized the jurors along racial lines. That almost certainly would disadvantage the prosecution, at least whenever there is a multiracial jury.

Charging, or failing to charge, a hate crime could place a prosecutor in a "catch-22" situation. The decision to charge or not charge a defendant with a bias crime could provoke anger in the victim's or the defendant's community (Fleisher 1994, p. 28). For example, the failure to bring a hate crime charge in the gang rape and near-fatal beating of the Central Park jogger led some observers to accuse the police and the mayor of adhering to a double standard in labeling hate crimes.

Hate crimes attract more media and community attention than ordinary crimes (see Chermak 1995, pp. 54–55). A prosecutor may desire such publicity in order to placate or attract the support of the victim's community. However, a prosecutor may wish to downplay the defendant's prejudice in order to avoid alienating members of the defendant's community.

2. *The Jury and Hate Crime Trials.* Selecting a jury for a hate crime trial presents unique challenges. How far should the prosecutor go on voir dire to determine whether a prospective juror is not himself or herself prejudiced against the victim's group and is willing and capable of finding the defendant to be prejudiced against the victim's group (Maldonado 1992/93, p. 559)? Some jurors who may be able to find that a defendant, a member of their same racial, ethnic, religious, or sexual orientation group, committed a garden-variety crime, may not be willing to find the defendant guilty of being a racist, anti-Semite, or other type of bigot. The juror, consciously or unconsciously, might

§ 241 was used to prosecute the Mississippi law enforcement personnel involved in the 1964 murders of civil rights workers Michael Henry Schwerner, James Earl Chaney, and Andrew Goodman (*United States v. Price*, 383 U.S. 787 [1966]).

see this as an indictment of his or her own prejudices (Jacobson 1977, p. 88; Barkan 1983, p. 28–44; Levine 1992, pp. 169–72).

3. *Proving Prejudice.* In some cases, evidence of bias motivation is "manifest."[15] For example, the defendant may have been screaming racial epithets at the time of the assault or robbery or when taken into custody may confess that his crime was racially motivated. However, even epithets at the crime scene will not invariably mean that the defendant was motivated by prejudice. For example, two individuals may have become embroiled in an argument over a parking place, the victim may have shouted an epithet, and the defendant may have retaliated with an epithet and a punch.

While prejudice may be manifest, it may have been triggered by an unplanned encounter, not by an ideologically driven determination to terrorize a specific racial, ethnic, or religious group (Jacobs 1992*b*, p. 58; Levin 1992/93, p. 167; Fleisher 1994, p. 11). One such case was *State v. Wyant*, 597 N.E.2d 450 (1992), in which the Ohio Supreme Court reversed the ethnic intimidation conviction of David Wyant. In May 1989, Wyant and his wife, both white, were renting a campsite. Jerry White and his girlfriend, both black, rented the campsite next to the Wyants'. There was no conflict between the two parties until late in the evening when Wyant complained to campground officials about loud music from White's campsite. A short time later, White and his girlfriend overheard Wyant saying, "We didn't have this problem until those niggers moved in next to us," "I ought to shoot that black mother [expletive]," "I ought to kick his black ass" (p. 450). On the basis of these statements (which were *overheard* by White, and not screamed in his face during a confrontation), Wyant was convicted of ethnic intimidation. The Ohio Supreme Court reversed on the ground that the statute, in effect, created a "thought crime" in violation of the First Amendment. It is questionable whether the Ohio court's decision is valid after the U.S. Supreme Court upheld Wisconsin's statute in *Mitchell.*

How much evidence is required to prove that a crime was motivated *in part* by prejudice? Would it be sufficient to show that the defendant

[15] In order to make hate crimes easier to prove, some commentators have proposed that in all violent interracial crimes, the burden of proving unbiased motive be shifted to the defendant (Fleischauer 1990, p. 701; *Harvard Law Review* 1988). The defendant would be presumed to have acted from a bias motive and would have to prove that he did not. Proponents of this policy usually suggest that it apply, in the interracial context, only to white defendants. No hate crime statute or proposed bills have included this proposal which, even under a liberal definition of affirmative action, would almost certainly be declared unconstitutional.

shouted a racial or religious slur as he fled the crime scene? In an attack on a Hispanic couple by a group of white youths who remained silent during the attack, would it be sufficient to present testimony from a witness who overheard the youths make ethnic slurs an hour (six hours? a day?) before or after the attack?

Where the offense involves more than one perpetrator, the problem of proving motive is more complex. What if only one member of the group shouted an epithet? Can that person's motivation be attributed to the codefendants? Accomplice liability typically requires that the accomplice desire the crime to be committed. Does that include the bias motivation (Fleisher 1994, p. 27)?

Most hate crime statutes do not require proof of *manifest* prejudice. Thus, where manifest prejudice was not evident at the crime scene, the prosecutor may attempt to prove prejudice based on the defendant's character, activities, and pronouncements. In order to prove the defendant's prejudice, a prosecutor may be tempted or pressured to delve into the defendant's beliefs and values, the publications he reads, the organizations to which he belongs, his activities, the backgrounds of his friends. In *People v. Aishman*, 19 Cal. Rep. 444 (1993), the prosecutor introduced as evidence of prejudice the fact that one of the defendants had a swastika and "Thank God I'm White" tattooed on his arms (1993, p. 447). Further, witnesses may be called on to testify about how the defendant told (or laughed at) racist or homophobic jokes, or whether he ever used racial slurs. In *Grimm v. Churchill*, 932 F.2d 674 (1991), the arresting officer testified that Grimm had a history of making racist remarks (pp. 675–76). Similarly, in *People v. Lampkin*, 457 N.E.2d 50 (1983), the prosecution presented as evidence racist statements that the defendant had uttered six years before the crime for which he was on trial (p. 50). In effect, the trial may turn into an inquisition on the defendant's character, or at least his values and beliefs.

When confronted with such evidence, a defendant may rebut the prosecution's allegations of prejudice by testifying, or having friends testify, that he is not prejudiced (Jacobs 1992/93, p. 551). This sort of rebuttal evidence may, in turn, lead to cross examinations like the following:

Q: [by the prosecutor]: And you lived next door to [a 65-year-old black neighbor of the defendant's] for nine years and you don't even know her first name?

A: No.

Q: Ever had dinner with her?

A: No.

Q: Never gone out and had a beer with her?
A: No.
Q: Never went to a movie?
A: No.
Q: Never invited her to a picnic at your house?
A: No.
Q: Never invited her to Alum Creek?
A: No. She never invited me nowhere.
Q: You don't associate with her, do you?
A: I talk to her when I can, whenever I see her out.
Q: All these black people that you have described that are your friends, I want you to give me one person, just one who was really a good friend of yours. (*State v. Wyant*, 597 N.E.2d 450 [1992])

Such testimony and cross examination may transform hate crime trials into character tests, which defendants will pass only if they are politically correct multiculturalists. The result of such inquisition-style hate crime trials may be increased polarization of the community and politicization of the criminal justice system. Ironically, the emphasis on hate crimes might generate more intergroup prejudice and conflict.

It is not surprising then that prosecutors infrequently bring hate crime charges. In Kings County (Brooklyn), New York, the Civil Rights Bureau of the district attorney's office received 169 complaints of bias motivated crimes in 1992 (Maldonado 1992/93, p. 555). Of these complaints, twenty-nine were prosecuted through disposition, or about 12 percent (p. 555). Maldonado attributes case mortality primarily to the difficulty of proving a nexus between the underlying crime and the bias motivation of the offender (p. 556).

C. *Sentencing Enhancement Statutes*

Hate crime laws that are formulated as sentencing enhancements, rather than as substantive offenses, need not be proved before a jury and therefore do not raise the problems discussed in the last section. Rules governing the admissibility of evidence, especially hearsay evidence, are less stringent at a sentencing hearing than at a trial. Indeed, courts have traditionally permitted the admission of associational and speech-related evidence at sentencing hearings where the evidence bears a direct relation to the crime charge (*Barclay v. Florida*, 1983, p. 939; *Dawson v. Delaware*, 112 S. Ct. 1093 [1992]; *Wisconsin v. Mitchell*, 113 S. Ct. 2194 [1993]).

The federal sentencing guidelines mandate an increased base-level offense score for the underlying crime when the offender had a bias motive. The defendant's prejudice must be shown by a preponderance of the evidence at the sentencing hearing.

VII. Sociopolitical Significance of Hate Crime Laws

Hate crime legislation should not be understood primarily as a crime control strategy. The United States is unlikely to produce equal opportunity predators by threatening hate crime prosecutions and aggravated sentences for criminal conduct motivated by prejudice. Moreover, the criminal justice system is unlikely to enforce these special laws vigorously for the reasons discussed in the last section. Their importance is greater as symbolic legislation than as crime control (Jacobs 1992/93, 1993*b*).

Civil rights legislation attempts to rectify past wrongs by codifying positive rights, and affirmative action extends preferences to members of historically discriminated against groups. Hate crime statutes transport the civil rights/affirmative action paradigm into the criminal law. The prejudice and discrimination that are condemned are not those of government or private employers but of criminals. Unlike civil rights legislation that makes otherwise lawful conduct (e.g., refusal to hire or promote) unlawful, hate crime laws enhance punishment for conduct that is already criminal. One further asymmetry with the standard civil rights model is that, in the hate crime context, minority group members, especially blacks and Hispanics, constitute a high proportion of offenders.

Politicians are easily convinced to support hate crime laws, because in passing such laws they believe they are sending a message of support to minority communities that demand such signals. They also send a more general message that they are morally correct individuals. Just as it does not take much political courage for politicians to denounce crime, it does not take courage, nor is it politically risky, for most politicians to denounce crime motivated by racism and religious prejudice. Only denunciation of prejudice against homosexuals seems politically risky. Thus, ironically, some politicians cannot or will not condemn crime motivated by prejudice against homosexuality, although this is a classic type of hate crime.

As the civil rights movement has become an entrenched feature of American politics, Americans have become more adept at asserting group rights. Increasingly, Americans find it in their interest to identify themselves as members of groups, especially victimized and disadvantaged groups, thereby establishing their eligibility for affirmative action and other special considerations (Epstein 1989, p. 20; Sykes 1992; Skerry 1993, pp. 6–7; Sleeper 1993, p. 1; Bernstein 1994). This "identity politics" makes "race, ethnicity, gender, and sexual orientation the primary lenses through which people view themselves and society" (Sleeper 1993, p. 1).

Making prejudice a key factor in categorizing and coding crime brings criminal justice politics closer to mainstream identity politics. Thus, it should not be surprising to find that some academic commentators advocate adoption of the affirmative action paradigm into criminal law so that white-on-black crime would be punished more severely than black-on-white crime. In support of such a proposal, Fleischauer (1990, p. 706), for example, argues that it is unfair to subject minorities to enhanced penalties "at a disproportionate rate compared to white offenders because it is in the nature of society for majorities to prosecute minorities more frequently and with more vigor than vice versa" (see also *Harvard Law Review* 1988). Other commentators go even further, proposing that in cases of white-on-black crime the white *defendant's prejudice be presumed* and the burden shifted to the white defendant to prove the absence of prejudice motivation. No jurisdiction has adopted these proposals, and in any event, they would be vulnerable to constitutional challenge under the Fourteenth Amendment's equal protection clause (Morsch 1991).

Hate crime laws can be criticized on the same grounds that affirmative action and identity politics are criticized: that such race-conscious laws and policies divide the society and destroy common ground. Twenty years ago most criminologists were probably uneasy about breaking down crime statistics sociodemographically. The thrust of the hate crime law movement is to further deconstruct crime along racial, ethnic, religious, gender, and sexual orientation fault lines as much as possible. The danger is that groups will start keeping score cards. That has already happened to some extent in New York City.

VIII. Summary and Conclusion

In most crimes, especially predatory crimes, the perpetrator and victim are members of the same group; at least that is true for racial groups. However, a minority of crime is committed by members of one racial, ethnic, religious, gender, and sexual orientation group against members of another, sometimes as an explicit expression of ideology and sometimes for ambiguous reasons, including conscious or subconscious prejudice. It may be convenient to lump all such racist, sexist, homophobic, misogynistic, and anti-Semitic conduct under the single label "hate crime," but obviously each of these abhorrent ideologies, forms of prejudice, and types of group-targeted aggression has its own etiology, sociology, and social psychology. Prejudice and motivation are both very complicated concepts. Social phenomena like criminal conduct motivated by anti-Semitic aggression and criminal conduct motivated by sexism cannot be adequately explained in the same general terms.

Until recently, intergroup crime and crime motivated by prejudice were not categories explicitly recognized by criminal law. In practice, of course, in different times and different places crimes by members of one group against another have been less vigorously investigated, prosecuted, and punished than "ordinary" crimes. However, until recently, the remedy for this type of discrimination was thought to be the evenhanded enforcement of generic criminal law. No doubt, to some extent, there has been improvement; for example, spouse abuse and gay bashing are now taken much more seriously by the police and the courts.

Recently, however, advocates for "minority" groups have pressed for special condemnation of intergroup and bias-motivated crime. They urge that bias-motivated crime be separately coded, counted, and reported. Moreover, they urge that bias-motivated crime be labeled, condemned, and punished independent of and more seriously than generic criminal conduct. Not all crime is equal, they argue; hate crime is worse than crimes attributable to run-of-the-mill antisocial motivations. Understood as symbolic politics, the new genre of hate crime laws makes sense, but it ought not to be assumed that such laws will contribute to a more just and harmonious society. Indeed, the formulation and implementation of hate crime laws themselves generate conflict and social strain.

The concept of hate crime is easy to grasp as an ideal type, but it is difficult to effectuate in a workaday criminal justice system. Most putative hate crimes are not ideologically motivated murders, although some of those do occur. Most are low-level crimes committed, like most crime, by nonideological young men who could be described as alienated, antisocial, impulsive, and frequently prejudiced. Whether it aids understanding of their conduct and of our society to brand them as bigots as well as criminals is not an easy question to answer.

Whether so branding them will improve intergroup relations generally is also an open question.

Beyond the problem of definition, labeling particular incidents as hate crimes bristles with subjectivity and potential for bias. Nevertheless, the very existence of the term, the attempt to measure the incidence of hate crime, and the prosecution and sentencing of some offenders under different types of hate crime statutes have already changed how Americans think about the crime problem. At a minimum, the new hate crime laws have contributed further to politicizing the crime problem.

Émile Durkheim and the sociologists and criminologists who have followed in his wake emphasized the social bonding effects of crime. According to Durkheim, in expressing their outrage at the criminal, the society affirms its commitment to common norms and culture (see Garland 1990). All this now may be changing. Rather than Americans pulling together and affirming their common ground by condemning criminal conduct, they may now increasingly see crime as a polarizing issue that pits one social group against another, thereby further dividing an already fractured society.

REFERENCES

Abramovsky, Abraham. 1992. "Bias Crime: A Call for Alternative Responses." *Fordham Urban Law Journal* 19:875–914.

Adorno, Theodor, Else Frenkel-Brunswick, Daniel J. Levinson, and R. Nevitt Sanford. 1950. *The Authoritarian Personality.* New York: Harper.

Alan-Williams, Gregory. 1994. *A Gathering of Heroes: Reflections on Rage and Responsibility.* Chicago: Academy Chicago Publishers.

Alfredo, Mirande. 1987. *Gringo Justice.* Notre Dame, Ind.: University of Notre Dame Press.

Allport, Gordon. 1954. *The Nature of Prejudice.* Cambridge, Mass.: Addison-Wesley.

American Psychological Association. 1984. *Final Report.* Task Force on the Victims of Crime and Violence. Washington, D.C.: American Psychological Association.

Ames, Jessie. 1942. *The Changing Character of Lynching.* Atlanta: Commission on Interracial Cooperation.

Anderson, Lorrin. 1990. "Crime, Race and the Fourth Estate." *National Review* (October 15), p. 52.

Andrist, Ralph K. 1964. *The Long Death: The Last Days of the Plains Indians.* New York: Collier.

Anti-Defamation League. 1987. *"Shaved for Battle": Skinheads Target America's Youth.* New York: Anti-Defamation League.

———. 1988. *Young and Violent: The Growing Menace of America's Neo-Nazi Skinheads.* New York: Anti-Defamation League.

———. 1989. *Combatting Bigotry on Campus.* New York: Anti-Defamation League.

———. 1990*a*. *Louis Farrakhan: The Campaign to Manipulate Public Opinion.* New York: Anti-Defamation League.

———. 1990*b*. *Liberty Lobby: A Network of Hate.* New York: Anti-Defamation League.

———. 1990*c*. *Neo-Nazi Skinheads: A 1990 Status Report.* New York: Anti-Defamation League.

———. 1991. *An ADL Special Report: The KKK Today: A 1991 Status Report.* New York: Anti-Defamation League.

———. 1992. *Hate Crimes Statutes: A 1991 Status Report.* New York: Anti-Defamation League.

———. 1994. *ADL Audit of Anti-Semitic Incidents for 1993.* New York: Anti-Defamation League.

———. 1995. *The Skinhead International: A Worldwide Survey of Neo-Nazi Skinheads.* New York: Anti-Defamation League

Bard, M., and D. Sangrey. 1979. *The Crime Victim's Book.* New York: Basic.

Barkan, Steven E. 1983. "Jury Nullification on Political Trials." *Social Problems* 31:28–44.

Barnes, Arnold, and Paul H. Ephross. 1994. "The Impact of Hate Violence on Victims: Emotional and Behavioral Responses to Attacks." *Social Work* 39(3):247–51.

Baron, Larry, and Murray A. Straus. 1989. *Four Theories of Rape in American Society.* New Haven, Conn.: Yale University Press.

Benedict, Helen. 1992. *Virgin or Vamp: How the Press Covers Sex Crimes.* New York: Oxford University Press.

Bennett, David H. 1988. *The Party of Fear: The American Far Right from Nativism to the Militia Movement.* New York: Vintage.

Berk, Richard A., Elizabeth A. Boyd, and Karl M. Hamner. 1992. "Thinking More Clearly About Hate Motivated Crimes." In *Hate Crimes: Confronting Violence against Lesbians and Gay Men,* edited by Gregory M. Herek and Kevin T. Berrill. London: Sage.

Bernstein, Richard. 1994. *Dictatorship of Virtue.* New York: Vintage.

Berrill, Kevin T. 1992. "Anti-Gay Violence and Victimization in the United States: An Overview." In *Hate Crimes: Confronting Violence against Lesbians and Gay Men,* edited by Gregory M. Herek and Kevin T. Berrill. London: Sage.

———. 1993. "Anti-Gay Violence: Causes, Consequences, and Responses." In *Bias Crime: American Law Enforcement and Legal Responses,* edited by Robert J. Kelly. Chicago: Office of International Criminal Justice.

Boskin, Joseph. 1976. *Urban Racial Violence in the Twentieth Century.* Beverly Hills, Calif.: Glencoe.

Box, Terry. 1993. "Hate Crimes against Whites Increase: Researchers, Observers Disagree on Meaning of Higher Numbers." *Dallas Morning News* (April 28), p. A1.

Brown, Dee. 1973. *Bury My Heart at Wounded Knee.* New York: Bantam.

Brownmiller, Susan. 1976. *Against Our Will: Men, Women and Rape.* New York: Bantam.

Burgess, A. W., and L. L. Holstrom. 1974. "Rape Trauma Syndrome." *American Journal of Psychiatry* 131:981–85.

Burk, R. A. 1972. "The Emergence of Muted Violence in Crowd Behavior: A Case Study of an Almost Race Riot." In *Collective Violence,* edited by J. F. Short and M. E. Wolfgang. Chicago: Aldine-Atherton.

Chaiken, Jan M., and Marcia R. Chaiken. 1983. "Crime Rates and the Active Criminal." In *Crime and Public Policy,* edited by James Q. Wilson. San Francisco: ICS Press.

Chavez, Lydia. 1994. "Crossing the Culture Line." *Los Angeles Times Magazine* (August 28), p. 22.

Chermak, Steven M. 1995. *Victims in the News: Crime and the American News Media.* Boulder, Colo.: Westview.

Cleary, Edward J. 1994. *Beyond the Burning Cross: The First Amendment and the Landmark R.A.V. Case.* New York: Random House.

Coates, James. 1987. *Armed and Dangerous: The Rise of the Survivalist Right.* New York: Hill & Wang.

Coldren, J. David. 1993. "Bias Crimes: State Policy Considerations." In *Bias Crime: American Law Enforcement and Legal Responses,* edited by Robert J. Kelly. Chicago: Office of International Criminal Justice.

Collins, Michael. 1992. "The Gay-Bashers." In *Hate Crimes: Confronting Violence against Lesbians and Gay Men,* edited by Gregory M. Herek and Kevin T. Berrill. London: Sage.

Crocker, Lawrence. 1992/93. "Hate Crime Statutes: Just? Constitutional? Wise?" *Annual Survey of American Law* 1992/93:485–507.

Daniels, Roger. 1978. *Anti-Chinese Violence in North America.* New York: Arno.

Debo, Angie. 1983. *A History of the Indians of the United States.* Norman: University of Oklahoma Press.

Desmond, Humphrey. 1912. *The A.P.A. Movement.* New York: Arno.

Dinnerstein, Leonard. 1987. *Uneasy at Home.* New York: Columbia University Press.

Egger, Steven A. 1990. "Serial Murder: A Synthesis of Literature and Research." In *Serial Murder: An Elusive Phenomenon,* edited by Steven A. Egger. New York: Praeger.

Ehle, John. 1988. *Trail of Tears: The Rise and Fall of the Cherokee Nation.* New York: Doubleday.

Ehrlich, Howard J. 1973. *The Social Psychology of Prejudice.* New York: John Wiley.

Elias, Robert. 1986. *The Politics of Victimization: Victims, Victimology and Human Rights.* New York: Oxford University Press.

Epstein, Joseph. 1989. "The Joys of Victimhood." *New York Times Magazine* (July 2), p. 20.

Federal Bureau of Investigation. 1990. *Hate Crime Data Collection Guidelines.* Washington, D.C.: U.S. Government Printing Office.

———. 1991. *Training Guide for Hate Crime Data Collection.* Washington, D.C.: U.S. Government Printing Office.

———. 1992*a*. *Hate Crime Statistics, 1990: A Resource Book.* Washington, D.C.: U.S. Government Printing Office.

———. 1992*b*. *Uniform Crime Reports: Crime in the United States—1991.* Washington, D.C.: U.S. Government Printing Office.

———. 1993. Press release. U.S. Dept. of Justice, January 1. Washington, D.C.: U.S. Government Printing Office.

———. 1994. *Hate Crime Statistics, 1992.* Washington, D.C.: U.S. Government Printing Office.

———. 1995. *Hate Crime Statistics, 1993.* Washington, D.C.: U.S. Government Printing Office.

Ferrell, Claudine L. 1986. *Nightmare and Dream: Anti-lynching in Congress, 1917-1922.* New York: Garland.

Finn, Peter, and Taylor McNeil. 1988. *Bias Crimes and the Criminal Justice Response: A Summary Report Prepared for the National Criminal Justice Association.* Cambridge, Mass.: Abt Associates.

Fleischauer, Marc L. 1990. "Teeth for a Paper Tiger: A Proposal to Add Enforceability to Florida's Hate Crimes Act." *Florida State University Law Review* 17:697–711.

Fleisher, Marc. 1994. "Down the Passage Which We Should Not Take: The Folly of Hate Crime Legislation." *Journal of Law and Policy* 2:1–53.

Forman, D. 1980. "Psychotherapy with Rape Victims." *Psychotherapy, Theory, Research, Practice* 17(3):304–11.

Freeman, Steven M. 1992/93. "Hate Crime Laws: Punishment Which Fits the Crime." *Annual Survey of American Law* 1992/93:581–85.

Garland, David. 1990. *Punishment and Modern Society.* Chicago: University of Chicago Press.

Garofalo, James, and Susan E. Martin. 1993. "The Law Enforcement Response to Bias-Motivated Crimes." In *Bias Crime: American Law Enforcement and Legal Responses,* edited by Robert J. Kelly. Chicago: Office of International Criminal Justice.

Gaumer, Craig Peyton. 1994. "Punishment for Prejudice: A Commentary on the Constitutionality and Utility of State Statutory Responses to the Problem of Hate Crimes." *South Dakota Law Review* 39:1–48.

Gellman, Susan. 1991. "Sticks and Stones Can Put You in Jail, But Can Words Increase Your Sentence? Constitutional and Policy Dilemmas of Ethnic Intimidation Laws." *UCLA Law Review* 39:333–96.

———. 1992/93. "Hate Crime Laws Are Thought Crime Laws." *Annual Survey of American Law* 1992/93:509–31.

Ginzburg, Ralph. 1962. *100 Years of Lynchings.* New York: Lancer.

Gioseffi, Daniela. 1993. *On Prejudice.* New York: Anchor.

Girgenti, Richard H. 1993. *A Report to the Governor on the Disturbances in*

Crown Heights: An Assessment of the City's Preparedness and Response to Civil Disorder, vol. 1. Albany: York State Division of Criminal Justice Services.

Gitlin, Todd. 1995. *The Twilight of Common Dreams: Why America Is Wracked by Culture Wars.* New York: Metropolitan.

Goldberger, David. 1992/93. "Hate Crimes Laws and Their Impact on the First Amendment." *Annual Survey of American Law* 1992/93:659–80.

Goleman, Daniel. 1990. "As Bias Crime Seems to Rise, Scientists Study Roots of Racism." *New York Times* (May 29), p. C1.

Gooding-Williams, Robert, ed. 1993. *Reading Rodney King, Reading Urban Uprising.* New York: Rutledge.

Greenawalt, Kent. 1992/93. "Reflections on Justifications for Defining Crimes by the Category of Victim." *Annual Survey of American Law.* 1992/93:617–28.

Griego, Tina. 1992. "King Case Aftermath." *Los Angeles Times* (May 2), p. A2.

Grimshaw, Allen. 1970. *Racial Violence in the United States.* Philadelphia: University of Pennsylvania Press.

Hamm, Mark S. 1993. *American Skinheads: The Criminology and Control of Hate Crimes.* Westport, Conn.: Praeger.

Hamner, Karl. M. 1992. "Gay-Bashing: A Social Identity Analysis of Violence Against Lesbians and Gay Men." In *Hate Crimes: Confronting Violence against Lesbians and Gay Men*, edited by Gregory M. Herek and Kevin T. Berrill. London: Sage.

Harry, Joseph. 1992. "Conceptualizing Anti-Gay Violence." In *Hate Crimes: Confronting Violence against Lesbians and Gay Men*, edited by Gregory M. Herek and Kevin T. Berrill. London: Sage.

Harvard Law Review. 1988. Note. "Combatting Racial Violence: A Legislative Proposal." *Harvard Law Review* 101:1270–86.

———. 1993. Note. "Hate Is Not Speech: A Constitutional Defense of Penalty Enhancement for Hate Crimes." *Harvard Law Review* 106:1314–31.

Hendrick, Burton. 1923. *The Jews in America.* New York: Doubleday.

Herek, Gregory M. 1992. "Psychological Heterosexism and Anti-Gay Violence: The Social Psychology of Bigotry and Bashing." In *Hate Crimes: Confronting Violence against Lesbians and Gay Men*, edited by Gregory M. Herek and Kevin T. Berrill. London: Sage.

Herek, Gregory M., and Kevin T. Berrill, eds. 1992. *Hate Crimes: Confronting Violence against Lesbians and Gay Men.* London: Sage.

Higham, Charles. 1985. *American Swastika.* New York: Doubleday.

Holmes, Ronald M., and J. DeBurger. 1988. *Serial Murder.* Newbury Park, Calif.: Sage.

Houston Chronicle. 1993. "First-Time FBI Report Reveals Prevalence of Malice." (January 11), p. 12.

Howard, Walter T. 1995. *Lynchings: Extralegal Violence in Florida during the 1930s.* London: Associated University Presses.

International Encyclopedia of the Social Sciences. 1st ed. 1968. New York: Macmillan.

Isolani, Paola A. Sensi, and Phylis Cancilla Martinelli. 1993. *Struggle and Success: An Anthology of the Italian Immigrant Experience in California.* New York: Center for Migration Studies.

Jacobs, James B. 1992*a*. "The New Wave of American Hate Crime Legislation." Report from the Institute of Philosophy and Public Policy, College Park, Md., 12:9–12.

———. 1992*b*. "Rethinking the Law against Hate Crimes: A New York City Perspective." *Criminal Justice Ethics* 11:55–61.

———. 1992/93. "Implementing Hate Crime Legislation: Symbolism and Crime Control." *Annual Survey of American Law* 1992/93:541–53.

———. 1993*a*. "Should Hate Be a Crime?" *Public Interest* 3-14.

———. 1993*b*. "The Emergence and Implications of American Hate Crime Jurisprudence." *Israel Yearbook on Human Rights* 22:113–39.

Jacobs, James B., and Barry Eisler. 1993. "The Hate Crime Statistics Act of 1990." *Criminal Law Bulletin* 29:99–123.

Jacobs, James B., and Jessica S. Henry. 1996. "The Social Construction of a Hate Crime Epidemic." *Journal of Criminal Law and Criminology* 86:366–91.

Jacobson, Garry J. 1977. "Citizen Participation in Policy-making: The Role of the Jury." *Journal of Politics* 39:73–88.

Jukes, Adam. 1993. *Why Men Hate Women.* London: Free Association Books.

Kelly, Robert J., ed. 1993. *Bias Crime: American Law Enforcement and Legal Responses.* Chicago: Office of International Criminal Justice.

Kiger, Kenna. 1990. "The Darker Figure of Crime: The Serial Murder Enigma." In *Serial Murder: An Elusive Phenomenon,* edited by Steven A. Egger. New York: Praeger.

Klanwatch. 1987. *"Move-In Violence": White Resistance to Neighborhood Integration in the 1980s.* Montgomery, Ala.: Southern Poverty Law Center.

———. 1989. *Intelligence Report #47, Hate Violence and White Supremacy—a Decade of Review, 1980–1990.* Montgomery, Ala.: Southern Poverty Law Center.

———. 1991. *The Ku Klux Klan: A History of Racism and Violence.* Montgomery, Ala.: Southern Poverty Law Center.

Lacey, Marc, and Paul Feldman. 1992. "Delays, Chaos Add to Woes in Solving Riot Homicides." *Los Angeles Times* (June 21), p. A1.

LaFave, Wayne, and Austin W. Scott. 1986. *Substantive Criminal Law,* vol. 1. St. Paul, Minn.: West.

Lawrence, Charles R. III. 1987. "The Id, the Ego and Equal Protection: Reckoning with Unconscious Racism." *Stanford Law Review* 39:317–88.

———. 1990. "If He Hollers Let Him Go: Regulating Racist Speech on Campus." *Duke Law Journal* 1990:431–83.

Lawrence, Frederick M. 1994. "The Punishment of Hate: Toward a Normative Theory of Bias-Motivated Crimes." *Michigan Law Review* 93:320–81.

Levin, Brian. 1992/93. "Bias Crimes: A Theoretical and Practical Overview." *Stanford Law and Policy Review* 4:165–81.

Levin, Jack, and Jack McDevitt. 1993. *Hate Crimes: The Rising Tide of Bigotry and Bloodshed.* New York: Plenum.

Levine, James P. 1992. "The Impact of Local Political Cultures on Jury Verdicts." *Criminal Justice Journal* 14:163–80.

Lorch, Donatella. 1992. "2 Crown Heights Deaths Are Still Deeply Mourned." *New York Times* (September 8), p. B3.

Lowenstein, Steven. 1989. *Frankfurt on the Hudson: The German-Jewish Community in Washington Heights.* Detroit: Wayne State University Press.

Madhubuti, Haki R., ed. 1993. *Why LA Happened: Implications of the '92 LA Rebellion.* Chicago: Third World Press.

Maffi, Mario. 1995. *Gateway to the Promised Land: Ethnic Cultures on New York's Lower East Side.* New York: New York University Press.

Maldonado, Migdalia. 1992/93. "Practical Problems with Enforcing Hate Crimes Legislation in New York City." *Annual Survey of American Law* 1992/93:555–61.

Markowitz, Fran. 1993. *Community in Spite of Itself: Soviet Jewish Emigres in New York.* Washington, D.C.: Smithsonian Institute Press.

Marovitz, William A. 1993. "Hate or Bias Crime Legislation." In *Bias Crime: American Law Enforcement and Legal Responses,* edited by Robert J. Kelly. Chicago: Office of International Criminal Justice.

Marx, Gary. 1986. "When Law and Order Works: Boston's Innovative Approach to the Problem of Racial Violence." *Crime and Delinquency* 32:205–23.

Matsuda, Mari J. 1989. "Public Response to Racist Speech: Considering the Victim's Story." *Michigan Law Review* 87:2320–81.

Mazon, Mauricio. 1984. *The Zoot-Suit Riots.* Austin: University of Texas Press.

McKinley, James C., Jr. 1990. "Tracking Crimes of Prejudice: A Hunt for the Elusive Truth." *New York Times* (June 29), p. A1.

McWilliams, Carey. 1944. *Prejudice—Japanese Americans: Symbol of Racial Intolerance.* Boston: Little, Brown.

Melillo, Wendy, and Hamil Harris. 1994. "Dissent Raised as Ex-Farrakhan Aide Returns to Howard U." *Washington Post* (April 20), p. B1.

Miller, Stuart. 1969. *The Unwelcome Immigrant.* Berkeley: University of California Press.

Mills, Nicolaus. 1994. "The Shame of 'Black Rage' Defense." *Chicago Tribune* (June 6), p. 13.

Morsch, James. 1991. "The Problem of Motive in Hate Crimes: The Argument against Presumptions of Racial Motivation." *Journal of Criminal Law and Criminology* 82:659–89.

National Academy of Sciences. 1996. Committee on Behavioral and Social Sciences and Education. Committee on Law and Justice. *Planning Meeting on Terrorism, Hate Crime, and Anti-Governmental Violence.* March 20. Washington, D.C.: National Academy of Sciences/National Research Council.

Newton, Michael, and Judy Ann Newton. 1991. *Racial and Religious Violence in America: A Chronology.* New York: Garland.

New York Police Department. 1991. Untitled document. Bias Incident Investigation Unit, September.

———. 1995. *Bias Incident Investigation Unit Year End Report—1995.*

Notman, M., and C. Nadelson. 1976. "The Rape Victim: Psychodynamic Considerations." *American Journal of Psychiatry* 133:408–12.

O'Brien, Gail Williams. 1989. "Return to 'Normalcy': Organized Racial Violence in the Post-World War II South." In *Violence in America,* vol. 2, edited by Ted Robert Gurr. London: Sage.

O'Sullivan, John. 1989. "Do the Right Thing—Suppress Crime: Racial Aspects of New York City Crime." *National Review* (October 13), p. 13.

Pachon, Harry. 1994. *New Americans by Choice: Political Perspectives of Latino Immigrants.* Boulder, Colo.: Westview.

Papajohn, George. 1993. "Korean Store Boycott Splits South-Siders." *Chicago Tribune* (December 28), p. 1.

Pendo, Elizabeth A. 1994. "Recognizing Violence against Women: Gender and the Hate Crime Statistics Act." *Harvard Women's Law Journal* 17:157–83.

Praeger, Dennis. 1993. "Blacks and Liberals: The Los Angeles Riots." *Current* (January), p. 11.

Prago, Albert. 1973. *Strangers in Their Own Land.* New York: Four Winds.

Redish, Martin H. 1992. "Freedom of Thought as Freedom of Expression." *Criminal Justice Ethics* 11:29–42.

Rieder, Jonathan. 1990. "Trouble in Store: Beyond the Brooklyn Boycott." *New Republic* (July 2), p. 16.

Rothschild, Eric. 1993. "Recognizing Another Face of Hate Crimes: Rape as a Gender-Bias Crime." *Maryland Journal of Contemporary Legal Issues* 4:231–85.

Rovella, David E. 1994. "Attack on Hate Crime Is Enhanced." *National Law Journal* (August 29), p. A1.

Rubin, Theodore Isaac. 1990. *Anti-Semitism: A Disease of the Mind.* New York: Continuum.

Sank, Diane, and David I. Caplan. 1991. *To Be a Victim: Encounters with Crime and Injustice.* New York: Plenum.

Santa Clara Law Review. 1994. Comment: "Substantive Penal Hate Crime Legislation: Toward Defining Constitutional Guidelines Following the *R.A.V. v. City of St. Paul* and *Wisconsin v. Mitchell* Decisions." *Santa Clara Law Review* 34:711–64.

Sargent, Lyman Tower, ed. 1995. *Extremism in America.* New York: New York University Press.

Saxton, Alexander. 1971. *The Invisible Enemy.* Berkeley: University of California Press.

Schmich, Mary. 1993. "Denny Case: Step Back or Justice?" *Chicago Tribune* (October 20), p. N1.

Schweitzer, Ruth E. 1986. *U.S. Internal Revenue Service, Illegal Tax Protester Information.* Washington, D.C.: U.S. Government Printing Office.

Schweitzer, Thomas A. 1995. "Hate Speech on Campus and the First Amendment: Can They Be Reconciled?" *Connecticut Law Review* 27:493–521.

Shay, Frank. 1938. *Judge Lynch: His First Hundred Years.* New York: Ives Washburn.

Simmel, Ernst, ed. 1946. *Anti-Semitism: A Social Disease.* New York: International Universities Press.

Skerry, Peter. 1993. "The New Politics of Assimilation." *City Journal* 3:6–7.

Skogan, W. G., and M. G. Maxfield. 1981. *Coping with Crime: Individual and Neighborhood Reactions.* Beverly Hills, Calif.: Sage.

Sleeper, Jim. 1990. *The Closest of Strangers: Liberalism and the Politics of Race in New York.* New York: W. W. Norton.

———. 1993. *In Defense of Civic Culture.* Washington, D.C.: The Progressive Foundation.

Smith, David Todd. 1994. "Enhanced Punishment under the Texas Hate Crimes Act: Politics, Panacea, or Pathway to Hell?" *St. Mary's Law Journal* 26:259–305.

Straus, Murray A., Richard J. Gelles, and Susan K. Steinmetz. 1980. *Behind Closed Doors: Violence in the American Family.* New York: Doubleday/Anchor.

Sykes, Charles. 1992. *A Nation of Victims.* New York: St. Martin's.

Takaki, Ronald. 1989. *Strangers from a Different Shore.* Boston: Little, Brown.

Toy, Eckard V., Jr. 1989. "Right-Wing Extremism from the Ku Klux Klan to The Order, 1915 to 1988." In *Violence in America,* vol. 2, edited by Ted Robert Gurr. London: Sage.

U.S. Commission on Civil Rights. 1992. *Civil Rights Issues Facing Asian Americans in the 1990s.* Washington, D.C.: U.S. Commission on Civil Rights.

U.S. Congress. 1987. *Anti-Asian Violence: Hearings before the Subcommittee on Civil and Constitutional Rights of the House Committee on the Judiciary.* 100th Cong., 1st Sess. Washington, D.C.: U.S. Government Printing Office.

U.S. Congress. House of Representatives Committee on the Judiciary. Subcommittee on Criminal Justice. 1986. *Ethnically Motivated Violence against Arab-Americans.* 99th Cong., 2d Sess. Washington, D.C.: U.S. Government Printing Office.

U.S. Senate. Senate Committee on the Judiciary. Subcommittee on the Constitution. 1988. *Hate Crime Statistics Act of 1988.* 100th Cong., 2d Sess. Washington, D.C.: U.S. Government Printing Office.

U.S. Senate. 1989. Senate Report No. 21. 101st Cong., 1st Sess. Washington, D.C.: U.S. Government Printing Office.

Van Til, William. 1959. *Prejudiced: How Do People Get That Way?* New York: Anti-Defamation League.

Walker, Samuel. 1994. *Hate Speech: The History of an American Controversy.* Lincoln: University of Nebraska Press.

Wang, Lu-in. 1995. *Hate Crimes Laws.* New York: Clark, Boardman, Callaghan.

Weiss, Joan. 1991. "Ethnoviolence: Impact and Response in Victims and the Community." In *Bias Crime: The Law Enforcement Response,* edited by Nancy Taylor. Chicago: Office of International Justice.

Welch, Richard F. 1994. "Unchallenged, Black Racism Grows." *Newsday* (February 10), p. 113.

Wilson, Laurie. 1993. "Scholars Say NY Attack Hard to Assess." *Dallas Morning News* (December 9), p. A14.

Wright, Kevin N. 1985. *The Great American Crime Myth.* New York: Praeger.

Yinger, John Milton. 1964. *Anti-Semitism: A Case Study in Prejudice and Discrimination.* New York: Anti-Defamation League.

Martin Daly and Margo Wilson

Crime and Conflict: Homicide in Evolutionary Psychological Perspective

ABSTRACT

Criminological theories are usually framed in sociological terms but always entail psychological assumptions. Psychological accounts, in their turn, entail assumptions about the adaptive "design" of evolved mental mechanisms and processes. Thus, explicit attention to recent theory and research on psychology and evolution can sometimes help criminologists generate productive hypotheses and avoid blind alleys. Homicide research is illustrative. Interpersonal conflicts are engendered by interactions among individuals whose psyches were designed by natural and sexual selection to make them effective competitors and effective nepotists (kin-benefactors). These considerations suggest numerous testable hypotheses about such matters as who is likely to kill whom, and how the demography of homicide perpetration and victimization is likely to vary among victim-killer relationships. An evolutionary psychological perspective inspires us to criticize recent criminological discussions of sex differences and age patterns in criminal offending, theories that contrast rational choice with emotional or impulsive behavior, and the medicalization of antisocial behavior as a pathology.

Criminological theory is overwhelmingly and appropriately framed in sociological terms, but it always entails assumptions or postulates about human desires, developmental susceptibilities, and social inferences. In other words, sociological concepts and theories rest on models of human psychology, models that are often implicit and unexamined (Mon-

Martin Daly and Margo Wilson are professors of psychology at McMaster University in Hamilton, Ontario, Canada. We thank John Monahan and Michael Tonry for comments on a draft of this essay and the Social Sciences and Humanities Research Council of Canada, the Harry Frank Guggenheim Foundation, and the Natural Sciences and Engineering Research Council of Canada for financial support.

0192-3234/97/0022-0002$02.00

ahan and Splane 1980) and sometimes obsolete. Attending to what psychologists have discovered about how people process information and select their actions can be a great aid to criminologists, including even those primarily interested in macrosocial phenomena.

Psychological explanations, in their turn, rest on models of the functional organization of the human animal, and these models of our evolved "human nature" also warrant scrutiny. Attending to what evolutionists have discovered about the process that designed the human mind can be a great aid to psychologists in their investigations of the mind's structure and operations (Barkow, Cosmides, and Tooby 1992). Our thesis, then, is that the conceptual framework of evolutionary psychologists can be a valuable aid to criminological theory and research if criminologists can forsake disciplinary parochialisms and reflex denunciations of "reductionism."

Evolutionary psychology's brand of reductionism is not simplistic. Quite the contrary, in fact, for it treats social influence as more complex than do prevailing criminological models. Seeing people as active agents with intricately structured information-processing abilities and self-interests, evolutionary psychologists are critical of approaches that treat them instead as little more than putty shaped by the statistical sum of their experiences. Influential treatments of the "subculture of violence" (e.g., Wolfgang and Ferracutti 1967) and of mass media effects on "imitative" violence (e.g., Phillips 1983; Baron and Reiss 1985), for example, are flawed by virtue of their reliance on an unrealistic, implicit model of the human animal as a passive recipient of cultural influence rather than its active interpreter (Daly and Wilson 1989). In these and other discussions of the social patterning of criminal violence, social influence is often conceptualized as the mere elicitation of an arbitrary, thoughtless conformity when the actual processes involved are likely to be subtler. A sensible man will be quicker on the trigger in what he perceives to be a relatively violent setting than in an apparently peaceful one, for example, not because he has become acculturated or has internalized local norms about the legitimacy of violence but because of a shift in the perceived risk of life-threatening action by antagonists. For this sort of reason, the positive feedback of violence on itself, which is often blithely attributed to imitation or contagion or the reinforcing of norms, may be mediated by processes quite different than these terms imply. A more satisfactory account of "subcultural" and "imitative" effects must incorporate a specific characterization of the psychological processes by which the effective variables influence individual actors. Nisbett and Cohen (1996) provide an outstanding example of such an approach with respect to regional differences in the legitimacy and prevalence of violence in the United States.

In this essay we outline an evolutionary psychological perspective on conflicts of interest and criminal violations of other people's interests, with principal reference to research on homicide. We argue that certain patterns in the incidence of conflict and crime are predictable consequences of psychological processes that have been designed by the evolutionary process of Darwinian selection to make individuals effective competitors and effective "nepotists" (kin-benefactors) in ancestral environments. We argue that this perspective sheds light on the roles of certain demographic and situational variables, some but not all of which criminologists already consider important as risk factors for crime perpetration and victimization. We discuss sex differences in crime in the light of evolutionary understandings of what the male-female phenomenon is fundamentally about, and we discuss age patterns in the light of evolutionary understandings of life span development. The school of criminological thought that is perhaps most congenial to this perspective is the "rational choice/routine activities" approach, but we suggest some caveats about "rationality." In conclusion, we offer some suggestions for research that will more explicitly acknowledge that emergent group-level phenomena are both the products of interactions of numerous actors and a crucial part of the social and material environment affecting those actors.

I. Crime and Conflict

"Crime" is a socially constructed category of variable-specific content: acts that are deemed crimes in one time or place may be legitimate in others. It does not follow, however, that the set of things called "crime" is arbitrarily constituted. There is considerable overlap in the content of criminal codes, both written and traditional, from around the world. The acts that are most consistently criminalized are concentrated in a few principal domains: certain acts of violence, certain sexual acts, certain acts of expropriation, and certain betrayals of the collectivity to rival collectivities. In sum, crime consists overwhelmingly of self-interested action conducted in violation (or reckless disregard) of the interests of others.

If criminal activity derives from interpersonal conflicts of interest, then criminological understanding would surely benefit from a sound theory of the fundamental nature of self-interests (Cohen and Machalek 1988; Daly and Wilson 1988*a*, 1988*b;* Vila 1994; Machalek 1995). Where do interests overlap and where do they conflict? What are the determinants of variable inclinations to challenge rivals or to expropriate material resources? What qualifies as a crucial resource anyway, and why are even immaterial social resources such as status perceived as limited and worth contesting? These are questions that are addressed at a fundamental level by the emerging synthesis of evolutionary psychology. Whereas "interests" and "conflict" are conceived as group-level phenomena by many criminologists, evolutionists see each person's interests as distinct and consider theories that analogize collectivities to individual actors to be flawed (see Sec. II*C* below).

The evolutionary conception of conflict is largely but not entirely a matter of resource competition. "Competition" refers to any conflict of interests in which one party's possession or use of a mutually desired resource precludes another party's possession or use of the same. This category clearly encompasses most of the criminal acts that are likely to be called "instrumental" or "rational," but it also includes crimes that might be deemed "expressive" or "irrational." Violence motivated by sexual rivalry is an obvious example. More subtle examples are the "face" and "status" disputes that constitute a very large proportion (perhaps the majority) of all U.S. homicides; the social resources contested in these cases are limited means to the end of more tangible resources (Wilson and Daly 1985). But not all conflicts are competitive according to the above definition. If a woman rejects one suitor for another, for example, then she and the spurned man have a conflict of interest, but they are not competitors, whereas the male rivals are. In general, competition is predominantly a same-sex affair because same-sex individuals are usually more similar in the resources they desire than opposite-sex individuals. There is a rich body of evolutionary theory, discussed below, concerning the ways in which sex, age, and other factors affect the intensity of competition, and this body of theory sheds light on the striking demographic patterning of crime.

Although we believe that an evolutionary psychological approach is of broad applicability to the study of crime, we focus here on homicide. Homicide is in several ways the best prototype of crime. It is a major crime in all codes, exemptions of various forms of justifiable homicide notwithstanding. It stands at or near the top of everyone's list of "serious" crimes. It is generally believed to be the most reliably detected and reported of crimes, hence the crime most amenable to unbiased analysis of its correlates and putative causes. Finally, homicides are drastic resolutions of interpersonal conflicts and thus afford a window on the variable incidence and intensity of such conflicts. It is this latter idea—that homicide can be treated as a sort of "conflict assay" for testing theoretical ideas about the factors exacerbating or mitigating interpersonal conflict in particular relationship categories, life stages, and circumstances—that has inspired most of our own research on homicide, some of which is reviewed below. But before we get to matters of criminological substance, a general introduction to evolutionary psychology is required.

II. Evolutionary Psychology

In criminology textbooks, the word "psychology" is used mainly with reference to personal attributes that differ among individuals, and especially those attributes that may be interpreted as abnormal deficits or pathologies. However, the study of stable individual differences, pathological or otherwise, constitutes only a small part of psychological science and not the part of greatest relevance for understanding crime as a social phenomenon.

A. Psychological Mechanisms and Processes Are Biological Adaptations

Psychological science is primarily a quest to discover the mechanisms and processes that produce behavior and to characterize them at a level of abstraction that applies to everyone (or at least to everyone of a given sex and life stage). Psychology is closely related to physiology and neuroscience, but it is distinguished by its focus on an informational level of description: its constructs include memory encoding and retrieval, attention processes, recognition and categorization, attitudes, values, self concepts, motives, and emotions. When postulating such constructs, psychologists aim for a level of abstraction at which historical, cultural, and ecological variability can be explained as the contingent products of consistent panhuman psychological processes responding to variable circumstances and experiences. "Anger," for example, is a motivational/emotional state that can be elicited in anyone, and that plays a role both in mobilizing physiological resources for violent action and in advertising one's likelihood of engaging in such action. More controversially, perhaps, we propose that "male sexual proprietariness" is a sexually differentiated motivational/cognitive subsystem of the human mind, with behavioral manifestations that are culturally and historically variable but are nevertheless predictably related to various aspects of the status and circumstances of the focal man, his partner, and his rivals. (This argument is developed in Sec. VIII below.)

Basic psychological constructs like "color vision" and "self esteem" and "anger" and "sexual proprietariness" are putative components of human nature. Insofar as they are complexly organized, they are almost certainly *biological adaptations:* attributes that are effectively organized, as a result of a long history of natural selection, to achieve some useful function such as respiration or image analysis or the vanquishing of rivals.

The proposition that some attribute is an adaptation is a hypothesis about special-purpose "design," suggesting avenues of further inquiry (Williams 1966). Generating hypotheses about what such enigmatic lumps of tissue as the heart or lungs or liver are designed to accomplish were essential first steps for investigating their physiology and pathologies (Mayr 1983). The same goes for the successful investigation of mental "organs": psychological mechanisms are designed to solve particular adaptive problems, and hypotheses about these adaptive functions give direction to the research enterprise in both obvious and more subtle ways (Daly and Wilson 1994*a*, 1995). A psychologist who assumes, for example, that the principal function of the psychophysiology of anger is to mobilize the organism for effective physical assaults will look for a somewhat different set of manifestations and social controls than another who instead assumes that anger functions primarily to threaten and deter so as to limit the costs of violent confrontations.

The unwitting "designer" of adaptations—the "blind watchmaker" in Dawkins's (1986) memorable phrase—is Darwinian selection, the process that created existing adaptations in each living species as solutions to recurring problems confronted by many generations of its ancestors. These evolved solutions necessarily entail contingent response to environmental features that were statistical predictors, on average, of the fitness consequences of alternative courses of action in the past. (Darwinian "fitness" refers to reproductive posterity, or, somewhat more precisely, to the average success of a given phenotypic design in promoting its proportionate prevalence by promoting the relative replicative success of its bearer's genes in competition with their alleles in the environments of natural selection.)

It follows that evolutionary psychologists see no distinction in kind between "psychological" and "biological" phenomena. Influences and processes, which are best characterized at a psychological level (e.g., in cognitive, interpretative, or experiential terms), are in incessant reciprocal interaction with the sorts of physiological states and processes commonly referred to as "biological" influences on behavior. Circulating blood levels of the male gonadal hormone testosterone, for example, have a variety of subtle effects on information processing and behavior, both by virtue of action in the central nervous system itself and by virtue of other peripheral effects, but testosterone levels are themselves affected by social experience and these effects are themselves affected by culturally specific considerations. A man's perception that he has won in some sort of competition can lead to rapid elevations of circulating testosterone, even if the "competitions" are as arbitrary as a coin toss (McCaul, Gladue, and Joppa 1992) or as cerebral as a chess game (Mazur, Booth, and Dabbs 1992). Moreover, in one experimental study, an insult that engendered a surge of testosterone in men raised in the "honor" culture of the south in the United States, in which retaliatory aggression is admired, had no such influence on men raised in the north, where it is not (Nisbett and Cohen 1996). Thus psychophysiological adaptations often entail contingent response not just to immediate circumstances but also to the cumulative consequences of experience, including the assimilation and internalization of local cultural norms.

Discussions of criminal violence are frequently couched in the language of *pathology*. This is an appropriate framework insofar as violence is associated with alcohol-induced psychoses, delusions, and organic defects, as may often be the case (e.g., Raine 1993; Giancola and Zeichner 1995; Aarsland et al. 1996), but the language of pathology can mislead. Violent behavior is abhorrent, but that does not mean that violence is a pathology (Monahan and Splane 1980; Cohen and Machalek 1994). Pathologies are failures of anatomical, physiological, and psychological adaptations as a result of mishap, senescent decline, or subversion by biotic agents with antagonistic interests, failures that reduce the adaptations' effectiveness in achieving the functions for which they evolved (Williams and Nesse 1991). Violence cannot in general be explained as a maladaptive byproduct of such failures since people and other animals possess complex psychophysiological machinery that is clearly designed *for* the production and regulation of violence.

The evidence of functional design in the psychophysiology of violence is diverse. In the first place, its elicitors are typically threats to survival and reproduction, and its effects are typically to counter those threats. Animals (including people) react violently to usurpation of essential resources by rivals, and they direct their violence against those rivals (Huntingford and Turner 1987; Archer 1988). Behavioral ecologists have analyzed the cost-benefit structure of confrontational violence in terms of the conditional determinants of the expected consequences of fight versus flight and of escalation (e.g., Andersson 1980; Enquist and Leimar 1990; Colegrave 1994), and they have assessed whether animals actually behave in ways that are contingent on available cues of the probable costs and benefits of alternative actions (e.g., Chase, Bartolomeo, and Dugatkin 1994; Pruett-Jones and Pruett-Jones 1994; Turner 1994; Kvarnemo, Forsgren, and Magnhagen 1995). These analyses leave little doubt that violent interactions are regulated with sensitivity to probable consequences.

In addition to contextual appropriateness, the motivational states of angry arousal entail postures appropriate for attack and defense and complex psychophysiological mobilization for effective violent action and for the temporary suppression of potential interference from other adaptations such as pain sensitivity. Animals exhibit diverse morphological structures that function solely or primarily as intraspecific weapons, and these are often sexually differentiated and characteristic of delimited life stages. There is neural machinery dedicated to aggression and this too is often sexually differentiated. Moreover, the sexual differentiation of physical aggression is itself variable across species, and the magnitude of sex differences in both overt weaponry and intrasexual aggressive behavior is systematically related to other variable aspects of social ecology (Daly and Wilson 1983). All of these facts testify to the potency of Darwinian selection in shaping the anatomy and psychology of intraspecific violence.

The misconception that human violence is merely pathological has perhaps been reinforced by studies linking it to disadvantaged backgrounds and environments. But these associations are by no means universal. In nonstate societies, like those in which the human psyche evolved, skilled violence was a prominent attribute of high-status men and a contributor to their success (Betzig 1986; Chagnon 1988, 1996). In modern state societies, the welfare of most people no longer depends on their own or their allies' violent capabilities, so violence is relatively rare and relatively likely to reflect psychological pathology. Nevertheless, disproportionate numbers of violent offenders are drawn from groups who lack access to the opportunities and protective state services available to more fortunate citizens, and who therefore find themselves in "self-help" circumstances much like those experienced by most of our human ancestors. It is not at all clear that violence in such circumstances is usefully deemed pathological. Moreover, even in other circumstances, and even where violence is associated with an organic defect, there remains a functional organization to its contingent controls.

B. Evolutionary Psychology Is Not a Monolithic Falsifiable Theory but a Framework for Generating Theories

Science is a self-correcting, cumulative enterprise whose practitioners routinely and appropriately try to formulate mutually exclusive alternative hypotheses and revise their models to accommodate unexpected findings. Ironically, however, when evolutionists engage in these ordinary scientific practices, they are apt to encounter accusations of engaging in untestable pseudoscience. A common misunderstanding, even among self-styled "evolutionary psychologists," is that "the evolutionary hypothesis" about sex differences or the age-crime relationship or whatever can and should be tested against "nonevolutionary" alternatives. But there is no single, privileged "evolutionary hypothesis" about any of these phenomena, and the only currently available alternative to the theory of evolution by selection is creationism, which *is* pseudoscience (see, e.g., Futuyma 1983). Evolution is "just a theory" in exactly the same sense as the atomic theory is just a theory. The proposition that the human animal and its psyche evolved under the influence of selection is a "fact" in the same sense (and as well established) as other scientific propositions at some remove from direct observation, such as the fact that brains process information or the fact that molecules are comprised of atoms. The alternatives to a particular evolutionary hypothesis are other evolutionary hypotheses.

Like other animals, human beings can be analyzed into subsystems that perform distinct tasks: respiration, learning, digestion, visual scene analysis, and so forth. These separate tasks are carried out by their separate bits of anatomical, biochemical, and psychological machinery, in the service of a functionally integrated, higher-order, organismic agenda. And what is that agenda? To manufacture additional, similar animals. This is the single superordinate "purpose" that natural selection, the process responsible for the fact that we possess complex adaptive attributes, designed them to achieve. We have placed the word "purpose" in quotation marks because it is important to stress that fitness is not literally an objective. The goals that animals (including people) have evolved to monitor and pursue are more immediate things like full bellies and sexual satisfaction.

Evolutionists often say that functionally integrated systems with many parts and actions constitute a "strategy." Elements in a particular flowering plant's "reproductive strategy," for example, might include sprouting in response to a threshold soil temperature, flowering at a certain day length, and maturing of the female parts of its hermaphroditic flowers before its male parts. The metaphorical nature of the language of strategy is obvious here; no one imagines that the plant has intentionality. Where this metaphor can be misleading is in the case of animals' evolved strategies since one may slip unwittingly from claims about what the organism is "designed" to achieve into claims about what it is "trying" to achieve. This is especially problematic in the case of the human animal.

In other words, the purpose-like functionality of adaptations invites an uncritical equation between intentions, goals, and ambitions, on the one hand, and adaptive functions, on the other. Consider the idea that sexual motivation has evolved "to" promote reproduction. Several writers have erroneously taken this to imply that people must have evolved to pursue reproductive ends with strategic flexibility, and that evolutionists should therefore expect contraception to be eschewed unless it can be used as a means of allocating reproductive efforts to increase the numbers or improve the circumstances of one's young. By similar logic, voluntary childlessness and vasectomy have been cited as evidence against "the evolutionary hypothesis." But it should be obvious that evolved adaptations can be expected to be reproductively effective only in environments that are not crucially different from those in which the relevant history of natural selection took place (Symons 1990; Tooby and Cosmides 1990*b*). Thus, even a convincing demonstration that the innovation of modern contraception has left people blithely pursuing reproductively ineffectual objectives would in no way challenge the proposition that human sexuality is a complex psychological adaptation for the promotion of fitness.

The point here is that fitness plays a different role in evolutionary theory from the role that homeostasis or self-esteem or other monitored target states play in physiological and psychological theories. When the fitness consequences of behavior are invoked to explain it, they are properly invoked not as wants or goals but as explanations of why particular proximal objectives and motivators have evolved to play their particular roles in the causal control of behavior, and why they are calibrated as they are. When male birds continuously follow their mates closely during the breeding season, for example, ornithologists interpret the behavior as *mate-guarding* and its fitness-promoting function as *paternity assurance.* These interpretations have inspired many testable hypotheses about the contingent causal control of behavior: mate-guarding has been found to vary in relation to several cues of the onset of female fertility, and to vary in relation to the proximity, abundance, and attractiveness of male rivals, for example, while the male's success in keeping his mate under guard has been found to be predictive of his subsequent level of participation in the care of his putative offspring (Davies 1992; Møller 1994). These facts were discovered as a direct result of theorizing that the adaptive function of the mate-guarding psychology of male birds resides in paternity assurance, and yet the bird neither knows nor cares about paternity per se.

Genetic posterity or fitness can be deemed the superordinate "purpose" of evolved psychologies, then, so long as the implication of functionality without intentionality is understood. But what use is it to identify superordinate purpose in this way? The very generality of the idea that reproductive posterity is the distal function of all adaptations may make it seem uselessly vague. Commanded by Darwinian gods to go forth and multiply, a dutiful Eve might sensibly ask, "But how, exactly?" So let's analyze Eve's task, from the top down rather than from respiration, et cetera, up.

People are manufactured out of other substances, so Eve's task immediately resolves itself into two major subtasks: garner the resources necessary for reproduction and convert those resources into more people. Moreover, making "more people" doesn't mean just *any* people. The specific adaptive attributes favored by selection are necessarily those that have somehow effectuated their own proliferation relative to alternative attributes within the same population. Thus, the people whose survival and reproduction our minds and bodies have evolved to promote are our descendants and other blood relatives. Although people often find common cause and cooperate with nonrelatives, and although there is a body of evolutionary theorizing concerned with such "reciprocal altruism" (Trivers 1971; Alexander 1987), shared interests and solidarity are most readily attained and maintained among blood kin. Moreover, all the males in a population have always been engaged in a sort of zero-sum game for the paternal half of the ancestry of future generations, while the females were playing a parallel game for the maternal half.

These considerations put a different gloss on the "two major subtasks" mentioned earlier. What people and other creatures must have evolved to do is to be effective competitors in intrasexual competition for essential reproductive resources in the social and material environments of selection, and to be effective "nepotists" in those environments (Hamilton 1964). And what they have certainly not evolved to do is to promote "the reproduction of their species," as a prominent misunderstanding of natural selection would have it.

C. Groups Are Not Individuals

Social scientists have repeatedly promulgated theories in which various characteristics of individuals—intentions and preferences, ambivalences, health and pathology, homeostatic regulation, and so forth—are attributed to collectivities. An evolutionary perspective suggests that such theorizing constitutes a weak metaphor, at best.

Evolutionary psychology and behavioral ecology began to flower only after a common fallacy, dubbed "greater goodism" by Cronin (1991), was dispelled. For 100 years after Darwin, most biologists had uncritically assumed that natural selection equips animals with the shared purpose of "the reproduction of the species." This assumption was wrong (Williams 1966).

Natural selection is a matter of differential reproductive success, and it has consistently favored *those individual attributes most effective in out-reproducing alternative attributes within the same population.* The attributes that succeed by this criterion are not necessarily those that will best promote the population's welfare or persistence. Decades of theoretical and empirical work on "levels of selection" in biology (see, e.g., Dawkins 1982, 1986; Cronin 1991) have confirmed and clarified why the individual organism is the primary locus of complex integrated self-interest in the hierarchy of life. (The reason why the main locus of integrated self-interest does not reside at a level *below* that of the individual is that the expected fitnesses of an individual's organs or cells or genes are for the most part isomorphic with the whole organism's expected fitness, so selection favors those suborganismic elements that maximize this quantity at the organismic level. There are, however, important exceptions at the genetic level [see, e.g., Cosmides and Tooby 1981; Dawkins 1982; Haig 1993].)

Attempts to understand the behavior of societies, classes, cohorts, and other collectivities confront a special problem. The human mind is marvelously adept at constructing mental models of the agendas and likely actions of intentional agents like ourselves. We apparently owe this talent to an evolved psychological mechanism, our so-called theory-of-mind module (e.g., Leslie 1992; Premack and Premack 1995). This extremely sophisticated cognitive device infers the idiosyncratic details and interconnections of the beliefs, plans, and intentions of each person we have to deal with, on the basis of that person's known history of actions and on the default assumption that his or her mind is like our own in its elements and rules but not in its detailed contents. The theory-of-mind module is essential for normal social functioning, and insight into its workings has been gained partly from study of the severe disability of those in whom it is defective or lacking, namely, autistics (Baron-Cohen 1995). It is obviously enormously useful to be able to anticipate the actions of other people by consulting a model of how what they know and don't know, what they want, and what they believe will interact and affect their actions. An apparent byproduct of this useful talent, however, is a (usually harmless) tendency to misapply the same sort of thinking to entities that are not intentional agents, such as computers or cars or "society."

In Canada, we are treated to an example of this sort of fallacious thinking whenever there is a multiparty election in which no party wins a majority of the parliamentary seats. Pundits can be counted on to explain that a disgruntled or skeptical public, trusting none of the contending parties to govern fairly or effectively, has expressed its preference for a minority government instead. We hope that the spuriousness and obfuscation produced by reifying the "body politic" is transparent in this case. The mere fact of a split vote provides no evidence about disgruntlement, skepticism, or trust on the part of anyone nor does the election of a minority government necessarily correspond to anyone's preferred result.

Social scientists are not immune to this sort of fallacious thinking. Treating "the patriarchy" as a cohesive, intentional agent, for example, clarifies nothing about conflict and power relations between the sexes while obscuring the relevance of men's conflicts with one another to their inclinations to control their wives coercively (see Sec. VIII below). Other cases are subtler. Discussions of "social disorganization," for example, may invoke the capacity of large amorphous segments of society, such as classes or subcultures, to "regulate themselves," piling one weak metaphor on another. Genuine "regulation" of perturbations is an attribute only of systems with a unity of purpose, an attribute "designed into" the system either by natural selection or by an intentional agent. "Social pathology" is similarly metaphorical, for as noted above, a genuine pathology is something that compromises a functionally united entity's capacity to do what it evolved to do.

Individual organisms and their constituent parts have evolved to do many specific things, but collectivities above the level of the individual organism are not, in general, specifically organized to accomplish anything in particular (Williams 1966). Clubs, political parties, and other human organizations formed for common goals are conspicuous exceptions to this generalization. But classes, subcultures, and societies are not. Applying individual-level concepts like desire or preference or pathology to group-level entities whose unity of purpose does not approach that of individual organisms virtually guarantees that their causal dynamics will be misrepresented. When one speaks of what "society" encourages or what "the patriarchy" schemes to achieve, for example, one obscures the complexity of social processes and the ubiquity of conflicts of interest. This is not to say that groups qua groups have no properties worth talking about. But group-level properties are emergent and distinct from those of their constituent individuals. A society or polity or occupational group or class does not have preferences or intentions or pathologies. It has institutions, balances of power, a greater or lesser degree of consensus on each issue, and a certain distribution of wealth, among other things.

D. Evolutionary Psychology Is Not Behavior Genetics

As we noted earlier, psychological science is primarily concerned with the mechanisms and processes that all normal individuals share, and this is equally true of evolutionary psychology. It is a fact that individuals respond differently to identical environmental inputs from the earliest developmental stages, and that some of that diversity is due to genetic differences. However, the notion that such genetic diversity is of central interest to evolutionists is a misconception.

Behavior genetics is the scientific discipline concerned with analyzing the degree to which behavioral differences between individuals within populations can be traced to genetic differences. This field has been largely isolated from evolutionary psychology (and behavioral ecology and sociobiology), whose main concerns are mental mechanisms and processes that are shared by all normal individuals, generating behavioral variation as contingent response, both immediate and enduring (developmental), to social and other environmental variation (Crawford and Anderson 1989; Daly 1996).

Confusion on this point derives largely from a mistaken belief that evolutionary psychological hypotheses imply that one should be able to discover genes "for" generating the proposed adaptations. Geneticists are able to identify genes that code "for" an attribute when some individuals have the gene and the condition while others do not, that is, when the attribute is "heritable." An example is the rare MOA1 gene associated with impulsive violence, discovered by Brunner et al. (1993). However, the adaptations of interest to evolutionary psychologists are typically universal, and there is no reason to expect that there will be detectable heritable variation in their expression. Thus, although it is often asserted that hypotheses about evolved adaptations imply that heritability should be appreciable and demonstrable (e.g., Sussman, Cheverud, and Bartlett 1995), just the opposite is true. A substantial amount of heritable variation is prima facie evidence that the attribute under consideration is selectively neutral and hence not an adaptation at all (Falconer 1960). It is no accident, for example, that the variable attribute of our eyes that is most highly heritable, namely the color of the iris, plays no part in vision.

Perhaps evolutionary adaptationist hypotheses are so often misconstrued as hypotheses about behavior genetics because they invoke hypothetical genes "for" behavioral and psychological attributes in their theories. The point of such theorizing is not, however, to trace observed behavioral variation to genetic differences. Rather, population genetical models are used to address how selection would be expected to shape a given trait if minor, rare heritable variants were to arise (as they evidently do with respect to almost any quantifiable trait), and to predict what forms and magnitudes of the selected traits would be expected to become species-typical over evolutionary time. But since selection is constantly removing suboptimal variants (such as the deficient MOA1 gene that Brunner et al. [1993] found in a single human lineage), the residual heritable variation of any trait with important fitness effects is likely to be negligible.

Thus notwithstanding the genetical language, both theory and research in evolutionary psychology and behavioral ecology are directed toward the discovery of species-typical adaptations, and these are often expressed as contingent decision rules. For example, "mate-guarding" behavior varies among the mated males of a given bird species (and, no doubt, among human males as well), and this variation is intelligible as the product of a common psychology with contingent decision rules: the males respond to "bachelor pressure" as cued by one's encounter rate with lone males and to various other "risk" factors (e.g., Møller 1994). For this reason, environmental rather than genetic sources of behavioral variation provide the crucial tests of evolutionary psychological hypotheses (Crawford and Anderson 1989).

III. Who Victimizes Whom?

The preceding introductory overview is all the evolutionary psychology one needs to approach some criminological issues in a fresh way. An exemplary topic is family violence (Daly and Wilson 1988*a*).

According to current understandings of the evolution of social motives and behavior, the basic appetites, aversions, motives, emotions, and cognitive processes characteristic of any species, including *Homo sapiens*, have been shaped by natural selection to produce social action that is effectively "nepotistic": action that promotes the persistence of the actor's genetic elements in future generations by contributing to the survival and reproduction of the actor's genetic relatives. It follows that the basic psychological processes underlying solidarity and conflict in any social species should include processes that typically function to engender discriminative behavior in relation to genetic relatedness, and such processes indeed abound. Theory and research are in accord: other things being equal, cues that are ordinarily indicative of genetic relationship may be expected to mitigate animal conflict, and there is abundant evidence that they do (see, e.g., Hepper 1991).

In light of the ubiquity of nepotistic solidarity in the animal kingdom, some prevailing notions about intrafamilial conflict and violence in the human animal seem more than a little odd. Freudians would have us believe that the urge to kill one's father is a universal element of the human male psyche, and the claims of some family violence researchers are scarcely less astonishing. According to Gelles and Straus (1985, p. 88): "With the exception of the police and the military, the family is perhaps the most violent social group, and the home the most violent social setting, in our society. A person is more likely to be hit or killed in his or her home by another family member than anywhere else or by anyone else." To an evolutionary psychologist, these assertions are too surprising to escape critical scrutiny.

The first concept needing scrutiny is "family." Following Marvin Wolfgang (1958), homicide researchers have typically partitioned the victim-killer relationship into three categories: stranger, acquaintance, and relative. However, the third of these is far too general, encompassing relationships whose qualitative distinctions greatly surpass those distinguishing "strangers" from "acquaintances." The evolutionary psychological basis of the parent-child relationship, for example, is different from that characterizing the marital relationship since parent and child are genetic relatives with an indissoluble overlap in their fitness prospects whereas a comparable overlap in the expected fitness of marriage partners is predicated on reproduction and sexual fidelity. It follows that the specific potential sources of conflict in these two "family" relationships are utterly different, and the risk that conflict will become violent is vastly different, too (Daly and Wilson 1988*a*, 1988*b*).

In addition to calling prevailing taxonomies of relationship into question, these considerations raise the issue of "opportunities" for violence as a result of routine activity patterns. In the report of a U.S. presidential commission on "causes and prevention of violence," Goode (1969, p. 941) posed the question, "Why do intimates commit violence against one another?" and replied, "Perhaps the most powerful if crude answer is that they are there." This appeal to differential opportunity is true as far as it goes, but it begs the question of whether relationships are differentially risky when opportunity is controlled. Goode implies that they are not, especially if the concept of opportunity is extended to encompass the intensity of interaction as well as its frequency: "Moreover, again crudely but reasonably, we are violent toward our intimates—friends, lovers, spouses—because few others can anger us so much. As they are a main source of our pleasure, they are equally a main source of frustration and hurt." Is such an analysis adequate? Or do the distinct sorts of "intimate" relationships differ in ways that are not simply a matter of differential opportunity, as an evolutionary theoretical analysis of relationships would lead us to expect? (Suspicion should be aroused by the omission of "children" from Goode's list of "intimates." His words surely apply to them at least as much as to "friends," but perhaps the distinctive quality of parent-child intimacy is too obvious to ignore.)

One way to try to control for opportunity is to assess the incidence of violence between members of the same household, using information on the living arrangements of the population-at-large to specify the universe of potential victim-offender pairs. Daly and Wilson (1982) performed such an analysis of homicides in Detroit, with the results portrayed in figure 1. Clearly, Goode's analysis was *not* adequate. Coresiding persons who were not genetic relatives experienced a ho-

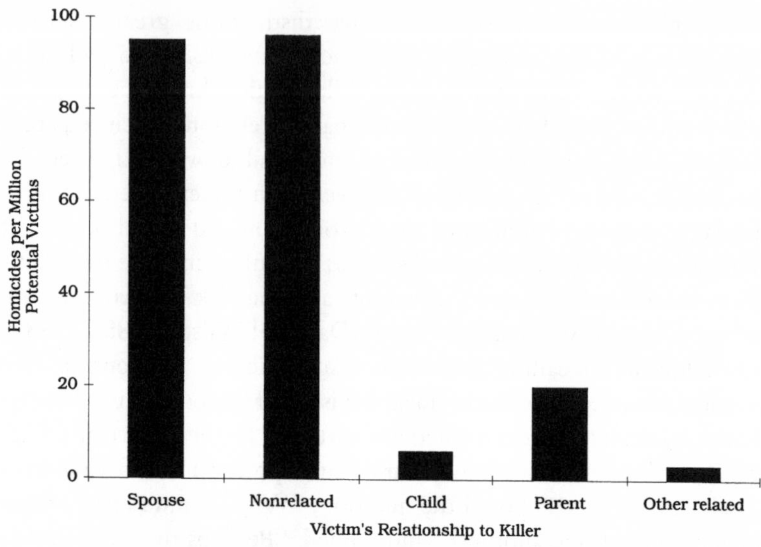

FIG. 1.—Rates of homicide in which victim and killer coresided in the same household in Detroit, 1972, by victim-killer relationship category. Note.—The 98 cases represent all solved within-household homicides known to the Detroit police. Denominators for rate determinations represent the numbers of coresiding dyads in the relevant category, in which the potential killer was an "adult" (age fourteen years or more) according to estimates from 1970 census information. "Parent" and "child" victims include steprelationships since these were not distinguishable from birth relationships in the household census data. Source.—Based on Daly and Wilson (1982).

micide rate more than eleven times greater than coresiding kin. Moreover, although so-called family homicide is seen to be mainly marital homicide, the risk incurred by other sorts of unrelated coresidents (roommates and boarders) was just as extreme and greatly exceeded the risk in more "intimate" family relationships, in apparent contradiction to Goode's invocation of intimates' special ability to evoke anger.

The more general points that figure 1 illustrates have been upheld in a variety of analyses of data from a variety of societies: kinship softens conflict, and the qualitative distinctions among relationships cannot be captured in simple dimensions like opportunity or intimacy (Daly and Wilson 1988*b*). The substance and intensity of conflicts are relationship-specific because particular social relationships—parent and child, spouses, unrelated friends, sexual rivals, and so forth—differ in their particular sources of potential and actual concordances and discrepancies in desired states of affairs.

Failures of reciprocation are common sources of conflict in virtually all relationships, for example, but not in the parent-child relationship, which is uniquely characterized by an unbegrudged one-way flow of resources. Instead, parent-offspring conflicts tend to revolve around an issue peculiar to that relationship, namely the allocation of parental resources among offspring (Trivers 1974); this insight predicts and explains much about the peculiar epidemiology of infanticide and other kinds of parentally perpetrated violence (Daly and Wilson 1988*a*, 1995). Other relationships have their characteristic conflicts, too. When men kill their brothers, the usual issue of contention is the partitioning of familial resources, whereas when they kill their brothers-*in-law*, other issues, especially the mistreatment of the person's sister by her husband, predominate (Daly and Wilson 1988*b*). And in violent marital conflict, the bones of contention, and hence the demographic risk markers, are different again (see Sec. VIII below).

IV. Sex Differences in Competition and Violence

Most lethal violence occurs not within the family but between unrelated acquaintances and strangers, and much of this violence arises in the context of competition for material goods and more intangible resources like face and status. Competition is predominantly a same-sex affair, and variations in rates of homicide involving unrelated same-sex persons can be considered a sort of assay of competition's local intensity (Daly and Wilson 1988*b*). Thus inequitable resource distribution obviously affects the local level of competition, and as we would expect, it is also a predictor of homicide rates (Krahn, Hartnagel, and Gartrell 1986; Hsieh and Pugh 1993), with same-sex nonrelative cases constituting the component of the homicide rate that varies most between times and places (Daly and Wilson 1988*b*). But whereas prevailing intensities of competition and gross rates of homicide are hugely variable in time and space, one difference is apparently universal: men kill unrelated men at vastly higher rates than women kill unrelated women, everywhere (see table 1).

Criminologists and other social scientists have offered a wide range of hypotheses to explain sex differences in the use of lethal violence. Unfortunately, most presuppose the psychic identity of the sexes and are clearly unsatisfactory. Many writers have attributed men's greater use of violence to some local aspect of one or another particular society, providing no candidate explanation for the phenomenon's cross-cultural generality (see Daly and Wilson 1988*b*, pp. 149–61). Others have invoked men's greater size and strength, but while this asymmetry

TABLE 1

Numbers of Same-Sex Homicides in Which Victim and Killer Were Unrelated: Various Studies

Location/Society	Periods of Study	Male	Female
Chicago	1965–81	7,439	195
Detroit	1972	316	11
Miami	1980	358	0
Canada	1974–83	2,387	59
England and Wales	1977–86	2,195	95
Scotland	1953–74	143	5
Iceland	1946–70	7	0
A Mayan village (Mexico)	1938–65	15	0
Bison-Horn Maria (India)	1920–41	36	1
Munda (India)		34	0
Oraon (India)		26	0
Bhil (India)	1971–75	50	1
Tiv (Nigeria)	1931–49	74	1
BaSoga (Uganda)	1952–54	38	0
Gisu (Uganda)	1948–54	44	2
BaLuyia (Kenya)	1949–54	65	3
Banyoro (Uganda)	1936–55	9	1
JoLuo (Kenya)	1949	22	2
Alur (Uganda)	1945–54	33	1
!Kung San (Botswana)	1920–55	12	0

NOTE.—Data are from Daly and Wilson (1990), who included both original tabulations and every published study that they were able to find meeting the following criteria: (1) that the data set comprise all homicides known to have occurred in a given jurisdiction rather than a selected subset and (2) that same-sex, nonrelative cases be identifiable. Victim and killer were unrelated cowives of a polygynous man in the single female-female case in each of the Maria, Bhil, Banyoro, and Alur data sets, as well as in one BaLuyia case and one JoLuo case; cowives were not deemed marital "relatives," because their relationship is analogous to that of unrelated male rivals, and hence were included.

may be relevant to differential use of violence against the opposite sex, it can hardly be said to predict or account for the sex difference portrayed in table 1; one might as readily have predicted that the group with the physical capacity to inflict the most damage (i.e., men) would be attacked least. What is too often missing from discussions of gendered behavior, including even those treatments that invoke "biological" (by which is usually meant hormonal) differences between the sexes, is any consideration of the different selection pressures confronting our male versus our female ancestors. When the zero-sum game that partitions paternal ancestry among males is played with different rules or parameters than the corresponding game among females, the selective process favors different attributes, including psychological attributes, in the two sexes.

Sex-differential violence against same-sex antagonists appears to be one of many manifestations of the fact that the human male psyche has evolved to be more risk-accepting in competitive situations than the female psyche (Wilson and Daly 1985; Daly and Wilson 1990, 1994*b*). Our sex difference in intrasexual violence is one we share with other species in which the variance in fitness (and the risk of complete reproductive failure) is greater among males than among females. The morphological, physiological, developmental, and psychological evidence that human beings evolved under chronic circumstances of a somewhat greater fitness variance in males than in females is abundant and consistent, and this sex difference in fitness variance apparently persists across the gamut of human societies (Daly and Wilson 1983). In hunting and gathering societies, which provide the best model of the social circumstances in which the human psyche's characteristics evolved, there is less disparity of wealth than in agricultural societies or modern nation states and marriage is mainly monogamous, but it is still the case that men are both more likely to have many surviving children than women and more likely to have none (Howell 1979; Hewlett 1988; Hill and Hurtado 1995). The natural selective link between such a mating system and sex differences in competitive violence is well understood and uncontroversial (Williams 1966; Trivers 1972; Daly and Wilson 1988*b*): basically, greater fitness variance selects for greater acceptance of risk in the pursuit of scarce means to the end of fitness. Furthermore, reckless life-threatening risk-proneness is especially likely to evolve where opting out of competition promises to yield no fitness at all and is therefore the natural selective equivalent of death (e.g., Rubin and Paul 1979).

This sketch of sex differences in competitiveness and violence and their evolutionary origins is not the last word on the subject, and we fully expect to see it developed in now unanticipated directions. However, it has essentially no chance of being drastically overturned, both because it is too well established in a nexus of coherent theory and supportive research, and because it is fully consistent with whatever facts the several disciplines that have concerned themselves with the sexes have been able to establish. This last criterion of what makes a theory tenable may seem hardly worth stating, for who would cling to a theory whose premises or predictions have been proven false? Alas, criminologists have sometimes done just that. Hagan's (1986, 1990) "power-control theory" of sex differences, for example, is explicitly premised on the behaviorist presumption that females and males react identically to contingencies and develop their differences only as a result of differential social treatment, although this presumption has long been rejected by those who study human sex differences and their development in childhood. There is remarkably little evidence that girls and boys *are* socialized differently with respect to such things as punishment or encouragement, despite hundreds of attempts to demonstrate such parental discrimination (Lytton and Romney 1991), but in a sense that is neither here nor there.

Regardless of whether sex-role socialization is a powerful force or an overrated one, it is clear that girls and boys *differ* in how they are affected by the *same* variations in experience (e.g., Bee et al. 1984; Flinn et al. 1996), even on the day of birth (e.g., Balogh and Porter 1986). This is hardly surprising given that the brains of human females and males differ in numerous anatomical and physiological details as a result of the effects of gonadal hormones at developmental stages ranging from before birth into adulthood (de Lacoste, Horvath, and Woodward 1991; Witelson 1991; Breedlove 1994; Gur et al. 1995). Moreover, besides their developmental ("organizing") influences, circulating levels of sex-typical hormones have a wide range of immediate ("activating") effects on emotion, mood, and cognition (e.g., Kimura and Hampson 1994; Sherwin 1994; Vangoozen et al. 1995).

For all these reasons, any theory that attributes sex differences merely to sex-biased treatment is a nonstarter. This is certainly not to say that "nature" triumphs over "nurture," a claim that is as simplistic and counterproductive as the reverse. The attributes of women and men and the magnitude and nature of their differences can undoubtedly be changed by a host of environmental manipulations, some odious, some justifiable. What is clear, however, is that the developmental processes by which the sexes come to exhibit psychological and behavioral differences in adulthood are much more intricate and interesting than the obsolete but enduring notion that differential socialization tells the tale. And thinking about how the selection pressures encountered by ancestral women and men are likely to have differed has proven to be a valuable aid to those interested in characterizing and explaining sex differences (e.g., Gaulin and Hoffman 1988; Daly and Wilson 1990; Buss et al. 1992; Symons 1995).

V. The Age-Crime Relationship

There is an age pattern in criminal violence that is almost as robust as the sex difference: rates of offending rise rapidly after puberty to a peak in young adulthood and then decline more slowly. Figure 2 illustrates this pattern with respect to same-sex nonrelative homicides in Canada, England and Wales, and Chicago.

Challenging the criminological community to explain this striking pattern, Hirschi and Gottfredson (1983, p. 554) asserted that "the age distribution of crime is invariant across social and cultural conditions," and that "the age distribution of crime cannot be accounted for by any variable or combination of variables currently available to criminology." A flurry of critical reactions ensued, including some unconvincing efforts to explain the pattern on the basis of received wisdom. Tittle (1988), for example, argued that the old standbys of "labeling theory" and "social control theory" could account for the age pattern perfectly well, but unfortunately, Gove (1985) had used the same "labeling theory" as Tittle to deduce precisely the opposite—that offending should increase throughout the life span. Arguably, what Tittle's and other ripostes to Hirschi and Gottfredson really show is that "labeling theory," "social control theory," "strain theory," and the like are not predictive theories at all but conceptual frameworks that one might cheerfully invoke in discussing the data however the chips might fall.

In our view, a more promising line of theory treats criminal offending as risk acceptance and treats life-span developmental change as adaptive modulation of risk acceptance. Wilson and Herrnstein (1985) have argued, with considerable evidentiary support, that engaging in predatory violence and other risky criminal activity is associated with having a short "time-horizon," such that one weighs the near future relatively heavily against the long term. The link with age has been illuminated by Rogers (1994), who has shown that life-span developmental changes in such time-horizons (more specifically, in the rates at which one "discounts" the future) are predictable products of natural selection. More remarkably, Rogers (1994) has predicted the expected form of evolved age patterns in time discounting on the sole basis of characteristic human schedules of age-specific fertility and mortality, and his predicted curve looks a lot like the "age-crime curve."

Three years after their initial salvo, Hirschi and Gottfredson (1986) expanded on their claim of an "invariant" age pattern in criminal offending. They argued that the observed age-crime relationship could not be attributed to a correlated factor of employment status, on the basis of evidence that working and nonworking teenagers incur similar arrest rates. They further denied that acquiring a mate is relevant to

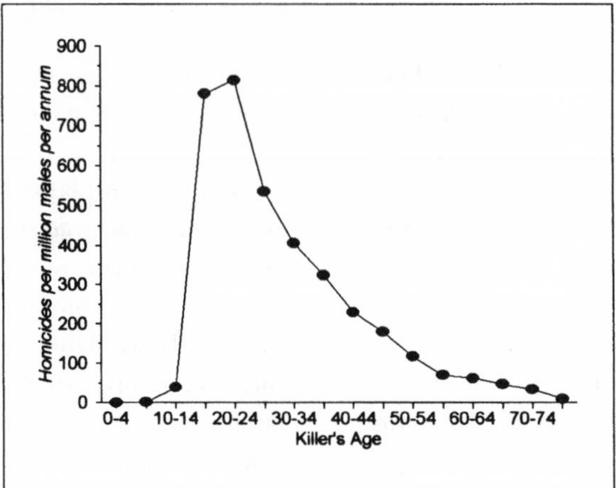

a, Chicago, 1965–89

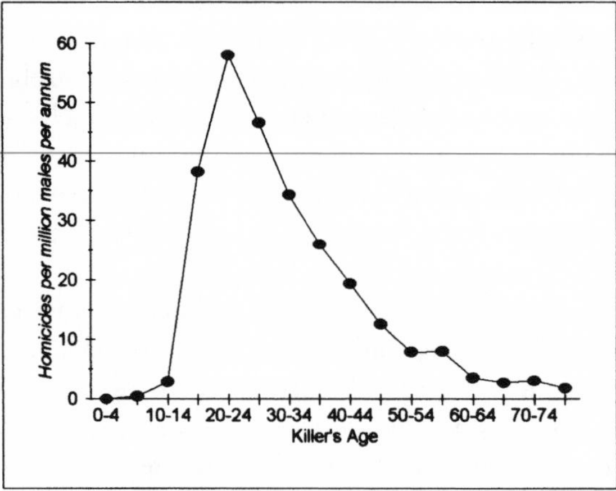

b, Canada, 1974–92

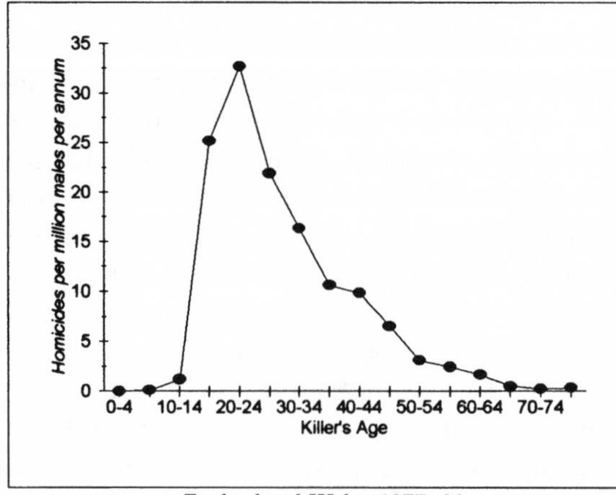

c, England and Wales, 1977–90

Fig. 2.—Age-specific rates at which males killed unrelated males in three data sets consisting of all homicides known to police. Source.—Based on Wilson and Daly (1994).

the adult diminution in offending, on the basis of evidence that delinquent boys are more, not less, likely to have girlfriends than their nondelinquent age-mates. And they denied that becoming a father plays any role either, although on this point they presented no evidence at all. They concluded that "change in crime with age apparently cannot be explained . . . by change in the social situation of people over the course of life" (1986, p. 67).

This argument is as provocative to evolutionary psychologists as to sociologists. If such psychological phenomena as "risk acceptance" and "time discounting" indeed mediate the age-crime curve and have been shaped by natural selection, we should expect them to be contingently responsive to social and material cues. Granted that Rogers's (1994) model suggests that an evolved schedule of life-span developmental change in time discounting might be manifest as age-related change in behavior even if social and material circumstances could be held constant. And granted, too, that young men are apparently specialized, both physically and psychologically, for competitive risk acceptance; male muscle strength and aerobic capacity, for example, rise and fall in a pattern rather like that of the age-crime curve, even when effects of exercise are controlled, and various sorts of voluntary risk-taking rise and fall similarly (review by Daly and Wilson 1990). Granting all that, it still does not follow that risk acceptance should have evolved to follow its life-span trajectory utterly unaffected by circumstantial cues of risk's costs and benefits. A married father, for example, has more to lose (and perhaps less to gain) in dangerous confrontations than does a childless bachelor of the same age, and we can think of no reason to imagine that the human psyche should have evolved to ignore such differences of personal circumstance.

So is Hirschi and Gottfredson's (1986) claim that changing social circumstances are irrelevant to the age-crime curve correct? Well, it is certainly overstated. In homicide, both employment status and marital status are indeed poor predictors of offense rates by teenagers, but they are very good predictors at subsequent ages (Wilson and Daly 1985; Daly and Wilson 1990). Figure 3 illustrates this point with respect to marital status, and as we predicted on evolutionary psychological grounds, being married is apparently pacifying. The hypothesis that being married reduces men's inclination to engage in violently dangerous risk-taking, rather than being an incidental correlate of other risk factors, is further supported by the finding that both divorced and widowed men exhibit elevated age-specific homicide rates like those of

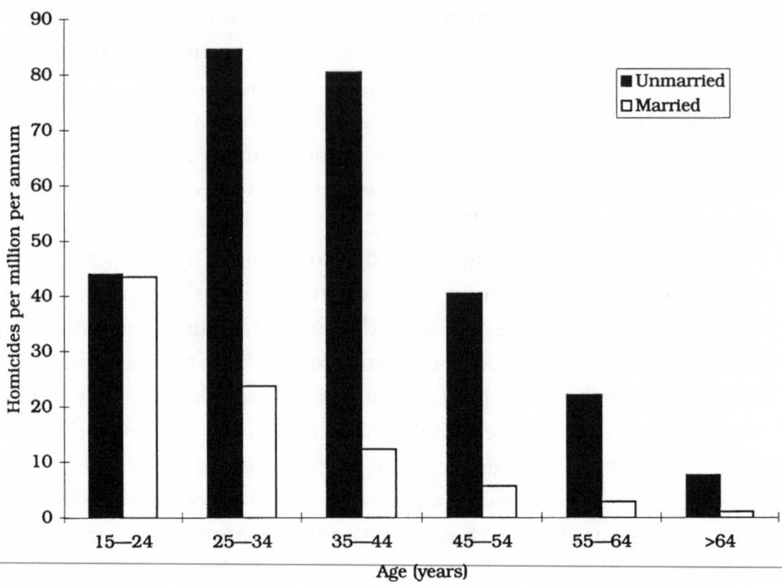

a

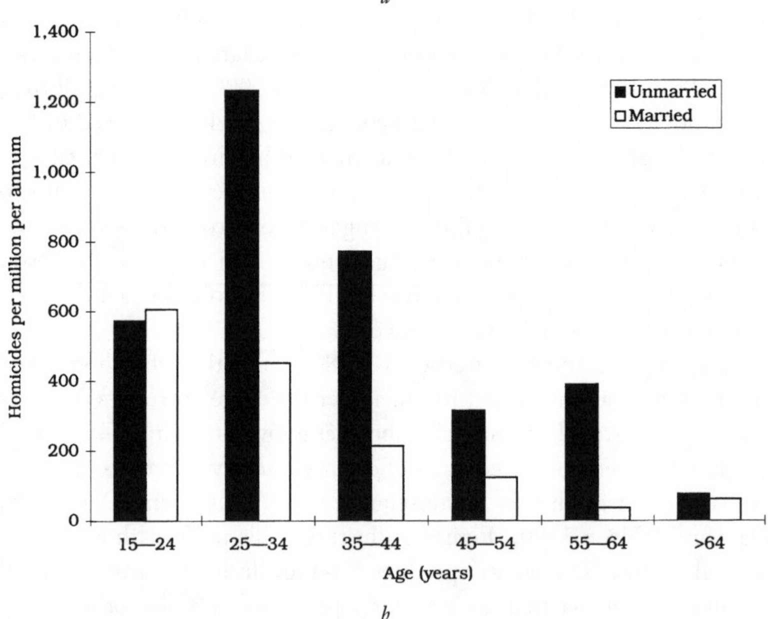

b

Fig. 3.—Age-specific rates of killing unrelated males by married men versus unmarried men in Canada in 1974–83 and Detroit in 1972. *a*, Canada; *b*, Detroit. Source.—Based on Daly and Wilson (1990).

never-married men (Daly and Wilson 1990). This and similar evidence with respect to nonlethal criminal offending (Kposowa, Singh, and Breault 1994; Farrington and West 1995) suggests that men who revert to unmarried status also revert to a mindset vis à vis risk acceptance that is more like that of bachelors than that of married men.

Marital status evidently matters, then. However, massive age effects persist in figure 3, and the same is true when one controls for the substantial effects of employment status (Wilson and Daly 1985). Rogers's (1994) theory of an evolved trajectory of life-span developmental change in discounting provides some reason to doubt that the age-crime relationship would disappear altogether even if one were to control for all relevant age-related changes in circumstances simultaneously. However, no such analysis is at present feasible, and no one knows how *much* of the age-related variability in crime will eventually prove to be attributable to age-related changes in social and material circumstances. What is already clear is that it must be a large fraction of the total.

There is irony in this story. Hirschi and Gottfredson proposed on the basis of limited evidence that the age-crime relationship is impervious to social factors and attributed it by default to "biology." But "biological" is not the antithesis of "social," quite the contrary, since social factors are the crucial proximate causes of behavioral variations in biological theories of social action. It was biological theorizing that made us suspicious of Hirschi and Gottfredson's claims: It seemed inconceivable that a social psyche that evolved by selection should be insensitive to such important modulators of one's cost-benefit situation as marital and employment statuses. And our selection-minded skepticism about Hirschi and Gottfredson's claims has proven to be sound.

VI. Evolutionary Psychology and "Rational Choice"

Rogers's (1994) future-discounting theory indicates that youthful risk-proneness and disdain for the future are predictable products of natural selection. One might call them "rational," which is not to say that we or most readers of this essay would deem them sensible. A rational choice makes sense given the actor's personal utilities, and as Gardner (1993, p. 71) notes, "The rational choice theory is not concerned with how people process information, and no-one claims that people make everyday choices by assigning numbers to outcomes and calculating utilities. The claim is that an outsider observing a sufficiently consistent pattern of choices could find numbers describing the person's values that would rationalize the choices." Nevertheless, hypotheses invoking "rational choice" are often marred, perhaps especially in economics and in criminology, by the theorists' uncritical adoption of a folk psychological conception of rationality and decision. A more subtle evolutionary psychological conception would better reflect the diversity of processes that mediate choices among behavioral alternatives and would be a boon to criminological discussion.

Evolutionists routinely model the costs and benefits of alternative decision rules about such matters as how many eggs a bird should lay before she begins incubating them, or when a plant or animal should stop channeling all its accrued energy into further growth and start putting some into reproduction. These determinations are aptly termed "decisions" insofar as they are complexly contingent on environmentally given information that imperfectly but usefully predicts relevant future conditions. To everyday folk psychology, this sounds like a metaphor, and perhaps a rather stretched metaphor at that. Genuine decisions are surely the products of deliberation by conscious human beings. Unfortunately for this folk conception, however, experimental psychologists have demonstrated repeatedly that people do not necessarily enjoy privileged insight into the determinants of their own decisions, and that the phenomenology of deliberation and reasoned choice can be illusory and reconstructive. Psychology experiments in which the causal determinants of some phenomenon or experience have been controlled by the experimenter elicit explanations from observers and from the decision makers themselves that are coherent and plausible but demonstrably incorrect (Nisbett and Wilson 1977; Nisbett and Ross 1980; Kahneman, Slovic, and Tversky 1982). For example, people might give an elaborate explanation for why they liked one film sequence more than another, when in fact their preferences were best accounted for by white noise levels manipulated by the experimenter. Moreover, in addition to leading us to misperceive the reasons for our actions, retrospective "theorizing" leads us to misrecall our pasts, sometimes dramatically (e.g., Ross 1989; Newman and Baumeister 1996).

The implication of these findings is certainly not that human decision making and the inferential procedures that inform it are inept, as has sometimes been implied. Our inference and choice procedures apparently deal with naturalistic inputs very well (Gigerenzer and Hoffrage 1995; Cosmides and Tooby 1996). Rather, the point we mean to stress is that neither decision processes themselves nor their logic and functionality are necessarily transparent to introspection. A great deal of inaccessible information processing by complex evolved machinery, designed by selection specifically to make such decisions, is involved.

This complex evolved machinery includes the emotions. Emotional states are functional operating modes whose specific elements are design features facilitating effective responses to the situations that arouse them (deSousa 1987; Frank 1988; Nesse 1990). An admonition like "don't get mad, get even" is therefore grounded in confusion: getting mad is a means to the end of getting even. If it were generally (or on average) the case that fear, anger, jealousy, and other emotional states interfered with our capacities to make decisions that furthered our interests, then we would have evolved to be affectless zombies. That we have not is testimony to the functionality of emotional states, as is the incapacity of people whose emotional mechanisms are operating abnormally (Nesse 1990).

Folk psychology's contrasting of reason versus emotion is thus a false antithesis, and it is an antithesis that has sown some mischief in criminology. Cusson's (1993) otherwise admirable discussion of the importance of fear during the commission of crimes, for example, is weakened by his conceiving of this emotional state simply as an impediment to decisive action rather than as an aid to prudent choice. And Katz's (1988) refreshingly novel treatise on the neglected thrills of crime commission is ultimately unenlightening because of its unsatisfactory framing as a challenge to rational choice theories.

Once the complexity of the psychological machinery generating even our "rational" choices is acknowledged, it no longer seems odd to speak of a physiological decision about when to ovulate, or to refer to choice points in growth and development, using the same language that we apply to the process that selects among behavioral options. In all these cases, some elaborate and only partially understood procedure, involving evolved information-processing machinery, the traces of individual experience, and contemporary extrinsic inputs, generates one choice rather than another. And if the deliberative homunculus of folk psychology seems not to be involved in deciding how much you will let your bone calcium be depleted during lactation, well, he contributes nothing toward a genuine explanation of how you decide what to eat or what to wear, either.

Consider, in this light, Gottfredson and Hirschi's (1990) critique of Wilson and Herrnstein (1985), whom they accused of embracing incommensurable ideas about crime and criminality. The latter authors had argued that delinquents are particularly apt to discount future consequences, a proposition that Gottfredson and Hirschi endorsed. But these critics maintained that Wilson and Herrnstein must then repudiate the "strain theory" that they allegedly also accept, in which "the potential delinquent looks into the future and sees dismal prospects. As a consequence, he turns to a life of crime designed to brighten these prospects. In other words, in strain theory the delinquent is especially future oriented as compared to the nondelinquent" (p. 114). According to Gottfredson and Hirschi, discounting the future is the antithesis of responding to one's prospects, dismal or otherwise. But to an evolutionary psychologist, predictive cues of dismal prospects are precisely the sorts of cues that would be expected to engender such discounting.

Continuing in the same vein, Gottfredson and Hirschi (1990) attack another ostensible contradiction in Wilson and Herrnstein's theorizing as follows: "The idea that offenders are likely to be concerned with equity is also contrary to the notion that they more heavily discount time: equity concerns, as described by Wilson and Herrnstein, require that the person compare his effort/reward ratio with the effort/reward ratios of others. . . . people who feel inequitably treated must have put forth the effort that justifies their feelings (otherwise we would be talking about envy). But people who discount the future do not exert themselves for uncertain future benefits, and the notion of inequity at the point of crime is therefore incompatible with the image of the offender at the point of criminality" (p. 114). One need not embrace Wilson and Herrnstein's analysis to recognize that these criticisms implicitly rely on a folk psychological conception of conscious deliberation. A young man need not engage in melancholy future-oriented contemplation to apprehend cues of dismal prospects, nor to increase his acceptance of risk in response. Indeed, we could substitute an insect, or a tree, for the young man in the last sentence. Folk conceptions of how it feels to deliberate about what to do next are superfluous distractions. The essential theoretical idea is adaptive adjustment of risk acceptance in response to relevant cues. Similarly, one need hardly cogitate about the future to be passionately concerned with equity, as is evident to any parent with two or more children (see Frank 1985).

One sort of information that ought to affect discounting of the future is information bearing on the likelihood that one *has* a future. Reason to doubt that you'll be alive tomorrow is reason to grab what you can today. Under rational choice, an increase in mortality in one's reference group increases the appeal of risky action in pursuit of quick returns, especially if the sources of that excess mortality are independent of the actors' choices. But what sort of evidence would bear on such risk adjustment? One possibility is some sort of semistatistical apprehension of the distribution of local life spans. This need not be so complex as it sounds. If both grandfathers of a young man were dead before he was born, and more than a couple of his primary school classmates are already dead too, and gray-haired men stand out in his neighborhood by virtue of their rarity, there may be something going on that he should attend to.

VII. Making Sense of Individual Differences

We have stressed that psychological theory and research have been more concerned with human nature than with human diversity (see also Monahan and Splane 1980). Nevertheless, such diversity exists and demands explanation. Much of it, but not all, depends on the contingent responsiveness of the psyche to differences in circumstance. In explaining and predicting the behavior of others, ordinary people rely on what they think they know about stable personal characteristics—whether someone is fair-minded or jealous or short-tempered or whatever—because such attributions appear to carry useful information about the reasons for past actions and the likelihoods of future actions. These imputations can be excessive or misguided, but the strategy is basically sound: stable individual differences really do account for a substantial proportion of behavioral diversity.

Why this should be so is a challenging question for evolutionists (Tooby and Cosmides 1990*a;* Buss 1991; Daly 1996). If selection favors an optimal species-typical design, what maintains such diversity? Why, for example, is variation in violent aggressivity largely a matter of personalities? Why should selection not have favored the single fittest available set of social psychological propensities, with the result that everyone's behavioral repertoire would include facultative violence in more or less similar response to more or less the same threats and challenges?

A partial answer is that people probably *are* alike in this regard to a much greater extent than is initially evident. Although people react differently to the same immediate situation, there may be greater consistency at the level of facultative developmental response to experiential contingencies. Certainly it is a fact that expertise based on experience makes violence more available as a social tool (e.g., Coie et al. 1991), and this makes sense insofar as expertise in the use of violence raises its effectiveness. Moreover, the information that is relevant for decision making in dangerous confrontations has greater time depth than just the immediate situation: how short one's temper "should" ideally be, for example, depends on statistical attributes of one's social milieu that can be induced only from cumulative experience over a long time (if at all). There is thus every reason to expect "personality" differences in how people react to a common immediate situation, even if their psyches respond to experience in exactly the same way.

There is considerable evidence that readiness to use violence is indeed developmentally labile, and some of this evidence suggests that this developmental lability may be functional for the actors in the manner just suggested. In a cross-cultural analysis of nonstate societies, Low (1989) has shown that it is specifically in societies that have repeatedly engaged in war in their recent history that parents and others inculcate aggressivity, strength, skilled use of weapons, and tolerance of pain in boys. In Western industrialized nations such as the United States, there is some evidence that people with childhood experience of violence, whether as victims or as witnesses, are likely to use violence (Widom 1989; Dodge, Bates, and Pettit 1990). Longitudinal studies of juvenile delinquents and career criminals reveal a prior history of various social transgressions including violence (e.g., Tonry, Ohlin, and Farrington 1991; Sampson and Laub 1993).

Psychiatrists have identified a personality type that is particularly likely to engage in violent aggressivity: the "antisocial personality." Diagnostic criteria include a history of conduct disorder prior to age fifteen and a continued pattern of "disregard for and violation of the rights of others" into adulthood (American Psychiatric Association 1994, p. 649). There are apparently a number of reliable risk factors associated with the development and maintenance of antisocial personality, including poverty, maleness, early maturity, poor school performance, parental criminal history, and psychopathology, and having a lone mother in loco parentis (e.g., Tonry, Ohlin, and Farrington 1991; Moffitt 1993). These risk factors largely overlap the risk factors for juvenile delinquency and violent crime (e.g., Wilson and Herrnstein 1985; Farrington 1991; Sampson and Laub 1993), and juvenile offenders and career criminals are indeed often diagnosed as antisocial personalities (Olweus, Block, and Radke-Yarrows 1986; Moffitt 1993). Moreover, these same risk factors characterize many urban communities with high rates of violence (Krahn, Hartnagel, and Gartrell 1986; Sampson 1991; Coulton et al. 1995). All of these considerations suggest that this "disorder" is largely a facultative developmental response to indicators of the futility of developing a more "prosocial" personality. (Which is not to deny that persons diagnosed with antisocial personality disorder are often dysfunctional. Insofar as the diagnosis is not merely pejorative, the individuals most likely to be so diagnosed may be those in whom the psychological mechanisms regulating violent behavior are not appropriately modulated by relevant context-specific cues because of "errors" in information-processing; see Dodge, Price, and Bachorowski 1990).

Notwithstanding the likely relevance of social environments to antisocial personality, there is also considerable evidence from twin and adoption studies that it is substantially heritable (Carey 1994; Gottesman and Goldsmith 1994; Lyons 1996). Hence the question raised earlier remains: why does genetic variability affecting traits like antisocial personality persist? Behavior geneticists have seldom considered their findings in the context of Darwinian selection, so the question has scarcely been addressed (but see Rowe 1994).

Possible answers to this puzzle appear to be few. One is that selection has been weak and the variability is (or was) effectively neutral with respect to fitness. This is perhaps especially plausible when the attributes in question develop as interactive products of particular genotypes and particular novel aspects of current environments. Sensitivity to novel chemical pollutants, for example, can be highly heritable, but the differential sensitivity of different genotypes will have been inconsequential in ancestral environments in which those chemicals did not exist. A second possibility is that selection pressures are heterogeneous in time, space, or both, so that no single optimal phenotype can become universal across the population's whole range of environments. Finally, perhaps the most interesting possibility in the present context is that of *frequency-dependent selection.*

A set of alternative types is said to incur frequency-dependent selection when their respective fitnesses vary systematically in relation to their relative numbers. In some animals, for example, there is a "rare male mating advantage" (Ehrman 1972) such that females prefer as mates whichever of two varieties of male is rarer in the local population, with the result that the rarer type outreproduces the commoner and neither is likely to go extinct. Mealey (1995) and accompanying commentaries discuss the possibility that "sociopaths"—an exploitative and often charming personality type, apparently lacking empathy—might be maintained analogously in human populations, with their success as deceivers tending to be inversely correlated with their prevalence.

It is theoretically possible that heritable diversity in violent aggressivity has been maintained in human populations by frequency-dependent selection, but we think it is unlikely. The routine occurrence of specialized warrior castes throughout human history (McCarthy 1993) may sound consistent with the idea that selection could have maintained multiple male types, but there is no particular reason to believe that the fitness benefits of being a warrior have been inversely related to their proportionate abundance. Furthermore, the degree of individual variability in violent experience and action that we see in contemporary mass society may be an evolutionary novelty because in the sort of nonstate societies in which we evolved, virtually all men were likely to have had sporadic experience of life-threatening interpersonal violence (Chagnon 1996). Heritable variation in violence in the modern world could thus be analogous to heritable variation in sensitivity to novel pollutants: a sort of previously neutral genetic diversity with novel expression.

VIII. Violence against Wives

Most of the criminal violence that we have considered thus far is perpetrated in the context of competition among men for material and social resources. But men also commit violence against women, including even their marriage partners. This sort of violence against "intimates" requires a different analysis. Wilson and Daly (1992*a*, 1993*a*) have proposed that violence against wives is largely to be understood as a reflection of sexually differentiated mental mechanisms of *sexual proprietariness*, which evolved in an ancestral social milieu in which assaults and threats functioned to deter wives from pursuing courses of action that threatened their husbands' fitness. The cognitive/emotional mental "module" of male sexual proprietariness responds to cues indicative of a risk of usurpation of the valued sexual relationship by rivals, cues that vary from indirect probabilistic indicators of such risk to irrefutable evidence.

As with other sorts of interpersonal conflicts, we can treat the relatively rare phenomenon of lethal violence against wives as a window on the broader phenomenon of marital conflict. This is not to suggest that uxoricides serve the killers' interests. We propose, instead, that they are epiphenomena: nonadaptive byproducts of masculine psychological processes, which evolved because of the utilities of their nonlethal manifestations. Neither do we suggest that man's violent capabilities and inclinations evolved in the specific context of marital conflict since violence and threat are effective means of coercive control in various relationships and contexts. However, by proposing that uxoricides are epiphenomena of male motives whose functions are coercion and deterrence, we do mean to imply that lethal and nonlethal violence against wives share commonalities of motive, of causal dynamics, of circumstance, of marital history, and of factors that exacerbate or mitigate the severity and frequency of assaults. This implication is for the most part supported by comparisons between uxoricide and nonlethal wife assault (Wilson, Johnson, and Daly 1995).

The ostensible motive in the majority of uxoricides is the husband's aggrieved intolerance of the real or imagined alienation of his wife, either through adultery or through her quitting the marriage. Daly and Wilson (1988*b*) reviewed several studies of well-described spousal homicide cases from a diversity of societies, and in each sample, such sexual proprietariness was apparently the primary motivational factor in over 80 percent of the cases; see also Allen (1990), Mahoney (1991), Campbell (1992*a*), Crawford and Gartner (1992), and Polk (1994). In studies of nonlethal violence against wives, ostensible rationales are more diverse than in the lethal cases, but the dominant motive is apparently the same. When asked what are the primary issues around which violent incidents occurred, both beaten wives and their assailants nominate "jealousy" above all else (Rounsaville 1978; Dobash and Dobash 1979, 1984; Brisson 1983).

The idea that the discovery of wifely infidelity is an exceptional provocation, which is likely to elicit a violent rage, is cross-culturally ubiquitous, perhaps universal (Daly and Wilson 1988*b*). Indeed, such a rage is widely considered so compelling as to mitigate the responsibility of violent cuckolds. In Anglo-American common law, for example, killing upon the discovery of a wife's adultery has been deemed to be the act of a "reasonable man" and to warrant a reduced penalty (Edwards 1954). Violent sexual jealousy is considered normal or at least unsurprising both in societies in which the cuckold's violence is seen as a reprehensible loss of control (e.g., Dell 1984) and in those where it is seen as a praiseworthy redemption of honor (e.g., Safilios-Rothschild 1969; Besse 1989; Chimbos 1993). While one may interpret these phenomena as indicative of the cross-cultural ubiquity of misogyny and patriarchy, such interpretations beg the question of the sources of the specific content of violent men's perceived grievances. Men are apparently much less likely to assault their wives for profligacy or stupidity or sloth, and they cannot invoke these failings as provocations in the courtroom. In fact, the only provocations that are invested with the same power as wifely adultery to mitigate a killer's criminal responsibility in our common-law tradition are physical assaults upon himself or a relative (see, e.g., Dressler 1982).

Granting the motivational relevance of jealousy to transitory rages and hence to the violent incidents themselves, however, one may still ask whether those husbands who are especially proprietary and controlling are also the husbands who are especially violent. Battered women often maintain that not only are their husbands violently jealous about interactions with other men, but that they are so controlling as to curtail the wives' contacts even with female friends and family (e.g., Hilberman and Munson 1978). In a 1993 survey, a national probability sample of over 12,000 Canadian women were asked about their experiences of sexual harassment, threats, and sexual and physical violence by marital partners and other men (Johnson and Sacco 1995). Those women whose husbands had assaulted them physically were especially likely to also affirm that their husbands engaged in various autonomy-limiting behaviors such as insisting on knowing the woman's whereabouts at all times, objecting to and curtailing social interactions outside the home, and exerting unilateral control on the family finances (Wilson, Johnson, and Daly 1995). The more serious the assaults, the more prevalent were these other controlling behaviors, so it appears that especially proprietary, controlling husbands are often also especially violent husbands.

Rather than wife assault being one of a set of alternative tactics of proprietary men, then, assault goes hand in hand with other means of control. There are undoubtedly stable individual differences ("personality" differences) between men in this regard, but much of the intrasocietal diversity in these correlated manifestations of male sexual proprietariness represents contingent response to circumstantial variables such as the parties' ages, material resources, and other considerations that are readily interpreted as valid indicators to the proprietary man of risk of loss of his wife (Wilson, Daly, and Wright 1993; Wilson, Johnson, and Daly 1995).

Violence against wives varies systematically between as well as within societies, and an evolutionary psychological perspective can shed light on both sorts of variability. Wherever social cues likely to activate male sexual proprietariness are salient, recurring, and prevalent, we may expect to see a high incidence of its manifestations. Jealousy and anger are linked in male sexual psychology, suggesting that cues of imminent threat of loss of sexual exclusivity entail some risk of violence everywhere (Daly and Wilson 1988*b*), but the prevalence and intensity of such violence may be expected to reflect local sanctions. Moreover, the target of a jealous man's ire may be the woman, the rival, or both, and again, this "decision" may be expected to reflect sanctions, as well as the social status of each party and the circumstances of the alleged trespass.

Some phenomena, such as age-related changes in fertility, are cross-culturally general and likely to account for within-society variability in more or less consistent ways; men are probably more jealous of wives who are young and attractive to other men than of older wives in all societies (Wilson and Daly 1993*a;* Wilson, Daly, and Scheib 1997). Moreover, a man is vulnerable to cuckoldry as a result of wifely infidelity only when his wife is fertile; while he may be concerned to protect a pregnant wife from various sorts of harms, he need not protect her from insemination by rivals. In a rare investigation of human mate-guarding, Flinn (1988) found that men indeed appear to be sensitive to such correlates of cuckoldry risk. Other potential cues of cuckoldry risk vary between societies. Cross-cultural variations in residential patterns, for example, are likely to be systematically related to husbands' perceptions of risk of alienation of wives: A man whose wife has been under continuous surveillance, either by himself or by trusted allies such as close kin, can be relatively confident; conversely, unmonitored absences may be deemed cause for concern (e.g., Fricke, Axinn, and Thornton 1993).

We expect that husbands' violence will prove to be more prevalent where it is more legitimate, for even if angry reactions are widespread and "automatic," enraged men are seldom impervious to social controls. Quantitative data bearing on this issue are sparse, but the ethnographic record appears to indicate that societies vary greatly in their incidences of severe wife assault, and that even vengeful husbands are sensitive to the probable costs of violence. Several authors have argued that wife battering is rarer or less severe in societies where wives retain close contact with their genealogical kin, whose proximity deters husbands from serious assaults (e.g., Campbell 1992*b;* Chagnon 1992; Draper 1992; Smuts 1992). Variation in the protection provided by male kin is apparently related to variable vulnerability of wives within societies, too, including even societies that are relatively matrilocal (H. Kaplan and K. Hill, personal communication 1990).

Factors such as the risk imposed by desperate, disenfranchised male rivals vary across societies and may therefore be expected to account for some of the between-society variance in proprietary manifestations. Accordingly, we expect the degree of coercive constraint of wives, including violence, to reflect cues of the local, contemporaneous intensity of male sexual competition and poaching. Such cues might include encounter rates with potential male rivals; whether they are encountered alone or in all-male groups as opposed to being accompanied by women (that is, cues of bachelor pressure); cues of the status, attractiveness, and resources (hence, mate value) of rivals relative to oneself and of other social groups or categories (lineages, castes, etc.) relative to one's own social group or category; and cues of local marital (in)stability. These are untested propositions, which we list in order to illustrate how adaptationist thinking can help generate hypotheses in cross-cultural research.

IX. Conclusion

In the preceding sections, we have tried to illustrate how adaptationist, selectionist thinking can be applied in criminological research. Even macrosocial phenomena are emergent from and partly to be understood in terms of the acts of individuals. Variations in the intensity of competition experienced by young men or in rates of violence against women, for example, are social phenomena that are affected by other group-level phenomena such as the population's age structure and local marital practices, but the links between these sociological phenomena will never be fully elucidated without consideration of the perceptual, inferential, and decision-making processes of individuals. This is "good reductionism" (Tooby and Cosmides 1992; Dennett 1995), and sociologists who study crime and justice already embrace it: Their theories are replete with psychological claims and assumptions, and appropriately so. What is perhaps less widely appreciated is that the relationship between evolutionary biology and psychology is to some degree analogous to that between psychology and sociology: The truths of the former, lower-level discipline are necessarily foundations of whatever we may hope to discover in the latter, with the result that theorizing at any one level is likely to be more efficient and fruitful the better informed the theorist is about current knowledge and ideas at the foundational level.

Consider again the idea that understanding violence against wives requires consideration of its utility as a means of coercive control. Men do not assault their wives merely because they have the opportunity, or merely because of inadequate sanctions, violent temperaments, or the effects of alcohol. These factors are important, but they do not account for the systematic patterning of violence against wives as a function of demographic and situational variables. Thinking of men's motives as evolved adaptations suggests that sexually proprietary inclinations will respond to demographic, social, and material indicators that are likely to be perceived by husbands as cues of risk of uxorial usurpation and loss of control. This line of thought led us to investigate the surprisingly neglected issues of the effects of estrangement (Wilson and Daly 1993*b*), the marriage partners' ages (Wilson, Johnson, and Daly 1995; Wilson, Daly, and Scheib 1997), and children of former unions (Daly and Wilson 1996) on rates of marital violence, and all of these have proven to be important risk factors. Thinking evolutionarily has also suggested several demographic and cross-cultural hypotheses that are still untested (Wilson and Daly 1992*b*, 1993*a*). However, it is no surprise to an evolutionist that additional factors that were already much discussed in the literature on violence against wives, such as the strength of legal sanctions and the degree of isolation from family and friends, are also important. A successful theory of the sources of variability in rates of violence against wives will have to be "vertically integrated" (Barkow, Cosmides, and Tooby 1992), incorporating multiple factors and levels of explanation.

So where can imminent progress in criminology be expected as a result of evolutionary insights? One promising area concerns socialization effects and the sources of individual differences. The presumption of potent parental influence that still dominates the social sciences has been falsified by research (e.g., Hetherington, Reiss, and Plomin 1994; Rowe 1994), and evolutionary psychological insights are leading to new ideas about when and to what degree familial environments are influential in child development (e.g., Sulloway 1996) and about the domains in which peer influence is likely to be prepotent (e.g., Harris 1995; Pinker 1997). It is also increasingly evident that genetic diversity within (not between) populations accounts for a large proportion of behavioral diversity, including criminal behavior (Carey 1994; Lyons 1996), but the meaning and implications of these findings remain obscure. Researchers with a professional interest in related topics such as "criminal careers" have mostly ignored these findings, perhaps out of a misplaced antipathy to biology, but the findings must be confronted and understood. Evolutionary psychology is not behavior genetics and does not in general predict heritable diversity, but it is essential for understanding the implications of the results of behavior geneticists. Testable hypotheses about what these results mean are now being formulated by evolutionary psychologists (Rowe 1994; Mealey 1995; Daly 1996).

We also expect evolutionary psychological theorizing to contribute increasingly to understandings of how aggregate sociological phenomena like crime rates are causally linked to their social determinants through the perceptions and inferences of individuals. What factors facilitate or dampen recklessness, competitive escalation, trust, coalitional solidarity, the social distance to which empathy and moral duty are extended, and so forth (Machalek and Cohen 1991; Wright 1994; Petrinovich 1995; Chagnon 1996)? Are the cognitive changes associated with hormonal fluctuations important, and what functions do they serve? Are the effects of age on risk taking mediated by changing inferential processes, changing priorities, or other changes? Are social comparison and inequity of greater salience to people in certain age-sex categories than to others? Might loyalties to gangs and other in-groups be better understood as manifestations of specialized social psychological processes adapted to the domains of kin group solidarity and coalitional aggression in social conditions without central authority? Do media portrayals distort unconscious inferences about the local prevalence of violence and crime, thus affecting behavioral thresholds, and if so, to exactly what aspects of these portrayals is the human mind most responsive? These are psychological questions, investigation of which will undoubtedly profit from evolutionary adaptationist thinking (Daly and Wilson 1989; Tooby and Cosmides 1992; Simpson and Kenrick 1997). Links to macrosocial phenomena such as variations in moral and legal codes have also begun to be elucidated (Alexander 1987; Nisbett and Cohen 1996).

That the human animal is a product of the process of evolution by selection is uncontroversial, but the implications of this fact for the social sciences are likely to be far-reaching (Dennett 1995). Evolutionary insights should not be viewed as alternatives to sociological and psychological analyses but as complementary components of a more complete understanding.

REFERENCES

Aarsland, Dag, J. L. Cummings, G. Yenner, and B. Miller. 1996. "Relationship of Aggressive Behavior to other Neuropsychiatric Symptoms in Patients with Alzheimer's Disease." *American Journal of Psychiatry* 153:243–47.

Alexander, Richard D. 1987. *The Biology of Moral Systems.* Hawthorne, N.Y.: Aldine de Gruyter.

Allen, Judith A. 1990. *Sex and Secrets: Crimes Involving Australian Women since 1880.* Melbourne: Oxford University Press.

American Psychiatric Association. 1994. *Diagnostic and Statistical Manual of Mental Disorders. Fourth Edition (DSM-IV).* Washington, D.C.: American Psychiatric Association.

Andersson, Malte. 1980. "Why Are There So Many Threat Displays?" *Journal of Theoretical Biology* 86:773–81.

Archer, John. 1988. *The Behavioural Biology of Aggression.* Cambridge and New York: Cambridge University Press.

Balogh, Rene D., and Richard H. Porter. 1986. "Olfactory Preferences Resulting from Mere Exposure in Human Neonates." *Infant Behavior and Development* 9:395–401.

Barkow, Jerome, Leda Cosmides, and John Tooby, eds. 1992. *The Adapted Mind.* New York: Oxford University Press.

Baron, J. N., and P. C. Reiss. 1985. "Same Time, Next Year: Aggregate Analyses of the Mass Media and Violent Behavior." *American Sociological Review* 50:357–63.

Baron-Cohen, Simon. 1995. *Mindblindness and the Language of the Eyes: An Essay in Evolutionary Psychology.* Cambridge, Mass.: MIT Press.

Bee, Helen L., Sandra K. Mitchell, Kathryn E. Barnard, Sandra J. Eyres, and Mary E. Hammond. 1984. "Predicting Intellectual Outcomes: Sex Differences in Response to Early Environmental Stimulation." *Sex Roles* 10:783–803.

Besse, Susan K. 1989. "Crimes of Passion: The Campaign against Wife Killing in Brazil, 1910–1940." *Journal of Social History* 22:653–66.

Betzig, Laura L. 1986. *Despotism and Differential Reproduction: A Darwinian View of History.* Hawthorne, N.Y.: Aldine.

Breedlove, S. Marc. 1994. "Sexual Differentiation of the Human Nervous System." *Annual Review of Psychology* 45:389–418.

Brisson, Norman J. 1983. "Battering Husbands: A Survey of Abusive Men." *Victimology* 6:338–44.

Brunner, Han G., M. Nelen, X. O. Breakefield, H. H. Ropers, and B. A. van Oost. 1993. "Abnormal Behavior Associated with a Point Mutation in the Structural Gene for Monoamine Oxidase A." *Science* 262:578–80.

Buss, David M. 1991. "Evolutionary Personality Psychology." *Annual Review of Psychology* 42:459–91.

Buss, David M., Randy J. Larsen, Drew Westen, and Jennifer Semmelroth. 1992. "Sex Differences in Jealousy: Evolution, Physiology, and Psychology." *Psychological Science* 3:251–55.

Campbell, Jacquelyn C. 1992*a*. "If I Can't Have You, No One Can: Issues of Power and Control in Homicide of Female Partners." In *Femicide*, edited by Jill Radford and Diana E. H. Russell. New York: Twayne.

———. 1992*b*. "Wife Battering: Cultural Contexts versus Western Social Sciences." In *Sanctions and Sanctuary: Cultural Perspectives on the Beating of Wives*, edited by Dorothy Counts, Judith K. Brown, and Jacquelyn C. Campbell. Boulder, Colo.: Westview.

Carey, Greg. 1994. "Genetics and Violence." In *Understanding and Preventing Violence: Biobehavioral Influences*, vol. 2, edited by A. J. Reiss, Jr., K. A. Miczek, and J. A. Roth. Washington, D.C.: National Academy Press.

Chagnon, Napoleon A. 1988. "Life Histories, Blood Revenge, and Warfare in a Tribal Population." *Science* 239:985–92.

———. 1992. *Yanomamö: The Last Days of Eden*. New York: Harcourt Brace Jovanovich.

———. 1996. "Chronic Problems in Understanding Tribal Violence and Warfare." In *Genetics of Criminal and Antisocial Behaviour* (CIBA Foundation Symposium 194), edited by Gregory R. Bock and Jamie A. Goode. Chichester, United Kingdom: John Wiley.

Chase, Ivan D., Costanza Bartolomeo, and Lee A. Dugatkin. 1994. "Aggressive Interactions and Inter-contest Interval: How Long Do Winners Keep Winning?" *Animal Behaviour* 48:393–400.

Chimbos, Peter D. 1993. "A Study of Patterns in Criminal Homicides in Greece." *International Journal of Comparative Sociology* 34:260–71.

Cohen, Larry E., and Richard Machalek. 1988. "A General Theory of Expropriative Crime: An Evolutionary Ecological Approach." *American Journal of Sociology* 94:465–501.

———. 1994. "The Normalcy of Crime. From Durkheim to Evolutionary Ecology." *Rationality and Society* 6:286–308.

Coie, John D., Kenneth A. Dodge, Robert Terry, and Virginia Wright. 1991. "The Role of Aggression in Peer Relations: An Analysis of Aggression Episodes in Boys' Play Groups." *Child Development* 62:812–26.

Colegrave, N. 1994. "Game Theory Models of Competition in Closed Systems: Asymmetries in Fighting and Competitive Ability." *Oikos* 71:499–505.

Cosmides, Leda, and John Tooby. 1981. "Cytoplasmic Inheritance and Intragenomic Conflict." *Journal of Theoretical Biology* 89:83–129.

———. 1996. "Are Humans Good Intuitive Statisticians after All? Rethinking Some Conclusions of the Literature on Judgment under Uncertainty." *Cognition* 58:1–73.

Coulton, Claudia J., Jill E. Korbin, Marilyn Su, and Julian Chow. 1995.

"Community Level Factors and Child Maltreatment Rates." *Child Development* 66:1262–76.

Crawford, Charles B., and Judith L. Anderson. 1989. "Sociobiology: An Environmentalist Discipline?" *American Psychologist* 44:1449–59.

Crawford, Maria, and Rosemary Gartner. 1992. *Woman Killing: Intimate Femicide in Ontario, 1974–1990.* Toronto: The Women We Honour Action Committee.

Cronin, Helena. 1991. *The Ant and the Peacock.* Cambridge: Cambridge University Press.

Cusson, Maurice. 1993. "Situational Deterrence: Fear During the Criminal Event." In *Crime Prevention Studies*, vol. 1, edited by Ronald V. Clarke. Monsey, N.Y.: Criminal Justice Press.

Daly, Martin. 1996. "Evolutionary Adaptationism: Another Biological Approach to Criminal and Antisocial Behaviour." In *Genetics of Criminal and Antisocial Behaviour* (CIBA Foundation Symposium 194), edited by Gregory R. Bock and Jamie A. Goode. Chichester, United Kingdom: John Wiley.

Daly, Martin, and Margo I. Wilson. 1982. "Homicide and Kinship." *American Anthropologist* 84:372–78.

———. 1983. *Sex, Evolution and Behavior*, 2d ed. Belmont, Calif.: Wadsworth.

———. 1988*a*. "Evolutionary Social Psychology and Family Homicide." *Science* 242:519–24.

———. 1988*b*. *Homicide.* New York: Aldine.

———. 1989. "Homicide and Cultural Evolution." *Ethology and Sociobiology* 10:99–110.

———. 1990. "Killing the Competition." *Human Nature* 1:83–109.

———. 1994*a*. "Evolutionary Psychology: Adaptationist, Selectionist and Comparative." *Psychological Inquiry* 6:34–38.

———. 1994*b*. "The Evolutionary Psychology of Male Violence." In *Male Violence*, edited by John Archer. London: Routledge.

———. 1995. "Discriminative Parental Solicitude and the Relevance of Evolutionary Models to the Analysis of Motivational Systems." In *The Cognitive Neurosciences*, edited by Michael Gazzaniga. Cambridge, Mass.: MIT Press.

———. 1996. "Evolutionary Psychology and Marital Conflict: The Relevance of Stepchildren." In *Sex, Power, Conflict: Feminist and Evolutionary Perspectives*, edited by David M. Buss and Neil Malamuth. New York: Oxford University Press.

Davies, Nicholas B. 1992. *Dunnock Behaviour and Social Evolution.* Oxford: Oxford University Press.

Dawkins, Richard. 1982. *The Extended Phenotype.* Oxford: Freeman.

———. 1986. *The Blind Watchmaker.* Harlow, United Kingdom: Longman.

de Lacoste, Marie-Christine, D. S. Horvath, and D. J. Woodward. 1991. "Possible Sex Differences in the Developing Human Fetal Brain." *Journal of Clinical and Experimental Neuropsychology* 13:831–46.

Dell, Susan. 1984. *Murder into Manslaughter.* Oxford: Oxford University Press.

Dennett, Daniel C. 1995. *Darwin's Dangerous Idea.* New York: Transaction.

deSousa, Ronald. 1987. *The Rationality of Emotions.* Cambridge, Mass.: MIT Press.

Dobash, Rebecca E., and Russell P. Dobash. 1979. *Violence against Wives.* New York: Free Press.

———. 1984. "The Nature and Antecedents of Violent Events." *British Journal of Criminology* 24:269–88.

Dodge, Kenneth A., John E. Bates, and Gregory S. Pettit. 1990. "Mechanisms in the Cycle of Violence." *Science* 250:1678–83.

Dodge, Kenneth A., Joseph M. Price, and Jo-Anne Bachorowski. 1990. "Hostile Attributional Biases in Severely Aggressive Adolescents." *Journal of Abnormal Psychology* 99:385–92.

Draper, Patricia. 1992. "Room to Maneuver: !Kung Women Cope with Men." In *Sanctions and Sanctuary: Cultural Perspectives on the Beating of Wives,* edited by Dorothy Counts, Judith K. Brown, and Jacquelyn C. Campbell. Boulder, Colo.: Westview.

Dressler, Joshua. 1982. "Rethinking Heat of Passion: A Defense in Search of a Rationale." *Journal of Criminal Law and Criminology* 73:421–70.

Edwards, J. L. 1954. "Provocation and the Reasonable Man: Another View." *Criminal Law Review,* pp. 898–906.

Ehrman, Lee. 1972. "Genetics and Sexual Selection." In *Sexual Selection and the Descent of Man, 1871–1971,* edited by Bernard Campbell. Chicago: Aldine.

Enquist, Magnus, and Olof Leimar. 1990. "The Evolution of Fatal Fighting." *Animal Behaviour* 39:1–9.

Falconer, Douglas S. 1960. *Introduction to Quantitative Genetics.* New York: Ronald.

Farrington, David P. 1991. "Psychological Contributions to the Explanation of Offending." *Issues in Criminological and Legal Psychology* 1:7–19.

Farrington, David P., and Donald J. West. 1995. "Effects of Marriage, Separation, and Children on Offending by Adult Males." *Current Perspectives on Aging and the Life Cycle* 4:249–81.

Flinn, Mark V. 1988. "Mate Guarding in a Caribbean Village." *Ethology and Sociobiology* 9:1–28.

Flinn, Mark V., Robert Quinlan, Mark Turner, Seamus A. Decker, and Barry G. England. 1996. "Male-Female Differences in Effects of Parental Absence on Glucocorticoid Stress Response." *Human Nature* 7:125–62.

Frank, Robert H. 1985. *Choosing the Right Pond.* New York: Oxford University Press.

———. 1988. *Passions within Reason: The Strategic Role of the Emotions.* New York: Norton.

Fricke, Tom, William G. Axinn, and Arland Thornton. 1993. "Marriage, Social Inequality, and Women's Contact with Their Natal Families in Alliance Societies." *American Anthropologist* 95:395–419.

Futuyma, Douglas J. 1983. *Science on Trial. The Case for Evolution.* New York: Pantheon.

Gardner, William. 1993. "A Life-Span Rational-Choice Theory of Risk Taking." In *Adolescent Risk Taking,* edited by Nancy J. Bell and Robert W. Bell. Newbury Park, Calif.: Sage.

Gaulin, Steven J. C., and Harol A. Hoffman. 1988. "Evolution and Development of Sex Differences in Spatial Ability." In *Human Reproductive Behaviour,* edited by Laura Betzig, Monique Borgerhoff Mulder, and Paul Turke. Cambridge: Cambridge University Press.

Gelles, Richard J., and Murray A. Straus. 1985. In *Crime and the Family,* edited by A. J. Lincoln and M. A. Straus. Springfield, Ill.: Thomas.

Giancola, Peter R., and Amos Zeichner. 1995. "An Investigation of Gender Differences in Alcohol-Related Aggression." *Journal of Studies in Alcohol* 56: 573–79.

Gigerenzer, Gerd, and Ulrich Hoffrage. 1995. "How to Improve Bayesian Reasoning without Instruction: Frequency Formats." *Psychological Review* 102:684–704.

Goode, William. 1969. "Violence among Intimates." In *Crimes of Violence,* vol. 13, edited by D. J. Mulvihill and M. M. Tumin. Washington, D.C.: U.S. Government Printing Office.

Gottesman, Irving I., and H. H. Goldsmith. 1994. "Developmental Psychopathology of Antisocial Behavior: Inserting Genes into Its Ontogenesis and Epigenesis." In *Threats to Optimal Development: Integrating Biological, Psychological, and Social Risk Factors,* edited by C. A. Nelson. Hillsdale, N.J.: Erlbaum.

Gottfredson, Michael R., and Travis Hirschi. 1990. *A General Theory of Crime.* Stanford, Calif.: Stanford University Press.

Gove, Walter. 1985. "The Effect of Age and Gender on Deviant Behavior: A Biopsychosocial Perspective." In *Gender and the Life Course,* edited by Alice S. Rossi. New York: Aldine.

Gur, R. C., L. H. Mozley, P. D. Mozley, S. M. Resnick, J. S. Karp, A. Alavi, S. E. Arnold, and R. E. Gur. 1995. "Sex Differences in Regional Cerebral Glucose Metabolism during a Resting State." *Science* 267:528–31.

Hagan, John. 1986. "The Unexplained Crimes of Class and Gender." In *Critique and Explanation,* edited by T. F. Hartnagel and R. A. Silverman. New Brunswick, N.J.: Transaction.

———. 1990. "The Structuration of Gender and Deviance: A Power-Control Theory of Vulnerability to Crime and the Search for Deviant Exit Roles." *Canadian Review of Sociology and Anthropology* 27:137–56.

Haig, David. 1993. "Genetic Conflicts in Human Pregnancy." *Quarterly Review of Biology* 68:495–532.

Hamilton, William D. 1964. "The Genetical Evolution of Social Behaviour," pts. 1 and 2. *Journal of Theoretical Biology* 7:1–52.

Harris, Judith R. 1995. "Where Is the Child's Environment? A Group Socialization Theory of Development." *Psychological Review* 102:458–89.

Hepper, Peter G., ed. 1991. *Kin Recognition.* Cambridge: Cambridge University Press.

Hetherington, E. Mavis, D. Reiss, and Robert Plomin, eds. 1994. *Separate Social Worlds of Siblings: The Impact of Nonshared Environment on Development.* Hillsdale, N.J.: Erlbaum.

Hewlett, Barry S. 1988. "Sexual Selection and Paternal Investment among Aka Pygmies." In *Human Reproductive Behaviour*, edited by Laura Betzig, Monique Borgerhoff Mulder, and Paul Turke. Cambridge: Cambridge University Press.

Hilberman, Elaine, and Kit Munson. 1978. "Sixty Battered Women." *Victimology* 2:460–70.

Hill, Kim R., and A. Magdalena Hurtado. 1995. *Aché Life History: The Ecology and Demography of a Foraging People.* Hawthorne, N.Y.: Aldine.

Hirschi, Travis, and Michael R. Gottfredson. 1983. "Age and the Explanation of Crime." *American Journal of Sociology* 89:552–84.

———. 1986. "The Distinction between Crime and Criminality." In *Critique and Explanation*, edited by Timothy F. Hartnagel and Robert A. Silverman. New Brunswick, N.J.: Transaction.

Howell, Nancy. 1979. *Demography of the Dobe !Kung.* New York: Academic Press.

Hsieh, Ching-Chi, and M. D. Pugh. 1993. "Poverty, Income Inequality, and Violent Crime: A Meta-analysis of Recent Aggregate Data Studies." *Criminal Justice Review* 18:182–202.

Huntingford, Felicity, and Angela Turner. 1987. *Animal Conflict.* London: Chapman & Hall.

Johnson, Holly, and Vincent Sacco. 1995. "Researching Violence against Women: Statistics Canada's National Survey." *Canadian Journal of Criminology* 37:281–304.

Kahneman, Daniel, Paul Slovic, and Amos Tversky, eds. 1982. *Judgment under Uncertainty.* New York: Cambridge University Press.

Katz, Jack. 1988. *Seductions of Crime.* New York: Basic.

Kimura, Doreen, and Elizabeth Hampson. 1994. "Cognitive Patterns in Men and Women Influenced by Fluctuations in Sex Hormones." *Current Directions in Psychological Science* 3:57–61.

Kposowa, Augustine J., Gopal K. Singh, and K. D. Breault. 1994. "The Effects of Marital Status and Social Isolation on Adult Male Homicides in the United States: Evidence from the National Longitudinal Mortality Study." *Journal of Quantitative Criminology* 10:277–89.

Krahn, Harvey, Timothy F. Hartnagel, and John W. Gartrell. 1986. "Income Inequality and Homicide Rates: Cross-National Data and Criminological Theories." *Criminology* 24:269–95.

Kvarnemo, Charlotta, Elisabet Forsgren, and Carin Magnhagen. 1995. "Effects of Sex Ratio on Intra- and Inter-Sexual Behaviour in Sand Gobies." *Animal Behaviour* 50:1455–61.

Leslie, Alan. 1992. "Pretense, Autism and the Theory-of-Mind Module." *Current Directions in Psychological Science* 1:18–21.

Low, Bobbi S. 1989. "Cross-Cultural Patterns in the Training of Children: An Evolutionary Perspective." *Journal of Comparative Psychology* 103:311–19.

Lyons, Michael J. 1996. "A Twin Study of Self-Reported Criminal Behaviour." In *Genetics of Criminal and Antisocial Behaviour* (CIBA Foundation

Symposium 194), edited by Gregory R. Bock and Jamie A. Goode. Chichester, United Kingdom: John Wiley.

Lytton, Hugh, and David M. Romney. 1991. "Parents' Differential Socialization of Boys and Girls: A Meta-Analysis." *Psychological Bulletin* 109:267–96.

Machalek, Richard. 1995. "Basic Dimensions and Forms of Social Exploitation: A Comparative Analysis." *Advances in Human Ecology* 4:35–68.

Machalek, Richard, and Larry E. Cohen. 1991. "The Nature of Crime: Is Cheating Necessary for Cooperation?" *Human Nature* 2:215–33.

Mahoney, Martha R. 1991. "Legal Images of Battered Women: Redefining the Issue of Separation." *Michigan Law Review* 90:1–94.

Mayr, Ernst. 1983. "How to Carry out the Adaptationist Program?" *American Naturalist* 121:324–34.

Mazur, Allan, Alan Booth, and James M. Dabbs, Jr. 1992. "Testosterone and Chess Competition." *Social Psychology Quarterly* 55:70–77.

McCarthy, Barry. 1993. "Warrior Values: A Socio-Historical Survey." In *Male Violence*, edited by John Archer. London: Routledge.

McCaul, Kevin D., Brian A. Gladue, and Margaret Joppa. 1992. "Winning, Losing, Mood, and Testosterone." *Hormones and Behavior* 26:486–504.

Mealey, Linda. 1995. "The Sociobiology of Sociopathy: An Integrated Evolutionary Model." *Behavioral and Brain Sciences* 18:523–41.

Moffitt, Terri. 1993. "Adolescence-Limited and Life-Course Persistent Antisocial Behavior: A Developmental Taxonomy." *Psychological Review* 100: 674–701.

Møller, Anders P. 1994. *Sexual Selection and the Barn Swallow*. Princeton, N.J.: Princeton University Press.

Monahan, John, and Stephanie Splane. 1980. "Psychological Approaches to Criminal Behavior." In *Criminology Review Yearbook*, vol. 2, edited by E. Bittner and S. Messinger. Beverly Hills, Calif.: Sage.

Nesse, Randolph M. 1990. "Evolutionary Explanations of Emotions." *Human Nature* 1:261–89.

Newman, Leonard S., and Roy F. Baumeister. 1996. "Toward an Explanation of the UFO Abduction Phenomenon: Hypnotic Elaboration, Extraterrestrial Sadomasochism, and Spurious Memories." *Psychological Inquiry* 7:99–197.

Nisbett, Richard E., and Dov Cohen. 1996. *Culture of Honor: The Psychology of Violence in the South*. Boulder, Colo.: Westview.

Nisbett, Richard E., and Lee Ross. 1980. *Human Inference: Strategies and Shortcomings of Social Judgment*. Englewood Cliffs, N.J.: Prentice Hall.

Nisbett, Richard E., and T. D. Wilson. 1977. "Telling More than We Can Know: Verbal Reports on Mental Processes." *Psychological Review* 84:231–59.

Olweus, Dan, J. Block, and Marian Radke-Yarrows, eds. 1986. *Development of Antisocial and Prosocial Behavior*. New York: Academic.

Petrinovich, Lewis. 1995. *Human Evolution, Reproduction, and Morality*. New York: Plenum.

Phillips, David P. 1983. "The Impact of Mass Media Violence on U.S. Homicide." *American Sociological Review* 48:560–68.

Pinker, Steven. 1997. *How the Mind Works.* New York: Norton.

Polk, Kenneth. 1994. *When Men Kill.* Cambridge: Cambridge University Press.

Premack, David, and Ann James Premack. 1995. "Origins of Human Social Competence." In *The Cognitive Neurosciences,* edited by Michael Gazzaniga. Cambridge, Mass.: MIT Press.

Pruett-Jones, Stephen, and Melinda Pruett-Jones. 1994. "Sexual Competition and Courtship Disruptions: Why Do Male Bowerbirds Destroy Each Other's Bowers?" *Animal Behaviour* 47:607–20.

Raine, Adrian. 1993. *The Psychopathology of Crime and Criminal Behavior as a Clinical Disorder.* San Diego, Calif.: Academic.

Rogers, Alan R. 1994. "Evolution of Time Preference by Natural Selection." *American Economic Review* 84:460–81.

Ross, Michael. 1989. "Relation of Implicit Theories to the Construction of Personal Histories." *Psychological Review* 96:341–57.

Rounsaville, Bruce J. 1978. "Theories in Marital Violence: Evidence from a Study of Battered Women." *Victimology* 3:11–31.

Rowe, David C. 1994. *The Limits of Family Influence: Genes, Experience, and Behavior.* New York: Guilford.

Rubin, P. H., and C. W. Paul. 1979. "An Evolutionary Model of Taste for Risk." *Economic Inquiry* 17:585–96.

Safilios-Rothschild, Constantina. 1969. "'Honor' Crimes in Contemporary Greece." *British Journal of Sociology* 20:205–18.

Sampson, Robert J. 1991. "Linking the Micro- and Macrolevel Dimensions of Community Social Organization." *Social Forces* 70:43–64.

Sampson, Robert J., and John H. Laub. 1993. *Crime in the Making: Pathways and Turning Points through Life.* Cambridge, Mass.: Harvard University Press.

Sherwin, Barbara B. 1994. "Estrogenic Effects on Memory in Women." *Annals of the New York Academy of Sciences* 743:213–31.

Simpson, Jeffrey, and Douglas Kenrick, eds. 1997. *Evolutionary Social Psychology.* Mahwah, N.J.: Erlbaum.

Smuts, Barbara. 1992. "Male Aggression against Women: An Evolutionary Perspective." *Human Nature* 3:1–44.

Sulloway, Frank J. 1996. *Born to Rebel: Radical Thinking in Science and Social Thought.* New York: Oxford University Press.

Sussman, Robert W., James M. Cheverud, and Thad Q. Bartlett. 1995. "Infant Killing as an Evolutionary Strategy: Reality or Myth?" *Evolutionary Anthropology* 3:149–51.

Symons, Donald. 1990. "Adaptiveness and Adaptation." *Ethology and Sociobiology* 11:427–44.

———. 1995. "Beauty Is in the Adaptations of the Beholder: The Evolutionary Psychology of Human Female Sexual Attractiveness." In *Sexual Nature, Sexual Culture,* edited by P. R. Abramson and S. D. Pinkerton. Chicago: University of Chicago Press.

Tittle, Charles R. 1988. "Two Empirical Regularities (Maybe) in Search of an Explanation: Commentary on the Age/Crime Debate." *Criminology* 26:75–85.

Tonry, Michael, Lloyd E. Ohlin, and David P. Farrington. 1991. *Human Development and Criminal Behavior.* New York: Springer-Verlag.

Tooby, John, and Leda Cosmides. 1990*a*. "On the Universality of Human Nature and the Uniqueness of the Individual: The Role of Genetics and Adaptation." *Journal of Personality* 58:17–67.

———. 1990*b*. "The Past Explains the Present: Emotional Adaptations and the Structure of Ancestral Environments." *Ethology and Sociobiology* 11:375–424.

———. 1992. "The Psychological Foundations of Culture." In *The Adapted Mind,* edited by Jerome Barkow, Leda Cosmides, and John Tooby. New York: Oxford University Press.

Trivers, Robert L. 1971. "The Evolution of Reciprocal Altruism." *Quarterly Review of Biology* 46:35–57.

———. 1972. "Parental Investment and Sexual Selection." In *Sexual Selection and the Descent of Man, 1871–1971,* edited by Bernard Campbell. Chicago: Aldine.

———. 1974. "Parent-Offspring Conflict." *American Zoologist* 14:249–64.

Turner, George F. 1994. "The Fighting Tactics of Male Mouthbrooding Cichlids: The Effects of Size and Residency." *Animal Behaviour* 47:655–62.

Vangoozen, Stephanie H. M., Peggy T. Cohenkettenis, Louis J. G. Gooren, Nico H. Frijda, and Nanne E. Vandepoll. 1995. "Gender Differences in Behavior: Activating Effects of Cross-sex Hormones. *Psychoneuroendocrinology* 20:343–63.

Vila, Bryan. 1994. "A General Paradigm for Understanding Criminal Behavior: Extending Evolutionary Ecological Theory." *Criminology* 32:311–59.

Widom, Cathy S. 1989. "The Cycle of Violence." *Science* 244:160–66.

Williams, George C. 1966. *Adaptation and Natural Selection.* Princeton, N.J.: Princeton University Press.

Williams, George C, and Randolph M. Nesse. 1991. "The Dawn of Darwinian Medicine." *Quarterly Review of Biology* 66:1–22.

Wilson, James Q., and Richard J. Herrnstein. 1985. *Crime and Human Nature.* New York: Simon & Schuster.

Wilson, Margo I., and Martin Daly. 1985. "Competitiveness, Risk-Taking and Violence: The Young Male Syndrome." *Ethology and Sociobiology* 6:59–73.

———. 1992*a*. "The Man Who Mistook His Wife for a Chattel." In *The Adapted Mind,* edited by Jerome Barkow, Leda Cosmides, and John Tooby. New York: Oxford University Press.

———. 1992*b*. "Who Kills Whom in Spouse Killings? On the Exceptional Sex Ratio of Spousal Homicides in the United States." *Criminology* 30:189–215.

———. 1993*a*. "An Evolutionary Psychological Perspective on Male Sexual Proprietariness and Violence Against Wives." *Violence and Victims* 8:271–94.

———. 1993*b*. "Spousal Homicide Risk and Estrangement." *Violence and Victims* 8:3–16.

———. 1994. "A Lifespan Perspective on Homicidal Violence: The Young Male Syndrome." In *Proceedings of the 2nd Annual Workshop of the Homicide Research Working Group*, edited by C. Rebecca Block and Richard L. Block. Washington, D.C.: National Institute of Justice.

Wilson, Margo I., Martin Daly, and Joanna E. Scheib. 1997. "Femicide: An Evolutionary Psychological Perspective." In *Feminism and Evolutionary Biology*, edited by Patricia A. Gowaty. New York: Chapman Hall.

Wilson, Margo I., Martin Daly, and Christine Wright. 1993. "Uxoricide in Canada: Demographic Risk Patterns." *Canadian Journal of Criminology* 35: 263–91.

Wilson, Margo I., Holly Johnson, and Martin Daly. 1995. "Lethal and Nonlethal Violence against Wives." *Canadian Journal of Criminology* 37:331–61.

Witelson, Sandra F. 1991. "Neural Sexual Mosaicism: Sexual Differentiation of the Human Temporo-Parietal Region for Functional Asymmetry." *Psychoneuroendocrinology* 16:131–53.

Wolfgang, Marvin E. 1958. *Patterns in Criminal Homicide*. Philadelphia: University of Pennsylvania Press.

Wolfgang, Marvin E., and Franco Ferracutti. 1967. *The Subculture of Violence*. London: Tavistock.

Wright, Robert. 1994. *The Moral Animal*. New York: Pantheon.

Neil Gilbert

Advocacy Research and Social Policy

ABSTRACT

Advocacy research—empirical investigations of social problems by people who are deeply concerned about those problems—has a long and honorable history, exemplified by the considerable influence of Michael Harrington's *The Other America* on federal antipoverty policies in the 1960s. Often, however, perhaps for understandable psychological reasons, advocacy has taken precedence to research, and results have been exaggerated or magnified. Claims in the 1980s, later irrefutably debunked, that 50,000 children are kidnapped each year by strangers, are one example. Other recent examples include wildly inflated estimates of the incidence of abuse of the elderly, sexual abuse of children, and rape. Exaggerated claims are eventually exposed but, when they deal with highly emotional subjects, can for a time powerfully shape media coverage and social policy. The trick—easier to say than do, but Harrington did it—is to be cautious and modest in making empirical claims and passionate and personal in expressing policy views.

Beginning with Charles Booth's (1892) large-scale survey of poverty in London during the 1880s, the development of social policy in industrial society has benefited from a long and honorable tradition of advocacy research—studies that seek to measure social problems, heighten public awareness of them, and recommend possible solutions. At the start of the twentieth century, studies intended to spur social reform in the United States focused on the problem of poverty and its connected miseries of slum housing, poor health, hunger, and child labor. Robert Hunter's book *Poverty*, first published in 1904, was an early classic in

Neil Gilbert is acting dean and Milton and Gertrude Chernin Professor of Social Welfare and Social Services at the University of California, Berkeley, School of Social Welfare. This essay is a revised and expanded version of material developed in his book *Welfare Justice: Restoring Social Equity* (New Haven, Conn.: Yale University Press, 1995).

0192-3234/97/0022-0004/$02.00

the advocacy research genre. Taking $460 a year as the poverty index for an average family of five in the Northern states and $300 a year in the South, Hunter estimated that at least 10 million Americans (about 13 percent of the population) lived in poverty. Noting that these indices of poverty were arbitrary, but not unreasonable, he proposed an agenda of social reforms that included increased public health measures, minimum wages, unemployment compensation, workers' disability insurance, and old-age pensions (Hunter 1965).

More than half a century later, in an era of relative prosperity, public concerns about poverty were revived by another study, Michael Harrington's (1962) classic *The Other America.* Harrington reviewed estimates that showed between 40 and 50 million Americans (20–25 percent of the population) living in poverty. He concluded that a national attack on poverty was necessary. Harrington's work is often credited with furnishing moral impetus, along with an empirical case, for the Johnson administration's "war on poverty" (Schlesinger 1965).[1] Harrington and Hunter came from the same breed of advocacy researchers. Both had spent time on the front lines as social workers and were drawn to socialism, and while well versed in the social sciences, their studies embodied a felicitous combination of reportage and analysis that was highly accessible to the general public. Indeed, it might be said that their prose was as persuasive as their numbers.

Reflecting on his approach to the study of poverty, Harrington offered a candid account of the style and nature of advocacy research: "If my interpretation is bleak and grim, and even if it overstates the case slightly, that is intentional. My moral point of departure is a sense of outrage, a feeling that it would be better to describe it in dark tones than to minimize it" (1962, p. 176). This is not to say, however, that his statistics were invented or misrepresented. Harrington explicitly identifies the assumptions and definitions that underlay his reading of the numbers. He readily admits that legitimate differences in point of view give rise to other definitions and interpretations, which yield different counts. And he reviews these alternative estimates of poverty in a balanced manner. Harrington explains that two principles guided his efforts to study *The Other America:* "To be as honest and objective as possible about the figures; to speak emotionally in the name of the common humanity of those who dwell in the culture of poverty" (Har-

[1] Harrington's study also sparked a proliferation of literature on the characteristics and conditions of poverty in the United States. Within several years of his work, half a dozen anthologies were published on the topic of poverty in America.

rington 1962, p. 177). Joining unbiased measurement with committed expression of concern, these principles reflected a standard of advocacy research at its best—a standard that has eroded since the 1960s as advocacy research activities multiplied with the development of federally funded programs for needy and oppressed groups.

After Harrington's study of poverty in the early 1960s, a notable rise in the volume of advocacy research was accompanied by changes in the style and focus of these efforts. As social rights for different interest groups expanded and public expenditures for new social programs climbed, an unprecedented level of federal funding became available to study the problems addressed by these programs and the groups affected by them. With millions in research funds distributed among federal agencies such as the Administration on Aging, the National Institute of Mental Health, the National Center on Child Abuse and Neglect, the Department of Housing and Urban Development, and the Children's Bureau, the research focus shifted from the poor to diverse constituencies of the oppressed and deprived who claimed entitlements to social protection. Included were women, gays and lesbians, ethnic minorities, children, and people who were elderly, homeless, disabled, or suffering various addictions.

Along with an infusion of research funds that began with the Great Society programs in the early 1960s, the expansion of social research gained impetus from computer technology and new analytic tools that promised to inform policy debates with useful data. These developments were quickened by the tremendous growth in the number of people professionally trained to conduct social science research (Aaron 1978). By the late 1960s, social scientists came to play an increasing role as advocates in the social policy arena—gaining, in Daniel Patrick Moynihan's words, "quite extraordinary access to power" (1969, p. 177).

With the rising output, advocacy researchers' efforts to measure those in need became more questionable and their prose less elegant. Estimates of need became more questionable, in part, because some of the emerging problems were harder to gauge than poverty. The measurement of homelessness does not lend itself to conventional social science sampling methods using telephone interviews or door-to-door surveys; unlike poverty, problems such as racial and gender discrimination, child abuse, elder abuse, and drug abuse involve crimes that are difficult to uncover by surveys. Also, the expansion of social welfare program benefits for various groups produced a certain amount of competition, increasing pressure to inflate evidence of the need for program support. Competition with other groups is less an issue in measuring the more inclusive problem of poverty. In figuring the national incidence of poverty, for example, Harrington was not concerned that an error in his calculations might show that the number of poor were 10 million less than he estimated. After all, he insisted, "give or take 10,000,000, the American poor are one of the greatest scandals of a society that has the ability to provide a decent life for every man, woman, and child" (Harrington 1962, p. 177). But as advocacy research has turned to problems that are more limited in scope than poverty, its function of promoting public awareness is being compromised by the growing tendency to magnify needs greatly while asserting the scientific validity of these large numbers.

This essay examines the methodology of advocacy research as it has been conducted in recent years, the tactics employed to legitimate these studies, and how policy deliberations have become muddled by vast and often questionable estimates of social ills promoted through advocacy research. Section I reviews how advocacy research overstates the magnitude of deeply disturbing problems—child kidnapping, child sexual abuse, elder abuse, and homelessness—by broadly framing their definitions to include an enormous number of cases, many—if not most—of which do not fit the conventional interpretation of the problem; these shockingly large numbers are picked up and amplified by the media, elevating public alarm to a point sometimes described as "moral panic." Section II offers an in-depth critique of advocacy research on rape, examining how estimates of the problem have been magnified by flawed research methods and misinterpretation of data. Drawing on the rape studies, Section III analyzes the tactics used by advocacy researchers to persuade policy makers and the media that this problem has reached epidemic proportions—claims of a "social epidemic" being one of the classic traits of willful moral panic (Cottino and Quirico 1995). Section IV explores the ideological forces and social factors in the 1990s cultural climate of strained gender relations that have contributed to public acceptance of advocacy research on rape. The final section examines how advocacy research distorts social policy deliberations.

I. Emotive Statistics and Moral Panics

In recent years the rising volume and declining quality of advocacy research has spawned the increasing use of emotive statistics—startling figures that purport to uncover "hidden crises" and "silent epidemics." These figures are regularly broadcast not only by the Oprah and Geraldo TV talk shows and printed in the *National Enquirer*, but they are also presented in steadier sources such as *Time*, the *New York Times*, and television network newscasts. A story in the *Los Angeles Times* (Trombley 1990, p. 1), for example, cites a study of 32,000 California children in which 25 percent of those surveyed reported that "they had gotten away from someone trying to kidnap them." Is it conceivable that one in four children or almost one child in every other family was a victim of attempted kidnapping? On a little reflection, most people would find it difficult to take these figures seriously. But not the University of Chicago professor of social work who conducted the study; in his view the survey results indicate that California's extensive statewide program to provide children with training to prevent sexual abuse "is effective in teaching youngsters how to deal with the threat of physical and sexual abuse" (Trombley 1990).

In the mid-1980s, fear of kidnappings had spiraled into what has been described in the literature on sociology of deviance and the media as a "moral panic"—a condition in which public perception of an evil threat is heightened to alarming proportions by media attention (Cohen 1972; Drotner 1992; McRobbie and Thornton 1995). In this instance, social anxiety was intensified by the widely publicized estimate that 50,000 children were being abducted by strangers annually. According to Child Find, an organization devoted to the plight of missing children, only 10 percent of these children were recovered by their parents, another 10 percent were found dead, and the remaining 40,000 cases per year continued to be missing. Prominently reported by the media, these figures first provided sensational headlines proclaiming a national crisis, and they later became grist for a Pulitzer Prize–winning analysis of the problem in the *Denver Post*, which criticized the risk of child abduction as wildly inflated. The *Post* revealed an astonishing discrepancy between the 50,000 estimate put forth by crusaders for missing children and the official number of FBI investigations of children abducted by strangers, which totaled sixty-seven cases in 1984 (Griego and Kilzer 1985).

A closer analysis of these figures by Best (1988) shows that, if the advocate's estimate of 50,000 was too high, the FBI count of sixty-seven cases was too low. The FBI's jurisdiction in kidnapping cases is limited to offenses that violate a federal statute, such as transporting a victim across state lines; only a fraction of the cases reported to local law enforcement authorities come under the Federal Kidnapping Statute. Examining data from a study by the National Center for Missing and Exploited Children, which included police records on every reported crime in 1984 that involved kidnapping or attempted kidnapping of children in Jacksonville, Florida, and Houston, Texas, Best demonstrates that a reasonable extrapolation of serious incidents would yield a nationwide estimate of 550 cases annually—a figure about eight times higher than the FBI count, but still one-ninetieth the incidence rate claimed by advocates.

In defining the serious incidents of stranger abductions, Best (1988) considered only those cases that involved either murder or a child's being missing for more than one day. This definition coincides with the image of child abduction originally portrayed by advocates who promulgated the figure of 50,000 missing children, which was widely publicized through the media by ABC news and other sources. Researchers at the National Center for Missing and Exploited Children (NCMEC) employed a broader definition that included attempted kidnappings and cases in which the victim is missing for less than twenty-four hours. Using the NCMEC definition to extrapolate a nationwide rate from the Jacksonville and Houston data yields an annual figure of 15,000 cases of stranger abduction. But as Best points out, in the enlarged definition subscribed to by NCMEC researchers, 97 percent of the cases involved a child missing for less than twenty-four hours, and over 60 percent of the cases were crimes of molestation (short-term abductions where the victim was moved to a different place). Indeed, local police classified only 15 percent of these cases as kidnappings or abductions. Sexual molestations are tragic for the victims, but a different crime from the kidnappings initially portrayed by advocates who claimed that 80 percent of abducted children continue to be missing each year.

By including cases in which most victims are missing less than one day, the broader definition of child kidnapping advanced by the NCMEC and other missing-children advocates generates a high incidence rate, which lends a sense of urgency for new policies to address the problem. Proposals for these policies typically focus on efforts to increase education, prevention, and social control. "Currently parents can choose among dozens of antikidnapping books, games, videotapes, ID kits, and other commercial products designed to educate children about the dangers of abduction. Most are reasonably priced, but it is more difficult to calculate the social costs of encouraging both children and adults to believe that terrifying crimes are commonplace. The missing-children movement also emphasizes the need for greater social control: schools should require detailed identification records for every student; police should have the power to hold runaways. . . . The unspeakable threat posed by the stranger abduction epidemic justifies these changes; the new policies' potential costs and dangers receive little attention" (Best 1988, p. 91).

As advocates for missing children seek to expand the definition of this terrible offense to include incidents of child sexual molestation, they enter the realm of what is widely perceived as a much larger problem. Estimates of missing children shrivel in comparison with those advanced by the movement to prevent child sexual abuse; the most frequently reported forecast is that one girl in three or four will be sexually molested before leaving high school, most often by a relative (Gilbert et al. 1989; Berrick and Gilbert 1991).[2] Briere and Runtz (1989, p. 65) offer a typical statement of the problem: "Sexual victimization of children by adults is now acknowledged to be a significant social problem in the United States. Most modern surveys of the prevalence of sexual abuse in the general population, for instance, indicate that 22 percent to 45 percent of adult women experienced some form of contact sexual victimization as children."

But unlike missing children, who are almost always reported to the authorities, child sexual abuse is a difficult problem to document. The estimated prevalence rates are considerably higher than one would infer from official figures on the number of child sexual abuse reports substantiated annually. In 1993, for example, approximately 140,000 cases of child sexual abuse were substantiated by child protective services agencies, which represented 2.1 victims per 1,000 children in the general population under 18 years of age (U.S. Department of Health and Human Services 1995). Although extremely serious, this annual incidence rate of .02 percent does not begin to yield a 25–33 percent prevalence rate over the course of childhood. Because many if not most incidents of child sexual abuse are never reported to the authorities,

[2] Continually recited by authorities in the field of child sexual abuse prevention, there is some evidence that these figures have had an effect on how the public perceives the magnitude of this problem. Surveys of parents in California reveal that a vast majority of respondents believed that 25 percent or more of all children were victims of child sexual abuse (Gilbert et al. 1989; Berrick and Gilbert 1991).

however, the official annual rates yield a fairly conservative estimate of the problem.[3]

Although the official reports underestimate the full extent of this problem, the highly publicized prevalence rates of 25–33 percent go to the other extreme. These figures come from surveys of adult women who were asked to recall if they had experienced any episodes of sexual abuse during childhood. Despite advocacy groups' claims about the enormous prevalence of child sexual abuse in the United States, an analysis of these surveys discloses more about the ambiguities of this problem than its magnitude.

Definitions of child sexual abuse include misbehaviors ranging from despicable violations that everyone would condemn to mild acts that many might find inappropriate or irritating but would not necessarily label as sexually abusive (Giovannoni and Becerra 1979; Ahn and Gilbert 1992). Different views of the full range of offenses that constitute child sexual abuse come to light in the results of fifteen surveys conducted since 1976, which attempt to estimate the prevalence of this problem. According to these surveys, the proportion of females sexually molested as children ranges from 6 percent to 62 percent of the population (for males, from 3 percent to 31 percent); half of the studies showed a female prevalence rate of 6 percent to 15 percent. Discrepancies among these findings are due in large part to differences in the researchers' operational definitions of sexual abuse, which include sexual propositions, exposure to an exhibitionist, unwanted touches and kisses, fondling, sexual intercourse, and other physical contact (Finkelhor et al. 1986).

Two of the largest and most widely cited surveys of the prevalence of child sexual abuse illustrate how expansively the problem is usually defined by advocacy researchers. Based on a survey of 930 women in San Francisco, Russell (1984) reports that 54 percent of her respondents were victims of incestuous or extrafamilial sexual abuse at least once before the age of eighteen. This prevalence rate reflects her definition of child sexual abuse, under which children who receive un-

[3] The fact that a case is substantiated does not always mean that behavior deemed as sexually abusive by the investigating authorities was motivated by sexual impulses on the part of the perpetrator and experienced by the child as emotionally or physically harmful. In some cultures it is considered generally permissible for family members to touch, even fondle, the sexual organs of babies and young children. Individuals from these groups have been charged with sexual abuse for behavior, such as touching a grandson's genitals, which they regard as an expression of pride rather than salaciousness (Ahn and Gilbert 1992).

wanted hugs and kisses and others who have not been touched at all (e.g., children who encounter exhibitionists) were classified as victims. Russell calculated a lower rate of 38 percent using a slightly narrower definition, which eliminated cases that did not involve physical contact. This narrower measure of sexual abuse included "unwanted sexual experiences ranging from attempted petting to rape" by persons outside the family and "any kind of exploitive sexual contact or attempted contact" by relatives. The information used to determine an episode of sexual abuse was composed of responses to fourteen screening questions such as, "Did anyone ever try or succeed in touching your breasts or genitals against your wishes before you turned 14?" "Did anyone ever feel you, grab you, or kiss you in a way you felt was threatening?" "At any time in your life has an uncle, brother, father, grandfather, or female relative ever had any kind of sexual contact with you?"

The supposedly more stringent definition of child sexual abuse actually stretches to cover everything from attempted petting and threatening kisses to any exploitive contact such as touching on the leg or other body parts to forced sexual intercourse, fellatio, and other forms of penetration. Claiming that Russell's research is one of the most accurate studies to date, Demause argues that it nevertheless substantially underestimates the true rate because many people do not consciously recall traumatic events before the age of five. According to Demause's (1991, p. 136) calculations, "The corrected incidence rates are at least 60 percent for girls and 45 percent for boys." His appraisal of the problem would have a sexually abused child in almost every family in the United States (or two abused children in every other family).

In the same vein as Russell's study, another major survey of child sexual abuse reported by Finkelhor et al. (1990) interviewed a sample of more than 2,600 men and women. Registering a prevalence rate somewhat lower than that of Russell's, Finkelhor and his colleagues found that 27 percent of women (and 16 percent of men) were sexually abused as children. The four screening questions used to detect abuse in this study are fewer in number than those employed by Russell but conceptually as indiscriminate. To illustrate the range of experiences merged under the definition of child sexual abuse, it is worth reporting these questions verbatim:

> When you were a child can you remember having any experience you would now consider as sexual abuse—like someone

> trying or succeeding in having any kind of sexual intercourse with you or anything like that?
>
> When you were a child can you remember having any experience you would now consider as sexual abuse involving someone touching you or grabbing you, or kissing you, or rubbing up against your body either in a public place or private—or anything like that?
>
> When you were a child can you remember any kind of experience that you would now consider sexual abuse involving someone taking nude photographs of you, or someone exhibiting parts of their body to you or someone performing some sex act in your presence—or anything like that?
>
> When you were a child can you remember any kind of experience that you would now consider sexual abuse involving oral sex or sodomy—or anything like that? (Finkelhor 1990, p. 18)

Positive responses to the first two questions—about someone trying or succeeding to have any kind of sexual intercourse or anything like that or any kind of touching, grabbing, and kissing or anything like that—accounted for nearly 90 percent of the acts defined as sexual abuse, with the remaining 10 percent involving exhibitionism.[4]

As these studies demonstrate, the most widely cited prevalence rates of child sexual abuse rest on responses to woolly questions such as, "Were you ever the victim of *attempted* petting?" "Did someone *try* or succeed in having *any kind* of sexual intercourse or *anything like that?*" "Did a relative ever have *any kind of sexual contact* with you?" "Did you receive a threatening kiss or an uncomfortable touch?" The basic problem with this research is that when one thinks of child sexual abuse, a single incident of attempted petting, a touch on the leg, a disagreeable kiss, and an unwanted pat on the buttock (or anything like that) is hardly what comes to mind. By designing research that lumps together possibly harmless behavior such as attempted petting with the

[4] Regarding the vagueness of wording and the judgments required by these questions, Finkelhor and colleagues (1990, p. 20) note: "Experiences *some* researchers might define as abuse could be left out because the respondents did not consider them as abuse. Other experiences of a minor nature that *many* researchers would exclude could have been counted because of a respondent's broad interpretation of the phrase, 'anything like that.' Unfortunately, no subsequent questions were asked about the sexual acts that could have been used to exclude experiences that did not meet researchers' criteria" (emphasis added). The qualifications "some" and "many" offer the only hint as to whether they believed that these questions were more likely to exaggerate or undercount rates of sexual abuse. About two-thirds of these incidents occurred only once, and 80 percent of the acts did not involve the use of force.

traumatic experience of child rape, advocates have inflated the estimates of child sexual abuse to critical proportions. Examining the prevalence surveys, Kutchinsky (1994, p. 12) "cannot help wondering why no attempt was made in these studies to single out the serious cases we are all interested in, the ones that are similar to those we see in the clinics or courts; those in which children have been victims of prolonged incest committed by a parent or a parent figure, or are forcibly molested, or abducted and abused, and so on."[5]

Following the approach of earlier surveys, recent research by advocates continues to expand the category of abuse by indiscriminately linking trivial, annoying, and impertinent acts with serious and terribly damaging sex crimes. Redefining child sexual abuse prevention programs as "victimization" prevention programs, Finkelhor, Asdigian, and Dziuba-Leatherman (1993) surveyed 2,000 children in an attempt to assess the prevalence of this problem and the effectiveness of prevention training. They report a 42 percent prevalence rate of "victimization" among the children surveyed. These "victimizations" included fights and attempted assaults by peers, gangs, or family members, kidnapping, and sexual abuse. Measures of sexual abuse involved positive responses to broadly worded questions such as, "Has there ever been a time when an older person tried to feel you, grab you, or kiss you in a sexual way that made you feel bad or afraid?" By equating school yard scraps, attempted fights, unwanted squeezes, and kisses that feel bad with kidnapping and rape of children, the researchers assemble a 42 percent "victimization" rate to construct a problem that affects almost every family in the country (and suggests a pressing need for more prevention programs). A closer look at the data reveals that when sexual abuse is separated out from other forms of victimization, the prevalence rate drops to 6 percent. And half of these involve attempted cases. Thus, the findings show an actual sexual abuse prevalence rate of 3 percent, which includes kisses and touches that felt bad. No explanation is offered for the discrepancy between this finding and the 27 percent prevalence rate of female child sexual abuse found in the 1990 survey (Finkelhor et al. 1990).

As the problems of child sexual abuse gained public notice and elicited new policies from state and federal government, advocates for the

[5] According to Kutchinsky's (1994, p. 12) reading, the data support conclusions that "the prevalence of single or episodic relatively serious events is in the neighborhood of 1 percent; and that prototype incest cases with small children being abused over several years by a parent run into a few cases per thousand."

elderly discovered that children were not the only victims of maltreatment. "A National Disgrace" was the title of the 1985 report issued by the Aging Committee's Subcommittee on Health and Long-Term Care. Citing research evidence that an estimated 4 percent of the elderly or 1 million older citizens are victims of abuse each year, the report maintained that "abuse of the elderly by their loved ones and caretakers existed with a frequency and rate only slightly less than child abuse" (Crystal 1987, p. 56).

One million victims is the kind of figure that attracts media attention, and the estimated incidence rate of 4 percent gained authority by frequent citation. But on closer inspection the figure evaporates into a haze of fuzzy calculations. The estimate is based on a survey of 433 elderly residents of Washington, D.C., of whom only seventy-three people (16 percent of the sample) responded. Such a low response rate immediately disqualifies any generalizations drawn from the results. As it turned out, three of the 73 respondents, or 4.1 percent, reported experiencing some form of psychological, physical, or material abuse. Advocates extrapolated from this small and unreliable sample to show that 1 million elderly people are victims of abuse, thereby constructing a national epidemic out of three incidents. Reviewing these "mythical numbers," Crystal (1987) points out that such findings stem from the strong interest among advocates for the elderly in keeping the victimization rate high—and from little interest in keeping it correct.[6]

In advocacy research, keeping the number high is often only part of the agenda. Beyond magnifying the size of their client group's problem to draw public attention, advocates habitually seek to define its essential characteristics. They tend not only to see their client group's problems as approaching epidemic proportions but to attribute the underlying causes to oppressive social conditions—such as sexism, racism, ageism, and capitalism—which can be corrected only through fundamental changes in society. Of course, there is a relation between the magnitude of a problem and the extent to which its cause is attributed to social forces or personal factors. If 4 percent of the labor force is unemployed, the workers without jobs are unskilled, unmotivated, or temporarily down on their luck; if the unemployment rate rises to 24

[6] Crystal (1987, p. 59) explains that the claims that "abuse of the elderly by their children or other family caretakers is increasing with epidemic proportions is particularly striking since fewer and fewer of the elderly are living with family at all . . . available evidence suggests that lack of a caretaker is a far more widespread problem than abuse by a caretaker."

percent, they are victims of a depression. If 5 percent of females are sexually abused as children, the offenders are sick deviants; if 50 percent of females are sexually abused as children, the problem is the way that males are regularly socialized to take advantage of females.

Along these lines, advocacy research dealing with homelessness has been concerned not only with inflating the estimates of the number of homeless but also with defining the nature of their problem. Advocates' estimates of the number of homeless in Chicago were nine times higher than the figures produced by repeated, carefully designed scientific surveys (Rossi, Fisher, and Willis 1986). Similarly, the National Coalition of the Homeless figured that there were 500,000 homeless children in the United States, a number ten times higher than the 35,000 calculated from the Urban Institute's national sample and the 40,000 estimated by a survey conducted by the U.S. Department of Housing and Urban Development (U.S. House Of Representatives, Committee on Ways and Means 1992). In assessing the cause of this problem, advocates take the large numbers as confirmation that the homeless are essentially victims of structural flaws and economic forces rather than personal deficiencies.[7] Examining the history of homelessness in America, for example, Miller concludes that causes for the current problem "can be found in the risks attendant on the wage labor system." As he sees it, "many members of the establishment would prefer to ignore a basic structural flaw in our socioeconomic system, whose correction would require a rethinking and reconstruction of the American system, and shift the blame for homelessness to the much smaller arena of mental health and care for the mentally ill" (Miller 1991, p. 162). The solution to the problem is employment. "Today's homeless," Miller explains, "need good jobs that pay decent wages. The homeless will work if they can find work" (p. 170).

This view of the homeless as people just like you and me, who for lack of a job find themselves on the streets, ignores compelling evidence to the contrary. Considerable information shows that between 40 percent and 66 percent of homeless adults suffer from significant alcohol problems (Rossi, Fisher, and Willis 1986; Wright 1988; Fischer and Breakey 1991); research findings also agree that between 33 percent and 50 percent of the homeless suffer from severe psychiat-

[7] In 1982, the Community for Creative Non-Violence made the highly publicized estimate that 2.2 million people (about 1 percent of the American population) were homeless. The empirical basis for this figure was never specified (Proch and Taber 1987).

ric disorders, such as schizophrenia (Burt and Cohen 1989; Fischer and Breakey 1991),[8] and various studies indicate that from 10 percent to 25 percent of homeless people are addicted to drugs (Wright 1988; Lubran 1990). Recognizing that alcoholism, mental illness, and drug abuse are not mutually exclusive problems, Baum and Burnes (1993) estimate that 65–85 percent of homeless adults suffer from at least one of these disabling conditions. Advocates, who wish to avoid blaming the victim, present the issue in terms of social and economic forces, which denies the essential nature of the personal problems afflicting most homeless people. Instead of solutions that emphasize employment and subsidized housing, Baum and Burnes's reading of the data shows that, above all, most homeless people require access to professional treatment and humane care.

Over the last decade, problems like stranger abduction, child abuse, elder abuse, and homelessness have been magnified by advocacy research. But these efforts are quite modest in comparison to the remarkably powerful campaign of advocacy research inspired by the rape crisis movement in the early 1990s.[9] According to the alarming accounts routinely voiced by some feminist groups, about one out of every two women will be victims of rape or attempted rape an average of two times in their lives, and many more will suffer other forms of sexual molestation. These claims are based on figures from several studies, among which the *Ms. Magazine* Campus Project on Sexual Assault, directed by Mary Koss, and Diana Russell's survey of sexual exploitation, are the largest, most widely disseminated, and frequently cited. Both studies were funded by the National Institute of Mental Health, endorsing these efforts with the imprimatur of a respected federal agency. Often quoted in newspapers and journals, on television, and

[8] As a result of the deinstitutionalization movement, the resident population in state hospitals declined from 475,000 in 1965 to 137,000 in 1980, and the rate is still falling (Applebaum 1987). Not only were a vast number of seriously mentally ill people discharged from these institutions over the last thirty years, but many others who would have been institutionalized during this period remained in the community. Some are in board-and-care facilities; others have drifted away to live on the streets. In an ironic conversion, the Keener Building on Wards Island in New York City became a men's shelter; originally a psychiatric hospital, it now provides refuge to some of the same people who previously would have received professional treatment and care at this facility.

[9] While some advocates deny the existence of the rape crisis movement, as two of its members, Collins and Whalen (1989, p. 61) explain: "The rape crisis movement was a radical feminist social issue that emerged in the early 1970s—feminist because the movement was conceived by women whose primary concerns focused on women's experiences, radical because it sought to dismantle the existing social order." By 1979 there were about 1,000 rape crisis centers that formed the organizational core of this movement (Amir and Amir 1979).

during the Senate reports (1991, 1993) on the Violence against Women Act, the findings from these studies have gained authority through repetition. Most of the time, however, those who cite the research findings take them at face value, understanding neither where the numbers come from nor what they actually represent. A critical analysis of these studies reveals how social scientists practice the craft of advocacy research, and why the media and the public are often deceived by these studies.

II. Rape Research: Examining the Facts

Advocacy research on rape benefits from a powerful aura of "scientific" inquiry. The findings are prefaced by sophisticated discussions of the intricate research methods employed and presented in a virtual blizzard of data supported by a few convincing case examples and numerous references to lesser-known studies. But footnotes do not a scholar make, and the value of quantitative findings depends on how accurately the research variables are measured, how well the sample is drawn, and the rigor with which the data are analyzed. Despite the respected funding source, frequent media acknowledgment, and an aura of scientific respectability, a close examination of the two most prominent studies on rape reveals serious flaws that cast grave doubt on their credibility.

The *Ms.* study directed by Koss involved a survey of 6,159 students at thirty-two colleges. As Koss operationally defines the problem, 27 percent of the female college students in her study had been victims of rape (15 percent) or attempted rape (12 percent) *an average of two times* between the ages of fourteen and twenty-one. Using the same survey questions, which she claims represent a strict legal description of the crime of rape, Koss calculates that during a twelve-month period 17 percent of college women were victims of rape or attempted rape and that more than one-half of these victims were assaulted twice (Koss, Gidycz, and Wisniewski 1987; Koss 1988; Warshaw 1988). If victimization continued at this annual rate over four years, we would expect well over half of the college women to suffer an incident of rape or attempted rape during that period, and more than one-quarter of them to be victimized twice.

There are several reasons for serious researchers to question the magnitude of sexual assault conveyed by the *Ms.* findings. To begin with, there is a notable discrepancy between Koss's definition of rape and the way most of the women she labeled as victims interpreted their experiences. When they were asked directly, 73 percent of the students whom Koss categorized as victims of rape did not think that they had been raped. This discrepancy is underscored by the subsequent behavior of a high proportion of those identified as victims, 42 percent of whom had sex again with the man who supposedly raped them. Of those categorized as victims of attempted rape, 35 percent later had sex with their purported offender (Koss, Gidycz, and Wisniewski 1987; Koss 1988).

Although the exact legal definition of rape varies by state, most definitions involve sexual penetration accomplished against a person's will by means of physical force or threat of bodily harm or when the victim is incapable of giving consent; the latter condition usually involves cases in which the victim is mentally ill, developmentally disabled, or intentionally incapacitated through the administration of intoxicating or anesthetic substances.

Rape and attempted rape were operationally defined in the *Ms.* study by five questions, three of which referred to the threat or use of "some degree of physical force." The other two questions, however, asked: "Have you had a man attempt sexual intercourse (get on top of you, attempt to insert his penis) when you didn't want to by giving you alcohol or drugs, but intercourse did not occur?" "Have you had sexual intercourse when you didn't want to because a man gave you alcohol or drugs?" (Koss, Gidycz, and Wisniewski 1987, p. 167; Koss 1988, p. 8). Forty-four percent of all the women identified as victims of rape and attempted rape in the previous year were so labeled because they responded positively to these awkward and vaguely worded questions. What does having sex "because" a man gives you drugs or alcohol signify? A positive response does not indicate whether duress, intoxication, force, or the threat of force were present, whether the woman's judgment or control were substantially impaired, or whether the man purposefully got the woman drunk in order to prevent her from resisting his sexual advances. Perhaps the woman was trading sex for drugs, or perhaps a few drinks lowered her inhibitions so that she consented to an act that she later regretted.[10] Koss's interpretation of the data assumes that a positive answer signifies the respondent engaged in sexual intercourse against her will because she was intoxicated to the

[10] In Prince George's County, Maryland, for example, where more than one in four allegations of rape in 1990–91 were unfounded (i.e., the women admitted their charges were false or the police found no evidence that a rape had occurred), the former head of criminal investigations concludes that this high rate of false reports is due in part "to frequent cases of sex-for-drug transactions gone sour" (Buckley 1992, p. B1).

point of being unable to deny consent (and that the man had administered the alcohol for this purpose). Although the question could have been clearly worded to denote "intentional incapacitation of the victim," only a mind reader could detect whether any affirmative response to the question as it stands corresponds to the legal definition of rape.

In an attempt to resolve this problem, Koss and Cook (1993*a*, p. 3) first take the question as originally reported, "Have you had sexual intercourse with a man when you didn't want to because he gave you drugs or alcohol?" and claim that it included the words "to make you cooperate." Rather than helping the case, however, this revised version suggests that instead of being too drunk to deny consent, the respondent actually cooperated in the act of intercourse after taking drugs and alcohol. After noting this criticism of their attempt to clarify the case by altering the original definition, Koss and Cook (1993*b*, p. 106) concede that "for the sake of discussion it is helpful to examine what happens to the prevalence figures when these instances are removed."[11] When the item dealing with drugs and alcohol is removed, according to Koss and Cook's revised estimates, the prevalence rate of rape and attempted rape declines by one-third.[12]

During Koss's (1990) testimony in the Senate Judiciary Committee Hearings on the Violence against Women Act, it emerged that three-quarters of the respondents classified as victims in the *Ms.* study did not think they had been raped. However, no questions were raised as to why all these other young college women would not know they had experienced the brutal and terrifying crime of rape. On how they did interpret the event, Koss (1990, p. 40) reports to the Senate Judiciary Committee: "Among college women who had an experience that met legal requirements for rape, only a quarter labeled their experience as rape. Another quarter thought their experience was some kind of crime, but not rape. The remaining half did not think their experience qualified as any type of crime."

A somewhat different account of how the students interpreted their experience had been published several years earlier by Koss and her colleagues (Koss et al. 1988). According to that report, 11 percent of

[11] Later, in an interview with Schoenberg and Roe (1993, p. 5), Koss acknowledged that the drug and alcohol questions, two of the five items used to define victims of rape and attempted rape, were ambiguous.

[12] From the form in which data are reported in Koss's earlier studies, it is not possible to verify this new prevalence estimate. But calculations that can be made from the original data show that the one-year incidence rate declines by about 44 percent when the item dealing with intercourse because of drugs or alcohol is removed.

the students said they "don't feel victimized," 49 percent labeled the experience "miscommunication," 14 percent labeled it "crime, but not rape," and 27 percent said it was "rape." Although there was no indication that other data might have been available on this question, three years later a surprisingly different distribution of responses was put forth. In answer to questions raised (Gilbert 1991*a*, 1991*b*) about the fact that most of the victims did not think they had been raped, Koss offered four new versions of the students' responses, in none of which did she mention that 49 percent thought it a matter of "miscommunication." First, in contrast to the data she originally published, Koss (1991*c*, p. 6) writes that the students labeled as "victims" viewed the incident as follows: "one quarter thought it was rape, one quarter thought it was some kind of crime but did not believe it qualified as rape, one quarter thought it was sexual abuse but did not think it qualified as a crime, and one quarter did not feel victimized."

In a later paper, Koss (1991*b*, p. 9) revised the gist of these new findings: "one quarter thought it was some kind of crime, but did not *realize* it qualified as rape; one quarter thought it was *serious* sexual abuse, but did not *know* it qualified as a crime" (emphasis added).

Two years later, yet another revision of these findings was published. Koss (1993) continued to deny that virtually one half of the students labeled their experience a case of "miscommunication"; she claimed instead that "only one in ten victims said she felt unvictimized by the experience. The remaining nine who felt victimized were split between those who thought their experience was rape (the 27 percent fraction Mr. Gilbert quotes), those who thought their experience was a crime but might not be called rape, and *those who thought their incident was extremely traumatic but* was not a crime" (emphasis added). Finally, in the fourth effort, Koss and Cook (1993*b*, p. 107) explain: "In fact, half the rape victims identified in the national survey considered their experience as rape or some crime similar to rape."

These inconsistencies aside, the additional data are difficult to interpret. If one-quarter thought their incidents involved a crime, but not rape, what kind of crime did they have in mind? Were they referring to illegal activity at the time such as underage drinking or taking drugs?[13]

[13] In reviewing the research methodology for the *Ms.* study, Koss (1988) and Koss, Gidycz, and Wisniewski (1987) explain that previous reliability and validity studies conducted on the ten-item Sexual Experience Survey instrument showed that few of the female respondents misinterpreted the questions on rape. Examining these earlier studies, however, one finds that the Sexual Experience Survey (SES) instrument originally referred to (Koss and Oros 1982) differed from the revised version used in the *Ms.* study

Despite Koss's elaboration on the data originally reported, in the first version of the findings 60 percent of the students either did not feel victimized or thought the incident was a case of miscommunication. Although in the second, third, and fourth versions Koss claims that many more of the students assessed the sexual encounter in negative terms, the fact remains that 73 percent did not think they were raped.

Although Koss did not examine the issue of miscommunication, findings by Sprecher et al. (1994) reveal the widespread extent of sexual miscommunication in dating relationships among college students. These researchers analyzed the experiences of college students from the United States, Russia, and Japan in regard to two forms of sexual miscommunication: token resistance (saying no, but meaning yes) and consent to unwanted sex (saying yes, but meaning no). The results of this study showed that 38 percent of the U.S. women reported engaging in token resistance to sex compared to 37 percent of the Japanese women and 59 percent of the Russian women, and that U.S. women indicated the highest rate (55 percent) of consent to unwanted sex compared to Russian (32 percent) and Japanese (27 percent) women.

With regard to the many students classified as victims in the *Ms.* survey who had sex again with the man who supposedly raped them, Koss (1988, p. 16) initially reported: "Surprisingly, 42 percent of the women indicated that they had sex again with the offender on a later occasion, *but it is not known if this was forced or voluntary;* most relationships (87 percent) did *eventually* break up subsequent to the victimization" (emphasis added). Three years later, in a letter to the *Wall Street Journal,* Koss claimed to know that the next instance of sexual intercourse with the same offender was likewise rape and that the relationship broke up not "eventually" (as do most college relationships) but immediately after the second rape. As she explained: "Many victims reacted to the first rape with self-blame and thought that if they tried harder to be clear they could influence the man's behavior. Only after the second rape did they realize the problem was the man, not themselves. Afterwards, 87 percent of the women ended the relationship with the man who raped them" (Koss 1991*a*, p. 21). Koss goes on to

---

in at least one important respect: the original SES instrument contained neither of the questions dealing with rape or attempted rape "because a man gave you alcohol or drugs." In a brief report on the assessment of validity, Koss and Gidycz (1985, p. 423) note: "To explore the veracity of the self-reported sexual experiences, the Sexual Experiences Survey (original wording) was administered to approximately 4,000 students," which suggests that the findings on validity would not include the vague items on "intentional incapacitation" absent from the original version of the SES instrument.

suggest that these students did not know they were raped since many of them were sexually inexperienced and "lacked familiarity with what consensual intercourse should be like."

These explanations are highly speculative. It is hard to imagine that so many college women, even if sexually inexperienced, are unable to judge if their sexual encounters were consensual. As for the victims blaming themselves and believing they might influence the man's behavior if they tried harder the second time, there are no data from the *Ms.* survey to substantiate this reasoning. Although research indicates there is a tendency for victims of rape to blame themselves (Craig 1990), there is no evidence that a sense of culpability induces them to have sex again with their assailant. Some battered wives do stay with their husbands under insufferable circumstances. But it is not apparent that the battered wife syndrome applies to a large proportion of female college students.

In a final attempt to explain the findings, Koss (1991*a*) asserts that most college women who are sexually violated by an acquaintance do not recognize themselves as victims of rape. She argues, "Many people do not realize that legal definitions of rape make no distinctions about the relationship between victim and offender." Contrary to this claim, findings from the Bureau of Justice Statistics (1989, 1991) suggest that the crime of being raped by an acquaintance may not be so difficult to comprehend; in recent years 33–45 percent of the women who said they were raped identified their assailant as an acquaintance.

Moving beyond the experiences of college students, Russell's study is another major source often quoted as evidence that rape has reached, as she describes it, "epidemic proportions throughout society" (Russell 1984, p. 57; 1991). In addition to reporting a child sexual abuse prevalence rate of 38–54 percent, Russell (1984) found that 44 percent of the women in her sample were victims of rape (26 percent) or attempted rape (18 percent) an average of twice in their life, and that many other women suffered experiences in marriage that, if not rape, were very close to it. As for the latter, if mutually desired intercourse and rape are placed at either end of a continuum, Russell (1982, p. 356) explains, "our study suggests that a considerable amount of marital sex is probably closer to the rape end of the continuum."

There are several fundamental problems with Russell's survey, which is based on interviews with a group of women in San Francisco. Although serious efforts were made to achieve a random sample of participants, the researchers were able to complete their interviews with only 930 people out of an original sample of 2,000. Thirty-six percent of the people contacted refused outright to participate in the study. Russell offers two somewhat different accounts of the inaccessibility of the other nonparticipants. In *Rape in Marriage* (Russell 1982, p. 31), she says, "Because of a high incidence of not-at-homes during the summer months when the interviews were conducted, and because of an unexpectedly large number of households in which no eligible women resided, the original sample of two thousand drawn by the methods described proved insufficient for obtaining one thousand completed interviews." Later, it appears that Russell really did not know the ("unexpectedly large") number of households in which no eligible women resided. As she describes the sampling difficulties in *Sexual Exploitation:* "Many of the households that were inaccessible or where no one was at home *might have been* households in which no eligible women lived (for example, there are a large number of male households in San Francisco)" (1984, p. 38, emphasis added).

For whatever reasons, more than 50 percent of the women in the sample did not participate in the interview survey. Properly executed interview surveys, according to the standard textbook criterion, should achieve a completion rate of 80 to 85 percent, which is the range usually required of surveys by Federal agencies (Rubin and Babbie 1989). It is very doubtful that the 930 participants who agreed to be interviewed for Russell's study can be considered a representative random sample of the women in San Francisco.

There is a more basic problem, however. After starting with a questionable sample, Russell goes on to claim that her respondents' sexual experiences not only reflect those of all the women in San Francisco but also are representative of the entire female population of the United States. A brief disclaimer to the effect that generalizing from the San Francisco sample "would be highly speculative" is quickly forgotten as, after adjusting her findings for age-specific probabilities, Russell (1984, p. 50) concludes: "It is indeed shocking that 46 percent of American women are likely to be victims of attempted rape or completed rape sometimes in their lives." She continues to share this conclusion with the media (Freedberg 1991). She also notes that these victims are likely to be attacked an average of two times. The fact that only 31 percent of the women in Russell's sample were married compared to a 63 percent marital rate nationally is one of many reasons that this national estimate drawn from the sexual experiences of the San Francisco sample is not simply highly speculative but scientifically groundless.

Beyond sampling bias there is the question of how rates of rape and attempted rape were measured. Russell's estimates are derived from responses to thirty-eight questions. Only one of these questions asked respondents whether they had been a victim of rape or attempted rape any time in their lives. Twenty-two percent of the sample, or one-half of women defined as victims by Russell, gave an affirmative answer to this question. Although the entire questionnaire is not reported, Russell offers an example of a typical question that was repeated several times in reference to strangers, acquaintances, and dates or lovers: "Have you ever had any unwanted sexual experiences including kissing, petting or intercourse with a date because you felt physically threatened?" If yes, "Did he either try or succeed in having any kind of sexual intercourse with you?" A considerable proportion of the cases counted as rape and attempted rape in this study are based on the researcher's interpretation of experiences described by respondents. In assessing the standards applied in these cases, one might bear in mind that it was even before Russell did this study that she claimed that "much of what passes for normal heterosexual intercourse would be seen as close to rape" (Russell 1975, p. 261). Although this analysis of sex relations is not as censorious as Andrea Dworkin's (1988), for whom all heterosexual sex is rape, it would seem to lean in that direction.

Using her San Francisco findings, Russell (1984) offers a detailed analysis to extrapolate, not only the lifetime probability, but the national incidence of rape and attempted rape in 1978. The incidence figure for rape in Russell's survey was 35 per 1,000 females; this includes cases of rape and attempted rape that occurred to residents of San Francisco, both inside and outside the city. According to Russell, "This is *24 times higher* than the 1.71 per 1,000 females reported by the Uniform Crime Reports" (Russell 1984, p. 46; she makes the same emphasis). On the basis of this calculation, Russell takes the 1978 Uniform Crime Report's figure of 67,131 for all the cases of rape and attempted rape in the United States and multiplies it by 24, which yields Russell's national estimate of 1.6 million incidents that year.

Faulty logic and poor arithmetic invalidate this analysis. First, the initial calculation (ironically italicized) is incorrect. The San Francisco rate of 35 per 1,000 is 20.5 times (not 24 times) higher than the Uniform Crime Report's 1.71 per 1,000. Ignoring, for a moment, this arithmetical error, the logic of the second calculation assumes a correspondence between the Uniform Crime Report rates for San Francisco and the nation. If Russell's sample had an incidence rate 24 times higher than the Uniform Crime Report's rate for San Francisco, we need only multiply the Uniform Crime Report's national rate by 24 to project the local difference on a national scale. However, those who study this subject know very well that the reported rates of rape are considerably higher for metropolitan areas than for the national population (Johnson 1980). Indeed, the Uniform Crime Report's total of 67,131 cases of rape and attempted rape in 1978 amounted to a national rate of 0.6 per 1,000 females, which was about one-third the rate of 1.7 per 1,000 females it showed for San Francisco (U.S. Bureau of the Census 1986). Thus, if we include the initial arithmetic error, Russell's national estimate of the incidence of sexual assault exaggerates by about 350 percent the figure that would result from simply an accurate reading of her own facts.

III. Promoting Advocacy Research: Tactics and the Media

The *Ms.* study by Koss and Russell's survey of sexual exploitation are highly sophisticated examples of advocacy research. Behind the veil of social science, elaborate research methods are employed to persuade the public and policy makers that a problem is vastly larger than is commonly recognized. This is done in several ways: first, by defining a problem so broadly that it forms a vessel into which almost any human difficulty can be poured; second, by measuring a group highly affected with the problem and then projecting the findings to society-at-large; third, by asserting that a variety of smaller studies and reports with different problem definitions, methodologies of diverse quality, and varying results form a cumulative block of evidence in support of current findings; fourth, by claiming that the publication of findings in professional journals attests to their validity; fifth, by employing what Best (1990) describes as "atrocity tales"—painfully detailed anecdotes that typify the human suffering caused by the problem but fail to give the slightest hint of its incidence in the population;[14] sixth, by changing

[14] Russell introduces her book *Sexual Exploitation* (1984) with a series of case studies of sexual abuse; her work *Rape in Marriage* (1982) also contains detailed descriptions of sexual molestations; Warshaw's (1988) book (which reports Koss's findings) uses numerous vignettes to illustrate acquaintance rape.

definitions and revising data in response to criticism in the hope that no one will examine the facts as originally reported; and, seventh, when all else fails, by regressing to ad hominem argument.[15]

Initially, the findings of advocacy research often receive a favorable reception from the media. With a lack of critical scrutiny, reporters at first rush to embrace advocates' claims about the magnitude and character of problems such as child abuse, homelessness, kidnapping, elder abuse, and rape. The various reasons for this willingness to suspend disbelief have to do with journalists, their public readership, and social scientists. As documented in *The Media Elite*, the majority of journalists hold distinctly liberal positions on political and social issues (Lichter, Rothman, and Lichter 1986). This viewpoint often translates into concerns about victims of oppression and social ills. "Afflict the comfortable and comfort the afflicted!" the edict of a distinguished professor of journalism at Columbia University, "could have been the school slogan," notes Gutmann (1993, p. 51). The message at Columbia, she explains, was that a viable story assignment for students "could combine any three from this list: Bronx, babies, community activists, crack, homelessness, social program that's losing its funding, single mothers, the Lower East Side, and AIDS—always AIDS." One need not examine the Columbia School of Journalism to recognize that as a rule journalists are quicker to report about experiences that are painful and sensational than about those that are comfortable and ordinary. One reason besides the tendency to publicize the plight of victims is that murder and mayhem attract public attention, for which the media compete. This is not a phenomenon unique to the United States. Discussing the role of the media in constructing moral panics, McRobbie and Thornton (1995, p. 570) explain, "As the British press become more competitive, one strategy for maintaining circulation figures is for the newspaper to cast itself in the role of moral guardian, ever alert to new possibilities for concern and indignation."

Advocacy research benefits from a felicitous union between journalists' inclinations to discover victims and their readerships' curiosities about the horrors of modern life, and it benefits from journalists' general inability to evaluate data that advocates feed to the press. Most

[15] Koss (1993), for example, unable to answer the questions raised and the discrepancies I documented in her research, takes the offensive: "I don't understand what Mr. Gilbert's academic affiliation as a professor of 'social welfare' means. All we have heard is what he is against. When is he going to share with us how he proposes to meet the legitimate needs for healing of sexually victimized women and children?"

journalists are not well versed in social science research methods. They gather and cross-check information by interviewing experts. Since advocates are frequently among the first to uncover and publicize information about emerging problems, in the initial stages of problem discovery they are the ones interviewed, and their data frame the issue.

A common tactic of advocacy researchers is to declare not only that their estimates are accurate but that they are well replicated in many other studies as well. In support of the *Ms.* survey findings, for example, Koss often adduces additional studies as sources of independent verification. But if the studies she usually cites are examined closely, very little confirmation is found. Some of these studies (e.g., Ageton 1983) use different definitions of forced sexual behavior (including verbal persuasion and psychological coercion) and involve small or nonrepresentative samples that are inappropriate as bases for making serious estimates about the size of the problem. Others are referred to without explanation or critical examination. Thus, for example, Koss and Cook (1993*b*) cite two studies using representative samples, which show the prevalence rate of rape for college students in the 12 percent range, a figure not too far from the 15 percent reported in the *Ms.* findings. One of these studies, conducted by Koss and Oros (1982), used the original version of the SES instrument to measure rape, which excluded items dealing with unwanted intercourse "because a man gives you drugs or alcohol." The second study (Yegidis 1986) defined rape as forced oral sex or intercourse, where the use of "force" included verbal persuasion. "This study showed," according to the researcher, "that most of the sexual encounters were forced through verbal persuasion-protestations by the male to 'go further' because of sexual need, arousal, or love." According to this definition, the conventional script of nagging and pleading—"Everyone does it," "If you really loved me, you'd do it," "I need it," "You will like it"—is transformed into a version of rape. After verbal persuasion, the form of "force" experienced most frequently by students was "use of alcohol or drugs," though the study neither elaborates on this category nor claims that it reflects intentional incapacitation of the victim (Yegidis 1986, p. 53).

As further evidence that their results are verified by other research, Koss and Cook (1993*b*, p. 110) refer to the National Victim Center (1992) study, noting that, "in a just released telephone survey of more than 4,000 women in a nationally representative sample, the rate of rape was reported to be 14 percent, although this rate excluded rapes of women unable to consent." This, of course, is close to the 15 percent rate claimed by the *Ms.* study. What Koss and Cook fail to tell the reader is that approximately 40 percent of the rapes reported in this study occurred to women between the ages of fourteen and twenty-four, resulting in about a 5 percent rape prevalence estimate for that age group.[16] According to Koss's findings in the *Ms.* study, 15 percent of college women are victims of rape between the ages of fourteen and twenty-one. Thus, for almost the same age cohort, the *Ms.* study found a rate of rape three times higher than that detected by the National Victim Center survey.

Some critical issues have also been raised about the National Victim Center (1992) survey. One of the four questions used to define rape in this study includes sexual penetration by a man's fingers, which does not reflect the legal definition of rape in most states.[17] Sommers (1994, p. 216) suggests that such rapes might include "cases in which a boy penetrated a girl with his finger against her will in a heavy petting situation. Certainly the boy behaved badly. But is he a rapist? Probably neither he nor his date would say so. Yet the survey seems to classify him as a rapist." Although the study director assured Sommers that responses to this item did not significantly affect the outcome, she wondered about that, since the study had found a large percent of rape among youngsters in the age group most likely to find themselves in a heavy petting situation. Further questions about the nature of the experiences defined as rape in the center's study are raised by the fact that almost one-half (49 percent) of those defined as rape victims said that they were not afraid of being seriously injured or killed during the incident.

Beyond knowing that one-half the victims were not afraid of being seriously injured, we do not know how the women defined the incidents because the researchers did not ask them directly whether they

[16] In fact, the rate of rape found in the National Victim Center (1992) study was 13 percent. Data on the victim's age at the time of rape are reported in the study grouped according to those less than eleven years old, eleven to seventeen years old, eighteen to twenty-four years old, and twenty-five and over. To calculate the percent of victims in the fourteen-to-twenty-four age cohort, I took a proportional rate of the eleven-to-seventeen-year-olds (18 percent) and added that to the 22 percent in the eighteen-to-twenty-four-year-old group. Since these data on the age of rape included cases in which some women were victimized more than once, the estimate assumes that the cases of multiple rapes were distributed proportionately among the age groups.

[17] When Schoenberg and Roe (1993, p. 5) inquired about this item, the study's director, Dean Kilpatrick, allowed that his definition "might be a tad broader" than the common legal standard.

had been raped. Regarding this omission, the research director explained that there was not enough time in the thirty-five-minute telephone survey to include this question (Schoenberg and Roe 1993). In an earlier survey conducted by the director of the 1992 National Victim Center study, respondents were classified as victims of rape if they had an experience in which someone used force or the threat of force to make them have sexual relations (including intercourse, oral and anal sex) against their will. That 1985 survey of 2,004 women found a rape prevalence rate of 5 percent, less than half the level of the 1992 findings (Kilpatrick et al. 1985). The findings from the 1985 survey are not mentioned in the 1992 report.

Koss and Cook also refer to Russell's (1984) study, which found a lifetime prevalence rate of rape that is twice as high as that found by the National Victim Center study. Despite the much higher prevalence rate, fewer than 1 percent of the rapes in Russell's sample were reported to have occurred when the victim was under eleven years of age, whereas 29 percent of the rapes reported in the National Victim Center study occurred during these childhood years. Continuing to claim that the *Ms.* survey's estimates of rape prevalence "are well-replicated in other studies," Koss (1991*c*) refers to Craig's (1990) discerning review of the literature to confirm the consistency of prevalence data on college students. This is a curious citation, for Craig holds a different opinion. She notes that the problems of definition "vary from use of force, to threat of force, to use of manipulative tactics such as falsely professing love, threatening to leave the woman stranded, or attempting to intoxicate the woman." Even when studies use the same general definitions, their authors often develop idiosyncratic measures to operationalize the terms—all of which leads Craig to conclude that "this lack of consistency limits the comparability of studies and makes replication of results difficult" (1990, p. 403).

What can be made of these vast discrepancies? Only by ignoring the relevant details can the results of studies such as these be construed as independent confirmation of the *Ms.* findings. Moreover, if the works of Koss, Russell, and others suggest that anywhere from 15 percent to 50 percent of women have been victims of rape and attempted rape, other studies—a "nonsupporting literature"—point to rates well below 10 percent. These studies with modest rates rarely make headlines. George, Winfield, and Blazer (1992), for example, found a 5.9 percent lifetime prevalence rate of sexual assault in North Carolina; this finding was based on responses to the broad question, "Has someone ever pressured you against your will into forced contact with the sexual parts of your body or their body?" While regional differences may account for some of the disparity between the *Ms.* findings and those of the Duke University team, it should be noted that in 1990 the rate of rapes reported to the police in North Carolina was 83 percent of the national average (author's calculation).

An even lower prevalence rate was detected by Riger and Gordon (1981), who report that, among 1,620 respondents, randomly selected in Chicago, San Francisco, and Philadelphia, only 2 percent had been raped or sexually assaulted in their lifetime. Riger and Gordon note, however, that among a small subsample of 367 respondents who were selected to be interviewed in-person and who were younger, wealthier, and better educated than those in the larger random sample, 11 percent mentioned ever having been raped or sexually assaulted. As already noted, Kilpatrick and his colleagues found a rape prevalence rate of 5 percent in a representative sample of 2,004 women (Kilpatrick et al. 1985). And in a survey conducted by Louis Harris and associates (1993), only 2 percent of a random sample of 2,500 women responded affirmatively to the question "In the last five years have you been a victim of rape or sexual assault?" Since "sexual assault" might be interpreted as applying to a wide range of experiences, we would expect the victims of rape to account for considerably less than the entire 2 percent.

The most startling disparity emerges when the *Ms.* study's findings on the annual incidence of rape and attempted rape is compared with the number of these offenses actually reported to the authorities on college campuses. Using her survey questions, Koss found that 166 women in 1,000 were victims of rape and attempted rape in just one year on campuses across the country (each victimized an average of 1.5 times). In sharp contrast, the FBI (1993) figures show that at 500 major colleges and universities with an overall population of 5 million students, only 408 cases of rape and attempted rape were reported to the police—less than one incident of rape and attempted rape per campus. The number yields an annual rate of .16 in 1,000 for female students, which is *1,000 times smaller* than Koss's finding. Although it is generally agreed that many rape victims do not report their ordeal because of the embarrassment and callous treatment frequently experienced at the hands of the police, no one to my knowledge publicly claims that the problem is 1,000 times greater than the cases reported to the po-

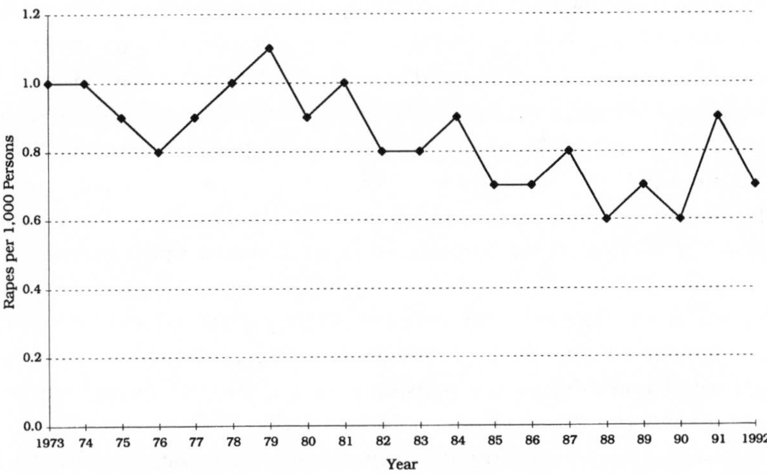

Fig. 1.—Rates of rape per 1,000 persons, age 12 or older, 1973–92. Source: Bureau of Justice Statistics (1993).

lice—a rate at which almost every women in the country would be raped at least once every year.

Finally, data collected annually by the Bureau of Justice Statistics (BJS) provide the most dependable figures on the changing rates of rape and attempted rape over the last two decades.[18] As Christopher Jencks (1991) points out, since the BJS surveys are conducted almost the same way every year, their biases are likely to be constant so that the data generated by these studies provide quite a reliable guide to trends in sexual assault over time (even if the magnitude is underestimated). As shown in Figure 1, the rates of rape and attempted rape

[18] The BJS surveys, which are actually conducted by the Census Bureau, interview a random sample of about 62,000 households every six months. The confidentiality of responses is protected by federal law, and response rates amount to 96 percent of eligible units. Up until 1992, the interview schedule included a series of screening questions such as, "Did anyone threaten to beat you up or threaten you with a knife, gun, or some other weapon?" "Did anyone try to attack you in some other way?" "Did you call the police to report something that happened to you that you thought was a crime?" "Did anything happen to you which you thought was a crime, but you did not report to the police?" After 1992, the screening questions in the redesigned BJS survey included a question asking whether any threats or attacks involved rape, attempted rape, or other type of sexual assault. A positive response to any of the screening items is followed up by asking, "What actually happened?" "How were you threatened?" "How did the offender attack you?" "What injuries did you suffer?" "When, where did it happen, what did you do?" and so forth (Bureau of Justice Statistics 1992, 1995).

rose somewhat from 1973 to 1979, then they declined and eventually leveled off after the mid-1980s. From its peak in 1979 to 1992, the incidence of rape and attempted rape declined by more than one-third; between 1985 and 1990 the rates fluctuated slightly, but the differences were not statistically significant (Bureau of Justice Statistics 1993). Starting in 1989, field tests were initiated to redesign the BJS survey by adding new questions in response to heightened interest in certain types of victimizations, particularly rape. The first findings from the redesigned survey were reported for 1993. Because of the redesign, the victimization rates for 1993 were not directly comparable to those derived from earlier surveys. However, to preserve the ability to detect annual changes during the transition period, one-half of the sampled households in 1992 were interviewed with the new survey instrument. Continuing the general trend shown in figure 1, a comparison of rates of rape per 1,000 persons for 1992–93 shows a 25 percent decline, though not statistically significant (Bureau of Justice Statistics 1993). Whether the focus is on the significant decline over the last decade or the steady state in recent years, the picture that emerges refutes advocates' accounts of an epidemic (Russell 1984, 1991).

As for the magnitude of the problem in recent times, BJS findings reveal that 140,100 people, or .7 people in 1,000, over twelve years of age were victims of rape or attempted rape in 1992, based on the old survey instrument. Using the new survey instrument, the rate of victimization more than doubled to 310,000 or 1.5 persons per 1,000 (Bureau of Justice Statistics 1994, p. 8). Although no trivial figure, the 1.5 persons per 1,000 rate is still lower than the rates claimed in the widely cited studies by Russell, Koss, and the National Victim Center.[19]

Despite this substantial rise in the incidence rate shown in official statistics, advocates continue to declare that rape is still underreported. Writing in the *New York Times*, Lynn Schafran, project director for the National Organization for Women Legal Defense and Education Fund, argues that the 1993 BJS figure of 310,000 rapes (160,000 completed and 150,000 attempted rapes) is less accurate than the annual

[19] In response to feminist concerns, the redesigned BJS survey also added a new category of victimization—"Sexual Assault." As defined by the survey: "Sexual assaults may or may not involve force and include such things as grabbing or fondling. Sexual assault also includes verbal threats." Of the 185,000 incidents of sexual assault reported in 1993, 141,000 involved sexual assaults without injury or verbal threats (Bureau of Justice Statistics 1995, pp. 9, 11).

rate of 683,000 completed rapes found in the National Victim Center Study (entitled "Rape in America"): "Although the redesigned Justice Department survey is a vast improvement," she explains, "its methodology is not as sophisticated as that used in the 'Rape in America' study" (Schafran 1995, p. A15).

In comparing the methodologies of the two studies for the *New York Times* readers, Schafran fails to mention that, as we already know, one of the four questions used to define a completed case of rape in the National Victim Center study (1992) involved sexual penetration by a man's fingers (not a legal definition of rape in most states) and that half of the respondents defined as victims of rape in this study were not afraid of being seriously injured during the incident in question. Nor does she mention that, although the survey sample was scientifically designed to allow for valid generalizations to the broader population, the accuracy of these generalizations was seriously undermined because nearly one-third of the scientifically designed sample did not participate in the second wave of interviews, from which the annual incidence rate of rape was calculated. The 3,220 study participants interviewed during the second wave amounted to only 68 percent of the original sample.[20] With a sample this size, the nationwide estimate of 683,000 rapes was based on twenty-three cases of rape uncovered in the interviews. The published results of this study, however, do not report how many of the twenty-three cases might have involved digital penetration by teenagers in a heavy petting situation.

Like other victimization surveys, the BJS studies have problems of subject recall, definition, and measurement, which—as Koss (1990) and others (Russell 1984; Jencks 1991) have pointed out—cause the amount of sexual assault to be underestimated. Less frequently pointed out is the fact that attempts to estimate the incidence of sexual assault are also contaminated by false reports of rape. According to the FBI (1993), for example, 8 percent of rapes reported to the police in 1992 were later deemed to be unfounded because the alleged victim recanted or investigators uncovered no evidence of a crime.

In light of these enormous discrepancies, the average layman and the social scientist must wonder what is really being measured here. To

[20] The description offered of this study's methodology creates an impression of a somewhat higher response rate. The researchers note that 85 percent of eligible respondents agreed to participate in the first wave of interviews and then indicate that the second wave of interviews reached 81 percent of the first wave respondents.

advocacy researchers these discrepancies represent inconvenient details to be swept under the carpet of "supporting literature." With neither the inclination nor the skill to systematically review and critically evaluate research literature, the media are easily deceived by claims of independent verification by other studies. Repeating Koss's claim, for example, in an article for *Newsweek*, Faludi (1993, p. 61) confidently asserts, "Numerous other studies bear these figures out." Among journalists there is much fuzzy thinking and writing on this matter. Pollitt, for one, writing in the *New Yorker* disregards serious concerns for detail and accuracy: "One in five, one in eight—what if it is only one in ten or one in twelve? Social science isn't physics. Exact numbers are important, and elusive, but surely what is significant here is that lots of different studies, with different agendas, sample populations, and methods tend in the same direction" (1993, p. 223). Pollitt fails to explain, however, what "direction" she is referring to—toward one in five or one in twelve.

Journalists also have a difficult time sorting out the numbers because activist constituencies lend vocal support to advocacy research claims. Reporters seeking to verify reports about the prevalence of rape, for example, will find many social workers and therapists in rape prevention centers and counseling programs ready to confirm the figures. These workers, of course, have a vested interest in increasing public funds to address the problem. But their support of advocacy numbers reflects more than simply an occupational stake in the problem. Working daily with women who have suffered dreadful sexual abuses, many therapists and social workers truly believe that the number of victims is huge as professed by advocacy studies. There is some evidence that their perceptions may be influenced not just by the stream of daily encounters with victims, but by personal experiences as victims themselves.[21] Thus, the initial absence of contradictory evidence and the presence of a constituency (often well organized) that will attest to the findings lend a degree of credibility to advocacy research.

Although the media initially tend to promote advocacy findings, most journalists—liberal tendencies and readers' curiosities aside—ul-

[21] A survey of graduate students in social work, guidance and counseling, education, and business reveals that social work students reported being sexually molested three times as often and counseling students twice as often as students in education or business (Russel et al. 1993).

timately are interested in the truth. When new data become available or advocacy claims stretch the suspension of disbelief so far that someone begins to wonder where these figures really came from, the media will challenge the numbers it originally promulgated.[22] Indeed, recent analyses suggest that moral panics are less monolithic than is implied by the initial conceptualization of this phenomenon. As McRobbie and Thornton (1995, p. 573) point out, "Moral panics are now continually contested."

In 1993 the media began to challenge advocacy research on rape; a *New York Times Magazine* cover story proclaimed, "RAPE HYPE BETRAYS FEMINISM." In a critical analysis of "rape-crisis feminists," Roiphe remembered a poster at college announcing that one in four women had been a victim of rape or attempted rape. "If I were really standing in the middle of an 'epidemic,' a 'crisis'—if 25 percent of my women friends were really being raped—wouldn't I know it?" she wondered (1993*a*, p. 26). Roiphe concludes, "These posters were not presenting facts. They were advertising a mood." It was a mood stirred considerably by earlier stories in the *New York Times* (Lewin 1991), *Time Magazine* (Gibbs 1991), and in many other dailies as well as television reports citing findings such as Koss's and Russell's as authoritative data. Roiphe's article was followed by a new round of reports on NBC television and PBS radio and in the press that presented a more critical assessment of the problem of rape on college campuses. Schoenberg and Roe's (1993) three-part series in the *Toledo Blade* offers an unusually thorough and insightful coverage of this issue. Not only do they dissect the exaggerated figures of advocacy researchers, Schoenberg and Roe also show that although poor and minority women are much more likely to be victims of rape than middle-class college students, their stories are seldom told.

Debunking advocacy research is almost as approved as promoting it. There are even eminent rewards, to wit, the Pulitzer Prize won for the *Denver Post* series debunking the estimates on missing children. In this manner, advocacy research is an excellent source of information for the media, often providing two lively stories—one with hype and the other with disputation.

[22] Dunn (1993) offers several telling examples of advocacy claims initially accepted and later refuted by the press. Cohen (1991) and Gutmann (1990) were among the first columnists to criticize advocacy findings on date rape.

IV. Ideological Currents and Social Factors

Advocacy research is not a phenomenon unique to studies of rape. It is practiced in a wide variety of substantive problem areas and supported by groups that, as Rossi (1987) suggests, share an "ideological imperative," which maintains that findings politically acceptable to the advocacy community are more important than the quality of research from which they are derived, playing fast and loose with the facts is justifiable in the service of a noble cause, and data and sentiments that challenge conventional wisdom are to be condemned or ignored. Indeed, the literature suggests that moral panics promoted by advocacy research not only involve the amplification of deviance but also serve as an ideological messenger. As McRobbie and Thornton point out, "It is only with theories of ideology that the idea of the media's moral panics as defining and distorting social issues gives way to a more integrated and connected understanding of the construction of meaning across the whole range of media forms and institutions" (1995, p. 562).

Although advocacy studies do little to elevate the standards of social science research, they sometimes serve a useful purpose in bringing grave problems to public attention. Among social activists, this is known as "consciousness-raising" and is deemed a respectable function of advocacy research. From this perspective radical feminists may claim a measure of success, when we consider the proliferation over the last decade of publicly subsidized rape crisis centers and rape prevention training programs, along with the growing support industry of consultants, books, videos, and other educational paraphernalia. One might say that, even if the rape research magnifies this problem in order to raise public consciousness, it is being done for a good cause, and in any case the difference is only a matter of degree. No matter how they are measured, rape and child sexual abuse are serious problems that create a great deal of human suffering. So why make an issue of the numbers?

But the issue is not that advocacy studies simply overstate the incidence of legally defined rape and child sexual abuse—it is the magnitude of this exaggeration and what it means. After all, the difference between boiling and freezing is only a matter of degree. In the case of sexual assault against women, advocacy research seeks to alter public consciousness more than raise it, by molding social perceptions of the basic nature of the problem and of what constitutes common experience in heterosexual relations.

If it is true that one-third of female children are sexually abused and almost half of all women will suffer an average of two incidents of rape or attempted rape sometimes in their lives, the almost ineluctable conclusion is that most men are pedophiles or rapists.[23] This view of men is repeatedly expressed by advocates in the child sexual abuse prevention movement and the rape crisis movement. As Russell puts it, "Efforts to explain rape as a psychopathological phenomenon are inappropriate. How could it be that all these rapes are being perpetrated by a tiny segment of the male population"? (1984, p. 65). Her explanation of "the truth that must be faced is that this culture's notion of masculinity—particularly as it is applied to male sexuality—predisposes men to violence, to rape, to sexually harass, and to sexually abuse children" (1984, p. 290). In a similar vein, Koss notes that her findings support the view that sexual violence against women "rests squarely in the middle of what our culture defines as 'normal' interaction between men and women" (1988, p. 23). And Wolf writes that "glamorized degradation has created a situation among the young in which boys rape girls and girls get raped *as a normal course of events*" (emphasis in original) (1991, p. 167). MacKinnon offers a vivid rendition of the theme that rape is a social disease afflicting most men. Writing in the *New York Times*, she advises that, when men charged with the crime of rape come to trial, the court should ask, "Did this member of a group sexually trained to woman-hating aggression commit this particular act of woman-hating sexual aggression"? (1991, p. 15).

Under the influence of such views, the sexual politics of advocacy research on violence against women demonizes men and defines the common experience in heterosexual relations as inherently menacing; here, men are characterized as a deviant class, the so-called folk devils of moral panics identified by Cohen (1972). When asked if college women should view every man they see as a potential rapist, a spokeswoman for the student health services at the University of California, Berkeley, responded, "I'm not sure that would be a negative thing" (Brydoff 1991, p. 1). This echoes the instruction supplied in one of the most popular college guidebooks on how to prevent acquaintance rape, which indicates that, since women cannot tell who has the potential for rape by simply looking, they should be on their guard with every man

[23] One explanation for this hostile view of male behavior is that it advances a radical feminist ambition to achieve absolute control in sexual relations. To further this objective, Podhoretz (1991, p. 34) explains, "It became necessary to delegitimize any instance of heterosexual coupling that starts with male initiative and involves even the slightest degree of female resistance at any stage along the way. Hence almost the entire range of normal heterosexual intercourse must be stigmatized as criminal, and both women and men must be educated to recognize it."

(Parrot 1988). Thus, a situation is created in which Menand observes, "The assumption that sexual relations among students at a progressive liberal-arts college should be thought of as per se fraught with the potential for violence is now taken for granted by about just everyone" (1994, p. 76).[24] The same message is being delivered to students at a very early age by sexual abuse prevention programs in the schools. Many of these programs make a point of teaching kids from the ages of three years and up that male family members, particularly fathers, uncles, and grandfathers, may sexually abuse children.[25]

At the same time that men are portrayed as dangerous predators, the most widely cited research on sexual violence conveys a view of women as helpless victims. In studies that claim to uncover the highest rates of rape, female subjects typically do not realize they have been raped, return to have sex again with the perpetrator because of guilt and self-doubt, are seen as substantially impaired by any amount of drinking, and are often psychologically coerced by men into having unwanted sex.[26] On the last point, Roiphe declares: "The idea that women can't withstand verbal or emotional pressure infantilizes them" (1993*b*, p. 67).

To protect women against nonphysical coercion and to empower those who might be hesitant to say no to sexual advances unless their oral permission is expressly requested, Antioch College has adopted a policy on sexual offense that maintains that anyone who initiates sexual activity must renew verbal consent as the couple moves to each new level of physical intimacy: "May I kiss you, now may I unbutton your blouse, now may I touch you here," and so on. But as Young (1992) points out, if failure to object to unwanted sex can be attributed to verbal intimidation or deficient will power, so can explicit consent. "Inevitably," she notes, "on the outer limits, this patronizing line of thinking reaches the conclusion that in our oppressive society, *there can be no*

[24] Experts on date rape advise college women to take their own cars on dates or to have a backup network of friends ready to pick them up, to stay sober, to inform the man in advance what the sexual limits will be that evening, and to prepare for the worst by taking a course in self-defense beforehand (Warshaw 1988). Separately, some of these instructions, such as staying sober, are certainly well advised. Collectively, however, this bundle of cautions transmits the unspoken message that dating men is a very dangerous affair.

[25] This is an example of the "new psychology," which Krauthammer (1993, p. 22) notes "is rooted in and reinforces current notions about the pathology of ordinary family life."

[26] According to the "feminist analysis of rape," as Koss and Harvey (1991, p. 125) explain, "women are socialized to be passive, good-willed, and compliant, and to assume the status of property."

consensual sex" (emphasis in the original). Indeed, according to Estrich (1987, p. 102), "Many feminists would argue that so long as women are powerless relative to men, viewing 'yes' as a sign of true consent is misguided." Estrich herself agrees that in sexual relations a woman's "yes" often may mean "no."

Besides attempting to portray normal sexual relations between men and women as inherently brutish, advocacy research on rape and child sexual abuse redefines these violations in ways that trivialize serious violence against women.[27] This is done by employing definitions that equate vicious and appalling acts of rape and child molestation with offenses such as attempted petting, unwanted kisses, touching a ten-year-old's breast, forced digital penetration in the midst of heavy petting, having intercourse after one's inhibitions are lowered by a few drinks and which is later regretted, and being coerced into sexual intercourse through verbal persuasion. This research strategy feeds off the suffering of real victims of sexual violence, whose stories are often used to illustrate the larger problem even though their painful experiences represent only a small fraction of the cases included in the problem definition.

Yet a puzzling question remains: if the popular estimates of rape are so greatly exaggerated compared to the relatively few cases reported to police and counselling centers, why have tens of thousands of female students on college campuses across the country marched by candlelight to "take back the night"? Something is going on here. Radical feminists and advocacy researchers, no doubt, take this anguished behavior as confirmation of widespread violence against college women. But there are several alternative explanations that suggest a climate heavily influenced by the social dynamics of fear, power, conflict, and sex.

A. Inflated Fear

The view of "take-back-the-night" protests as confirmation of an epidemic of rape can, of course, be turned on its head. Claims that 33 percent of children are sexually abused, 25 percent of students will be

[27] Thus, Gillian Greensite, founder of the Rape Prevention Education program at the University of California, Santa Cruz, writes that the seriousness of rape "is being undermined by the growing tendency of some feminists to label all heterosexual miscommunication and insensitivity as acquaintance rape" (Greensite 1991, p. 15). Recall that 49 percent of the students whom Koss defined as victims of acquaintance rape labeled their experience as miscommunication.

victims of rape or attempted rape and 50 percent of women will be raped sometime during their lifetime have gained a degree of legitimacy and authority through repetition by public officials, journalists, TV reporters, and well-known advocates with access to the media. Rather than responding to real violence against women on campus, these demonstrations may reflect a level of fear inflated by the exaggerated reports of violence, which create a premonition of danger that is vastly out of proportion to the actual risks of campus life. According to Roiphe (1993*b*, p. 58), a significant number of students are walking around with the alarming belief that 50 percent of women are raped. "This hyperbole," she notes, "contains within it a state of perpetual fear."

B. Power of Victimization

One might argue, however, that demonstrations to take back the night are incited less by irrational fear than by the sense of righteousness and power that often accompany the invocation of victim status. "Even the privileged," as Sykes (1992, p. 12) tells us, "have found that being oppressed has its advantage. On campuses of elite universities, students quickly learn the grammar and protocols of power—that the route to moral superiority and premier griping rights can be gained most efficiently through being a victim—which perhaps explains academia's search for what one critic calls the 'unified field theory of oppression.' "

C. Increased Gender Conflict

Over the last few decades more women have entered college and joined the paid labor force than ever before. In 1960, most women were married before their twenty-first birthday (Smith 1994). Today, at that age they are competing with men for graduate school slots in almost every field and for jobs throughout the economy. An unprecedented number of women have also become heads of single-parent families, to which absent fathers often contribute minimal (if any) support. These developments enlarge occasions for friction and resentment in economic and social relations between the sexes, particularly among the college-aged group. The anxieties and animosities expressed in rallies to take back the night, in part, may reflect a real increase in tensions between men and women. This explanation suggests that "sexual assault" has come to represent a broad and vaguely formulated category of offenses, which ranges from rape to the incivilities of heightened gender conflict in social and economic relations.

D. Sexual Turmoil

Explanations that refer to fear, power, and conflict downplay the extent to which sexual activities influence the highly emotional responses to the threat of rape on campus. Sexual relations between young men and women, never exactly serene, have become more troublesome and confused in recent times. This is because there is more of it to manage, sex has become more dangerous, and it is harder to say no. Since 1960, as the median age for premarital intercourse declined and the median age at first marriage rose, the period of premarital sexual activity has grown from an average of one to 7.5 years for women (Smith 1994). The sexual revolution in the late 1960s discounted the moral strictures against premarital sex. Without the shield of morality, it became more socially awkward to avoid having sex in situations where one's feelings were ambiguous or even strongly negative (Decter 1972). (It is easier to assert morality and say no because premarital sex is wrong than to say no for all the other reasons: "I don't love [or even like] you enough," "You don't seem to love me enough," "I am not ready yet," and so forth.) Shortly after the time span for sexual activity began to increase and the shield of morality fell, the risks of contracting AIDS and other sexually transmitted diseases rose to alarming levels.

These explanations are not mutually exclusive. They describe a cultural climate of strained gender relations under which advocacy research has been relatively successful in furthering the sexual politics of radical feminism. This politics is based on several convictions: that violence is the norm in heterosexual relations, that all women are oppressed and deserve special treatment by government, and that from an early age women need to be empowered by publicly supported training and prevention programs. This agenda coincides with the interests of sexual abuse prevention professionals—therapists, counselors, sensitivity trainers, and consultants—who have developed a small industry of workshops, courses, videos, self-defense training, and publications for schools and colleges.[28] This agenda does not serve the in-

[28] The fact that many of these professionals support the claims of advocacy research may reflect more than an occupational stake in the problem. As already noted, there is some evidence that their reading of the data may be influenced by personal experiences as victims (Russel et al. 1993).

terests of poor women, minorities, teenage boys, and other groups most in need of social protection from violence.

That agenda has framed public discourse on violence against women since the 1980s. During the last few years, however, there has been a mounting challenge to this perspective from other quarters of the feminist movement. Roiphe (1993*a*) and Guttman (1990) were among the first to question the sexual politics of the rape crisis feminists. In 1993 the Women's Freedom Network was organized by a prominent group of feminist thinkers, including Mary Ann Glendon, Elizabeth-Fox Genovese, Jeane Kirkpatrick, Edith Kurzweil, Sally Pipes, Virginia Postrel, Christina Sommers, Rita Simon, and Cathy Young. Among the principles to which this group subscribes is the belief that "the rhetoric of victimization trivializes real abuse, demeans women, and promotes antagonism instead of real partnership between men and women" (Women's Freedom Network 1994, p. 1). This school of thought poses an alternative perspective on violence against women, one which promises to render a more rigorous account of the problem and more balanced policy solutions than those advanced by advocacy research.

V. Inflated Measures Distort Social Policy

In advocacy research, vivid anecdotes of real victims are traded on to support fragile numbers. But when policy implications are drawn from these advocacy studies, the real victims are betrayed by what Sykes (1992, p. 19) calls "a victimist version of Gresham's Law: Bogus victims drive out genuine victims."

In the deliberations on federal policy regarding violence against women, advocacy research on rape was accepted almost at face value. In the opening statement during Senate hearings on the Violence against Women Act in 1990, Chairman Joseph Biden explained: "One out of every four college women will have been attacked by a rapist before they graduate, and one in seven will have been raped. Less than 5 percent of these women will report these rapes to the police. Rape remains the least reported of all major crimes. . . . Dr. Koss will tell us today the actual number of college women raped is more than fourteen times the number reported by official governmental statistics. Indeed, while studies suggest that about 1,275 women were raped at America's three largest universities last year, only three rapes—only three—were reported to the police" (U.S. Senate 1991, p. 3). Without a blink, the panel was informed that unreported rapes of college women are more than twenty times, more than fourteen times, and more than four hundred times the number of incidents reported to the police. In fact, as noted earlier, according to Koss's figures the unreported rate is about a thousand times higher than the rate of rape and attempted rape reported on college campuses.[29]

Expert opinions solicited for the hearings reinforced the figures presented by Chairman Biden as authoritative measures of rape, which came directly from the *Ms.* study. The first professionals testifying before the committee were introduced as "two nationally prominent experts in this field. . . . Ms. Warshaw is the author of the foremost book published on acquaintance rape and the attitudes that lead to it, entitled *I Never Called It Rape.* And Dr. Koss has studied the incidence and prevalence of rape more extensively than any other social scientist in this country" (U.S. Senate 1991, p. 27). Warshaw (1988) is a journalist, and the full title of her book is *I Never Called It Rape: The Ms. Report on Recognizing, Fighting, and Surviving Date and Acquaintance Rape* (with an afterward by Koss, who directed the *Ms.* study).

Due to the credibility attributed to advocacy research, under Title IV (Safe Campuses for Women) the Violence against Women Act of 1993 proposed to appropriate $20 million for rape education and prevention programs to make college campuses safe for women. Extrapolating from the 408 reported cases of rape and attempted rape on campuses among 5 million college students in 1992 yields approximately 1,000 reported incidents among all colleges in the United States. The appropriation proposed under Title IV thus amounted to $20,000 per case reported in the previous year (U.S. Senate 1993).

[29] In comparing Koss's claim to the number of actual reports, it should be noted that organized efforts have been made to facilitate reporting by college students. During the last decade, rape crisis counseling and supportive services have been established on most major campuses. Highly sensitive to the social and psychological violations of rape, these services offer a sympathetic environment in which victims may come forward for assistance, without having to make official reports to the police. Reliable data on how many rape victims these programs serve are difficult to obtain. But individual accounts suggest that the demand is not excessive. The director of counseling services at Lafayette College, for example, reports having counseled over five years about a dozen students who confided that they were sexually assaulted (Forbes and Kirts 1993). Offering an account of a typical Saturday night at the Rape Crisis Center at Columbia University, Hellman (1993, p. 37) reports: "Nobody called; nobody came."

Whatever the value of these programs, the cost is remarkably high compared to the funds allocated per reported cases of rape off college campuses; among those cases, poor and minority women are vastly overrepresented (Bureau of Justice Statistics 1992). According to the FBI (1993) data, there were altogether 109,062 reported cases of rape and attempted rape in 1992. Based on these rates, to make the rest of society as safe as college campuses would require an expenditure of over $2 billion on educational and prevention programs (or more than twice the appropriations proposed under all five titles of the act combined). Compared to the $20 million designated for college campuses (a rate of $20,000 per reported case), the Violence against Women Act proposed to appropriate $65 million (a rate of approximately $650 per reported case) for prevention and education programs to serve the broader community (U.S. Senate 1993).[30] Under this arrangement, a disproportionate sum would be distributed for education and prevention programs on college campuses, where most victims, according to the *Ms.* study, do not know they have been raped. And comparatively meager resources would be invested in similar programs for low-income and minority communities, where authentic victims need all the help society can afford to offer. Although the final version of the Violence against Women Act, passed as part of the 1994 Crime Bill, did not contain funding for prevention efforts on college campuses, this is an example of how proposals based on advocacy research can muddle social policy deliberations.

It is difficult to criticize advocacy research without giving an impression of caring less about the problem under consideration than do those who are engaged in magnifying its size. But one may be deeply concerned about problems such as rape, child abuse, and homelessness yet still wish to see a rigorous and objective analysis of their dimensions. Advocacy research that uncovers a problem, measures it with reasonable accuracy, and brings it to public attention performs a valuable service by raising public consciousness. The current trend in advocacy research is to inflate problems and redefine them in line with the advocates' ideological preferences. The few impose their definition of social ills on the many—seeking to incite moral panics. This type of advocacy research invites social policies that are likely to be neither effective nor fair.

[30] While prevention and education funds are disproportionately targeted to college campuses, an appropriation of $100 million is earmarked for "high density crime areas" for

REFERENCES

Aaron, Henry. 1978. *Politics and the Professors: The Great Society in Perspective.* Washington, D.C.: Brookings Institution.

Ageton, S. 1983. *Sexual Assault among Adolescents: A National Study.* Final Report to the National Institute of Mental Health. Washington, D.C.: National Institute of Mental Health.

Ahn, Helen, and Neil Gilbert. 1992. "Cultural Diversity and Sexual Abuse Prevention." *Social Service Review* 66(3):410–27.

Amir, D., and M. Amir. 1979. "Rape Crisis Centers: An Arena for Ideological Conflicts." *Victimology* 4:247–57.

Applebaum, Paul. 1987. "Crazy in the Streets." *Commentary* 83(5):37.

Baum, Alice, and Donald Burnes. 1993. "Facing the Facts about Homelessness." *Public Welfare* 51(2):20–27.

Berrick, Jill Duerr, and Neil Gilbert. 1991. *With the Best of Intentions: The Sexual Abuse Prevention Movement.* New York: Guilford.

Best, Joel. 1988. "Missing Children, Misleading Statistics." *Public Interest* 92(Summer):84–92.

———. 1990. *Threatened Children: Rhetoric and Concern about Child-Victims.* Chicago: University of Chicago Press.

Booth, Charles. 1892. *Life and Labour of People in London.* London: Macmillan.

Briere, John, and Marsha Runtz. 1989. "University Males' Sexual Interest in Children: Predicting Potential Indices of 'Pedophilia' in a Nonforensic Sample." *Child Abuse and Neglect* 13(1):65–75.

Brydoff, Carol. 1991. "Professor Rape Figures Are Inflated." *Oakland Tribune* (March 30), p. 1.

Buckley, Stephen. 1992. "Unfounded Reports of Rape Confound Area Police Investigations." *Washington Post* (June 27).

Bureau of Justice Statistics. 1989. *Criminal Victimization in the United States, 1987.* Washington, D.C.: U.S. Government Printing Office.

———. 1991. *Criminal Victimization in the United States, 1989.* Washington, D.C.: U.S. Government Printing Office.

———. 1992. *Criminal Victimization in the United States, 1990.* Washington, D.C.: U.S. Government Printing Office.

———. 1993. *Criminal Victimization in the United States, 1992.* Washington, D.C.: U.S. Government Printing Office.

———. 1994. "Crime Rates Essentially Unchanged Last Year." Report. Washington, D.C.: Bureau of Justice Statistics, October 30.

———. 1995. "Violence against Women: Estimates from the Redesigned Survey." Special report. Washington, D.C.: Bureau of Justice Statistics, August.

Burt, Martha, and Barbara Cohen. 1989. *America's Homeless: Numbers, Characteristics, and Programs That Serve Them.* Washington, D.C.: Urban Institute.

Cohen, Richard. 1991. "Surveying Rape." *Washington Post* (May 19), p. 18.

---

the purposes of expanding police protection, implementing prosecution policies, and improving data collection systems.

Cohen, Stanley. 1972. *Folk Devils and Moral Panics.* London: MacGibbon & Kee.

Collins, Barbara, and Mary Whalen. 1989. "The Rape Crisis Movement: Radical or Reformist?" *Social Work* 34(1):61–65.

Cottino, A., and M. Quirico. 1995. "Easy Target and Moral Panic: The Law on Drug Addiction No. 162 of 1990." *Scandinavian Journal of Social Welfare* 4:108–13.

Craig, Mary. 1990. "Coercive Sexuality in Dating Relationships: A Situational Model." *Clinical Psychology Review* 10:395–423.

Crystal, Stephen. 1987. "Elder Abuse: The Latest 'Crisis.'" *Public Interest* 88(Summer):56–66.

Demause, Lloyd. 1991. "The Universality of Incest." *Journal of Psychohistory* 19(2):123–64.

Decter, Midge. 1972. *The New Chastity and Other Arguments against Women's Liberation.* New York: Coward, McCann, & Geoghegan.

Drotner, K. 1992. "Modernity and Media Panics." In *Media Cultures: Reappraising Transnational Media*, edited by M. Skovmand and K. Schrode. New York: Routledge.

Dunn, Katherine. 1993. "Fibbers." *New Republic* (June 21), pp. 18–19.

Dworkin, Andrea. 1988. *Letters from a War Zone.* London: Secker & Warburg.

Estrich, Susan. 1987. *Real Rape.* Cambridge, Mass.: Harvard University Press.

Faludi, Susan. 1993. "Victimization Is No Fantasy." *Newsweek* (October 25), p. 61.

Federal Bureau of Investigation. 1993. *Crime in the United States: Uniform Crime Reports, 1992.* Washington, D.C.: U.S. Government Printing Office.

Finkelhor, David, Sharon Araji, Larry Baron, Angela Browne, Stefanie Peters, and Gail Wyatt. 1986. *A Sourcebook on Child Sexual Abuse.* Beverly Hills, Calif.: Sage.

Finkelhor, David, Nancy Asdigian, and Jennifer Dziuba-Leatherman. 1993. *The Effectiveness of Victimization Prevention Instruction: An Evaluation of Children's Responses to Actual Threats and Assaults.* Durham: University of New Hampshire, Family Research Laboratory.

Finkelhor, David, Gerald Hotaling, I. A. Lewis, and Christine Smith. 1990. "Child Abuse in a National Survey of Adult Men and Women: Prevalence, Characteristics, and Risk Factors." *Child Abuse and Neglect* 14:19–28.

Fischer, Pamela, and William Breakey. 1991. "The Epidemiology of Alcohol, Drug, and Mental Disorders among Homeless Persons." *American Psychologist* 46(November):1115–28.

Forbes, Karen, and Donald Kirts. 1993. "Letter to the Editor." *Lafayette* (October 29), p. 5.

Freedberg, L. 1991. "Rape Expert Accuses UC of Barring Her Lecture." *San Francisco Chronicle* (November 9), p. 14.

George, Linda, Idee Winfield, and Dan Blazer. 1992. "Sociocultural Factors in Sexual Assault: Comparison of Two Representative Samples of Women." *Journal of Social Issues* 48(1):105–25.

Gibbs, Nancy. 1991. "When Is It Rape?" *Time* (June 3), pp. 48–54.

Gilbert, Neil. 1991*a*. "The Phantom Epidemic of Sexual Assault." *Public Interest* 103(Spring):54–65.

———. 1991*b*. "The Campus Rape Scare." *Wall Street Journal* (June 27), p. 10.

Gilbert, Neil, Jill Duerr Berrick, Nicole LeProhn, and Nina Nyman. 1989. *Protecting Young Children from Sexual Abuse: Does Preschool Training Work?* Lexington, Mass.: Lexington Books.

Giovannoni, Jeanne, and Rosiana Becerra. 1979. *Defining Child Abuse.* New York: Free Press.

Greensite, Gillian. 1991. "Acquaintance Rape Clarified." *Student Guide, University of California at Santa Cruz* (Fall).

Griego, Diana, and Louis Kilzer. 1985. "Truth about Missing Kids: Exaggerated Statistics Stir National Paranoia." *Denver Post* (May 12), pp. 1A, 12A.

Gutmann, Stephanie. 1990. "How Date Rape 'Education' Fosters Confusion, Undermines Personal Responsibility and Trivializes Sexual Violence." *Reason* (July), pp. 22–27.

———. 1993. "The Breeding Ground." *National Review* (June 21), pp. 47–55.

Harrington, Michael. 1962. *The Other America: Poverty in the United States.* New York: Macmillan.

Harris, Louis, and Associates. 1993. *The Commonwealth Fund Survey of Women's Health.* New York: Commonwealth Fund.

Hellman, Peter. 1993. "Crying Rape: The Politics of Date Rape on Campus." *New York* (March 8), pp. 32–37.

Hunter, Robert. 1965. *Poverty: Social Conscience in the Progressive Era*, edited by Peter d'A. Jones. New York: Harper Torchbook Edition. (Originally published 1904. New York: Macmillan.)

Jencks, Christopher. 1991. "Is Violent Crime Increasing?" *American Prospect* 4(Winter):98–109.

Johnson, Allan. 1980. "On the Prevalence of Rape in the United States." *Signs* 6(1):137–45.

Kilpatrick, Dean, Connie Best, Lois Veronen, Angelynne Amick, Lorenz Villeponteaux, and Gary Ruff. 1985. "Mental Health Correlates of Criminal Victimization: A Random Community Survey." *Journal of Consulting and Clinical Psychology* 53(6):866–73.

Koss, Mary. 1988. "Hidden Rape: Sexual Aggression and Victimization in a National Sample of Students in Higher Education." In *Rape and Sexual Assault II*, edited by A. W. Burgess. New York: Garland Publishing.

———. 1990. "Testimony in Senate Hearings on Women and Violence." In *Women and Violence: Hearings before the Committee on the Judiciary, United States Senate, 101st. Congress, Second Session, Part 2.* Washington, D.C.: U.S. Government Printing Office.

———. 1991*a*. "Letter to the Editor." *Wall Street Journal* (July 25), p. 21.

———. 1991*b*. "Rape on Campus: Facing the Facts." Photocopy.

———. 1991*c*. "Statistics Show Sexual Assaults Are More Prevalent than Many Realize." *Los Angeles Daily Journal* (July 17), p. 6.

———. 1993. "Letters to the Editor." *Wall Street Journal* (August 3), p. A15.

Koss, Mary, and Sarah Cook. 1993*a*. "Facing the Facts: Date and Acquaintance Rape." Tucson: University of Arizona. (Final draft of chapter prepared for *Current Controversies on Family Violence*, edited by Richard Gelles and Donileen Loseke [Beverly Hills, Calif.: Sage].)

———. 1993*b*. "Facing the Facts: Date and Acquaintance Rape." In *Current Controversies on Family Violence*, edited by Richard Gelles and Donileen Loseke. Beverly Hills, Calif.: Sage.

Koss, Mary, Thomas Dinero, Cynthia Seibel, and Susan Cox. 1988. "Stranger and Acquaintance Rape: Are There Differences in the Victims' Experience?" *Psychology of Women Quarterly* 12:1–24.

Koss, Mary, and Christine Gidycz. 1985. "Sexual Experiences Survey: Reliability and Validity." *Journal of Consulting and Clinical Psychology* 53:422–23.

Koss, Mary, Christine Gidycz, and Nadine Wisniewski. 1987. "The Scope of Rape: Incidence and Prevalence of Sexual Aggression and Victimization in a National Sample of Higher Education Students." *Journal of Consulting and Clinical Psychology* 55:162–70.

Koss, Mary, and Mary Harvey. 1991. *The Rape Victim*. Newbury Park, Calif.: Sage.

Koss, Mary, and Cheryl Oros. 1982. "The Sexual Experiences Survey: A Research Instrument Investigating Sexual Aggression and Victimization." *Journal of Consulting and Clinical Psychology* 50:455–57.

Krauthammer, Charles. 1993. "Defining Deviancy Up." *New Republic* (November 22), pp. 21–25.

Kutchinsky, Berl. 1994. "The Prevalence and Incidence of Child Sexual Abuse: The Child Sexual Abuse Panic." Paper presented at the Conference on Evolution of Sexual Abuse Prevention Programs. Berlin, January 20–21.

Lewin, Tamar. 1991. "Tougher Laws Mean More Cases Are Called Rape." *New York Times National* (May 27), p. 8.

Lichter, Robert, Stanley Rothman, and Linda Lichter. 1986. *The Media Elite*. Bethesda, Md.: Adler & Adler.

Lubran, Barbara. 1990. "Alcohol and Drug Abuse among the Homeless Population: A National Response." In *Treating Alcoholism and Drug Abuse among Homeless Men and Women: Nine Community Demonstration Grants*, edited by Milton Argeriou and Dennis McCarty. Binghampton, N.Y.: Haworth.

MacKinnon, Catherine. 1991. "The Palm Beach Hanging." *New York Times* (December 15), p. 15.

McRobbie, Angela, and Sarah Thornton. 1995. "Rethinking 'Moral Panic' for Multi-mediated Social Worlds." *British Journal of Sociology* 46(4):559–74.

Menand, Louis. 1994. "Behind the Culture of Violence." *New Yorker* (March 14), pp. 74–85.

Miller, Henry. 1991. *On the Fringe: The Dispossessed in America*. Lexington, Mass.: Lexington Books.

Moynihan, Daniel P. 1969. *Maximum Feasible Misunderstanding*. New York: Free Press.

National Victim Center. 1992. *Rape in America: A Report to the Nation*. Arlington, Va.: National Victim Center.

Parrot, Andrea. 1988. *Acquaintance Rape and Sexual Assault Prevention Training Manual.* Ithaca, N.Y.: Cornell University.

Podhoretz, Norman. 1991. "Rape in Feminist Eyes." *Commentary* (October), pp. 29–35.

Pollitt, Katha. 1993. "Not Just Bad Sex." *New Yorker* (October 4), pp. 222–23.

Proch, Kathleen, and Merlin Taber. 1987. "Helping the Homeless." *Public Welfare* 45(2):5–9.

Riger, Stephanie, and Margaret Gordon. 1981. "The Fear of Rape: A Study of Social Control." *Journal of Social Issues* 37(4):71–92.

Roiphe, Katie. 1993*a*. "Date Rape's Other Victim." *New York Times Magazine* (June 13), pp. 26–28, 40–41.

———. 1993*b*. *The Morning After: Sex, Fear, and Feminism on Campus.* Boston: Little, Brown.

Rossi, Peter. 1987. "No Good Applied Social Research Goes Unpunished." *Society* 25(1):73–79.

Rossi, Peter, Gene Fisher, and Georgianna Willis. 1986. *The Condition of the Homeless in Chicago.* Amherst: University of Massachusetts, Social and Demographic Research Institute.

Rubin, Alan, and Earl Babbie. 1989. *Research Methods for Social Work.* Belmont, Calif.: Wadsworth Publishing.

Russel, Robin, Phyllis Gill, Ann Coyne, and Jane Woody. 1993. "Dysfunction in the Family of Origin of MSW and Other Graduate Students." *Journal of Social Work Education* 29(1):121–29.

Russell, Diana. 1975. *The Politics of Rape.* New York: Stein & Day.

———. 1982. *Rape in Marriage.* New York: Macmillan.

———. 1984. *Sexual Exploitation: Rape, Child Sexual Abuse, and Workplace Harassment.* Beverly Hills, Calif.: Sage.

———. 1991. "The Epidemic of Sexual Violence against Women: A National Crisis." Seabury Lecture, University of California at Berkeley, November 25.

Schafran, Lynn. 1995. "Rape Is Still Underreported." *New York Times* (August 26).

Schlesinger, Arthur M., Jr. 1965. *A Thousand Days: John F. Kennedy in the White House.* Boston, Mass.: Houghton Mifflin Co.

Schoenberg, Nara, and Sam Roe. 1993. "Rape: The Making of an Epidemic." *Toledo Blade* (October 10), pt. 1, pp. 1, 8; (October 11), pt. 2, pp. 1, 5; (October 12), pt. 3, pp. 1, 4.

Smith, Tom. 1994. "American Sexual Behavior." In *Sexuality and American Social Policy: The Demography of Sexual Behavior,* edited by Jayne Garrison, Mark Smith, and Douglas Besharov. Menlo Park, Calif.: Kaiser Family Foundation.

Sommers, Christina. 1994. *Who Stole Feminism?* New York: Simon & Schuster.

Sprecher, Susan, Elaine Hatfield, Anthony Cortese, Elana Potaoiva, and Anna Levitskaya. 1994. "Token Resistance to Sexual Intercourse and Consent to Unwanted Sexual Intercourse: College Students' Dating Experiences in Three Countries." *Journal of Sex Research* 31(2):125–32.

Sykes, Charles. 1992. *A Nation of Victims.* New York: St. Martins.

Trombley, William. 1990. "Budget Cloud Brings Gloom to Successful State Program." *Los Angeles Times* (July 2), p. 1.

U.S. Bureau of the Census. 1986. *Statistical Abstract of the United States, 1978.* Washington, D.C.: U.S. Government Printing Office.

U.S. Department of Health and Human Services, National Center on Child Abuse and Neglect. 1995. *Child Maltreatment 1993: Reports from the States to the NCCAN.* Washington, D.C.: U.S. Government Printing Office.

U.S. House Of Representatives, Committee on Ways and Means. 1992. *The Green Book: Overview of Entitlement Programs.* Washington, D.C.: U.S. Government Printing Office.

U.S. Senate. 1991. *Women and Violence Hearing before the Committee on the Judiciary.* 101st Congress, 2d session, pt. 2. Washington, D.C.: U.S. Government Printing Office.

———. 1993. *S.11 Violence against Women Act 1993.* 103rd Congress, 1st session. Washington, D.C.: U.S. Government Printing Office.

Warshaw, Robin. 1988. *I Never Called It Rape: The Ms. Report on Recognizing, Fighting, and Surviving Date and Acquaintance Rape.* New York: Harper & Row. (Afterword by M. Koss.)

Wolf, Naomi. 1991. *The Beauty Myth.* New York: Morrow.

Women's Freedom Network. 1994. "Statement of Purpose." *Women's Freedom Network Newsletter* 1(1):1.

Wright, James. 1988. "The Worthy and Unworthy Homeless." *Society* 25(5): 69.

Yegidis, Bonnie. 1986. "Date Rape and Other Forced Sexual Encounters among College Students." *Journal of Sex Education and Therapy* 12:51–54.

Young, Cathy. 1992. "Women, Sex, and Rape." *Washington Post* (May 31), p. C1.

Joan Petersilia

Probation in the United States

ABSTRACT

Probation officers supervise two-thirds of all correctional clientele in the United States. But despite the unprecedented growth in probation populations over the past decade, probation budgets have not grown. The result is that U.S. probation services are underfunded relative to prisons and serious felons often go unsupervised, encouraging offender recidivism and reinforcing the public's view that probation is too lenient and lacking in credibility. Yet, there is much unrealized potential in probation. Recent research shows that probation programs, if properly designed and implemented, can reduce recidivism and drug use. Moreover, certain probation programs are judged by offenders to be more punitive than short prison terms, and the public seems increasingly willing to support intermediate sanctions for nonviolent offenders. Experimentation and evaluation are needed to determine whether adequately funded probation systems can protect society and rehabilitate offenders.

Probation is the most common form of criminal sentencing in the United States. The American Correctional Association (1995) defines it as: "A court-ordered dispositional alternative through which an adjudicated offender is placed under the control, supervision and care of a probation staff member in lieu of imprisonment, so long as the probationer meets certain standards of contact."

The Bureau of Justice Statistics reports that just over 3 million

Joan Petersilia is professor of criminology, law, and society in the School of Social Ecology, University of California at Irvine. For helpful suggestions, she is very grateful to John DiIulio and the other members of the Brookings Institution's Study Group on Crime Policy. Special thanks are extended to Patrick Langan, senior statistician at the Bureau of Justice Statistics, for helping to locate sometimes obscure sources of probation data.

0192-3234/97/0022-0005$02.00

adults were under state or federal probation at year end 1995, and that probationers made up 58 percent of all adults under correctional supervision (Bureau of Justice Statistics 1996*a*). The number is so large that the U.S. Department of Justice estimates that nearly 2 percent of all U.S. adult citizens are under probation supervision on any one day. And the population continues to rise—increasing 4 percent in 1994 and almost 300 percent over the past ten years (Bureau of Justice Statistics 1996*a*).

Despite wide usage, probation is often the subject of intense criticism. It suffers from a "soft on crime" image and, as a result, maintains little public support. Probation is often depicted as permissive, uncaring about crime victims, and committed to a rehabilitative ideal that ignores the reality of violent, predatory criminals.

Their poor (and some believe, misunderstood) public image leaves probation agencies unable to compete effectively for scarce public funds. Nationally, probation receives less than 10 percent of state and local government corrections funding, even though they supervise two out of three correctional clients (Petersilia 1995*b*).

As a result of inadequate funding, probation often means freedom from supervision. Offenders in large urban areas are often assigned to 100-plus caseloads, in which meetings occur at most once a month, and employment or treatment progress is seldom monitored. As long as no rearrest occurs, offenders can successfully complete probation whether or not conditions have been fully met or court fees paid (Langan 1994). Such "supervision" not only makes a mockery of the justice system but leaves many serious offenders unsupervised.

But while current programs are often seen as inadequate, the *concept* of probation has a great deal of appeal. As Judge Burton Roberts, Administrative Judge of the Bronx Supreme and Criminal Courts, explained: "Nothing is wrong with probation. It is the *execution* of probation that is wrong" (cited in Klein 1997, p. 72).

Scholars and citizens agree that probation has many advantages over imprisonment, including lower cost, increased opportunities for rehabilitation, and reduced risk of criminal socialization. And with prison crowding a nationwide problem, the need for inexpensive and flexible community punishment options has never been greater. Probation leaders (Corbett 1996; Nidorf 1996), policy makers (Bell and Bennett 1996), and scholars (Clear and Braga 1995; Tonry and Lynch 1996) are now calling for "reforming," "reinvesting," and "restructuring" probation.

But exactly *how* would one go about reforming probation? Some are beginning to offer suggestions. There is a general trend toward greater judicial involvement in monitoring probation conditions. In many jurisdictions, judges have established special drug courts. Here, judges identify first-time drug offenders, sentence them to participate in drug testing and rehabilitation programs, and then personally monitor their progress. If the offender successfully completes the program, he or she is not incarcerated and in some jurisdictions (e.g., Denver, Colorado), the conviction is expunged from the official record. Research on drug courts has been limited, but some studies have shown reductions in recidivism (Goldkamp 1994) and increased offender participation in treatment (Deschenes, Turner, and Greenwood 1995).

Other judges have decided on an individual basis to impose probation sentences that are more punitive and meaningful. As part of his sentencing an offender for molesting two students, a judge in Houston, Texas, forced a sixty-six-year-old music instructor to give up his $12,000 piano and post a sign on his front door warning children to stay away. State District Judge Ted Poe also barred the teacher from buying another piano and even from playing one until the end of his twenty-year probation (Mulholland 1994).

But meting out individualized sentences and personally monitoring offenders takes time, and judges' court calendars are crowded. James Q. Wilson of UCLA has suggested enlisting the police to help probation officers monitor offenders, particularly for the presence of weapons (Wilson 1995). He recommends giving each police patrol officer a list of people on probation or parole who live on that officer's beat and then rewarding the police for making frequent stops to insure that the offenders are not carrying guns or violating other statutes. Police in Redmond, Washington, have been involved in such an experiment since 1992, and while the program has not been formally evaluated, the police believe it has resulted in reduced crime (Morgan and Marris 1994).

But closer monitoring of probationers addresses only half the problem. The more difficult problem is finding jail and prison capacity to punish violators once they are discovered. Closely monitoring drug testing, for example, leads to many positive drug tests (Petersilia and Turner 1993). Most local jails do not have sufficient space to incarcerate all drug users because a greater priority is to have space for violent offenders. The result is that probationers quickly learn that failing a drug test, or violating other court-ordered conditions, has little consequence.

Oregon is trying to rectify this problem by imposing a swift and certain, but short (two to three days), jail sentence on *every* probationer who tests positive for drugs (Parent et al. 1994). The notion is that the offender will find the term disruptive to his normal life and be deterred from further drug use. Sanctions are gradually increased upon each subsequent failed drug test according to written department policy, and after three failed tests, the probationer is sent to prison. An evaluation of the program by the National Council on Crime and Delinquency (Baird, Wagner, and DeComo 1995) shows encouraging results in terms of increased offender participation in treatment and lowered recidivism while under supervision.

Unfortunately, debating the merits of these or other strategies is severely limited because we know so little about current probation practice. Assembling what is known about U.S. probation practices, so that public policy can be better informed, is the main purpose of this essay.

Together, the data in this essay show that probation is seriously underfunded relative to prisons—a policy that is not only short-sighted but also dangerous. Probationers in urban areas often receive little or no supervision, and the resulting recidivism rates are high for felons. But prison crowding has renewed interest in community-based sanctions, and recent evaluative evidence suggests that probation programs—properly designed and implemented—can be effective on a number of dimensions, including reducing recidivism.

There are several steps to achieving greater crime control over probationers. First, we must provide adequate financial resources to deliver programs that have been shown to work. Successful probation programs combine *both* treatment and surveillance and are targeted toward appropriate offender subgroups. Current evidence suggests that low-level drug offenders are prime candidates for enhanced probation programs. We must then work to garner more public support by convincing citizens that probation sanctions are punitive and convincing the judiciary that offenders will be held accountable for their behavior. Over time, probation will demonstrate its effectiveness, both in terms of reducing the human toll that imprisonment exacts on those incarcerated and reserving scarce resources to ensure that truly violent offenders remain in prison.

Section I begins by describing U.S. juvenile and adult probation data sources, explaining briefly why the topic has received relatively little attention. Section II presents a brief history of probation in the United States, highlighting important milestones. Section III summarizes probation in modern sentencing practice, discussing how the probation decision is made, the preparation of the presentence investigation, and the setting and enforcement of probation conditions. This section also describes the organization and funding of U.S. probation departments. Section IV describes current probation population characteristics. It reviews the growth in probation populations and what is known about offenders' crimes, court-ordered conditions, and supervision requirements. It also presents data detailing how the granting of probation varies across jurisdictions. Section V is devoted to assessing probation outcomes, reviewing recidivism and alternative outcomes measures. Section VI outlines several steps to reviving probation and achieving greater crime control over probationers.

I. Sources of Probation Information

Probation receives little public scrutiny, not by intent but because the probation system is so complex and the data are scattered among hundreds of loosely connected agencies, each operating with a wide variety of rules and structures. The term "probation" has various meanings within multiple areas of corrections, and the volume and type of offenders on probation are quite large and varied. Whereas one agency may be required to serve juvenile, misdemeanant, and felony offenders, another agency may handle only one type of offender. In some locations, probation officers run detention facilities and day-reporting centers, and in still others they supervise pretrial offenders or even parolees and run school-based prevention programs.

Virtually all probation information is national in scope and collected by agencies within the Office of Justice Programs, U.S. Department of Justice. There are only a few states (e.g., Minnesota, Vermont, North Carolina) that collect more detailed data on probationers, and very few probation agencies maintain their own research units. As a result, most states cannot describe the demographic or crime characteristics of probationers under their supervision. For example, California—which supervises nearly 300,000 adult probationers—is unable to provide the gender, age, or crime convictions of its probationers to the annual probation survey carried out by the Bureau of Justice Statistics (Maguire and Pastore 1995).

A. Juvenile Probationers

Information on the number of youth placed on probation comes from the *Juvenile Court Statistics* series. This annual series collects information from all U.S. courts with juvenile jurisdiction. Sponsored by the Office of Juvenile Justice and Delinquency Prevention (OJJDP) and analyzed by the National Center for Juvenile Justice (NCJJ), it describes the numbers of youth granted probation, as well as their underlying crimes and demographic characteristics (see Butts et al. 1995).

In 1992, the OJJDP sponsored a nationwide survey of juvenile probation departments, collecting information on departments' size, organization, and caseload size. Results of this survey are contained in Hurst and Torbet (1993).

B. Adult Probationers

Nearly all existing national data describing adult probationers comes from two statistical series sponsored by the Bureau of Justice Statistics (BJS), the statistical arm of the U.S. Department of Justice (DOJ). The first series, *Correctional Populations in the United States*, collects annual counts and movements from all federal, state, and local adult probation agencies in the United States. Probationer information includes race, sex, and ethnicity, and the numbers on probation for felonies, misdemeanors, and driving while intoxicated. Data on the type of discharge are also obtained (i.e., successful completion, incarcerated). This information has been collected by the Department of Justice since the mid-1970s.

The second series is the *National Judicial Reporting Program* (NJRP), a biennial sample survey, which compiles information on the sentences that felons receive in state courts nationwide and on the characteristics of the felons. The latest information is reported in *State Court Sentencing of Convicted Felons, 1992* (Langan and Cohen 1996) and is based on a sample of 300 nationally representative counties. The information collected on convicted felons includes their age, race, gender, prior criminal record, length of sentence, and conviction offense.[1]

Data on the organization of adult probation departments have been sporadically collected over the years by the National Institute of Justice (Comptroller General of the United States 1976; Nelson, Ohmart, and Harlow 1978; Allen, Carlson, and Parks 1979), the National Association of Criminal Justice Planners (Cunniff and Bergsmann 1990; Cunniff and Shilton 1991), the National Institute of Corrections (National Institute of Corrections 1993), and the Criminal Justice Institute (Camp and Camp 1995). The Criminal Justice Institute is a private,

[1] In 1992, BJS conducted the National Survey of Adults on Probation, the first-ever survey which will obtain detailed information on the backgrounds and characteristics of a national sample of probationers. The results will be available in spring 1997.

nonprofit organization that since 1990 has been publishing selected probation data in *The Corrections Yearbook: Probation and Parole.*

The National Institute of Justice (NIJ), the research arm of the U.S. Department of Justice, has sponsored nearly all of the basic and evaluation research conducted to date on adult probation. In recent years, these efforts have focused primarily on evaluating the effects of intermediate sanctions, programs that are more severe than routine probation but do not involve incarceration (for a review, see Tonry and Lynch 1996).

Beyond these minimal data, there is little systematic information on probation. We know almost nothing, for example, about the over 1 million adult misdemeanants who are placed on probation—what were their crimes, what services did probation provide, and how many are rearrested? And except for the studies mentioned above, we do not have that type of information about adult felons or juveniles either. There are serious gaps in our knowledge, and what does exist is not easily accessible or summarized.

II. The Origins and Evolution of Probation

To understand current probation practice, one must appreciate its historical roots. Probation in the United States began in 1841 with the innovative work of John Augustus, a Boston bootmaker who was the first to post bail for a man charged with being a common drunk under the authority of the Boston Police Court. Mr. Augustus was religious, a man of financial means, and had some experience working with alcoholics. When the man appeared before the judge for sentencing, Mr. Augustus asked the judge to defer sentencing for three weeks and release the man into Augustus's custody. At the end of this brief probationary period, the offender convinced the judge of his reform and therefore received a nominal fine. The concept of probation had been born (Dressler 1962).

From the beginning, the "helping" role of Augustus met with the scorn of law enforcement officials who wanted offenders punished, not helped. But Augustus persisted, and the court gradually accepted the notion that not all offenders needed to be incarcerated. During the next fifteen years (until his death in 1859), Augustus bailed out over 1,800 persons in the Boston courts, making himself liable to the extent of $243,234 and preventing those individuals from being held in jail to await trial. Augustus is reported to have selected his candidates carefully, offering assistance "mainly to those who were indicted for their first offense, and whose hearts were not wholly depraved, but gave promise of better things" (Augustus 1939). He provided his charges with aid in obtaining employment, an education, or a place to live, and also made an impartial report to the court.

Augustus reported great success with his charges, nearly all of whom were accused or convicted of violating Boston's vice or temperance laws. Of the first 1,100 offenders he discussed in his autobiography, he claimed only one had forfeited bond and asserted that, with help, most of them eventually led upright lives (Augustus 1939).

Buoyed by Augustus's example, Massachusetts quickly moved into the forefront of probation development. An experiment in providing children services (resembling probation) was inaugurated in 1869. In 1878, Massachusetts was the first state formally to adopt a probation law for juveniles. Concern for mitigating the harshness of penalties for children also led to the international development of probation (Hamai et al. 1995).

Public support for adult probation was much more difficult to come by. It was not until 1901 that New York passed the first statute authorizing probation for adult offenders, over twenty years after Massachusetts passed its law for juvenile probationers (Latessa and Allen 1997). By 1956, all states had adopted adult and juvenile probation laws.

John Augustus's early work provided the model for probation as we know it today. Virtually every basic practice of probation was conceived by him. He was the first person to use the term "probation"—which derives from the Latin term *probatio*, meaning a "period of proving or trial." He developed the ideas of the presentence investigation, supervision conditions, social casework, reports to the court, and revocation of probation. Unfortunately for such a visionary, Augustus died destitute (Dressler 1962).

Initially, probation officers were volunteers who, according to Augustus, needed to just have a good heart. Early probation volunteer officers were often drawn from Catholic, Protestant, and Jewish church groups. In addition, police were reassigned to function as probation officers while continuing to draw their pay as municipal employees. But as the concept spread and the number of persons arrested increased, the need for presentence investigations and other court investigations increased, and the volunteer probation officer was converted into a paid position (Dressler 1962). The new officers hired were drawn largely from the law enforcement community—retired sheriffs and policemen—and worked directly for the judge.

Gradually the role of court support and probation officer became synonymous, and probation officers became "the eyes and ears of the local court." As Rothman observed some years later, probation developed in the United States very haphazardly and with no real thought (Rothman 1980, p. 244). Missions were unclear and often contradictory, and from the start there was tension between the law enforcement and rehabilitation purposes of probation (McAnany, Thomson, and Fogel 1984). But most important, tasks were continually added to probation's responsibilities, while funding remained constant or declined. A 1979 survey (Fitzharris 1979) found that probation departments were responsible for more than fifty different activities, including court-related civil functions (e.g., step-parent adoption investigations, minority age marriage investigations).

Between the 1950s and 1970s, U.S. probation evolved in relative obscurity. But a number of reports issued in the 1970s brought national attention to the inadequacy of probation services and their organization. The National Advisory Commission on Criminal Justice Standards and Goals (1973, p. 112) stated that probation was the "brightest hope for corrections" but was "failing to provide services and supervision." In 1974, a widely publicized review of rehabilitation programs purportedly showed probation's ineffectiveness (Martinson 1974), and two years later the U.S. Comptroller General's Office released a report concluding that probation as currently practiced was a failure and that the U.S. probation systems were "in crisis" (Comptroller General of the United States 1976, p. 3). They urged that "since most offenders are sentenced to probation, probation systems must receive adequate resources. But something more fundamental is needed. The priority given to probation in the criminal justice system must be reevaluated" (Comptroller General of the United States 1976, p. 74).

In recent years, probation agencies have struggled—with continued meager resources—to upgrade services and supervision. Significant events in the development of U.S. probation are summarized in table 1. Important developments have included the widespread adoption of case classification systems and various types of intermediate sanctions (e.g., electronic monitoring, intensive supervision). These programs have had varied success in reducing recidivism, but the evaluations have been instructive in terms of future program design.

III. Probation and Modern Sentencing Practice

Anyone who is convicted, and many of those arrested, come into contact with the probation department. Probation officials, operating with a great deal of discretionary authority, significantly affect most subse-

TABLE 1

Significant Events in the Development of U.S. Probation

Year	Event
1841	John Augustus introduces probation in the United States in Boston.
1878	Massachusetts is first state to adopt probation for juveniles.
1878–1938	Thirty-seven states, the District of Columbia, and the federal government pass juvenile and adult probation laws.
1927	All states but Wyoming have juvenile probation laws.
1954	All states have juvenile probation laws.
1956	All states have adult probation laws (Mississippi becomes the last state to pass authorizing legislation).
1973	National Advisory Commission on Criminal Justice Standards and Goals endorses more extensive use of probation.
1973	Minnesota first state to adopt Community Corrections Act; 18 states follow by 1995.
1974	Martinson's widely publicized research purportedly proves that probation does not work.
1975	U.S. Department of Justice conducts the first census of U.S. probationers.
1975	Wisconsin implements first probation case classification system; American Probation and Parole founded.
1976	U.S. Comptroller General's study of U.S. probation concludes it is a "system in crisis" due to inadequate funding.
1982	Georgia's intensive supervision probation program claims to reduce recidivism and costs.
1983	Electronic monitoring of offenders begins in New Mexico, followed by larger program in Florida.
1985	RAND releases study of felony probationers showing high failure rates; replications follow, showing that probation services and effectiveness vary widely across nation.
1989	General Accounting Office survey shows all 50 states have adopted intensive probation and other intermediate sanction programs.
1991	U.S. Department of Justice funds nationwide intensive supervision demonstration and evaluation.
1993	Program evaluations show probation without adequate surveillance and treatment is ineffective, but well-managed and adequately funded programs reduce recidivism.

Source.—Compiled by the author.

quent justice processing decisions. Their input affects not only the subsequent liberties offenders will enjoy, but their decisions influence public safety, since they recommend (within certain legal restraints) which offenders will be released back to their communities, and judges usually accept their sentence recommendations.

A. Probation's Influence throughout the Justice System

As figure 1 shows, probation officials are involved in decision making long before sentencing, often beginning from the time a crime comes to the attention of the police. They usually perform a personal investigation to determine whether a defendant will be released on his own recognizance or bail. Probation reports are the primary source of information the court uses to determine which cases will be deferred from formal prosecution. If deferred, probation officers will also supervise the diverted offender, and their recommendation will be primary to the decision whether the offender has successfully complied with the diversionary sentence and, hence, that no formal prosecution will occur.

For persons who violate court-ordered conditions, probation officers are responsible for deciding which violations will be brought to the court's attention and what subsequent sanctions to recommend. When the court grants probation, probation staff have considerable discretion about which court-ordered conditions to enforce and monitor. And even when an offender goes to prison, the offender's initial security classification (and eligibility for parole) will be based on information contained in the presentence investigation. Finally, when the offender is released from jail or prison, probation staff often provide his or her community supervision.

No other justice agency is as extensively involved with the offender and his case as is the probation department. Every other agency completes its work and hands the case over to the next decision maker. For example, the police arrest offenders and hand them over to the prosecutor who files charges and then hands them to the judge who sentences and then transfers them to the prison authorities who confine—but the probation department interacts with all of these agencies, provides data that influence each of their processing decisions, and takes charge of the offender's supervision at any point when the system decides to return the offender to the community (of course, for parolees, parole officers usually assume this function). Figure 1 highlights the involvement of probation agencies throughout the justice system, showing its integral role to custody and supervision.

B. The Presentence Investigation Report

When most people think of probation, they think of its *supervision* function. But providing law enforcement agencies and the courts with necessary information to make key processing decisions is the other

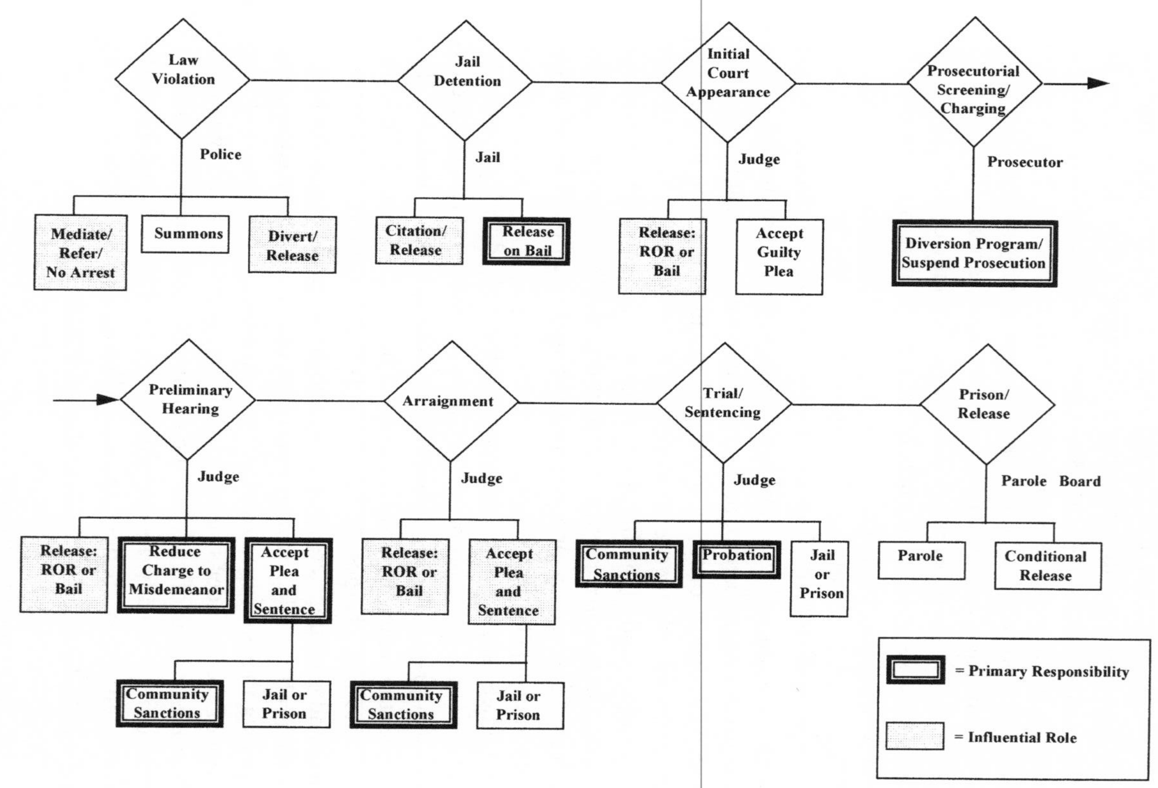

Fig. 1.—Probation's involvement in the criminal justice system. Source.—Adapted from Wilkinson (1995).

major function of probation, commonly referred to as probation's *investigation* function.

From the point of arrest, information about the offender's crime and criminal background is accumulated and eventually presented to the court if the case proceeds through prosecution and sentencing. This formal document is known as the presentence investigation (PSI) or presentence report (PSR).

The PSI is a critically important document, since over 90 percent of all felony cases in the United States are eventually resolved through a negotiated plea (Bureau of Justice Statistics 1995), and the court's major decision is whether imprisonment will be imposed. A survey by the National Institute of Corrections found that half of all states require a PSI in all felony cases; the PSI is discretionary for felonies in another sixteen states. Only two states require a PSI prior to disposition in misdemeanor cases (National Institute of Corrections 1993). Where PSIs are discretionary, the option of requesting them usually rests with the courts.

Research has repeatedly shown that the judge's knowledge of the defendant is usually limited to the information contained in the PSI and, as a result, there is a high correlation between the probation officer's recommendation and the judge's sentence. Research by the American Justice Institute (1981), for example, using samples from representative probation departments throughout the United States, found that recommendations for probation were adopted by the sentencing judge between 66 and 95 percent of the time.

The PSI typically includes information on the seriousness of the crime, the defendant's risk, the defendant's circumstances, a summary of the legally permissible sentencing options, and a recommendation for or against prison. If recommending prison, the PSI recommends sentence length; and if recommending probation, the PSI recommends sentence length and the conditions to be imposed.

Some have noted that the introduction of sentencing guidelines—which require calculations based on details of the crime and prior criminal record—have increased the importance of the PSI and the role and responsibility of the probation officer, particularly at the federal level (McDonald and Carlson 1993).

While the PSI is initially prepared to aid the sentencing judge, once prepared it becomes a critically important document to justice officials throughout the system, as well as the basis of most criminological research studies. As Abadinsky noted, its most common uses are serving as the basis for the initial risk/needs classification probation officers use to assign an offender to a supervision caseload and treatment plan, assisting jail and prison personnel in their classification and treatment programs, furnishing parole authorities with information pertinent to consideration for parole and release planning, and providing a source of information for research studies (Abadinsky 1997, p. 105).

C. Factors Influencing Who Gets Probation versus Prison

The most important purpose of the PSI is to assist in making the prison/probation decision. Generally speaking, the more serious the offender, the greater likelihood of a prison term. But exactly what crime and offender characteristics are used by the court to assess "seriousness?"

Petersilia and Turner (1986) analyzed the criminal records and case files of approximately 16,500 males convicted of selected felony crimes in one of seventeen California counties in 1980. We coded detailed information about the offenders' crimes, criminal backgrounds, and how their cases were processed (e.g., private or public attorney). The purpose was to identify the factors that distinguished who was granted probation (with or without a jail term) and who was sentenced to prison among offenders convicted under the same penal code section, in the same county, and in the same year. We found that an offender was more likely to receive a prison sentence if he had two or more conviction counts (i.e., convicted of multiple charges), had two or more prior criminal convictions, was on probation or parole at the time of the arrest, was a drug addict, used a weapon during the commission of the offense, or seriously injured the victim.

For all offenses except assault, offenders having three or more of these characteristics had an 80 percent or greater probability of going to prison in California, regardless of the type of crime of which they were currently convicted (Petersilia and Turner 1986).

After controlling for these "basic factors," the researchers also found that having a private (vs. public) attorney could reduce a defendant's chances of imprisonment (this was true except for drug cases, where attorney type made no difference). Obtaining pretrial release also lessened the probability of going to prison, whereas going to trial increased that probability (Petersilia and Turner 1986, p. xi).

But while such factors predicted about 75 percent of the sentencing decisions in the study, they did not explain the remainder. Thus, Petersilia and Turner (1986) concluded that in about 25 percent of the cases studied, those persons sent to prison could not be effectively distinguished in terms of their crimes or criminal backgrounds from those receiving probation. These data suggest that many offenders who are granted felony probation are indistinguishable in terms of their crimes or criminal record from those who are imprisoned (or vice versa).

D. Setting and Enforcing Probation Conditions

For offenders granted probation, the court decides what conditions will be included in the probation contract between the offender and the court. In practice, when sentencing an offender to probation, judges often combine the probation term with a suspended sentence, under which the judge sentences a defendant to prison or jail and then suspends the sentence in favor of probation. In this way, the jail or prison term has been legally imposed but is held in abeyance to be reinstated if the offender fails to abide by the probation conditions (Latessa and Allen 1997). Offenders are presumed to be more motivated to comply with conditions of probation by knowing what awaits should they fail to do so.

In addition to deciding whether to impose a sentence of incarceration and then "suspend" it in favor of probation (or sentence to probation directly), the judge makes a number of other highly important, but discretionary, decisions. He must decide whether to impose a jail term along with probation. This is commonly referred to as "split sentencing"; nationally, probation is combined with a jail term in 26 percent of felony cases (Langan and Cohen 1996). Some states use split sentencing more frequently. For example, 60 percent of persons sentenced to probation in Minnesota are required to serve some jail time (Minnesota Sentencing Guidelines Commission 1996), as are nearly 80 percent of felons in California (California Department of Justice 1995). The average jail sentence for felony probationers is seven months, while the average length of felony probation is forty-seven months (Bureau of Justice Statistics 1995).

It is the judge's responsibility to enumerate the conditions the probationer must abide by in order to remain in the community. The conditions are usually recommended by probation officers and contained in the PSI. But they may also be designed by the judge, and judges are generally free to construct any terms of probation they deem necessary. Judges also often authorize the setting of "such other conditions as the probation officer may deem proper to impose" or may leave the mode of implementation of a condition (such as method of treatment) to the discretion of the probation officer.

The judge's (and probation officer's) required conditions usually fall into one of three realms. *Standard conditions* imposed on all probationers include such requirements as reporting to the probation office, notifying the agency of any change of address, remaining gainfully employed, and not leaving the jurisdiction without permission. *Punitive conditions* are usually established to reflect the seriousness of the offense and increase the intrusiveness and burdensomeness of probation. Examples are fines, community service, victim restitution, house arrest, and drug testing. *Treatment conditions* are imposed to force probationers to deal with a significant problem or need, such as substance abuse, family counseling, or vocational training.

The U.S. Supreme Court has held that probation should not be considered a form of "prison without walls" but, rather, a period of conditional liberty that is protected by due process (McShane and Krause 1993, p. 93). In that vein, the courts have ruled that probation conditions must not infringe on the basic rights of the person being supervised. Case law has established that there are four general elements in establishing the legal validity of a probation condition. Each imposed probation condition must serve a *legitimate purpose*—must either protect society or lead to the rehabilitation of the offender; must be *clear*—with language that is explicit, outlining specifically what can or cannot be done so that the average person can know exactly what is expected; must be *reasonable*—not excessive in its expectations; and must be *constitutional*—while probationers do have a diminished expectation of certain privileges, they retain basic human freedoms such as religion, speech, and marriage.

In legal terms, the probation conditions form a contract between the offender and the court.[2] The contract, at least theoretically, states the conditions the offender must abide by to remain in the community. The court requires that the probation officer provide the defendant with a written statement setting forth all the conditions to which the sentence is subject. The offender signs the contract, and the probation officer is the contract's "enforcer," responsible for notifying the court when the contract is not being fulfilled.

[2] An excellent discussion of the legal bases for probation and enforcing probation conditions can be found in Klein (1997).

Should a defendant violate a probation condition at any time prior to the expiration of his term, the court may, after a hearing pursuant to certain rules (which include written notification of charges), continue him on probation, with or without extending the term or modifying or enlarging the conditions, or revoke probation and impose any other sentence that was available at the initial sentencing (e.g., prison or jail).

As mentioned previously, a suspended sentence is often imposed along with probation, and on revocation the judge may order the original sentence carried out. When a suspended sentence is reinstated, the judge may decide to give credit for probation time already served or may require that the complete original incarceration term be served.

Over the years, the proportion of probationers subject to special conditions has increased (Clear 1994). The public's more punitive mood, combined with availability of inexpensive drug testing and a higher number of probationers having substance abuse problems, contribute to the increased number of conditions imposed. More and more stringent conditions increase the chances of failure (Petersilia and Turner 1993). According to BJS, the percentage of offenders successfully completing their probation terms is falling. In 1986, 74 percent of those who exited probation successfully completed their terms; in 1992, the figure was 67 percent, and by 1994, it had dropped to 60 percent (Langan 1996).

Langan and Cunniff's (1992) study of felons on probation showed that 55 percent of the offenders had some special condition (beyond the standard conditions) added to their probation terms (shown in fig. 2), the most common being drug testing. Further analysis by Langan (1994) showed that many probationers failed to satisfy their probation-ordered conditions. He found that half of probationers simply did not comply with the court-ordered terms of their probation, and only 50 percent of known violators went to jail or prison for their noncompliance. Langan concluded (1994, p. 791) that "sanctions are not vigorously enforced."

Taxman and Byrne (1994), reanalyzing a national sample of felons placed on probation and tracked by BJS for two years (Dawson 1990), discovered that even probation absconders (i.e., those who fail to report) often are not punished. They found that, on any one day, about 10–20 percent of adult felony probationers were on abscond status, their whereabouts unknown. While warrants were usually issued for

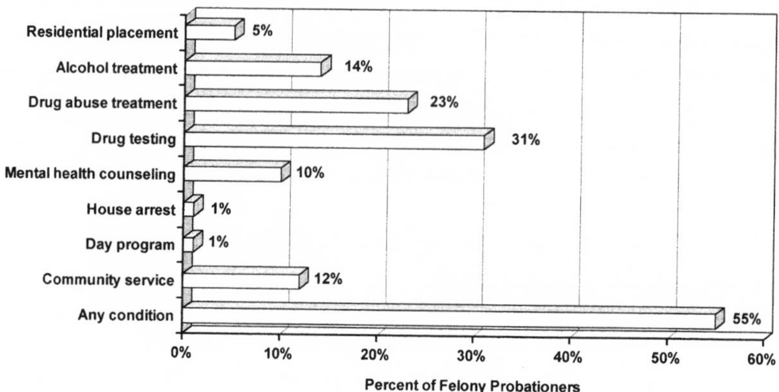

FIG. 2.—Special conditions imposed on adult felony probationers. Source.—Langan and Cunniff (1992).

their arrest, no agency actively invests time finding the offenders and serving the warrants. They concluded that, practically speaking, as long as they are not rearrested, offenders are not violated.

Even though many court-ordered conditions are not actively enforced, the probation population is so large that revoking even a few percent of them or revoking all those who are rearrested can have a dramatic impact on prison admissions. Current estimates are that between 30 and 50 percent of all new prison admissions are probation and parole failures (Parent et al. 1994). Texas, for example, reported that approximately two-thirds of all prison admissions in 1993 were either probation or parole violators. In Oregon, the figure was over 80 percent and in California over 60 percent (Parent et al. 1994).[3]

Due to the scarcity of prison beds, policy makers have begun to wonder whether revoking probationers and parolees for technical violations (i.e., infractions of conditions, rather than for a new crime) makes sense. While it is important to take some action when probation violations are discovered, it is not obvious that prison is always the best response.

Several states, trying to reserve prison beds for violent offenders, are now structuring the courts' responses to technical violations. Missis-

[3] California reports that more than 60 percent of its prison admissions each year are probation and parole violators, but a recent analysis by Petersilia (1995*a*) found that "true" technical violators (those returned for rule infractions rather than new crimes) made up only 4 percent of total admissions in 1991.

sippi and Georgia use ninety-day boot camp programs housed in separate wings of the state prison for probation violators (Grubbs 1993; Prevost, Rhine, and Jackson 1993). While empirical evidence is scant as to the effects of these programs, many officials believe that the programs increase the certainty of punishment, while reserving scarce prison space for the truly violent (Rhine 1993).

E. Probation Caseloads and Contact Levels

The most common measure of probation's workload is caseload size—the number of offenders assigned to each probation officer. Published reports normally divide the number of probation department employees or line officers by the number of adult probationers under supervision to indicate average caseload size. Over the years probation caseloads have grown from what was thought in the mid-1970s to be an ideal size of 30:1 (President's Commission on Law Enforcement and Administration of Justice 1967) to the early 1990s, when the average adult regular supervision caseload is reported to be 117:1 (Camp and Camp 1995).

The adult figure is misleading and vastly overstates the number of officers available for offender supervision. First, as Cunniff and Bergsmann showed, not all probation employees or even line officers are assigned to offender supervision. Cunniff and Bergsmann (1990) found that in a typical U.S. probation department only 52 percent of staff are line officers; 48 percent are clerical, support staff, and management. Such high clerical staffing (23 percent) is required because a third to a half of all clerical personnel type PSIs for the court. Of line probation officers, *only about 17 percent of them supervise adult felons.* The remaining officers supervise juveniles (half of all U.S. adult probation departments also have responsibility for supervising juveniles), and 11 percent prepare PSIs. These figures were nearly identical to those found in the NIC national survey of probation departments (National Institute of Corrections 1993).

There were an estimated 50,000 probation employees in 1994 (Camp and Camp 1995). If 23 percent of them (or 11,500 officers) were supervising 2,962,166 adult probationers, then the average U.S. adult probation caseload in 1994 was 258 offenders per line officer.

A recent survey (Thomas 1993) of juvenile probation officers responsible for supervision showed that U.S. juvenile caseloads range between two and 200 cases, with a typical (median) active caseload of

TABLE 2

Felony Probationers' Initial Supervision Levels

Supervision Level	Prescribed Number of Contacts	Percent of Caseload
Intensive	9 per month	10
Maximum	3 per month	32
Medium	1 per month	37
Minimum	1 per 3 months	12
Administrative	None required	9

Source.—Langan and Cunniff 1992.

forty-one. The optimal caseload suggested by juvenile probation officers was thirty cases.

Of course, offenders are not supervised on "average" caseloads. Rather, probation staff use a variety of risk and needs classification instruments to identify offenders needing more intensive supervision or services. Developing these "risk/need" classification devices occupied probation personnel throughout the 1970s, and their use is now routine throughout the United States (for a review, see Clear 1988). Unfortunately, while risk assessments can identify offenders more likely to reoffend, funds are usually insufficient to implement the levels of supervision predicted by classification instruments (Jones 1996).

Recent BJS data show that 95 percent of all U.S. adult probationers are supervised on regular caseloads, about 4 percent are on intensive supervision, and about 1 percent are on specialized caseloads such as electronic monitoring or boot camps (Brown et al. 1996). Again, however, these numbers do not tell much about the actual contact levels received by felons. The best data on this subject come from the Langan and Cunniff (1992) study tracking felony probationers. They report that about 10 percent of *felony* probationers are placed on intensive caseloads, for which administrative guidelines suggest probation officers should have contact with probationers nine times per month (table 2). The authors note that the initial classification level does not necessarily mean that offenders received that level of service but, rather, that they were assigned to a caseload having that administrative standard.

The Langan and Cunniff (1992) study also provides information on supervision levels relative to conviction crimes and county of conviction. They report that across all the sites and felony crimes studied, about 20 percent of adult felony probationers are assigned to caseloads requiring *no* personal contact.

In large urban counties the situation is particularly acute and the average caseload size noted above does not convey the seriousness of the situation. Consider, for example, the Los Angeles County Probation Department, the largest probation department in the world. In 1995, its 900 line officers were responsible for supervising 88,000 adult and juvenile offenders. Since the mid-1970s, county officials have repeatedly cut the agency's budget, while the number of persons granted probation and the number of required presentence investigations have grown (Nidorf 1996).

As a result, 66 percent of all probationers in Los Angeles in 1995 were supervised on "automated" or banked caseloads (Petersilia 1995*b*)—no services, supervision, or personal contacts are provided. Probationers are simply required to send in a preaddressed postcard once or twice a month reporting on their activities. A more detailed study found that nearly 10,000 violent offenders (convicted of murder rape, assault, kidnap, and robbery) are being supervised on any given day by probation officers in Los Angeles, and half are on "automated minimum" caseloads with no reporting requirements (Los Angeles County Planning Committee 1996).

F. *The Organization of Probation*

Probation is administered by more than 2,000 separate agencies, and there is no uniform structure (Abadinsky 1997). Probation is a state and local activity with the federal government providing technical support, data gathering, and funding for innovative programs and their evaluation. As the National Institute of Corrections (NIC) recently observed, "Probation was established in nearly as many patterns as there are states, and they have since been modified by forces unique to each state and each locality" (1993, p. v). The result is that probation services in the United States differ in terms of whether they are delivered by the executive or the judicial branch of government, how services are funded, and whether probation services are primarily a state or a local function. While a detailed discussion of these issues is beyond the scope of this essay, interested readers are referred to the NIC (1993) report *State and Local Probation Systems in the United States: A Survey of Current Practice.*

1. *Centralized or Decentralized Probation?* The centralization issue concerns the location of authority to administer probation services.

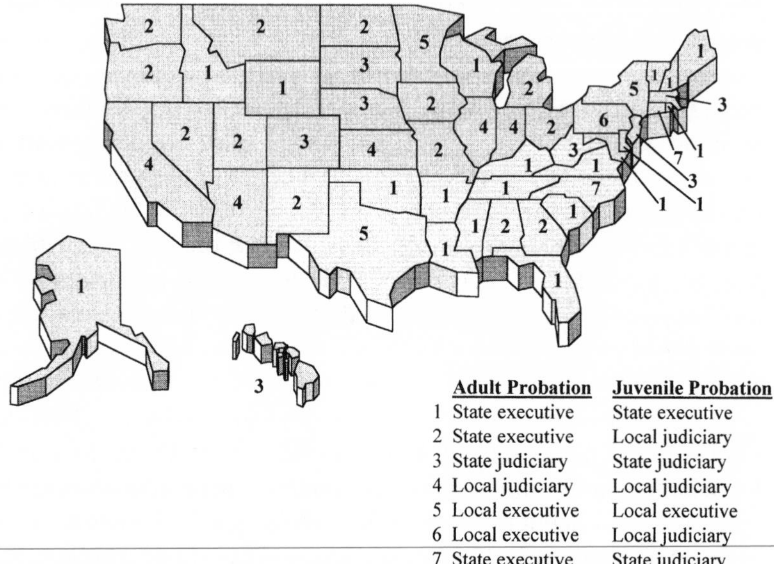

FIG. 3.—Jurisdictional arrangements for probation, by state. Source.—American Correctional Association (1995).

Proponents of probation argue that judicially administered probation (usually on a county level) promotes diversity. Nelson et al. (1978) suggest that an agency administered by a city or county instead of a state is smaller, more flexible, and better able to respond to the unique problems of the community. And because decentralized probation draws its support from its community and local government, it can offer more appropriate supervision for its clients and make better use of existing resources. It is also argued that if the state took over probation it might be assigned a lower level of priority than if it remained a local, judicially controlled service.

Over time adult probation services moved from the judicial to the executive branch and are now located in the judicial branch in only one-quarter of the states (see fig. 3). However, more than half of the agencies providing juvenile probation services are administered on the local level. (Fortunately, parole administration is much less complex: one agency per state and always in the executive branch.)

The trend in adult probation is toward centralization, with authority for a state's probation activities placed in a single statewide administrative body (National Institute of Corrections 1993). In 1996, three-quarters of all states located adult probation in the executive branch, where services and funding were centralized. Proponents of this approach assert that all other human services and correctional subsystems are located within the executive branch; program budgeting can be better coordinated; and judges, trained in law, not administration, are not well equipped to administer probation services (Abadinsky 1997, p. 35). Even in those states with county-based probation systems, states have usually created an oversight agency for better coordination and consistency of services—California is currently the only state operating probation locally without a state oversight agency (Parent et al. 1994).

As Clear and Cole (1997) point out, there is no optimal probation organization. In jurisdictions with a tradition of strong and effective local probation programming, decentralized services make sense. In states that typically have provided services through centralized, large-scale bureaucracies, perhaps probation should be part of such services. As probation receives greater attention—and its services and supervision are more closely scrutinized—the issue of who oversees probation and who is responsible for standards, training, and revocation policy will become central in the years ahead.

2. *Probation Funding.* Probation funding has long been recognized as woefully inadequate.

a. *State versus County Funding.* While states have become more willing to fund probation, counties still provide primary funding for probation in twelve states, although some of these agencies also receive significant state support. In NIC's 1993 survey, California counties received the least amount of state assistance, ranging from a low of 9 percent in Los Angeles and San Diego to a high of 14 percent in San Francisco. Counties in Texas received some of the largest shares of state assistance (Dallas received 50 percent of its operating budget from the state) (National Institute of Corrections 1993).

Some states have used other means to upgrade the quality of probation services and funding. Community Corrections Acts (CCAs) are mechanisms by which state funds are granted to local governments to foster local sanctions to be used in lieu of state prison. By 1995 eighteen states had enacted CCAs, and the evidence suggests that CCAs have encouraged some good local probation programs but have been less successful at reducing commitments to state prison or improving coordination of state and local programs (Parent 1995; Shilton 1995). Still, interest in the CCA concept—and other state "subsidies" to upgrade probation—is growing across the United States.

Arizona probation probably has the best current system. In 1987, the state legislature established a statutory standard that felony probation caseloads not exceed sixty offenders to one probation officer. And state funding was allocated to maintain that level of service. As a result, probation departments in Arizona are nationally recognized to be among the best, providing their offenders with both strict surveillance and needed treatment services.

b. *Annual Costs per Probationer.* The *Corrections Yearbook* reports that the annual amount spent for probationers on supervision in the United States ranged from $156 in Connecticut to $1,500 in the federal system. The average of the forty-four reporting states was $584 per probationer, per year (Camp and Camp 1995). But such numbers are nearly meaningless since we do not know what factors were considered in calculating them. One system may compute the average cost per offender per day on the basis of services rendered and officers' salaries, while others may divide the total operating budget by the number of clients served. Still others may figure into the equation the costs of various private contracts for treatment and drug testing. There is no standard formula for computing probationer costs, but funds are known to be inadequate.

Since its beginnings, probation has continually been asked to take on greater numbers of probationers and conduct a greater number of presentence investigations, all while experiencing stable or declining funding. As Clear and Braga recently observed: "Apparently, community supervision has been seen as a kind of elastic resource that could handle whatever numbers of offenders the system required it to" (Clear and Braga 1995, p. 423).

From 1977 to 1990, prison, jail, parole, and probation populations all about tripled in size. Yet only spending for prisons and jails increased. In 1990, prison and jail spending accounted for two cents of every state and local dollar spent—twice the amount spent in 1977. Spending for probation and parole accounted for two-tenths of one cent of every dollar spent in 1990—unchanged from 1977 (Langan 1994). Today, although two-thirds of all persons convicted are handled in the community, only about one-tenth of the correctional budget goes to supervise them.

c. *Fines and Fees.* As conditions of probation, many jurisdictions are including various offender-imposed fees which, when collected, are used to support the probation department. Fees are levied for a variety of services, including the preparation of presentence reports, electronic monitoring, work release programs, drug counseling, and regular probation supervision. By 1992, more than half of the states allowed probation departments to charge fees to probationers, ranging from $10 to $40 per month, usually with a sliding scale for those unable to pay (Finn and Parent 1992).

Finn and Parent (1992) in an NIJ study of fines found that despite a common perception of the criminal as penniless and unemployable, most offenders on probation who have committed misdemeanors—and even many who have committed felonies—can afford modest monthly supervision fees. Texas, for example, has been highly successful in generating probation fees. Probationers there are required to pay a standard monthly fee of $10 plus $5 for the victims' fund. In 1990, Texas probation agencies spent about $106 million to supervise probationers but collected more than $57 million in fees—about one-half the cost of basic probation supervision (Finn and Parent 1992, p. 12).

Taxpayers applaud such efforts, and they may also teach offenders personal responsibility, but the practice causes dilemmas concerning whether to revoke probation for nonpayment. The courts have ruled that probation cannot be revoked when an indigent offender has not paid his fees or restitution (*Bearden v. Georgia* 1983).

IV. Who Is on Probation?

Probation was never intended to serve as a major criminal sanction. It was designed for first-time offenders who were not deeply involved in crime and for whom individualized treatment and casework could make a difference. But, as shown below, things have changed considerably.

A. Profile of Persons Placed on Probation

The Bureau of Justice Statistics recently reported that U.S. judges sentence 80 percent of adults convicted of misdemeanors to probation or probation with jail and about 60 percent of adults convicted of felonies—or fully two-thirds of all persons convicted of a crime (Bureau of Justice Statistics 1996*a*). As a result, BJS estimated that a record number of 3,096,529 adults were on probation at year end 1995, an increase of 4 percent over the previous year (see fig. 4).

Figure 4 also shows a consistent 3 : 1 ratio between probationers and

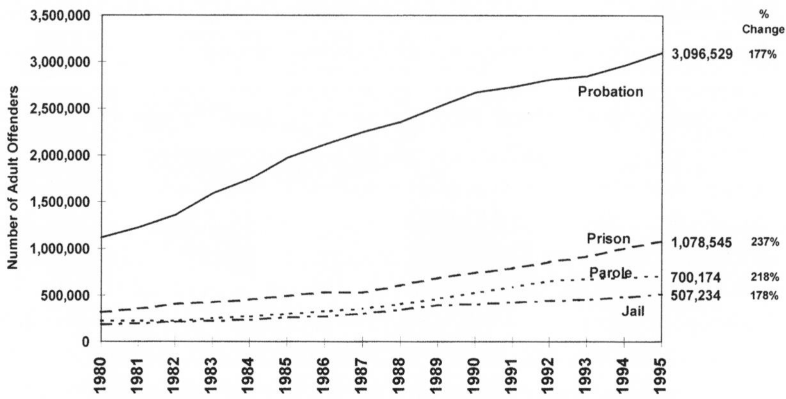

FIG. 4.—Adults in prison, jail, probation, parole, 1980–95. Source.—Bureau of Justice Statistics (1996*b*).

prisoners over the past decade. An interesting recent analysis by Zvekic (1996) shows that the United States and other Western European countries' preference for probation compared with prison is not shared by some other countries, most notably Japan, Israel, and Scotland. For example, the ratio of imprisonment to probation in Japan is 4:1.

The Bureau of Justice Statistics also reports that the southern U.S. states generally have the highest per capita ratio of probationers—reporting 1,846 probationers per 100,000 adults at year end 1995 (Bureau of Justice Statistics 1996*a*). In terms of sheer numbers of probationers, Texas has the largest adult probation population (about 396,000), followed by California (about 277,000). In Texas, 3.1 percent of all adults were on probation at year end 1995 (Bureau of Justice Statistics 1996*a*).

If probation were being used primarily as an alternative to incarceration, one might expect to find that the states that imposed more probationary sentences would have lower than average incarceration rates and vice versa. This is not the case. Generally, states with a relatively high per capita imprisonment rate also have a relatively high per capita use of probation. Texas, for example, had the highest state imprisonment rate in the nation in 1995 (Bureau of Justice Statistics 1996*b*) and the highest rate of probation impositions. Similarly, Southern states generally place persons on probation at a high rate, and they also generally incarcerate more than the rest of the nation (Klein 1997).

Half of all offenders on probation in 1995 had been convicted of a

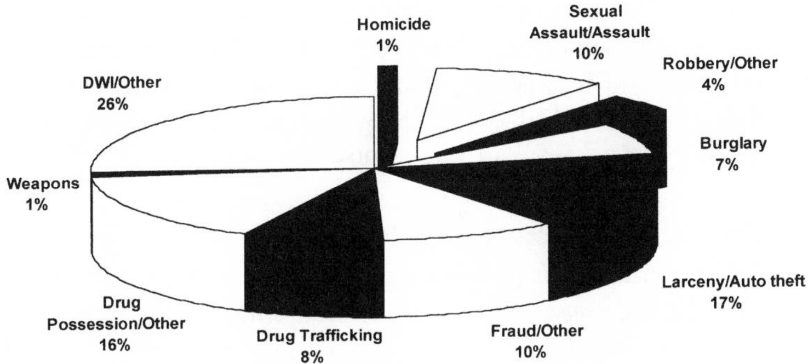

FIG. 5.—Adults on probation by conviction crime type. Source.—Bureau of Justice Statistics (1992).

felony and a quarter of a misdemeanor. One in every six had been convicted of driving while intoxicated—which could be either a felony or misdemeanor (Bureau of Justice Statistics 1996*a*).

The average age of adult state probationers nationwide in 1995 was twenty-nine years; women made up 21 percent of the nation's probationers, a larger proportion than for any other correctional population. Approximately 64 percent of adults on probation were white, and 34 percent were black. Hispanics, who may be of any race, represented 14 percent of probationers (Bureau of Justice Statistics 1996*a*). These percentages have remained relatively constant since BJS began collecting the data in 1978 (Langan 1996).

While BJS does not routinely collect data on the conviction crimes of probationers, such information was obtained for a nationally representative sample of adult probationers (felons and misdemeanors combined) (Bureau of Justice Statistics 1992). The conviction crimes of adult probationers are shown in figure 5.

While we know less about the characteristics of juvenile probationers, Butts et al. (1995) report that 35 percent (520,500) of all formally and informally handled delinquency cases disposed by juvenile courts in 1993 resulted in probation. Probation was the most severe disposition in over half (56 percent) of adjudicated delinquency cases, with annual proportions remaining constant for the five-year period 1989–93.

Figure 6 shows the growth in juvenile probation populations, as well as their underlying offenses. It is important to remember that this growth in juvenile probation populations has occurred even though a greater number of serious juveniles are being waived to adult court for prosecution and sentencing (Butts et al. 1995). Judicial waivers increased 68 percent between 1988 and 1992, although waivers to adult court are estimated to be less than 2 percent of all cases filed in juvenile court (Howell, Krisberg, and Jones 1993).

B. The Variability and Prevalence of Probation Sentencing

The decision to grant probation is highly discretionary within certain legal boundaries, and practices vary considerably within and among states. Cunniff and Shilton (1991), in a study of over 12,000 cases sentenced to probation in 1986 in thirty-two large jurisdictions, found that the percent of all sentences involving probation in the participating jurisdictions ranged from 30 percent in New York County (Manhattan) to 75 percent in Hennepin County (Minneapolis).

Cunniff and Shilton (1991) suggest that some of the variation is due to sentencing laws under which these jurisdictions function and their justice environments. They report that courts in determinate sentencing states (with no parole board) tend to use probation more frequently than courts in indeterminate sentencing states (with parole boards). Presumably, in indeterminate states, parole boards will release the less serious and less dangerous offenders—thus reducing length of prison time served for less serious offenders early. But in determinate sentencing states, prison terms are fixed and parole boards have little ability to reduce the lengths of stay courts impose. Apparently, judges are

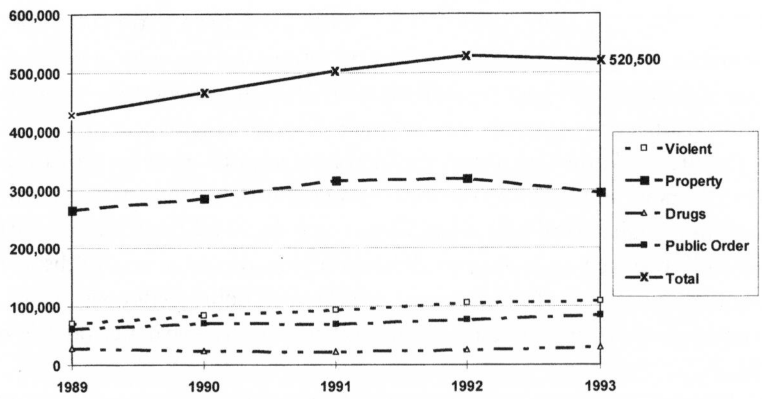

Fig. 6.—Number of juveniles in the United States sentenced to probation, by year and crime. Source.—Butts et al. (1995).

less willing to sentence to prison when lengths of sentences are fixed.

Studies have also shown that judges are more willing to place felons on probation when they perceive that the probation department can monitor the offender closely and that community resources are sufficient to address some of the offender's underlying problems (Frank, Cullen, and Cullen 1987). Minnesota, Washington, and Arizona—the three states identified by Cunniff and Shilton (1991) as using probation most frequently—are well known for delivering good probation supervision and having adequate resources to provide treatment and services.

Some of the variability in granting probation, however, must also be due to the underlying distributions of offense categories within these jurisdictions. For example, it may be that the robberies committed in one location are much less serious than those committed in another. However, reanalysis of a data set collected by RAND researchers, where offense seriousness was statistically controlled, still revealed a wide disparity among jurisdictions in their use of straight probation (i.e., without a jail term). Klein and his colleagues examined adjudication outcomes of defendants from fourteen large urban jurisdictions across the country in 1986; all of the defendants were charged with stranger-to-stranger armed robberies and residential burglaries (Klein et al. 1991). The granting of straight probation, even for felons convicted of similar crimes, varied substantially across the nation, particularly for burglary (see fig. 7). The figures for the California counties are particularly low because California commonly uses split sentences (probation plus jail) for felony crimes.

This demonstrated variability in the granting of probation is important, as it suggests that the underlying probation population and the services they need and supervision risks they pose are vastly different, depending on the jurisdiction studied.

As noted above, states vary considerably in their usage of probation. The main reason is that there are no national guidelines for granting probation or limiting its use. Rather, generally speaking, the court is supposed to grant probation when the defendant does not pose a risk to society or need correctional supervision, and if the granting of probation would not underrate the seriousness of the crime (American Bar Association 1970). Until recently, in most states those broad guidelines were interpreted with great variability.

States have, however, recently been redefining categories of offense that render an offender ineligible for probation and identifying offend-

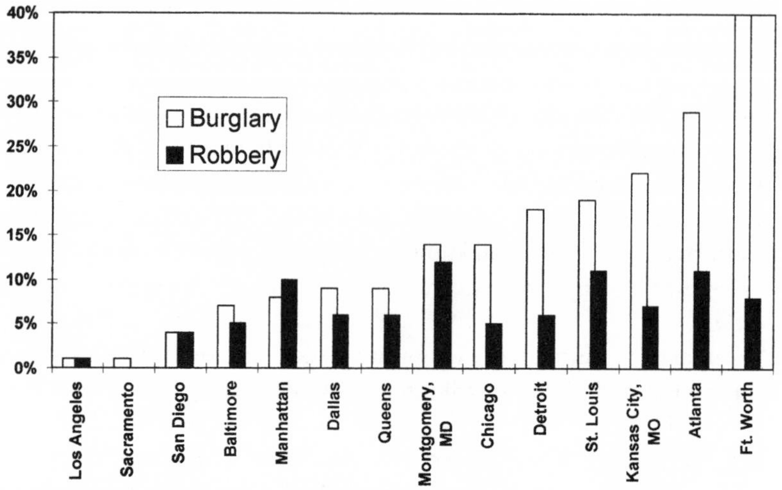

FIG. 7.—Percent of convicted residential burglars and armed robbers granted straight probation. Source.—Klein et al. (1991).

ers who are low risk and *should* be sentenced to probation. Recent mandatory sentencing laws such as "three strikes and you're out" have been motivated, in large part, by a desire to limit judicial discretion and the court's ability to grant probation to repeat offenders (Greenwood et al. 1994).

The public perceives that the justice system is too lenient, and when certain statistics are publicized, it appears that way. But, as in other matters involving justice data, the truth is more complicated, and it all depends on which populations are included in the summary statistics.

Roughly two-thirds of all adult convicted felons are granted probation. Hence, the common observation that "probation is our nation's most common sentence." Many use this finding to characterize U.S. sentencing practices as lenient (Bell and Bennett 1996). But felony probation terms typically include jail, particularly for offenses against persons. The BJS recently reported that overall 71 percent of convicted felons were sentenced to incarceration in a state prison or local jail, and just 29 percent were sentenced to straight probation (see table 3).

V. Does Probation Work?

The most common question asked about probation is, "Does it work?" And, by "work" most mean whether the person granted probation has

TABLE 3

Felony Sentences Imposed by State and Federal Courts, by Offense, United States, 1990 (%)

	% of Felons Sentenced to:				
		Incarceration			
Most Serious Conviction Offense	Total	Total	Prison	Jail	Straight Probation
Violent offenses:					
Murder/manslaughter	100	95	91	4	5
Rape	100	86	67	19	14
Robbery	100	90	74	16	10
Aggravated assault	100	72	45	27	26
Other violent offenses	100	67	42	25	33
Property offenses:					
Burglary	100	75	54	21	25
Larceny	100	64	39	25	36
Motor vehicle theft	100	75	46	29	25
Other theft	100	62	38	24	38
Fraud/forgery	100	52	32	20	48
Fraud	100	46	25	21	54
Forgery	100	59	40	19	41
Drug offenses:					
Possession	100	64	35	29	36
Trafficking	100	77	51	26	23
All offenses	100	71	46	25	29

Source.—Langan and Perkins (1994).

Note.—For persons receiving a combination of sentences, the sentence designation came from the most severe penalty imposed—prison being the most severe, followed by jail, then probation.

refrained from further crime or reduced his or her recidivism. Recidivism is currently the primary outcome measure for probation, as it is for all corrections programs.

A. Offender Recidivism

We have no national information on the overall recidivism rates of juvenile probationers, and we know only the "completion rates" for adult misdemeanants. This omission is very important to note, since summaries of probation effectiveness usually report the recidivism rates of *felons* as if they represented the total of the probation population, and adult felons make up only 42 percent of the total probation population (Maguire and Pastore 1995). Failure to make this distinc-

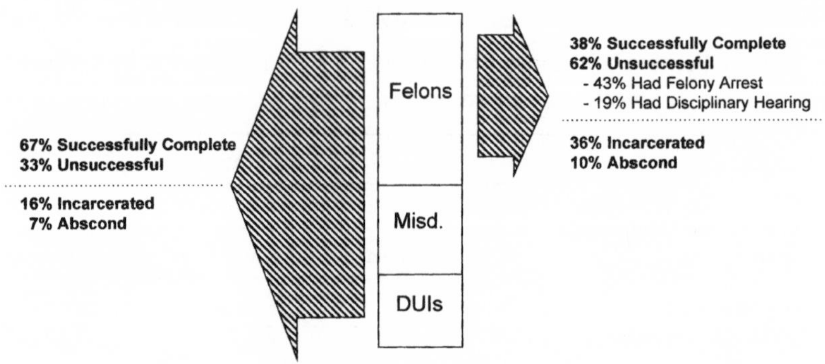

Fig. 8.—Adult probation recidivism outcomes. Sources.—Bureau of Justice Statistics (1992, 1995).

tion is why profoundly different assessments have been offered as to whether probation "works."

For example, a recent review of community corrections by Clear and Braga suggests that adult probation is very successful. They write: "Studies show that up to 80 percent of all probationers complete their terms without a new arrest" (Clear and Braga 1995, p. 430). But Langan and Cunniff, summarizing data from the same source, conclude: "Within 3 years of sentencing, while still on probation, 43 percent of these felons were rearrested for a crime within the state. Half of the arrests were for a violent crime (murder, rape, robbery, or aggravated assault) or a drug offense (drug trafficking or drug possession). The estimates (of recidivism) would have been higher had out-of-state arrests been included" (Langan and Cunniff 1992, p. 5).

How can these respected scholars summarize the evidence so differently? The difference is that Clear and Braga are summarizing probation completion rates (not rearrests) for the *entire* adult felon and misdemeanant population—and most misdemeanants complete probation, whereas Langan and Cunniff are referring to rearrests and including only adult *felons*—many of whom are rearrested. In most writings on probation effectiveness the *felon* recidivism rates are presented as representing the entirety of the probation population. Figure 8 shows adult probationer recidivism outcomes for 1992, separately for felons versus the entire population.

In reality then there are two stories about probationer recidivism rates. Recidivism rates are low for the half of the population that is placed on probation for a misdemeanor—data suggest that three-quarters successfully complete their supervision. Of course, previous data have shown that misdemeanants typically receive few services and little supervision; either they presented little risk of reoffending or they were "rehabilitated" as a result of their own efforts or being placed on probation served some deterrent function and encouraged them to refrain from further crime.

One might then question the wisdom of placing such low-risk persons on probation in the first place, given that probation departments are strapped for funds. Even if such persons do not receive direct supervision, there are transactional costs to their being on probation (e.g., staff training, administrative costs, office space for files).

More important, when these offenders do commit new crimes, probation is blamed for not providing adequate supervision and preventing their recidivism. Such bad publicity further tarnishes probation's image. Recently, the failure to carry out court-ordered supervision has served as legal grounds for successfully suing probation departments that failed adequately to supervise offenders who subsequently recidivated; this is referred to as "negligence in supervision" (for a discussion, see del Carmen and Pilant 1994).

The other story is that for *felons* placed on probation, recidivism rates are high, particularly in jurisdictions that use probation extensively, where offenders are serious to begin with, and where supervision is minimal. In 1985, RAND researchers tracked a sample of 1,672 felony probationers sentenced in Los Angeles and Alameda Counties in 1980 for a three-year period. Over that period, 65 percent of the probationers were rearrested, 51 percent were reconvicted, and 34 percent were reincarcerated (Petersilia et al. 1985).

Other agencies replicated the RAND study, and the results showed that recidivism rates for felony probationers varied greatly from place to place, depending on the seriousness of the underlying population characteristics, the length of follow-up, and the surveillance provided. Geerken and Hayes (1993) summarized seventeen follow-up studies of adult felony probationers and found that felony rearrest rates ranged from 12 to 65 percent. Such wide variation in recidivism is not unexpected, given the wide variability in granting probation and monitoring court-order conditions.

B. *Predicting Probationer Recidivism*

Several studies have examined probationers' backgrounds and criminal records in order to identify those characteristics that are associated with recidivism (e.g., Petersilia et al. 1985; Petersilia and Turner 1993;

Langan 1994). The results are consistent across studies, and Morgan (1993) recently summarized them as follows: *the kind of crime conviction and extent of prior record:* offenders with more previous convictions and property offenders (burglary as compared to robbery and drug offenders) showed higher rates of recidivism; *income at arrest:* higher unemployment/lower income are associated with higher recidivism; *household composition:* persons living with spouse, children, or both have lower recidivism; *age:* younger offenders have higher recidivism rates than older offenders; *drug use:* probationers who used heroin had higher recidivism rates.

In Petersilia and Turner (1986), although these factors were shown to be correlated with recidivism, the ability to *predict* recidivism was limited. Knowing the above information and using it to predict which probationers would recidivate and which would not resulted in accurate predictions only about 70 percent of the time. The probation programs the offender participated in, along with factors in the environment in which he was supervised (family support, employment prospects), predicted recidivism as much or more than the factors present prior to sentencing and often used in recidivism prediction models. Despite the ambition to predict offender recidivism, available data and statistical methods are insufficient to do so at this time.

C. *Comparing Probationer and Parolee Recidivism*

Proponents of probation often argue that although probationer recidivism rates may be unacceptably high, parolee recidivism rates are even higher. To buttress their arguments they usually compare the recidivism rates of all released prisoners with the recidivism rates of all probationers to show the greater benefits of probation versus prison. Generally—and not surprisingly—the probationers' recidivism rates are lower compared with prisoner recidivism rates. But this conclusion rests on flawed methodology, since there are basic differences between probationers and prisoners as groups, and these differences influence recidivism.

Petersilia and Turner (1986) conducted a study using a quasi-experimental design that incorporated matching and statistical controls to analyze the issue of comparative recidivism rates. They constructed a sample of 511 prisoners and 511 felony probationers who were comparable in terms of county of conviction, conviction crime, prior criminal record, age, and other characteristics, except that one group went to prison and the other was placed on felony probation. In the two-year follow-up period, 72 percent of the prisoners were rearrested, as compared with 63 percent of the probationers; 53 percent of the prisoners had new filed charges, compared with 38 percent of the probationers; and 47 percent of the prisoners were incarcerated in jail or prison, compared with 31 percent of the probationers. However, although the prisoners' recidivism rates were higher than the probationers', their new crimes were no more serious, nor was there a significant difference in the length of time before their first filed charges (the average was about six months for both groups).

This study suggests that prison might have made offenders more likely to recidivate than they would have without the prison experience, although only a randomly designed experiment—where identically matched offenders are randomly assigned to prison versus probation—could confidently conclude that, and as yet none has been conducted.

D. Other Probation Outcome Measures

Another way to examine probation effectiveness is to look at the contribution of those on probation to the overall crime problem. The best measure of this comes from BJS's *National Pretrial Reporting Program*, which provides data on the pretrial status of persons charged with felonies collected from a sample which is representative of the seventy-five largest counties in the nation. The most recent BJS data are from 1992 and are contained in Reaves and Smith (1995). Figure 9 shows that of all persons arrested and charged with felonies in 1992, 17 percent of them were on probation at the time of their arrest.

From other BJS data, we can determine what percentages of offenders in different statuses were on probation or parole at the time of their arrest (fig. 10). Of those in prison during 1991 (Bureau of Justice Statistics 1993) and included in the BJS nationally representative *Survey of State Prison Inmates*, 29 percent were on probation at the time of the offense which landed them in prison. The BJS further reports that 31 percent of persons on death row in 1992 reported committing their murders while under probation or parole supervision (Bureau of Justice Statistics 1994).

Practitioners have expressed concern about the use of recidivism as the primary, if not sole, measure of probation's success (Boone and Fulton 1995). They note that crime is the result of a long line of social ills—dysfunctional families, economic and educational deprivation, and so on—and that these social problems are beyond the direct in-

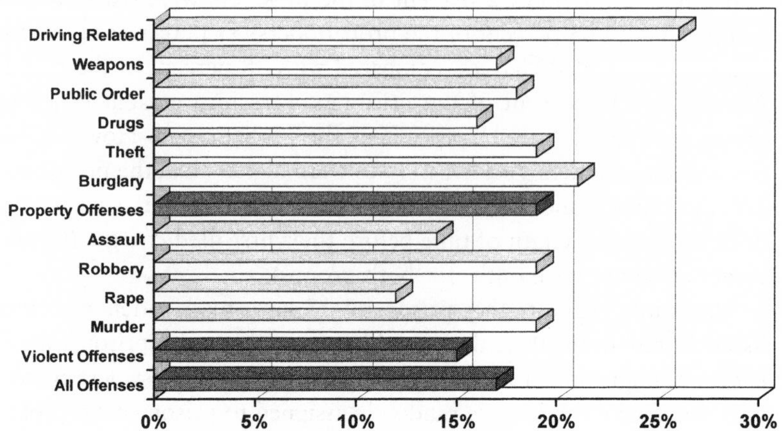

FIG. 9.—Percent of felony arrestees on probation at time of arrest, by crime type. Source.—Reaves and Smith (1995).

fluence of probation agencies. Moreover, using recidivism as the primary indicator of probation's success fails to reflect the multiple goals and objectives of probation, and it serves further to erode the public's confidence in probation services, since correctional programs, by and large, have been unable significantly to reduce recidivism.

The American Probation and Parole Association (APPA), the na-

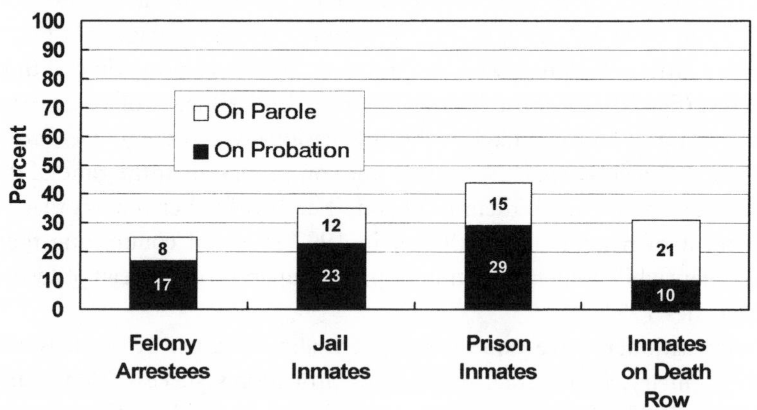

FIG. 10.—Percent of offenders on probation or parole at time of offense. Sources.—Beck (1991); Bureau of Justice Statistics (1993, 1994*a*); Reaves and Smith (1995).

tional association representing U.S. probation officers, argues that recidivism rates measure just one probation task while ignoring others such as preparing presentence investigations, collecting fines and fees, monitoring community service, and coordinating treatment services (Boone and Fulton 1995). There has been some exploration of how community corrections outcomes might appropriately be measured (Petersilia 1993).

The APPA has urged its member agencies to collect data on alternative outcomes, such as amount of restitution collected, number of offenders employed, amount of fines/fees collected, hours of community service, number of treatment sessions, percent financial obligation collected, enrollment in school, days employed, educational attainment, number of days drug-free. Some probation departments have begun to report such alternative outcomes measures to their constituencies and believe it is having a positive impact on staff morale, public image, and funding (Griffin 1996).

VI. How Can Probation Be Revived?

Probation finds itself in an awkward position in the United States. It was originally advanced by progressive reformers who sought to help offenders overcome their problems and mitigate the perceived harshness of jails and prisons. The public is now less concerned with helping offenders than with public safety and deserved punishment. But the public's tough-on-crime stance has caused jail and prison crowding nationwide, and the costs of sending a greater number of convicted offenders to prison have proven prohibitively expensive.

The public has now come to understand that not all criminals can be locked up, and so renewed attention is being focused on probation. Policy makers are asking whether probation can implement less expensive but more credible and effective community-based sentencing options. No one advocates the abolition of probation, but many call for its reform. But how should that be done?

A. Implement Quality Programming for Appropriate Probation Target Groups

Probation needs first to regain the public's trust that it can be a meaningful, credible sanction. During the past decade, many jurisdictions developed "intermediate sanctions" such as house arrest, electronic monitoring, and intensive supervision as a response to prison crowding. These programs were designed to be community-based sanctions that were tougher than regular probation but less stringent and expensive than prison (Gowdy 1993; Clear and Braga 1995; Tonry and Lynch 1996).

The program models were plausible and could have worked, except for one critical factor: they were usually implemented without creating organizational capacity to ensure compliance with the court-ordered conditions. Intermediate sanctions were designed with smaller caseloads enabling officers to provide both services and monitoring for new criminal activity, but they were not given the resources needed to enforce the sanctions or provide necessary treatment.

When courts ordered offenders to participate in drug treatment, for example, many probation officers could not ensure compliance because local treatment programs were unavailable (Petersilia and Turner 1993). Programs that were available often put offenders at the back of the waiting list. Similarly, when courts ordered fines or restitution to be paid or community service to be performed, the order often was ignored because of a lack of personnel to follow through and monitor such requirements (Petersilia and Turner 1993). Over time, what was intended as tougher community corrections in most jurisdictions did not materialize, thereby further tarnishing probation's image.

As Andrew Klein, former chief probation officer in Quincy, Massachusetts, put it: "Unenforced sanctions jeopardize any sentence, undermining its credibility and potential to address serious sentencing concerns . . . they are like sentences to prison with cell doors that do not lock and perimeter gates that slip open. The moment the word gets out that the alternative sentence or intermediate sanction is unmonitored is the moment the court loses another sentencing option" (Klein 1997, p. 311).

While most judges still report being willing to use tougher, community-based programs as alternatives to routine probation or prison, most are skeptical that the programs promised "on paper" will be delivered in practice (Sigler and Lamb 1994). As a result, some intermediate sanction programs are beginning to fall into disuse (Petersilia 1995*b*).

But not all programs have had this experience. In a few instances, communities invested in intermediate sanctions and made the necessary treatment and work programs available to offenders (Klein 1997). And, most important, the programs worked: in programs where offenders received *both* surveillance (e.g., drug tests) and participated in relevant treatment, recidivism was reduced 20–30 percent (Petersilia and Turner 1993). Recent program evaluations in Texas, Wisconsin, Oregon, and Colorado have produced similarly encouraging results (Clear and Braga 1995). Even in a national BJS probation follow-up study by Langan (1994), it was found that if probationers were participating in or making progress in treatment programs, they were less likely to have a new arrest (38 percent) than either those drug offenders who had made no progress (66 percent) or those who were not ordered to be tested or treated (48 percent).

There now exists solid empirical evidence that ordering offenders into treatment and requiring them to participate reduces recidivism (Anglin and Hser 1990; Lipton 1995; Gendreau 1996). So, the first order of business must be to allocate sufficient resources so that the designed programs (incorporating both surveillance and treatment) can be implemented. Sufficient monetary resources are essential to obtaining and sustaining judicial support and achieving program success.

High-quality probation supervision costs money, and we should be honest about that. We currently spend about $200–$700 per year, per probationer for supervision (Camp and Camp 1995). Even in the better-funded richer probation departments, the average annual amount spent on probation supervision is well below $1,000 per probationer (Abadinsky 1997). It is no wonder that recidivism rates are so high. Effective substance abuse treatment programs are estimated to cost at least $12,000–$14,000 per year (Lipton 1995). Those resources will be forthcoming only if the public believes the programs are both effective and punitive.

Public opinion is often cited by officials as the reason for supporting expanded prison policies. According to officials, the public demands a "get-tough-on-crime" policy, which is synonymous with sending more offenders to prison for longer terms (Bell and Bennett 1996). We must publicize recent evidence showing that offenders—whose opinion on such matters is critical for deterrence—judge some intermediate sanctions as *more* punishing than prison. Surveys of offenders in Minnesota, Arizona, New Jersey, Oregon, and Texas reveal that when offenders are asked to equate criminal sentences, they judge certain types of community punishments as *more* severe than prison (Crouch 1993; Petersilia and Deschenes 1994; Spelman 1995; Wood and Grasmick 1995).

One striking example comes from Marion County, Oregon. Selected nonviolent offenders were given the choice of serving a prison term or returning to the community to participate in the Intensive Supervision

Probation (ISP) program, which imposed drug testing, mandatory community service, and frequent visits with the probation officer. About a third of the offenders given the option to choose between ISP or prison chose prison. When Minnesota inmates and corrections staff were asked to equate a variety of criminal sentences, they rated three years of intensive supervision probation as equivalent in punitiveness to one year in prison (Petersilia and Deschenes 1994).

What accounts for this preference of prison over community-based penalties? Why should anyone prefer imprisonment to remaining in the community—no matter what the conditions? Some have suggested that prison has lost some of its punitive sting and, hence, its ability to scare and deter. Possessing a prison record may not be as stigmatizing as in the past, because so many of the offenders' peers (and family members) also have "done time." Further, about a quarter of all U.S. black males will be incarcerated during their lives, so the stigma attached to having a prison record is not as great as it was when it was relatively uncommon (Mauer and Huling 1995). And the pains associated with prison—social isolation, fear of victimization—seem less severe for repeat offenders who have learned how to do time.

Far from stigmatizing, prison evidently confers status in some neighborhoods. Jerome Skolnick of the University of California at Berkeley found that for drug dealers in California, imprisonment confers a certain elevated "home boy" status, especially for gang members for whom prison and prison gangs can be an alternative site of loyalty (Skolnick 1990). And according to the California Youth Authority, inmates steal state-issued prison clothing for the same reason. Wearing it when they return to the community lets everyone know they have done "hard time" (Petersilia 1992).

The time an offender can be expected to serve in prison has also decreased—latest statistics show that the average U.S. prison term for those released to parole is seventeen months (Maguire and Pastore 1995). But more to the point, for less serious offenders, the expected time served can be much less. In California, for example, more than half of all offenders entering prison in 1990 were expected to serve six months or less (Petersilia 1992). Offenders on the street may be aware of this, perhaps because of the extensive media coverage such issues receive.

For convicted felons, of course, freedom is preferable to prison. But the type of probation program being advocated here—combining heavy doses of surveillance and treatment—does not represent freedom. Such programs may have more punitive bite than prison. Consider a comparison between Contra Costa (California) County's Intensive Supervision Program (ISP) for drug offenders, which was discontinued in 1990 due to a shortage of funds, with what drug offenders would face if imprisoned:

1. *ISP.* Offenders are required to serve at least one year on ISP. In addition to twice weekly face-to-face contacts, ISP includes a random drug testing hotline, Saturday home visits, weekly narcotics anonymous meetings, special assistance from police to expedite existing bench warrants, and liaison with the State Employment Development Department. To remain on ISP, offenders must be employed or in treatment, perform community service, pay victim restitution, and remain crime- and drug-free.

2. *Prison.* A sentence of twelve months will require that the offender serve about half of that. During his term, he is not required to work nor will he be required to participate in any training or treatment, but may do so if he wishes. Once released, he will probably be placed on routine parole supervision, where he might see his officer once a month.

It is important to publicize these results, particularly to policy makers, who say they are imprisoning such a large number of offenders because of the public's desire to get tough on crime. But it is no longer necessary to equate criminal punishment solely with prison. The balance of sanctions between probation and prison can be shifted, and at some level of intensity and length, intermediate punishments can be the more dreaded penalty.

Once the political support and organizational capacity are in place, offender groups need to be targeted that make the most sense, given our current state of knowledge regarding program effectiveness (for a recent review, see Harland 1996). Targeting drug offenders makes the most sense for a number of reasons. Drug offenders were not always punished so frequently by imprisonment. In California, for example, just 5 percent of convicted drug offenders were sentenced to prison in 1980, but by 1990 the number had increased to 20 percent (Petersilia 1992). Large-scale imprisonment of drug offenders has only recently taken place, and there is some new evidence suggesting that the public seems ready to accept different punishment strategies for low-level drug offenders.

A 1994 nationwide poll by Hart Research Associates reported that Americans understand that drug abuse is not simply a failure of will-power or a violation of criminal law. They now see the problem as far more complex, involving not only individual behavior but also fundamental issues of poverty, opportunity, and personal circumstances. The Drug Strategies report (Falco 1995) reports that nearly half of all Americans have been touched directly by the drug problem: 45 percent of those surveyed in the 1994 Hart poll said that they knew someone who became addicted to a drug other than alcohol. This personal knowledge is changing attitudes about how to deal with the problem: seven in ten believe that their addicted acquaintance would have been helped more by entering a supervised treatment program than by being sentenced to prison.

It appears that the public wants tougher sentences for drug traffickers and more treatment for addicts—what legislators have instead given them are long sentences for everyone. The Drug Strategies group, which analyzed the Hart survey, concluded that "public opinion on drugs is more pragmatic and less ideological than the current political debate reflects. Voters know that punitive approaches won't work" (Falco 1995).

Another recent national telephone survey confirms these findings (Flanagan and Longmire 1996), concluding that respondents favored treatment rather than punishment as the best alternative to reduce the use of illegal drugs and that Americans want to see a change in drug control strategy (Cintron and Johnson 1996). Public receptiveness to treatment for addicts is important, because those familiar with delivering treatment say that is where treatment can make the biggest impact.

A recent report by the prestigious Institute of Medicine (IOM) of the National Academy of Sciences recommends focusing on probationers and parolees to curb drug use and related crime (Institute of Medicine 1990). They noted that about one-fifth of the estimated population needing treatment—and two-fifths of those clearly needing it—are under the supervision of the justice system as parolees or probationers. And since the largest single group of serious drug users in any locality comes through the justice system every day, the IOM concludes that the justice system is one of the most important gateways to treatment delivery and that we should be using it more effectively.

Moreover, research has shown that those under corrections supervision stay in treatment longer, thereby increasing positive treatment outcomes. The claim that individuals forced into treatment by the courts will not be successful has not been borne out by research; just the opposite is true. Research at UCLA and elsewhere has provided strong evidence not only that drug abuse treatment is effective but also that individuals coerced into treatment derive as many benefits as those who enter voluntarily (Anglin and Hser 1990). The largest study of drug treatment outcomes found that justice system clients stayed in treatment longer than clients with no justice system involvement and, as a result, had higher than average success rates (Institute of Medicine 1990). The evidence suggests that drug treatment is effective for both men and women, whites and minority ethnic groups, young and old, and criminal and noncriminal participants.

However, as noted above, good-quality treatment does not come cheap. But in terms of crime and health costs averted, it is an investment that pays for itself immediately. Researchers in California recently conducted an assessment of drug treatment programs and identified those that were successful, concluding that it can now be "documented that treatment and recovery programs are a good investment" (Gerstein et al. 1994). The researchers studied a sample of 1,900 treatment participants, followed them up for as much as two years of treatment, and studied participants from all four major treatment modalities (therapeutic communities, social models, outpatient drug free, and methadone maintenance).

Gerstein et al. (1994, p. 33) conclude: "Treatment was very cost beneficial: for every dollar spent on drug and alcohol treatment, the state of California saved $7 in reductions in crime and health care costs. The study found that each day of treatment *paid for itself on the day treatment was received*, primarily through an avoidance of crime. The level of criminal activity declined by two-thirds from before treatment to after treatment. The greater the length of time spent in treatment, the greater the reduction in crime. Reported criminal activity declined before and after treatment as follows: mean number of times sold or helped sell drugs (−75 percent), mean number of times used weapon/physical force (−93 percent), percent committing any illegal activity (−72 percent), and mean months involved in criminal activity (−80 percent)."

Regardless of type of treatment modality, reduction in crime was substantial and significant (although participants in the social model recovery programs had the biggest reduction). In the California study, the most effective treatment programs cost about $12,000 per year, per client (Gerstein et al. 1994). UCLA researchers recently concluded: "It seems that drug abuse treatment mandated by the criminal justice system represents one of the best and most cost-effective approaches to breaking the pernicious cycle of drug use, criminality, incarceration, and recidivism" (Prendergast, Anglin, and Wellisch 1995).

In sum, there are several steps to achieving greater crime control over probationers and parolees. First, adequate financial resources must be provided to deliver programs that have been shown to work. Successful programs combine *both* treatment and surveillance and are targeted toward appropriate offender subgroups. Current evidence suggests that low-level drug offenders are prime candidates for the intermediate sanction programs considered here. Then support must be garnered, convincing the public that the probation sanction is punitive and convincing the judiciary that offenders will be held accountable for their behavior.

Of course, there is much more to reforming the probation system than simply targeting low-level drug offenders for effective treatment, but this would be a start. We also need to seriously reconsider probation's underlying mission, administrative structure, and funding base. And, we need to fund a program of basic research to address some of probation's most pressing problems.

B. Make Probation a Priority Research Topic

Basic research on probation has diminished in recent years, except for evaluations on intermediate sanctions funded by NIJ. While these early evaluations are instructive, their results are by no means definitive. The programs have mostly been surveillance-oriented and have focused primarily on increasing drug testing and face-to-face contacts with offenders. They have incorporated little treatment or employment training. Most intermediate sanction programs targeted serious, career criminals with lengthy histories of crime and substance abuse. As noted in this essay, there is some supportive evidence that intermediate sanctions incorporating treatment in addition to surveillance activities do produce lower recidivism. It is also possible that had these programs been targeted toward less serious offenders or earlier in their criminal careers the results might have been more encouraging. There is reason to continue experimenting with community-based sanctions, varying target populations, program elements, setting, and point in the criminal career for intervention.

This essay has also highlighted the importance of technical violations in community supervision. Probation and parole officers spend most of their time monitoring the technical conditions imposed by the courts (such as no alcohol or drug use). When violations are discovered, additional time is spent in processing the paperwork necessary to revoke offenders. Many of those offenders are revoked to prison, most of them for violations of the "no drug use" condition, as detected through urine testing. Such revocations will undoubtedly increase as urinalysis testing for drugs becomes less expensive and more widespread.

This begs an important question: what purpose is served by monitoring and revoking persons for technical violations, and is the benefit worth the cost? If technical violations identify offenders who are "going bad" and likely to commit crime, then we may well wish to spend the time uncovering such conditions and incarcerating those persons. However, if technical violators are simply troubled, but not criminally dangerous, then devoting scarce prison resources to this population may not be warranted. Despite the policy significance of technical violations, little serious research has focused on this issue. As the cost of monitoring and incarcerating technical violators increases, research must examine its crime control significance.

There is also the ongoing debate about who is in prison and whether there exists a group of prisoners who, based on crime and prior criminal records, could safety be supervised in the community. Proponents of alternatives argue that over the past decade the use of imprisonment expanded vastly and, as a result, that many low-level offenders are now in prison. They contend that many (if not most) prisoners are minor property offenders, low-level drug dealers, or technical violators—ideal candidates for community-based alternatives. Those who are against expanding prison alternatives disagree, citing data showing that most prisoners are violent recidivists with few prospects for reform.

It is likely that the truth lies somewhere in between and that the differences in the numbers cited depend on how one aggregates the data and what data set one chooses to analyze. It is likely that historical sentencing patterns have resulted in vastly different populations being incarcerated in different states. Research examining the characteristics of inmates in different states (by age, criminal record, and substance abuse history) is necessary to clarify this important debate. It is also critical that we conduct better follow-up studies (ideally, using experimental designs) of offenders who have been sentenced to prison as opposed to various forms of community supervision. By tracking similarly situated offenders, sentenced differently, we will be able to refine our recidivism prediction models and begin to estimate more accurately the crime and cost implications of different sentencing models.

We also need to move away from the fragmentary studies of individual agencies and toward more comprehensive assessment of how probation departments and other justice agencies influence one another and together influence crime. Decisions made in one justice agency have dramatic workload and cost implications for other justice agencies and for later decisions (such as probation policy on violating technicals). To date, these systemic effects have not been well studied, and much benefit is likely to come from examining how various policy initiatives affect criminal justice agencies, individually and collectively. Generating more arrests will not necessarily result in more convictions and incarcerations if prosecutors and corrections (either by policy or budget constraints) do not follow through with convictions and incarcerations. Many past probation reforms—implemented by well-meaning probation staff—have been undermined by the failure of other justice system agencies to cooperate in the program.

The issues presented above are only a few of the salient themes that should be pursued to improve understanding of the nation's probation system. Probation has much untapped potential and, with research and program attention, can become an integral part of our nation's fight against crime.

REFERENCES

Abadinsky, Howard. 1997. *Probation and Parole: Theory and Practice.* Englewood Cliffs, N.J.: Prentice-Hall.

Allen, Harry, Eric W. Carlson, and Evalyn C. Parks. 1979. *Critical Issues in Adult Probation.* Washington, D.C.: U.S. Department of Justice, National Institute of Law Enforcement and Criminal Justice.

American Bar Association. 1970. *Standards Relating to Probation.* Chicago: American Bar Association.

American Correctional Association. 1995. *Probation and Parole Directory, 1995–1997.* Lanham, Md.: American Correctional Association.

American Justice Institute. 1981. *Presentence Investigation Report Program.* Sacramento, Calif.: American Justice Institute.

Anglin, Douglas, and Yih-Ing Hser. 1990. "Treatment of Drug Abuse." In *Drugs and Crime*, edited by Michael Tonry and James Q. Wilson. Vol. 13

of *Crime and Justice: A Review of Research*, edited by Michael Tonry and Norval Morris. Chicago: University of Chicago Press.

Augustus, John. 1939. "A Report of the Labors of John Augustus, for the Last Ten Years, in Aid of the Unfortunate." Boston: Wright & Hasty. Reprinted as John Augustus, *First Probation Officer*. New York: New York Probation Association.

Baird, Christopher, Dennis Wagner, and Robert DeComo. 1995. *Evaluation of the Impact of Oregon's Structured Sanctions Program*. San Francisco: National Council on Crime and Delinquency.

Beck, Allen J. 1991. *Profile of Jail Inmates, 1989*. Washington, D.C.: U.S. Department of Justice, Bureau of Justice Statistics.

Bell, Griffin B., and William J. Bennett. 1996. *The State of Violent Crime in America*. Washington, D.C.: Council on Crime in America.

Boone, Harry N., and Betsy A. Fulton. 1995. *Results-Driven Management: Implementing Performance-Based Measures in Community Corrections*. Lexington, Ky.: American Probation and Parole Association.

Brown, Jodi M., Darrell K. Gilliard, Tracy L. Snell, James J. Stephan, and Doris James Wilson. 1996. *Correctional Populations in the United States, 1994*. Washington, D.C.: U.S. Department of Justice, Bureau of Justice Statistics.

Bureau of Justice Statistics. 1992. *Census of Probation and Parole, 1991*. Washington, D.C.: U.S. Department of Justice.

———. 1993. *Survey of State Prison Inmates, 1991*. Washington, D.C.: U.S. Government Printing Office.

———. 1994. *Capital Punishment, 1992*. Washington, D.C.: U.S. Government Printing Office.

———. 1995. *Correctional Populations in the United States, 1992*. Washington, D.C.: U.S. Government Printing Office.

———. 1996*a*. *Correctional Populations in the United States, 1995*. Washington, D.C.: U.S. Department of Justice Press Release, June 30.

———. 1996*b*. *Prison and Jail Inmates, 1995*. Washington, D.C.: U.S. Government Printing Office.

Butts, Jeffrey, Howard Snyder, Terrence Finnegan, and Anne Aughenbaugh. 1995. *Juvenile Court Statistics 1992*. Washington, D.C.: Office of Juvenile Justice and Delinquency Prevention.

California Department of Justice. 1995. *Crime and Delinquency in California, 1994*. Sacramento: California Department of Justice, Bureau of Criminal Statistics and Special Services.

Camp, George M., and Camille Camp. 1995. *The Corrections Yearbook 1995: Probation and Parole*. South Salem, N.Y.: Criminal Justice Institute.

Cintron, Myrna, and W. Wesley Johnson. 1996. "The Modern Plague: Controlling Substance Abuse." In *Americans View Crime and Justice: A National Public Opinion Survey*, edited by Timothy J. Flanagan and Dennis R. Longmire. Thousand Oaks, Calif.: Sage.

Clear, Todd. 1988. *Statistical Prediction in Corrections*. Research in Corrections Monograph. Washington, D.C.: National Institute of Corrections.

———. 1994. *Harm in American Penology*. Albany, N.Y.: State University of New York Press.

Clear, Todd, and Anthony A. Braga. 1995. "Community Corrections." In *Crime*, edited by James Q. Wilson and Joan Petersilia. San Francisco: Institute for Contemporary Studies.

Clear, Todd R., and George C. Cole. 1997. *American Corrections*, 4th ed. Belmont, Calif.: Wadsworth.

Comptroller General of the United States. 1976. *State and County Probation: Systems in Crisis, Report to the Congress of the United States.* Washington, D.C.: U.S. Government Printing Office.

Corbett, Ronald P. 1996. "When Community Corrections Means Business: Introducing 'Reinventing' Themes to Probation and Parole." *Federal Probation* 60(1):36–42.

Crouch, Ben. 1993. "Is Incarceration Really Worse? Analysis of Offenders' Preferences for Prisons over Probation." *Justice Quarterly* 10:67–88.

Cunniff, Mark, and Ilene R. Bergsmann. 1990. *Managing Felons in the Community: An Administrative Profile of Probation.* Washington, D.C.: National Association of Criminal Justice Planners.

Cunniff, Mark, and Mary Shilton. 1991. *Variations on Felony Probation: Persons under Supervision in 32 Urban and Suburban Counties.* Washington, D.C.: U.S. Department of Justice.

Dawson, John. 1990. *Felony Probation in State Courts.* Washington, D.C.: U.S. Department of Justice, Bureau of Justice Statistics.

del Carmen, Rolando V., and James Alan Pilant. 1994. "The Scope of Judicial Immunity for Probation and Parole Officers." *Perspectives* 18(4):14–21.

Deschenes, Elizabeth, Susan Turner, and Peter Greenwood. 1995. "Drug Court or Probation: An Experimental Evaluation of Maricopa County's Drug Court." *Justice System Journal* 18(1):55–73.

Dressler, David. 1962. *Practice and Theory of Probation and Parole.* New York: Columbia University Press.

Falco, Malthea. 1995. *Keeping Score: What We Are Getting for Our Federal Drug Control Dollars.* Washington, D.C.: Drug Strategies.

Flanagan, Timothy J., and Dennis R. Longmire. 1996. *Americans View Crime and Justice: A National Public Opinion Survey.* Thousand Oaks, Calif.: Sage.

Finn, Peter, and Dale Parent. 1992. *Making the Offender Foot the Bill: A Texas Program.* Washington, D.C.: U.S. Department of Justice, National Institute of Justice.

Fitzharris, Timothy L. 1979. *Probation in an Era of Diminishing Resources.* Foundation for Continuing Education in Corrections. Sacramento: California Probation, Parole, and Correctional Association.

Frank, J., F. Cullen, and J. Cullen. 1987. "Sources of Judicial Attitudes toward Criminal Sanctioning." *American Journal of Justice* 11:17–36.

Geerken, Michael, and Hennessey D. Hayes. 1993. "Probation and Parole: Public Risk and the Future of Incarceration Alternatives." *Criminology* 31(4): 549–64.

Gendreau, Paul. 1996. "The Principles of Effective Intervention with Offenders." In *Choosing Correctional Options That Work: Defining the Demand, Then Evaluating the Supply*, edited by Alan Harland. Thousand Oaks, Calif.: Sage.

Gerstein, Dean, R. A. Johnson, H. J. Harwood, D. Fountain, N. Suter, and

K. Malloy. 1994. *Evaluating Recovery Services: The California Drug and Alcohol Treatment Assessment.* Sacramento: State of California, Department of Alcohol and Drug Programs.

Goldkamp, John. 1994. "Miami's Treatment Drug Court for Felony Misdemeanants." *Prison Journal* 73:110–66.

Gowdy, Voncile. 1993. *Intermediate Sanctions.* Washington, D.C.: U.S. Department of Justice, National Institute of Justice.

Greenwood, Peter, C. Peter Rydell, Allan F. Abrahamse, Jonathan P. Caulkins, James Chiesa, Karyn E. Model, and Steve Klein. 1994. *Three Strikes and You're Out: Estimated Benefits and Costs of California's New Mandatory-Sentencing Law.* Santa Monica, Calif.: RAND.

Griffin, Margaret. 1996. "Hunt County, Texas Puts Performance-Based Measures to Work." *Perspectives:* 9–11.

Grubbs, John. 1993. "Handling Probation and Parole Violators in Mississippi." In *Reclaiming Offender Accountability: Intermediate Sanctions for Probation and Parole Violators,* edited by Edward Rhine. Laurel, Md.: American Correctional Association.

Hamai, K., R. Ville, R. Harris, M. Hough, and Ugljesa Zvekic, eds. 1995. *Probation Round the World.* London: Routledge.

Harland, Alan. 1996. "Correctional Options That Work: Structuring the Inquiry." In *Choosing Correctional Options That Work: Defining the Demand and Evaluating the Supply,* edited by Alan Harland. Thousand Oaks, Calif.: Sage.

Howell, James C., Barry Krisberg, and Michael Jones, eds. 1993. "Trends in Juvenile Crime and Youth Violence." In *Serious, Violent and Chronic Juvenile Offenders: A Sourcebook.* Thousand Oaks, Calif.: Sage.

Hurst, H., and Patricia Torbet. 1993. *Organization and Administration of Juvenile Services: Probation, Aftercare, and State Institutions for Delinquency Youth.* Washington, D.C.: U.S. Department of Justice, Office of Juvenile Justice and Delinquency Prevention.

Institute of Medicine, Committee for the Substance Abuse Coverage Study. 1990. "A Study of the Evolution, Effectiveness, and Financing of Public and Private Drug Treatment Systems." In *Treating Drug Problems,* vol. 1, edited by D. R. Gerstein and H. J. Harwood. Washington, D.C.: National Academy Press.

Jones, Peter R. 1996. "Risk Prediction in Criminal Justice." In *Choosing Correctional Options That Work: Defining the Demand and Evaluating the Supply,* edited by Alan Harland. Thousand Oaks, Calif.: Sage.

Klein, Andrew R. 1997. *Alternative Sentencing, Intermediate Sanctions, and Probation.* Cincinnati: Anderson.

Klein, Stephen, Patricia Ebener, Allan Abrahamse, and Nora Fitzgerald. 1991. *Predicting Criminal Justice Outcomes: What Matters?* Santa Monica, Calif.: RAND, R-3972.

Langan, Patrick. 1994. "Between Prison and Probation: Intermediate Sanctions." *Science* 264:791–93.

———. 1996. Personal communication. Washington D.C.: U.S. Department of Justice, Bureau of Justice Statistics.

Langan, Patrick A., and Robyn L. Cohen. 1996. *State Court Sentencing of Con-*

victed Felons, 1992. Washington D.C.: U.S. Department of Justice, Bureau of Justice Statistics.

Langan, Patrick A., and Mark A. Cunniff. 1992. *Recidivism of Felons on Probation, 1986–89.* Washington, D.C.: U.S. Department of Justice, Bureau of Justice Statistics.

Langan, Patrick A., and Craig A. Perkins. 1994. *Felony Sentences in the United States, 1990.* Washington, D.C.: U.S. Department of Justice, Bureau of Justice Statistics.

Latessa, Edward J., and Harry E. Allen. 1997. *Corrections in the Community.* Cincinnati: Anderson.

Lipton, Douglas S. 1995. *The Effectiveness of Treatment for Drug Abusers under Criminal Justice Supervision.* Washington, D.C.: U.S. Department of Justice, National Institute of Justice.

Los Angeles County Planning Committee. 1996. *Managing Offenders in Los Angeles County.* Los Angeles: Los Angeles County Planning Committee.

Maguire, Kathleen, and Ann L. Pastore, eds. 1995. *Sourcebook of Criminal Justice Statistics, 1994.* Washington D.C.: U.S. Department of Justice, Bureau of Justice Statistics.

Martinson, Robert. 1974. "What Works? Questions and Answers about Prison Reform." *Public Interest* 35:22–54.

Mauer, Marc, and Tracy Huling. 1995. *Young Black Americans and the Criminal Justice System: Five Years Later.* Washington, D.C.: The Sentencing Project.

McAnany, Patrick, Doug Thomson, and David Fogel. 1984. *Probation and Justice: Reconsideration of Mission.* Cambridge, Mass.: Oelgeschlager, Gunn & Hain.

McDonald, D. C., and K. E. Carlson. 1993. *Sentencing in the Federal Courts: Does Race Matter?* Washington, D.C.: U.S. Department of Justice, Bureau of Justice Statistics.

McShane, Marilyn, and Wesley Krause. 1993. *Community Corrections.* New York: Macmillan.

Minnesota Sentencing Guidelines Commission. 1996. *Sentencing Practices: Highlights and Statistics Tables.* St. Paul: Minnesota Sentencing Guidelines Commission.

Morgan, Kathryn. 1993. "Factors Influencing Probation Outcome: A Review of the Literature." *Federal Probation* 57(2):23–29.

Morgan, Terry, and Stephen Marris. 1994. "Washington's Partnership between the Police and Community Corrections: A Program Worth Emulating." *Perspectives:* 28–30.

Mulholland, David. 1994. "Judges Finding Creative Ways of Punishing." *Wall Street Journal* (May 24), B1.

National Advisory Commission on Criminal Justice Standards and Goals. 1973. *Corrections.* Washington, D.C.: U.S. Government Printing Office.

National Institute of Corrections. 1993. *State and Local Probation Systems in the United States: A Survey of Current Practice.* Washington, D.C.: National Institute of Corrections.

Nelson, E. Kim, Howard Ohmart, and Nora Harlow. 1978. *Promising Strategies in Probation and Parole.* Washington, D.C.: U.S. Government Printing Office.

Nidorf, Barry. 1996. "Surviving in a 'Lock Them Up' Era." *Federal Probation* 60(1):4–10.

Parent, Dale, Dan Wentwork, Peggy Burke, and Becky Ney. 1994. *Responding to Probation and Parole Violations.* Washington, D.C.: U.S. Department of Justice, National Institute of Justice.

Parent, Dale G. 1995. "Community Corrections Acts: A Recap." *Overcrowded Times* 6(5):1, 9–11.

Petersilia, Joan. 1992. "California's Prison Policy: Causes, Costs, and Consequences." *Prison Journal* 72(1):8–36.

———. 1993. "Measuring the Performance of Community Corrections." In *Performance Measures for the Criminal Justice System.* Washington, D.C.: U.S. Department of Justice, Bureau of Justice Statistics.

———. 1995*a*. "How California Could Divert Nonviolent Prisoners to Intermediate Sanctions." *Overcrowded Times* 6(3):4–8.

———. 1995*b*. "A Crime Control Rationale for Reinvesting in Community Corrections." *Prison Journal* 75(4):479–96.

Petersilia, Joan, and Elizabeth Piper Deschenes. 1994. "Perceptions of Punishment: Inmates and Staff Rank the Severity of Prison versus Intermediate Sanctions." *Prison Journal* 74:306–28.

Petersilia, Joan, and Susan Turner. 1986. *Prison versus Probation in California: Implications for Crime and Offender Recidivism.* Santa Monica, Calif.: RAND.

———. 1993. "Intensive Probation and Parole." In *Crime and Justice: A Review of Research,* vol. 17, edited by Michael Tonry. Chicago: University of Chicago Press.

Petersilia, Joan, Susan Turner, James Kahan, and Joyce Peterson. 1985. *Granting Felons Probation: Public Risks and Alternatives.* Santa Monica, Calif.: RAND, R-3186-NIJ.

Prendergast, Michael, Douglas Anglin, and Jean Wellisch. 1995. "Treatment for Drug-Abusing Offenders under Community Supervision." *Federal Probation* 59(4):66–75.

President's Commission on Law Enforcement and Administration of Justice. 1967. *The Challenge of Crime in a Free Society.* Washington, D.C.: U.S. Government Printing Office.

Prevost, John P., Edward Rhine, and Ronald Jackson. 1993. "The Parole Violations Process in Georgia." In *Reclaiming Offender Accountability: Intermediate Sanctions for Probation and Parole Violators,* edited by Edward Rhine. Laurel, Md.: American Correctional Association.

Reaves, Brian A., and Pheny Z. Smith. 1995. *Felony Defendants in Large Urban Counties, 1992.* Washington, D.C.: U.S. Department of Justice, Bureau of Justice Statistics.

Rhine, Edward, ed. 1993. *Reclaiming Offender Accountability: Intermediate Sanctions for Probation and Parole Violators.* Laurel, Md.: American Correctional Association.

Rothman, David J. 1980. *Conscience and Convenience: The Asylum and Its Alternatives in Progressive America.* Boston: Little, Brown.

Shilton, Mary K. 1995. "Community Corrections Acts May Be Rx Systems Need." *Corrections Today* 57(1):32–36, 66.

Sigler, Robert, and David Lamb. 1994. "Community Based Alternatives to Prison: How the Public and Court Personnel View Them." *Federal Probation* 59(2):3–9.

Skolnick, Jerome. 1990. "Gangs and Crime Old as Time: But Drugs Change Gang Culture." *Crime and Delinquency in California, 1989.* Sacramento, Calif.: California Department of Justice, Bureau of Criminal Statistics.

Spelman, William. 1995. "The Severity of Intermediate Sanctions." *Journal of Research in Crime and Delinquency* 32:107–35.

Taxman, Faye S., and James Byrne. 1994. "Locating Absconders: Results from a Randomized Field Experiment." *Federal Probation* 58(1):13–23.

Thomas, Douglas. 1993. *The State of Juvenile Probation, 1992: Results of a Nationwide Survey.* Washington, D.C.: U.S. Department of Justice, Office of Juvenile Justice and Delinquency Prevention.

Tonry, Michael, and Mary Lynch. 1996. "Intermediate Sanctions." In *Crime and Justice: A Review of Research*, vol. 20, edited by Michael Tonry. Chicago: University of Chicago Press.

Wilkinson, Reginald. 1995. *Community Corrections: A Vital Link.* Columbus: Ohio Department of Corrections.

Wilson, James Q. 1995. "Crime and Public Policy." In *Crime*, edited by James Q. Wilson and Joan Petersilia. San Francisco: Institute for Contemporary Studies.

Wood, Peter B., and Harold G. Grasmick. 1995. "Inmates Rank the Severity of Ten Alternative Sanctions Compared to Prison." *Journal of the Oklahoma Criminal Justice Research Consortium* 2:30–42.

Zvekic, Ugljesa. 1996. "Probation in International Perspective." *Overcrowded Times* 7(2):5–8.

Kathleen Daly and Michael Tonry

Gender, Race, and Sentencing

ABSTRACT

Race and gender pose empirical and policy problems that are both similar and different for the U.S. criminal justice system. They are similar in that blacks and women occupy subordinate social and economic positions in American life, and their interests are less likely to be represented in the justice system than are those of white men. They are different in that blacks are overrepresented in arrest statistics and jail and prison populations while women are underrepresented. If over- (or under-) representation is assumed to result from similar effects of bias and subordination, the two patterns are hard to explain. The empirical literature on criminal courts reveals policy dilemmas in achieving "just" sentencing practices. Blacks (and especially black men) may be more likely than white men or women to benefit from tightly limited discretion and limited individualization of sentencing whereas women (both black and white) may be more likely to benefit from broader discretion and greater individualization. Future policies will need to confront the competing demands of justice that race and gender pose in the official response to crime.

On June 30, 1995, federal and state prisons in the United States held 1,104,074 sentenced prisoners. Black men and women, who are 12 percent of the general population, were 51 percent of prisoners. Women of all racial and ethnic groups, who are 51 percent of the general population, were 6 percent (Bureau of Justice Statistics 1995*b*).

Racial and ethnic disproportionalities in those charged, convicted,

Kathleen Daly is associate professor, School of Justice Administration, Faculty of Humanities, Griffith University, Queensland, Australia. Michael Tonry is Sonosky Professor of Law and Public Policy, University of Minnesota Law School.

0192-3234/97/0022-0006$02.00

and sentenced for crime in the United States have received renewed attention in recent years. Reports by The Sentencing Project, which showed that in 1990 and 1995, respectively, 23 and 32 percent of black men aged twenty to twenty-nine were in jail or prison or on probation or parole, received front-page attention in newspapers and electronic media. So did estimates from the National Center on Institutions and Alternatives, which showed that in 1991 in Baltimore and Washington, D.C., respectively, 56 and 42 percent of black men aged eighteen to thirty-five were under some form of criminal justice system control (Tonry and Hamilton 1997).

Gender disproportionalities, while receiving relatively less media or political attention, are as great as or greater than those for race. For example, in 1995 the male incarceration rate for state and federal prisons, 789 per 100,000, was sixteen times the female rate of 47 per 100,000. In 1993, the black incarceration rate, 1,471 per 100,000, was seven times the white rate of 207 per 100,000 (Bureau of Justice Statistics 1995*a*, 1995*b*).

At every stage of the justice system for which national data are available, the 51 percent of Americans who are female make up 6–14 percent of those prosecuted or confined in adult institutions. By contrast, the 12 percent of Americans who are black make up 40–54 percent of court and confinement populations. For example, the female share of convictions in state felony courts in 1990 was 14 percent; the black share, 47 percent (Bureau of Justice Statistics 1993*a*, p. 16).[1] The female share of jail inmates in 1994 was 10 percent; the black share, 44 percent (Bureau of Justice Statistics 1995*c*). The female share of new court commitments to prisons in 1991 was 9 percent; the black share, 54 percent (Maguire and Pastore 1994, p. 625). Just over 1 percent of those on death row in 1993 were female; 41 percent were black (Bureau of Justice Statistics 1994*d*, table 6).[2]

These data suggest distinctive influences of gender and race on patterns of lawbreaking and on the state's response to crime, yet racism and sexism are often decried in the same sentence as variants of the same problem: white men's social, economic, and political dominance over less powerful women and minority group men. This has led some to adopt the simple working hypothesis of racial and gender discrimi-

[1] The black/white composition of felony court defendants varies by the source of data used (discussed below).

[2] An additional 8 percent were Hispanic.

nation: institutions of criminal justice operate in ways that favor the interests of whites over blacks (or other minority groups) and of men over women.

The cross-sectional data portray a more complicated pattern. Race operates as the hypothesis predicts: blacks are overrepresented in arrest, court, and prison populations. But women, members of the socially subordinate gender group, are underrepresented in arrest, court, and prison populations. Although the hypothesis holds *within* gender groups—that is, among both male and female prisoners, 65 percent are members of racial or ethnic minority groups (Bureau of Justice Statistics 1995*a*, p. 9)—it cannot explain the disproportionate presence of men under formal criminal justice control.

The demography of crime and punishment poses challenges to feminist and nonfeminist explanations of crime and punishment. Feminist theorists have yet to explain why, if men have more power than women, men are at greater risk to be under criminal justice control. Nonfeminist theorists have yet to explain why, if disadvantaged members of society are most likely to be under criminal justice control, far fewer disadvantaged women than disadvantaged men are affected.[3]

This essay reviews race and gender patterns in adult arrest and imprisonment statistics, but our focus is on the criminal courts and the transformation of sentencing policy in the 1970s. We are interested in understanding why sentencing reform unfolded as it did and with what consequences for contemporary justice system practices, including dramatic increases in imprisonment for members of all race and gender groups. We are also interested in the varied ways that race and gender work in the criminal process and in criminological discourse.

Sentencing and its reform can be seen as one component of a criminal justice system that operates as a "social ordering practice" (Garland 1990; Lacey 1994, pp. 28–35). Sentencing, and punishment more generally, contain symbolic and instrumental elements. The justice system produces a good deal of injustice, but some of its elements are positive, indeed indispensable. Moreover, the rhetoric of sentencing reform must be set alongside the practices: the two do not necessarily coincide. For example, the rhetorical focus of sentencing reform in the 1970s was on "just deserts," but utilitarian considerations could not be

[3] This claim is contextual (i.e., within a neighborhood or city) and historically and culturally specific. It would be wrong to assume that women are (or will be) more law-abiding than men (or less likely to be criminalized) across time, place, nation, and culture.

avoided or eliminated. The story of sentencing reform was (and is) partly about "doing justice" better and partly about relegitimating the state's power to punish in a society rife with "background conditions of inequality and injustice" (Lacey 1994, p. 33).

Beginning in the early 1970s and with the stated aim of reducing race and class disparities in the justice system, sentencing reformers advocated strong equality policies, often expressed in terms of "just deserts" or proportionality theories that emphasized the current offense and the defendant's criminal history as the primary criteria for sentencing. The central rationale was that the broad discretionary power permitted in indeterminate sentencing systems was exercised in ways unfavorable to poor and minority defendants; in particular, by allowing officials to take into account a defendant's biographical information (e.g., education, employment prospects, and familial circumstances), it was believed that white and middle-class defendants were advantaged over others.

Throughout the debates on sentencing reform, the presumptive sentencing subject was male: women and gender differences were not featured. What might explain this silence? First, like their academic counterparts, criminal justice policy makers would argue that "there were too few women" to warrant inquiry on the gendered dynamics of crime and crime control. This seems curious in that men are no less gendered than women. However, because women are the marked gender category, when the question of "gender" enters criminological discourse, attention centers on "women's issues" or "the female offender." As the unmarked gender category, men are "the norm," the universal nongendered offender. Second, in feminist criminological and legal inquiry, and in feminist activism during the 1970s and 1980s, attention was paid primarily to violence against women. By contrast, research on women's lawbreaking and its response were (and remain) less developed. Third, even for those with research and policy interests in gender, courts, and prisons, it was difficult to know *how* to engage in policy debates; it was not clear what to recommend.[4]

The early sentencing reform movement in the United States emerged from a race-centered civil rights movement and from the prisoners' rights movement that began in the 1960s (e.g., American

[4] Examples of dilemmas and ambivalences surrounding feminist engagement with criminal justice are given by Chesney-Lind (1991), on whether to push for building a women's prison or not, and by Daly (1992) and Howe (1990) on how to represent women lawbreakers and prisoners.

Friends Service Committee 1971; Messinger and Johnson 1978). During 1965 to 1975, 96–97 percent of prisoners were men, and approximately 40 percent were black. Sentencing became the object of reformers' attention not only because of widespread interest in sentencing processes per se but because of concern for racial injustices in sentencing. Thus, sentencing reform, which developed from the civil rights movement and was motivated by concerns for fairness to prisoners, was primarily focused on eliminating racial bias and primarily committed to values of equal treatment. Without giving it much attention, sentencing reformers assumed that the logics of racial and gender injustice were similar, requiring similar methods of redress.

In every jurisdiction that changed its sentencing policies and attempted to establish sentencing guidelines, three propositions were taken as self-evident. First, race and gender were believed to be illegitimate considerations in sentencing. Second, other factors like education and employment were considered to be forbidden or discouraged because they would work systematically and directly to the detriment of poor defendants and, because proportionately more blacks than whites were poor, indirectly to the detriment of black defendants. Third, because most judges then (as now) were white men, it was assumed that, if given broad discretion, they would be influenced by conscious or unconscious prejudice toward members of minority groups. Thus, it was decided that sentencing should be based on the nature and seriousness of the crime and that judicial discretion should be tightly constrained.

Gender was largely absent from the debates and calculations: if race was a forbidden consideration, so self-evidently was gender. Equal treatment was (and is) a seductive criminal justice ideology; there appeared to be no legal or policy alternative. An immediate difficulty arose, however, from reviews of the statistical research literature (Blumstein et al. 1983; Nagel and Hagan 1983). After controlling for the defendant's prior record of arrests or convictions, and the type and severity of the convicted charge, women's sentences appeared to be less severe than men's. If future sentences were to be based on past average sentences for men or on an average of men's and women's sentences (no jurisdiction considered using average sentences for women), the policy choice was between "equal treatment" (i.e., using past averages and applying them both to men and women) or "special treatment" (i.e., preserving a two-track system in which it appeared that women were sentenced less severely).

Every jurisdiction we are aware of, including Minnesota, Pennsylvania, Washington, Oregon, Kansas, North Carolina, and the federal sentencing commission, opted for equal treatment. They used the seriousness of the current offense and measures of previous lawbreaking to set sentencing standards. This translated to harsher sentences for women. In Minnesota, policy makers were conscious of the trade-offs. They decided that it was preferable to endorse the symbolism of gender-neutral equal treatment than to be concerned with potential increases in sentences for women (Parent 1988). An evaluation of the first three years of implementing the guidelines suggests that gender disparities in sentencing were reduced and that women's sentences became more severe (Knapp 1984). Monitoring data from most guideline systems show the same pattern of increased sentencing severity for women (e.g., Bogan and Factor 1995, p. 13).

While race- and gender-based disparities may be reduced with "equal treatment" sentencing policies, there are negative consequences, as well. First, the decision to restrict sentencing criteria to current and past lawbreaking makes it difficult for judges to mitigate sentences to take account of offenders' personal circumstances. Since relatively few felony defendants come from middle-class backgrounds and close to half are black, an equal treatment policy disadvantages those poor, minority defendants whose lives show some social and economic success. Second, it is difficult for judges to tailor sentences to the distinctive demands of justice that are linked to racial, class, and gender differences. Race and gender relations have different histories and logics; at the same time, criminal justice policies may also suffer from viewing race and gender as being on separate tracks. By separate-track thinking, we mean policies that address what are seen as *special or unique problems* of minority group members *or* of women. How to imagine the *intersections* of racial-ethnic and gender relations, while also appreciating their different logics and demands of justice, will continue to pose dilemmas for crime and justice policy.

This essay examines the sentencing literature with the following questions in mind. What does the research show? How are race and gender conceptualized in the criminal process? What are the policy implications of theory and research in this area? The essay has five parts. The first summarizes data on arrest, confinement, and sentencing trends by race and by gender over the past two decades. The second surveys the statistical literature on race and gender disparities in sentencing; the third reviews several theoretical perspectives that have been proposed for thinking about race-gender intersectionalities; and the fourth considers racial and gender politics in sentencing reform. The last offers recommendations for policy and future research. Before turning to these discussions at the beginning of Section I we discuss problems with terms such as "race," "crime," and "justice" and the limits of available data.

I. Race and Gender in Official Statistics

As anthropologists have long emphasized, "race" does not exist, that is, "there are no clearly isolatable populations of human beings that vary from one another significantly on . . . physical dimensions" (Meneses 1994, p. 139). Race refers instead to socially and historically constructed categories and identities. Like ethnicity and cultural identity, race may be best understood as a "means of group formation rather than the cause of it" (p. 141) (see also Georges-Abeyie 1989; Roediger 1991; Hall 1992; Frankenberg 1993; Ang 1995). However much anthropologists, historians, and biological scientists (among others) may stress that race, as a set of biological categories for human populations, does not exist, or that ethnic identities are actively constructed without clear origins or consistent elements, it is difficult to convince people of these ideas. Meneses (1994, p. 139) suggests that the reason is that people hold a "firm commitment to a folk theory of race . . . because of the convenience of marking ethnic groups . . . with physical features and because the symbolism of common ancestry . . . is powerful to maintain ethnic group coherence." In addition to fixed notions of "race," in the United States, the "black-white" racial dualism obscures a more complex picture of racial and ethnic relations, especially the relational histories of Hispanic Americans, Native Americans, African Americans, and Asian Americans to each other (Mann 1993; Martinez 1993; Takaki 1993; Omi and Winant 1994).

There is a sharp disjuncture between a contextual and socially constructed understanding of race and ethnicity and how statistical data on crime, courts, and prisons are gathered. Statistical categorization presumes a fixed quality or "essence" to racial and ethnic differences, when such differences are more fluid. But even if one wanted to work with extant statistical categories, the data on racial and ethnic categories may be available in some sources (e.g., arrest and prison populations) but fragmentary or absent in others (e.g., victimization and national court data). This makes comparisons across data sources difficult. Another major problem is that, with some exceptions, crime and justice system data lack measures of class standing; thus, analyses use "race" as a surrogate for discussing class and crime, when a more satisfactory approach would be to analyze class and race together. Despite these recognized problems, we use the national data available to us and the folk theory of race on which the data are based: black and white as dichotomous race groups, and without reference to class standing.

"Male" and "female" have a more secure biological referent, and the statistical categorization of gender groups is somewhat less contentious than that for race and ethnicity (but for feminist challenges, see Gatens [1996]). Yet serious problems remain. Arrest and court data examine race and gender separately, but not together. This is a major problem because the most interesting analytical and political questions center on the *intersections* of race and gender, not merely the separate categories of "black," "white," "male," and "female."

Crime and justice system data are limited by the very terms in which these phenomena are counted and explained: crime is a state-created definition and phenomenon. That is not to say that harms of various types are not "real" or that people do not suffer them, but that certain harms are more easily counted and detected than others (common law crimes compared with various organizational and occupational crimes, or crimes between strangers compared with crimes between intimates) and that certain offenses become a targeted focus of policing and criminal justice activity. The historical shifts in the meaning and content of particular crime categories, themselves heterogeneous groupings of diverse harms, must always be kept in mind.

Although this essay does not address the sociological and philosophical literature on crime, punishment, and justice, we find Hudson's (1996, pp. 151–52) distinction between punishment and justice a useful one. She argues that "punishment cannot be a synonym for 'justice' ": whereas the former concerns the infliction of pain, the latter concerns "the balance between individual freedom and social responsibility [and] . . . the fair distribution of the rights and responsibilities of citizenship." When we use the phrase "the distinctive demands of justice," we have in mind a meaning of justice as the "right" response to the particulars of the harm and the case. We argue that race and gender relations have different histories and logics, and by that we refer to the mechanisms and practices by which racial and gender oppression are structured, enacted, reproduced, and challenged. Ultimately, more "just" decisions in individual cases (or across groups of cases) would address these broader configurations of inequality. Current sentencing policy remains rooted in notions of individual responsibility, denying the larger societal inequalities and histories of race and gender relations. Within these narrowly circumscribed terms, however, there remain competing demands of racial and gender justice, which scholars and policy makers have not yet addressed.

A. Arrests

Because arrests are the starting point of the criminal process, they set basic patterns on which later official decisions embroider. They also provide the first indication that patterns of lawbreaking differ for blacks compared with whites and for women compared with men, even though blacks and women both occupy subordinated social positions. Arrests do not give an optimal picture of criminal behavior, and no one is sure how good a picture they do give. Some unlawful behavior results in people being taken into custody, and some takings into custody result in arrests being officially entered in police records. Policies and conventions governing such decisions vary over time and place; arrest data are as much a measure of official behavior as of criminal behavior.

Thus, when examining gender, race, and arrest statistics over time, it is unclear whether apparent shifts in the black or female share of arrests reflect "real" changes in lawbreaking or changes in police responses to crime. Varied data sources suggest that there are "real" race and gender differences in crime involvement, especially with street forms of violent crime (blacks higher and women lower) and elite or white-collar forms of property crime (men and whites higher) (see Blumstein 1982; Daly 1989*c;* Harris and Meidling 1994; Tonry 1995, pp. 49–80). However, cross-national trend data on gender and arrests suggest that enhanced police record-keeping practices, coupled with credit-based currency systems, can explain increases in women's arrests for the less serious forms of property crime and fraud (Steffensmeier, Allan, and Streifel 1989; Steffensmeier 1993, 1995).

1. *Gender and Arrests.* The data on gender and arrests show three patterns (table 1, pts. A–C).[5] First, arrest rates for women are lower than for men. For all offenses combined, men's arrest rates are over four times greater than women's. Second, men's and women's arrest

[5] Our tables are similar to Steffensmeier's (1993, 1995) method of arraying gender and arrest data in that we group the offense categories to reflect similar clusters of behavior rather than by index and nonindex offenses. Our rates of arrest differ from his, however, in that our base is the entire U.S. population whereas his is the population aged ten through sixty-four years. Also, when calculating the female (and black) shares of arrests, we use the raw numbers, not the arrest rates as Steffensmeier does. Readers will notice slight differences in our calculations as a result.

TABLE 1

Gender and Arrests

A. Women's Arrest Rates per 100,000, by Offense, Ranked from Most to Least Frequent, 1994

Rank and Number of Arrests	Rate per 100,000 Female Population	Offense
Moderate:		
546,304	410	All other offenses (except traffic)
411,331	309	Larceny-theft
Moderate-low:		
185,111	139	Simple assault
184,160	138	Drug abuse violations
153,382	115	Driving under the influence
130,239	98	Fraud
Low:		
74,696	56	Aggravated assault
66,271	50	Public drunkenness
53,313	40	Prostitution
33,424	25	Burglary
33,305	25	Vandalism
33,206	25	Forgery and counterfeiting
20,559	15	Motor vehicle theft
18,057	14	Stolen property
13,591	10	Robbery
Very low:		
4,783	4	Embezzlement
2,460	2	Arson
1,839	1	Homicide
2,372,426	1,475	All offenses

B. Men's Arrest Rates per 100,000, by Offense, Ranked from Most to Least Frequent, 1994

Rank and Number of Arrests	Rate per 100,000 Male Population	Offense
Very high:		
2,499,796	1,967	All other offenses (except traffic)
High:		
934,186	735	Drug abuse violations
926,151	729	Driving under the influence
824,980	649	Larceny-theft
806,770	635	Simple assault
Moderate:		
505,149	398	Public drunkenness
475,167	374	Disorderly conduct
375,020	295	Aggravated assault
341,177	268	Liquor laws
286,502	225	Burglary
226,274	178	Vandalism

TABLE 1 (*Continued*)

B. Men's Arrest Rates per 100,000, by Offense, Ranked from Most to Least Frequent, 1994

Rank and Number of Arrests	Rate per 100,000 Male Population	Offense
200,513	158	Fraud
196,232	154	Weapons
Moderate-low:		
145,701	115	Motor vehicle theft
133,388	105	Robbery
116,873	92	Stolen property
Low:		
74,991	59	Sex offenses
73,000	57	Offenses against family and children
59,797	47	Forgery and counterfeiting
33,505	26	Prostitution
29,460	23	Rape
16,958	13	Vagrancy
16,658	13	Homicide
14,304	11	Arson
9,504,762	7,480	All offenses

C. Female Share of Arrests, 1975, 1980, 1990, 1994, in Percent

	1975	1980	1990	1994
All offenses	16	16	18	20
Index offenses only:				
Violent index	10	10	11	14
Property index	22	21	25	27
Offenses against the person:				
Homicide	16	13	10	10
Aggravated assault	13	12	13	17
Simple assault	14	14	16	19
Major property:				
Robbery	7	7	8	9
Burglary	5	6	9	10
Stolen property	11	11	12	13
Minor property:				
Larceny-theft	31	29	32	33
Fraud	34	41	44	39
Forgery	29	31	35	36
Embezzlement	31	29	41	41
Drinking, drugs, public order:				
Public drunkenness	7	8	10	12
Driving under the influence	8	9	13	14
Drug abuse violations	14	13	17	17
Disorderly conduct	18	16	19	21
Prostitution	74	70	64	61

TABLE 1 (*Continued*)

D. Offenses Showing the Largest Increase in Women's and Men's Total Arrests, 1975 and 1994

	1975	1994	Rate of Increase (in Percent)
Women:			
Simple assault	48,745	185,111	280
Aggravated assault	26,394	74,696	183
Liquor laws	38,124	83,275	118
Fraud	50,004	130,239	130
All other (except traffic)	167,465	546,304	226
Drug abuse violations	70,060	184,160	163
Men:			
Simple assault	303,903	806,770	165
Aggravated assault	175,823	375,020	113
Liquor laws	228,933	341,177	49
Fraud	96,249	200,513	108
All other (except traffic)	870,289	2,499,796	187
Drug abuse violations	438,129	934,186	113

SOURCES.—For pts. A and B: Federal Bureau of Investigation (1995), table 42; U.S. Department of Commerce (1996), table 12. For pt. C: Federal Bureau of Investigation (1976), table 38; (1981), table 35; (1991), table 37; (1995), table 42. For pt. D: Federal Bureau of Investigation (1976), table 38; (1995), table 42.

NOTE.—The arrest rate is calculated from FBI data on arrests by sex and census data on population by sex (female population = 133,265,000; male population = 127,076,000). The total amounts for both women and men do not equal the amounts shown in columns; some arrest categories are omitted.

rates are high for driving under the influence, larceny-theft, and a residual set of "other offenses," and they are low for homicide, embezzlement, and arson. Gender differences are evident in the middle ranges: men's arrest profile contains a higher share of arrests for major forms of violent and property crime, whereas women's contain a higher share of arrests for more minor forms of property crime. Third, while the female share of overall arrests is lower than men's, this share has increased from 16 to 20 percent from 1975 to 1994. For both men and women, arrest rates have increased most for simple and aggravated assault, the residual "other offense" category, drug law violations, and fraud. The female share of arrests for serious violent offenses (homicide, aggravated assault, and robbery) was 12 percent in 1975 and 1990, rising to 14 percent in 1994.

2. *Race and Arrests.* When arrests for blacks and whites are com-

pared, three patterns stand out (table 2, pts. A–C). First, arrest rates for blacks are higher than for whites. For all offenses combined, they are nearly four times higher. Second, blacks' and whites' arrest rates are high for drug law violations, simple assault, larceny-theft, and a residual set of "other offenses." They are relatively lower for arson, embezzlement, and homicide. There are significant differences. Disorderly conduct and aggravated assault are high-arrest rate offenses for blacks, whereas driving under the influence is for whites. Third, the overall black share of arrests has risen from 25 percent of arrests in 1974 and in 1980 to 31 percent in 1994. During the past two decades, the black share of arrests for most offenses has moved up or down by only a few percentage points. The major exception is drug law violations: whereas the black share of arrests for this offense category was 20 percent in 1975, it was 41 percent in 1990, dropping a bit to 38 percent in 1994.

3. *Gender, Race, and Arrests.* Scholars draw from the Federal Bureau of Investigation's Uniform Crime Reports data, National Crime Victimization Survey data, and adolescents' self-reported involvement in crime and delinquency to analyze race and gender together. This body of research shows that women are less likely than men to be involved in crime but that black women's involvement is higher than white women's (Young 1980; Lewis 1981; Mann 1984; Laub and McDermott 1985; Chilton and Datesman 1987; Hill and Crawford 1990; Simpson 1991). Several studies suggest that, in similar crime situations, black women are more likely to be arrested than white women (Visher 1983; Smith, Visher, and Davidson 1984). The race-gender hierarchy from most to least likely to be arrested for common crime (or to be perceived as an offender) is black men, white men, black women, and white women. Black-white differences for men and women in rates of arrest (or perceived race of offender for National Crime Victimization Survey data) are especially strong for violent crime, but less so for property crime.

B. Confinement in Prisons and Jails

The number of sentenced prisoners in state and federal prisons in the United States has increased dramatically in the past fifteen years. In 1980, there were about 330,000 prisoners. By the end of 1995 there were 1,078,000, more than three times as many (Bureau of Justice Statistics 1996). Data on admissions to state prisons reveal three changes since 1980. First, court commitments are a decreasing share of prison

TABLE 2

Race and Arrests

A. Black Arrest Rates per 100,000, by Offense, Ranked from Most to Least Frequent, 1994

Rank and Number of Arrests	Rate per 100,000 Black Population	Offense
Very high:		
1,092,034	3,342	All other offenses (except traffic)
Very high–high:		
429,479	1,315	Drug abuse violations
407,231	1,246	Larceny-theft
341,941	1,047	Simple assault
High:		
199,094	609	Disorderly conduct
176,062	539	Aggravated assault
Moderate:		
120,640	369	Fraud
107,347	329	Driving under the influence
97,867	300	Burglary
96,200	294	Drunkenness
89,232	273	Robbery
87,531	268	Weapons
66,544	204	Motor vehicle theft
59,083	181	Vandalism
57,575	176	Liquor laws
54,601	167	Stolen property
Moderate-low:		
32,001	98	Forgery and counterfeiting
30,860	94	Prostitution
30,242	93	Offenses against family and children
Low:		
12,419	38	Rape
10,420	32	Homicide
3,853	12	Arson
3,816	12	Embezzlement
3,705,713	11,342	All offenses

B. White Arrest Rates per 100,000, by Offense, Ranked from Most to Least Frequent, 1994

Rank and Number of Arrests	Rate per 100,000 White Population	Offense
High:		
1,891,312	874	All other offenses (except traffic)
Moderate:		
932,802	431	Driving under the influence
796,212	368	Larceny-theft
677,025	313	Drug abuse violations

TABLE 2 (*Continued*)

B. White Arrest Rates per 100,000, by Offense, Ranked from Most to Least Frequent, 1994

Rank and Number of Arrests	Rate per 100,000 White Population	Offense
625,689	289	Simple assault
460,300	213	Drunkenness
390,326	180	Disorderly conduct
352,683	163	Liquor laws
Moderate-low:		
264,466	122	Aggravated assault
215,363	99	Burglary
205,362	95	Fraud
Low:		
193,538	89	Vandalism
121,834	56	Weapons
95,216	44	Motor vehicle theft
77,709	36	Stolen property
62,300	29	Sex offenses
59,127	27	Forgery and counterfeiting
58,427	27	Offenses against family and children
55,055	25	Robbery
53,819	25	Prostitution
Very low:		
16,683	8	Rape
12,555	6	Arson
7,705	4	Homicide
7,600	4	Embezzlement
7,894,414	3,647	All offenses

C. Black Share of Arrests, 1975, 1980, 1990, 1994, in Percent

	1975	1980	1990	1994
All offenses	25	25	29	31
Index offenses only:				
Violent index	47	44	45	45
Property index	31	33	30	30
Offenses against the person:				
Homicide	54	48	55	56
Aggravated assault	40	36	38	39
Simple assault	34	32	34	35
Major property:				
Robbery	59	58	61	61
Burglary	28	29	30	31
Stolen property	34	32	41	41
Minor property:				
Larceny-theft	31	31	31	33
Fraud	29	30	33	37

TABLE 2 (*Continued*)

C. Black Share of Arrests, 1975, 1980, 1990, 1994, in Percent

Forgery	33	33	34	34
Embezzlement	31	24	32	33
Drinking, drugs, public order:				
Public drunkenness	19	16	18	17
Driving under the influence	13	11	9	10
Drug abuse violations	20	24	41	38
Disorderly conduct	30	30	32	33
Prostitution	54	53	39	36

D. Offenses Showing the Largest Increase in Blacks' and Whites' Total Arrests, 1975 and 1994

	1975	1994	Rate of Increase (in Percent)
Blacks:			
Drugs	96,660	429,479	344
All other	267,294	1,092,034	309
Simple assault	113,608	341,941	201
Fraud	40,476	120,640	198
Aggravated assault	71,360	176,062	147
Vandalism	25,149	59,083	135
Whites:			
Simple assault	217,481	625,689	188
All other	696,160	1,891,312	172
Aggravated assault	105,226	264,466	151
Fraud	99,972	205,362	105
Drugs	383,649	677,025	76
Weapons	69,843	121,834	74

Sources.—For pts. A and B: Federal Bureau of Investigation (1995), table 42; U.S. Department of Commerce (1996), table 12. For pt. C: Federal Bureau of Investigation (1976), table 38; (1981), table 35; (1991), table 37; (1995), table 42. For pt. D: Federal Bureau of Investigation (1976), table 39; (1995), table 43.

Note.—The arrest rate is calculated from FBI data on arrests by race and census data on population by race (black population = 32,672,000; white population = 216,470,000). The total amounts for both blacks and whites do not equal the amounts shown in columns; some arrest categories are omitted.

admissions (70 percent in 1992) whereas "conditional release violators" (those who left prison as parolees or by other types of release involving community supervision) form an increasing share (from 17 percent in 1980 to 30 percent in 1992). Second, court commitments have increased dramatically for drug offenses, rising from about 2 percent to 10 percent of drug arrests (Bureau of Justice Statistics 1994*a*,

TABLE 3

Rates per 100,000 of Federal and State Sentenced Prisoners, by Gender and Race, 1980–1993

		Men		Women	
Year	Total*	White	Black	White	Black
1980	139	168	1,111	6	45
1984	187	228	1,459	9	63
1990	297	339	2,376	19	125
1993	359	398	2,920	23	165
Rate of increase, (in percent) 1980–1993	158	137	163	283	267

Source.—Adapted from Bureau of Justice Statistics (1994*a*), p. 9.
*Total includes prisoners of other racial-ethnic groups.

p. 8). In 1980, 7 percent of new court commitments were for drug offenses; in 1992, it was 31 percent. Third, the black share of those imprisoned has increased from 44 percent in 1980 to 47 percent in 1994; for women, from 4 percent to 6 percent. While the rate of increase in incarceration has been greatest for black and white women, their increased numbers are a small portion of the overall growth in the size of the prison population, which has been shouldered disproportionately by black men.

Table 3 shows incarceration rates by race and gender for state and federal prisoners from 1980 to 1993. Black men's incarceration rate was six times that of white men's in 1980, seven times that in 1990, and eight times that in 1993. Black women's incarceration rate was seven times that of white women's in 1980 and in 1993. Gender differences within racial groups are even more pronounced. Black men's incarceration rate was eighteen times that of black women in 1993 (it was twenty-five times that of black women in 1980). White men's incarceration rate was seventeen times that of white women in 1993 (it was twenty-eight times that of white women in 1980).

For men and women in prison in 1991, the median age is thirty to thirty-one years (table 4). Nearly two-thirds are members of minority groups (black, Hispanic, Native American, and Asian), and most have not graduated from high school. Over half the women and 32 percent of the men were unemployed at the time of arrest. More imprisoned

TABLE 4

Demographic, Offense, and Criminal History Profiles of Men and Women in State Prisons in 1991 and Jails in 1989 (in Percent)

	In Prison		In Jail	
	Men	Women	Men	Women
Median age (in years)	31	30	28	28
Race/ethnicity:				
White, non-Hispanic	35	36	39	38
Black, non-Hispanic	46	46	42	43
Hispanic	17	14	17	16
Other	2	4	2	3
Education:				
Eighth grade or less	20	16	16	12
Some high school	46	46	38	38
High school graduate or more	34	28	46	50
Prearrest employment:				
Employed	69	47	68	38
Unemployed, looking	16	19	20	28
Unemployed, not looking	15	34	12	34
Offense:				
Violent	47	32	24	13
Property	25	29	30	32
Drugs:				
Possession	7	12	9	15
Trafficking	13	20	12	17
Public order	7	6	23	19
Other	1	1	2	4
Criminal history:				
Not sentenced to probation or incarceration before	19	28	22	31
Previously sentenced for violent offense	50	26	31	16
Previously sentenced for nonviolent offense	31	46	47	52
Level of conviction:				
No prior record	20	29	22	33
One conviction	19	22	21	20
Two or more convictions	61	49	57	47

Sources.—Prison data for 1991 are adapted from Bureau of Justice Statistics (1994*b*), pp. 2–4. Jail data for 1989 are adapted from Bureau of Justice Statistics (1992), pp. 3–6.

Note.—The sample sizes on which these percents are based may vary depending on whether there is complete information. For prison data, the *N* of women and men is about 38,700 and 670,000, respectively. For jail, the *N* is for all inmates, convicted and not convicted. In 1989, that was about 36,500 women and 344,500 men.

men (close to half) were in prison for violent offenses than were women (one-third). More imprisoned women (one-third) were in for drug offenses than were men (20 percent), although just five years earlier, drug offenses accounted for 11 and 8 percent, respectively, of the offenses for which women and men were incarcerated. More incarcerated men (50 percent) than women (26 percent) had been previously convicted of a violent offense, and more men (61 percent) than women (49 percent) had two or more previous convictions.

In addition to those in prison, there were 507,000 people in U.S. jails in 1995 (Bureau of Justice Statistics 1996). Forty-five percent were convicted and serving sentences; the rest were awaiting trial. The number of adults in local jails more than doubled from 1983 to 1995, and the increases were greater for women than men. A 1989 survey of inmates in local jails reveals a profile with some similarities and differences from that of prison inmates (table 4). Women were then 9 percent of jail inmates; most men and women (62 percent) were members of minority groups (black, Hispanic, and Native American/Asian), and half of women and 46 percent of men had completed high school or more. Compared to the prison population, fewer men and women were in jail for violent offenses; they were more likely to be jailed for public order offenses. Like women prisoners, jailed women were less likely than their male counterparts to have been sentenced before and less likely to have been sentenced for a violent crime.

C. Criminal Courts

Compared with data gathered on arrests, on jail and prison inmates, and on federal criminal courts, a national reporting system for state criminal courts has taken longer to develop. Four sources are available, although two have ended recently. These are the Prosecution of Felony Arrests (PFA), Offender-Based Transaction Statistics (OBTS), the National Judicial Reporting Program (NJRP), and the National Pretrial Reporting Program (NPRP).

The PFA is a county-level program; the OBTS, state-level. Both began in the late 1970s and ended in the early 1990s. The PFA data set includes a varied number of urban felony courts (ranging from fourteen to thirty-seven), which volunteered to report information on cases from arrest to disposition (Boland, Brady, et al. 1983; Boland, Conly, et al. 1990). The PFA statistics give the estimated percent of felony arrests dismissed and prosecuted, the percent of cases going to trial, and the kinds of sentences imposed. Outcomes are not disaggregated by race or gender.

State participation in the OBTS was voluntary; thus, the completeness of data varies by state.[6] The OBTS contains information on outcomes from arrest to sentencing. While the gender and race composition of those prosecuted is reported, sentencing outcomes are not disaggregated by race or gender.

After several pilot efforts (see, e.g., Bureau of Justice Statistics 1987), the NJRP began in 1986 with a sample of state courts in 100 counties; the sample expanded to state courts in 300 counties in 1988. The NJRP gathers information on sentences for convicted defendants only. To supplement the NJRP, the NPRP, which began in 1988, gathers data on the pretrial status of defendants. The NPRP uses a sample of the seventy-five largest urban counties, whereas the NJRP uses both a national sample and courts serving the seventy-five largest urban counties. (We refer to the latter two NJRP samples as the "national" and "urban-county" samples, respectively.) The data from the NJRP provide the only national source of information on felony court sentences for race and gender groups.[7]

We have described these sources of court data in some detail because, depending on which source is consulted, the race and gender profile varies. Table 5 shows the black and female shares of cases in 1990, drawing from three data sources: the OBTS (table 5, pt. A), NJRP urban county sample (table 5, pt. B), and NJRP national sample (table 5, pt. C). In all three samples, 14–15 percent of the defendants were women. However, the black share of defendants is greater in the NJRP urban-county sample (table 5, pt. B; 55 percent) than in the OBTS national sample (table 5, pt. A; 41 percent) or NJRP national

[6] An early OBTS report described sentencing practices for thirteen states during 1979–82 (Bureau of Justice Statistics 1984). Disposition data from five states were reported for 1983–86 (Bureau of Justice Statistics 1989*b*); fourteen for 1988 (Bureau of Justice Statistics 1991); and eleven for 1990 (Bureau of Justice Statistics 1994*c*). A bureau senior statistician says that the OBTS series data generally reflect justice system practices in California because of its population in comparison to other OBTS states (Langan 1995).

[7] Bureau of Justice Statistics researchers suggest that comparisons of 1986 and 1990 using the national data should be made with care because the 1986 sample comes from only 100 counties. They recommend comparisons using the urban county samples (Bureau of Justice Statistics 1993*b*, p. 7). We prefer the national sample for two reasons: it has data for 1986, and it disaggregates sentences by race and gender. One problem is that the 1986 data provide less detailed offense categories than those in later years. This can be circumvented by selecting offense categories common to 1986 and subsequent years.

TABLE 5

Black and Female Percentages of Defendants Prosecuted in Felony Courts in 1990 as Estimated from Three National Sources of Data

A. Offender-Based Transaction Statistics Data for 1990 from 11 States

No. Prosecuted	Black Female Share	White Female Share	Black Male Share	White Male Share	Other Share
518,929	6	8	35	50	1

B. National Judicial Reporting Program Data for 1990, Sample of 75 Urban Counties

All Offenses	Black Female Share	White Female Share	Black Male Share	White Male Share	Other Share
50,444	8	7	47	37	2

C. National Judicial Reporting Program Data for 1990, National Sample of 300 Counties

All Cases (Estimated)	Female Share	Male Share	Black Share	White Share	Other Share
713,000	14	86	47	52	1

Sources.—In pt. A, Offender-Based Transaction Statistics data are from Bureau of Justice Statistics (1994*c*), p. 3. In pt. B, National Judicial Reporting Program data are from Bureau of Justice Statistics (1993*c*), p. 3. In pt. C, National Judicial Reporting Program data are from Bureau of Justice Statistics (1993*a*), p. 16.

Note.—"Other Share" = Native American and Asian men and women. The 11 states in pt. A are Alabama, Alaska, California, Idaho, Minnesota, Missouri, Nebraska, New Jersey, New York, Vermont, and Virginia.

sample (table 5, pt. C; 47 percent). It is not surprising that the urban-county sample has a higher percent of blacks because of the demographics of urban populations. What is important is that the race and gender composition of defendants in state felony courts is characterized accurately.

In light of the differences in how court data have been gathered, an accurate analysis of sentencing trends cannot be stitched together with OBTS data from the early 1980s and NJRP data from the mid-1980s onward. We therefore focus on the 1986 and 1990 NJRP national sample data (see tables 6–8). From 1986 to 1990, the female share of defendants remained the same (13–14 percent). The black share in-

TABLE 6

The Female and Black Shares of Those Convicted in Felony Courts, 1986–90, Using the National Judicial Reporting Program National Sample

	Female Share		Black Share	
	1986	1990	1986	1990
All felonies (in percent)	13	14	40	47
Homicide	9	10	46	56
Rape	1	1	37	33
Robbery	6	6	53	63
Aggravated assault	9	9	44	44
Burglary	4	5	38	42
Larceny	20	18	38	42
Drug sales ("trafficking")	14	15	48	57
Other felonies	17	10	37	33

Sources.—For 1986, Bureau of Justice Statistics (1990), p. 3; for 1990, Bureau of Justice Statistics (1993*a*), p. 16.

Note.—The 1986 and 1990 data are not strictly comparable in that more detailed offense categories are available in 1990. Thus, the "other felonies" share drops in 1990. In 1986, the larceny category included both larceny and fraud, but in 1990 larceny and fraud were separated.

creased from 40 to 47 percent (table 6), with the largest increases being for homicide (46 to 56 percent), robbery (53 to 63 percent), and drug sales (48 to 57 percent). (The Bureau of Justice Statistics uses the term "drug trafficking," but we use "drug sales" or "selling drugs.") Within race and gender groups, the drug sales share of court convictions increased from 13 to 20 percent of men's convictions, 15 to 22 percent of women's, 10 to 17 percent of whites', and 14 to 25 percent of blacks' (see table 7).

Turning to the sentences received (table 8, pts. A and B), several caveats are in order. First, although the severity of the offense and the defendant's prior record are typically the strongest factors, sentencing is based on a complex mix of case and biographical elements. Second, the averages reported for length of sentence combine defendants who pleaded guilty and those who were found guilty at trial. Defendants convicted at trial are likely to receive more severe sentences than those pleading guilty; previous research suggests that gender and race groups may have different mixes of trial and guilty plea sentences.[8]

[8] Zatz (1987, pp. 79–80) finds that black offenders were less likely to resolve their cases through plea bargaining than whites. Daly (1994*a*, p. 19) estimates a higher plea-bargaining rate for women (97 percent) than men (92 percent).

TABLE 7

The Distribution of Convicted Offenses, by Gender and Race, 1986–90, Using the National Judicial Reporting Program National Sample

	Men		Women		Black		White	
	1986	1990	1986	1990	1986	1990	1986	1990
Homicide, rape, robbery, aggravated assault	20	17	9	8	22	17	17	15
Burglary, larceny, motor vehicle theft	35	28	30	24	34	25	37	30
Drug sale	13	20	15	22	14	25	10	17
Other felonies	32	35	46	46	30	33	36	38

Sources.—For 1986, Bureau of Justice Statistics (1990), p. 3; for 1990, Bureau of Justice Statistics (1993*a*), p. 17.

Note.—All percents sum to 100. Only those offense categories that can be compared for 1986 and 1990 are shown, leaving a large "other felonies" category. The estimated number of convictions in 1986 was 582,764; in 1990, 829,344.

From 1986 to 1990, the percent of defendants receiving a prison or jail sentence rose a little from 67 to 71 percent, although the average (mean) sentence length was largely unchanged (fifty-eight to fifty-two months). In 1986, there was a 20 percentage point "gender gap" in incarceration: 70 percent of men were sentenced to prison or jail compared with 50 percent of women. That gap decreased to 17 percentage points in 1990. For men, the likelihood of imprisonment rose most sharply for drug sales (65 to 79 percent) with only slight increases for most other offenses. For women, increases were also strongest for drug sales (from 53 to 69 percent), although also sizable for aggravated assault and robbery.

Compared with the incarceration gender gap, that for race was smaller: in 1986 and 1990, the incarceration rate for blacks was 2–3 percentage points higher than for whites. For blacks, increases in incarceration were marked for drug sales (up from 67 to 78 percent) and aggravated assault (66 to 75 percent). For whites, incarceration sentences for drug sales rose from 56 to 77 percent. The "race gap" in incarceration for drugs thus declined from an 11-percentage-point difference in 1986 to near parity in 1990.

All groups in 1990 were more likely to receive an incarceration sentence than in 1986, but as table 8, part B, shows, the mean sentence length dropped substantially for whites (sixty-two to forty-five

TABLE 8

Sentences Imposed on Convicted Defendants, by Gender and Race, 1986–90, Using the National Judicial Reporting Program National Sample

	All		Men		Women		Black		White	
	1986	1990	1986	1990	1986	1990	1986	1990	1986	1990
A. Percent receiving an incarceration (prison or jail) sentence:										
All offenses	67	71	70	74	50	57	69	75	66	73
Homicide	95	95	95	96	95	88	95	95	94	96
Rape	88	86	88	86	75	84	91	89	89	87
Robbery	87	90	89	91	69	79	88	92	89	91
Aggravated assault	71	72	74	75	44	58	66	75	73	76
Burglary	74	75	74	78	70	65	74	82	72	78
Larceny and motor vehicle theft	64	65	67	70	49	49	69	70	61	69
Drug sale	64	77	65	79	53	69	67	78	56	77
B. For those sentenced to prison and jail, the mean length of sentence imposed (in months):										
All offenses	58	52	60	54	42	36	59	58	62	45
Homicide	213	233	217	234	168	173	220	233	228	206
Rape	129	128	129	128	124	75	170	157	123	98
Robbery	124	97	128	98	85	48	111	99	162	85
Aggravated assault	66	52	66	52	71	42	72	57	59	44
Burglary	57	61	57	62	54	45	57	63	62	55
Larceny and motor vehicle theft	31	33	32	35	29	23	36	40	31	29
Drug sale	42	52	42	52	43	44	38	56	46	41

Sources.—For the "all offenses" category for 1986, Bureau of Justice Statistics (1989*a*), pp. 2, 4. For the "all offenses" category for 1990, Bureau of Justice Statistics (1993*b*), pp. 6, 7. For disaggregation for 1986, Bureau of Justice Statistics (1990), pp. 5, 6. For disaggregation for 1990, Bureau of Justice Statistics (1993*a*), pp. 19–22.

Note.—"All offenses" includes offenses not listed here. The mean length of sentence imposed includes trials and guilty pleas. The percent of men receiving an incarceration sentence for drug sale in 1986 is corrected from that reported in Bureau of Justice Statistics (1990), p. 5 (66 percent). The sentence lengths reported for women for 1990 in Bureau of Justice Statistics (1993*a*), p. 21, are in error. The ones shown here are correct (Patrick Langan, personal communication, January 1995).

months), but not for blacks (down one month). Average sentence lengths for men and women declined by six months between 1986 and 1990. The gender gap in length of sentence in both years was eighteen months with the largest gaps for homicide and robbery. As Part B of table 8 also shows, the racial gap in length of sentence, though negligible in 1986, widened in 1990. The largest black-white gaps were for those sentenced for rape and aggravated assault.

Because there have been significant shifts in sentencing for drug selling, we examine them for race and gender groups (table 9). From 1986 to 1992, the percentage of drug sale cases receiving an incarceration sentence increased from 64 to 75 percent, the average sentence length increasing eight months. While the race gap in proportions receiving an incarceration sentence closed for both men and women, the race gap in sentence length reversed by 1992: it was twenty-six and twelve months longer, respectively, for black men and black women compared with their white counterparts. The gender gap for blacks and whites receiving incarceration sentences is still wide (at 14–15 percentage points), as is the gender gap in length of sentence for black defendants.

The arrest, court, and incarceration data show that for all race and gender groups, drug-related offenses have become an increasing share of arrests and felony court cases, and they have become increasingly subject to sentences of incarceration. In a very short period of time, jail and prison populations have ballooned with inmates serving time for drug-related offenses. What, then, is happening in felony courts? We turn to that research literature to see if it suggests patterns of racial and gender bias.

II. Research on Race and Gender in Criminal Courts

Statistical sentencing studies show that the strongest and most consistent predictors of outcomes are the severity of the offense charged and the defendant's criminal history. By comparison, defendant attributes such as race, gender, or age do not exert as strong or as consistent effects. While statistical studies can provide important information on the court process, they do not give the whole picture. Such studies show whether average sentences are more or less severe for some groups, after controlling for levels of offense severity, criminal history, and other variables, than for other groups. However, a finding of no group differences (no "race" or "sex effects") does not mean that race and gender do not powerfully influence the criminal process and the experiences of victims, offenders, attorneys, and judges.

TABLE 9

Sentencing for Drug Sale, by Gender and Race, 1986–92, Using the National Judicial Reporting Program National Sample

A. Percent Receiving Incarceration Sentences and Length of Sentence

For All Groups	1986	1992
Percent of drug sale cases receiving incarceration	64	75
Length of incarceration (in months)	42	50

	Black Men		Black Women		White Men		White Women	
	1986	1992	1986	1992	1986	1992	1986	1992
Percent of drug sale cases receiving incarceration	69	80	56	66	56	82	55	67
Length of incarceration sentence (in months; prison and jail)	39	61	27	43	42	35	61	31

B. Gender and Race Gaps in Incarceration Sentences Imposed and Length of Sentences*

	1986	1992
Gender gap, incarceration sentence imposed:		
Blacks	13	14
Whites	1	15
Gender gap, length of sentence imposed:		
Blacks	12	18
Whites	19†	4
Race gap, incarceration sentence imposed:		
Men	13	2†
Women	1	1†
Race gap, length of sentence imposed:		
Men	3†	26
Women	34†	12

Source.—Data were provided by Patrick Langan (Bureau of Justice Statistics).

* Unless otherwise indicated, the size of the gap shows the more severe sanction for men than women, and for blacks than whites.

† More severe for women than men, or for whites than blacks.

The following review of the court literature focuses on court *outcomes*, not on the *processes* that led to those decisions. Specifically, we are not reviewing the body of observational and interview studies that explore "the [ethnographic] jungle" of legal decision making (Hawkins 1986, p. 1242). We are also passing over research on court organizational and political contexts (e.g., Eisenstein and Jacob 1977; Blumberg 1979; Nardulli, Eisenstein, and Flemming 1988) and sociohistorical analyses of the relationship between punishment and social structure (see Melossi and Pavarini 1981; Garland 1990, 1991; Melossi 1990; Bridges and Beretta 1994; Howe 1994).

A. *Race and the Criminal Courts*

Those new to the criminal court literature find it hard to believe that statistical sentencing studies normally do not find "race effects" favoring whites (for reviews, see Kleck [1981]; Hagan and Bumiller [1983]; Wilbanks [1987]). How could it be that black men and women are 50 percent of those *inside* prison but only 12 percent of those *outside* without something questionable taking place in the criminal courts? Racial disparities have been documented for capital punishment in the South before the *Furman v. Georgia* decision in 1972 (Kleck 1981). With the reintroduction of the death penalty in the late 1970s, legal claims have centered on race-of-victim discrimination and the victim-offender relationship, not the defendant's race alone (see Baldus, Woodworth, and Pulaski 1990).

Kleck's (1981) review of studies up through the 1970s found that, of twenty-three that controlled in some way for the defendant's prior record, 56 percent found no "race effects" favoring whites. "Mixed effects," defined as one-third to one-half of the study outcomes finding race effects favoring whites, were apparent in 35 percent of studies. The remaining two of the twenty-three studies (or 9 percent) found race effects favoring whites (table 10). More recent appraisals of the literature have produced contention about the quality and interpretation of evidence (see, e.g., Blumstein et al. 1983, chap. 2; Kempf and Austin 1986; Wilbanks 1987; MacLean and Milovanovic 1990; Myers 1993; Reiner 1993; Smith 1994). Spohn (1994, p. 249) depicts researchers as falling into two camps: those arguing that racial disparity has declined and its importance is negligible compared to other case factors, and those arguing that disparity has not declined but is more difficult to detect.

Zatz (1987), a member of the latter camp, identifies four research

TABLE 10

Findings of "Race Effects" and "Sex Effects" in Sentencing, in Percent (Excluding Studies of the Death Penalty)

	Race and Sentencing (Kleck 1981)		Gender and Sentencing (Daly and Bordt 1995)	
Do Effects Favor Whites or Women?	All Studies (N = 40)	Control for Prior Record (N = 23)	All Cases (N = 50)	Control for Prior Record (N = 38)
Yes	20	9	52	45
Mixed*	30	35	24	29
No	50	56	24	26

* "Mixed" refers to cases where one-third to one-half of the outcomes showed effects favoring whites (Kleck) or women (Daly and Bordt).

waves on race and sentencing: studies conducted up to the mid-1960s (wave 1), those in the late 1960s and 1970s (wave 2), studies in the 1970s and 1980s (wave 3), and those in the 1980s (wave 4). Wave 1 is characterized by findings of "overt discrimination against minority defendants" (Zatz 1987, p. 70). Reanalysis of these studies during wave 2 showed that, except for the imposition of the death penalty in the South, initial findings of disparity resulted from unsophisticated statistical analyses that, among other problems, lacked controls for criminal history. Wave 3 research used data from courts in the late 1960s and 1970s, and with more sophisticated analyses found evidence of "both overt and more subtle forms of bias against minority defendants . . . in some social contexts" (Zatz 1987, p. 70). In wave 4, studies did not find overt forms of bias, but subtle forms were apparent.

One of Zatz's major points—that court processing is "systematically biased due to institutionalized discrimination" (p. 81) so that the effect of race may be "indirect" or "subtle" (rather than overt) through routine court practices—anticipates a mode of analysis we consider later. Another of Zatz's points—that studies of court process may themselves be stacked against a finding of racial disparity—can be summarized here: statistical analyses may do a poor job of modeling adjudication processes and detecting various forms of disparity because they focus on discrete outcomes rather than on cumulative and structural effects of disadvantage.

B. Gender and the Criminal Courts

Compared to race effects, sex effects are more often found in statistical sentencing studies. Reviews of the literature up to the early 1980s (Parisi 1982; Nagel and Hagan 1983) found that gender differences more often arose in the pretrial release and sentencing decisions, but not in other court contexts.

A more recent appraisal of statistical sentencing by Daly and Bordt (1995) analyzed fifty unique data sets from studies published through mid-1990. They found that, of thirty-eight cases that controlled in some way for prior record, 26 percent found no sex effects, 29 percent found mixed effects, and 45 percent found effects favoring women (table 10). Statistical procedures mattered: multivariate analyses that controlled for a variety of variables, especially prior record, attenuated findings of sex effects. But even with such controls, sex effects were common.

Because the quality of the studies varied, a quality score was assigned and used to weight the cases. An analysis of the weighted sample showed that sex effects were more likely when the court analyzed was a felony court, when the jurisdiction was urban, and when a single jurisdiction was studied. Sex effects were more likely for the "in-out" (incarceration or not) decision than for sentence length. The magnitude of the gap for the in-out decision was explored in the higher-quality studies: after statistical controls were introduced, the gap ranged from 8 to 25 percentage points. As to temporal effects, there appeared to be no relationship between the time period of data collection and findings of sex effects. Sex effects were as evident in more recent court disposition data sets (1976 to 1985) as in those prior to 1976. (Note that subsequent studies of jurisdictions with sentencing guidelines are few in number and that they show mixed findings: sex effects in imprisonment were evident in Pennsylvania and the federal system [Steffensmeier, Kramer, and Streifel 1993; Nagel and Johnson 1994] but not in Minnesota [Miethe and Moore 1985].)

Although the race and sentencing literature rarely grapples with gender (beyond introducing sex as a control variable), the gender and sentencing literature has been more attentive to race. The very first multivariate study of gender and race in sentencing was published only a decade ago (Gruhl, Welch, and Spohn 1984). That and subsequent quantitative studies generally find gender differences within race groups but not racial or ethnic differences within gender groups (see the review in Daly [1989*b*] and studies by Kruttschnitt [1980–81, 1982*a*, 1982*b*]; Mann [1984]; Spohn, Welch, and Gruhl [1985]; and Bickle and Peterson [1991]). From the handful of studies available, it appears that the gender gap may be widest or more often statistically significant for black defendants.

C. *Is the Statistical Sentencing Literature Misleading?*

The race and sentencing literature suggests that race has little effect on sentencing outcomes whereas the gender and sentencing literature suggests that gender bias is present but apparently working to women's advantage. Is there something wrong with these studies?

Sample selection bias is a major statistical concern; earlier screening processes in the handling of black and white cases may attenuate findings of race effects at later stages of court processing (Klepper, Nagin, and Tierney 1983). If, for example, prosecutors screened out more of the less serious white than black robbery cases at an earlier stage, the white robbery cases remaining would be, on average, more serious than the black robbery cases. A finding of "no race effects" at sentencing in this jurisdiction might be interpreted as indicating that black and white cases were treated the same, yet it does not reflect the cumulative advantage accorded whites (i.e., a higher rate of case dismissal or charge reduction).

Other related concerns are how race operates indirectly in the sentencing process (e.g., via the bail decision or type of attorney representing the defendant), how race interacts with case factors (e.g., the type of offense charged and prior record; see Zatz [1984, 1985]), how race affects sentencing for certain types of defendants or victim-offender relations, and how race differences may depend on characteristics of courts and communities (for reviews, see Reiner [1993]; Myers [1994]; and Spohn [1994]).

Statistical controls themselves may also render important race-linked sentencing elements invisible. One example is the policy decision embodied in the federal sentencing guidelines (and in some states) to impose more severe penalties on those convicted of crack compared with powdered cocaine. Because crack is more often sold by blacks, and powder by whites, the harshest penalties were largely experienced by blacks (see McDonald and Carlson [1993] and Tonry [1995, pp. 188–90] for more discussion). Thus, depending on how a study is conducted, a multivariate analysis may not pick up the embeddedness of race or ethnicity in offense and statutory severity categories.

For gender, the statistical problems are the same, but the gender-embeddedness in offense variables may be even more pronounced. Specifically, the sources of variation in the character and content of men's and women's offenses and their criminal histories may be especially poorly measured. For example, suppose that male crack dealers typically dealt in larger quantities than female dealers. This might occur if men typically held higher positions in distribution networks or if more women sold small quantities to support a habit. Even a statistical analysis that controlled for many variables, including the statutory code of the conviction offense, might show that men were sentenced more harshly than women. Unless data were also available on drug quantities and on individuals' drug trafficking roles, the analysis might well (but wrongly) conclude that women were sentenced more leniently than men for these drug charges.

From Uniform Crime Report arrest data and NJRP felony court data, we know that the female share of arrests or court cases for serious interpersonal violence is low. It has been asserted, more generally, that across the spectrum of lawbreaking, women engage in less serious forms of crime and play less culpable roles than men (see, e.g., Steffensmeier 1980). Perhaps because the claim that women's lawbreaking is less serious than men's seems so self-evident, there have been few studies that have documented gender variation in crime contexts and content. They include Daly and Wilson (1987), Jurik and Gregware (1991), and Polk and Ranson (1991) on homicide, and Daly (1989*c*) for selected white-collar offenses.

Recent research suggests that, with better information on the nature of the offense and the defendant's prior criminal history, statistical sex effects are eroded. For example, Steffensmeier, Kramer, and Streifel (1993, p. 437) found that by introducing more precise control variables, the magnitude of sex effects in the decision to incarcerate was reduced from about 20 to 9 percentage points. Daly's (1994*a*) multivariate analysis of felony court sentences in New Haven, Connecticut, found a gender gap of 17 percentage points in the decision to incarcerate, but in a subsequent analysis of a smaller, deep sample of forty pairs of men and women, who were convicted of similar statutory offenses, there were negligible (though not entirely absent) gender disparities.

From Daly and Bordt's (1995) review, we learned that sex effects were more evident in felony courts than in courts prosecuting less serious offenses or a mix of felonies and misdemeanors. This implies that sources of variation in men's and women's offenses are poorly measured for the more serious types of crimes. That inference was borne out in the New Haven felony court studied by Daly (1994*a*): while 48 percent of the forty pairs in the deep sample committed crimes of comparable seriousness, 40 percent of men's offenses were more serious than the women's, and 12 percent of the women's were more serious than the men's.[9] In courts that dispose of the less serious types of offenses (e.g., Feeley 1979; Eaton 1986), there appears to be less statistical evidence of leniency toward women. One reason may be the kinds of offenses handled and how variation in seriousness is "controlled for" in a statistical sense.

There is, of course, more to the story of gender and sentencing than the need to improve statistical procedures. Like race and sentencing, but in a different way, the added question is how gender-linked criteria are embedded in decisions and whether such criteria are warranted or not (see also Raeder 1993; Nagel and Johnson 1994; Daly 1995; *Federal Sentencing Reporter* 1995). One example is a defendant's ties to and responsibilities for others, which may be used to mitigate sentences for *familied* defendants (those caring for or supporting others) and especially familied women (Eaton 1986; Daly 1987*a*, 1987*b*, 1989*a*, 1989*b*). Federal judges' concerns for not incarcerating "good family men" were apparent in preguidelines interviews with judges (Wheeler, Mann, and Sarat 1988). The logic in both instances is consequentialist and materialist: by separating mothers (or fathers) from families, children (or other dependents) lose sources of care and economic support. Women, more often than men, are involved in day-to-day care for others, and, depending on the offense and prior criminal history, they may benefit from this decision criterion.

A second gender-linked criterion is women's greater reform potential. Our review of jail and prison profiles showed that women do not return to court on new offenses as often as men do. We cannot be sure, of course, what part of men's more enhanced criminal histories and higher rates of recidivism is explained by state actors' behavior (e.g., the police or parole officials), by that of male lawbreakers, or by a combination of the two. We are somewhat more sure that court officials assume that women are more easily deterred than men and that women

[9] These summary percents can give the misleading impression that judgments of seriousness can be made easily across diverse harms. They cannot. Four chapters in Daly (1994*a*) discuss how to quantify and compare criminal acts for the deep sample of forty matched pairs. Gender differences in seriousness were most striking for the robbery and interpersonal violence cases and less so for the larceny and drug offense cases.

will make greater efforts to reform themselves (Daly 1987*a*, 1989*a*, 1994*a*).

The statistical literature can therefore mislead in several ways: it can suggest that race differences are absent when they are present and that gender differences are strongly present when they are absent. Race- and gender-linked elements in criminal law, coupled with utilitarian and consequentialist decision-making, add both statistical and conceptual complications. Race and gender may be embedded in criminal law in ways that they should not be, and race and gender may be embedded in decision-making processes in ways that may be warranted and unwarranted.

III. Conceptualizing Race and Gender in Court Practice

Theoretical discussions of race and sentencing have drawn largely from conflict and labeling-interactionist perspectives. Both assume that relations of inequality and disadvantage in the wider society will be reproduced and reenacted, and perhaps amplified, in the criminal court (for classical statements, see Schur 1971; Quinney 1974). Thus, the *simple hypothesis of discrimination* is that minority group members will experience harsher outcomes than do majority group members. Today, that hypothesis has been transformed to a context-dependent one as scholars argue for more sophisticated ways to detect and identify racial disparity. Such attempts to transform and reconfigure conflict and labeling-interactionist theories will continue to run into problems, however, without a better appreciation of how relations of race and ethnicity operate in criminal law and justice system processes.

One problem is an overly simplified dual model of majority-minority relations (i.e., advantaged/disadvantaged). How can a dual model be used to analyze the experiences of several racial and ethnic minority groups? Leiber's (1994) analysis of Native American, African American, and white youth at several stages of juvenile court process is instructive. He proposes that, while "Native Americans and African Americans are disproportionately two of the poorest, least educated, and most highly unemployed groups in the U.S. . . . the conditions of Native Americans are described as the most appalling" (Leiber 1994, p. 260). Thus, Leiber takes the simple hypothesis of discrimination and heaps a second layer of disadvantage for Native Americans. But when he reviews the sparse literature on Native Americans and the justice system, he questions whether his assumption of double disadvantage is correct. He finds that "stereotypes associated with [Native Americans charged with] drug or alcohol offenses . . . may affect the likelihood of receiving either harsher or more lenient outcomes" (p. 262), and he further suggests that African-American youth may be viewed as more "dangerous" in comparison to Native Americans. Specifying the direction of court leniency or harshness is not straightforward in a multiethnic frame (see also Hagan 1977).

For gender and sentencing, the simple hypothesis of discrimination is rarely used. Because bivariate outcomes show that women are "favored," the hypothesis that women's disadvantage in the wider society reproduces itself in the criminal court has not made sense. In its place have been several ad hoc efforts to explain apparent leniency toward women when it occurred: first came chivalry (Pollak 1950); then, judicial paternalism toward women (Nagel and Weitzman 1971). Next, perhaps to generate a sense of debate, Simon (1975) suggested that some women might be treated leniently and others harshly (or as "evil women") if they violated certain "sex-role stereotypes." Despite efforts to clarify the meaning of chivalry, paternalism, and evil women (see Moulds 1980; Nagel and Hagan 1983), these concepts lack an empirical referent and analytic bite.

Kruttschnitt (1980–81, 1982*a*, 1982*b*, 1984) and Kruttschnitt and Green (1984) developed more sophisticated arguments that drew from Black's (1976) ideas on law and social control. She suggested that, because women were more subject to informal social control in their lives than men (via their dependency on others or the state), they would be subject to less formal social control. Subsequent work by Daly (1987*a*, 1987*b*, 1989*a*, 1989*b*) outlined and tested a social control/social costs framework. Daly noted that, although Kruttschnitt's social control formulation explained variation in the treatment among men or women, it could not explain differential treatment between them; further, Daly argued that women's caretaking responsibility for others was the more crucial source of informal social control than their dependency on others. These arguments attempted to clarify how economic support and care for others could produce variable responses both among and between men and women. One as yet unsettled policy question is whether this family-based logic is acceptable.

More recent work by Steffensmeier, Kramer, and Streifel (1993) and Daly (1994*a*) centers on gender differences in the social organization of lawbreaking and criminal history, in addition to elements of women's past and present lives that, in comparison to men, make women appear to be less blameworthy, more conforming, and better prospects for reform. Apparent "sex effects" seen in previous studies can be viewed as arising from inadequate control variables and as warranted or explicable in light of court officials' consequentialist logic. In exploring the intersection of race and gender, Daly (1994*a*) found that black men stood out as the defendant group most at risk to receive the heaviest penalties. Their biographies were least likely to be constructed with a blurred boundaries theme of victimization and criminalization, they were most likely to be categorized as troublemakers or as committed to street life, and they were least likely to be seen as reformable.

The simple hypothesis of discrimination, founded on the dualism of advantaged-disadvantaged defendants, has proved unsatisfactory in understanding race, gender, and criminal process. Part of the problem is that the kinds of offenses subject to arrest and prosecution in state courts ensnare a predominantly disadvantaged population. To explain how court officials exercise discretion toward this already marginalized group requires a consideration of the cues and categories that officials use in assessing defendants' danger to others, of their conventionality and indispensability for families, and of their desire to change and "help themselves." A defendant's prior record, which is a powerful cue for officials in differentiating the amount of respect that defendants hold for the law and their degree of commitment to the "street life," may override individual circumstances that sometimes mitigate sentences.

Three broad modes of conceptualizing race and gender in criminal law and justice system practices have been adopted by social science and sociolegal scholars. These are law and practices as racist/sexist, white/male, and racialized/gendered (Daly [1994*b*], adapting in part from Smart [1992]).[10] Virtually all empirical work on race and gender disparities (and our assessment of it) is framed within a racist/sexist perspective in that the research centers on whether sanctions are applied differently across varied racial-ethnic, gender groups. However, a new generation of feminist and critical race scholars has raised questions about the limits this conceptualization imposes on theory, research, and policy; they are more likely to embrace the latter two modes.

[10] Reiner (1993) and Smith (1994) discuss other ways of analyzing racial discrimination. Their comparison and ours is similar in emphasizing the limitations of individual-based models and the need to consider the disparate impact of law and policies on disadvantaged groups. Our analysis departs from theirs, however, in that they fail to address the different demands of justice that a joint consideration of race and gender raise.

A. Sexist/Racist Modes

Analysts using a practices-as-racist-and-sexist perspective focus on ways of exposing differential treatment and eradicating it. Differential treatment is seen as synonymous with discrimination. The concern is that racial and ethnic minority group men and all women may be allocated fewer resources, may be judged by different standards, and may be denied opportunities. The corrective is "race-blind" and "gender-blind" justice that treats all those before the court equally.

Critical race theorists challenge this position because, as they point out, racial dominance can be achieved in at least two ways: in an older form, by overtly racist practices, and in a newer form, by practices that are ostensibly race-neutral. As Cook (1992, p. 1007) explains, the former "predicate[s] subordination on difference," and the latter "predicate[s] subordination on sameness." Likewise, feminist legal theorists have criticized older, overtly sexist, and newer ostensibly gender-neutral practices (MacKinnon 1987; Fineman 1991; Vogel 1993). Critical and feminist theorists are therefore more likely to adopt one of the other two conceptualizations.[11]

B. White/Male Modes

Practices-as-white-and-male proponents assume that the point of view of criminal law and justice system practices is white, middle-class, and male (Greene 1990, 1993; Roberts 1991; Austin 1992; Peller 1993). The precise elements of a "white point of view" (often referred to as "institutionalized racism") have not been clarified for justice system practices to the same extent that the "male point of view" has. One problem is that "whiteness" has both class and cultural dimensions. It includes notions of what constitutes appropriate dress, demeanor, ways of speaking, and child-rearing practices; it means believing that existing rules and authorities are legitimate and fair.

When practices-as-white-and-male proponents claim that law has a "point of view," the claim may be easily denied by law and its agents as outside the realm of acceptable legal discourse. That is because the claim undermines the principles on which law and normal science are built: objectivity and neutrality—the reputedly unbiased "view from nowhere" (Bordo 1990, p. 133). One way to reveal the "point of view" of law is to show that apparently neutral laws or practices can have a

[11] Liberal feminists would be more comfortable with the practices-as-racist-and-sexist formulation.

disparate effect. Examples include the following: white/male justice cannot "hear" or empathize with stories of harm (Culp 1992; Daly 1994*b*); white/male justice overcriminalizes (the War on Drugs is a current example; see Tonry [1995, chap. 3] and discussion below); and white/male justice expects lawbreakers easily to conform to conventional behavior patterns and norms (Carlen 1988; Finnegan 1990; Austin 1992).

There are several problems with the justice-as-white-and-male position. First, it may be misleading to assume that white men "benefit or are celebrated in a rehearsal of practices that claim universality" (adapting from Smart [1992, p. 34]). Second, the argument may be unduly color-coding and gendering practices that are also linked to nation, culture, and class. Third, there are no coherent or unified conceptions of black, multiethnic, or feminist justice waiting in the wings to replace current laws and practices.

C. *Racialized/Gendered Modes*

The practices-as-racialized-and-gendered position assumes that race and gender relations structure criminal law and justice system practices so profoundly that legal subjects are saturated with racializing and gendered qualities. Majority group members do not always benefit, nor are women and minority group men always subordinated. Rather than analyzing race-ethnic or gender variability in justice system outcomes, the focus instead is on how race-ethnicity and gender are brought forth as racialized and gendered subject positions by criminal law and justice system practices. In taking this perspective, scholars analyze how criminal law and justice system practices may only be able to "see and think a gendered [and racialized] subject" (Smart 1992, p. 34).

One problem with the law-and-practices-as-racialized-and-gendered position is that it may produce knowledge that appears to be useless for changing policy or directing social change more generally. It is one thing to appreciate how people and texts are drenched in racialized and gendered codes and metaphors but quite another to know what to do with that knowledge. The position is important, however, for challenging the idea that race or gender are attached to people's bodies as a natural or stable characteristic (see Lubiano 1992). There is also an openness to seeing how minority group members can construct racialized and gendered identities that both subvert and confirm dominant group members' expectations.

While differences in theory and method may divide traditional and more critical sociolegal scholars, there is a shared interest in redressing patterns of racial and gender injustice. All three modes have strategic value, even if the first is the most practical and familiar for those in the policy world. For example, one may only be able to argue from a practices-as-racist position in a legal brief claiming discrimination against blacks in the imposition of the death penalty (Baldus, Woodworth, and Pulaski 1990, 1994). Legal arguments from a practices-as-male position can be effective, however, in challenging the presumptively "gender-free world" of the federal sentencing guidelines (Raeder 1993), and analyses from a practices-as-racialized-and-gendered position reveal that gender (and race) relations are constitutive of law (Smart 1989). Empirical studies of race and gender in the criminal process, which are typically framed within the racist/sexist mode, could be more effective by revealing the point of view of criminal law and justice system practices, including the disparate effect of particular laws and policies.

IV. Race and Gender Politics in Sentencing Reform

Although in the previous section we used race/gender as an analogous couplet, the histories and logics of the social relations themselves differ. Before drawing out the implications of that point for sentencing reform, we discuss how black feminist scholars have theorized the race/gender relation.[12]

A. Black Feminist Challenges

One classic black feminist reaction to the literary and historical literature of the 1960s and 1970s sets the stage: "All the women are white, all the blacks are men, but some of us are brave" (Hull, Scott, and Smith 1980). The point is that separate theorizing "about race" or "about gender" does not resonate with the history or experiences of black women. The second and perhaps more crucial point is that white people are racialized, and men, gendered. Thus, while "blacks" and "women" are marked as being on the subordinate side of race and gender relations, there is more to race and gender than a discussion of its subordinated members (see, e.g., Frankenberg [1993] on whiteness and Jefferson [1994] and Messerschmidt [1993] on masculinity). In particular, many black feminists named a theoretical construct of class-race-

[12] Black feminist scholarship in the United States and elsewhere is prodigious, although little of it has moved into criminology (for reviews, see Rice 1990; Daly 1993; Daly and Stephens 1995).

gender to argue that these three relations were connected and intersecting, and unless all were considered, an understanding of inequality was incomplete (see, e.g., Crenshaw 1989; Collins 1990; hooks 1990).

From a black feminist perspective, the ways that sentencing reform has been discussed will invite the refrain "but some of us are brave." When sentencing reformers discuss race, they invariably focus on white and racial-ethnic minority group men. When they discuss gender, they do not differentiate by race or ethnicity.

B. Sentencing Reform

As race and gender politics unfolded in sentencing reform, race was structured by presumptive masculinity, and gender, when it was discussed, was nonracialized. American sentencing reform in the 1970s was spawned by and wholly constructed through a race- (and, to some degree, class-) based politics. When women entered the frame, sentencing reformers were hemmed in by a "strong equality" stance that had emerged from these politics.

A partial and highly schematic history of punishment in the United States would go this way. In the last quarter of the nineteenth century, an optimistic rehabilitation-oriented ethos emerged based on individualized treatment and a forward-looking approach to punishment. Indeterminate sentences allowed for discretion by judges, probation officers, and parole boards to decide whether and when individuals were reformed or not a threat to community safety. These practices became politicized in the late 1960s. Of concern were apparent abuses of state officials' powers of arrest, prosecution, and sentencing; class-based disparities in criminal law; and racial disparities in sentences received and time spent incarcerated. Radical and liberal commentators called for limits on officials' discretionary power and, in sentencing, a shift away from the highly individualized model to stronger versions of equality and equal treatment. The call for change was interpreted by state legislatures, sentencing commissions, and a National Academy of Science panel (Blumstein et al. 1983) as a call for justice systems explicitly to abjure race- or class-linked factors such as employment status or familial situation as sentencing criteria.

From the initial premise that race- (and to a lesser degree, class-) linked factors should not be allowed to affect decisions in prejudicial ways, it was an easy slide to say that the focus of punishment ought to be the act, not the actor. That was the move to just deserts, which promised a measure of equal treatment for those committing like offenses. That policy, along with other nondesert approaches (such as mandatory minimums), were established during the 1970s and 1980s within a general context of a rising tide of punitiveness.

This demand for strong versions of equality in justice systems resonated with how racial justice has been conceived historically in U.S. liberal law: "equal justice under the law." Initially embodied in the three Reconstruction Amendments in the late 1860s, the racial justice demand was keyed to black men (for the Fourteenth and Fifteenth Amendments, though not the Thirteenth). However, when women (or gender difference) are discussed (then and today), the justice demand shifts to a more weakened equality standard and a greater acceptance of difference.[13] More specifically, in crime and justice, it has been easier to discuss differences in the kinds and qualities of crimes that men and women commit and in the kinds of justice system responses that may be more appropriate for women than it is to discuss differences ordered by race or ethnicity. As but one example, reformatories and prisons were expressly built for men and for women, but not for whites and blacks.

What happened then when sentencing reformers considered women in sentencing policy? As enumerated by Blumstein et al. (1983, p. 114), if the aim was to "equalize sentences," there were these options: to punish women more like men, to punish men more like women, or to shift both groups to achieve an average of past sentencing practices (split-the-difference). Of these, only one—to punish men more like women—optimally combines principles of parsimony and proportionality. That option was not acceptable at the time: it would have made the sentencing system appear "too lenient." Instead, sentencing reformers decided that if strong versions of equality were to be applied to men, then they should also be applied to women. In practical terms, this meant that black men should be punished no more than white men for "like crimes" and that all women would face harsher penalties (like men's or split the difference) than before.

[13] These different justice demands are evident in the U.S. Supreme Court's use of different standards in deciding whether sex- or race-based classifications in work, education, housing, voting, etc., are constitutional, although these have not been applied to criminal justice policy except in challenges to the death penalty. Sex-based classifications have been permitted a more relaxed standard (intermediate scrutiny) than have race-based classifications (strict scrutiny). We agree with Rhode's (1987, p. 21) observation that less attention should be given to "women's and minorities' respective places in an oppression sweepstakes" and more to "the continuities and discontinuities in various patterns of discrimination."

An ironic result of sentencing reform is that in the name of a restricted notion of equality with men, more women (especially black women) are being incarcerated than ever before. And in the name of racial justice in the criminal process, more black men are being incarcerated than ever before. Sentencing reformers vastly underestimated the electorate's susceptibility to law-and-order appeals and the harsher penalties imposed on (and served by) offenders.

C. A Policy Dilemma

Were we advocates on behalf of disadvantaged groups of accused men, especially those who are members of racial and ethnic minority groups, we might endorse a strong version of equality in sentencing, perhaps with some allowance for their "good works" as fathers or community members (see Tonry 1995). But were we policy advocates on behalf of all accused women, we would not endorse strong equality for several reasons. First, any equality model is bound to be male-centered, taking men's circumstances, motives, and actions as the norm for crime and punishment. Second, women generally have more to gain from an individualized model, which focuses on future-oriented criteria such as having responsibilities for others and reform potential.

Imagine now that we are advocates for both groups. We find ourselves looking in two directions at the same time: toward seeing justice as equality (or "equal treatment"), on the one hand, and seeing justice as a response to individual (though often gender-linked) differences, on the other. Sentencing reformers faced this dilemma, and they decided to apply the distinctive demands of racial justice and racial redress to those for gender. That stance, coupled with the War on Drugs and the law-and-order campaigns of the 1980s, has yielded dramatically increasing incarceration rates.

V. Recommendations for Policy and Future Research

How should policy makers respond? How might they think differently about sentencing? We offer these recommendations for policy and future research.

First, policy makers need to rethink the aims and purposes of punishment. One way to do that is to contemplate women as sentencing subjects. As an initial step, we might imagine a form of gender neutrality that is female-normed, and we might fashion an equal treatment punishment scheme in which women, not men, are the standard. For example, if statistical averages of previous sentencing outcomes are used to guide future sentencing policy, policy makers should consider using women's, not men's, outcomes as the base. Research is needed that examines the varied circumstances and contexts of women's lawbreaking and the points at which they are both similar and different from men's lawbreaking. Variation in women's responses to sanctions or the threat of sanctions also need to be studied. We know that, on average, women are less likely to be repeat offenders and to return to prison. This should matter in devising sanctions and in fashioning sentencing policy. By disrupting the image of men as presumptive sentencing subjects, we may see some men's lawbreaking in a different, perhaps more sympathetic light, and we can revisit questions of what is just and humane punishment.

Second, policy makers must consider ways of shifting public opinion away from extraordinarily harsh punishment schemes. For two decades in the United States, there has been unremitting pressure for increases in penalties and no pressure for decreases. Liberals and radicals who were involved in the early sentencing reform movement envisaged not only a more equitable sentencing policy but one that reduced the use of incarceration as a crime control measure. However, the punitive tide has continually risen since the mid-1970s. As a result, while there has been increasing fiscal and political support for expanding the criminal justice system, there has been less for education, housing, and social welfare. Research in other countries suggests that the U.S. criminal justice system is more punitive than elsewhere. Comparative research needs to be brought into the policy debates in the United States; in that way, decreases in levels of punishment will not be seen as concessions to soft-hearted liberals but, rather, as a more rational allocation of resources. Research on alternatives to the criminal justice system, including alternatives to incarceration, must document promising approaches with a strong visual and economic message to policy makers and citizens.

Third, policy makers must address the foreseeable distributive effects of policies. If these have a disparate effect on particular groups, the policies need to be rethought. One way to inspire such rethinking is the tool of rebuttable presumption. That is, unless disparate-effect-causing policies can be shown to achieve important public policy goals, the policies should be reconsidered. The most dramatic example of *not* considering the disparate-effect-causing effects of a particular criminal justice policy was the War on Drugs. Because visible drug dealing is found in inner city areas, it was foreseeable that tactical policies aimed at substantial arrests and incarceration of drug dealers would yield a sharp increase in the numbers of minority group prisoners. This might have been justifiable it there had been reason to expect that drug use or trafficking would diminish as a result, but there was little reason to believe those things would happen (Wilson 1990; Tonry 1995, chap. 3). There is an important role for research that can forecast the future distributive effects of policies, under varied conditions.

Fourth, researchers need to fashion better methods of assessing justice system practices. That will entail an understanding of how justice "gets done," including practitioners' understandings of the "right response" and ways to evaluate those activities that are empathetic and critical. The just deserts movement sought to reduce disparity in sentencing those convicted of "like crimes" and with similar criminal histories. In seeking to eradicate sources of decision makers' prejudice, such policies unwittingly removed the positive uses of their discretion. Legislating justice from a distance and not consulting closely with practitioners themselves were mistakes. Likewise, assessing justice from a distance and not paying close attention to how justice "gets done" are mistakes. Statistical evidence alone is not sufficient in evaluating sentencing practices, nor is recourse to celebrated cases of unjust decisions. A more complete measure of justice would contain a moral dimension, and it would permit oscillation between logicoscientific and narrative modes of reasoning (Daly 1994*a*, chaps. 1 and 12).

Finally, policy makers need to wrestle with the fact that practices that are race- and gender-neutral, as well as those that are overtly prejudiced, can produce injustice. Further, there is a need to consider the distinctive demands of justice that multiple inequalities—of class, race-ethnicity, gender, and age—produce. A justice system that is based on an imperative of uniformity (or equal treatment) will produce injustice, as will one based on an imperative of individuality (or individualized treatment). Striking a balance between the two appears the only route, but in taking this tack, state authorities will be assailed for both lacking a standard and imposing just one standard. We should expect that the practices of doing justice will produce destabilization and incoherence. Better to acknowledge the limits of doing justice in an unequal society, even as one imagines a different world. In the interim, the principles that may best guide policy makers are responses that cause least harm and a parsimonious use of penal law and the machinery of criminal justice.

REFERENCES

American Friends Service Committee. 1971. *Struggle for Justice: A Report on Crime and Punishment in America.* New York: Hill & Wang.

Ang, Ien. 1995. " 'I'm a Feminist But . . .': 'Other' Women and Postnational Feminism." In *Transitions,* edited by Barbara Caine and Rosemary Pringle. St. Leonards, New South Wales: Allen & Unwin.

Austin, Regina. 1992. " 'The Black Community,' Its Lawbreakers, and a Politics of Identification." *Southern California Law Review* 65:1769–1817.

Baldus, David C., George Woodworth, and Charles A. Pulaski, Jr. 1990. *Equal Justice and the Death Penalty.* Boston: Northeastern University Press.

———. 1994. "Reflections on the 'Inevitability' of Racial Discrimination in Capital Sentencing and the 'Impossibility' of Its Prevention, Detection, and Correction." *Washington and Lee Law Review* 51(2):359–430.

Bickle, Gayle S., and Ruth D. Peterson. 1991. "The Impact of Gender-Based Family Roles in Criminal Sentencing." *Social Problems* 38(3):372–94.

Black, Donald. 1976. *The Behavior of Law.* New York: Academic Press.

Blumberg, Abraham. 1979. *Criminal Justice: Issues and Ironies.* 2d ed. New York: New Viewpoints.

Blumstein, Alfred. 1982. "On the Racial Disproportionality of United States' Prison Populations." *Journal of Criminal Law and Criminology* 73:1259–81.

Blumstein, Alfred, Jacqueline Cohen, Susan E. Martin, and Michael H. Tonry, eds. 1983. *Research on Sentencing: The Search for Reform.* Vols. 1 and 2. Washington, D.C.: National Academy Press.

Bogan, Kathleen, and David Factor. 1995. "Oregon Guidelines 1989–1994." *Overcrowded Times* 6(2):1, 13–15.

Boland, Barbara, Elizabeth Brady, Herbert Tyson, and John Bassler. 1983. *The Prosecution of Felony Arrests, 1979.* Washington, D.C.: Institute for Law and Social Policy.

Boland, Barbara, Catherine H. Conly, Paul Mahanna, Lynn Warner, and Ronald Sones. 1990. *The Prosecution of Felony Arrests, 1987.* Cambridge, Mass.: Abt Associates, Inc.

Bordo, Susan. 1990. "Feminism, Postmodernism, and Gender Scepticism." In *Feminism/Postmodern,* edited by Linda J. Nicolson. New York: Routledge.

Bridges, George S., and Gina Beretta. 1994. "Gender, Race, and Social Control: Toward an Understanding of Sex Disparities in Imprisonment." In *Inequality, Crime, and Social Control,* edited by George S. Bridges and Martha A. Myers. Boulder, Colo.: Westview Press.

Bureau of Justice Statistics. 1984. *Sentencing Practices in 13 States.* Washington, D.C.: U.S. Department of Justice, Bureau of Justice Statistics.

———. 1987. *Sentencing Outcomes in 28 Felony Courts, 1985.* Washington, D.C.: U.S. Department of Justice, Bureau of Justice Statistics.

———. 1989*a. Felony Sentences in State Courts, 1986.* Washington, D.C.: U.S. Department of Justice, Bureau of Justice Statistics.

———. 1989*b. Criminal Cases in Five States, 1983-86.* Washington, D.C.: U.S. Department of Justice, Bureau of Justice Statistics.

———. 1990. *Profile of Felons Convicted in State Courts, 1986.* Washington, D.C.: U.S. Department of Justice, Bureau of Justice Statistics.

———. 1991. *Tracking Offenders, 1988.* Washington, D.C.: U.S. Department of Justice, Bureau of Justice Statistics.

———. 1992. *Women in Jail 1989.* Washington, D.C.: U.S. Department of Justice, Bureau of Justice Statistics.

———. 1993*a*. *National Judicial Reporting Program, 1990.* Washington, D.C.: U.S. Department of Justice, Bureau of Justice Statistics.

———. 1993*b*. *Felony Sentences in State Courts, 1990.* Washington, D.C.: U.S. Department of Justice, Bureau of Justice Statistics.

———. 1993*c*. *Felony Defendants in Large Urban Counties, 1990.* Washington, D.C.: U.S. Department of Justice, Bureau of Justice Statistics.

———. 1994*a*. *Prisoners in 1993.* Washington, D.C.: U.S. Department of Justice, Bureau of Justice Statistics.

———. 1994*b*. *Women in Prison 1991.* Washington, D.C.: U.S. Department of Justice, Bureau of Justice Statistics.

———. 1994*c*. *Tracking Offenders, 1990.* Washington, D.C.: U.S. Department of Justice, Bureau of Justice Statistics.

———. 1994*d*. *Capital Punishment 1993.* Washington, D.C.: U.S. Department of Justice, Bureau of Justice Statistics.

———. 1995*a*. *Prisoners in 1994.* Washington, D.C.: U.S. Department of Justice, Bureau of Justice Statistics.

———. 1995*b*. "State and Federal Prisons Report Record Growth during Last 12 Months." Press release, December 3. Washington, D.C.: U.S. Department of Justice, Bureau of Justice Statistics.

———. 1995*c*. *Jails and Jail Inmates, 1993-94.* Washington, D.C.: U.S. Department of Justice, Bureau of Justice Statistics.

———. 1996. "Almost 1.6 Million Men and Women in the Nation's Prisons and Jails." Press release, August 18. Washington, D.C.: U.S. Department of Justice.

Carlen, Pat. 1988. *Women, Crime and Poverty.* Philadelphia: Open University Press.

Chesney-Lind, Meda. 1991. "Patriarchy, Prisons, and Jails: A Critical Look at Trends in Women's Incarceration." *Prison Journal* 71(1):51–67.

Chilton, Roland, and Susan K. Datesman. 1987. "Gender, Race, and Crime: An Analysis of Urban Arrest Trends, 1960–1980." *Gender and Society* 1: 152–71.

Collins, Patricia Hill. 1990. *Black Feminist Thought.* London: Unwin Hyman.

Cook, Anthony E. 1992. "The Spiritual Movement towards Justice." *University of Illinois Law Review*, pp. 1007–20.

Crenshaw, Kimberele. 1989. "Demarginalizing the Intersection of Race and Sex: A Black Feminist Critique of Antidiscrimination Doctrine, Feminist Theory, and Antiracist Politics." *University of Chicago Legal Forum*, pp. 139–67.

Culp, Jerome M. 1992. "You Can Take Them to Water but You Can't Make Them Drink: Black Legal Scholarship and White Legal Scholars." *University of Illinois Law Review*, pp. 1021–41.

Daly, Kathleen. 1987*a*. "Structure and Practice of Familial-Based Justice in a Criminal Court." *Law and Society Review* 21(2):267–90.

———. 1987*b*. "Discrimination in the Criminal Courts: Family, Gender, and the Problem of Equal Treatment." *Social Forces* 66(1):152–175.

———. 1989*a*. "Rethinking Judicial Paternalism: Gender, Work-Family Relations, and Sentencing." *Gender and Society* 3(1):9–36.

———. 1989*b*. "Neither Conflict nor Labeling nor Paternalism Will Suffice: Intersections of Race, Ethnicity, Gender, and Family in Criminal Court Decisions." *Crime and Delinquency* 35(1):136–68.

———. 1989*c*. "Gender and Varieties of White-Collar Crime." *Criminology* 27(4):769–94.

———. 1992. "Women's Pathways to Felony Court: Feminist Theories of Lawbreaking and Problems of Representation." *Southern California Review of Law and Women's Studies* 2(1):11–52.

——-. 1993. "Class-Race-Gender: Sloganeering in Search of Meaning." *Social Justice* 20(1–2):56–71.

———. 1994*a*. *Gender, Crime, and Punishment.* New Haven, Conn.: Yale University Press.

———. 1994*b*. "Criminal Law and Justice System Practices as Racist, White, and Racialized." *Washington and Lee Law Review* 51:431–64.

———. 1995. "Gender and Sentencing: What We Know and Don't Know from Empirical Research." *Federal Sentencing Reporter* 8(3):163–68.

Daly, Kathleen, and Rebecca Bordt. 1995. "Sex Effects and Sentencing: A Review of the Statistical Literature." *Justice Quarterly* 12(1):143–77.

Daly, Kathleen, and Deborah J. Stephens. 1995. "The 'Dark Figure' of Criminology: Toward a Black and Multi-ethnic Feminist Agenda for Theory and Research." In *Engendering Criminology: International Feminist Perspectives on the Transformation of a Social Science*, edited by Frances Heidensohn and Nicole Rafter. Milton Keynes: Open University Press.

Daly, Martin, and Margo Wilson. 1987. *Homicide.* New York: Aldine de Gruyter.

Eaton, Mary. 1986. *Justice for Women?* Philadelphia: Open University Press.

Eisenstein, James, and Herbert Jacob. 1977. *Felony Justice: An Organizational Analysis of Criminal Courts.* Boston: Little, Brown.

Federal Bureau of Investigation. 1976. *Crime in the United States—1975.* Washington, D.C.: U.S. Government Printing Office.

———. 1981. *Crime in the United States—1980.* Washington, D.C.: U.S. Government Printing Office.

———. 1991. *Crime in the United States—1990.* Washington, D.C.: U.S. Government Printing Office.

———.1995. *Crime in the United States—1994.* Washington, D.C.: U.S. Government Printing Office.

Federal Sentencing Reporter. 1995. "Thematic Issue: Gender and Sentencing." Vol. 8, no. 3.

Feeley, Malcolm M. 1979. *The Process Is the Punishment.* New York: Russell Sage.

Fineman, Martha. 1991. *The Illusion of Equality.* Chicago: University of Chicago Press.

Finnegan, William. 1990. "Out There." *New Yorker*, pt. 1 (September 10), pp. 51 ff., and pt. 2 (September 17), pp. 60 ff.

Frankenberg, Ruth. 1993. *White Woman, Race Matters.* Minneapolis: University of Minnesota Press.

Garland, David. 1990. *Punishment and Modern Society.* Chicago: University of Chicago Press.

——. 1991. "Sociological Perspectives on Punishment." In *Crime and Justice: A Review of Research*, vol. 14, edited by Michael Tonry. Chicago: University of Chicago Press.

Gatens, Moira. 1996. *Imaginary Bodies: Ethics, Power, and Corporeality*, chap. 1. New York: Routledge.

Georges-Abeyie, Daniel E. 1989. "Race, Ethnicity, and the Spatial Dynamic: Toward a Realistic Study of Black Crime, Crime Victimization, and Criminal Justice Processing of Blacks." *Social Justice* 16:35–54.

Greene, Dwight L. 1990. "Drug Decriminalization: A Chorus in Need of Masterrap's Voice." *Hofstra Law Review* 18:457–500.

———. 1993. "Justice Scalia and Tonto, Judicial Pluralistic Ignorance, and the Myth of Colorless Individualism in Bostick v. Florida." *Tulane Law Review* 67:1979–2062.

Gruhl, John, Susan Welch, and Cassia Spohn. 1984. "Women as Criminal Defendants: A Test for Paternalism." *Western Political Quarterly* 37:456–67.

Hagan, John. 1977. "Finding 'Discrimination': A Question of Meaning." *Ethnicity* 4:167–76.

Hagan, John, and Kristin Bumiller. 1983. "Making Sense of Sentencing: A Review and Critique of Sentencing Research." In *Research on Sentencing: The Search for Reform*, vol. 2, edited by Alfred Blumstein, Jacqueline Cohen, Susan E. Martin, and Michael H. Tonry. Washington D.C.: National Academy Press.

Hall, Stuart. 1992. "What Is This 'Black' in Black Popular Culture?" In *Black Popular Culture*, edited by Gina Dent. Seattle: Bay Press.

Harris, Anthony R., and Lisa R. Meidling. 1994. "Criminal Behavior: Race and Class." In *Criminology*, 2d ed., edited by Joseph F. Sheley. Belmont, Calif.: Wadsworth.

Hawkins, Keith. 1986. "On Legal Decision-Making." *Washington and Lee Law Review* 43(4):1161–242.

Hill, Gary D., and Elizabeth M. Crawford. 1990. "Women, Race and Crime." *Criminology* 28:601–26.

hooks, bell. 1990. *Yearning: Race, Gender, and Cultural Politics.* Boston: South End Press.

Howe, Adrian. 1990. "Prologue to a History of Women's Imprisonment: In Search of a Feminist Perspective." *Social Justice* 17(2):5–22.

———. 1994. *Punish and Critique: Towards a Feminist Analysis of Penality.* New York: Routledge.

Hudson, Barbara A. 1996. *Understanding Justice.* Bristol, Pa.: Open University Press.

Hull, Gloria T., Patricia Bell Scott, and Barbara Smith, eds. 1980. *All the*

Women Are White, All the Blacks Are Men, but Some of Us Are Brave. Westbury, N.Y.: Feminist Press.

Jefferson, Tony. 1994. "Theorizing Masculine Subjectivity." In *Just Boys Doing Business?* edited by Tim Newburn and Elizabeth A. Stanko. New York: Routledge.

Jurik, Nancy C., and Peter Gregware. 1991. "A Method for Murder: The Study of Homicides by Women." In *Perspectives on Social Problems,* vol. 4, edited by James Holstein. Westport, Conn.: JAI.

Kempf, Kimberly L., and Roy L. Austin. 1986. "Older and More Recent Evidence on Racial Discrimination in Sentencing." *Journal of Quantitative Criminology* 2(1):29–48.

Kleck, Gary. 1981. "Racial Discrimination in Criminal Sentencing: A Critical Evaluation of the Evidence with Additional Evidence on the Death Penalty." *American Sociological Review* 46:783–805.

Klepper, Steven, Daniel Nagin, and Luke-Jon Tierney. 1983. "Discrimination in the Criminal Justice System: A Critical Appraisal of the Literature." In *Research on Sentencing: The Search for Reform,* vol. 2, edited by Alfred Blumstein, Jacqueline Cohen, Susan E. Martin, and Michael H. Tonry. Washington, D.C.: National Academy Press.

Knapp, Kay. 1984. *The Impact of the Minnesota Sentencing Guidelines—Three Year Evaluation.* St. Paul: Minnesota Sentencing Guidelines Commission.

Kruttschnitt, Candace. 1980–81. "Social Status and Sentences of Female Offenders." *Law and Society Review* 15:247–65.

———. 1982*a*. "Women, Crime, and Dependency." *Criminology* 19:495–513.

———. 1982*b*. "Respectable Women and the Law." *Sociological Quarterly* 23: 221–34.

———. 1984. "Sex and Criminal Court Dispositions: The Unresolved Controversy." *Journal of Research in Crime and Delinquency* 21:213–32.

Kruttschnitt, Candace, and Donald E. Green. 1984. "The Sex-Sanctioning Issue: Is It History?" *American Sociological Review* 49:541–51.

Lacey, Nicola. 1994. "Introduction: Making Sense of Criminal Justice." In *Criminal Justice,* edited by Nicola Lacey. New York: Oxford University Press.

Langan, Patrick. 1995. Personal communication with authors, January.

Laub, John H., and Joan M. McDermott. 1985. "An Analysis of Serious Crime by Young Black Women." *Criminology* 23:81–98.

Leiber, Michael J. 1994. "A Comparison of Juvenile Court Outcomes for Native Americans, African Americans, and Whites." *Justice Quarterly* 11(2): 257–79.

Lewis, Diane. 1981. "Black Women Offenders and Criminal Justice: Some Theoretical Considerations." In *Comparing Female and Male Offenders,* edited by Marguerite Q. Warren. Beverly Hills, Calif.: Sage.

Lubiano, Wahneema. 1992. "Black Ladies, Welfare Queens, and State Minstrels: Ideological War by Narrative Means." In *Race-ing Justice, Engendering Power: Essays on Anita Hill, Clarence Thomas, and the Construction of Social Reality,* edited by Toni Morrison. New York: Pantheon Books.

MacKinnon, Catharine. 1987. *Feminism Unmodified.* Cambridge, Mass.: Harvard University Press.

MacLean, Brian D., and Dragan Milovanovic, eds. 1990. *Racism, Empiricism, and Criminal Justice*. Vancouver: Collective Press.

Maguire, Kathleen, and Ann L. Pastore. 1994. *Sourcebook of Criminal Justice Statistics—1993*. Washington, D.C.: U.S. Department of Justice, Bureau of Justice Statistics.

Mann, Coramae Richey. 1984. "Race and Sentencing of Female Felons: A Field Study." *International Journal of Women's Studies* 7:160–72.

———. 1993. *Unequal Justice: A Question of Color*. Bloomington: Indiana University Press.

Martinez, Elizabeth. 1993. "Beyond Black/White: The Racisms of Our Time." *Social Justice* 20:22–34.

McDonald, Douglas C., and Kenneth E. Carlson. 1993. *Sentencing in the Federal Courts: Does Race Matter?* Washington, D.C.: U.S. Department of Justice.

Melossi, Dario. 1990. *The State of Social Control: A Sociological Study of Concepts of State and Social Control in the Making of Democracy*. Cambridge: Polity.

Melossi, Dario, and Massimo Pavarini. 1981. *The Prison and the Factory: Origins of the Penitentiary System*. Totowa, N.J.: Barnes & Noble Books.

Meneses, Eloise Hiebert. 1994. "Race and Ethnicity: An Anthropological Perspective." *Race, Sex and Class* 1(2):137–46.

Messerschmidt, James W. 1993. *Masculinities and Crime*. Lanham, Md.: Rowman & Littlefield.

Messinger, Sheldon, and Phillip Johnson. 1978. "California's Determinate Sentencing Laws." In *Determinate Sentencing: Reform or Regression*, edited by National Institute of Justice. Washington, D.C.: U.S. Government Printing Office.

Miethe, Terance D., and Charles A. Moore. 1985. "Socioeconomic Disparities under Determinate Sentencing Systems: A Comparison of Preguideline and Postguideline Practices in Minnesota." *Criminology* 23:337–63.

Moulds, Elizabeth. 1980. "Chivalry and Paternalism: Disparities of Treatment in the Criminal Justice System." *Western Political Quarterly* 31:416–30.

Myers, Martha. 1994. "The Courts: Prosecution and Sentencing." In *Criminology*, 2d ed., edited by Joseph F. Sheley. Belmont, Calif.: Wadsworth.

Myers, Samuel L., Jr. 1993. "Racial Disparities in Sentencing: Can Sentencing Reforms Reduce Discrimination in Punishment?" *University of Colorado Law Review* 64:781–808.

Nagel, Ilene, and John Hagan. 1983. "Gender and Crime: Offense Patterns and Criminal Court Sanctions." In *Crime and Justice: An Annual Review of Research*, vol. 4, edited by Michael Tonry and Norval Morris. Chicago: University of Chicago Press.

Nagel, Ilene H., and Barry L. Johnson. 1994. "The Role of Gender in a Structured Sentencing System: Equal Treatment, Policy Choices, and the Sentencing of Female Offenders under the United States Sentencing Guidelines." *Journal of Criminal Law and Criminology* 85(1):181–221.

Nagel, Stuart, and Lenore Weitzman. 1971. "Women as Litigants." *Hastings Law Journal* 23:171–81.

Nardulli, Peter F., James Eisenstein, and Roy B. Flemming. 1988. *The Tenor of Justice*. Urbana: University of Illinois Press.

Omi, Michael, and Howard Winant. 1994. *Racial Formation in the United States.* 2d ed. New York: Routledge.

Parent, Dale. 1988. *Structuring Sentencing Discretion: The Evolution of Minnesota's Sentencing Guidelines.* Stoneham, Mass.: Butterworth.

Parisi, Nicolette. 1982. "Are Females Treated Differently? A Review of the Theories and Evidence on Sentencing and Parole Decisions." In *Judge, Lawyer, Victim, Thief,* edited by Nicole Hahn Rafter and Elizabeth Anne Stanko. Boston: Northeastern University Press.

Peller, Gary. 1993. "Criminal Law, Race, and the Ideology of Bias: Transcending the Critical Tools of the Sixties." *Tulane Law Review* 67:2231–52.

Polk, Kenneth, and D. Ranson. 1991. "Patterns of Homicide in Victoria." In *Australian Violence: Contemporary Perspectives,* edited by Duncan Chappell, Peter Grabosky, and Heather Strang. Canberra: Australian Institute of Criminology.

Pollak, Otto. 1950. *The Criminality of Women.* Philadelphia: University of Pennsylvania Press.

Quinney, Richard. 1974. *Critique of Legal Order: Crime Control in Capitalist Society.* Boston: Little, Brown.

Raeder, Myrna. 1993. "Gender and Sentencing: Single Moms, Battered Women, and Other Sex-Based Anomalies in the Gender Free World of the Federal Sentencing Guidelines." *Pepperdine Law Review* 20(3):905–90.

Reiner, Robert. 1993. "Race, Crime and Justice: Models of Interpretation." In *Minority Ethnic Groups in the Criminal Justice System,* edited by Loraine R. Gelsthorpe. Cropwood Conference Series no. 21. Cambridge: Institute of Criminology.

Rhode, Deborah. 1987. "Justice, Gender, and the Justices." In *Women, The Courts, and Equality,* edited by Laura L. Crites and Winifred L. Hepperle. Newbury Park, Calif.: Sage.

Rice, Marcia. 1990. "Challenging Orthodoxies in Feminist Theory: A Black Feminist Critique." In *Feminist Perspectives in Criminology,* edited by Loraine Gelsthorpe and Allison Morris. Philadelphia: Open University Press.

Roberts, Dorothy E. 1991. "Punishing Drug Addicts Who Have Babies: Women of Color, Equality, and the Right of Privacy." *Harvard Law Review* 104:1419–82.

Roediger, David R. 1991. *The Wages of Whiteness: Race and the Making of the American Working Class.* London: Verso.

Schur, Edwin. 1971. *Labeling Deviant Behavior.* New York: Harper & Row.

Simon, Rita. 1975. *Women and Crime.* Lexington Mass.: Lexington Books.

Simpson, Sally S. 1991. "Caste, Class, and Violent Crime: Explaining Difference in Female Offending." *Criminology* 29:115–35.

Smart, Carol. 1989. *Feminism and the Power of Law.* New York: Routledge.

———. 1992. "The Woman of Legal Discourse." *Social and Legal Studies* 1: 29–44.

Smith, David J. 1994. "Race, Crime, and Criminal Justice." In *The Oxford Handbook of Criminology,* edited by Mike Maguire, Rod Morgan, and Robert Reiner. Oxford: Clarendon Press.

Smith, Douglas A., Christy Visher, and Laura Davidson. 1984. "Equity and Discretionary Justice: The Influence of Race on Police Arrest Decisions." *Journal of Criminal Law and Criminology* 75:234–49.

Spohn, Cassia. 1994. "Race and Social Control." In *Inequality, Crime, and Social Control,* edited by George Bridges and Martha Myers. Boulder, Colo.: Westview.

Spohn, Cassia, Susan Welch, and John Gruhl. 1985. "Women Defendants in Court: The Interaction between Sex and Race in Convicting and Sentencing." *Social Science Quarterly* 66:178–85.

Steffensmeier, Darrell J. 1980. "Assessing the Impact of the Women's Movement on Sex-Based Differences in the Handling of Adult Criminal Defendants." *Crime and Delinquency* 26(3):344–57.

———. 1993. "National Trends in Female Arrests, 1960–1990: Assessment and Recommendations for Research." *Journal of Quantitative Criminology* 9(4):411–41.

———. 1995. "Trends in Female Crime: It's Still a Man's World." In *The Criminal Justice System and Women,* 2d ed., edited by Barbara Raffel Price and Natalie J. Sokoloff. New York: McGraw-Hill.

Steffensmeier, Darrell, Emilie Allan, and Cathy Streifel. 1989. "Modernization and Female Crime: A Cross-National Test of Alternative Explanations." *Social Forces* 68:262–83.

Steffensmeier, Darrell, John Kramer, and Cathy Streifel. 1993. "Gender and Imprisonment Decisions." *Criminology* 31(3):411–46.

Takaki, Ronald. 1993. *A Different Mirror: A History of Multicultural America.* Boston: Little, Brown.

Tonry, Michael. 1995. *Malign Neglect—Race, Crime, and Punishment in America.* New York: Oxford.

Tonry, Michael, and Kathleen Hatlestad. 1997. *Sentencing Reform in Overcrowded Times—a Comparative Perspective.* New York: Oxford University Press.

U.S. Department of Commerce. 1996. *Statistical Abstract of the United States—1996.* Washington, D.C.: U.S. Government Printing Office.

Visher, Christy. 1983. "Gender, Police Arrest Decisions, and Notions of Chivalry." *Criminology* 21:5–28.

Vogel, Lise. 1993. *Mothers at Work: Maternity Policy in the U.S. Workplace.* New Brunswick, N.J.: Rutgers University Press.

Wheeler, Stanton, Kenneth Mann, and Austin Sarat. 1988. *Sitting in Judgment.* New Haven, Conn.: Yale University Press.

Wilbanks, William. 1987. *The Myth of a Racist Criminal Justice System.* Pacific Grove, Calif.: Brooks/Cole.

Wilson, James Q. 1990. "Drugs and Crime." In *Drugs and Crime,* edited by Michael Tonry and James Q. Wilson. Vol. 13 of *Crime and Justice: A Review of Research,* edited by Michael Tonry and Norval Morris. Chicago: University of Chicago Press.

Young, Vernetta. 1980. "Women, Race and Crime." *Criminology* 18:26–34.

Zatz, Marjorie S. 1984. "Race, Ethnicity, and Determinate Sentencing: A New Dimension to an Old Controversy." *Criminology* 22(2):147–71.

———. 1985. "Pleas, Priors and Prison: Racial/Ethnic Differences in Sentencing." *Social Science Research* 14:169–93.

———. 1987. "The Changing Forms of Racial/Ethnic Biases in Sentencing." *Journal of Research in Crime and Delinquency* 24(1):69–92.

Mark H. Moore and Stewart Wakeling

Juvenile Justice: Shoring Up the Foundations

ABSTRACT

America's juvenile justice system is besieged by critics from both ends of the political spectrum—from the Left for its intrusiveness, its unfairness, and its failure to provide needed services and from the Right for its failure to hold offenders accountable and to protect society. The juvenile courts' traditional *parens patriae* premise has been undermined, and the courts' credibility has declined. Its likeliest successors are abolition or "criminalization" of the juvenile court or its subsumption into family courts with broad mandates. The latter is the more promising, perhaps reconceptualized as courts for "bankrupt families," which encompass juvenile crime as merely one of their major subjects.

The signs are everywhere that the mandate for the nation's juvenile courts and juvenile justice systems has been badly eroded. Repeated attacks from all sides of the political spectrum have done the job. The Left has criticized the juvenile court for intruding into matters beyond its proper domain (Krisberg and Austin 1993), for abusing the rights of those who come before it (Feld 1993*a*), and for failing to provide the kind of services that could be counted on to deflect children from future criminal careers (Schwartz 1989). The Right has attacked the court's unwillingness to hold young offenders accountable for their crimes and its failure to make dispositions that could protect the com-

Mark H. Moore is Daniel and Florence V. Guggenheim Professor of Criminal Justice Policy and Management at the John F. Kennedy School of Government, Harvard University. Stewart Wakeling is senior program associate in the Program in Criminal Justice Policy and Management at the John F. Kennedy School of Government, Harvard University.

0192-3234/97/0022-0007$02.00

munity from youthful predators in the short as well as the long run (Springer 1986; DiIulio 1995).

These attacks have undermined both political and legal support for the current system. In the political system, ordinary citizens grumble, the media fulminate, policy elites argue among themselves, and legislators propose new legislation to reform the court (Butterfield 1996). Within the legal system, higher courts find reasons to interfere with and transform the operations of the juvenile court (Feld 1993*a*). The net result has been a dramatic shrinkage in the size of the court's discretion and jurisdiction—sure signs of an institution headed toward bankruptcy (Snyder and Sickmund 1995; Butterfield 1996).

To stand tall and cast a long shadow, public enterprises need strong foundations. But public enterprises in democracies are not rooted in earth and concrete. They are, instead, founded on the shifting sands of public aspirations. Their survival, their standing, and ultimately, their effectiveness depend on steady, enthusiastic support for what they do. This, in turn, is built on shared understandings and commitments to the purposes the public enterprises are meant to serve and the particular means considered appropriate and effective in serving their ends. In short, the foundations of public enterprises lie in their mandates for action (M. Moore 1990, 1995).

Not all mandates are equally valuable in guiding and sustaining public enterprises. Some are durable, widely supported, coherent, precise, easy to implement, and focus the institution on important, contemporary problems. These provide a firm, valuable foundation. Others are fickle, hotly debated, inconsistent, hard to operationalize, or increasingly irrelevant (Hargrove and Glidewell 1990). These do less well in legitimating and guiding public enterprises. Thus to build a strong public enterprise, one must do the political work required to forge a strong mandate for action. This is partly a matter of advocacy—of trying to build support for a particular public enterprise through education and persuasion. But it sometimes means responding and adapting to powerful currents that are running in the society (M. Moore 1995).

At any given moment, mandates for action can be found in important formal documents: in the statutes that establish a public enterprise, in the court decisions that qualify and adapt the statutes in response to particular cases, in the policies promulgated by those who oversee or manage the enterprise, in the standard operating procedures that govern day-to-day operations of the system. Such structures give a consistent, recognizable shape to the enterprise and prevent it from changing too rapidly or departing too far from its original purpose.

But other factors operate less formally and more dynamically to shape the future of the effort. After all, public discussion about the enterprise does not stop when the enabling legislation is passed; it continues. Problems with the ways in which the existing institution operates become the focus of political criticism. New methods for achieving old goals are proposed and implemented. And new problems, more or less central to the original purposes of the enterprise, come to the fore. The ongoing policy discussion about the operational weaknesses, desirable innovations, and new problems not only animate the present but also threaten to transform the formal structures relied on to constitute and control the enterprise in the future. Thus in seeking to interpret an enterprise's existing or emergent mandate for action, these dynamic factors, too, must be considered. These observations seem fundamental to any serious, contemporary analysis of the nation's juvenile court and juvenile justice system.

The question for this essay is whether a new, widely supported mandate for the juvenile court and juvenile justice system can be generated, and if so, for what purposes? The method will be first to clear away some preliminary matters having to do with defining the body of law that is to be administered through the juvenile court, the institutions that lie within the domain of the juvenile justice system, and the important social problems the juvenile court and juvenile justice system are supposed to solve. Then, we examine the mandate for the juvenile justice system as it has developed both historically and cross-sectionally across the states and consider the contemporary and future problems that the juvenile justice system must face if it is to be valuable to society. Two broadly different paths for the development of the juvenile court and the juvenile justice system are sketched and roughly evaluated. One, pushed by a public focus on juvenile crime, follows the path toward a "criminalized" juvenile court. The other, animated by heightened public concerns about "family values," works toward a broader conception of a "family court." This article closes with reflections on the kinds of investments that would be needed in the system's operational capacities if it were to fulfill either of these plausibly valuable future mandates.

I. Defining the Boundaries of Juvenile Justice

To fix conceptions, it is useful to start with a definition of the particular social institutions included within the "juvenile justice system" and to describe the kinds of problems those institutions are expected to handle. This exercise is not just a technical problem of definition; it goes to the heart of what the enterprise of juvenile justice is expected to be. Yet this important strategic problem presents itself first as a technical, definitional problem.

A. *What Institutions Constitute the Juvenile Justice System?*

At the center of the juvenile justice system is the juvenile or family court. Typically, the juvenile or family court is a specialized unit within a larger state court system (Rubin and Flango 1992; Page 1993). The need for such a court is established in the first instance by the existence of a body of law (both statutory and common) that gives the state jurisdiction over certain matters involving families and juveniles such as abuse and neglect of children, so-called status offenses such as truancy and incorrigibility, and the crimes committed by youthful offenders (Areen 1978; Humm et al. 1994; Mnookin and Weisberg 1995). The particular form that a juvenile or family court takes is determined in the second instance by a legislative or administrative decision about how best to organize the work of a state court system (Katz and Kuhn 1991; Rubin and Flango 1992; Page 1993).

1. *The Jurisdiction of the Juvenile Court.* Appendix A sets out a list of the kinds of legal matters that can come before a state court and that represent candidate elements of the jurisdiction of a juvenile or family court. Typically, jurisdiction over these matters is distributed across probate courts, family courts, and juvenile courts by administrative decisions made by state court systems according to their judgments about what particular organizational arrangement could be expected to produce both substantive justice and administrative efficiency in court operations.

The fact that the juvenile or family court is constituted from the wide body of law regulating families and children carved up among courts to achieve the administrative purposes of the court raises the first and most interesting question about the definition of the juvenile justice system: namely, should we think of the entire body of law that regulates the behavior of families and children as part of the juvenile justice system or only that part that is explicitly given over to the institution that states define as the juvenile court? And, if a state has both a juvenile and family court (as well as perhaps a probate court), should we include all these courts in our definition of the juvenile justice system, or only one or two, and if so, which ones?

This question is important for the obvious reason that the laws, and the administrative decisions to assign certain kinds of cases to certain kinds of courts, define the immediate boundaries of the work of the juvenile justice system. But it is also important for the less obvious reason that the reach of the juvenile justice system into social life, the kinds of dispositions it might make, and the kinds of expertise it might require to make just and efficacious decisions differ considerably depending on what particular laws we decide to administer through the juvenile justice system. It is one thing to imagine that the only laws being administered are those governing the state's responses to crimes committed by young offenders, but quite another to imagine that the juvenile justice system includes laws regulating divorce, child custody, responsibility for orphans, child abuse and neglect, and domestic violence among adults who are responsible for children.

2. *Functional Operations: Nomination, Adjudication, and Disposition.* As a practical matter, of course, the wide array of possible jurisdictions has been narrowed to a smaller number of possible choices. Most states have opted for a court organization that divides this wide jurisdiction into either a probate court (dealing with matters of divorce, child custody, and the like) or a juvenile court (dealing with offenses committed by young offenders, status offenses, and some kinds of abuse and neglect) or a family court (dealing with the same matters as the juvenile court plus selected other matters involving family relations such as divorce, child custody, etc.) (Katz and Kuhn 1991; Rubin and Flango 1992; Page 1993).

Even this limited amount of variation is enough to present problems, however. Once one begins thinking about the institutions that determine what cases get brought into the juvenile justice system, and what institutions are involved in the dispositions made by the juvenile justice system, even the relatively limited variation still produces very different conceptions of the boundaries of the juvenile justice system.

Consider, for example, the institutions that are potentially important in *identifying or "nominating" cases* for consideration by the juvenile justice system (M. Moore et al. 1987). In the case of a "juvenile court system" with its predominant orientation to crimes committed by or against children, attention is drawn naturally toward the police (and those who mobilize the police) as the most important intake mechanism. In the case of a "family court," with its predominant orientation to intrafamily relationships, attention is turned away from the police toward individual family members who might themselves bring matters before the court.

Consider also the institutions that would be important in *the dispositions of the cases* made by the court. In the case of the "juvenile court system," attention is naturally drawn to the institutions and programs managed by the state's juvenile correctional agency. In the case of a "family court system," attention is more likely to be focused on the court's decisions about how relationships within the family are to be constituted in the future and the array of social services that is to be provided to families to allow them to function more effectively.

Finally, at the edges of the system, consider the institutions that might be considered important in *preventing the circumstances and events that bring cases into the juvenile justice system.* In the case of the "juvenile court system," the focus might be on institutions such as families, schools, and recreational and employment opportunities for young people as important in preventing delinquency. In the case of the "family court system," the focus might be on one of these key institutions for preventing delinquency explicitly and how it might be made to function more effectively by the provision of such things as jobs for adults, health and welfare benefits, parental training, and day care for children.

So what particular body of law is being administered through the juvenile justice system has important implications for what particular institutions are importantly engaged in its operations. One way to visualize the complexity of the system is to start with the idea that the laws define certain "matters" (i.e., events or circumstances) that involve the responsibilities of families and children toward one another and toward the wider society that may legally become the focus of public state action (Minow 1987). The whole set of such events and circumstances that occur in the world constitutes the potential jurisdiction of the juvenile justice system. (We understand that we are drawing a wide boundary here.)

Of course, only some portion of all the real events and circumstances that could, in principle, become part of the juvenile justice system will actually do so. The institutions that determine which potential cases become cases in the juvenile justice system could be thought of as part of the "nominating" and "gatekeeping" subsystem. Included here would be not only the police who decide whether and how to respond to juvenile offenses but also social service agencies that must decide whether to report instances of abuse and neglect, even parents who must decide whether to ask for court assistance in controlling a rebellious teenager (M. Moore et al. 1987).

Those potential cases that are plucked out of ordinary social life and become part of a legal proceeding would then be subject to the "court processing" part of the system. Court processing would include the development of relevant facts and analyses for the court to use in its consideration of the case. It would also include appearances before the court of those who were considered parties to the case. And, it would include a disposition of the case that directed different parties to do different things. The quality of this court processing could be judged against standards of justice and fairness, on the one hand, and efficiency and effectiveness in achieving particular purposes, on the other.

The dispositions made by the court would then be carried out (more or less reliably) by those who were directed to do something. Many (but by no means all) of these dispositions would be carried out by youth corrections agencies. Many others (but by no means all) would be implemented by state-financed social service agencies. Some would be carried out simply by the parents, children, and other private caretakers who came before the court to have their cases heard and left with a new understanding of their rights and responsibilities toward one another.

To the extent activities and agencies designed to *prevent* juvenile delinquency or family dysfunction were considered part of the juvenile justice system, important parts of the juvenile justice system could include the voluntary efforts of parents, children, and neighbors on one hand and the tax-financed services of government social service, educational, and recreational agencies on the other (DeJong 1994; National Crime Prevention Council 1994). Figure 1 offers a crude graphic idea of the broad conception of the juvenile justice system (M. Moore et al. 1987). This is proposed as an alternative to the usual conception of the juvenile justice system as a "case flow management system." In the conception presented here, the laws governing families and children set the context for public action to deal with problems of family and children. The courts that enforce these laws are seen as "linebackers" or "backstops" to the ordinary operations of the private, informal institutions and the formal public agencies that shape the daily conditions under which children are being raised. The private, helping institutions are grouped on the left of the diagram. The public, obliging

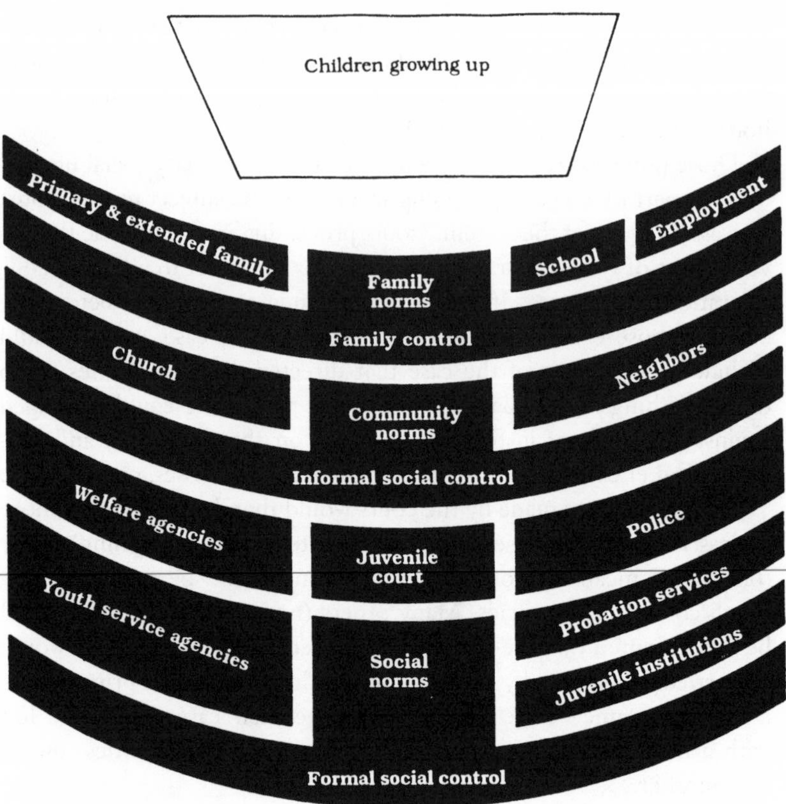

FIG. 1.—The court as backstop and linebacker: an alternative view of the juvenile justice system. Source: M. Moore et al. (1987).

institutions are grouped on the right. The institutions that are in regular daily contact with the children (such as parents, day care, schools) are placed in the front of the process of raising children. The institutions that are only occasionally and intermittently engaged with specific children (such as neighbors, police) are placed further back as the "linebackers" to deal with events and circumstances that breach the capacities of the front line agencies to handle them.

In this diagram, the process of nominating cases involves taking a case from the front line and requesting aid from the back lines. Often the response of the back line is simply to push the case back into the front lines without further action. Other times, it is to push the case back into the front lines with specific orders that particular agencies on the front line take particular actions. On rare occasions, it is to remove the child to the care of youth correctional agencies.

This, of course, represents the broadest definition of the institutions of the juvenile justice system—so broad, in fact, that the boundary between juvenile justice and all of society has begun to blur. Of course, the institutions of the juvenile justice system can be defined far more narrowly. Yet what is surprising is the extent to which the combination of existing laws regulating families and children, concern for the processes by which some of the legally liable cases show up as real cases before the court, recognition that many of the most important dispositions made by the courts engage private and public social service agencies, and curiosity about the prospects for preventing juvenile delinquency and family dysfunction forces an analyst to widen the boundaries of the juvenile justice system. Perhaps more focus can be gained if attention is turned away from the institutions that constitute the juvenile justice system and toward the problems society is trying to solve through the operations of the juvenile justice system.

B. *To What Problems Is the Juvenile Justice System an Answer?*

Most citizens view the juvenile and family court as an institution designed primarily to deal with crimes committed by young offenders. This is not surprising. Juvenile crimes are by far the largest part of the juvenile and family court's caseload (Snyder and Sickmund 1995). It is also the portion of the court's caseload that is most salient to the public and most unambiguously a public issue. For both reasons, most citizens tend to view the juvenile court as a specially designed criminal court to deal with young offenders. They also tend to evaluate it in these terms. This is unfortunate, for in most states, juvenile and family courts include two other important jurisdictions: abuse and neglect of children, and status offenses (Katz and Kuhn 1991; Rubin and Flango 1992; Page 1993). Each of these represents a somewhat different problem that society looks to the juvenile and family court to solve.

1. *Juvenile Crime.* The juvenile and family court is most commonly associated in the public mind with responding to juvenile crime and youthful offenders. The public understands that this is the most important jurisdiction of the court. They want a just and effective response to such crime. And, to some degree, they recognize that society's response to juvenile crimes should be different from the response to adult crime (Schwartz, Guo, and Krebs 1992). What seems to have

been lost, however, is the rationale for treating young offenders differently than adult offenders.

The distinction between adult and juvenile offenders has long existed in the law. Under the English common law, children under the age of seven could not be found guilty of crimes because they were considered incapable of forming the requisite criminal intent (Radzinowicz and Hood 1986). They were, in some sense, constitutionally innocent (despite their ability to inflict harm). But the notion that young offenders differed from adult offenders was significantly expanded in the statutes that established juvenile and family courts, gave them jurisdiction over crimes committed by young offenders, and transformed what had previously been viewed as "crimes" into instances of "delinquency" (M. Moore et al. 1987).

Both the original reason for distinguishing adults from children and the more recent extension of this idea are based on the idea that children differ from adults in ways that are relevant to the just and effective response to crimes committed by them. The most important way in which children differ from adults is that they are "in the process of becoming adults" rather than fully developed—a state that Zimring (1982) has described as "semiautonomous." Their moral characters are not fully developed. They remain vulnerable to external influences from peers. Their conduct is still being regulated to some extent by adults who are responsible for them. For all these reasons, their actions are not fully theirs and do not reliably reflect their intentions or character.

This view has important implications for a just and effective social response to crimes they commit. Because they are not fully developed as moral agents, it would be *unjust* to hold them strictly accountable for criminal offending. They are only partially responsible. Because they are still malleable, it might be *practically useful* to make investments in their future development rather than to consign them to the ranks of the unredeemable. Indeed, to the extent that they have been victims of private and social neglect in the past, they may even have some moral if not legal right to demand that society provide for them the kind of care, supervision, and instruction that is necessary to help them reach the status of competent adulthood (American Bar Association 1993; Carnegie Task Force on Meeting the Needs of Young Children 1994). Thus, for reasons of both justice and practical efficacy, the argument is that society should treat youthful offenders as "delinquents" rather than young "criminals." It follows that one important task of the juvenile court is to fashion the appropriately different response to juvenile offenses and young criminal offenders; the response that would be more just (in the sense that it accommodated their partial guilt) and more effective (in the sense that it exploited their malleability to minimize the chance that they would become repeat offenders).

It is worth noting that the conception of what constitutes a just and effective response to youthful offenders seems to be changing. The changes began with criticisms focused on the ways in which the court processed juvenile offenses. In *In re Gault*, 387 U.S. 1 (1967), the Supreme Court ruled that, if young offenders faced dispositions of their cases in the juvenile court that could not be reliably distinguished from simple incarceration, as a constitutional matter they were entitled to the same due process protections that adults charged with crimes in the adult courts enjoyed. This began the process of what Feld (1993*b*) has described as the "criminalization" of the juvenile court.

More recently, society seems to be less inclined to extend the presumption of a kind of innocence to young offenders that the original conception of the juvenile court seemed to mandate. By reducing the age of jurisdiction of the court, and by developing automatic or discretionary mechanisms for transferring juvenile cases to the adult courts, society is saying that it sees in many juvenile offenders the same kind of moral culpability, and the same kind of social interest in exercising effective control over the offenders, as apply to adult offenders (Feld 1988). And, insofar as society supports dispositions such as youthful "boot camps" that are long on mechanisms of accountability and control and short on the educational and counseling services that could build dispositions and capabilities for citizenship, it seems that Americans are abandoning the original idea of making a different kind of response to young offenders in the interests of both justice and efficacy (Cronin 1994).

In any case, responding justly and effectively to crimes committed by young offenders remains one of the most important problems to which society expects the juvenile justice system to respond. To the extent that its response departs from contemporary views about what constitutes a just and effective response to these crimes, the legitimacy of the court is undermined. And it is probably the court's seeming inability to accomplish this goal, combined with growing fears of youth violence, that has most undermined its current standing (Bragg 1994; DiIulio 1995).

2. *Abuse and Neglect of Children.* Despite the importance and salience of the court's jurisdiction over crimes committed by youthful offenders, this remains but one of the problems society relies on the court to resolve. In many states, the juvenile or family court also has jurisdiction over cases involving the abuse and neglect of children (Katz and Kuhn 1991; Rubin and Flango 1992; Page 1993). Viewed from one perspective (the one that views the juvenile court primarily as a specially designed criminal court to deal with crimes committed by children), the inclusion of child abuse and neglect within the purview of the juvenile court seems odd, even anomalous. After all, these are crimes committed by adults *against* children, not crimes committed *by* children. As crimes committed by adults, why not treat them in the context of the adult criminal court? Does it not demean the significance of these cases as adult offenses to keep them in the juvenile court?

The reason that these cases are often heard in juvenile and family courts rather than adult criminal courts, of course, is that the state has a concern about the present and future conditions under which children will be raised as well as an interest in adjudicating the guilt or innocence of adult offenders. That concern seems more consistent with the procedures and capabilities of the juvenile or family court than with those of the adult court. The future of the child will always be close to the center of the juvenile court's concerns. It has the license to investigate the totality of circumstances surrounding the instances of abuse and neglect, not just the question of guilt and innocence. And most important, the juvenile court can face the trade-off between the state's interest in criminal prosecution of the caretakers accused of abuse and neglect *and* the creation of an effective nexus of care and supervision around the juvenile victims. In short, because the state is concerned with family relations and the future of the child as well as with criminal dispositions in cases of abuse and neglect, it makes sense to handle these cases in courts that are competent to deal with these concerns.

3. *Status Offenses and "Children in Need of Supervision."* In many states, juvenile and family courts also retain a third jurisdiction: one that covers so-called status offenses such as truancy, incorrigibility, and promiscuity. This jurisdiction has also long seemed anomalous to those who viewed the juvenile or family court as essentially a specially designed criminal court to deal with crimes committed by children (Andrews and Cohn 1974). The reason is that, while it is true that this

jurisdiction focuses on acts committed *by* children (rather than by adults against children as in the case of abuse and neglect), the particular acts that are the focus of the court's concern seem to be better described as ongoing statuses than acts and, further, that neither the acts nor the statuses would be viewed as crimes if adults committed them.

To many commentators, the fact that youth faced court intervention in such circumstances revealed an unjust discrimination against children: they faced legal liabilities that did not attach to adults (Feld 1993*a;* Krisberg and Austin 1993). This seemed discriminatory on its face. Add to that the observation that the legal liability attached to vaguely described statuses rather than specifically described acts and the stage was set for a vigorous attack on the propriety of this particular jurisdiction.

These criticisms were powerful enough in some jurisdictions to eliminate the court's jurisdiction over these matters. In many other states, however, the cases were simply renamed. Instead of thinking about these as cases of "delinquency" that attached guilt and stigma to children, they were viewed as "child in need of supervision" cases in which any notion of child misconduct was downplayed, and the focus was placed instead on what could be done to improve the circumstances under which the child was being raised (Feld 1993*a;* Krisberg and Austin 1993).

It is important to consider why these cases remain within the jurisdiction of the juvenile court given that they do not describe crimes committed by children. One answer is simply that there are many children whose parents cannot or will not exercise effective control over, or provide sufficient care to, their children. The result is that children do things that are less than crimes but are nonetheless somewhat offensive to society. More important, these same acts are dangerous to the child's future as a resourceful citizen. Thus, legal authority and state courts are brought into play to help society find a just and effective response to these unfortunate circumstances. Despite the wish to keep these cases out of the courts, some keep appearing because society demands that the court act to assign responsibility for the care of the child.

There is an important question about both the justice and efficacy of the court's responses in these cases. It often seems unjust for the court to take legal action in cases where children have done nothing that would be considered a crime if an adult committed the offense. But one way to rationalize this jurisdiction is to take seriously the notion that children *do* occupy a different legal status than adults. One feature of that unique legal status is the privilege of reduced liability for criminal offenses. That is an implication of treating crimes as delinquency rather than criminal offenses. Another feature of their status, however, is that, as children, they have some special responsibilities that do not attach to adults. This is the flip side of their special privileges. Arguably, some of those special responsibilities would be to avoid actions that could jeopardize the process of becoming responsible adults. That could, in turn, mean that they would be responsible for continuing to accept the supervision and instruction of their parents (incorrigibility), and for going to school (truancy), and for avoiding fatherhood and pregnancies (promiscuity). Thus it might be just for children to have special responsibilities as well as special privileges as a feature of their unique legal status in society.

Whether the court can make an effective response to these circumstances is less clear. It may be that court interventions that take the form of requiring children to recognize these special responsibilities are ineffective. The court's response may be equally ineffective when it requires parents and caretakers to exercise more effective supervision over the children. Perhaps the capacity of the court effectively to oblige parents and children to take action in support of the development of the child is weak or counterproductive. This might be particularly true when the problem is that the parents and caretakers need help in discharging their responsibilities (rather than simply being reminded of what their responsibilities are) and where public resources or capabilities to provide needed assistance are inadequate. In short, the effectiveness of such interventions may depend crucially on the supply of services to struggling families as well as on the court's power to impose obligations. In any case, these problems remain a part of the court's jurisdiction.

C. *Toward a Coherent Theory of the Juvenile Court's Jurisdiction*

This discussion suggests that, in thinking about a proper and useful mandate for the juvenile and family court, everything would be much easier if it were thought of primarily, or even exclusively, as a specially designed criminal court to deal with youthful offenders—one in which the responses to young offenders could be tailored to the fact that they were less morally culpable and better able to change than adult offenders. There is a simplicity and coherence to this idea that is easy to comprehend. It has the additional virtue of focusing attention on the jurisdiction of the court that is most salient and most obviously public.

The situation becomes far more complicated, however, when society looks to the court to respond also to problems such as abuse and neglect and status offenses. Abuse and neglect seem anomalous because they are crimes committed *against* rather than *by* children. Status offenses seem anomalous because they describe acts that are not crimes if committed by adults.

Yet, despite the anomalous status of these events in the conception of the juvenile court as a special criminal court to deal with crimes committed by children, they generally remain part of the court's jurisdiction. Indeed, if anything, these cases are becoming more important as families and other structures for supervising and caring for children erode, and there is increasing interest in finding ways to prevent as well as respond to juvenile criminal offending. Thus, in constructing a coherent mandate for the court, it becomes important to consider whether some concept can be developed that embraces these apparently diverse problems.

There is such a conception. It views the juvenile and family court less as a *criminal* court specially designed to deal with the problems of crimes committed by children and more as a *civil* court overseeing the conditions under which children are being raised. If the court were seen in this light, it would make perfect sense for the court to have jurisdiction over abuse and neglect and status offenses since these are obviously and importantly about constructing arrangements that can provide minimal levels of care and supervision over children. Thus, these apparently anomalous jurisdictions could be rationalized.

Even more important, however, adopting this perspective could importantly transform and rationalize current responses to *juvenile crime*. If a special court is needed to respond to crimes committed by juveniles because children are viewed as less able to form criminal intent and more able to profit from efforts made to deflect them from a future life of crime, and if an important part of the apparatus for accomplishing these results includes parents and other caretakers who were supposed to be providing effective care and supervision of the children who have emerged as criminal offenders, then it makes sense to respond to crimes committed by young offenders as events that were importantly influenced by the conditions under which children were being raised as well as by the criminal inclinations of the young offender. Delinquency cases would be viewed in the context of the same questions about the adequacy of the arrangements for raising children that are raised by cases of abuse and neglect as well as status offenses. In each case, parents and caretakers would be parties to the proceedings. In each case, the concern would be less about specific events and whether particular individuals had or had not committed criminal acts than about the conditions under which children were being raised.

In short, if the juvenile or family court were seen as a civil court overseeing the conditions under which children were being reared rather than as a criminal court responding to young offenders, each component of its current jurisdiction could be understood and rationalized as part of a coherent whole. If, however, influenced by the importance and salience of the court's jurisdiction over juvenile crime, the court were seen as a special agency to deal with crimes committed by children, the rationale for having it also deal with abuse and neglect and status offenses is lost. Of course, there is nothing that says that these other problems could not be included within the court's jurisdiction opportunistically or because they did not fit anywhere else. But the court's foundations might be made stronger if there were a consistent and coherent rationale for all its work. Whether this would be a valuable and feasible mandate for the court is yet to be tested.

II. The Evolving Mandate for Juvenile Justice

In Section I, we noted some of the difficulties in deciding what institutions should be considered part of the juvenile justice system and in constructing a coherent rationale for the different kinds of problems society relies on those institutions to solve. We noted that viewing the juvenile justice system as consisting primarily of a court designed to respond to juvenile crime, and doing so through a set of dispositions managed by some kind of youth correctional system, had the advantage of being consistent with our images of the adult criminal justice system. However, it also had disadvantages: failing to account for all the institutions that could be considered part of the juvenile justice system, leaving as anomalous some important parts of the juvenile court's jurisdiction, and leaving potentially important opportunities for crime prevention unexploited. This discussion suggested the range of possibilities for a different but equally coherent mandate for action. In this section, we ask two more concrete, empirical questions: how have states acted over the last few decades to adapt the mandate of the juvenile and family court, and which of the problems to which the court could conceivably respond are becoming increasingly urgent?

A. Trends in Legislation Affecting the Juvenile Justice System

A straightforward way to examine the evolving mandate for juvenile justice is to look closely at the statutes that authorize the enterprise. Since 70 percent of the statutes seem to be modeled on the original 1899 Illinois statutes, it is useful to begin there (Bleich 1986).

1. *The Original Legislative Mandate.* The key provisions of this statute include the following:

> Section 1: . . . For the purposes of this act, the words "dependent child" and "neglected child" shall mean any child who for any reason is destitute or homeless or abandoned; or dependent upon the public for support; or has not proper parental care or guardianship; . . . or whose home by reason of neglect, cruelty or depravity on the part of its parents, guardians or other person in whose care it may be, is an unfit place for such a child. . . . The words "delinquent child" shall include any child under the age of 16 years who violates any law of this state, or any city or village ordinance. . . .
>
> Section 7: . . . When any child under the age of 16 years shall be found to be dependent or neglected within the meaning of this act, the court may make an order committing the child to the care of some suitable State institution, or to the care of some reputable citizen of good moral character, or the care of some training school . . . , or to the care of some association willing to receive it.

The focus of this statute on the conditions under which children were being raised, treating crimes by children as instances of delinquency and removing children from dangerous home environments, established the basic conception of the *parens patriae* model of the juvenile court. This conception proved widely popular; within twelve years, twenty-five states had copied it. By 1925, its overall philosophy and specific provisions could be found in forty-eight of the fifty states (Krisberg and Austin 1993, p. 30).

2. *Criticisms of the* Parens Patriae *Court.* The initial, nearly universal enthusiasm for this conception of the juvenile court has not, unfortunately, stood the test of time. Criticisms from both the Left and the Right of the political spectrum about both the justice and effectiveness of the court have eroded this mandate.

The political Left attacks the fairness of the court by pointing to its overly broad and ambiguous jurisdiction, its cavalier approach to the due process rights of those who appear before it, and its apparently discriminatory practices (Schwartz 1989; Feld 1993*a;* Krisberg and Austin 1993). It attacks the effectiveness of the court by claiming that premature court involvement "labels" youth, thereby hardening their identification with deviant subcultures and harming their prospects for successful development (Schwartz and Skolnick 1964; Schur 1971). Finally, the Left attacks the hypocrisy of justifying broad state powers to intervene in the lives of children in terms of a broad public interest in fostering the healthy development of children, when the state has consistently shown itself to be unwilling to provide the financial resources required to achieve that goal (Minow 1987). The Left's agenda for the juvenile court, then, is to shrink its jurisdiction, focus it narrowly on the most flagrant juvenile crimes and instances of abuse and neglect, provide adequate due process protections to those who come before it, and ensure the quality of the services made available to those who face the court.

The political Right's criticism focuses on its leniency with juvenile offenders. In their view, it is unjust to excuse the criminal conduct of children on grounds of immaturity or social deprivation. It is right to hold them accountable. Indeed, it is not only right to do so, it may be necessary to facilitate the moral development of young offenders and to protect the community in both the short and long run. Thus, many on the Right recommend the abolition of the juvenile court's jurisdiction in favor of adult court processing (Dawson 1990).

3. *A Potential Synthesis: The Criminalized Juvenile Court.* Standing in the middle of this fray, it is hard to see the way forward. Yet, when one stands a bit above the tumult, one can see points of agreement and sense at least one possible future for the juvenile justice system. The Left and Right agree on the following points: that the principal focus of the juvenile court should be on crimes committed by children, that status offenses and ambiguous cases of abuse and neglect should be excluded from the court's jurisdiction as unnecessary distractions and unnecessary extensions of state power, and that children should be guaranteed due process protections. In effect, both Left and Right agree that juvenile offenses could be handled more justly and effectively in a straightforward "justice" court for young offenders (M. Moore et al. 1987). To the extent that society wanted to continue to concern itself with other matters signaling family dysfunction (such as status offenses or uncertain conditions of abuse and neglect), it could create some different kind of forum that would make less extensive use of state authority.

Washington State pointed toward this conception of juvenile justice with a statute passed in 1977. That statute divides the domain of juvenile justice into two large components: crimes committed by children, and everything else. With respect to crimes committed by children, the process is highly formalized with due process protections, clear penalties for given offenses, and extensive prosecutorial involvement. With respect to "everything else," emphasis is placed on informal processing (Schneider and Schram 1983).

The basic appeal of this approach is clear. It moves the unfamiliar and discredited idea of a *parens patriae* juvenile court into a more comfortable niche in the public's mind—a criminal court for youthful offenders. It appeals to the Left because it narrows the court's jurisdiction, "constitutionalizes" its procedures, and strips away the hypocrisy of paternalism that often does nothing more than provide a cover for racism. It appeals to the Right because it promises to hold juvenile offenders accountable for their crimes and emphasizes the community's interests in secure dispositions.

4. *Limitations of the Criminalized Juvenile Court.* Despite the apparent appeal of the criminalized juvenile court, few states have followed Washington's lead. The problem is apparently *not* the basic appeal of dealing more harshly with juvenile crime. That interest is strong and growing stronger. Appendix B shows the jurisdictional approaches taken in the fifty states and the District of Columbia. Other states have established concurrent juvenile and adult court jurisdiction over some crimes and allowed either juvenile court judges or prosecutors from the adult system to decide in which court to proceed. Figure 2 summarizes state laws on minimum ages of offenders over whom juvenile court jurisdiction can be waived to permit adult court prosecution. So why have more states not transformed their juvenile courts and juvenile justice systems in the way that Washington did?

An answer to this question requires a more fine-grained, state-by-state analysis of the politics of juvenile justice than can be presented here. But an initial hypothesis is that the Washington statute fails to deal with two important problems that remain important to citizens and their representatives in legislatures and executive branch agencies.

The first is that, at the extreme, the idea of "criminalizing" the juvenile court leads eventually to an argument for its abolition. If society makes juvenile crime the principal focus of the juvenile court and "constitutionalizes" its procedures, the distinction between the adult

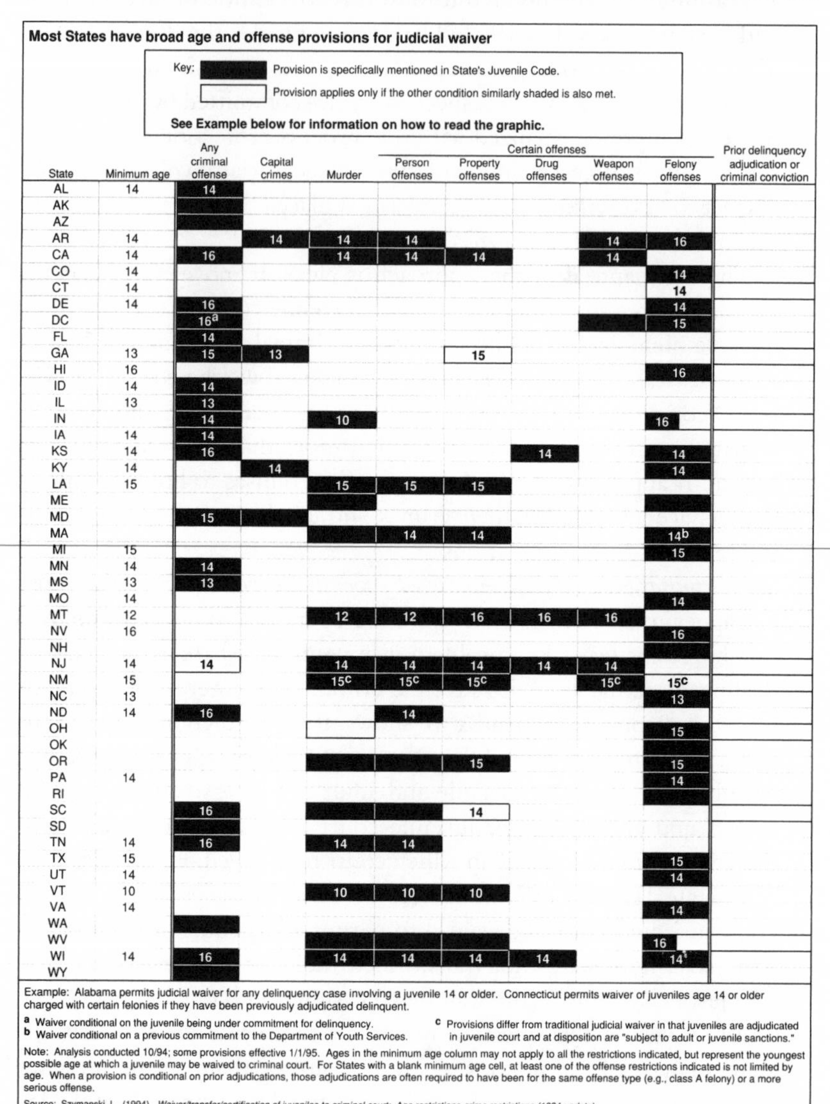

Most States have broad age and offense provisions for judicial waiver

Key: ■ Provision is specifically mentioned in State's Juvenile Code.
□ Provision applies only if the other condition similarly shaded is also met.

See Example below for information on how to read the graphic.

State	Minimum age	Any criminal offense	Capital crimes	Murder	Certain offenses: Person offenses	Certain offenses: Property offenses	Certain offenses: Drug offenses	Certain offenses: Weapon offenses	Felony offenses	Prior delinquency adjudication or criminal conviction
AL	14	14								
AK		■								
AZ		■								
AR	14		14	14	14			14	16	
CA	14	16		14	14	14		14		
CO	14								14	
CT	14								14	□
DE	14	16							14	
DC		16[a]						■	15	
FL		14								
GA	13	15	13			15				□
HI	16								16	
ID	14	14								
IL	13	13								
IN		14		10					16	□
IA	14	14								
KS	14	16					14		14	
KY	14		14						14	
LA	15			15	15	15				
ME				■					■	
MD		15	■							
MA				■	14	14			14[b]	
MI	15								15	
MN	14	14								
MS	13	13								
MO	14								14	
MT	12			12	12	16	16	16		
NV	16								16	
NH									■	
NJ	14	14		14	14	14	14	14		□
NM	15			15[c]	15[c]	15[c]		15[c]	15[c]	□
NC	13								13	□
ND	14	16			14					□
OH				□					15	□
OK									■	
OR				■	■	15			15	
PA	14								14	
RI									■	
SC		16		■	■	14				□
SD		■								
TN	14	16		14	14					
TX	15								15	
UT	14								14	
VT	10			10	10	10				
VA	14								14	
WA		■								
WV				■	■	■			16	□
WI	14	16		14	14	14	14		14	□
WY		■								

Example: Alabama permits judicial waiver for any delinquency case involving a juvenile 14 or older. Connecticut permits waiver of juveniles age 14 or older charged with certain felonies if they have been previously adjudicated delinquent.

[a] Waiver conditional on the juvenile being under commitment for delinquency.
[b] Waiver conditional on a previous commitment to the Department of Youth Services.
[c] Provisions differ from traditional judicial waiver in that juveniles are adjudicated in juvenile court and at disposition are "subject to adult or juvenile sanctions."

Note: Analysis conducted 10/94; some provisions effective 1/1/95. Ages in the minimum age column may not apply to all the restrictions indicated, but represent the youngest possible age at which a juvenile may be waived to criminal court. For States with a blank minimum age cell, at least one of the offense restrictions indicated is not limited by age. When a provision is conditional on prior adjudications, those adjudications are often required to have been for the same offense type (e.g., class A felony) or a more serious offense.

Source: Szymanski, L. (1994). *Waiver/transfer/certification of juveniles to criminal court: Age restrictions-crime restrictions (1994 update).*

FIG. 2.—State laws on minimum ages of offenders over whom juvenile court jurisdiction can be waived to permit adult court prosecution. Source: Szymanski (1994).

and juvenile court gets very fine indeed. Perhaps the juvenile court jurisdiction should be eliminated altogether.

That is, in fact, what two long-term observers of the juvenile justice system have recently concluded (Hirschi and Gottfredson 1993). Of course, they are in favor of remaking the adult criminal court in the image of the juvenile court's concerns with individualized treatment of offenders and detailed investigations of the backgrounds of offenders and the circumstances of crimes in the interest of making just and effective dispositions. In this respect they might be seen as *extending* the juvenile court to cover adult crimes. But the key point is that they think the only viable future of the juvenile court is to merge with the adult criminal court.

That conception seems to go too far for most state lawmakers. They seem to want to retain some special jurisdiction for the juvenile court—some way of responding to crimes committed by children between the ages of ten and sixteen that are not serious offenses. In this respect, the old mandate for the juvenile court remains alive, even if weakened.

The second, larger problem is that there is some important work society wants the juvenile court to do that is not fully captured by the concept of juvenile crime. Nor is it handled adequately when the concept is enlarged to include crimes committed *against* children (such as abuse and neglect). That work consists of dealing with "minor" family problems that signal greater problems in the future: parents who are absent, parents who are mildly but chronically neglectful or only intermittently abusive, children who have run away. These cases all grow out of situations in which the structures society is relying on to care for, protect, and supervise children have begun to deteriorate but have not yet collapsed into outright criminality by the parents or children.

It is significant that even the Washington statute does not eliminate state jurisdiction over these matters. They are simply diverted to more "informal" processing. It is also significant that, despite several decades of lobbying to eliminate "status offenses" from the law and from the jurisdiction of the juvenile and family court, most states retain the legal power to act in circumstances where children are without parents or behaving in ways that endanger their futures, and most states keep those cases within the jurisdiction of the juvenile or family court (Schneider and Schram 1983). The need for the state to act in the messy, difficult circumstances where children are at risk because families are collapsing is, apparently, the court's tar baby: it cannot seem to free itself from becoming society's agent in dealing with these sad and difficult situations.

Indeed, public concern about families and the conditions under which children are being raised and the desire to act on such conditions through laws and obligations as well as through social service institutions seem to be increasing rather than decreasing. Three important political movements are sustaining (or increasing) the focus on the conditions under which children are being reared.

One is the intense political concern that focuses on holding parents accountable for the misbehavior of their children. In the last few years almost half of all states have passed "parental responsibility" laws that compel parents of young offenders to attend counseling or education programs (Egan 1995; Applebome 1996). These laws reflect the public's concern that the family breakdowns that contribute to juvenile crime cannot be addressed without the active involvement of parents, whether it be voluntary or coerced.

The second is in the growing public concern about the effectiveness of family preservation programs. Public officials are increasingly concerned that family preservation programs neither protect children nor improve the conditions under which they are being raised. Many states are reviving policies that quickly remove children from high-risk families and place them in foster care (Dugger 1991, 1993; Firestone 1996). Public officials and other experts have also proposed reviving the use of orphanages and "inner-city kibbutzim" in which to raise children from high-risk or struggling families (Wilkerson 1994; Purnick 1996).

Behind these concerns lies a third: the sense that the family has weakened as a social institution and that the nation is now threatened by "kids having kids." This is variously seen as a problem tied to frequent divorces, working mothers, and latchkey children or as a problem of pregnancies and births among unmarried, young, urban poor people. However it is viewed, concern about recommitting the society to "family values"—the idea that family members have responsibilities to one another and to society that must be fulfilled if society is to flourish and be just—is an important feature of current politics (Whitehead 1993). To the extent that the nation's juvenile and family courts are involved with cases in which issues about the extent to which particular individuals are or are not living up to their responsibilities within the family (and, therefore, to the broader society), one can expect the debate over the future of juvenile justice to channel these broader concerns.

These issues—parental responsibility, family preservation, and family values—prevent the politics of juvenile justice from focusing too narrowly on juvenile crime. Indeed, it hardly seems accidental that just when the debate about the future of juvenile justice seemed to turn decisively in the direction of focusing on the control of juvenile crime through criminal court processes, society rediscovered its concerns about runaway children and the overall state of the family. Society does not seem to be able to disentangle the concern about juvenile crime from its concerns about how children are being raised. The interesting question here seems to be how these issues can be integrated in a political/legislative mandate for the court.

5. *An Alternative: The "Family Court Model."* The original legislation that authorized broad public interventions to save children and society from the consequences of inadequate parenting still survives, but in altered form. Society has come to be more cynical about the state's motives for intervention, more attentive to the rights of children and parents, and more skeptical about the capacity of the state to achieve the practical goals of restoring family functioning and reducing juvenile recidivism.

New legislation designed to enhance the accountability of juvenile offenders by exposing them to the rigors of the adult court or by importing into the juvenile justice system many of the features of the adult criminal court presents a serious alternative to the *parens patriae* court. Such legislation satisfies some who believe that these changes will improve society's response to the most important part of the juvenile court's mandate, namely, to deal justly and effectively with juvenile crime. But it worries others who believe that the adult criminal court model is both an unjust and ineffective response to juvenile crime and that, by emphasizing the juvenile crime aspects of the court's jurisdiction, other important problems that could offer useful points of intervention to reduce juvenile crime (such as child abuse and neglect) will be neglected.

A third alternative may now be coming into view: the family court model. The first family court was established in Cincinnati, Ohio in 1914—fifteen years after the establishment of the juvenile court, and relatively late in the Progressive Era (Katz and Kuhn 1991; Page 1993). There the concept died until 1959 when it was resurrected by the National Council on Crime and Delinquency, the National Council of Juvenile and Family Court Judges, and the United States Children's Bureau. They published a "Standard Family Court Act" that set out a vision of a family court (Katz and Kuhn 1991; Page 1993). In 1961, Rhode Island enacted portions of that vision into law. Hawaii followed in 1965 with an even more ambitious version of the law.

The basic concept is that states should establish a special court (ideally, through constitutional amendment or statute rather than administrative decision) whose jurisdiction would embrace all those legal matters that involve relationships within the family and between the family and the state (Katz and Kuhn 1991; Page 1993; Shepherd 1993; Town 1994). The National Council of Juvenile and Family Court judges recommends that the following should be included within the jurisdiction of the family court:

> 13. A state's family court statute should include provisions determined by Symposium Conferees to be essential as follows: (a) an establishment clause which proports [*sic*] statewide effect; (b) Supreme Court authority to adopt rules of procedure relating to the family court; (c) a provision defining jurisdiction as profferred in recommendations 14–17; and (d) court authority to transfer jurisdictions as appropriate.
>
> 14. Family court jurisdiction should include all divorce/dissolution matters and anything attendant thereto, including marital property distribution, separation and annulment, child custody orders which include modification and visitation, Uniform Child Custody Jurisdiction Act cases, support and Uniform Reciprocal Enforcement of Support Act cases.
>
> 15. Family court jurisdiction should include all child dependency related matters including abuse and neglect, including termination of parental rights, family violence including protective orders, children and persons in need of services (CHINS and PINS) and adoption.
>
> 16. Family court jurisdiction should include all delinquency proceedings and juvenile traffic matters including driving while intoxicated offenses. Status offenses including liaison with public education districts relative to truancy matters should also be included.
>
> 17. Family court jurisdiction should include adult and juvenile guardianships and conservatorships, mentally retarded and mental health matters including civil commitment and confinement, legal–medical issues, e.g., right to die, abortion and living wills, paternity, emancipation and name change. (National Council of Juvenile and Family Court Judges 1989)

Their aim is to be ambitious; to err on the side of too much rather than too little. As one report put it: "The primary indicator of the establishment of a comprehensive family court is the placement of cases involving both juvenile delinquency and divorce within one single court system" (Page 1993, p. 8). The same report also noted that the farthest reaches of jurisdiction of family court extended to a concurrent jurisdiction with the criminal court, not only over cases involving intrafamilial violence, but over *any* crimes committed by family members (Page 1993). This would, in effect, force society to think about the consequences *for the family* of imprisoning fathers who also happened to be armed robbers or drug dealers.

The reasons for giving the court such a wide jurisdiction are partly philosophical and partly practical. On the philosophical side, the basic idea is to recover the idea of the family as an important social institution in whose operations society and the state not only have an interest but also a right to intervene. Of course, society has long understood that the family is an important social institution. It is at once an arena within which individuals live their lives and enjoy their rights and a complex productive system that has a profound effect on the life chances of those within its embrace—particularly the children. What has been disputed is whether society as a whole, and the state in particular, has any justification for interfering in family relations. Indeed, the tradition in liberal societies has been to set families aside as largely immune from public intervention. In this view, the family is a private institution that has rights to autonomy and privacy that kept it sacrosanct from state intrusion and which, in any case, performed best for the society if left alone (Zimring 1982).

Recently, however, that conception has gradually eroded as society has found reasons to be concerned about conditions within the family. One part of that concern has focused on the extent to which the rights of children and women were adequately protected within families. When it seemed plausible that the individual rights of any family member, but particularly women and children, were being abused within the family, the state would intervene to protect their individual rights. In effect, the state intervened to ensure justice *within* families as well as *between* the family and the state and, in so doing, changed the relationship between the family and the state (Zimring 1982). Instead of being immune to public inspection and regulation, the family became subject to it.

A second part of the concern has been that families were failing to perform important social functions, in particular, raising children. A part of this instrumental concern about the performance of families in raising children can be captured in the concern for protecting children's rights. To the extent that society believes children have particular substantive rights to such things as food, clothing, shelter, protection from abuse and neglect by their caretakers, effective adult supervision, reliable mentoring, good-quality education, and employment opportunities, society's interest in providing these things to children could be viewed as the vindication of a right in a just society rather than particular substantive interests that society decided to pursue through the instrumentalities of government (Minow 1987). But even if these things were not viewed as rights, society might well have an interest in trying to produce them. After all, future criminal conduct is the most obvious way neglected children can repay society for its neglect. To avoid future drug abuse, unwanted pregnancies, and economic dependency, society could act to provide for the well-being of children even if it did not treat such benefits provided to children as rights the children had not only vis-à-vis their caretakers but also, in their default, the state.

So society has acted. It has extended aid of various kinds to families and children. The extension of aid has raised some important questions on the part of clients as to the terms on which such aid is provided: what must they reveal about themselves and do to "qualify" for the aid (Mead 1986; Ellwood 1988; Johnson 1996)? For its part, the citizens and the state have often looked for ways to limit their obligations to families and to find others (such as "deadbeat dads") with whom they might share the burdens of caring for the failing families (Whitehead 1993; Dao 1995). Many of these issues have been litigated and have thereby entangled the state and the court even more deeply into the affairs of families. Moreover, in these cases, the interest of the state seems to have widened from a concern for protecting the rights of individual family members to a substantive concern that relationships within families be constituted in ways that are effective in achieving substantive results—such as operating in "the best interests of the child." This, too, has broken down the sharp boundary that was once thought to exist between families and the state.

Family courts, then, seem partly to be an expression of society's consistent and now increasing interests in helping families to function well. Society's interests are partly to ensure justice—that is, to ensure not only that families enjoy the rights they have vis-à-vis society but also that they live up to their obligations—and to ensure that relationships within the family are as just as those relationships between the society and the family (Oshima 1987). But society's interests are also in achieving important practical results: for example, to do what it can to help families raise children.

Judge Robert Page recently summarized these trends in the following terms:

> The movement toward individualism or self-realization tended to undermine the thought of the family as a collective unit. The women's movement emphasizes the value of women as individuals apart from the collective value of the family, as does the children's rights movement. The improved status of all family members as individuals has also increased the demand for more responsive laws and a better judicial system to most effectively resolve their disputes. Legislatures have responded with increased legislation involving family relationships. . . . These new laws . . . have substantially increased the workload and focus upon courts deciding intrafamilial disputes. . . . The increasing realization of the importance of these courts . . . and their emergence as a respected judicial system . . . [have put the lights on] a heretofore darkened area of the courthouse. With the increased status comes the increased demand for a responsible and effective system. (Page 1993, pp. 3–4)

No one wants to go back to the days when conditions within families remained largely invisible to the outside world and when, within that darkness, the rights of women and children could be abused. But having intervened in the domestic context to protect these rights, and to provide services to help the family function well, the state now finds itself having to deal with many more family issues. Perhaps it can learn more quickly how to do this if it creates a court that can embrace the full extent of the laws now regulating intrafamily relations. In any case, it is worth reminding ourselves that a family is more than the bundle of individual rights held by individual family members as individual members of the society, and it is worth asking ourselves what bundles of reciprocal rights and responsibilities distributed across family members define a "well-governed" family—one that not only meets its obligations to its various members, but also works reasonably well in achieving its important social purposes.

The practical argument for a family court is that a court that could look at all the legal matters involving a single family could do its job more efficiently, effectively, and fairly than a court system that tried to deal with different issues in different courts (Katz and Kuhn 1991; Rubin and Flango 1992; Page 1993; Shepherd 1993; Town 1994). Through consolidation, the courts could prevent "forum shopping" by family members disappointed in court decisions. Through consolidation, the courts could also gain whatever benefits would come in terms of justice or practical effect from seeing each individual matter before the court in light of the overall family situation as it was revealed through the investigation into the different matters before the court. Through consolidation, a significant amount of duplication of effort in creating basic information about the family situation could be avoided, to the advantage of both the family (who would be less intruded on) and the court (which would have to spend less time gathering the information). And through consolidation, greater consistency across cases involving both the same family and different families could be attained.

These arguments have been sufficient to persuade many states to adopt family court legislation and for many others to experiment with the idea (Shepherd 1993). Appendix C shows the status of the family court concept across the nation as of 1995. Beyond the boundaries of the United States there have been family court innovations in New Zealand, Canada, and Poland (J. Waterhouse and L. Waterhouse 1983; Mitchell 1990).

6. *Concerns about the Family Court Model.* Although the basic concept of a family court has enjoyed significant support and popularity, some important concerns remain. These include uncertainty about the sources, extent, and efficacy of the court's legal authority over children, parents, and other public caretakers, the availability of social services to support the work of the court, and some technical and administrative questions about the sorts of information systems that would provide the necessary basis for making improved dispositions.

Perhaps the greatest uncertainty about the family court model is the sources, extent, and practical efficacy of its authority over family members, parents, and other caretakers. This uncertainty is crucial, for it strikes at what is fundamental to the family court concept: namely, the idea that family members have responsibilities (as well as rights) toward one another, that the reliable execution of these responsibilities (and vindication of the rights) will allow the family to perform minimally satisfactorily in both the short and long run, and that it is the court's job to ensure that these responsibilities (and rights) are lived up to in daily life. If the court, in fact, lacks these powers, or if, as a practical matter, the powers turn out to be useless in trying to restore family functioning, then much of the promise of the family court is lost.

Note that the question of whether the court has authority over caretakers really divides itself into two parts. One is whether the family court has powers over *parents;* the second is whether the court has power over other caretakers who have assumed responsibility for the conduct and care of children, including other private individuals who have volunteered their efforts, private individuals and agencies paid by government with tax dollars to perform this job, or tax-financed, civil service staffed public agencies. In today's world, where in-home placements are being sustained only through a continued supply of intensive social services, and where many more children are in out-of-home placements, the question whether the court has power over publicly supported agencies often seems more significant than whether it has power over parents, though both are important.

There is little doubt, of course, about the power of the state over parents or public caretakers when the cases involve the abuse and neglect of children. In these cases, no one doubts the interest of the state or the propriety of its focus on the parents and caretakers even if the proper response to the cases remains unclear. It is their conduct that has brought the case before the court.

Greater doubt attaches to the propriety and effectiveness of making caretakers parties before the court in cases involving either crimes or status offenses. The justification for such practices is the simple notion that, because children are supposed to be in the care and custody of their parents, their parents and caretakers share some of their guilt when they offend. This idea was explicit in colonial practices that allowed parents to be placed in public stocks for the misconduct of their children (Bremner et al. 1974). And it has enjoyed a recent public resurgence in Oregon, where a statute was passed that made parents responsible for the conduct of their children and exposed them to fines if the children misbehaved (Egan 1995). Moreover, one could argue that, insofar as society is currently committed to making the "least restrictive" disposition in juvenile delinquency cases (and therefore implicitly relying on parents and caretakers to shoulder the burden of effectively supervising young offenders), it is implicitly relying on the principle that parents and caretakers should be held accountable for the actions of their children and wards (Institute of Judicial Administration, American Bar Association Joint Commission on Juvenile Justice Standards 1980). And, to the extent that the United States begins to adopt the practice of "family group conferences" pioneered in New Zealand for adjudicating and disposing of juvenile cases, the principle that parents and caretakers should be parties before the court in juvenile cases is being implicitly embraced (D. Moore 1993). In these respects, then, the concept of parental or caretaker responsibility seems well established.

But the idea that parents and caretakers should be parties before the court in delinquency and status offense cases and that they should be subject to court authority as part of the disposition the court makes strikes many as bizarre. After all, it is the conduct of the children that brought them before the court. Why is the court focusing on the parents?

Family court judges themselves report they are uncertain about whether they have the authority to order parents to take specific actions in disposing of juvenile delinquency cases and, if so, what the source of their power might be. A recent survey found that 76 percent of the judges surveyed thought they had the power to enforce an order to parents in delinquency cases through their contempt powers, 61 percent thought they could review treatment orders involving parents, but only 50 percent thought they could order protections and restraints, and only 26 percent thought parents would be subject to criminal sanctions for failure to meet the obligations ordered by the court (National Council of Juvenile and Family Court Judges 1989, app. A, pp. 25–31).

The situation changes, to some degree, when the guardian of the child is not the parent but is instead a foster parent or an agency of the state. The situation is easier since the court is less obviously intruding into a private institution. The line between public and private has already been blurred, if not erased. The question then becomes whether one branch of government—the judicial—can compel other branches of government—the legislative or the executive—to behave in particular ways with respect to whole classes of children or a particular child. This important "separation of powers" question has not been fully adjudicated (Chayes 1976; Nagel 1978; Horowitz 1983). It is clear that, on occasion, a court can order an agency to provide services to individual children. It is also clear that, on occasion, a court can place a social service agency into receivership if it is failing to protect the constitutional rights of its clients (Cooper 1988). But what remains unclear is whether the court can write orders for each individual child and have the cumulative total of those orders bind the legislature to fund and the executive to provide. Arguably, such orders constitute the court's judgment about what justice requires for individual children. That judgment ought to have some kind of standing in the minds of legislators and executive branch officials. But it is not clear that the judicial views can overwhelm judgments of legislators or elected chief executives and their appointed commissioners about the level of supervision and care to be publicly supplied to children.

This brings us to the second principal concern about the family court: the availability of sufficient social services to achieve the purposes of the court. Many are dissatisfied with the prospects of a court that only imposes obligations on parents and children and does little to help them. While such a court could satisfy the desire to hold individuals accountable for meeting minimal standards as a parent, caretaker, or child, it would not necessarily achieve the desired results of producing well-functioning family systems unless the parents and children *responded* to the imposition of authority with improved behavior. That, in turn, may only be possible if they are provided with some material assistance.

Material assistance to struggling families may be both substantively and symbolically important. The substantive importance lies in the value that the assistance has in solving problems that now beset the family, for example, enough day care to relieve stress, or sufficient treatment to reduce drug and alcohol abuse. The symbolic importance lies in the fact that, by providing aid, society shows its continued concern for the family. It cannot be accused of merely "scapegoating" or "blaming the victim." The symbolic effect may have material consequences for the motivation of the family to improve. In any case, if providing services is an important part of the court's success in restoring family functioning, then it is obvious that the overall availability of such services and their particular availability to court-referred families becomes key to the success of the family court model.

It is in this key domain that family court judges voice their greatest degree of dissatisfaction. The same survey that reported judicial uncertainty about their power to order parents and public caretakers to provide services also found that 75 percent of the judges thought that their greatest problem was to "assure the availability of appropriate sanctions, service, or treatment resources." Importantly, the judges found this limitation more significant in dealing with delinquency and status offense cases than in cases involving abuse and neglect (National Council of Juvenile and Family Court Judges 1989, app. A, pp. 23–24).

This is also the area in which the states that have actually established family courts have experienced the greatest problems and frustrations. In Rhode Island, the state that has had the longest experience in operating a unified family court system, family court judges and social service administrators agree that the unified court works much better for the children and families that come before it (Wakeling 1995). Yet, the principal problem they have encountered is that the court's operations have made the lives of social service administrators far more difficult. With judges ordering high levels of services for particular cases that come before them (and case workers playing the system to advantage their clients' prospects for services over others who are not court-involved), it is hard for social service administrators to ensure that their services are being fairly distributed according to their definitions of who needs services. In effect, a principle of bureaucratic rationality governing the fair and efficient delivery of overall services is coming into conflict with a judicial determination of what justice demands in individual cases. That problem could be solved if there were enough resources for all. But in a world in which resources are scarce, conflicts arise, and losses are incurred from one standpoint or the other.

In Hawaii, the situation seems somewhat better (Wakeling 1995). There are fewer conflicts between judges and social service agencies. The reason seems to be that the judges, social service administrators, and caseworkers act more as partners in the design and delivery of social services as part of the court's dispositions. They understand both the overall limitations of the social service system, the needs of the particular cases now before the judges, and the needs of other cases that are not now before the judge but are also in desperate straits. It also helps that Hawaii has in the past invested heavily in social service systems and, as a consequence, has a relatively large and diverse system. And it helps that many family court judges have acted as advocates in the political process for increasing investments in social service systems. The extent to which the better situation in Hawaii is explained by the larger supply of social services will probably be tested in the future as Hawaii is forced to cut back on social services due to unprecedented budget deficits. It may be that the situation there will come to more closely resemble that of Rhode Island.

The dissatisfaction of the judges with the availability of services to support troubled families and children both nationwide and in selected family court states is echoed by many others who see a huge gap between the needs of the nation's families and children and the limited availability of public programs (American Bar Association 1993; Carnegie Task Force on Meeting the Needs of Young Children 1994; Weissbourd 1996). If the aggregate, national picture is one of struggling families and limited social services, then it is not surprising that the courts find it hard to stimulate the appropriate supply of services in the disposition of the cases that come before them.

Why there is such a shortfall between responsible estimates of need and the supply of services is, of course, the subject of intense political discussion. One might consider this discussion well beyond the concerns of an essay focused on developing a proper mandate for the juvenile justice system. Yet there might be an important link.

The political argument for expanded social services is implicitly made on three different grounds. One is simple charity and compassion: the suffering of the families and children is great; it would be a virtue for society to alleviate it. A second is an appeal to enlightened self-interest: if society does not act now to deal with the plight of families and children, there will be a huge price to pay later on in terms of increased criminality and other social ills. The third is a general claim about justice: a just society would recognize that children have substantive rights to be cared for decently and act to ensure that such care would be provided. In many ways, this third ground is the most demanding claim. Yet there often seems to be little to back it up.

It is here that the nation's family and juvenile court judges could potentially have an effect. They could commit themselves to writing down dispositions of individual cases that come before them in terms of what they think justice requires *without being constrained by the availability of resources.* They could define these dispositions as the "just dispositions." The "real dispositions" would be the ones that were actually administered in the constrained circumstances the judges encountered. Each year, the courts could add up the total discrepancies between what the "just disposition" required and what the "real disposition" actually provided and describe the difference between the two as a measure of the extent to which society was doing injustice to its family and children. That shortfall could be reported publicly without further comment. The legislature and the executive could do whatever they wanted with this information, but instead of being an abstract concept, the idea of what justice requires for family and children would have become quite concrete and particular.

The power of the claim that the aggregate total of the court's "just dispositions" represents an accurate picture of what justice requires society to do on behalf of family and children depends crucially on the quality of the dispositions the court can make. Society must believe that the family and juvenile court judges are making dispositions in individual cases that accurately reflect proper ideas of what family members owe to one another and what society owes to the family and its individual members. Moreover, it helps in legitimating these decisions if society also believes that the dispositions made will be instrumentally valuable in achieving practical social purposes—such as preventing future criminality by neglected and abused children. This is where the third concern about the family court arises: namely, in its technical capacity to produce just and effective dispositions in individual cases.

A host of technical problems beset family courts in making just and effective dispositions. It is by no means clear that the law has developed adequately in this domain for family court judges to have a clear conception of any of the important rights (and responsibilities) they are supposed to be protecting (and enforcing). What children really are entitled to from their private and public caretakers remains unclear. What duties parents owe society in caring for their children is also unclear (Minow 1987). Nor is it clear that our knowledge about how to intervene in the lives of family and children to help them function more effectively is well established. We do not really know whether it is helpful or harmful to future family functioning to have the court threaten or actually intervene in family matters. Nor do we know how to assemble different kinds of services in appropriate combinations to achieve the aims of the family court.

These facts, no doubt, account for some of the frustration experienced by those states that have committed themselves to family courts. Although much of the frustration that Rhode Island and Hawaii have experienced seems linked to the absence of both general legal authority and social service resources to accomplish the job, there is also evidence of frustration with the adequacy of the technical legal and substantive infrastructure for doing the job (Wakeling 1995). As a legal doctrine, family courts can commit themselves to the principles of "family maintenance" and "permanency planning," and it seems reasonable to suppose that these principles reasonably guide the courts to just and effective dispositions in dependency cases (Fraser, Pecora, and Haapala 1991). But the case law that would provide instruction about how to balance conflicting rights and interests in hard cases and the social science evidence that not only demonstrates that these approaches work but also tells us what specific dispositions designed to be consistent with these principles should be are both sketchy and contradictory at present.

There is even a fundamental conceptual problem in thinking through what a "case" and what a "family" means in the context of a family court and how the structure and function of a family could be assessed to support findings and dispositions in the family court. Consider, first, what is meant by a "case" in the family court.

At one level, the answer is perfectly obvious: a case is a legal matter pending before the court. It could be a divorce petition, an allegation of abuse and neglect, a truancy, or a burglary committed by a youthful offender. The case is resolved when the court decides what is to be done with the matter before it: whether the divorce will be granted, the abuse and neglect proven and sanctioned or dismissed, and so on. Yet, in making each of these decisions, the court is typically not trying to assess simply whether an act occurred and whether the accused did it but instead to find out a great deal about the family circumstances that gave rise to the incident that brought the matter before the court (M. Moore et al. 1987, pp. 14–20). Moreover, the court is supposed to see this particular legal matter in the context of all other pending (and presumably prior) legal matters involving the family in the interest of making a more accurate and comprehensive assessment of the circumstance (Rubin and Flango 1992; Page 1993). And, once it makes a particular decision about a particular legal matter, that disposition will probably require some ongoing monitoring to see that it is carried out and what the effect on family circumstances turns out to be. Thus, a case is not a discrete event fixed in time and space to be responded to with a particular decision that ends the case; a case is an ongoing relationship between the family and the court where particular incidents give the court an occasion to review the overall performance of the family.

Consider, next, what is meant by a "family." At one level, again, this seems straightforward: a family is a caretaker for the children for whom the caretaker is responsible. But consider what that means in the concrete circumstances of today. Suppose there is a woman who is the natural mother of four children, and the court-appointed caretaker for two others. Suppose, further, that the four natural children have two different fathers. Suppose still further that much of the care of the six children for whom the woman is responsible is provided by the woman's mother and a sixteen-year-old girl who has come to live with the woman because her mother was once a friend. In such a circumstance, if one tried to define the family in terms of family function, one would say that one was looking at a woman trying to support six children with the (intermittent) help of their two other natural parents, her mother, and a neighbor. But one could also define family from the point of view of each individual child. Viewed from that perspective, we would be looking at six different families in this one setting.

This could be seen as a mere semantic problem, but it goes deeper than that. To the extent that a family court is trying to improve family functioning with respect to the raising of children, it has to be able to look at the quality of family functioning from the perspective of each individual child. That means that it has to look at the quality of care and supervision that comes to a child not only from his or her primary caretaker, but also from the wider nexus of caretakers wrapped around the child. It may "take a village to raise a child," but it is up to the court to know what particular parts of the village are committed to dealing with an individual child.

Now consider what it would mean to do an investigation to support a disposition. An investigation might well begin with an effort to ascertain whether a particular juvenile offense, or a particular instance of abuse or neglect, did or did not occur and who committed it. Yet, the investigation would soon start ranging well beyond this narrow question. In investigating the particular offense, it would seek to understand the context in which the offense occurred because that would be a more reliable way to understand how the family was functioning and to guide an appropriate disposition. The investigation would then reach beyond the boundaries of the current incident and the context that led up to it and determine the extent to which parties to the current investigation had other matters pending before the court, either now or in the past. The aim would be to support accurate judgments about how well a particular nexus of care, supervision, and investment was working to support the development of the child whose current condition and future prospects formed the heart of the court's concerns.

This sort of investigation may require the skills of both police investigators and social workers. The interpretation of the data collected from the investigation would require the skills of social workers who knew what sorts of relationships sustained over time would be most valuable to the future development of the child. The design of a just and effective disposition in response to the circumstances observed requires the skills of both social workers and judges. Whether the skills to conduct such investigations, make such interpretations, and propose appropriate dispositions really exist is quite uncertain. Yet, the success of the family court concept depends crucially on the existence of such capabilities, for without them the promise that the family court's interventions could be more effective than those of a more traditional court seems hollow.

B. *Trends in Social Conditions Affecting the Work of the Juvenile Justice System*

History seems to have brought society to a place where it is considering two broadly different paths for the juvenile justice system to follow. One is toward a "criminalized juvenile court." The other is toward a "family court." In trying to determine which should be embraced in the future, one can look to political and legal trends as we have been doing. It is in these domains that society's collective aspirations can be found. The alternative is to look out to the tasks that society will be relying on the juvenile justice system to perform in the future. That is the task of this section.

The most obvious and important thing to say about the tasks before the juvenile justice system is simply that over the next decade or two there is going to be a great deal of work for it to do no matter how we define its purposes. Demographic trends show increases in the population of concern to the juvenile justice system—both the twelve- to sixteen-year-olds who might become offenders and the younger children who might be victims of abuse and neglect (Snyder and Sickmund 1995, p. 2). The demographic data also suggest significant increases in families with problems that might bring them to the juvenile court (Snyder and Sickmund 1995, p. 6). Abuse and neglect continue to be reported at increasing rates; many of the cases are serious enough to reach the juvenile court but not serious enough to reach the adult court (National Center on Child Abuse and Neglect 1995). Foster care is increasing (U.S. House of Representatives, Committee on Ways and Means 1994; Tatara 1996). So are families with limited parental resources (Annie E. Casey Foundation 1996; Weissbourd 1996). In essence, society has a great deal of child rearing to do, and the private and public institutions available to do it are quite limited.

This suggests to us that the embrace of the criminalization of the juvenile court would be a mistake. It puts the emphasis on the wrong problem. It leaves too many problems and too many public concerns neglected. The alternative approach, to strengthen our focus on the dependency jurisdiction through the further development of the family court, is the right way to go. The difficulty with this idea, however, is that it seems open-ended and unfamiliar.

III. Conclusion: A Court for Superintending "Family Bankruptcies"

Society is now vigorously debating the future of the juvenile justice system. The debate is, perhaps, overly influenced by the need to respond to crimes committed by young offenders and by the compelling analogy of the adult criminal court. The easiest way for society to think about the issue of juvenile justice and the future of the juvenile court is to think in terms of strengthening the juvenile court as a special kind of criminal court to deal with crimes committed by youthful offenders. That is the path that leads to a "criminalized" criminal court.

A harder way to think about it is to face up to the broader problems that society is trying to solve at least partly through the operations of the juvenile or family court. The broader problems have to do with the conditions under which children are now being raised. These are the conditions that are signaled by such matters as divorce, child custody, visitation rights, child support payments, conditions under which welfare benefits are provided to poor families, and "permanency planning" in foster care placements, and by juvenile crimes, abuse and neglect of children, and status offenses.

Different concerns could motivate society to look at these broader problems. It could be a simple desire to alleviate the pain and suffering of children. It could be a practical interest in preventing future criminal offending by neglected children. It could be a belief that children have rights to care, protection, and effective mentoring that society has to meet if their parents will not. These are values that are potentially at stake in the political discussion about the future of juvenile justice and the juvenile court, but they tend to get pushed off the stage by other more urgent and familiar concerns with responding to criminal offending by children.

Part of the reason that these values get pushed off the stage is that these concerns seem softer and less urgent than the problems of juvenile crime. But another important reason is that society is not sure that it has the right, or can plausibly have an effect on, these broader conditions. It has become sufficiently frustrated with the *parens patriae* model of the juvenile court that anything that resembles this model must be considered suspect. The vision of the "family court" is, unfortunately, sufficiently close to that model that its prospects suffer from the defects of its predecessor. To give the "family court model" a chance in the debate about the future of the juvenile court, a fresh way of looking at such a court has to be invented.

A. The Family Court as a Family Bankruptcy Court

One idea that might be helpful in making the case for the "family court" model would be to liken it to "bankruptcy" courts (Jordan and Warren 1985; Practising Law Institute 1988). In essence, the family court model would be proposed as a court designed to oversee families that were going "bankrupt" in the sense that they seemed to be failing to meet their obligations to their creditors—that is, the wider society that is counting on them to do the job of raising children well.

The signs that a family is headed toward bankruptcy are present when the family declares itself "bankrupt," or when society has concrete evidence indicating that things are not going well with respect to the child rearing. These conditions are written into the codes defining the jurisdiction of the family court. They include situations where parents have divorced, failed to make child support payments, or have otherwise disappeared from the child's life; where parents and other caretakers have abused and neglected their children in physically more drastic ways; where children are committing crimes against other citizens; and where children are engaged in conduct that is particularly dangerous for their future development such as engaging in drug use or behaving in ways that can produce unwanted pregnancies.

Faced with such signs of "bankruptcy," the family court could intervene in two different ways broadly analogous to the options facing a bankruptcy court. It can decide to "liquidate" the bankrupt enterprise and transfer the child to the care and custody of someone other than the current caretakers. Or, it can decide to "restructure." It can explain to the "creditors" (such as the victims of juvenile crime or the citizens who are outraged by parental abuse and neglect) that, while they have reason to feel betrayed by the family's current conduct, they would not be particularly well served by insisting that the family be broken apart.

Instead, they would be better served if they could give the family room to begin functioning again.

To ensure that the interests of these creditors are protected, the court will order the family to behave in particular ways, will provide assistance of various kinds, and will keep monitoring conditions to ensure that the family is successfully emerging from bankruptcy. In defining and enforcing these obligations, the court would be well served by someone operating in the role of a "special master" in a bankruptcy case. This role could be assumed by a social worker, a court probation officer, or even a case manager for a youth correctional agency.

There is an important difference between the image of a court that superintends family bankruptcies and the *parens patriae* court. Like the *parens patriae* court, the family bankruptcy court retains a broad jurisdiction. The crucial difference, however, is that the relationship between the court and the child remains a mediated one. The court does not assume direct responsibility and control over the child; it holds private and public caretakers, and the children, responsible for living up to their duties to one another, and makes available to these parties the services that the state is willing to provide to support their work.

B. Jurisprudential Axioms Supporting the Family Bankruptcy Court

To accept this analogy, society would have to come to accept some uncomfortable but important truths about the relationship between families, children, and the wider society. Specifically, it would have to acknowledge three jurisprudential axioms defining the proper relationships among families, children, and society.

The first axiom is that, despite its desire to leave most of the child-rearing work to families, society as a whole has a widely acknowledged, broad responsibility for rearing its children. Put more provocatively, in the end child rearing is a public responsibility.

This may seem startling since, for the most part, the state does not participate in or interfere with child-rearing practices. Generally speaking, the responsibility for raising children rests with parents, and many discharge their duties tolerably well. That is fortunate since it allows the state to achieve the dual objective of protecting the privacy and autonomy of families and assuring the proper development of its future citizens. This state of affairs also makes it seem as though the state had few legitimate interests or concerns about the quality of child rearing.

What makes this axiom a plausible one, however, is that, where there is a significant and obvious default of the private responsibilities of caring for children, society, in the form of its legal institutions, inevitably and invariably steps in. When a child lacks a legal guardian, the court appoints one. When a marriage with children breaks up, the state decides who will have custody. When parents attack a child, the state steps in to prevent future occurrences.

The second axiom is closely related to the first: parents, legal guardians, and other public caretakers of children have responsibilities to the broader society. They are not entirely autonomous. Put more provocatively, the family (and its various substitutes) are (at least to some degree) the agents of society in raising children.

This, too, may seem surprising—even outrageous. We are accustomed to thinking of families as being autonomous and granted great deference in child rearing. And so they are. The point is simply that, even with this wide deference, families remain under some degree of supervision and restraint by the state. Minimal standards for care exist implicitly in the laws defining abuse and neglect. They are also present in the standards regulating the conduct of those public agencies that assume responsibility for children. If the standards are violated, the caretakers—whether private or public—will come under public scrutiny. If the violation is serious enough, the court will seek to reconstitute the arrangements for caring for children to ensure that children receive the required minimum care, supervision, and training. It is in this sense that caretakers are agents for society.

The third axiom is that the just and effective public response to breakdowns in child-rearing arrangements includes not only the vindication of children's rights and the provision of public services but also the imposition of duties on caretakers and children. Often people imagine that the only proper and just response to breakdowns in child rearing is to provide material assistance to the child or his caretakers in the form of increased financial assistance, more social work counseling, or enhanced educational opportunities for the child. Such assistance may well be important, not only for its own sake, but also in establishing an effective working relationship in which struggling parents and children come to believe that society has not entirely abandoned them. But it is also important to keep in mind that a just and effective response to breakdowns in child rearing could include reminding both caretakers and children of their duties to the broader society. This could be described as holding parents and children accountable for the performance of their duties and could well be part of a just and effective response to signs of failure in child rearing.

C. Investments Required to Support the Family Bankruptcy Court

Acceptance of these basic axioms would provide much of the justification for proceeding with the development of the family court as the future of juvenile justice. But, to make the court work reliably, a great deal of additional work must be done on the basic technical infrastructure of the court. This includes working out in more detail than has so far been done what these axioms mean in particular cases. It also means developing the social science base that can guide the court to effective as well as just dispositions. And it means investing in a wide array of social services. Even with all this, it is by no means certain that the family court model could succeed.

Why, then, does it seem important—even urgent—for society to get on with the business of developing this family court model? The simple answer is that society's stakes in ensuring the quality of child rearing are very large even if largely unacknowledged. A society that neglects its children cannot hope to succeed. Nor can it claim to be either just or virtuous. And a society that has given up trying to succeed, and to be just and virtuous, is a society that is headed for bankruptcy itself.

The ancient philosophers always thought that the quality of relations in a society depended crucially on the quality of relationships within its constitutive parts—particularly the family (Aristotle 1995). More recently, we have acted as though we could take quality in family relations for granted. But the price of that has been the neglect of families that need both to be reminded of their importance to the society and given assistance in helping them meet their responsibilities. That is a particularly urgent task today, and a task that must be met in trying to produce justice for families and children and, through that, justice for the broader society.

APPENDIX A

Candidate Subject Matter Jurisdiction for Family and Juvenile Courts

Abuse and neglect
Adoption
Alimony
Child custody and visitation
Child support
Consent to marriage by minors
Dissolution of marriage (including divorce, annulment, separate maintenance, etc.)

Domestic violence
Spousal abuse
Elder abuse
External review of children in placement
Juvenile delinquency
Management of minors' funds
Palimony
Paternity
Spousal abuse
Status offenses (including children or families in need of supervision, incorrigibility, truancy, runaways, dependent and neglected, etc.)
Termination of parental rights

Adult criminal (intrafamilial)
Appeals of agency decisions affecting children
Commitment to mental health facilities or institutions
Competency
Motor vehicle offenses of minors

SOURCE.—Page (1993).

APPENDIX B

Juvenile Court Transfer Provisions

Waiver only:
- Arizona
- California
- Iowa
- Maine
- Massachusetts
- Missouri
- Montana
- New Jersey
- North Dakota
- Oregon
- South Carolina
- Tennessee
- Texas
- Virginia
- West Virginia
- Wisconsin

Exclusion only:
- New York

Concurrent jurisdiction only:
- Nebraska

Waiver and exclusion:
- Alabama
- Alaska
- Connecticut
- Delaware
- Hawaii
- Idaho
- Illinois
- Indiana
- Kansas
- Kentucky
- Maryland
- Minnesota
- Mississippi
- Nevada
- New Mexico
- North Carolina
- Ohio
- Oklahoma
- Pennsylvania
- Rhode Island
- Washington

Waiver and concurrent exclusion:
- Arkansas
- Colorado
- District of Columbia
- Florida
- Michigan
- New Hampshire
- South Dakota
- Wyoming

All three mechanisms:
- Georgia
- Louisiana
- Utah
- Vermont

Source.—Snyder and Sickmund (1995).

Note.—Analyses were conducted October 1994; some provisions were effective January 1, 1995.

APPENDIX C

Family Court Status in the United States

Not Present (25):
- Alaska
- Arizona

- Arkansas
- Georgia
- Idaho
- Indiana
- Iowa
- Louisiana
- Maine
- Massachusetts
- Michigan
- Montana
- Nebraska
- New Hampshire
- New Mexico
- North Carolina
- North Dakota
- Ohio
- Oklahoma
- South Dakota
- Tennessee
- Texas
- West Virginia
- Wisconsin
- Wyoming

Present (12):
- Connecticut
- Delaware
- District of Columbia
- Hawaii
- Nevada
- New Jersey
- New York
- Pennsylvania
- Rhode Island
- South Carolina
- Vermont
- Virginia

Experiment (3):
- California
- Illinois
- Kentucky

Under Development (1):
- Florida

Recently Enacted (1):
- Missouri

Actively Considering (6):
- Colorado
- Kansas

Maryland
Oregon
Utah
Washington
Specific District/Circuit (3):
Alabama
Minnesota
Mississippi

Source.—National Center for Juvenile Justice (1995).

REFERENCES

American Bar Association Presidential Working Group on the Unmet Legal Needs of Children and Their Families. 1993. *America's Children at Risk: A National Agenda for Legal Action.* Chicago: American Bar Association.

Andrews, R. Hale, and Andrew H. Cohn. 1974. "Ungovernability: The Unjustifiable Jurisdiction." *Yale Law Journal* 83:1383–1409.

Annie E. Casey Foundation. 1996. *Kids Count Data Book: State Profiles of Child Well-Being.* Baltimore: Annie E. Casey Foundation.

Applebome, Peter. 1996. "Holding Parents Responsible as Children's Misdeeds Rise." *New York Times* (April 10), p. A1.

Areen, Judith C. 1978. *Family Law.* Mineola, N.Y.: Foundation Press.

Aristotle. 1995. *The Politics,* translated by Ernest Barker. New York: Oxford University Press.

Bleich, Jeffrey. 1986. "An Analysis of Juvenile Justice Statutes: Philosophies and Trends." Unpublished manuscript. Cambridge, Mass.: Harvard University.

Bragg, Rick. 1994. "Where a Child on the Stoop Can Strike Fear." *New York Times* (December 2), p. A1.

Bremner, R. H., J. Barnard, T. K. Hareven, and R. Mennel, eds. 1974. *Children and Youth in America.* Cambridge, Mass.: Harvard University Press.

Butterfield, Fox. 1996. "States Revamping Laws on Juveniles as Felonies Soar." *New York Times* (May 12), p. A1.

Carnegie Task Force on Meeting the Needs of Young Children. 1994. *Starting Points: Meeting the Needs of Our Youngest Children.* New York: Carnegie Corporation of New York.

Chayes, Abram. 1976. "The Role of the Judge in Public Law Litigation." *Harvard Law Review* 89:1281.

Cooper, Phillip J. 1988. *Hard Judicial Choices: Federal District Court Judges and State and Local Officials.* New York: Oxford University Press.

Cronin, Roberta C. 1994. *Boot Camps for Adult and Juvenile Offenders: Overview and Update.* Washington, D.C.: National Institute of Justice, Office of Justice Programs.

Dao, James. 1995. "Plan Links Child Support to Licenses." *New York Times* (August 7), p. B1.

Dawson, Robert O. 1990. "The Future of Juvenile Justice: Is It Time to Abolish the System?" *Journal of Criminal Law and Criminology* 81:136–55.

DeJong, William. 1994. *Preventing Interpersonal Violence among Youth: An Introduction to School, Community, and Mass Media Strategies.* Washington, D.C.: National Institute of Justice, Office of Justice Programs.

DiIulio, John J. 1995. "The Coming of the Super-predators." *Weekly Standard* 1:23–28.

Dugger, Celia W. 1991. "A Quandary for System." *New York Times* (October 5), p. 23.

———. 1993. "Program to Preserve Families Draws Child-Welfare Debate." *New York Times* (August 6), p. A1.

Egan, Timothy. 1995. "When Young Break the Law, a Town Charges the Parents." *New York Times* (May 31), p. A1.

Ellwood, David T. 1988. *Poor Support: Poverty in the American Family.* New York: Basic.

Feld, Barry C. 1988. "The Juvenile Court Meets the Principle of Offense: Punishment, Treatment, and the Difference It Makes." *Boston University Law Review* 68:821–915.

———. 1993*a*. *Justice for Children: The Right to Counsel and the Juvenile Courts.* Boston: Northeastern University Press.

———. 1993*b*. "Criminalizing the American Juvenile Court." In *Crime and Justice: A Review of Research*, vol. 17, edited by M. Tonry. Chicago: University of Chicago Press.

Firestone, David. 1996. "Giuliani Seeks Tough Laws to Help Abused Children." *New York Times* (February 2), p. B6.

Fraser, M. W., P. J. Pecora, and D. A. Haapala. 1991. *Family in Crisis: The Impact of Intensive Family Preservation Services.* New York: Walter de Gruyter.

Hargrove, E. C., and J. C. Glidewell. 1990. *Impossible Jobs in Public Management.* Lawrence: University Press of Kansas.

Hirschi, Travis, and Michael Gottfredson. 1993. "Rethinking the Juvenile Justice System." *Crime and Delinquency* 39(2):262–71.

Horowitz, Donald L. 1983. "Decreeing Organizational Change: Judicial Supervision of Public Institutions." *Duke Law Journal* 1983:1265.

Humm, S. Randall, et al., eds. 1994. *Child, Parent, and State: Law and Policy Reader.* Philadelphia: Temple University Press.

Institute for Judicial Administration, American Bar Association Joint Commission on Juvenile Justice Standards. 1980. *Juvenile Justice Standards.* Cambridge, Mass.: Ballinger.

Johnson, Dirk. 1996. "One Mother's Ordeal with Life on Welfare." *New York Times* (July 31), p. A10.

Jordan, Robert, and William Warren. 1985. *Bankruptcy.* Mineola, N.Y.: Foundation Press.

Katz, S., and J. Kuhn. 1991. *Recommendations for a Model Family Court: A Report from the National Family Court Symposium.* Pittsburgh, Pa.: National Center for Juvenile Justice.

Krisberg, B., and J. Austin. 1993. *Reinventing Juvenile Justice.* Newbury Park, Calif.: Sage.

Mead, Lawrence M. 1986. *Beyond Entitlement: The Social Obligations of Citizenship.* New York: Free Press.

Minow, Martha. 1987. "The Public Duties of Families and Children." In *From Children to Citizens,* vol. 2, *The Role of the Juvenile Court,* edited by Francis X. Hartmann. New York: Springer-Verlag.

Mitchell, Ann. 1990. "Family Courts in Europe." *Family Law* 20:389.

Mnookin, Robert H., and D. Kelly Weisberg. 1995. *Child, Family, and State: Problems and Materials on Children and the Law.* Boston: Little, Brown.

Moore, David B. 1993. "Shame, Forgiveness, and Juvenile Justice." *Criminal Justice Ethics* 12:3–25.

Moore, Mark H. 1990. "What Sort of Ideas Become Public Ideas?" In *The Power of Public Ideas,* edited by Robert B. Reich. Cambridge, Mass.: Harvard University Press.

———. 1995. *Creating Public Value: Strategic Management in Government.* Cambridge, Mass.: Harvard University Press.

Moore, Mark H., Thomas Bearrows, Jeffrey Bleich, Francis X. Hartmann, George L. Kelling, Michael Oshima, and Saul Weingart. 1987. *From Children to Citizens,* vol. 1, *The Mandate for Juvenile Justice.* New York: Springer-Verlag.

Nagel, Robert F. 1978. "Separation of Powers and the Scope of Federal Equitable Remedies." *Stanford Law Review* 30:661.

National Center on Child Abuse and Neglect. 1995. *Child Maltreatment: Reports from the States to the National Center on Child Abuse and Neglect.* Washington, D.C.: U.S. Government Printing Office.

National Council of Juvenile and Family Court Judges. 1989. "Curriculum Enhancement Project." *Juvenile and Family Court Journal* 40:1–21, appendices.

National Crime Prevention Council. 1994. *Preventing Violence: Program Ideas and Examples.* Washington, D.C.: National Crime Prevention Council.

Oshima, Michael W. 1987. "Toward a Jurisprudence of Children and Families." In *From Children to Citizens,* vol. 2, *The Role of the Juvenile Court.* New York: Springer-Verlag.

Page, Robert. 1993. "Family Courts: An Effective Judicial Approach to the Resolution of Family Disputes." *Juvenile and Family Court Journal* 44:3–59.

Practising Law Institute. 1988. *The Basics of Bankruptcy and Reorganization.* New York: Practising Law Institute.

Purnick, Joyce. 1996. "Ex-Prosecutor Builds a Case for Children." *New York Times* (February 12), p. B1.

Radzinowicz, Leon, and Roger Hood. 1986. *A History of English Criminal Law and Its Administration from 1750,* vol. 5, *The Emergence of Penal Policy.* Agincourt, Ontario: Carswell Company Ltd.

Rubin, Ted, and Victor E. Flango. 1992. *Court Coordination of Family Cases.* Williamsburg, Va.: National Center for State Courts.

Schneider, Anne Larason, and Donna D. Schram. 1983. *An Assessment of Juvenile Justice System Reform in Washington State.* Vol. 10. Eugene, Oreg.: Institute of Policy Analysis.

Schur, E. 1971. *Labelling Deviant Behavior.* Englewood Cliffs, N.J.: Prentice-Hall.

Schwartz, Ira. 1989. *(In)justice for Juveniles.* Lexington, Mass.: Lexington Books.

Schwartz, I., S. Guo, and J. Krebs. 1992. *Public Attitudes toward Juvenile Crime and Juvenile Justice: Implications for Public Policy.* Ann Arbor: University of Michigan, Institute for Social Research.

Schwartz, R., and J. Skolnick. 1964. "Two Studies of Legal Stigma." In *The Other Side,* edited by H. Becker. Glencoe, Ill.: Free Press.

Shepherd, Robert E. 1993. "The Unified Family Court: An Idea Whose Time Has Finally Come." *Juvenile Justice* 8:37–39.

Snyder, H., and M. Sickmund. 1995. *Juvenile Offenders and Victims: A National Report.* Washington, D.C.: Office of Juvenile Justice and Delinquency Prevention.

Springer, C. E. 1986. *Justice for Juveniles.* Washington, D.C.: U.S. Department of Justice, Office of Juvenile Justice and Delinquency Prevention.

Szymanski, L. 1993. *Waiver/Transfer/Certification of Juveniles to Criminal Court: Age Restrictions-Crime Restrictions (1992 Update).* Pittsburgh: National Center for Juvenile Justice.

Tatara, Toshio. 1996. "U.S. Child Substitute Care Flow Data for FY 94 and Current Trends in the State Child Substitute Care Populations." *VCIS Research Notes* 12:1–14.

Town, Michael A. 1994. *The Unified Family and Juvenile Court: Quality Justice for America's Families and Children.* Photocopy. Honolulu: Family Court, First Circuit.

U.S. House of Representatives, Committee on Ways and Means. 1994. *1994 Green Book: Background Material and Data on Programs within the Jurisdiction of the Committee on Ways and Means.* Washington, D.C.: U.S. Government Printing Office.

Wakeling, Stewart. 1995. Confidential interviews. June–July.

Waterhouse, John, and Lorraine Waterhouse. 1983. "Implementing Unified Family Courts: The British Columbian Experience." *Canadian Journal of Family Law* 4:153–71.

Weissbourd, Richard. 1996. *The Vulnerable Child.* Reading, Mass.: Addison-Wesley.

Whitehead, Barbara Dafoe. 1993. "Dan Quayle Was Right." *Atlantic Monthly* (April), pp. 47–84.

Wilkerson, Isabel. 1994. "Doing Whatever It Takes to Save a Child." *New York Times* (December 30), p. A1.

Zimring, Frank. 1982. *The Changing Legal World of Adolescence.* New York: Free Press.

Julian V. Roberts

The Role of Criminal Record in the Sentencing Process

Men's evil manners live in brass: Their virtues we write in water. (Shakespeare, *Henry VIII*, act 4, scene 2, line 45)

ABSTRACT

An offender's criminal history plays an important role in sentencing in all jurisdictions. Statutory enhancements for repeat offenders exist in most countries, and there is widespread public support for harsher penalties for recidivists. Advocates of general or specific deterrence support a recidivist premium on the grounds that recidivists are more likely to reoffend and need stronger disincentives. Incapacitationists argue that longer detention is required for offenders with a greater likelihood of reoffending. Most desert-based theorists support a limited sentencing discount for first offenders. State and federal sentencing guideline systems in the United States attach great importance to criminal history information, but there is considerable diversity in the way in which different systems define and limit the use of previous convictions. This essay explores a number of important policy issues relating to the use of criminal history information, including definitions of what should be included in a criminal record, the use of juvenile adjudications, the duration of previous convictions, and the question of whether previous criminal misconduct should ever be completely effaced. As well, a number of alternative ways of conceptualizing criminal history are explored. Throughout this essay, the focus is on the sentencing guideline systems in the United States, although many of these issues also apply to other jurisdictions.

Julian Roberts is professor of criminology at the University of Ottawa. I would like to express my gratitude to Andrew Ashworth, Michael Tonry, Andrew von Hirsch, and the anonymous reviewers from the *Crime and Justice* series for their comments on an earlier draft of this essay. I would also like to acknowledge the cooperation of the many sentencing commissions across the United States that sent me information about their guideline systems.

0192-3234/97/0022-0001$02.00

Consider the case of an offender being sentenced, under the Minnesota sentencing guidelines, of aggravated robbery. The prescribed range of sentence for a first offender is forty-four to fifty-two months. But if he has two prior convictions for this offense, the guidelines specify a range of eighty-four to ninety two months.[1] What justification exists for the harsher sentence? Because the individual failed to "learn" from the sentences previously imposed? Because the crime itself is somehow more serious in light of the offender's criminal history? To prevent him from committing further crimes at least while incarcerated? To deter him from committing further burglaries? To deter other potential burglars? To punish him further for defying the authority of the court that sentenced him in the past? These questions all relate to criminal record and the sentencing process.

Prior convictions play a vital yet variable role in the sentencing systems of most Western nations. After the seriousness of the crime, the criminal history of the offender is the most important determinant of sentence severity in common-law jurisdictions. Evidence of the importance of criminal record is to be found in statutory sentencing enhancements for recidivists, case law decisions affirming sentencing differentials between defendants with different criminal histories, and in sentencing practices in trial courts.

Criminal record influences the treatment of offenders throughout (and beyond) the criminal justice system. For example, twenty-four states require or permit criminal records to be considered in bail decisions (Bureau of Justice Statistics 1993). As well, criminal record affects correctional classifications, disciplinary proceedings in prison, and parole eligibility dates (see Farrell and Swigert 1978; Horan, Myers, and Farnworth 1982; Bureau of Justice Statistics 1991; Hebenton and Thomas 1993).[2] A criminal record also carries implications for the offender that extend far beyond the expiry of the sentence (e.g., Damaska 1968; Gardiner 1972; Reed and Nance 1972; Davis 1980). Besides the stigma of carrying a criminal record (which may itself provoke further offending), individuals with criminal records are restricted from participating fully in civic life in a number of ways. As Moore notes: "people

[1] Two criminal history points are scored for each prior offense at seriousness level 7; see Minnesota Sentencing Guidelines Commission (1993).

[2] This is particularly true in states such as Illinois where passage of the Illinois Uniform Conviction Information Act (in 1991) has permitted even members of the public to have access to conviction records maintained by the Illinois State Police. These rap sheets contain more than just convictions; they also include arrest records for any given individual (see Owens 1994).

with criminal records are deprived of many sorts of civil liberties: they cannot serve on juries, they cannot hold government offices, they cannot even lead a Cub Scout pack" (Moore 1989, p. 177). However, the most frequent, and yet controversial, use of criminal history records by the courts is in connection with sentencing. The focus of this essay is on the role of criminal record in sentencing and, in particular, in the American sentencing guideline systems.

An offender's prior crimes are also important to lay conceptions of justice and perceptions of offenders. Public views of wrongdoing are influenced by information about an individual's past conduct, whether relating to the discipline of children or the sentencing of offenders. Not surprisingly then, much of the recent crime control debate in the United States, Canada, Great Britain, and Australia has centered on crime by recidivists. Evidence of the depth of feeling in the United States on this issue is to be found in the widespread support for "three strikes and you're out" laws in Washington, California, and other states. Such a provision was incorporated in the 1994 federal crime bill, and similar provisions have found support in Australia and Canada (e.g., Frieberg 1995; Roberts 1995). In 1995, the British home secretary introduced similar "three strikes" legislation for habitual burglars and hard drug dealers (*Guardian Weekly* 1995). As adopted in the state of Washington, conviction for a serious offense for the third time results in the imposition of a mandatory life sentence without the possibility of early release on parole (see Boerner 1995). Habitual or recidivist offender statutes also can be found throughout the United States and in other jurisdictions around the world (see Proband 1994). Finally, proposals have recently been advanced in several countries to restrict legal aid to accused persons without a criminal record (Roberts 1995). The seriousness of crimes committed by recidivists clearly touches nerves among politicians and the general public.

Public and professional opposition to reform of statutes relating to criminal record provides evidence of how deeply ingrained the recidivist premium is in our societies. In England and Wales, the relationship between criminal record and sentencing was the subject of vigorous debate following passage of the 1991 Criminal Justice Act.[3] Section

[3] There has been ambivalence in England surrounding the use of criminal record. For some motoring offenses, for example, there is a milder version of the three-strikes provision. Each offense results in the loss of a number of points, and once a certain threshold is reached, the motorist is "out" of circulation. In contrast, other less serious offenses such as illegal parking and regulatory offenses can be committed repeatedly without any increment in the penalty imposed.

29(1) of that statute limited the court's ability to incorporate previous convictions into the sentence: while the absence of a criminal record led to a mitigated sentence, the presence of priors did not, under the provisions of the act, lead to a harsher disposition. The effect would have been to restrict the ability of judges to sentence an offender on the basis of prior convictions. This provision was criticized by newspapers and criminal justice professionals, including the lord chief justice (see Wasik 1993). Adverse public and media reaction played a role in provoking the revision of the criminal record provision of that statute.[4]

It is surprising that the role of criminal history in sentencing has not generated more scholarly attention. The considerable literature on sentencing guidelines in the United States (e.g., von Hirsch, Knapp, and Tonry 1987; Champion 1989; Doob 1995) has focused on issues such as the effects of the guidelines. A recent survey of experience with sentencing commissions (Tonry 1993) identified criminal history measures as an important evolutionary issue in the field of guidelines. This then is the point of departure for this essay, which, after describing the historical antecedents of sentencing premiums for recidivists, focuses on the role of criminal record in U.S. sentencing guideline systems. Although an offender's past crimes importantly affect his treatment by the criminal justice system, there is considerable variability in the way that different jurisdictions define criminal record and respond to recidivist offenders.

Throughout this essay, I attempt to relate the practice of using criminal record to the underlying sentencing theories. A number of important principles emerge from those theories. Both statewide and federal sentencing guideline systems have attempted to ensure that the practical use of criminal record is consistent with principles derived from sentencing theories. However, a clear tension exists between the principles guiding criminal history information and the way in which criminal record actually affects sentencing decisions.

This essay is an attempt to understand both the way in which criminal record affects sentencing decisions in the United States (and elsewhere) and to explore the theoretical justifications. Why do we punish

[4] The criminal history provisions of the 1991 act have been replaced by a less restrictive formulation the exact consequences of which are unclear at present. It is clear that the original intention of the act, to restrict the use of criminal record in sentencing decisions, has been undermined (see Ashworth and Gibson 1994; Wasik and von Hirsch 1995).

people repeatedly for the same criminal conduct? Is it not a case of double punishment? And if such a practice is theoretically justified, what principles should regulate the use of criminal record? Many questions recur in the area. Should juvenile adjudications count against adult offenders? How should we define a criminal record? By previous arrests or just convictions? Should the nature of the relationship between the previous and current offending be relevant, or should all priors count equally no matter if they are very different from the offense of current conviction? What role does the factor of time play? That is, should the weight of a previous conviction decline if the offender lives a crime-free life? At what point should previous convictions cease to count against a defendant? Should they ever cease to count? Finally, are there other ways of conceptualizing criminal record that do not connote, to quite the same degree, the notion of repeated punishment for the same offense? Although relevant to the American guideline systems, all these questions have application to the sentencing process in other countries as well.

Increasing public, professional, and scholarly attention to the concept of criminal record and its relevance for the sentencing process means that policies relating to criminal history will become more subtle and sophisticated as time passes. The principal constraint on the evolution of criminal history measures would appear to be an understandable desire on the part of sentencing commissions to keep their sentencing guidelines as simple and comprehensible as possible.

Section I briefly reviews statutory sentencing enhancements for recidivist offenders. It also provides historical precedents and discusses public perceptions of the role of criminal record and the nature and extent of criminal recidivism. Section II examines definitions of the recidivist premium and different theoretical justifications for it. This section explores important policy questions relating to the use of criminal record, such as how to define criminal history, whether juvenile adjudications should count at the adult level, and whether (and after what period of time) criminal records should become extinct. Throughout this discussion, I attempt to relate the practical use of criminal record information to the utilitarian or desert-based theories that justify their usage. Section III reviews data on sentencing practices in several jurisdictions and provides quantitative data on the impact of criminal record in sentencing guideline systems in the United States. Section IV proposes some alternative ways in which criminal record could be taken into account by the sentencing process. Section V draws some conclusions about the role of criminal record in the sentencing process.

I. Statutory Sentencing Premiums for the Recidivist Offender

For as long as countries have had formal legal systems, there is evidence that crimes by recidivists have been seen as deserving harsher punishments than crimes by first offenders. Modern research on public attitudes toward punishment shows that the general public likewise sees recidivist crimes as warranting severer sanctions.

A. Historical Evidence of the Recidivist Premium

Statutory sentencing enhancements for recidivist offenders go back millennia. Durham (1987) cites biblical examples of special sanctions for repeat offenders. Ancient Hebrew laws prescribed particular terms of imprisonment for several cases, including a murderer who commits the same crime for a third time (see Drapkin 1989). In classical Athens, perjury led to the imposition of financial penalty, but if it were a third conviction, the penalty would be far more severe: loss of civic rights. Classical philosophers refer to the role of criminal antecedents. Plato, for example, discusses the disposition of the criminal; although he does not make it explicit, it is clear that he would regard repetition as evidence of "incurability," which would result in different treatment (see Mackenzie 1981, chap. 11).

As early as the late seventeenth century, an offender's criminal history appears to have had an effect on sentencing patterns. Shoemaker's analysis of sentencing decisions in London and Middlesex led him to conclude that "the age, social status, attitude and previous criminal history of the accused played a crucial role in shaping sentencing decisions" (Shoemaker 1991, p. 190; see also Beattie 1986). However, it was not until official record keeping became more systematic that an offender's prior crimes came to count heavily against him in subsequent sentencing proceedings. To that point, unless the offender had committed his previous offenses in the same area, it was likely that his prior misconduct would remain hidden. By the nineteenth century, statutory recidivist premiums had become highly punitive.[5] The In-

[5] There is also historical evidence that defendants have long appealed for lenient treatment on the basis of the *absence* of previous misconduct. Thus records in early seventeenth-century Maryland recount the trial of one John Goneere, who admitted having perjured himself but asked the court for mercy because this was the first time he had transgressed in this way (see Semmes 1970).

dictable Offences Bill, introduced in England in 1843, provided a mandatory minimum sentence for recidivists. The result was very punitive sentences for persistent petty offenders, a pattern that persists to this day (see Ashworth 1992, pp. 157–58).[6] The Indictable Offences Bill stated that "Every one who, under the provisions hereinafter contained is liable to an increased punishment upon a conviction after a previous conviction shall, if sentenced to penal servitude, be sentenced to penal servitude for not less than seven years" (House of Commons 1879, p. 2).[7]

Today, most jurisdictions employ explicit statutory sentencing enhancements for recidivist offenders, although there is considerable variation in the magnitude of the recidivist premium, the profile of the offender targeted, and the manner in which the premium is administered. Some criminal codes tie a recidivist premium to a particular sentencing goal. For example, the Indian Penal Code justifies enhanced sentences for recidivist property crime on the grounds that offending of this nature warrants greater deterrent treatment than the conventional penalty structure provides (see Nigam 1965). Penal codes in other countries are less explicit about the relationship between sentencing purpose and criminal history. In Ghana, a minimum five-year term is imposed when an adult offender has two or more previous convictions (see Seidman 1966). Even in those countries that do not provide a specific statutory enhancement for recidivists (as in the case of Romania), the importance of criminal record is noted in the penal code: "The penalty is established by considering . . . the state of recidivism" (Article 80; see Kleckner 1976). Likewise in China, Article 61 defines a "repeating offender" and notes that such a person will be "punished severely." The penal codes of some countries express the recidivist premium as a function of the severity of the previous sentence. The Turkish code provides specific guidance for judges in terms of the magnitude of the increments: if the new crime is dissimilar to the previous offense, the recidivist premium is one-sixth of the sentence.[8]

[6] For example, in 1872 William Crosley was convicted of stealing two pecks of potatoes. His previous convictions resulted in the imposition of seven years' penal servitude and seven years of police supervision (see Emsley 1987).

[7] Evidence of differential treatment of recidivists is found in legal statutes that exclude such offenders from lenient treatment. In England, benefit of clergy, which permitted persons charged with a clergyable offense to escape capital punishment, was available only to first offenders (Stephen 1883).

[8] The importance of criminal record is not restricted to existing criminal codes. Grygier's "Social Protection Code," which purports to advance a new model of criminal

In contemporary America, most states have statutes that provide for enhanced sentences for offenders with prior convictions (see Bureau of Justice Statistics [1991], table 8, for a complete list as of the late 1980s). For example, Section 667 of the California Penal Code enhanced a felon's prison term by five years for each serious prior felony conviction. In Alabama, a class A felony conviction, with at least one prior felony resulted in a sentence of fifteen years to life (Shane-Dubow, Brown, and Olsen 1985, p. 14). Many states have long authorized the sentencing of persistent recidivists to enhanced terms as career criminals or habitual criminals. Kentucky, for example, provides enhanced prison terms for persistent felony offenders—those who have one or more prior felony convictions within periods specified by the statute. These statutes can be very punitive. In *Rummel v. Estelle*, 100 U.S. 113 (1980), for example, the U.S. Supreme Court upheld the constitutionality of a sentence of life imprisonment for a third, and minor, property offense (see Davis [1992] for discussion of issues arising from the *Rummel* decision). Repetitive offender statutes are increasing in number and scope. A 1985 survey showed that repeat or habitual offender laws had recently been strengthened in thirty-three states (see Shane-Dubow, Brown, and Olsen 1985).[9] Clearly, then, an offender's past crimes have long been part of the legal culture relating to punishment. It also appears that criminal record is critical to lay perceptions of crime and punishment.

B. Criminal Record and Public Opinion

Most sentencing systems attempt to keep in step with community values. Many make explicit reference to the link between sentencing practices and public opinion. For example, Judge William Wilkins, the former chairman of the U.S. Sentencing Guidelines Commission, stated that "public input has played a pivotal role in the formulation of the guidelines" (Bureau of Justice Statistics 1987, p. 7). And further,

---

justice (Grygier 1977), also has a section on recidivist penalties. Criminal record is treated as an aggravating circumstance that results in an upgraded penalty.

[9] In addition to statutory definitions of specific penalties, the recidivist premium also appears in statutes relating to parole. Some jurisdictions deny recidivists the opportunity of conditional release on parole. In Canada, the penalty for second-degree murder is life imprisonment without parole for at least ten years, although in practice almost all offenders obtain release on parole at the ten-year mark. However, according to Section 742 (a.1) of the Canadian *Criminal Code*, defendants convicted of second-degree murder and who have a previous murder conviction are sentenced to the penalty reserved for offenders convicted of first-degree murder: imprisonment for twenty-five years without the possibility for parole.

"enhancing a defendant's sentence on the basis of criminal history . . . is consistent with public perceptions of crime seriousness" (Wilkins 1992, p. 577). It is therefore worth asking whether systematic research supports this assertion.

In general, prior misconduct seems to play an important role in everyday perceptions of wrongdoing.[10] This is borne out in the results of systematic research on the issue. A number of studies in the United States have compared public sentencing preferences in cases involving first offenders and recidivists. Fichter and Veneziano (1988) report data from a Missouri survey that compared "sentences" imposed on one of two offender profiles: a burglar with no priors or a burglar with two previous convictions. The percentage of respondents favoring a sentence of state prison rose from 12 percent to 60 percent when the burglar had a criminal record (see also Mande and English 1989). These data, however, do not indicate whether public support for increased penalties for recidivists results from a view that first offenders deserve a discount or a view that penalties should become steadily harsher as the criminal record lengthens.[11]

Part of the explanation for public support of the use of criminal record may be that an offender's criminal record is seen as affecting the seriousness of the crime. Although desert theorists see a clear distinction between crime seriousness and criminal history, research by Monahan and Ruggiero (1980) clearly shows that for the public the two concepts are interdependent. Subjects were asked to state how much punishment an offender deserved, as well as how much punishment was warranted on utilitarian grounds (i.e., to prevent crime). There were two kinds of offenders: first offenders and recidivists. Not surprisingly, perhaps, when the offender was a recidivist, subjects felt that a longer sentence was required in order to protect society from further offending. However, subjects also felt that the recidivist *deserved* more punishment than the first offender, regardless of the issue

[10] The laws of most sports incorporate recidivist premiums. For example, in soccer, a second transgression worthy of a yellow card results in the player being ejected from the game. The exception to this rule appears to be ice hockey, in which "tariff" penalties are imposed regardless of the number of previous penalties. There are, of course, noncriminal contexts in which no leniency is extended to first offenders or no recidivist premiums exist. These include parking violations, library fines, and so forth.

[11] The public also see previous convictions as being relevant to parole release. When a sample of Canadians were asked to identify the most important factors that should be kept in mind when granting an inmate parole, the number of previous convictions was second in importance only to the seriousness of the crime for which the inmate was currently imprisoned.

of future offending. These results suggest that public perceptions of appropriate sentencing are influenced by the extent of the offender's record, possibly by enhancing the seriousness of the offense.

What else explains the strong degree of public support for the recidivist premium? Public views may be based in part on an exaggerated perception of the extent to which the average offender has a criminal history. As with other criminal justice statistics (see Roberts [1992] for a review of this literature), the public has an overly pessimistic view of the proportion of offenders who have criminal records. Stalans and Diamond (1990) compared the perceptions of members of the public with actual court data and found that most respondents believed that the average burglar had been convicted of at least two prior burglaries, while court data showed that a significant proportion of convicted offenders had no record of prior offending. The American public would probably be surprised to learn that data from state guideline systems show that the majority of offenders occupy the least serious criminal history categories. For example, data from Oregon show that 85 percent of offenders sentenced in 1992 had no prior felony conviction (Oregon Criminal Justice Council 1993, table 10). In the state of Washington, there are ten categories of criminal history, yet almost two-thirds of offenders fall into the first, least serious levels (Washington State Sentencing Guidelines Commission 1992*b*, table 3). At the federal level, almost two-thirds of offenders sentenced in 1989–90 fell into the least serious criminal history category (U.S. Sentencing Commission 1991, table 11).

The public also appear to overestimate the likelihood of future offending. A Canadian survey found that the public systematically overestimated the recidivism rates of various categories of offenders. For example, while the official rate of recidivism for sex offenders at the time the survey was conducted was 13 percent, the average public estimate of the rate was 58 percent. Although the recidivism rate for violent offenders was 16 percent, most people estimated the rate to be much higher, in excess of 60 percent (Roberts and White 1986).[12]

[12] Official recidivism rates clearly underestimate the actual rate at which offenders reoffend, as some reoffending remains undetected. For this reason, subjects in the study were asked about official reconviction rates. It is still possible that respondents were nevertheless thinking of *all* recidivism officially recorded or otherwise. The public believes that reoffending closely matches past offending. The public estimated that, of violent offenders who had a record, the previous conviction was likely to be a crime of violence in over 80 percent of cases. The reality is otherwise. Recent data from the state of Washington show that, for the category "violent sex offenders," only 8 percent had a prior violent offense (Washington State Sentencing Guidelines Commission 1992*b*).

However, careful and recent research in the United States demonstrates that there are important limits on the public's support for "three strikes" sentencing laws. Finkel et al. (1996) found that, while the public endorsed the use of criminal record in the sentencing process, this support did not extend to those laws that demand very harsh penalties for crimes committed by recidivists. Rossi, Berk, and Campbell (1996) conducted a large representative survey of the American public and concluded that "there did not seem to be widespread support for habitual offenders sentencing such as is usually found in 'three-strikes-you're out' legislation" (p. 9). Thus the public are likely to disapprove of legislation that condemns an offender to a lengthy prison term for a relatively minor felony simply because he has committed two prior serious felonies. For example, in 1995 an offender was sentenced to twenty-five years to life in California for stealing a pizza. Although only a petty theft felony, it was his third conviction, with two serious priors. The public would appear to favor harsh recidivist statutes only if the third, triggering offense is very serious in nature (see Roberts [1996] for discussion of public attitudes regarding the use of criminal record in the sentencing process).

II. Defining the Role of Criminal Record

Differential sentencing as a function of an offender's criminal record can be described as either a discount (for first offenders) or a premium (for recidivists). Discounts can be justified on the rationale that a first offense was an aberration or an out-of-character misjudgment and thus deserving of less than normal punishment or less likely to be predictive of future offending. Premiums can be portrayed as warranted either because the subsequent offense is inherently more serious, on various rationales, or because utilitarian crime prevention concerns justify a harsher sentence.

If recidivists are punished more severely than first offenders, is this sentencing differential a *discount* for first offenders or a *premium* for those with prior criminal involvement? It is a puzzle with parallels in other areas of sentencing. Offenders who plead guilty—particularly early in the criminal justice process—generally receive more lenient sentences than offenders who are convicted after a trial (Ashworth 1992). Is this a discount for the admission of culpability (and, perhaps, the expression of remorse) or an additional penalty imposed on defendants who assert their constitutional rights to a trial? Some people would say that there is no difference between the two and that it matters little how the difference is described. I would argue that, if a tariff is clearly established for a particular offense, and if the rate for first offenders is below that tariff, then it is most appropriate to call this arrangement a first offender discount and not a recidivist premium. From the offender's perspective it may matter little whether it is called a first offender discount or a recidivist premium because the result is the same: more punishment for subsequent convictions. This view may underestimate the importance to offenders of a justification of their sentences. There may also be an important symbolic message conveyed by stressing the notion of a discount rather than a premium. Under a discount, first offenders are being rewarded for a crime-free past. Under a premium, offenders are punished additionally for offending that has already resulted in punishment.

Consider the sentencing of two defendants convicted of a serious felony. Assume that their profiles are comparable in all respects save their prior records: one is a first offender; the other has four prior convictions for armed robbery within the past five years. Assume further that the sentencing guidelines prescribe a sentence length range of two to four years for a felony at this level of seriousness. If the first offender receives a sentence of one year (departures being allowed), while the recidivist receives a three-year term, this is surely an example of a first offender discount that has been denied the recidivist to reflect his status as a repeat offender. Now consider a third defendant, identical in all respects to the first two save for the fact that he has a longer criminal history than either. This individual has eight priors for robbery over the previous five years. If the judge imposes a four-year term, this is a recidivist premium because an additional distinction has been made between recidivists with differing criminal histories.

Two analogies may help to clarify the point. First, some European countries such as France and Belgium periodically extend amnesties to inmates to mark the ascension to power of a new president or monarch or to celebrate a national holiday, such as Bastille Day. If recidivists were excluded from such an amnesty, would it be called a recidivist premium? Surely not, as the consequence would be not the imposition of *additional* punishment for recidivists but, rather, the denial of a privilege. Second, immigration authorities in some countries occasionally offer an amnesty to illegal immigrants who, if they come forward, can become legitimate landed immigrants. If the amnesty is not extended to illegal immigrants who have previously been deported and yet who have returned (illegally) to the country, is this a punishment premium for repetitive wrongdoing? I would argue that this too is an example of clemency extended to "first offenders" and not a recidivist premium per se. (See von Hirsch [1985], p. 88, for further discussion of this issue.)

III. The Role of Criminal Record in Sentencing Theory and Practice

Is it necessary to justify sentencing differentials on the basis of prior offending? Some readers would take it to be self-evident that sentences should become harsher as a function of the extent of the offender's criminal history. For example, Kirkpatrick, in discussing Oregon's guidelines, asserts that "greater severity is justified when the offender has been convicted previously but has continued to engage in criminal conduct" (Kirkpatrick 1992, p. 701). Similarly, several state guidelines manuals affirm the importance of criminal history as an enhancement, without stating exactly *why* sentences should be harsher for recidivists.

For example, the statement of purpose and principles contained in the Oregon Sentencing Guidelines Implementation manual states that "the appropriate punishment for a felony conviction should depend on the seriousness of the crime of conviction when compared to all other crimes and the offender's criminal history" (Oregon Criminal Justice Council 1989, p. 5). In North Carolina, the sentencing laws enacted in 1993 "classify felons based on the severity of their crime and on the extent and gravity of their criminal record" (North Carolina Sentencing and Policy Advisory Commission 1993, p. 1). In this respect, criminal history is treated in the same way as crime seriousness: harsher penalties are justified for more serious crimes, as well as for offenders with longer records. In my view, the issue of criminal record requires additional justification in terms of sentencing purposes. It is insufficient merely to assume, for the purposes of sentencing, the significance of a criminal record. Few people would disagree with the proposition that the severity of sentences should reflect the seriousness of the crimes for which they were imposed.[13] There is far less agreement about the relevance of criminal record, as I hope to demonstrate in this essay.

[13] A great deal of empirical research (e.g., Blumstein and Cohen 1980) has demonstrated that the principle of proportionality, according to which the severity of sentences reflects the seriousness of the crimes for which they are imposed, underlies public views of sentencing.

A. *Justifying the Use of Criminal History Information*

A moral issue lies at the heart of the relationship between sentencing and criminal record. As Fletcher notes: "There are serious ethical issues in punishing a person more severely on the basis of past crimes already once punished" (Fletcher 1978, p. 466). If a defendant has already discharged the previous sentence of the court, is he not being sentenced a second time for the same criminal conduct? Some jurists argue that increased penalties because of prior crimes conflict with the principles underlying legal doctrines of double jeopardy. Many affirm that the recidivist premium is nothing less than additional punishment for a prior offense (see, e.g., the discussion in Fletcher 1982; Monahan 1982; Dormont 1991). The constitutions of many countries contain provisions that prohibit double punishment. According to Section 11 (h) of the Canadian Charter of Rights and Freedoms, any person "has the right . . . if finally found guilty and punished for the offence, not to be tried or punished for it again." If an offender receives a much harsher penalty on the grounds that he has offended (and been punished) in the past, is this not punishment a second time for the same criminal conduct? (From this perspective, the potential for increased penalties occasioned by prior crimes can be viewed as akin to an inchoate sentence, similar to a suspended sentence. If the offender remains law-abiding, no further penalty will ensue. However, in the event that a reconviction occurs, the previous crime will now have an effect, although that effect is hidden within a fresh sentence, as an enhancement rather than an independent disposition.)

The consequences for the defendant of a recidivist premium can be far-reaching. In some cases the recidivist premium means that a defendant who otherwise would receive a noncustodial penalty is incarcerated, not for the seriousness of his current conduct, but for crimes committed earlier. In other cases, the recidivist premium can mean the addition of years of extra time to an offender's custodial term. On what theoretical grounds then, can additional punishment of an offender for actions already paid for in the past be justified? The principal sentencing purposes consider an offender's criminal history to be relevant to the sentencing decision, although the justifications, and the consequences for the defendant, vary widely.

1. *Utilitarian Sentencing Purposes.* For the utilitarian purposes of special deterrence and incapacitation, the link between past and future offending is unambiguous: previous criminal conduct is predictive of future offending. Research on the prediction of criminal behavior has

repeatedly demonstrated criminal record to be the single best predictor of future offending (e.g., Gabor 1986; Champion 1994). Although other variables—including social characteristics such as age, gender, and employment status—are related to recidivism risk, the relationship between recidivism and criminal record is strongest. Advocates of special deterrence would argue that the existence of a fresh conviction is prima facie evidence that the previous sentence "failed" to have the desired effect, presumably because it was too lenient. Accordingly, recidivists should receive harsher sentences because they have not learned their lessons.

As far as general deterrence is concerned, the link between criminal record and sentence severity is more tenuous, although some advocates of this sentencing purpose argue that a message needs to be conveyed to other, potential recidivists, and this message consists of the imposition of a harsher sentence. Van den Haag, for example, states that "there is no reason why the punishment threatened for committing a second offense should not exceed that threatened for the first" (van den Haag 1978, p. 132) and that "the punishment threatened for committing a second offense should exceed that threatened for the first" (van den Haag 1986, p. 88). In short, the utilitarian sentencing agenda attempts to reduce the incidence of crime through the imposition or threat of punishment and criminal record is seen as being directly relevant to this aim.

2. *Desert Theories of Sentencing.* Desert theories of sentencing emphasize the seriousness of the criminal conduct and the culpability of the offender. The probability of future offending is of limited relevance. Popular conceptions of desert theories would appear to rule out the use of criminal history information, as the focus is on the offense of conviction, and not previous criminal conduct. Nevertheless, desert theorists such as Andrew von Hirsch, Martin Wasik, Andrew Ashworth, and Hyman Gross, do see a limited role for criminal history information.[14] They argue that everyday moral judgments incorporate the notion of leniency toward people who transgress for the first time. According to this view, a lapse into criminality after a lifetime of law-

[14] Marc Ouimet (1989, n.d.) argues that a recidivist premium is justified from a desert perspective in order to preserve proportionality in sentencing. Just as rich defendants should pay a higher monetary fine than less wealthy offenders, so it is with imprisonment: those who have already served several terms of custody "need" harsher penalties on subsequent occasions. This is a harsh view of desert and implies that offenders become progressively desensitized to the rigors of imprisonment. To my knowledge there is no evidence that a third period of imprisonment is less harsh than the first.

abiding conduct should be responded to with a certain degree of tolerance.[15] The result is a first-offender discount (but not a recidivist premium). As Wasik and von Hirsch note: "A first offender, after being confronted with censure or blame, is capable—as a reasoning human being presumed capable of ethical judgements—of reflecting on the morality of what he has done and making an extra effort to show greater restraint. What we do, in granting the discount [to first offenders] is to show respect for this capacity—and thereby give the offender a so-called 'second chance.' With repetitions, however, the discount should begin to diminish and eventually disappear" (Wasik and von Hirsch 1995, p. 410; see also Gross 1979; von Hirsch 1982, 1985). Recidivists can make no such appeal for leniency, and accordingly the full force of the sentence should be imposed.

This perspective on the role of prior convictions is consistent with the "progressive loss of mitigation" model that operates in most common-law jurisdictions, such as Canada and England and Wales (Ashworth 1992). Mitigation is accorded first offenders—or those who are practically first offenders—but this leniency is progressively withdrawn. The word "progressive" implies that this loss is a gradual process. The extinction of mitigation in practice is not that progressive; after three convictions, first offender status appears to be lost, and the offender faces the full brunt of the sentencing tariff. In contrast to the position taken by Wasik and von Hirsch, other theorists point out the difficulties in justifying even a limited role for criminal record in the sentencing decision (see Fletcher 1978, pp. 463–66; Singer 1979, chap. 5; Durham 1987). According to their view, prior criminality should not be considered at all in determining how much punishment an offender deserves for the current offense.

Thus, while desert proponents agree on one conclusion (no version of desert theory would support a recidivist premium in which the severity of the sentence increases as a direct function of the number of previous convictions), there is disagreement as to whether a sentencing discount should be extended to first offenders. Figure 1 presents graphic representations of the desert-based and utilitarian positions regarding the role of criminal record in determining the severity of sentence.

[15] These notions are not new: over a century ago, Cox noted that, "for he who has had so emphatic a warning as a trial, a conviction and punishment can plead none of the excuses which may be properly urged in behalf of first offenders" (Cox 1877, pp. 146–47).

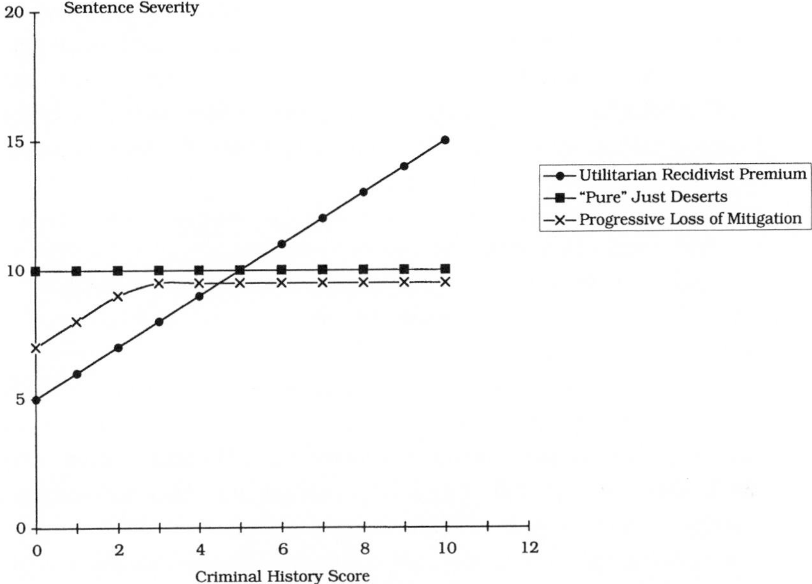

FIG. 1.—Sentence severity as a function of criminal history score: theoretical curves

Other theories of punishment also address the issue of criminal record. These cannot all be reviewed here, but one can be used for illustration. Adler advances a theory of punishment that turns on the issue of rights. According to his "rectification" theory, someone who commits a crime has "expanded the sphere of liberty . . . by arrogating excess liberties" (Adler 1991, p. 3). Following this theory, recidivists should be punished more severely because their current offending (their recidivism) has canceled or, to use Adler's phrase, "denatured the punishment for the first offense" (p. 170). It is clear then that almost all theories of sentencing or punishment grapple directly with the issue of a recidivist premium, with most supporting some kind of sentencing differential as a function of the number or nature of previous convictions.

American sentencing guidelines systems have developed the most detailed policies concerning the use of prior record of any common-law sentencing systems. Criminal history plays a central role in all state systems as well as in the federal guidelines. Only the American systems lay out in an explicit manner the ways in which criminal history information is to be used. Any attempt to understand the use of criminal history in jurisdictions such as Canada or England and Wales would have to rely on inferences on the basis of sentencing statistics and decisions in the case law. Although there are important common characteristics of all guidelines systems, the diversity of approach to criminal record found in the United States illustrates the subtleties and complexities of the issue and the different approaches that have evolved.

B. *Justifying the Premium*

Which sentencing purposes are cited by the guideline systems in the United States to justify sentencing differentials between offenders with varying criminal histories?

1. *Federal Guidelines.* The federal guidelines manual is one of the few that ties criminal record explicitly to the goals of sentencing (see Roberts [1994] for a more detailed discussion). The federal commission decided against endorsing a single sentencing rationale or even a hierarchy of purposes. Instead, the commission appeals to the principal sentencing purposes and then relates criminal record to these goals. The federal sentencing guidelines manual asserts that a defendant's criminal record is directly relevant to considerations of desert *and* crime control: "A defendant with a record of prior criminal behavior is more culpable than a first offender and thus deserving of greater punishment. General deterrence of criminal conduct dictates that a clear message be sent to society that repeated criminal behavior will aggravate the need for punishment with each occurrence. To protect the public from further crimes of the particular defendant, the likelihood of recidivism and future criminal behavior must be considered. Repeated criminal behavior is an indicator of a limited likelihood of successful rehabilitation" (U.S. Sentencing Commission 1992, p. 267).

2. *State Systems.* All state systems take account of prior crimes, but no system offers a fully articulated reason for doing so. In order to understand the sentencing philosophy underlying the state systems, it is sometimes necessary to go to the enabling statute that created the guidelines. Many state guideline system manuals omit reference to the purposes of sentencing. In the absence of an explicit rationale, some states provide a statement of purpose, although this is not always particularly informative. In Oregon, the statement of purpose is that "the primary objectives of sentencing are to punish each offender appropriately" (Oregon Criminal Justice Council 1993, p. 4). The Oregon manual further states that "From a 'just deserts' perspective, repeat criminal conduct after punishment for prior convictions warrants increasingly severe responses. . . . Historically and logically, an offender

with a criminal record deserves more punishment for a subsequent crime than an offender without a record" (Oregon Criminal Justice Council 1989, p. 50).

In several states the relevance of criminal record is asserted without any justification. For example, the Minnesota manual states that "the purpose of the sentencing guidelines is to establish rational and consistent sentencing standards which reduce sentencing disparity and ensure that sanctions following conviction of a felony are proportional to the severity of the offense of conviction and the extent of the offender's criminal history" (Minnesota Sentencing Guidelines Commission, 1993, p. 1). And the Sentencing Reform Act in the state of Washington was designed to "ensure that the punishment for a criminal offense is proportionate to the seriousness of the offense and the offender's criminal history" (Washington State Sentencing Guidelines Commission 1992*a*, p. II-6).

Some states make a clear distinction between crime seriousness and the dangerousness of the offender. For example, the Utah guidelines note that "the underlying philosophy of the guidelines is that sentences should be proportionate to the seriousness of the offense for which the offender is convicted . . . the risk that offender poses to society as inferred from offender's criminal history is also a major consideration" (Utah Commission on Criminal and Juvenile Justice 1994, p. 2). In contrast, other states combine the issues of desert and dangerousness into a single concept. As the North Carolina Sentencing and Policy Advisory Committee noted: "The severity of the sentence should reflect the extent and gravity of the offender's prior criminal behavior. Such behavior is viewed as a measure of culpability or blameworthiness and also as a predictor of future criminal conduct" (North Carolina Sentencing and Policy Advisory Committee 1993, p. 17). Guidelines manuals in other states (e.g., Kansas, Pennsylvania, Florida) eschew all mention of sentencing purposes, launching instead directly into the mechanics of computing criminal history scores. In the absence of any such statement of sentencing purpose, it is hard to know whether the criminal history information is being used in a principled way or which theoretical justifications are being invoked.

IV. Policy Issues Relating to the Role of Criminal Record

Criminal record is not a unidimensional dichotomous variable. Nor is it simply a matter of counting prior convictions. Criminal history can be defined in many different ways, and a full appreciation of the concept—whether from the perspective of desert or dangerousness—requires a multidimensional approach. A series of important policy questions has confronted sentencing commissions in the United States. These include the following: how to define previous criminal conduct, whether the elapsed time between convictions should count, and whether the degree of similarity between the episodes of offending and the seriousness of previous behavior is relevant. (See Wasik [1987] for a thorough discussion of English case law relating to eight quantitative and qualitative factors relevant to criminal record.) These issues have been discussed for over twenty years now, but there is still no consensus on how they should be resolved (see Wilkins et al. [1976] and Kress [1980] for earlier writings). Different commissions have resolved these policy questions in quite different ways.

Central to any commission's deliberations is the question of operational simplicity. It would be straightforward to devise a criminal history scheme with points for the number, nature, similarity, and recency of prior offending, but one consequence would be a wide range of criminal history scores. As the potential range of criminal history scores increases, so does the number of criminal history categories, and this in turn increases the number of cells within a two dimensional sentencing grid (assuming a narrow range of points per criminal history category). For example, the federal grid contains six criminal history categories and generates 258 cells in the matrix. Criminal history points range from 0 (criminal history category 1) to 13 or more (category 6). Increasing the number of criminal history categories would mean a large and unwieldy guidelines grid.

Of course, the number of criminal history categories can always be constrained by aggregating offenders with criminal history scores within a range. First offenders might be defined as criminal history scores of zero to three; the next category as criminal history scores from four to seven and so on. The effect of this aggregation is however to lose the very sensitivity that a complex criminal history computation was designed to create. For this reason, commissions have attempted to strike a balance between incorporating a number of variables (such as seriousness of previous convictions) without creating a criminal history calculation that would be excessively complicated.

A. Definitions of Criminal History: Previous Arrests, Convictions, or Sentences

The general concept of criminal history can be deconstructed into a number of different yet overlapping elements, including the number, recency, seriousness, and similarity of prior arrests or convictions. As well, the concept of prior criminality can be approached by means of the previous sentencing record, including (but not restricted to) the number, recency, and duration of custodial terms. When different elements are combined within some kind of point system, arbitrary decisions have to be taken regarding equivalences. For example, how many misdemeanors are the equivalent in terms of seriousness of one prior felony? Should any number of repetitive yet minor crimes such as theft ever carry the same weight in a criminal history index as a violent felony such as rape? How many nonviolent crimes are the equivalent in terms of criminal history of a crime of violence? How many convictions resulting in a community-based sanction are the equal of a one-year period of custody? These are some of the vexed questions that confront a sentencing commission attempting to derive a measure of prior criminal activity.

The concept underlying these different measures of record is that of offense seriousness. An alternate way of gauging the seriousness of an offender's criminal history would be to employ a direct measure of crime seriousness based on one of the scales of crime seriousness that have been developed (e.g., Rossi et al. 1974). This approach has not yet been employed. One of the advantages would be greater uniformity between jurisdictions in measurement of criminal history.

The most basic issue is exactly what kinds of previous contact with the criminal justice system should be counted. First, however, it is worth returning briefly to the level of theory. Different sentencing theories would use different definitions of prior offending. Utilitarian theories concerned with risk should be highly sensitive to the nature of prior offending and its relationship to current offending. Incapacitative sentencing strategies are particularly concerned with offending that suggests either a career criminal or a pattern of repetitive offending. Desert theories however, would be less interested in the nature of prior offending than the severity, which can be gauged (and is, at the federal level) in terms of previous sentencing decisions.

The primary issue then that confronts a sentencing commission is to decide what determines an offender's criminal history score. An important central dichotomy is whether the criminal history calculation should reflect previous convictions or previous sentences. The federal guidelines count previous sentences rather than previous convictions. Three criminal history points are scored for a prior sentence of imprisonment exceeding thirteen months, two points for each prior sentence of imprisonment of at least sixty days, and one point for every other prior sentence. The justification for using periods of custody as a measure of criminal history is that variations in offense definition preclude valid comparisons of previous convictions from different jurisdictions. The goal of this approach is to devise a criminal history score that reflects the seriousness of the prior offending. Two offenders with previous felony convictions may have committed crimes of different seriousness. Counting the mere existence of a prior felony will not capture this variability. However, the duration of previous periods of incarceration can be taken (according to advocates of this criminal history measure) as a proxy for crime seriousness.

Nevertheless, there are also several disadvantages with the federal system of scoring previous sentences. The principal is that the use of prior sentences can undermine the incapacitative effectiveness of the guideline system. Consider two offenders, each of whom has two prior felonies. One individual has two priors for robbery; the other has two priors for criminal sexual conduct. The periods of custody were approximately the same for both offenders. The current offense of conviction for both defendants is sexual assault. The data on criminal specialization are rather mixed; however, some offenses show a more specialized pattern of recidivism than others. Recidivists in these categories are more likely to commit crimes similar to those for which they have already been convicted (see Champion [1994] for a review), but this would be missed by a system that did not take the nature of the priors into account but just the duration of previous imprisonment.

A second disadvantage of counting previous sentences of imprisonment is that criminal history scores reflect a previous sentencing judge's perception of the seriousness of the prior offense, and this may or may not adequately reflect the seriousness of the crime. In short, previous sentences are a very poor proxy for the seriousness of prior offending.

Finally, there is a clear loss of precision in a system that uses the number of previous custodial terms rather than the statutory definition of crime seriousness or even the length of prior terms of custody. Consider the case of two offenders sentenced in 1980. Defendant A received a twelve-year term; defendant B a fourteen-month term. In 1995 the two are resentenced. On this occasion their criminal history scores will be identical (three points for a previous custodial sentence in excess of thirteen months). This makes little sense from the perspective of desert or dangerousness.

For these (as well as other reasons), the state guideline systems have rejected the use of prior sentences in favor of an index of previous criminality based on the number and nature of previous convictions (see Parent [1987] for a discussion of the choice between prior convictions and prior sentences in Minnesota). The scope of the definition of prior record used in Florida is typical of many state systems: " 'Prior record' is defined as any past criminal conduct resulting in conviction occurring prior to the commission of the primary offense. 'Conviction' is defined as the determination of guilt resulting from plea or trial, regardless of whether adjudication was withheld or imposition of sentence was suspended. Prior record includes all prior Florida, federal, out-of-state, military and foreign convictions as well as convictions for violation of municipal or county ordinances that are supported by a state statute" (Florida Sentencing Guidelines Commission 1991, p. 10). Guideline systems have also steered clear of using prior arrests as an index of previous offending. Although the number of prior arrests may be a significant predictor of recidivism, guideline systems restrict the definition of previous offending to convictions. Central to the objections to use of prior arrests is the notion that the defendant's guilt has simply been alleged and not determined in a judicial proceeding. (Not all scholars would agree with this exclusion. For example, van den Haag [1986], p. 89, writes that, "in sentencing, previous arrests as well as prior convictions may be regarded as aggravating factors.") Finally, there is some research evidence that suggests that adding arrests to the criminal history calculation would provide little additional predictive power beyond that which is achieved by counting convictions alone (Wilkins et al. 1976, p. 28).

A guideline system that simply assigned criminal history scores on the basis of the raw number of previous convictions would be crude, indeed, and would not follow theoretical principles relating to desert or dangerousness. However, the guideline systems do not simply count the number of previous convictions recorded; various weighting schemes are introduced so that the seriousness of the prior criminal conduct also determines the final criminal history score. Perhaps the most popular weighting concerns the presence of violent crimes in the criminal history of the offender.

1. *Person versus Property Offending.* Most state guideline systems assign greater weight to crimes of violence. Prior felony convictions in Pennsylvania, for example, are assigned one, two, or three criminal history points. Three points are assigned for the most serious offenses

against the person, including murder, manslaughter, rape, involuntary deviate sexual intercourse, kidnapping, arson endangering persons, and robbery in which injury is threatened or inflicted (Pennsylvania Commission on Sentencing 1988). Similarly, in Oregon and Kansas, the highest criminal history category includes offenders whose criminal history includes three or more person felonies, the second highest category includes two person felonies, and so on (see Oregon Criminal Justice Council 1989; Kansas Sentencing Commission 1993). However, not all states follow this rule: in Michigan, the greatest number of criminal history points is awarded to defendants with high severity convictions. These include offenses against the person (e.g., assault, homicide) and property (e.g., larceny) (see Michigan Sentencing Guidelines Advisory Committee 1988).

2. *Offense Definitions.* A second way in which guideline systems take into account the gravity of the criminal record is to weight felonies more heavily than misdemeanors and more serious felonies more heavily than less serious felonies. The Minnesota guidelines provide a good example. Offenses are banded into ten levels of crime seriousness. Criminal history scores reflect the seriousness level of the prior offending. Thus prior felonies at the lowest level of seriousness (severity level 1 or 2) generate one-half a criminal history point, while prior felonies at the highest levels (8–10) result in the accretion of two full points to the offender's criminal history score.

Another way in which guideline systems reflect the seriousness of prior offending concerns the problem of the persistent petty offender. If the criminal history calculation mechanically assigned a point (or even half a point) for misdemeanors, some offenders would end up with high criminal history scores as a result of repetitive but minor crimes. The solution adopted in the state of Minnesota is to place a limit of a single point on the consideration of misdemeanors in the criminal history score. Likewise in Kansas, misdemeanors have a very limited effect on the criminal history computation. First offenders or defendants with only one prior misdemeanor constitute the first of nine criminal history categories. Category 2 is for defendants with two or more misdemeanors, but thereafter the number of misdemeanors does not result in promotion to a higher criminal history level.

B. *Regulating the Use of Juvenile Records*

A critical question for many offenders with respect to the reach of guideline systems is whether juvenile records should count in sentencing proceedings at the adult level. Is it appropriate that juvenile records extinguish for the purposes of sentencing at the adult level? On this question, desert and utilitarian theorists would probably agree that these records should stay alive. There seems little justification from the perspectives of deterrence or incapacitation for expunging a juvenile record when the offender reaches the age of majority. Indeed, utilitarian sentencing theorists would consider the juvenile offense record to be a critical indicator of the likelihood of further offending. A sixteen-year-old who commits several burglaries has a higher probability of recidivism than a sixteen-year-old with no priors. Desert theorists should also have difficulty with a system that completely erased records at the age of majority. Sentencing adults who have a significant juvenile record as first offenders is tantamount to offering a double discount: the offender received a discount at the juvenile level (first juvenile offense) and should not now be accorded a second completely fresh start. Both utilitarian and desert theorists would also agree that the juvenile priors should not carry the same weight as adult previous convictions. Insofar as juvenile records are concerned, the difference between utilitarian and desert theories relates to the slope of effect on sentence severity. Utilitarians would use juvenile convictions to augment sentence lengths for adults over a sustained period of time, whereas, from a desert perspective, the juvenile record should serve only to disentitle an adult of first-offender status, but its influence should not extend much further than this.

The criminal justice systems in other countries have demonstrated a reluctance to use juvenile infractions in sentencing proceedings at the adult level. For example, the Young Offenders Act in Canada regulates the use of juvenile convictions in the following way. If a juvenile offender commits no further offense prior to attaining the age of majority, the convictions under the Young Offenders Act will be expunged. As with similar legislation elsewhere, this provision of the Young Offenders Act recognizes the limited accountability of young offenders and reflects the different model of criminal justice that applies to juvenile offenders. If juvenile convictions carried the same weight as adult convictions in sentencing proceedings, this would be contrary to the notion of processing young offenders within a separate justice system.

If juvenile records are ignored, or their effect is significantly reduced, how much predictive power is sacrificed in terms of adult reoffending? On the face of things, a significant predictor of recidivism is being underused or totally lost. According to a large-scale Bureau of

Justice Statistics study (see Champion 1994), the presence of juvenile offenses was one of the most significant predictors of adult reconviction. However, this predictive power assumes that systematic juvenile statistics are available and the use of juvenile records does not come without a price.

The question of whether to include juvenile records and, if so, how to weight them in the computation of a criminal history score has been given considerable attention by sentencing commissions across the United States. As with other issues relating to criminal record there is variability in the way in which different systems use juvenile records. There appears to be little consensus among practitioners: prosecutors and law enforcement officials in general are likely to vigorously endorse the use of juvenile records in adult sentencing proceedings. Defense counsel (and most academics) are likely to oppose the use of such information (see Falvey [1982], pp. 262–64, and Parent [1987] for discussion of the Minnesota experience in this regard). As Greenwoood, Abrahamse, and Zimring (1984) note: "The hazard is that the unsubstantiated arrest information could foster incorrect predictions of subsequent criminality" (p. vii).

The arguments against the use of juvenile records in adult sentencing proceedings turn not so much on a principled argument of nonrelevance but, rather, on recognition that the administration of juvenile justice fails to accord the young offender the same degree of protection that is offered to offenders at the adult level. The full due process protections that are accorded adult offenders are not generally extended to juveniles (Dormont 1991). There has also been recognition by several guidelines commissions and scholars that the poor state of juvenile record information systems (relative to comparable systems at the adult level) would result in inequities of application if all juvenile adjudications were included (Griswold 1985). Since disparity reduction is a principal expressed aim of all guideline systems, there has been a tendency to count only the most serious juvenile convictions. For example, according to the Pennsylvania prior record arrangements, "the juvenile adjudications of delinquency which may be counted are strictly limited. The commission concluded that it would be unfair to count prior juvenile crimes committed by the defendant when he was very young, or when the juvenile crimes were not very serious" (Pennsylvania Commission on Sentencing 1988, p. 47). This means that only felony crimes or weapons misdemeanors are counted, and then only if the crime was committed when the defendant was at least fourteen years of age.

For these reasons, sentencing commissions have sought to effect a balance between the extremes of completely disregarding previous juvenile convictions and assigning them the same weight as previous adult convictions. Unlike some other issues relating to criminal record, there is a degree of consensus. Almost all the sentencing guideline systems count some juvenile adjudications. However, relative to previous adult convictions, the juvenile priors play a limited role in subsequent sentencing hearings. The American guidelines systems typically employ prior juvenile convictions in complex ways that reflect the defendant's current age, the time since the previous (juvenile) infractions, as well as the seriousness of the juvenile offending. The Minnesota guidelines provide a good example of a system in which juvenile records play a role in sentencing at the adult level, but one that is carefully circumscribed.

In Minnesota, juvenile convictions are included primarily to target offenders whose criminal careers became clear at the juvenile level (Minnesota Sentencing Guidelines Commission 1993). The focus is on serious crimes. Thus only juvenile offenses that would have been felonies if committed at the adult level are included in the criminal history score computation. There is also an age-related exclusion: juvenile offenses committed before the offender's sixteenth birthday are excluded from consideration. In addition, prior juvenile adjudications receive a differential weighting: two juvenile offenses are required to equal one point on the criminal history score. Since partial points are not counted, the practical effect of this is to give juvenile offenders a second chance: a single juvenile conviction will not result in an enhanced sentence for the adult offender. The result appears to have been a reduction in the variability surrounding usage of juvenile records.

Other sentencing guidelines systems follow the same general approach, namely of counting juvenile adjudications, but with strict limiting standards. The guidelines in Florida, for example, count *all* prior juvenile convictions but only if they occurred within a three-year period preceding the commission of the primary offense. This three-year period is considerably shorter than the period of eligibility that applies to adult priors (ten years—see Florida Sentencing Guidelines Commission 1991). In Kansas, the age of the offender is the determining factor. Juvenile adjudications extinguish once the adult offender reaches twenty-five years of age. However, there is also a threshold of seriousness: this decay mechanism does not apply to juvenile adjudications that would constitute a violent felony (Kansas Sentencing Commission 1993).

Some state commissions have chosen to include juvenile offenses within the criminal history score calculation because to act otherwise would create inequities. The Pennsylvania commission consulted extensively with criminal justice professionals and state legislators and held public hearings on the topic. The manual states the result of those consultations: "It [the commission] concluded that it would be inequitable for defendants with serious juvenile records to be treated the same as defendants who were first offenders" (Pennsylvania Commission on Sentencing 1988, p. 47). Nevertheless, the Pennsylvania guidelines, like those found in Minnesota, also carefully circumscribe the use of juvenile adjudications. Once again the seriousness of the prior offending is relevant, although in Pennsylvania the issue of seriousness also applies to the current offense. Thus only a felony or certain weapons misdemeanors are considered serious enough to count, and then only when the current adult offense is itself a felony (Pennsylvania Commission on Sentencing 1988). The age of the offender at the time of the juvenile offending is relevant. Pennsylvania only includes juvenile delinquent acts that occurred after the defendant turned fourteen (Pennsylvania Commission on Sentencing 1988).

A seriousness threshold is also present in the federal guidelines, although, consistent with other aspects of those guidelines, seriousness is defined by reference to the severity of the sentence previously imposed (rather than by offense definition, such as felony or misdemeanor). Thus, only those juvenile adjudications that resulted in adult sentences of imprisonment for a term in excess of thirteen months or resulted in imposition of an adult or juvenile sentence or release from confinement of that sentence within five years of the defendant's commencement of the current offense are counted (U.S. Sentencing Commission 1992). Finally, a limited number of states such as Alaska do not use juvenile convictions in setting the presumptive sentence for adult offenders (Alaska Sentencing Commission 1991, p. 16).

The importance of targeting repetitive violent offenders is clear from the juvenile record provisions in many states. Juvenile records are always counted, or weighted more heavily, if the juvenile conviction is for a violent felony and the instant offense is also a crime of violence.

Under the Washington guidelines, prior violent felony convictions at the juvenile level receive the same weight as prior violent adult felonies, if the current offense is a crime of violence (Washington State Sentencing Guidelines Commission 1992*a*, p. II-56). Finally, some states explicitly ignore the juvenile criminal history. Alaska, for example, does not use juvenile convictions in setting the presumptive sentence (Alaska Sentencing Commission 1991, p. 16).

C. The Relationship between Previous and Current Offending

Another issue that should be relevant to sentencers concerns the relationship between the nature of the previous and current offending. The similarity of the previous conviction to the current offense should be relevant to the recidivist premium. As with many others, this question returns us to the sentencing theories. Utilitarians should be interested in the pattern of similarity from conviction to conviction. Repetitive offending—six robbery priors—provides utilitarians with the justification for an incapacitative sentence on the grounds that the defendant is, or is about to become, a career criminal. According to desert theory, the issue of similarity is of less importance. The disentitlement to a first-offender discount should be unaffected by whether the offender has been convicted of similar offenses in the past. This said, similarity of previous to current offending is an important issue for almost all American guideline systems. The defendant with similar priors receives an escalated progress along the criminal history dimension of most sentencing grids.

The federal guidelines, however, pay no attention to the degree of similarity between previous and current offending. Dissimilar priors have the same effect as similar priors, provided they resulted in comparable terms of custody. There is no mechanism to discount prior unrelated offenses or to enhance the recidivist premium for highly similar prior offenses, although the rules for sentencing departures include reference to similarity of previous conduct. An asymmetry exists in this respect: evidence of *similar* adult criminal conduct *not* resulting in a conviction can be used to justify an upward departure (although dissimilar previous conduct cannot be used to justify a downward departure) (U.S. Sentencing Commission 1992, Sec. 4A1.3 [e]).

Many state guideline systems are sensitive to the relationship between previous and current offense. The Washington guidelines typify a system that weighs prior convictions more heavily if they indicate a pattern of offending. If an offender has several previous convictions involving violence, these will count most heavily when the current offense is also a crime of violence. The same is true for burglary, drug offenses, and violent traffic offenses (Washington State Sentencing Guidelines Commission 1992*a*, p. II-56). The result is that recidivists who commit the same kind of offense will move more rapidly across the criminal history scale.

This use of criminal history represents a departure from systems that simply enhance sentences as a function of the number, seriousness, or recency of priors. It suggests a greater orientation toward incapacitation and recidivism risk and less concern with simply punishing recidivist offenders more harshly. Underlying the Washington model is an assumption that, all things being equal, an offender with two prior burglary convictions is more likely to commit further burglaries than an offender with two prior felonies of a different nature. This raises the question of specialization in offending: To what extent do criminal histories follow an offense-specific path?

Data on this question are mixed. Blumstein et al. (1986) found evidence of specialization, but there was also considerable variation in the extent of this specialization among offense types. Thus offenders convicted of offenses involving drugs or fraud were the most highly specialized. There were also significant interactions between offense types and offender characteristics such as race. Auto theft, for example, was a highly specialized offense among black offenders. These researchers concluded that "most active offenders engage in a considerable variety of crime types, with a somewhat greater tendency for offenders to repeat the same crime or to repeat within the group of property crimes or the group of violent crimes" (Blumstein et al. 1986, p. 5).

Recent research (Champion 1994) supports this notion of specialization in offending patterns. However, data from the state of Washington fail to sustain an image of specialized recidivism. Offenders convicted of a violent offense were more likely to have a nonviolent previous conviction than a violent prior (33 percent had a prior nonviolent offense compared to 22 percent with a prior violent offense of any kind; see Washington State Sentencing Guidelines Commission [1992*b*], table 8). Of the violent sex offenders, only 6 percent had a prior conviction for a violent sex offense. The most frequent prior offense category for sex offenders was nonviolent crimes (15 percent); fully 67 percent had no prior offense. Even the drug offenders were more likely to have a non-drug-related offense in their record than a prior drug offense (19 percent vs. 6 percent). Similar results emerge from research in other jurisdictions. For example, Farrington (1991) reports British data showing limited specialization for violent offenders. Bottomley and Pease show that when there was a reconviction it was more likely to be for a different offense (Bottomley and Pease 1986, p. 108). For the present, then, a system that bases its criminal history calculations on a model of criminal behavior that reflects offense-specific specialization is going to result in some overprediction: offenders with previous convictions involving violence are going to pay a heavier price in terms of their criminal history score than is justified in light of the actual probability of further *violent* offending.

D. *Custody Status at the Time of the Offense*

One feature of the criminal history provisions of many guideline systems concerns the offender's custody status at the time the current offense was committed. This variable affects large numbers of offenders: almost half the offenders committed to state prisons in 1986 were on parole or probation at the time of admission (Bureau of Justice Statistics 1990). Being on pretrial release, probation, or on parole at the time of offending inflates the criminal history score in most states (as well as at the federal level), and this provokes a more punitive response. What is the theoretical justification for this? In Minnesota, Parent notes that "the theory was that an offender deserved greater punishment if he committed a new crime before completing service of a previous sentence" (Parent 1987, p. 70). Many people would agree with this statement, but it is an assertion more than a justification and fails to explain *why* the criminal history calculation should be affected. After all, the crime is no more serious because the offender's parole has been breached. The justification must lie in notions of culpability or defiance of lawful authority. Although it may make little practical difference to the offender how his sentence is enhanced, one might ask what relation there is between the defendant's custody status at the time of the offense and his criminal history.

Why should the offender's criminal history score per se be inflated because he was on parole? Being on parole surely sheds no light on the number or nature of his previous convictions. One response concerns the notion of defiance of authority (see Fletcher 1978): the offender is defying authority on two grounds, first, because of the recidivism and, second, because the recidivism occurs while another sentence is still being discharged. Another response might be that the offender is abusing a privilege. He has been offered a mitigated sentence (diversion or early release from confinement) and has abused the opportunity offered to him. Neither response touches the issue of criminal history per se. It would seem more reasonable to impose a more severe penalty for reasons to do with the failure to complete a previous sentence. A custody status premium would appear to be justified according to utilitarian sentencing purposes: just as a protracted delay between the current and previous offending indicates a lower probability of recidivism, a brief interval between episodes suggests that reoffending is more likely. Thus reductivist theories would advocate a custody status premium while desert theorists would not (but see von Hirsch 1993).

How do guideline systems handle this issue? The federal guidelines are particularly sensitive to an offender's custody status at arrest. Under the federal system, if the defendant committed the current offense while under some form of criminal justice custody status from a previous conviction, he receives two criminal history points (U.S. Sentencing Commission 1992). Since any prior sentence in excess of thirteen months results in the accretion of three points, committing an offense while on parole has two-thirds the incremental power of a prior sentence of, say, five years.

In Minnesota, criminal history scores are increased by a point if the offender was on probation or parole or in prison following a felony at the time the new felony was committed (Minnesota Sentencing Guidelines Commission 1993, p. 10). Elsewhere this provision has less influence. Under the North Carolina guidelines, there is a legal status enhancement, albeit of a modest magnitude. A prior felony (class A) conviction generates ten criminal history points. A single additional point is added if the offense was committed while the offender was on probation, parole, or postrelease supervision, or while serving a sentence of imprisonment, or while escaping custody (see North Carolina Sentencing and Policy Advisory Commission 1994, table 1).

Some state systems ignore the legal status of the defendant at the time of the arrest. According to the Pennsylvania guidelines, whether the defendant was on bail, probation, or parole or even whether he had just escaped from custody at the time of the offense of current conviction has no effect on the criminal history score. The Pennsylvania manual's commentary notes that this decision was taken because including these as factors in criminal history calculations would have two negative effects. First, defendants who had already had their parole revoked would in effect be penalized twice for the same behavior. Second, including legal status factors in the criminal history score calculation may inhibit prosecutors from "pursuing other courses of action against the defendant on the theory that these factors would be included in determining the sentence on new crimes" (Pennsylvania Commission on Sentencing 1988, p. 48).

E. Elapsed Time between Current and Previous Convictions

There are several reasons why the length of time between the current and the previous conviction might be taken into account in any guideline scheme that prescribes a premium for recidivists. As the interval between episodes of offending increases, the probative value of criminal history as a predictor of future behavior declines. This result has emerged from research on criminal recidivism, which shows that those offenders who are going to recidivate will do so within three years of release from prison (Beck and Shipley 1987). The difference in recidivism risk between an offender with a clean record for, say, thirteen years and a first offender is minimal. Thus advocates of incapacitation should find diminishing predictive utility in previous convictions as the interval of time between the last and the latest conviction increases. As well, desert theorists would argue that a significant interval of time between current and previous conviction would undermine the plausibility of the claim that the current offense is characteristic of the individual (see von Hirsch 1991). Sentencing theorists of all stripes, then, agree that the relevance of a previous conviction declines over time. At some point the prior offending should become extinct for the purposes of future sentencing. The American Bar Association endorsed such a position in its standards relating to sentencing procedures when it stated that any additional term of imprisonment used to reflect prior offending should only include criminality occurring less than five years since the offense of conviction (American Bar Association 1968, p. 161). There is another reason for allowing the importance of priors to decay over time: it offers offenders an incentive to refrain from further offending.

In this section, I examine two questions relating to this issue. The first concerns the existence of a recency premium: do recent priors count more than older previous convictions? Second, is there a point at which previous criminal conduct ceases to count against the defendant, who thereafter is treated as a first offender in any subsequent sentencing proceedings? There is considerable variability in the way in which different guideline systems respond to these issues. American guideline systems do not generally employ a structure in which the power of priors declines over time until they cease to count at all. The terminology used by several guideline manuals is misleading in this respect. By talking about the "decay" of priors, the manuals imply a slow, degenerative effect. In reality there is no decay but, rather, an abrupt extinction of priors once a certain period is reached, usually ten years (e.g., Michigan) or fifteen years (federal sentencing guidelines). This point has been made by Parent in his analysis of the criminal history provisions of the Minnesota guidelines (see Parent 1987, p. 67).

1. *The Federal Guidelines.* According to the federal guidelines, criminal history scores are inflated if the current conviction was recorded within a short space of following the most recent prior offense. Thus under the federal system, two points are added to the criminal history score if the defendant committed any part of the current offense less than two years following release from prison on a prior conviction (U.S. Sentencing Commission 1992, p. 267). This criminal history enhancement shows the asymmetry of guideline systems. Very recent priors carry more weight, but old convictions still within the time period are not discounted.

2. *State-Level Systems.* Most states do not consider "recency" as a continuous variable. Instead, there is a window of time within which previous convictions are equally weighted. This is curious, for, as the Minnesota guidelines manual acknowledges, "The Commission decided it was important to consider not just the total number of felony sentences and stays of imposition, but also the age of the sentences and stays of imposition. A person who was sentenced for three felonies within a five-year period is more culpable than one sentenced for three felonies within a twenty-five year period" (Minnesota Sentencing Guidelines Commission 1993, p. 8). That said, the Minnesota guidelines assign comparable criminal history scores to offenders with different criminal history profiles, so long as both offenders' felony priors are within the fifteen-year period of eligibility. Even the Oregon guidelines, which have sophisticated and articulated criminal history mechanisms taking into account both quantitative and qualitative aspects of prior offending, are insensitive to the *length* of time between episodes of offending (see Oregon Criminal Justice Council 1989, pp. 50–57). Under some (but not all) of the state systems, criminal history is thus transformed into a simple dichotomous variable (within or without the statute of limitation) rather than a more complex continuous one.

The Utah guidelines provide an example of a system that incorporates a true decay provision. The criminal history assessment assigns two points for each prior felony conviction (each separate criminal incident). Thus an offender with three prior felonies has an initial score of six points. However, one point is subtracted for each consecutive year of arrest-free street time that has elapsed since the individual was arrested. As the guidelines manual notes: "The purpose is to reward those offenders who have changed their lives" (Utah Commission on Criminal and Juvenile Justice 1994, p. 13). This provision cannot efface the felony criminal history; the reduction for arrest-free time is restricted to half of the total number of criminal history points (Utah Commission on Criminal and Juvenile Justice 1994, p. 9). However, this mechanism is more sophisticated and sensitive to the issue of crime-free time than those in other states.

Finally, this discussion illustrates a general lesson in the use of criminal record as an aggravating factor in sentencing hearings. Many of the criminal history computational procedures are based to a degree on considerations of simplicity of application. The "decay" provision in the state of Minnesota, for example, includes all previous convictions within the fifteen-year capture period. This means that a one-year-old previous felony carries the same weight in terms of aggravating the current sentence as a fourteen-year-old prior. On either utilitarian or desert grounds, this seems inappropriate. However, it does have the advantage of being simple. The Minnesota Sentencing Guidelines Manual acknowledges as much when it states that "it [the fifteen-year rule] has the over-riding advantage of accurate and simple application" (Minnesota Sentencing Guidelines Commission 1993, p. 9). Clearly, the rule is straightforward; what is less clear is why simplicity should override other considerations.

F. Capture Period: How Long Should Previous Convictions Count against a Defendant?

Another temporal issue concerns the duration of criminal record for the purposes of sentencing. It would be a harsh sentencing system that held an individual's previous convictions against him indefinitely regardless of the length of the period of crime-free behavior that had accumulated or the seriousness of the prior convictions. But at what point should priors cease to count? Most American guideline schemes define a period within which priors will count against a defendant. This period in most states exceeds by a considerable margin the relevant periods established in other countries. In Canada, as well as England and Wales, a period of more than five years undermines the relevance of previous convictions for the purposes of subsequent sentencing (Ruby 1994) although an offender's record will always be available to the court, even after a pardon has been granted.

As with other aspects of criminal record, there is often an interaction between the seriousness of the prior offending and the time to decay: more serious priors take longer to extinguish. For example, according to Section 4A1.2 (e) of the federal guidelines, previous sentences in excess of thirteen months will count against a defendant unless they were imposed more than fifteen years prior to the current offense. (If the previous sentence was for a shorter duration, the period of inclusion is ten years.) The Minnesota guidelines employ a similar period of time. Under the Pennsylvania and Kansas systems, all previous convictions are inexpiable: there is no time limit. In some states, the duration and the existence of a "statute of limitation" depends on the seriousness of the priors. In the state of Washington, for example, the most serious felonies and sex offense felonies are always counted against the defendant. Less serious felony convictions are counted unless the offender has spent ten years in the community without further felony convictions. The least serious (class C) felony convictions are not included if there has been a five-year felony-free period and traffic convictions are not included if the offender has no subsequent serious traffic or felony convictions over the same period. Once these periods have elapsed, the previous convictions cannot be resurrected to justify further recidivist premiums.

As with other policy issues relating to criminal record, there is considerable variability in the statute of limitation for prior convictions. For example, under the federal sentencing guidelines, prior adult felonies follow a two-step system. The inclusion period is ten years for prior felonies resulting in a prison term in excess of two months and fifteen years for previous convictions resulting in a sentence of imprisonment exceeding thirteen months (see U.S. Sentencing Commission 1992, p. 4.2). In Florida and Michigan, the period of inclusion is ten years (Florida Sentencing Guidelines Commission 1991, p. 10; Michigan Sentencing Guidelines Advisory Committee 1988, p. 3), while in Minnesota it is fifteen years (Minnesota Sentencing Guidelines Commission 1993, p. 6). However, in several other states, the period of inclusion is indefinite. Thus, in North Carolina, "All prior convictions are counted, even if there has been a crime-free period between the prior convictions and the instant offense" (North Carolina Sentencing and Policy advisory Commission 1993, p. 18). In the state of Kansas, there is no decay factor applicable to adult convictions; all prior adult felony convictions are scored (Kansas Sentencing Commission 1993, p. 19).

Why does the statute of limitation vary with the seriousness of the offense? Why is it that some guideline systems efface certain offenses (following a crime-free period) but not others? The rationale is not self-evident. An offender who serves a four-year term for a serious felony has "paid the price" as surely as an offender who has served four one-year terms for less serious crimes. Yet they are treated differently under some guideline systems. The justification cannot be found in either desert theory or the concept of dangerousness. A violent felony conviction twenty years ago carries little weight in terms of offender culpability for the current offense. Nor does it add much in terms of additional predictive value for subsequent offending. Surely this feature of some guidelines suggests that criminal record carries additional implications for the recidivist. It implies that recidivists should continue to be punished indefinitely, even in the absence of any justification articulated in the guidelines manuals.

G. Purging the Past: The Question of Expiation

As Moore (1989, p. 7) notes, pardoning offenders is "a practice common to all cultures and all periods of history." He cites pardon provisions for all formal constitutions around the world (with the sole exception of the People's Republic of China). Pardons are usually defined as executive acts of clemency (as in the United States) or specific benefits relating to previous convictions for which offenders apply (as in Canada). Underlying the notion of a pardon, however, is the concept that prior misconduct will henceforth have limited or no consequences for the individual receiving the pardon. The related concept with regard to the U.S. guideline systems is that of "expungement." There are several arguments for having an expungement mechanism, for closing the door on at least some forms of previous criminal conduct. The first and most obvious is to prevent offenders from paying repeatedly for the same crime in the absence of any justification on the grounds of desert or dangerousness. In this respect, there seems no reason for previous convictions to remain active indefinitely. An offender with two convictions recorded twenty years prior to the current offense is not, all else being equal, a greater risk for recidivism than a first offender. Nor is a desert theorist likely to find grounds to distinguish two such individuals in terms of their relative culpability.

The second reason for expunging priors is to offer ex-offenders some positive reward for abstaining from criminal behavior. Sentencers who hope to change the behavior of the offender should incorporate positive reinforcements within their sentencing decisions. According to the utilitarian perspective, the recidivist premium is designed to prevent crime through deterrence or incapacitation of the offender. A washout provision provides some *positive* reinforcement: the offender can earn back his or her status as a citizen without a criminal history. Sentencing theorists have generally not addressed the psychological or social benefits of earning (by maintaining a crime-free period) a clean record, but the issue is worthy of attention.[16]

Underlying utilitarian justifications of the recidivist premium is the notion that greater punishments are necessary to deter offenders who were not deterred in the past by the severity of the previous sentence. Advocates of deterrence rely on the apprehension of punishment to inhibit future offending. But human motivation is responsive to more than just punishment; positive reinforcement is a more potent motivator. In practice, the recidivist premium is unidirectional: offenders pay for previous criminal conduct, but they receive limited rewards for periods of crime-free living. If the aim is to reduce recidivism through the imposition of enhanced penalties for recidivists, perhaps more incentives should be offered to encourage law-abiding conduct. Offenders with records should be able to regain their status as first offenders through protracted periods of crime-free conduct, although, as previously noted, this is not possible in all states. A final reason for providing an explicit mechanism to expunge criminal records concerns sentencing aims that attempt to restore the offender to the community. The process of restoration cannot be complete so long as an offender's criminal record remains alive.

Should an expiation mechanism encompass all crimes, or are some inexpiable? In all likelihood, there would be overwhelming public op-

[16] Some people would argue that a crime-free period expunges more than just the record, it might even erase unserved sentences. Britain's infamous train robber Ronald Biggs served one year of a thirty-year sentence before escaping to South America. He then passed a thirty-year crime-free period in Brazil and was recently quoted as saying: "I believe I have wiped the slate clean" (*Guardian Weekly* 1994). Her Majesty's Government takes a different view: if Biggs were to return to England, he would be required to resume serving the sentence interrupted by his escape in 1964.

position to the total expungement of a murder conviction. The public might be willing to countenance erasing a fifteen-year-old robbery conviction, but a murder is harder to efface from the community's memory. Indeed, the very nature of the mandatory life sentence imposed in so many jurisdictions attests to the unique nature of a murder. This crime would appear to be an exception.

V. The Use of Criminal History Information in Guideline Systems

There is virtually no literature on the practical consequences of different approaches to the incorporation of criminal history information in sentencing policies. A sizable research literature demonstrates that the extent of criminal history is strongly predictive of sentence severity. However, there has been little writing that considers the different weights assigned criminal history in different sentencing systems. This section offers a number of analyses of those differences.

At this point I attempt to quantify the effects of criminal records on sentencing patterns in various states and at the federal level. First, however, the findings of empirical research on the effects of criminal history on sentencing patterns warrant mention.

A. Criminal Record and Sentencing Research

What does the sentencing literature say about the use of criminal history information at the trial court level? Do judges follow a just deserts sentencing strategy, giving primary weight to the gravity of the current offense but taking some account of past criminality, or do they pursue a utilitarian model, in which the extent of an offender's criminal record is directly correlated with the severity of sanction imposed? Sentencing statistics are inconclusive. An overlooked weakness of analyses of sentencing practices is the correlational nature of the data. Some researchers have assumed that an association between sentence length and the severity of criminal history reflects the causal effect of criminal record. But crimes committed by recidivists may differ in many respects that might explain sentencing differentials between recidivists and first offenders.

Crimes committed by recidivists may be more serious or may result in more harm than crimes committed by first offenders (or people with minimal prior criminal activity). Bank robberies committed by professionals may result in greater loss than robberies committed by neophytes. Compared with first-time offenders, recidivists might be more likely to carry arms or to threaten victims with serious harm. Indeed, it might be reasonable to expect recidivists to adopt a more rigorous approach to the commission of crime on the grounds that they must be aware that apprehension and conviction is a definite possibility. To the extent that recidivists are mindful of the consequences of their criminal records on subsequent sentencing decisions, they may also have a greater incentive to avoid rearrest. These caveats accepted, sentencing statistics from several countries reveal a pattern that is highly suggestive of a powerful recidivist premium that follows a utilitarian model. This finding is one of the most robust in the sentencing literature.

American data show incarceration rates in 1986 for three groups of offenders in federal courts as follows: no priors, 58 percent; prior misdemeanors, 62 percent; and prior felonies, 81 percent (Bureau of Justice Statistics 1990). Earlier research by Green (1961) of sentencing patterns in Philadelphia revealed a similar pattern of incarceration rates as a function of prior felony convictions: none, 14 percent; one, 27 percent; two, 36 percent; three, 32 percent; and four or more, 51 percent. Research on predicting sentencing patterns reveals the importance of criminal record as a determinant of the sentencing decision. For example, Sutton (1978) found that prior record was more strongly related than any other variable to the nature of the sanction imposed (see also Burke and Turk 1975; Tiffany, Avichai, and Peters 1975; Neubauer 1979; Myers and Talarico 1987; Albonetti 1991). Similar results emerge from research involving juvenile records. For example, Greenwood, Abrahamse, and Zimring (1984) found that young adult offenders with extensive juvenile records were sentenced more severely than comparable offenders with shorter records.

Comparable findings emerge from empirical research on sentencing patterns elsewhere. In Canada, the Law Reform Commission released data showing incarceration rates of 15 percent, 45 percent, 57 percent, 70 percent, and 80 percent for groups of offenders with, respectively, no priors, one, two, three, and four previous indictable convictions (Law Reform Commission of Canada 1976).[17] Hogarth (1971) conducted an in-depth examination of sentencing practices from a different methodological perspective and reached the same result: the most statistically significant predictor of sentence length was the number of

[17] These were the last published sentencing statistics broken down by the criminal history of the offender.

previous convictions. Data from the United Kingdom cited by Fitzmaurice and Pease (1986) reveal the same pattern of incarceration rates as found in North America: no priors, 3 percent; one, 12 percent; two to four priors, 26 percent; and five or more priors, 47 percent. Data from the Australian state of Victoria showed incarceration rates of 9 percent, 16 percent, and 37 percent for groups of defendants with no, "a few," or "many" priors (Victorian Sentencing Committee 1988). These sentencing statistics suggest that, in practice, judges are following a utilitarian model and not the just deserts model that results in the progressive loss of mitigation: sentence severity is strongly correlated with the number of previous convictions. In jurisdictions in which case law endorses the principle of progressive mitigation, these statistics demonstrate a divorce between rhetoric and reality.

The absence of systematic sentencing guidelines in countries such as Canada or England makes it hard to estimate the magnitude of the recidivist premium. The only sources of information are sentencing statistics and case law decisions. As noted above, the former can be rather ambiguous guides to the effect of prior record while the latter are nowhere nearly systematic enough to provide a reliable estimate of the magnitude of the premium. The sentencing guideline systems in the United States, though, are quite explicit.

Previous convictions have an important influence on the "in/out" decision—whether the offender is incarcerated or given a community-based sanction. In Minnesota, for example, there are seven criminal history categories. The effect of criminal history on whether the offender receives a presumptive stayed sentence (with a noncustodial sanction as a condition of probation) or a presumptive period of imprisonment depends on the seriousness of the offense of conviction. For crimes at the lowest severity level, six or more criminal history points are required to propel the defendant over the dispositional line and into the custodial category. However, a criminal history score of only three points is required to result in a presumptive period of imprisonment at offense severity level 6. Frase (1993) provides evidence of the importance of criminal record in determining whether the defendant receives a custodial sentence: record was the most significant predictor of custody even in the desert-oriented guideline system in Minnesota (see Frase 1993, p. 315). However, the more important effect of criminal record, and one that is quantifiable, concerns the effects of previous convictions on the duration of custodial terms.

The power of prior offenses can be conveyed by calculating a recidi-

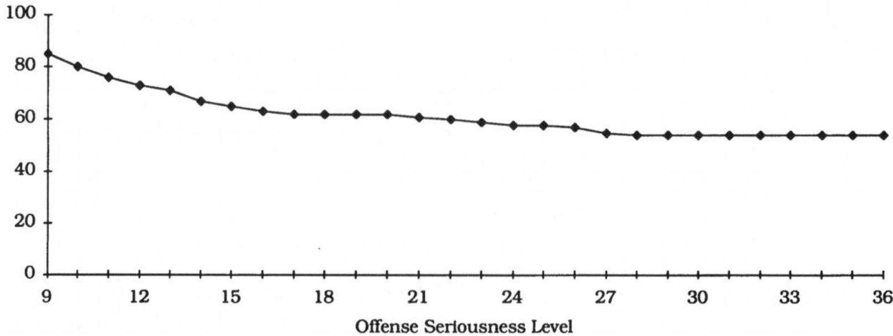

FIG. 2.—Federal guidelines: recidivist premium as a function of offense seriousness. Source: I computed these values from the U.S. Sentencing Commission (1992).

vism index that expresses the longest sentence length possible (i.e., upper limit of the most serious criminal history category) as a percentage of the shortest sentence possible (i.e., lower limit of the first offender criminal history category). To take the same example, a sentencing guideline row with upper and lower bounds of twelve and six months, respectively, generates a recidivism premium index of 200 percent.

Aggregating across levels of offense seriousness results in a recidivism premium of 281 percent in the federal sentencing guidelines grid. Thus averaged across the entire grid, the most punitive guideline range is almost three times as long as the most lenient sentence that can be imposed on first offenders convicted of the same offense. However, like most aggregate statistics, this one can be misleading: it masks a high degree of variation across levels of offense seriousness. The effect of criminal record expressed as a percentage of the highest criminal history category sentence declines as the seriousness of the offense of conviction increases. Thus criminal record accounts for fully 85 percent of the most severe guideline sentence for offenses at crime seriousness level 9. This percentage declines progressively as the offense seriousness category increases: at seriousness level 20, this recidivism premium is 61 percent. The index eventually reaches a "floor" of 54 percent for offenses at crime seriousness level 28 and higher (see fig. 2).

The reason for this pattern would appear to be a desire to constrain the effect of criminal record when the guideline sentence lengths become particularly long. If the same percentage were applied at offense seriousness level 27, the range would run from 70 months to over 500 months (instead of 162). Although understandable from a practical point of view, the consequence, however, is a paradox. As the current offense becomes more serious, the effect of criminal record (in proportional terms) declines.[18] One obvious reason for this is that the amount of additional time imposed (the recidivist premium) in absolute terms is much greater at the higher levels.

B. State Systems

There is considerable range in the recidivist premium in different state systems. In most states, however, criminal record accounts for well over half the sentence lengths that can be imposed on offenders in the highest criminal history category. In Alaska, for example, criminal record accounts for 85 percent of the highest criminal history category sentence length (collapsing across levels of crime seriousness). The percentage varies with the seriousness of the offense: thus the presumptive term for class A felonies ranges from five years for a first felony conviction to fifteen for more than two felony priors, but the range of sentence can run from 2.5 years (first felony conviction) to 20 years (three or more felony convictions).

For almost all state guideline systems, at the highest criminal history levels at least, the offender's criminal record is a more powerful determinant of sentence severity than the seriousness of the offense. One exception is Minnesota, where even at the highest level criminal history, criminal record still accounts for less than half the sentence length. Table 1 summarizes the recidivist premiums in a number of states and in the federal system. Exact comparisons between jurisdictions are not possible due to differences in offense definitions and other factors. This table makes some limited comparisons for the most serious offense class in each guideline system. In addition to the criminal history ranges, two versions of the recidivist premium are presented: the percentage of the highest criminal history category sentence length accounted for by criminal record and the most severe sentence expressed as a function of the least severe.

As can be seen in table 1, offenders in the most serious criminal history category pay a heavy price for their previous convictions: over half

[18] As Andrew Ashworth (personal communication, fax, March 21, 1994) notes, the phenomenon of prior record having proportionately less effect on sentence severity for very serious crimes also applies to mitigating factors. It would appear that, as the crime gets more serious, sentencing systems are less inclined to consider offender characteristics of any kind, whether in mitigation or aggravation. Manslaughter would appear to be an exception to this rule.

TABLE 1

Recidivist Ranges and Premiums: Examples from Some American Guideline Systems

Jurisdiction	Most Serious Offense Class*	Recidivist Range (in Months)	Recidivism Ratio†	Recidivism Premium (in Percent)‡
Delaware	Class B felony	24–240	10.0:1	90
Florida	Category 1	60–360	6.0:1	83
Michigan	Homicide level 2	48–180	3.75:1	73
Pennsylvania	10	36–120	3.33:1	70
Alaska§	Class A	60–180	3.00:1	67
Tennessee	Felony class A	162–432	2.66:1	63
North Carolina	B	144–360	2.50:1	60
Washington	14	240–548	2.28:1	56
Oregon	11	121–269	2.22:1	55
Kansas	Level 1 (nondrug)	92–204	2.21:1	55
Federal guidelines	36	188–405	2.15:1	54
Minnesota	10	299–433	1.44:1	31

Source.—Relevant federal and state sentencing guidelines manuals.

* Excludes offenses which result in life imprisonment.

† Ratio of longest guideline sentence (highest criminal history score) to shortest guideline range (first-offender criminal history score).

‡ Percentage of sentence length highest criminal history score that is accounted for by the criminal record dimension.

§ Presumptive sentence range used; minimum-maximum penalty range is greater.

the sentence lengths are due to the influence of criminal record in all the guideline systems except the state of Minnesota. The actual percentage varies from 31 percent in Minnesota up to 90 percent in Delaware. This table also shows that, in these states, the longest sentence possible as a function of criminal record is at least twice the shortest sentence possible and can rise to ten times the shortest sentence length in Delaware.

Although several sentencing guideline systems appeal to just deserts as a justification for enhanced sentencing as a function of criminal history, it is clear that the use of criminal record is not consistent with desert theory. One practical consequence of this is that proportionality based on the seriousness of the offense becomes greatly weakened. For example, in Minnesota an offender with a high criminal history score (category 6) who is now sentenced for first-degree assault receives a presumptive sentence length in excess of the presumptive sentence imposed on a first offender convicted of murder (150 months).

C. The Snowballing Effect of Criminal Record on Sentence Severity

It is also important to bear in mind the cumulative effect of criminal record on sentencing patterns. Consider an offender who is sentenced under the federal guidelines for three offenses over a ten-year period. The crimes were all at offense seriousness level 15. Further assume that he receives the midpoint sentence from each appropriate criminal history category. Thus he will be sentenced to twenty-one months, thirty-four months, and forty-two months for the three consecutive offenses. On the latter two occasions he is sentenced as a recidivist (criminal history categories 4 and 5, respectively). The first conviction alone therefore cost him an additional thirteen months on the second sentence and eight months on the third sentencing hearing. After three sentencing hearings his first conviction has cost him the additional equivalent (in sentence length) of the time imposed for the first offense by itself. In any subsequent sentencing hearings, the first offense will cost even more, and the recidivism premium will rise still further. Put another way, in this example the recidivism premium has the effect in terms of custodial time of the first offense. This point is important because analyses based on comparisons between different criminal history categories fail to account for the cumulative effects of criminal history on sentence severity.

In addition to the recidivist premium across criminal history levels, many guideline systems have special offender categories or career criminal enhancements that result in even harsher penalties. Under the federal sentencing guidelines, there are three special categories of recidivist offender. Thus an offender is defined as a career offender if he is at least eighteen years of age at the time of the offense, has been convicted of a felony involving violence or drugs, and has at least two prior felony convictions involving violence or drugs. A defendant convicted of possession of a controlled substance with two priors is labeled a career offender and is assigned to the highest criminal career category.

D. Increments in Premiums

What consequences does the recidivist premium have across different categories of criminal history? If the guideline systems were founded on utilitarian principles, one would expect to see the premium changing with the number of priors. That is, if the guidelines were truly risk-driven, the recidivist premium would follow actuarial predictions of reoffending. Instead, criminal records in most systems produce

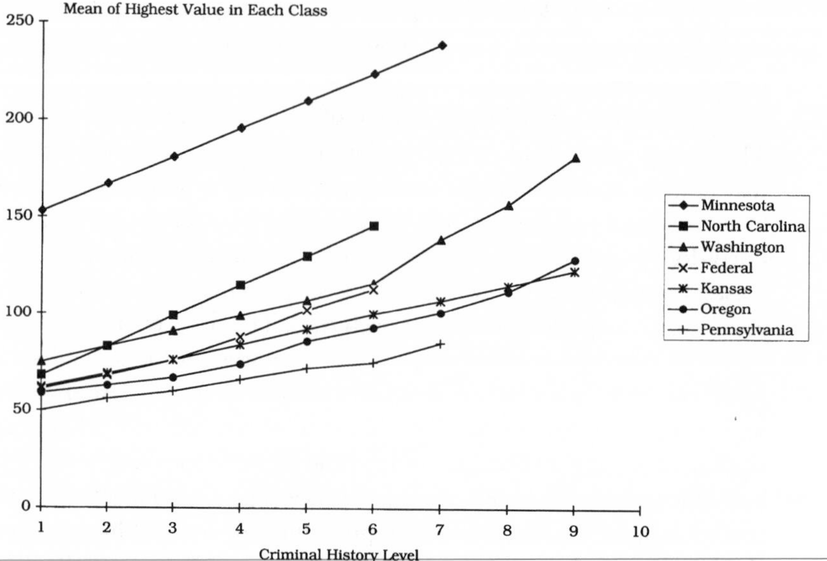

FIG. 3.—Recidivist premiums from selected U.S. guideline systems. Note: These data are derived from state and federal guideline systems. The base of each curve reflects the first offender presumptive sentence length averaged across offense seriousness levels. The apex of each individual graph reflects the highest criminal history score, averaged across offense seriousness levels.

a monotonic increase in sentence severity as a function of increasing criminal history scores. Figure 3 presents a plot of recidivist increments in a number of states and at the federal level. While the slopes vary (reflecting the differential power of criminal record), the increments in sentence length from one criminal history category to another are fairly constant, of the magnitude of approximately 10 percent from one category to the next. The difference between first offenders and those in the next criminal history category is no greater than the difference between, say, criminal history categories 3 and 4. For example, under the federal sentencing guidelines, there is an average 11 percent increment in sentence length from criminal history category 1 to category 2. The increment from category 3 to category 4 is of the same magnitude.

E. Prescribed versus Actual Premiums

The data discussed to this point are theoretical in nature: they are derived from presumptive guideline ranges prescribed by the sentencing guideline manuals. But departures are allowed, and there is also room for variation within a guideline range. The recidivist premium actually imposed by judges may be different from the theoretical recidivist premium. Data on this issue are available from the federal system. Comparison of the projected and actual sentencing trends from the federal system provide insight into the way in which judges respond to the variable of criminal history. Judges have the capacity to attenuate the effect of an offender's criminal record on sentence severity. There is some evidence that this is the case. This can be shown by comparing the range in average sentence lengths collapsed across all levels of offense seriousness. The range derived from the federal guidelines grid is 54 months (criminal history category 1) to 102 months (average of criminal history category 6). The range of actual sentence lengths is more constrained: 57 months for offenders in category 1 and only 84 months in criminal history category 6.

Similar trends can be seen at the state level. Data on incarceration rates from Oregon show less variation between criminal history categories than would be expected in light of the architecture of the grid itself. There are nine categories of criminal history in the Oregon grid. The observed imprisonment rate for category E was 22 percent, while the incarceration rate for the most serious criminal history category was not significantly higher (36 percent; see Mosbaek 1993). This difference between the expected and the observed criminal history increments suggests some reluctance on the part of the judiciary to impose the full recidivist premium permitted by the guidelines.

F. Risk

Most sentencing guideline systems have a strong utilitarian orientation: the recidivist premium is justified in terms of providing additional deterrence or incapacitation. The reality of the guideline systems, however, is that they prescribe linear increments in punishment for progressively longer criminal histories. The disregard for factors that may interact with the number (or seriousness) of prior convictions suggests that risk per se is not the central concern of the recidivist premium. Rather, the systems appear to have invented a degradation of desert theory. According to this view, repeat offenders are simply more culpable than first offenders, and their increments of additional culpability are viewed as being a direct linear function of the number of previous convictions. The sentencing guideline systems appeal to principles of desert theory claiming that recidivist offenders deserve harsher punishments, the argument being that culpability increases as a function of the number of priors. But this is an incorrect interpretation of desert theory. No desert theorist supports a sentencing premium of this nature. In short, the architecture of the guidelines systems suggests that the recidivist premium is justified not only by the mixture of desert and dangerousness but also by a notion of punitiveness.

If the guidelines ignore factors that are clearly related to utilitarian reductivist sentencing goals, how risk-driven are they? Consider an analogy of automobile insurance. Companies that insure motorists against accidents are also concerned with risk—risk of future accidents that will provoke additional claims. As with criminal behavior, the best predictor of future claims is the number of past accidents or traffic violations. But when automobile insurance premiums are compared to recidivist prison terms, the analogy breaks down and may shed some light on the true nature of sentence premiums for criminal recidivism. Any insurance company that adopted a premium schedule to match that prescribed by a sentencing guideline system would soon be seeking Chapter 11 protection. A progressive increment of approximately 10 percent would not reflect risk at all. Accident risk is simply not distributed in such a predictable manner. And so automobile premiums in the insurance industry follow a very different pattern.

The guideline systems, then, are not primarily risk-driven: they simply prescribe a more severe penalty each time an offender acquires additional convictions. The effect is to create a system in which *all* recidivists pay a certain premium independent of their actual risk of future offending. To complete the automobile analogy, this is the equivalent of making all "recidivist" drivers pay a certain premium regardless of the empirical probabilities that they will be involved in further accidents. Thus with each additional claim, motorists would pay an additional compounding premium of 10 percent.

What would a recidivist premium look like that was truly risk-driven? In order to be wholly risk-sensitive, the system would have to derive from a detailed empirical analysis of recidivist weights that would reflect the empirical likelihood of reoffending. Consider a defendant who has three priors for offenses of varying seriousness and who is now being sentenced for burglary. Computer analysis, similar to multiple regression analysis, could generate this offender's probability of reoffending and match a recidivist sentencing premium to the risk score.

Why is it that the sentencing guideline systems have not adopted a recidivist premium that is more sensitive to other risk factors, including social characteristics? There are several sound reasons for avoiding social characteristics. First, there is the obvious question of resources. Many guideline systems are very sensitive to costs. This is reflected in the fact that guideline ranges in some systems are responsive to prison populations. A system that attempted to consider all factors empirically related to recidivism risk would be expensive as well as cumbersome. The research facility of such a commission would necessarily be very substantial.

A second reason for excluding risk factors other than criminal record is that these factors are likely to be sociodemographic variables that many guideline systems eliminate from consideration a priori on grounds of equity. Unemployed offenders are a greater recidivism risk than those with steady jobs, yet to consider employment status within a recidivism risk calculus with effects on sentence severity would favor employed, often more privileged and affluent offenders over others less fortunate. There would also be conflicts between risk and justice. Consider the variable of age. One of the most robust findings in the criminology literature is that the risk of reoffending declines significantly after offenders reach their mid-twenties (Farrington 1986; Champion 1994). A recidivism premium that was sensitive to the defendant's age would decline for offenders in their forties and fifties. The result would be a much lower recidivist premium for older offenders. Most people would find this proposal unacceptable on grounds of equity.

VI. Alternate Models of Criminal Record

As noted in earlier sections of this essay, a central problem associated with recidivist sentencing premiums is a moral one: offenders are being repeatedly punished for the same criminal conduct. Are there ways in which this can be avoided? Few publications have explored ways around the problem, but alternative conceptualizations are possible. In this section, I briefly explore three alternatives. At the heart of each alternate conceptualization is a desire to incorporate criminal history information to a limited degree, but without provoking the notion of double punishment.

A. Flat Recidivist Premiums

One problem with the use of criminal record within a two-dimensional matrix is that the magnitude of the premium is determined by the severity of the ultimate penalty, which itself will reflect the seriousness of the current offense. While this is an obvious point, the consequences have not been fully explored. Consider the following example of sentencing under the federal sentencing guidelines. Four years ago, two first offenders were sentenced as codefendants in a robbery case. Today they appear independently for sentencing on fresh charges but which differ in seriousness. One defendant is now sentenced for a seriousness level 13 offense, while the second is sentenced for an offense at seriousness level 33. The robbery committed four years earlier will now cost the first defendant an additional three months, but the same previous offending will cost the other offender an additional twenty months. This may strike some as being inequitable. After all, their criminal histories are identical.

The problem can be circumvented by divorcing the recidivist premium from the seriousness of the current conviction through the imposition of a flat recidivist premium for each previous conviction regardless of the nature (i.e., the seriousness) of the current offense. For example, the recidivist tariff for robbery could be set at three months. Under this revised scheme the current sentences for both offenders would rise by the same increment. In this way the recidivist premium and the current penalty would be clearly distinguished. This approach was taken by early recidivist legislation in England. According to the Prevention of Crime Act of 1908, the court awarded two sentences in the case of recidivists: a penalty for the offense of conviction and an independent penalty for being a recidivist (see Sharpe 1990; Ashworth 1992).

Unfortunately, this scheme creates another problem. Specifically, if a defendant has committed a very serious crime in the past and is now to be sentenced for a less serious offense, the flat (and in this case, high) tariff for recidivism would result in the imposition of a lengthy prison term for a crime of low seriousness. For example, if an offender had a prior conviction for manslaughter and were now sentenced for a minor theft, the weight of the prior, serious crime would result in a disproportionately harsh penalty for the theft.[19] Placing a cap on the recidivist premium—for example, preventing the premium from exceeding 50 percent of the tariff for the current offense—solves this new problem but leads inevitably back to a system where the same pre-

[19] This is why the American Bar Association proposed as part of its standards that any increased term imposed to reflect previous criminality should be related in severity to the sentence otherwise provided for the new offence (American Bar Association 1968, Sec. 3.3[a]i.).

vious conviction now results in a differential premium if offenders are now convicted of crimes of differing seriousness. Some state guideline systems are sensitive to this problem. In the state of Washington, for example, a defendant convicted of a serious crime of violence will receive three points for each prior conviction of this kind. However, if the offense of conviction is less serious than this, the guidelines discount the offender's criminal history score.

Compromise solutions are also possible. One would involve the creation of bands of recidivist premiums. The sentencing guidelines of most American states use bands of offense seriousness. In a similar way, there could be bands of recidivist premiums. For instance, there might be a three-month recidivist premium on current sentences under two years, six months for sentences between two and four years, and so on. This kind of system would incorporate advantages of the flat rate and the percentage approach.[20]

B. *The Recidivist Premium as a Partly Suspended Sentence*

Is there a way around the moral dilemma that recidivists are being repeatedly punished for the same offense? One alternative proposal would be to convert the recidivist premium into a partly suspended sentence. Imagine an offender sentenced to forty months imprisonment for burglary. A portion of this sentence (perhaps a tithe of the total custodial term) would be suspended but with clear direction as to the conditions that would involve execution. The offender would then serve thirty-six months (minus any good time or time in the community under parole supervision). In the event of a subsequent reconviction he would receive whatever new sentence was imposed *plus* the additional four months that had been suspended. A portion of this new custodial term would also be suspended and reactivated in any subsequent sentencing hearings, and so on. Such a scheme has several advantages. First, the recidivist component is not so much punishment a second time for the same offense but a conditional benefit (suspension of part of the sentence) extended to the offender and withdrawn in the event of reconviction. Second, in jurisdictions without formal guidelines (such as England and Wales and Canada) it would make the consequences of further offending that much more salient to the offender. At some point (perhaps after ten years) the suspended portion of the sentence would extinguish.

[20] This compromise approach was suggested to me by Andrew Ashworth.

Consider the case of a second-time offender who receives a period of imprisonment because he is a recidivist. The additional time is supposed to serve some deterrent effect, but the individual may not even be aware of the magnitude of the recidivist premium or of the extent of the enhanced sentence that he will acquire in the event of subsequent offending. A partly suspended sentence would make the full consequences of future offending that much clearer to the offender. There is also some incentive to the offender who can avoid paying the full penalty by refraining from further offending. This concept could be tied to the notion of decay of effect. Those guideline systems that incorporate a decay provision do not follow a degenerative model but simply cease to count a prior conviction if a lengthy period has elapsed, usually ten or fifteen years. If the recidivist premium became a form of partly suspended sentence, the amount of time that was suspended could slowly decay, thereby providing the offender with the means of purging part of the penalty by simply avoiding further offending.

C. Relating Criminal History to Parole Eligibility Dates

A second possibility for jurisdictions that retain parole release is to tie the previous convictions to parole eligibility dates. This was formerly the procedure in some states, including Arkansas (see Shane-Dubow, Brown, and Olsen 1985), and in some countries, such as Finland.[21] If first offenders are eligible for parole after having served, for example, one third of the custodial term (as in Canada), recidivists could receive a deferred parole date with the delay to parole eligibility being a direct function of the number of priors. Inmates with very long records might not be eligible for parole until the 75 percent mark. In this way recidivists would not pay an additional price for past offending but would be denied a discount (in terms of time served) offered to inmates with less extensive criminal histories. Those who regard release on parole as resentencing will see little merit in this proposal: it will simply mean transferring the recidivist premium from the hands of the judge to a parole statute. For those who regard the parole release as a privilege accorded certain inmates by a decision-making body independent of the sentencing process, the proposal may have some merit. This proposal may also receive the approbation of the public, who probably disapprove of recidivists obtaining parole at the same

[21] In Finland, first offenders can obtain parole after having served one-half of the custodial term, while recidivists must await the lapse of two-thirds of the sentence (see Joutsen 1989; Tornudd 1994).

point as first offenders. It may also appeal to offenders who may well perceive the recidivist premium at sentencing to consist of additional punishment for crimes for which they have already paid the price. Staggered parole eligibility dates may be less likely to provoke the perception of injustice.

VII. Conclusions

Consistent with sentencing practices in other countries, all guideline systems in the United States assign a critical role to an offender's criminal record, albeit with considerable variation in the details. Most guideline systems use a sentencing grid in which criminal history is one of the two dimensions. The various guidelines appeal to a variety of sentencing purposes to justify the recidivist premium. These justifications include both desert and utilitarian goals. Examination of the guidelines reveals that the recidivist premium is inconsistent with a desert-based theory of sentencing, which would permit only a very limited discount for first offenders or people with very short (or very old) criminal histories. Guideline developers appear to have developed their own version of desert theory in which recidivist offenders are more culpable than first offenders and this culpability is a direct function of the number of previous convictions or, in the case of the federal guidelines, the severity of previous sentencing decisions.

Researchers in the United States (Wheeler, Mann, and Sarat 1988) and the United Kingdom (Wasik 1987) suggest that judicial reasoning is more subtle and sophisticated than the guideline systems. For example, Wheeler, Mann, and Sarat (1988, p. 186) argue that "common law sentencers make qualitative judgements while guideline sentencers count points." This would appear to be a misrepresentation of the complexities involved in American guideline systems. As well, the guideline systems have the great advantage of generating more consistency and fairness. The use of a sentencing grid ensures that criminal record will be interpreted more consistently and with more clarity than in a system that does not use such a device. The consequence is undoubtedly more equity in the application of criminal history information.

Nevertheless, it is clear that the treatment of criminal record by the guideline systems may well become more complex in terms of some of the issues explored in this essay. Criminal history measures are still evolving. In general, sentencing commissions have adopted fairly simple definitions of criminal history. The effect of a crime-free period is one example of this. Rather than weighting prior convictions by the amount of elapsed time between the last and current conviction, most systems simply count all convictions within a ten- or fifteen-year period. There are sound reasons for this, one of which is ease of application, thereby reducing the likelihood of errors of application (see Blumstein et al. 1983, p. 24). The cost, however, of this simplicity is a loss of discrimination between offenders of variable culpability or recidivism risk.

In all probability, a decade from now guideline systems in the United States will use more complex rules to regulate the use of criminal history. These may include more sensitive temporal measures in which the weight of a previous conviction decays over time, sliding scales of recidivist premiums in which the power of the premium more closely mirrors the degree of specialization shown in the offender's criminal career, and perhaps the limited use of social characteristics such as age and the provision of more opportunities for the offender to earn back his or her status as a nonoffender.

Finally, in those jurisdictions in which there is no statute of limitation or expungement mechanism, the criminal justice system is creating an ever-growing number of people with criminal records. According to a 1992 survey, state criminal history databases contain records for almost 50 million people (Bureau of Justice Statistics 1992). In Canada, 10 percent, or almost 3 million people, have criminal records (Correctional Services Canada 1994). Data from England and Wales show that fully 40 percent of men in Britain have a criminal record by the time they reach the age of forty (Barclay 1993). Absent a mechanism for expiation, people with criminal records can never shake off their past offending. This may be the most important deficiency of the use of criminal record in the sentencing process.

REFERENCES

Adler, J. 1991. *The Urgings of Conscience: A Theory of Punishment.* Philadelphia: Temple University Press.

Alaska Sentencing Commission. 1991. *1991 Annual Report to the Governor*. Anchorage: Alaska Sentencing Commission.

Albonetti, C. 1991. "An Integration of Theories to Explain Judicial Discretion." *Social Problems* 38:247–65.

American Bar Association. 1968. *Project on Minimum Standards for Criminal Justice: Standards Relating to Sentencing Alternatives and Procedures.* New York: Institute of Judicial Administration.

Ashworth, A. 1992. *Sentencing and Criminal Justice.* London: Weidenfeld & Nicolson.

Ashworth, A., and B. Gibson. 1994. "The Criminal Justice Act 1993." *Criminal Law Review* (February), pp. 99–112.

Barclay, G. 1993. *Digest 2: Information on the Criminal Justice System in England and Wales.* London: Home Office, Research and Statistics Department.

Beattie, J. 1986. *Crime and the Courts in England, 1660–1800.* Princeton, N.J.: Princeton University Press.

Beck, A., and B. Shipley. 1987. *Recidivism of Young Parolees.* Washington, D.C.: U.S. Department of Justice, Bureau of Justice Statistics.

Blumstein, A., and J. Cohen. 1980. "Sentencing of Convicted Offenders: An Analysis of the Public's View." *Law and Society Review* 14:223–61.

Blumstein, A., J. Cohen, S. Martin, and M. Tonry, eds. 1983. *Research on Sentencing: The Search for Reform.* 2 vols. Washington, D.C.: National Academy Press.

Blumstein, A., J. Cohen, J. Roth, and C. Visher, eds. 1986. *Criminal Careers and "Career Criminals."* Washington, D.C.: National Academy Press.

Boerner, D. 1995. "Sentencing Policy in Washington." *Overcrowded Times* 6(3):1, 9–12.

Bottomley, K., and K. Pease. 1986. *Crime and Punishment: Interpreting the Data.* Milton Keynes: Open University Press.

Bureau of Justice Statistics. 1990. *Compendium of Federal Justice Statistics, 1986.* Washington, D.C.: U.S. Department of Justice, Bureau of Justice Statistics.

———. 1991. *Statutes Requiring the Use of Criminal History Record Information.* Washington, D.C.: Government Printing Office.

———. 1992. *Survey of Criminal History Information Systems.* Washington, D.C.: U.S. Department of Justice, Bureau of Justice Statistics.

———. 1993. *Use and Management of Criminal History Record Information: A Comprehensive Report.* Washington, D.C.: U.S. Department of Justice, Bureau of Justice Statistics.

Burke, P., and A. Turk. 1975. "Factors Affecting Postarrest Dispositions: A Model for Analysis." *Social Problems* 22:313–32.

Champion, D., ed. 1989. *The U.S. Sentencing Guidelines: Implications for Justice.* New York: Praeger.

Champion, D. 1994. *Measuring Offender Risk: A Criminal Justice Sourcebook.* Westport, Conn.: Greenwood.

Correctional Services Canada. 1994. *Basic Facts about Corrections in Canada.* Ottawa: Minister of Supply and Services Canada.

Cox, E. 1877. *The Principles of Punishment: As Applied in the Administration of the Criminal Law, by Judges and Magistrates.* London: Law Times Office.

Damaska, M. 1968. "Adverse Legal Consequences of a Conviction and Their Removal." *Journal of Criminal Law and Criminology* 59:542–68.

Davis, M. 1992. "Just Deserts for Recidivists." In *To Make the Punishment Fit the Crime: Essays in the Theory of Criminal Justice.* Boulder, Colo.: Westview.

Davis, R. 1980. "The Mark of Cain: Some Subliminal Effects of the Criminal Process." *Saskatchewan Law Review* 44:219–60.

Doob, A. 1995. "The United States Sentencing Commission's Guidelines: If You Don't Know Where You Are Going, You May Not Get There." In *The Politics of Sentencing Reform*, edited by C. Clarkson and R. Morgan. Oxford: Oxford University Press.

Dormont, D. 1991. "For the Good of the Adult: An Examination of the Constitutionality of Using Prior Juvenile Adjudications to Enhance Adult Sentences." *Minnesota Law Review* 75:1769–1805.

Drapkin, I. 1989. *Crime and Punishment in the Ancient World.* Toronto: Lexington Books.

Durham, A., III. 1987. "Justice in Sentencing: The Role of Prior Record of Criminal Involvement." *Journal of Criminal Law and Criminology* 78:614–43.

Emsley, C. 1987. *Crime and Society in England, 1750–1900.* London: Longman.

Falvey, W. 1982. "Defense Perspectives on the Minnesota Sentencing Guidelines." *Hamline Law Review* 5:257–70.

Farrell, R., and V. Swigert. 1978. "Prior Offense Record as a Self-fulfilling Prophecy." *Law and Society* 12:437–53.

Farrington, D. 1986. "Age and Crime." In *Crime and Justice: An Annual Review of Research*, vol. 7, edited by M. Tonry and N. Morris. Chicago: University of Chicago Press.

———. 1991. "Childhood Aggression and Adult Violence: Early Precursors and Later Life Outcomes." In *The Development and Treatment of Childhood Aggression*, edited by D. Pepler and K. Rubin. Hillsdale, N.J.: Erlbaum.

Fichter, M., and C. Veneziano. 1988. *Criminal Justice Attitudes: Missouri.* Jefferson City: Missouri Department of Corrections.

Finkel, N., S. Maloney, M. Valbuena, and J. Groscup. 1996. "Recidivism, Proportionalism and Individualized Punishment." *American Behavioral Scientist* 39:474–88.

Fitzmaurice, C., and K. Pease. 1986. *The Psychology of Judicial Sentencing.* Manchester: Manchester University Press.

Fletcher, G. 1978. *Rethinking Criminal Law.* Boston: Little, Brown.

———. 1982. "The Recidivist Premium." *Criminal Justice Ethics* 1:54–59.

Florida Sentencing Guidelines Commission. 1991. *Florida Sentencing Guidelines. Scoresheet Preparation Manual.* Tallahassee, Fla.: Office of the State Courts Administrator.

Frase, R. 1993. "Implementing Commission-Based Sentencing Guidelines: The Lessons of the First Ten Years in Minnesota." *Cornell Journal of Law and Public Policy* 2:279–337.

Frieberg, A. 1995. "Sentencing and Punishment in Australia." *Overcrowded Times* 6:1, 11–15.

Gabor, T. 1986. *The Prediction of Criminal Behaviour.* Toronto: University of Toronto Press.

Gardiner, L. 1972. *Living It Down: The Problem of Old Convictions.* London: Stevens & Sons.

Green, E. 1961. *Judicial Attitudes in Sentencing.* London: Macmillan.

Greenwood, P., A. Abrahamse, and F. Zimring. 1984. *Factors Affecting Sentence Severity for Young Adult Offenders*. Santa Monica: Calif.: RAND.

Griswold, D. 1985. "Florida's Sentencing Guidelines: Progression or Regression?" *Federal Probation* 2:25–32.

Gross, H. 1979. *A Theory of Criminal Justice*. New York: Oxford University Press.

Grygier, T. 1977. *Social Protection Code: A New Model of Criminal Justice*. London: Sweet & Maxwell.

Guardian Weekly. 1994. (March 25), p. 24.

———. 1995. "Judge Scorns Howard's Jail Package." *Guardian Weekly* (October 22).

Hebenton, B., and T. Thomas. 1993. *Criminal Records: State, Citizen and the Politics of Protection*. Aldershot: Avebury.

Hogarth, J. 1971. *Sentencing as a Human Process*. Toronto: University of Toronto Press.

Horan, P., M. Myers, and M. Farnworth. 1982. "Prior Record and Court Processes: The Role of Latent Theory in Criminology Research." *Sociology and Social Research* 67:40–58.

House of Commons. 1879. *Indictable Offenses Bill and Related Statutes*. London: House of Commons.

Joutsen, M. 1989. *The Criminal Justice System of Finland: A General Introduction*. Helsinki: Finnish Department of Justice.

Kansas Sentencing Commission. 1993. *Kansas Sentencing Guidelines: Desk Reference Manual*. Topeka: Kansas Sentencing Commission.

Kirkpatrick, L. 1992. "Mandatory Felony Sentencing Guidelines: The Oregon Model." *University of California Davis Law Review* 25:695–714.

Kleckner, S. 1976. *The Penal Code of the Romanian Socialist Republic*. London: Sweet & Maxwell.

Kress, J. 1980. *Prescription for Justice: The Theory and Practice of Sentencing Guidelines*. Cambridge, Mass.: Ballinger.

Law Reform Commission of Canada. 1976. *Studies on Imprisonment*. Ottawa: Canadian Government Publishing Centre.

Mackenzie, M. 1981. *Plato on Punishment*. Berkeley and Los Angeles: University of California Press.

Mande, M., and K. English. 1989. *The Effect of Public Opinion on Correctional Policy: A Comparison of Opinions and Practice*. Boulder: Colorado Department of Public Safety.

Michigan Sentencing Guidelines Advisory Committee. 1988. *Michigan Sentencing Guidelines*. 2d ed. St. Paul, Minn.: West Publishing Company.

Minnesota Sentencing Guidelines Commission. 1993. *Minnesota Sentencing Guidelines and Commentary*. St. Paul: Minnesota Sentencing Guidelines Commission.

Monahan, J. 1982. "The Case for Prediction in the Modified Just Desert Model of Criminal Sentencing." *International Journal of Law and Psychiatry* 5:103–13.

Monahan, J., and M. Ruggiero. 1980. "Psychological and Psychiatric Aspects of Determinate Sentencing." *International Journal of Law and Psychiatry* 3:105–16.

Moore, K. 1989. *Pardons: Justice, Mercy and the Public Interest.* Oxford: Oxford University Press.

Mosbaek, C. 1993. *Third Year Report on Implementation of Sentencing Guidelines: 1992.* Oregon: Oregon Criminal Justice Council.

Myers, M., and S. Talarico. 1987. *The Social Contexts of Criminal Sentencing.* London: Springer-Verlag.

Neubauer, D. 1979. *America's Courts and the Criminal Justice System.* North Scituate, Mass.: Duxbury.

Nigam, R. 1965. *Law of Crimes in India.* Vol. 1, *Principles of Criminal Law.* London: Asia Publishing House.

North Carolina Sentencing and Policy Advisory Commission. 1993. *Report to the 1993 Session of the General Assembly of North Carolina.* Raleigh: North Carolina Sentencing and Policy Advisory Commission.

———. 1994. *Summary of New Sentencing Laws and the State-County Criminal Justice Partnership Act,* revised. Raleigh: North Carolina Sentencing and Policy Advisory Commission.

Oregon Criminal Justice Council. 1989. *Oregon Sentencing Guidelines Implementation Manual.* Portland, Oreg.: Portland State University, School of Urban and Public Affairs.

———. 1993. *Third Year Report on Implementation of Sentencing Guidelines. 1992.* Portland, Oreg.: Portland State University, School of Urban and Public Affairs.

Ouimet, M. 1989. "Tracking Down Penal Judgement: A Study of Sentencing Decision-Making among the Public and Court Practitioners." Ph.D. dissertation, Rutgers University.

Ouimet, M. n.d. *Just Deserts and Prior Criminal Convictions: An Alternative Explanation.* Montreal: University of Montreal, School of Criminology.

Owens, J. 1994. "Criminal History Records: Keeping Track." *Compiler* (Summer), pp. 4–16.

Parent, D. 1987. *Structuring Criminal Sentences: The Evolution of Minnesota's Sentencing Guidelines.* Toronto: Butterworth Legal Publishers.

Pennsylvania Commission on Sentencing. 1988. *Sentencing Guidelines Implementation Manual.* 3d ed. State College: Pennsylvania Commission on Sentencing.

Proband, S. 1994. "Habitual Offender Laws Ubiquitous." *Overcrowded Times* 5(1):7.

Reed, J., and D. Nance. 1972. "Society Perpetuates the Stigma of a Conviction." *Federal Probation* 2:27–31.

Roberts, J. V. 1992. "Public Opinion, Crime, and Criminal Justice." In *Crime and Justice: A Review of Research,* vol. 16, edited by M. Tonry. Chicago: University of Chicago Press.

———. 1994. "The Role of Criminal Record in the Federal Sentencing Guidelines." *Criminal Justice Ethics* 13:21–30.

———. 1995. *Public Knowledge of Crime and Justice.* Ottawa: Department of Justice Canada.

———. 1996. "Public Opinion and the Role of Criminal Record in the Sentencing Process." *American Behavioral Scientist* 79:488–500.

Roberts, J., and N. White. 1986. "Public Estimates of Recidivism Rates: Consequences of a Criminal Stereotype." *Canadian Journal of Criminology* 28: 229–41.

Rossi, P., R. Berk, and A. Campbell. 1995. "Popular Views of Sentencing Federal Criminals." Unpublished manuscript. Amherst: University of Massachusetts, Department of Sociology.

Rossi, P., E. Waite, C. Bose, and R. Berk. 1974. "The Seriousness of Crimes: Normative Structure and Individual Differences." *American Sociological Review* 39:224–37.

Ruby, C. 1994. *Sentencing.* 4th ed. Toronto: Butterworths.

Seidman, R. 1966. *A Sourcebook of the Criminal Law of Africa.* London: Sweet & Maxwell.

Semmes, R. 1970. *Crime and Punishment in Early Maryland.* Montclair, N.J.: Patterson Smith.

Shane-Dubow, S., A. Brown, and E. Olsen. 1985. *Sentencing Reform in the United States: History, Content and Effect.* Washington, D.C.: U.S. Department of Justice.

Sharpe, J. 1990. *Judicial Punishment in England.* London: Faber & Faber.

Shoemaker, R. 1991. *Prosecution and Punishment: Petty Crime and the Law in London and Middlesex, c. 1660–1725.* Cambridge: Cambridge University Press.

Singer, R. 1979. *Just Deserts: Sentencing Based on Equality and Desert.* Cambridge, Mass.: Ballinger.

Stalans, L., and S. Diamond. 1990. "Formation and Change in Lay Evaluations of Criminal Sentencing: Misperception and Discontent." *Law and Human Behavior* 14:199–214.

Stephen, K. 1883. *A History of the Criminal Law of England.* New York: Franklin.

Sutton, P. 1978. *Variations in Federal Criminal Sentences: A Statistical Assessment at the National Level.* Washington, D.C.: U.S. Department of Justice.

Tiffany, L., Y. Avichai, and G. Peters. 1975. "A Statistical Analysis of Sentencing and Federal Courts: Defendants Convicted after Trial, 1967–1968." *Journal of Legal Studies* 4:369–90.

Tonry, M. 1993. "Sentencing Commissions and Their Guidelines." In *Crime and Justice: A Review of Research*, vol. 17, edited by Michael Tonry. Chicago: University of Chicago Press.

Tornudd, P. 1994. "Sentencing and Punishment in Finland." *Overcrowded Times* 5:1–16.

U.S. Department of Justice. 1987. "Federal Sentencing Guidelines: Answers to Some Questions." NIJ Report no. 205. Washington, D.C.: U.S. Government Printing Office.

U.S. Sentencing Commission. 1991. *The Federal Sentencing Guidelines: A Report on the Operation of the Guidelines System and Short-Term Impacts on Disparity in Sentencing, Use of Incarceration, and Prosecutorial Discretion and Plea Bargaining.* Washington, D.C.: U.S. Sentencing Commission.

———. 1992. *Sentencing Commission Guidelines Manual.* Washington, D.C.: U.S. Sentencing Commission.

Utah Commission on Criminal and Juvenile Justice. 1994. *Utah Sentence and Release Guidelines.* Salt Lake City: Utah Commission on Criminal and Juvenile Justice.

van den Haag, E. 1978. "Punitive Sentences." *Hofstra Law Review* 7:123–38.

———. 1986. "On Sentencing." In *Punishment and Privilege,* edited by W. Groves and G. Newman. New York: Harrow & Heston.

Victorian Sentencing Committee. 1988. *Report of the Victorian Sentencing Committee.* Vol. 3. Melbourne: Victorian Attorney-General's Department.

von Hirsch, A. 1982. "Constructing Guidelines for Sentencing: The Critical Choices for the Minnesota Sentencing Guidelines Commission." *Hamline Law Review* 5:165–215.

———. 1985. "Previous Convictions." In *Past or Future Crimes.* New Brunswick, N.J.: Rutgers University Press.

———. 1991. "Criminal Record Rides Again." *Criminal Justice Ethics* 4:2–56.

———. 1993. *Censure and Sanctions.* Oxford: Clarendon.

von Hirsch, A., K. Knapp, and M. Tonry. 1987. *The Sentencing Commission and Its Guidelines.* Boston: Northeastern University Press.

Washington State Sentencing Guidelines Commission. 1992*a. Implementation Manual—1992.* Olympia: Washington State Sentencing Guidelines Commission.

———. 1992*b. A Statistical Summary of Adult Felony Sentencing: Fiscal Year 1992.* Olympia: Washington State Sentencing Guidelines Commission.

Wasik, M. 1987. "Guidance, Guidelines and Criminal Record." In *Sentencing Reform: Guidance or Guidelines?* edited by M. Wasik and K. Pease. Manchester: Manchester University Press.

———. 1993. "England Repeals Key Provisions of '91 Sentencing Reform Legislation." *Overcrowded Times* 4(4):1, 16–17.

Wasik, M., and A. von Hirsch. 1995. "Section 29 Revised: Previous Convictions in Sentencing." *Criminal Law Review* (June), pp. 409–18.

Wheeler, S., K. Mann, and A. Sarat. 1988. *Sitting in Judgement: The Sentencing of White-Collar Criminals.* New Haven, Conn.: Yale University Press.

Wilkins, L., J. Kress, D. Gottfredson, J. Calpin, and A. Gelman. 1976. *Sentencing Guidelines: Structuring Judicial Discretion. Final Report of the Feasibility Study.* Washington, D.C.: Law Enforcement Assistance Administration.

Wilkins, W. 1992. "The Federal Sentencing Guidelines: Striking an Appropriate Balance." *University of California Davis Law Review* 25:571–86.

Richard S. Frase

Sentencing Principles in Theory and Practice

ABSTRACT

In Norval Morris's "limiting retributivist" theory of punishment, considerations of "just deserts" set upper and occasionally lower limits on sentencing severity. Other purposes, including general deterrence, considerations of equality, and "parsimony," provide the necessary "fine-tuning." Proponents of just deserts, such as Andrew von Hirsch, give much greater weight to retributive and equality values and would allow almost no role for other sentencing goals in the determination of the severity of individual sentences. The relative severity of sentences must be closely linked to desert, and parsimony should only be considered in determining issues such as the overall severity of the sentencing scale. Minnesota's sentencing guidelines, in effect since 1980, are based on a theory of just deserts, but also give substantial weight to utilitarian sentencing purposes. This was true even of the original guidelines and is more true today. The theory of punishment that has evolved is quite similar to Morris's theory and quite different from von Hirsch's. Minnesota's fifteen-year experience with guidelines shows that Morris's theory of punishment is both theoretically sound and practically viable.

Norval Morris's theory of punishment is a theory of "limiting retributivism," in which concepts of "just deserts" set upper and occasionally lower limits on sentencing severity; within these broad outer limits, other purposes and principles provide the necessary "fine-tuning."

Richard S. Frase is Benjamin N. Berger Professor of Criminal Law at the University of Minnesota Law School. A preliminary version of this article was presented at a conference in honor of Norval Morris, entitled "Crime, Punishment, and Mental Health: Soundings for the Twenty-first Century," held at the University of Chicago Law School on October 28–29, 1994.

0192-3234/97/0022-0008$02.00

Such other purposes and principles include not only traditional crime-control purposes (deterrence, incapacitation, and rehabilitation) but also considerations of equality (uniformity) and a concept Morris calls "parsimony": a preference for the least severe alternative that will achieve the purposes of the particular sentence. However, Morris rejects coerced rehabilitation as a reason for imprisonment or for extending a prison term. He also rejects basing the type or duration of sentences on individual predictions of dangerousness, except in very limited situations. His later writings express strong support for sentencing guidelines, provided such guidelines are flexible, and prescribe intermediate sanctions as well as prison terms.

Proponents of just deserts, such as Andrew von Hirsch, give much greater weight to retributive and equality values. Indeed, von Hirsch would allow almost no role for other sentencing goals in the determination of individual sentences. Von Hirsch agrees with Morris that sentencing severity, and especially the use of incarceration, are excessive in the United States; however, von Hirsch believes that the concept of parsimony should only be used to determine absolute, not relative, sentencing severity (e.g., the maximum and minimum extremes of the punishment scale) and should not be considered at a case-specific level. Like Morris, he favors sentencing guidelines and believes that they should promote broader use of intermediate sanctions; but von Hirsch insists that the severity of sentences for different offenders must be closely linked to their deserts.

Minnesota's sentencing guidelines, in effect since 1980, are widely believed to be based primarily on a just-deserts sentencing theory. In fact, however, the guidelines have always given substantial weight to all traditional sentencing purposes: not only retribution and equality, but also crime-control goals and parsimony (especially in the use of state prison terms). This hybrid theory is evident even at the level of theory and formal rules; it is even more evident in practice.

Section I of this essay describes Morris's theory of punishment as it has evolved over the years. Section II summarizes von Hirsch's critique of key aspects of Morris's theory and presents the responses Morris has made, or which could be made, to those criticisms. In Section III, I describe the theory of punishment which has evolved under the Minnesota guidelines, both in theory and in practice. Section IV reviews and discusses the many ways in which the guidelines have implemented Morris's approach. Even the differences between the Minnesotan and Morris theories generally reflect practical considerations which Morris has often noted. I conclude that Minnesota's experience demonstrates the wisdom of Morris's theory of punishment, which is both theoretically sound and (as proved in Minnesota) practically viable over a substantial period of time.

I. Morris's Theory of Punishment

In his first book, *The Habitual Criminal*, published in 1951, Morris noted that the theories of criminal punishment being applied by judges and legislators were neither coherent nor stable over time (quoting a 1902 criminal law text, making the same point) (Morris 1951, p. 8). However, Morris insisted that specific purposes *are* being applied, consciously or not, and that an effort must be made to define them more precisely, to avoid the "fortuitousness" of widely disparate sentences imposed by different judges in similar cases (Morris 1951, p. 9). Two years later, Morris again noted that courts "have failed to develop any agreed principles or practices and that consequently judicial sentencing lacks uniformity and equality of application, is considerably capricious, and can be shown to fit neither the crime nor the criminal" (Morris 1953, p. 186). Morris presented sentencing data documenting the extent of existing disparities and proposed a number of reforms.

Thus at the outset of his career, Morris identified and began to address the interrelated problems of sentencing disparity and the conflicting purposes of, and at, sentencing. His earliest works also show his strong belief in the importance of relating sentencing theory to sentencing practice—"the actual functioning" of penal sanctions (Morris 1951, p. 16). Morris is an empiricist and a realist; he wants to know how judges and other practitioners think and act. Armed with this information, sentencing theory may reflect the accumulated wisdom of the past and may also avoid imposing highly unpopular rules which will only be circumvented in practice.

In his early critique of sentencing disparity, and also in some of his proposals for reform, Morris foreshadowed the revolution that would later transform the American sentencing process. Although most of his early reform proposals were intended to improve the quality of sentencing within the traditional "indeterminate" model (e.g., improved presentence investigations), several of his suggested reforms involved procedures that would later become central features of sentencing guidelines. Thus Morris assumed that sentences should be subject to appellate review (although at that time, such review was minimal in the British Commonwealth system and almost unheard of in the United

States). He also insisted that trial courts should give reasons for their sentences, if an appeal was filed, and that the appeals court should likewise state reasons for its judgment. Morris further suggested that trial judges be provided with data on sentences imposed (by offense, offender age, and offender prior record), so that the judges could "see clearly where they stand in relation to their brethren" (Morris 1953, p. 200).

Morris's own theory of punishment began to emerge in his 1964 book, *Studies in Criminal Law*, coedited with Colin Howard. In an essay by Morris, entitled "Penal Sanctions and Human Rights," Morris argued that "power over a criminal's life should not be taken in excess of that which would be taken if reform were not considered one of our purposes" (Morris and Howard 1964, p. 175). Morris was thus one of the first mainstream writers to suggest the empirical and moral defects of the "rehabilitative ideal" of coerced, prison-based treatment linked to the timing of parole release (see also Allen 1964, pp. 25–41; Allen 1981). In addition, Morris's essay explicitly linked retributive sentencing goals to the human rights of defendants and implied that such rights place firm upper limits on the severity of punishments imposed to achieve crime-control purposes (Bottoms 1995, pp. 19, 22–23).

Morris continued his attack on the rehabilitative ideal in his 1970 book, *The Honest Politician's Guide to Crime Control* (Morris and Hawkins 1970, chap. 5). Morris questioned whether in-prison treatment programs are effective and argued strongly in favor of community-based sentencing and treatment. He also advocated much broader use of fines, in lieu of short custodial terms, and argued against statutes that impose mandatory minimum prison terms or place arbitrary limitations on probation eligibility (Morris and Hawkins 1970, pp. 112–13, 115–24, 141–43; see also Morris 1977*a*, p. 150; Morris 1977*b*, pp. 279–80; Morris and Hawkins 1977, pp. 60–61; Morris 1993, p. 310).

A. Emergence of Morris's Limiting Retributive Theory

A more comprehensive theory of punishment was presented in 1974 in *The Future of Imprisonment*. Morris's theory was further developed in his 1976 lecture, "Punishment, Desert, and Rehabilitation" (Morris 1977*a*); in his 1982 book, *Madness and the Criminal Law;* and in his 1990 book (with Michael Tonry), *Between Prison and Probation: Intermediate Punishments in a Rational Sentencing System.*

In *The Future of Imprisonment*, Morris attempted to reconcile the numerous and often conflicting purposes of punishment within a theory of "limiting" retributivism, in which retributive or "just-deserts" values set upper, and occasionally lower, limits on the nature and severity of punishment. Although these principles were specifically addressed to the question of whether a prison term should be imposed, Morris indicated that they should also apply, "with suitable modifications," to prison duration and to other sentencing issues (Morris 1974, p. 59). His later writings on punishment have generally addressed both prison commitment and prison duration issues.

Morris's upper limits of desert are strict and explicit: "No sanction should be imposed greater than that which is 'deserved' for the last crime, or series of crimes" being sentenced (Morris 1974, pp. 60, 73–77). However, he strongly emphasized that courts are permitted, but *not* obligated, to impose the maximum which the offender deserves (Morris 1974, p. 75).

In later writings, Morris extended the concept of desert to include at least some offender-based factors, especially the defendant's prior record of convictions (Morris 1982, pp. 151–52, 162–63, 184–86; Morris 1992, p. 145).[1] Morris has also distinguished between the "societal" and "individual" faces of desert (Morris 1982, p. 161). The former determines the absolute upper and lower desert limits and "is a reflection of society's official view of what the criminal deserves; it is not finely tuned." However, within these outer limits, additional moral distinctions, based on the facts of the particular case, may be considered, along with other punishment goals and factors (Morris 1977*b*, pp. 275, 280–81; Morris 1982, pp. 151–52, 161, 168–69).

Morris's concept of "societal" desert was perhaps originally intended to correspond to the absolute upper and lower limits set by the legislature, for each offense, within which courts may consider the aggravating and mitigating circumstances of the particular case ("individual" desert). In a sentencing guidelines system such as Minnesota's (where presumptive sentencing ranges are often narrower than the statutory range), a second level of "societal" desert might be recognized: courts could routinely and somewhat loosely consider case-specific desert within the presumptive sentence range but would have to meet more exacting standards in order to "depart" and impose a sentence closer to the statutory minimum or maximum.

In Morris's view, desert sometimes also sets lower limits on punish-

[1] This article, although published in 1992, was based on Morris's 1982 Cardozo Lecture to the Association of the Bar of New York City.

ment (i.e., minimum severity requirements); in his words, the sentence must not "depreciate the seriousness" of the current offense (Morris 1974, pp. 60, 78–79). This language was taken from the Model Penal Code (American Law Institute 1962, § 7.01(c)). Although Morris usually refers to this as a retributive concept (Morris 1974, p. 78; Morris 1977*a*, pp. 157–58; Morris 1982, p. 198), the code's language is also consistent with a long-term deterrent or norm-reinforcing function. Morris seemed to agree, noting that such minimum severity limits are needed because "[t]he criminal law has general behavioral standard-setting functions; it acts as a moral teacher" (Morris 1974, p. 78). In any case, whether for retributive reasons, norm-reinforcement, or both, Morris felt that strict lower limits on sentencing severity are only sometimes required (citing, as one example, a case of spousal homicide, where a prison term might be required even if the offender is no longer dangerous, and even if granting probation would not cause an immediate jump in homicide rates) (Morris 1974, p. 78). Finally, as noted earlier, Morris has consistently opposed mandatory minimum prison terms and arbitrary limits on probation eligibility (Morris and Hawkins 1970, pp. 141–43).

Within the upper and lower limits of desert, Morris envisioned a range of "not undeserved" penalties. In later writings, he characterizes these ranges as "overlapping and quite broad" (Morris 1982, p. 151). He also explicitly differentiated his own views from other desert-based theories by distinguishing between purposes of punishment which are "defining," those which are "limiting," and those which are only "guiding" principles (Morris 1977*a*, pp. 140–42; Morris 1982, pp. 182–87). Morris suggested that deterrent purposes could precisely define the proper punishment, but only if we knew much more than we now do about the deterrent effects of punishment. As for desert, however, he argued that this concept is inherently too imprecise (and perhaps also too lacking in political and philosophical consensus; Morris and Tonry 1990, pp. 86–89) to precisely define the sentence; it can only establish rough outer limits, an allowable sentencing range, beyond which penalties would be widely seen as clearly *undeserved* (i.e., either excessively severe or excessively lenient) (Morris 1977*a*, pp. 158–59; Morris 1982, pp. 198–99; Morris and Tonry 1990, pp. 104–5). Within those broad ranges of desert, other punishment goals, acting as "guiding principles," will interact to "fine-tune" the sentence. A guiding principle is defined as "a general value which should be respected unless other values sufficiently strongly justify its rejection in any given case" (Morris 1977*a*, p. 142).

B. The Role of Various Nonretributive Sentencing Factors

What, then, are the "guiding principles" in Morris's theory, which provide the necessary fine-tuning between retributive upper and lower limits, and what precise role does each play?

1. *Rehabilitation.* Morris was an early critic of the "rehabilitative ideal" of coerced, in-prison treatment linked to the timing of parole release (Morris 1964, p. 175). He greatly expanded on this critique in later writings (Morris and Hawkins 1970, chap. 5; Morris 1974, pp. 12–27; Morris 1977*a*, p. 139; Morris and Hawkins 1977, chap. 6). First, he argued, postprison risk cannot reliably be predicted based on in-prison behavior. Moreover, coerced in-prison treatment programs waste resources on unamenable subjects, while encouraging feigned cooperation which may actually preclude genuine reform. Finally, returning to the human rights theme of his earlier writings, Morris argued that such coercive treatment would be morally wrong even if it were effective.

Thus Morris concluded that rehabilitation is not a reason either to impose or to extend a prison sentence; furthermore, all in-prison treatment programs must be entirely voluntary and not linked to the timing of release. However, the inmate may be compelled to participate in such a treatment program long enough to "know what it is about" (Morris 1974, pp. 18–19). Moreover, Morris has long been a strong advocate of community treatment and apparently does not object to conditioning the terms of probationary or parole release on participation in an appropriate community-based treatment program—at least one "closely and directly" related to the conviction offense (Morris and Hawkins 1970, pp. 112–13, 118–24; Morris 1974, pp. 34, 42–43; Morris and Tonry 1990, pp. 186–203, 206–12).

2. *Incapacitation.* Morris's second guiding principle, proposed in *The Future of Imprisonment*, was similarly in conflict with traditional goals and practices of indeterminate sentencing. Morris was opposed to basing prison commitment, duration, and release decisions on individualized assessments of the defendant's degree of "dangerousness" (Morris 1974, pp. 62–73; Morris 1977*b*, pp. 276–77). Again, Morris argued that we lack the ability accurately to predict future behavior and are very likely to err on the side of massive overprediction and

overincarceration. The latter excesses occur because of the vague and expansive nature of the notion of "dangerousness." There are also strong political and bureaucratic pressures to err on the side of detention (since "only" criminals are being unnecessarily detained, and their very detention prevents us from knowing which ones would have been safe to release—what Morris calls the "mask of overprediction") (Morris 1974, p. 68). Thus Morris concluded: "Prediction of future criminality is an unjust basis for determining that the convicted criminal should be imprisoned . . . or for prolonging its term" (Morris 1974, pp. 59–60, 66).

Morris acknowledged, however, that the fear of crime *in general* (not just fear of what this particular defendant will do in the future) may help to determine the retributive upper limits of punishment. Such fear might be based on the frequency and distribution of that type of crime, "a few sensational events," "a wave of widely reported crimes," and even the "brutal or mitigating details" of the current offense (Morris 1974, p. 76; see also Morris 1982, pp. 161–62). Morris would also permit parole decisions to be based on actuarial predictions (i.e., "base expectancy rates" of parole success, for various offender categories) (Morris 1977*a*, p. 148) and would allow "anamnestic" predictions (based on the defendant's past behavior) to influence conditions of parole release (Morris 1974, p. 34).[2]

In later writings, Morris—always the realist—recognized that individualized predictions of dangerousness *will* be made, whether they are formally permitted or not (Morris 1992, p. 139). He therefore sought to define the narrow conditions under which such predictions might be a fair and effective basis for prison commitment and duration decisions. In particular, he argued that sentencing severity may be increased (up to the retributive maximum) if "reliable actuarial data" indicate that the defendant's risk of assaultive behavior is "substantially" higher than that of other offenders with very similar prior records and current offenses (Morris 1982, pp. 166–72; Morris 1992, pp. 138–47; see also Morris and Miller 1985; and Miller and Morris 1986). However, Morris felt that these conditions would rarely be met. Indeed, it

[2] However, Morris favored a fixed duration of parole, rather than the traditional "unexpired term" concept under which the "best risks" (those released earliest) have the longest period of supervision, while the worst risks (those released late, or after "maxing out") have little or no parole aftercare (Morris and Hawkins 1970, pp. 113, 142).

seems likely that they will *never* be met, since the only "reliable actuarial data" likely to be available would be for groups of offenders with similar prior record and current offense—without distinguishing, as Morris requires, among offenders *within* each such group.

3. *Failure of Prior, Lesser Penalties; Categoric Recidivist Enhancements.* In *The Future of Imprisonment,* Morris argued that increased severity (up to the retributive maximum) is appropriate when "other less restrictive sanctions have been frequently or recently applied to this offender" (Morris 1974, pp. 60, 79–80). Morris seemed to base this provision on retributive grounds—when "lesser sanctions have been appropriately applied and contumaciously ignored . . . the criminal law must keep its retributive promises" (Morris 1974, pp. 79–80).[3] However, such increases in punishment might also be justified on a theory of special deterrence (also sometimes referred to as specific or individual deterrence) (Zimring and Hawkins 1973, pp. 72–74, 224): if the offender did not "get the message" before, increased severity is needed to "get his attention" (or perhaps, to counteract particularly strong temptation). So viewed, special deterrence will sometimes raise the necessary and appropriate penalty above the retributive minimum required.

The imposition of greater severity in such cases might also be justified on grounds of prevention (i.e., incapacitation) of high-risk defendants. Although Morris rejected incarceration based on individualized predictions of dangerousness, he approved of parole release decisions based on actuarial (group, or categoric) predictions of risk. He has also stated that prior convictions are a legitimate reason for sentence enhancement—not only for reasons of desert but also because of the recidivist's statistically greater likelihood of reoffending: "The best predictor of future criminality is past criminality" (Morris 1982, pp. 162–63).

4. *General Deterrence.* Morris felt that we lack the necessary data to permit general deterrence to serve as a "defining" goal which would precisely calibrate punishment in each case (Morris 1977*a*, pp. 140–42; Morris 1982, pp. 182–83). However, within the retributive upper and lower limits, Morris viewed general deterrence as an appropriate

[3] For discussions of various retributive justification for the increased punishment of recidivists, see von Hirsch (1981*a*); von Hirsch (1985, pp. 77–91); Ashworth (1992, pp. 147–50).

guiding factor. Thus he would permit sentencing severity to be increased (up to the retributive maximum) if such an increase "is necessary to achieve socially justified deterrent purposes, and the punishment of this offender is an appropriate vehicle to this end" (Morris 1974, pp. 60, 79).

In particular, Morris approved of the practice of imposing additional severity "to capture public attention and to deter such behavior by a dramatic punishment"—what Morris calls "exemplary" sentences (Morris 1977*a*, pp. 151–53; Morris 1982, pp. 187–88). As one example, he cites a British judge's imposition of four-year prison terms (at least double the term normally imposed for the offense) for racially motivated attacks (the Notting Hill cases). Another of his examples is Chicago's annual pre-Christmas crackdown on drunk drivers, designed to counteract the increased incidence of this crime during the holiday period.

Morris would also allow sentences to be mitigated for deterrent purposes—overall, or by some random process of selection—if the crime in question could be controlled effectively by very minor or occasional penalties. His favorite example is federal income tax enforcement (Morris 1974, p. 79), especially for certain, highly risk-averse offenders. Thus of "six Denver doctors" accused of tax fraud, only some need be prosecuted and imprisoned to achieve adequate deterrence (Morris 1977*a*, pp. 153–56; Morris 1982, pp. 189–92). Given the perennial lack of resources to fully enforce all criminal laws, Morris suggests that selective enforcement and mitigated punishment are a practical necessity; however, for reasons of "parsimony" he would advocate deterrent selectivity even if resources were adequate to permit more frequent and severe punishment (Morris 1977*a*, pp. 156–58; Morris 1982, pp. 189–90).

5. *Equality (or Uniformity).* Morris accords the goal of uniformity in sentencing a lower priority than do many just-deserts theorists (and also, perhaps, many supporters of sentencing guidelines). In Morris's view, the goal of equality in punishment is an important consideration in fine-tuning the sentence, "but it is by no means a categorical imperative . . . the principle of equality—that like cases should be treated alike—is . . . only a guiding principle which will enjoin equality of punishment unless there are other substantial utilitarian reasons to the contrary" (e.g., "exemplary" deterrent enhancement, or "parsimonious" deterrent mitigation) (Morris 1982, pp. 160, 198; see also Morris 1977*a*, pp. 137, 142). Morris acknowledges "the long tradition of jus-

tice as equality" (Morris 1982, p. 204) and also recognizes that equality is an especially important value in the American context (Morris 1982, p. 180). Nevertheless, he argues that, within the range of "not undeserved" penalties, punishment can be unequal—and even, in some sense, "unfair"—and yet still be "just" (Morris 1977*a*, pp. 151–63; Morris 1982, pp. 187–92).

Morris points to a number of traditional law enforcement and sentencing practices that are flatly inconsistent with a very restrictive requirement of equality. In particular, he cites the use of selective prosecution, exemplary sentences, and deterrent parsimony; the grant of leniency to defendants who turn state's evidence; the traditional pardon and amnesty powers; and the use of early parole release to avoid prison overcrowding. Morris recognizes that equality values are traditionally viewed as strongest at the point of sentencing and are weaker both in the earlier, police- and prosecutor-controlled stages and in the later correctional processes. Nevertheless, he believes that, in light of such substantial (and, perhaps, inevitable) systemwide inequality, the sentencing process cannot, and should not, attempt to observe strict equality constraints (Morris 1982, pp. 206–8). This conclusion also follows from his strong belief in the concept of "parsimony," which "overcomes the principle of equality" (Morris 1977*a*, p. 154; Morris 1982, p. 191).

6. *Parsimony.* In *The Future of Imprisonment*, Morris argued that one of the most important guiding principles of sentencing is that "[t]he least restrictive (punitive) sanction necessary to achieve defined social purposes should be imposed" (Morris 1974, p. 59). Morris found direct support for this principle in the American Bar Association's Sentencing Standards (American Bar Association 1968, § 2.2)[4] and implicit support in recent National Crime Commission proposals and in the Model Penal Code's general presumption in favor of probation (American Law Institute 1962, § 7.01). He further argued that important analogues of the principle can be found in cases interpreting the prohibition of cruel and unusual punishments (since "any punitive suffering beyond societal needs is what, in this context, defines cruelty") and in mental health and juvenile justice dispositional standards (Morris 1974, pp. 60–62).

For Morris, the principle of parsimony "is both utilitarian and hu-

[4] The principle is also found in the second and third editions of these standards (American Bar Association 1979, § 18-2.2; American Bar Association 1993, §§ 18-2.4 and 18-6.1).

manitarian" (Morris 1974, p. 61). The concept has long been a central tenet of utilitarian philosophy. As Michael Tonry points out, writers at least as far back as Jeremy Bentham (1789) argued that "punishment itself is an evil and should be used as sparingly as possible . . . 'it ought only to be admitted in as far as it promises to exclude some greater evil' " (Tonry 1994, p. 63, quoting Bentham). Parsimony is also perhaps a necessary (or at least a natural) corollary of a theory of limiting retributivism; if judges are permitted broad rather than narrow ranges of "just" punishment, some overarching principle such as parsimony is needed to give them more guidance, or at least a more precise "starting point."

Broader sentencing ranges, combined with the principle of parsimony, permit and encourage the exercise of mercy. As Morris eloquently put it, "justice and mercy both have roles in the criminal justice system; mercy cannot be precisely quantified and institutionalized or it ceases to be mercy and becomes leniency; mercy is the trump that can capture equality's ace and allow punishment at the bottom range of a deserved punishment" (Morris 1982, p. 180). Parsimony in the use of custodial sentences also permits the preservation of the defendant's social ties (Morris 1974, pp. 8, 75) and the avoidance of needless suffering and expense (Morris 1977*a*, p. 154). In any event, Morris argued, the ability to grant case-level mitigation of punishment, without strict desert or equality constraints, is a necessary and inevitable feature of our chronically overloaded and underfunded criminal justice system (Morris 1977*a*, pp. 156–58; Morris 1982, p. 190).

To summarize, Morris believed that judges should use the *lower* end of the range of "deserved" punishments as a starting point and should increase that penalty only if (and only to the extent that) one or more of his other "guiding" factors requires increased severity in the particular case. Thus the specific sentence would be determined by whichever factor required the greatest severity (general deterrence, failure of prior lesser penalties, and [very rarely] actuarially based predictions of dangerousness).

Case-specific ("individual") desert considerations are also relevant. Morris would probably say that case-specific desert imposes strict upper limits on punishment (i.e., that it lowers the maximum severity that may be imposed for utilitarian reasons). However, given his general view that lower desert limits are more flexible, he might argue that only cases of exceptionally aggravated culpability should serve to raise the judge's "starting point" (i.e., the minimum of the statutory or guidelines range), before consideration of utilitarian goals.

It is not clear exactly how Morris's guiding principle of equality is reconciled with the principle of parsimony, since the two will often be in conflict. However, if the presumption in favor of the least severe sentence is a *strong* presumption, and if judges thus usually sentence near the bottom of the "not-undeserved" range, then sentences will tend to be fairly uniform among offenders whose cases fall into the same range. Morris probably did expect that sentences would cluster near the bottom of the desert range—if only for lack of sufficient utilitarian justification for raising them higher; he has often argued that criminal laws and punishments have very little effect on crime rates (Morris 1977*b*, pp. 267–69; Morris 1993, p. 309).

7. *Rewarding Defendant Cooperation (Especially Guilty Pleas).* As everyone familiar with American criminal courts knows, the most important "guiding" factor in sentencing is often the defendant's plea. Morris expressed dislike for the exchange of "concessions" for guilty pleas (Morris 1974, p. 52) and the resulting coercion, overcharging, and distortion of the sentencing process (Morris 1977*a*, p. 147; Morris and Hawkins 1977, pp. 57–58). But Morris is a realist and recognizes the practical reasons that underlie the grant of leniency to defendants who "cooperate." His proposed alternative to traditional plea bargaining is a pretrial "settlement" conference, attended by the judge, prosecutor, defense attorney, defendant, and victim (Morris 1974, pp. 50–57; see also Heinz and Kerstetter 1979, passim, reporting on the successful implementation of Morris's proposal in Dade County, Florida). This procedure is intended to better regulate the process; however, it appears to assume considerable flexibility in sentencing and does not rule out charge and/or sentence mitigations resulting from the conference.

For similar practical reasons, Morris recognized the need to grant good-conduct ("good-time") reductions of prison terms to encourage cooperation and maintain order (Morris 1974, p. 49; Morris 1977*b*, p. 277). He also appeared to approve of the occasional grant of even earlier release, where necessary to avoid or lessen serious prison overcrowding problems (Morris 1982, p. 189).

It is not clear how the cooperation mitigations noted above should be incorporated into Morris's desert-range-with-parsimony theory. If such mitigations are not to undercut essential (nothing-less-will-do) crime control measures, it would seem necessary to initially add some additional severity (within desert limits) to what the latter measures minimally require, in order to leave room for cooperation-rewarding mitigations. For example, prison terms would need to be increased by the maximum good-time credits prisoners may earn.

C. *Morris on Sentencing Guidelines*

Morris opposed legislatively drafted determinate sentencing reforms, when they were first proposed and enacted in the mid-1970s (Morris 1977*a*, pp. 149, 164; Morris 1977*b*, pp. 272–81). He recognized (as he had since 1951) that sentencing disparity is a serious problem but felt that the solution was not to impose excessive legislative rigidity; the necessary "fine-tuning" of the sentence must be done by the trial court (Morris 1977*b*, pp. 272–75). Thus he preferred to continue on the path of criminal law reform (recodification; statutory guiding principles) inspired by the Model Penal Code (Morris 1977*b*, pp. 275–76). At the same time, Morris strongly advocated two reforms which subsequently became essential features of most sentencing guidelines systems: the requirement that trial judges state reasons for their sentences and appellate review of sentences (Morris 1977*a*, pp. 149–50, 164–65; Morris 1977*b*, pp. 275–76; Morris and Hawkins 1977, pp. 59–60). Morris hoped that these reforms would facilitate the gradual evolution of binding precedents on frequently occurring issues—what he termed a "common law of sentencing."

Morris gave qualified support to the earliest federal bills calling for the creation of a sentencing commission to promulgate guidelines—provided that such guidelines retained sufficient judicial discretion (Morris 1977*a*, pp. 149–50, 165; Morris 1977*b*, pp. 276, 281–85). His support was due in part to the fact that these bills included requirements of trial court reasons and appellate review. However, Morris may also have recognized the value of having an independent commission make case-level sentencing policy. In *The Future of Imprisonment*, Morris had identified an important "latent" function of the parole board: the precise timing of prison release could be determined at a time and place removed from the "emotional intensity" and the "searchlight of public attention" that often attends the trial and initial (maximum) sentence determination (Morris 1974, pp. 36–37, 39, 48). Later, in *Madness and the Criminal Law*, Morris noted a similar problem with legislative control over case-level sentencing severity: political pressures to be "tough on crime" inevitably cause legislators to set penalties based on the "worst" case of each type (Morris 1982, p. 158).

Thus if parole-release discretion were to be eliminated, under sentencing guidelines,[5] and prisoners were then expected to serve most of the sentence imposed by the court, the shorter (but "real-time") presumptive sentences must be set by a body independent of the legislature. This "insulation" argument subsequently became, and remains, one of the major justifications for commission-based sentencing guidelines (Frase 1991*a*, pp. 729–30).

In his later writings, Morris gave much stronger support to the new (commission-based) sentencing guidelines movement (Morris 1982, pp. 172–76; Morris and Tonry 1990, pp. 48–49; Morris 1993, p. 307, 309). Nevertheless, he has criticized state and federal guidelines for putting too much emphasis on prison sentences, without enough attention to the wide variety of "intermediate" sanctions more restrictive than straight probation (Morris and Tonry 1990, pp. 37–42; Morris 1993, pp. 307–8, 310).

In his book written with Michael Tonry, *Between Prison and Probation*, Morris proposed to replace the "two-zone" systems found in most state guidelines grids (presumed prison; presumed probation) with a system employing multiple presumptions and multiple sanction types (Morris and Tonry 1990, chap. 3). For example, he expressed strong support for the "four-zone" system proposed by the District of Columbia Sentencing Guidelines Commission: the least serious group of offenders receive only community-based sanctions (e.g., probation, fine, restitution, and/or community service); cases in the second, more serious, group may receive either a community sentence or custody, with a rebuttable presumption in favor of the former; for the third group, judges would have the same choices, but without the presumption; in the most serious cases, a custodial sentence was specified (Morris and Tonry 1990, pp. 60, 77).

To further guide judges, and encourage the use of noncustodial sanctions, Morris and Tonry proposed the development of a system of "interchangeable" punishments (Morris and Tonry 1990, pp. 75–81, 90–92). Judges would first decide the primary purposes to be served by that offender's sentence; the judge would then select a package of

[5] Except for the latent function noted in text, Morris was quite willing to abolish parole release discretion. He felt that such discretion could not be justified by the need to make individualized assessments of reform and/or dangerousness (which he rejected) and was not needed to maintain prison discipline, maximize deterrence, avoid prison overcrowding, or rectify unjust disparities; each of the latter functions could be better served by other means (or were not being effectively served by parole discretion in any case) (Morris 1977*b*, pp. 276–79).

sanctions designed to achieve those purposes (and no more severe than necessary to do so) (Morris and Tonry 1990, pp. 90–92). Similarly situated offenders (i.e., those with similar conviction offense and prior record) would receive sanction combinations roughly equal in their overall punitiveness. This would be achieved by means of "equivalency scales," defining the relative severity of different sanction types (Morris and Tonry 1990, pp. 92–108)—for example, two months of home detention equals one month of imprisonment.

Very serious cases were excluded from the proposal above, for both theoretical and practical reasons (Morris and Tonry 1990, pp. 78–79, 123). In such cases, any sentence other than prison would depreciate the seriousness of the offense (thus violating Morris's retributive minimum); also, such offenders are likely to be violent, and thus in need of custodial restraint. As a practical matter, it is difficult to enforce community-based sanctions equivalent in severity to very long prison terms (Morris and Tonry 1990, p. 173). At the other end of the severity spectrum, "trifling" cases were also excluded (Morris and Tonry 1990, p. 79)—presumably because principles of parsimony call for nothing more severe than straight probation.

D. *Summary*

Morris's theory of punishment is both principled and pragmatic. Some features are based on strong normative arguments. However, as foreshadowed in his first book, he has also very deliberately tried to fashion a theory that is congruent with the widely held values and practices of judges and other system actors. In opting for a hybrid theory, seeking to balance conflicting punishment goals, case-specific factors, and practical realities, Morris recognized (quoting H. L. A. Hart) that "the pursuit of one aim may be qualified by the pursuit of others"; in the end, he concluded, "there is no universal formula . . . penal policy always represents a choice among a plurality of aims and objectives and every decision we reach may be attended by some disadvantages" (Morris and Hawkins 1970, p. 123).

II. Von Hirsch's Critique, and Morris's Response

Von Hirsch is probably the best-known American advocate of the "just-deserts" model of sentencing (von Hirsch 1976, 1981*a*, 1981*b*, 1985, 1992, 1993), and he has frequently criticized Morris's theory of punishment. In this section, I outline the general principles of von Hirsch's own theory, summarize his major objections to Morris's views, and consider the responses that Morris has made, or which could be made, to these criticisms.

A. *Summary of von Hirsch's Sentencing Theory*

In Morris's terms, von Hirsch is a "defining" retributivist: desert and equality goals define, within narrow limits, the precise degree of punishment severity which each offender must receive, relative to other offenders. Von Hirsch believes that the criminal law is primarily and essentially a "blaming" institution and that criminal penalties properly convey "censure" to the offender as well as the public (von Hirsch 1976, chap. 8; von Hirsch 1985, chap. 3; von Hirsch 1993, passim). Such expressions of blame serve to recognize the importance of the individual and societal rights violated by the offense and also confirm the offender's responsibility by addressing him or her as a responsible moral agent, capable of understanding right and wrong (von Hirsch 1992, p. 67). In such a system, the relative severity of sanctions imposed on different offenders must be closely correlated with the relative blameworthiness of these offenders (the requirement of "ordinal proportionality"), and equally culpable offenders must receive equally severe sanctions (the requirement of "parity") (von Hirsch 1985, p. 40; von Hirsch 1992, p. 79).

The concept of "ordinal" proportionality deals with issues of *relative* severity—the rank order and spacing of severity increments of penalties, for offenses of increasing seriousness. Von Hirsch distinguishes sharply between ordinal proportionality and "cardinal proportionality"—the determination of *absolute* degrees and types of severity (von Hirsch 1985, pp. 39–40; von Hirsch 1992, pp. 83–84). For von Hirsch, there are at least two important issues of cardinal proportionality which must be addressed in any punishment system: the definition of the upper and lower extremes ("anchoring points") of the punishment scale (e.g., death, and/or the maximum prison term; suspended sentence, or other least severe authorized penalty) (von Hirsch 1985, pp. 92–94; 1992, pp. 75–79, 83–85); and the exact placement of lines dividing different zones or types of punishment (e.g., the point at which incarceration is the appropriate disposition rather than some relatively severe noncustodial penalty) (von Hirsch 1981*b*, pp. 787–89).[6]

[6] A third issue is treated by von Hirsch in a manner somewhat similar to questions of cardinal desert. That issue is whether "hard treatment" such as prison is the required means with which to express censure or whether more symbolic, verbal denunciation is sufficient. Von Hirsch believes that this choice is not determined by the logic of desert

Von Hirsch views the requirements of cardinal desert as much less constraining than those of ordinal desert. Like Morris's view of desert generally, von Hirsch feels it is difficult to say exactly what absolute degree or type of severity each offender deserves; but we can at least say that some penalty scales are clearly too severe or too lenient in the type or degree of sanctions (von Hirsch 1985, pp. 43–46). Given this greater degree of uncertainty, von Hirsch would allow the legislature or sentencing commission to consider nonretributive goals—including crime control, parsimony, and available resources—when deciding issues of cardinal proportionality (von Hirsch 1985, p. 45; von Hirsch 1987*b*, pp. 94–95; von Hirsch 1992, pp. 83–84). But he would rarely allow either crime-control or parsimony goals to affect the ordinal proportionality decisions made by the legislature or sentencing commission, nor would he allow such goals to be considered by judges on a case-specific basis (von Hirsch 1985, pp. 40–46).

B. Von Hirsch's Critique of Morris's Theory

Von Hirsch finds Morris's sentencing theory vague, unfair, and likely to produce unduly severe results (von Hirsch 1981*b*, pp. 772–89; von Hirsch 1984, pp. 1094–1110; von Hirsch 1985, pp. 38–46, 139–46; von Hirsch 1992, pp. 89–90; von Hirsch 1993, pp. 64–68).[7] His specific questions and criticisms are summarized below.

Just how broad are the desert ranges, he asks—except for very serious offenses, would anything from a suspended sentence to the statutory maximum prison term be permitted? Does desert "substantially constrain" the sentence, or is it "relegated to the margins?" (von Hirsch 1981*b*, p. 785). Furthermore, how are these ranges set? What specific factors should legislators or guidelines commission members consider, in setting anchoring points or range widths? How are courts supposed to apply Morris's numerous but conflicting "guiding principles," to determine the precise sentence within the range?

Von Hirsch also questions the precise meaning of "mercy," which Morris says his broader ranges permit. Von Hirsch believes that this concept may be closely related to "desert"; if so, he argues, it does not operate within desert limits but rather serves to define the truly deserved sentence (von Hirsch 1984, pp. 1107–8).

---

and (like the two "cardinal" desert issues noted in text) depends instead on crime-prevention needs (von Hirsch 1992, pp. 73–74).

[7] See also von Hirsch (1994, pp. 39–49) and von Hirsch (1995, pp. 160–61, 163–64, n. 32), criticizing this author's previous writings defending Morris's limiting retributive theory, as adopted in Minnesota.

Similarly, what is "parsimony"? If this is simply the traditional utilitarian goal of maximizing efficiency (no more expense, pain, or other "cost" than is necessary to achieve all legitimate utilitarian purposes), then it is a *consequence* of pursuing utilitarian goals, not a justification for choosing or preferring such goals. Although admitting that Morris himself avoids such circular reasoning, von Hirsch notes that other advocates of parsimony have not (von Hirsch 1984, p. 1107).

Von Hirsch also faults Morris for using current or past sentencing practices (e.g., the imposition of exemplary sentences) to argue for his theory: "Citing the *existence* of a sentencing practice does not demonstrate the *justice* of that practice" (von Hirsch 1984, p. 1104; emphasis in original).

Von Hirsch and Morris are in fundamental disagreement on the meaning of "justice" and "fairness." In von Hirsch's view, Morris's limiting retributive theory would allow routine imposition of unequal penalties on equally culpable offenders and would even permit less severe punishment to be given to more culpable offenders (von Hirsch 1984, pp. 1102–3; von Hirsch 1992, p. 76; von Hirsch 1994, p. 45; von Hirsch 1995, pp. 163–64, n. 32). This is simply too unfair, and it violates the basic premises of criminal law as a "blaming" institution. Von Hirsch is also critical of Morris's willingness to give prior convictions a significant role in defining the outer limits of desert; in von Hirsch's view, the proper role of criminal history is quite modest (von Hirsch 1985, pp. 77–91; von Hirsch 1994, pp. 39–40).

Finally, von Hirsch questions whether application of a limiting retributive theory, even one which included Morris's principle of parsimony, would promote lower, more reasonable degrees of sentencing severity (von Hirsch 1984, pp. 1104–7; von Hirsch 1985, pp. 140–46; von Hirsch 1993, pp. 67–68; von Hirsch 1994, pp. 43–46). Von Hirsch appears to agree with Morris that sentencing severity, and especially the use of incarceration, is excessive in the United States. However, von Hirsch believes that sufficient leniency can be achieved without sacrificing ordinal proportionality and parity, by simply lowering the upper and lower anchoring points of the punishment scale and encouraging judges to forgo custodial penalties in favor of noncustodial, intermediate sanctions of approximately equal severity (von Hirsch, Wasik, and Greene 1989, pp. 599, 604–6; von Hirsch 1992, pp. 80, 92–93).

Von Hirsch feels that giving judges a broad sentencing range may actually invite excessive punishment, not parsimony—judges may choose sentences closer to the maximum end, and legislators or sentencing commissioners may feel freer to increase these maxima than they would under a more "defining" desert scheme. In any case, lowering sentences for some offenders almost inevitably means raising them for others. "*Parsimony for whom?*" von Hirsch asks; the offenders receiving increased punishment will not appreciate the parsimony extended to others (von Hirsch 1984, pp. 1106–7; emphasis in original).

C. *Morris's Response to von Hirsch's Criticisms*

Morris has not written a comprehensive rejoinder to von Hirsch's criticisms, although he has responded specifically to some of them (Morris 1982, pp. 202–5; Morris and Tonry 1990, pp. 84–90). The summary below is based on the latter responses; on arguments Morris has indirectly aimed, over the years, at von Hirsch's theory; and on my assessment, based on all of Morris's work, of the additional arguments Morris could make to round out his reply.

On the initial question of range width, and the relative importance of desert and nondesert goals, Morris agrees that the very "modest" role of desert, under the American Bar Association's second edition of its sentencing standards (American Bar Association 1979), goes too far; Morris favors stronger desert constraints, in "an ordered system of justly deserved punishments" (Morris 1982, p. 203). In his later writings, Morris gave strong support to sentencing guidelines, particularly the Minnesota version. This implies that his suggested ranges are comparable in width to the cells on the Minnesota guidelines grid. At one point, in discussing how a sentencing commission might set presumptive terms for second-offense purse snatchers, Morris suggested that a range running from probation to six-months' custody would be appropriate (Morris 1982, pp. 194–96).[8]

Von Hirsch finds Morris's praise of the Minnesota guidelines curious, since he feels that these guidelines "come close to adopting the desert parity that Morris wishes to reject" (von Hirsch 1984, p. 1100, n. 29). To this, Morris might reply (having read Sec. III below), that the Minnesota guidelines do not, in fact, give "desert parity" nearly as big a role as von Hirsch claims. He would also point out that even von Hirsch allows *some* flexibility in the application of his ordinal proportionality principle: sanctions for equally culpable offenders need only

[8] See also Morris and Tonry (1990), p. 90 (of three like-situated offenders, one might appropriately receive a six-month prison term; the second, a substantial fine; and the third, required participation in a drug treatment program).

be "approximately" equivalent in severity (von Hirsch 1992, pp. 80, 92–93), and the gradations (spacing) of penalties for crimes of increasing severity "are likely to be matters of inexact judgment" (von Hirsch 1992, p. 83).

As to the method by which desert ranges would be defined, Morris implies that this is ultimately a political decision, which could be made in a variety of ways, including public or judicial surveys and legislative or sentencing commission deliberation and consensus building (Morris and Tonry 1990, p. 85). It would also seem that Morris (or the sentencing commission) could employ von Hirsch's own methods of ordinal ranking and spacing to produce one series of proportioned *upper* limits (Tonry 1994, p. 80), tied to appropriate desert-based categories of conviction offense and prior record, and a second series of proportioned *lower* limits (at least for those offenses deemed serious enough to require minimum desert standards). Finally, as previously discussed, Morris's theory does provide considerable guidance to judges in picking the precise sentence within the outer limits of desert: judges should start at the bottom of the range and increase severity only to the extent needed to meet all appropriate utilitarian and case-specific desert needs.

On the meaning and importance of "mercy," Morris might agree that this is sometimes related to desert (and he agrees that such case-specific desert factors have a role to play in fine-tuning the sentence). However, Morris would also say that von Hirsch leaves insufficient room for appropriate exercise of case-level mercy that is *unrelated* to desert—for example, the traditional pardon and amnesty power, and the grant of early release to relieve prison overcrowding. Another example of undeserved mercy, discussed by Morris, is the parable of the prodigal son (Morris 1982, pp. 205–6). Morris argued that there are useful sentencing analogies to the theological issues of repentance, forgiveness, and divine mercy illustrated by the parable. The theme of forgiveness is also emphasized in Morris's proposal to include the victim in a pretrial settlement conference (Morris 1974, pp. 56–57). In retrospect, it seems that Morris anticipated the development of the theory of restorative justice, which emphasizes the importance of defendant acceptance of responsibility, victim forgiveness, and victim-offender reconciliation (Cragg 1992, passim, but esp. pp. 204–17).

Morris would also argue that judges must have broad discretion to mitigate sentencing severity if (as von Hirsch himself advocates) courts are to make greater use of intermediate sanctions. As a practical matter, any theory requiring rigid "equality of suffering" among offenders with similar offense and prior record precludes frequent substitution of noncustodial sanctions—for example, lengthy community service obligations are difficult to enforce (Morris and Tonry 1990, pp. 168–69, 173). A rigid theory of equality and desert thus forces judges to impose needless and expensive incarceration that serves no social good other than to provide symbolic denunciation (and, perhaps, "misery-loves-company" satisfaction). As discussed more fully below, Morris gives little weight to the latter grounds. In his more recent writings, von Hirsch seems to agree that relaxing desert constraints would facilitate substitution of noncustodial penalties (von Hirsch 1992, pp. 92–93). However, he appears unwilling to accept any major departures from his central principles of parity and ordinal desert.

As for von Hirsch's point that the existence of a practice does not necessarily prove its validity, Morris would almost certainly agree. However, he might counter that the existence of a widespread practice often says something about our basic moral and societal values, which is why philosophers (including von Hirsch himself; von Hirsch 1981*a*, pp. 595–613) traditionally have cited everyday concepts and practices to illustrate fundamental moral principles. Morris would also point out that the abstract justice or logic of a theory does not guarantee that judges and other practitioners will accept it in practice. Morris recognized that these system actors are strongly committed to pursuing a variety of sentencing goals and will never accept a pure, one-dimensional retributive theory (Morris and Tonry 1990, pp. 87–88). If such a theory were forced on them, they would use their remaining, unregulated discretionary powers to undercut it (Morris 1982, p. 158; Morris 1992, p. 139).

Morris also questions the internal logic and persuasiveness of von Hirsch's theory. Von Hirsch concedes that "cardinal" desert is difficult to precisely define; Morris questions whether "ordinal" desert is really so different. For Morris, "judgments of comparable [i.e, *ordinal*] culpability are enormously difficult to make," given the imprecision of offense categories and criminal history records, the ambiguities of social deprivation, and other factual and moral uncertainties (Morris and Tonry 1990, p. 87). How—other than by simply assuming it—can von Hirsch be so sure that ordinal ranking and spacing decisions permit a high degree of societal consensus and precision as to desert? And how can he categorically rule out any consideration of nondesert factors, in making ordinal decisions?

Indeed, is the cardinal/ordinal distinction even that clear? Von Hirsch considers a guidelines commission's decision about where to draw the "in/out" line (presumptive prison/presumptive probation) to be an example of cardinal (absolute) desert, thus permitting much greater flexibility and the consideration of nondesert factors. But in practice, the imposition of a prison sentence often results in a major "step-up," at least in symbolic denunciation (and often also in actual severity), when compared to the most severe nonprison sanction. Thus wherever the in/out line is drawn, it is likely to violate von Hirsch's requirements for precise ordinal *spacing*—increased severity directly proportional to increased blame.

Morris might also question von Hirsch's assumption that the sentencing process is a "blaming" or "censuring" institution (and therefore by its very nature, must impose penalties conforming to strict standards of ordinal desert). This essential premise seems somewhat at odds with von Hirsch's view that "cardinal" issues may be strongly influenced by crime-control purposes. Decisions on cardinal issues—the absolute severity and the form of punishments—determine the basic parameters of any system of criminal sanctions; if such fundamental issues are closely linked to utilitarian concerns, how can von Hirsch insist that punishment is still "essentially" or "primarily" a blaming institution?

Morris further questions von Hirsch's arguments based on "fairness." Morris freely admits that his theory allows equally blameworthy defendants to receive unequal degrees of severity and thus permits the more blameworthy to receive less punishment. This much is implicit in any system of broad, overlapping desert ranges (although Morris's examples of overlapping ranges are for offenses of fairly similar severity—murder and manslaughter; rape and aggravated assault; Morris 1982, p. 151). But such "failures" of ordinal proportionality are not necessarily either substantial in degree or routine, as von Hirsch asserts. Morris's principle of parsimony, combined with his recognition of equality as an important guiding factor, are intended to result in *most* defendants receiving punishment near the bottom of their desert range; thus most sentences will be roughly proportionate to (ordinal) desert.

More fundamentally, however, Morris questions von Hirsch's assumption that equality values trump all other concerns. Although equality is an important goal of sentencing, few people believe it is the *only* goal (Morris and Tonry 1990, pp. 86–87, 89). As discussed more fully in Section III below, Morris's assumptions about popular notions of equality and "fairness" seem to be borne out, at least in Minnesota; the people of that state have, for over fifteen years, accepted a guidelines sentencing system with much greater departures from ordinal desert than von Hirsch would allow. Different sentences for two offenders of equal blame are apparently seen as "fair," provided there are good (nondesert) reasons for unequal treatment, and provided further that the differences are not too great, or too often linked to *bad* reasons (e.g., racial bias).

The latter problem is, of course, a very legitimate concern. Although von Hirsch has not specifically accused Morris of promoting or tolerating invidious distinctions, Morris himself recognizes that a broader sentencing range, with discretion to be selectively lenient, risks allowing distinctions to be made along race and class lines. But he argues that if discretion is denied, to minimize the potential for bias, the alternative in practice will often simply be to impose uniformly *severe* penalties on all offenders, with no evidence that society or anyone else is benefited (Morris 1982, pp. 158–59).

Morris could also easily defend his conception of desert, as allowing substantial weight to be given to the defendant's criminal record. He notes that criminal history is "the second most significant factor in defining the amount of punishment in all existing systems of criminal punishment" and has a legitimate role for reasons of both crime control and desert (Morris 1982, pp. 162–63); it thus should be, and will always be, a major factor. Other retributive theorists have also been willing to give criminal history a greater role than does von Hirsch (Bottoms 1995, p. 22, n. 17, citing Andrew Ashworth 1992).

Finally, Morris disagrees that sufficient parsimony can be provided simply by lowering the anchoring points on the punishment scale. Given the political pressures they face, legislators are very unlikely to do this (Morris 1982, pp. 157–58), and beyond a certain point, neither is an independent (but politically appointed) sentencing commission. Thus power to grant case-level leniency, without strict desert and equality constraints, is essential. Such power is particularly critical if, as so often happens, the legislature also fails to provide enough prison space and other resources to accommodate the scale it has enacted. Moreover, case-level mitigations will continue to be granted by prosecutors through their charging and plea-bargaining discretion, even—indeed, *especially*—if such power is denied to judges (Morris 1982, p.

158). Morris feels that this power is better shared with judges and brought out in the open; if dealt with openly and honestly, principles can be developed to provide guidance, and judges can be encouraged to state reasons for their decisions. Morris has long been a foe of hypocrisy and secrecy and prefers an open and honest approach. As he once said, in arguing to decriminalize "victimless" crimes, "what is required is better regulation . . . *it is impossible to regulate behavior that is prohibited*" (Morris and Hawkins 1977, p. 21; emphasis in original).

Another defect of von Hirsch's approach is that, given his strict "ordinal proportionality" requirements—including proportional *spacing* of penalties—it is impossible for the legislature or sentencing commission to lower penalties for less serious offenses (e.g., to stay within available resources) without also lowering penalties for more serious offenses; simply lowering the "low" end of the grid would change the spacing, thus violating ordinal proportionality (or at least, whatever proportionality assessments underlay the original grid). Similarly, sentences could not be raised for violent offenders, without raising the entire penalty scale. Yet sentencing systems need to be able to respond to major changes in the type or volume of crime and to give priority, in the allocation of scarce resources, to more serious crimes. States should not have to raise or lower the entire penalty scale to respond to these needs. Von Hirsch would probably view such constraints as a "plus," assuming that the legislature, reluctant to raise the entire scale, would keep all penalties low and "parsimonious." Morris would reply that a far more likely scenario is to raise all penalties, with the expectation of massive (but selective and inconsistent) mitigation of sanctions for less serious offenders.

Morris would also insist that his theory would not, as von Hirsch claims, lead to greater sentencing severity. Judges could not routinely sentence close to the maximum of desert without violating Morris's central principle of parsimony. Legislatures could, of course, unwisely raise the maximum and/or minimum desert-range limits, just as they could raise von Hirsch's cardinal "anchoring points." Whether they would feel freer to do this in a system of broad ranges is speculative, and cannot be answered in the abstract, for all jurisdictions (see Sec. III below). It should also be recognized that if only the range maximums were raised, judges would remain free (and, under the parsimony principle, would be expected) to continue to sentence most cases near the bottom end of the desert range.

D. *Summary*

Von Hirsch and Morris appear to agree on several important points: first, that the concept of desert is very important; second, that the pre-guidelines systems of "indeterminate sentencing" gave far too great a role to offender-based rehabilitative and incapacitative goals; and third, that parsimony is important—sentencing severity, and especially the use of incarceration, are excessive in the United States.

However, von Hirsch and Morris disagree strongly on the details of a system of desert-oriented sentences, designed to limit unjustified disparity and promote parsimony. As frequently happens in such debates, the two writers often talk past each other because of their fundamentally different assumptions (Tonry 1994, pp. 77–79). Morris values, and wants to accommodate, a much broader range of sentencing goals, and he is also very concerned with how well his proposed principles will be accepted (and consistently applied) in practice. Von Hirsch is striving to create a logical and coherent sentencing theory, without much regard for either the value of nondesert goals or how well his theory accords with traditional practices. These two authors also seem to have very different ideas of what is intuitively "fair." Of the two, Morris would seem to be more attuned to what people actually think is fair, at least in Minnesota.

III. The Minnesota Sentencing Guidelines, in Theory and Practice[9]

The Minnesota Sentencing Guidelines Commission adopted retribution (just deserts) as its primary sentencing goal (Minnesota Sentencing Guidelines Commission 1980, p. 9; Minnesota Sentencing Guidelines Commission 1984, pp. v, 10–14). However, the original 1980 version of the guidelines also gave substantial emphasis to utilitarian goals, which had strong legislative support. The role of nonretributive purposes has grown in the fifteen years since the guidelines became effective, but the changes have been gradual, and usually built on themes that were clearly present in the original guidelines and enabling legislation. Just deserts continues to play a very important role in Minnesota sentencing, but its role is more accurately described as a "limiting" one: defining the maximum sentence severity in almost all cases and, for the most serious cases (about one-fifth of the annual caseload), specifying relatively flexible standards of minimum severity.

[9] An earlier version of this section of the article appeared in Frase (1994).

In this section of the essay, I first examine the Minnesota legislature's original intent regarding sentencing goals. I then present a brief summary of how the guidelines work, describe how the Minnesota Sentencing Guidelines Commission carried out its statutory mandate, and analyze the commission's original intent (including what it *did*, as well as what it said it was doing). Finally, I discuss how punishment theory under the guidelines has evolved over time, addressing the sentencing purposes implicit in appellate case law interpreting the guidelines, significant legislative and commission actions since 1980, and the actual sentencing practices of trial judges and attorneys.

A. The Original Legislative Intent

The 1978 guidelines enabling statute (1978 Minn. Laws, chap. 723) contained no explicit statement of sentencing theory and imposed relatively few specific mandates. The Minnesota legislature simply directed the newly created commission to promulgate guidelines (regulating both the decision to impose state imprisonment and the duration of such imprisonment), based on "reasonable offense and offender characteristics," while taking into "substantial consideration" two factors: "current sentencing and releasing practices" and "correctional resources, including but not limited to the capacities of local and state correctional facilities." The commission was also permitted (but was not required) to develop guidelines regulating the conditions of nonprison sentences.

The enabling statute abolished parole release discretion and substituted a limited reduction (up to one-third off the pronounced sentence) for good behavior in prison. This earned good-time reduction then constitutes a period of parole-type postrelease supervision (the supervised release term). The statute also implied that denial of good-time reductions could only be based on disciplinary violations, not failure to participate in or cooperate with in-prison treatment programs (since all such programs were to become voluntary).[10] Finally, the statute requires sentencing judges to provide written reasons when they depart from the guidelines, and both defendants and the prosecution are given the right to appeal any sentence (whether or not it is a departure).

It seems clear that a major purpose of the statute was to reduce sen-

[10] Since 1993, inmates may lose good-time credits if they refuse to work or participate in treatment programs. See Sec. IIIC2 below.

tencing discretion, thus promoting greater uniformity of sentences, but what broader purposes did the legislature want such sentences to serve? Did it intend to move toward a "just-deserts" model, with sharply reduced emphasis on rehabilitation, incapacitation, and deterrence? The legislative preference for greater uniformity does not, by itself, imply a strong emphasis on retributive values: reduced case-level discretion limits the ability of courts to "fine-tune" their assessments not only of each offender's treatment needs and dangerousness but also of his or her precise deserts (Frase 1991*b*, p. 332).

Von Hirsch has argued that the Minnesota enabling statute "suggests no particular rationale" or choice between sentencing purposes (von Hirsch 1987*a*, p. 65). However, on closer inspection it appears that the legislature *did* take a position, albeit an imprecise one (Frase 1993*b*, pp. 347–49). First, the legislature left unchanged several references to utilitarian goals and offender-based sentencing, contained in the state's criminal code. Second, the enabling statute directed the guidelines commission to give "substantial consideration" to existing sentencing and releasing practices, which suggests limited change in preexisting norms and therefore substantial continued emphasis on the utilitarian goals which had dominated preguidelines sentencing.

Of course, the statute did limit the pursuit of utilitarian goals (especially rehabilitation and incapacitation) in several ways: discretionary parole release was abolished, and all prison treatment programs were made voluntary. But the statute did not forbid consideration of the offender's treatment needs or dangerousness when determining whether to impose a prison term, nor did it preclude the imposition of conditions of probation or supervised release designed to promote rehabilitation or public safety. Thus although individualized parole-risk assessments and coerced "cure" in prison were both abandoned, probation-risk assessments and required treatment in the community were not necessarily rejected.[11]

Nor does the legislative history of the enabling statute evince an intent to emphasize retribution, abandon utilitarian goals, or dramatically change any existing sentencing norms. The 1978 act was the culmination of several years of legislative ferment over the sentencing reform issue, reflecting increasing dissatisfaction with indeterminate sentencing, but disagreement over what to do about it (Parent 1988,

[11] Goodstein (1983), p. 494, noting the early emergence of the practice of setting mandatory treatment conditions of supervised release (the Minnesota guidelines "parole" term).

pp. 21–27; Frase 1993*b*, pp. 347–49). Sentencing purposes were rarely debated as such; whatever consensus there was at that time seemed to focus on abolishing the parole board and increasing the uniformity of sentences, while at the same time avoiding any overall increase in sentencing severity and prison populations.

It thus appears that the most probable legislative purposes in enacting the 1978 enabling statute were, first, to sharply limit judicial and parole discretion in the pursuit of all of the traditional purposes of punishment, without abandoning any of those purposes, or strongly preferring some over others; second, to emphasize that state prison sentences are imposed primarily to achieve retribution, deterrence, and incapacitation, and not to achieve forced rehabilitation (i.e., rehabilitation is to be pursued primarily outside of prison); third, to consider other changes in sentencing policy, without departing too much from existing practices; and, fourth, to recognize, while pursuing the goals above, that punishment (especially prison) is expensive and that overcrowding of prisons and other resources must be avoided even if this limits the achievement of certain punishment goals.

B. The Sentencing Commission's Original Intent—the Meaning of "Modified Just Deserts" in Minnesota

Pursuant to the statutory mandate described above, the Minnesota Sentencing Guidelines Commission developed a set of guidelines in the form of a two-dimensional matrix (Minnesota Sentencing Guidelines Commission 1980, p. 30). The current grid, shown in figure 1, was last revised in 1989 (Minnesota Sentencing Guidelines Commission 1995*b*, § IV). There are ten categories of increasing offense severity running down the vertical axis of the grid, and seven defendant criminal history categories (from zero to six or more points) running across the horizontal axis.

The numbers in each cell are presumptive prison durations, in months. Offenders with low to medium criminal history scores, convicted of lower severity offenses, are recommended to receive probation, accompanied by a stayed (suspended) prison term of a specified number of months; for more serious offenses or criminal history scores, the recommended sentence is an executed prison term within a narrow specified range (e.g., forty-four to fifty-two months, at severity level 7, with zero criminal history).

The boundary between presumptive stayed and presumptive executed prison terms is shown on the grid by a heavy black line known

Severity Levels of Conviction Offense		Criminal History Score						
		0	1	2	3	4	5	6 or more
Sale of a Simulated Controlled Substance	I	12 *	12 *	12 *	13	15	17	19 *18-20*
Theft Related Crimes ($2,500 or less) Check Forgery ($200-$2,500)	II	12 *	12 *	13	15	17	19	21 *20-22*
Theft Crimes ($2,500 or less)	III	12 *	13	15	17	19 *18-20*	22 *21-23*	25 *24-26*
Nonresidential Burglary Theft Crimes (over $2,500)	IV	12 *	15	18	21	25 *24-26*	32 *30-34*	41 *37-45*
Residential Burglary Simple Robbery	V	18	23	27	30 *29-31*	38 *36-40*	46 *43-49*	54 *50-58*
Criminal Sexual Conduct 2nd Degree (a) & (b)	VI	21	26	30	34 *33-35*	44 *42-46*	54 *50-58*	65 *60-70*
Aggravated Robbery	VII	48 *44-52*	58 *54-62*	68 *64-72*	78 *74-82*	88 *84-92*	98 *94-102*	108 *104-112*
Criminal Sexual Conduct, 1st Degree Assault, 1st Degree	VIII	86 *81-91*	98 *93-103*	110 *105-115*	122 *117-127*	134 *129-139*	146 *141-151*	158 *153-163*
Murder, 3rd Degree Murder, 2nd Degree (felony murder)	IX	150 *144-156*	165 *159-171*	180 *174-186*	195 *189-201*	210 *204-216*	225 *219-231*	240 *234-246*
Murder, 2nd Degree (with intent)	X	306 *299-313*	326 *319-333*	346 *339-353*	366 *359-373*	386 *379-393*	406 *399-413*	426 *419-433*

FIG. 1.—Minnesota Sentencing Guidelines grid, effective August 1, 1989. Source: Minnesota Sentencing Guidelines Commission (1995*b*). Note: Presumptive sentence lengths are in months. An asterisk (*) = one year and one day. Italicized numbers within the grid range denote the range within which a judge may sentence without the sentence being deemed a departure. Under state statutes, first-degree murder has a mandatory life sentence.

as the "disposition line." Cases falling in cells above the line generally receive presumptive probation sentences (a few cases above the line have presumptive prison-commit sentences; most of the latter involve repeat sex offenders or use of a dangerous weapon, which are subject to mandatory minimum prison terms under state statutes).

Additional guidelines rules specify when consecutive prison sentences may be imposed; list permissible and impermissible bases for departure from presumptive disposition, duration, and consecutive-sentence rules; define a general departure standard ("substantial and compelling circumstances"); and suggest (but do *not* regulate by presumptive rules) a wide variety of possible conditions of stayed prison sentences. Such conditions may include up to one year of confinement in a local jail, home detention, electronic monitoring, intensive probationary supervision, required appearances at a day-reporting center, inpatient or outpatient treatment, restitution, fines, community service, or (with certain limitations, discussed below) any combination of the above conditions (Minnesota Sentencing Guidelines Commission 1995*b*, § III.A.; Minn. Stat. Annot. § 609.135).[12]

1. *The Sentencing Commission's Key Policy Choices.* The commission chose to adopt a "prescriptive" rather than a "descriptive" approach to guidelines drafting (Minnesota Sentencing Guidelines Commission 1980, pp. 2–3; Minnesota Sentencing Guidelines Commission 1984, pp. v, 8–14). Thus the new guidelines were intended to change, not simply model and perpetuate, past judicial and parole decisions. Although prior practices were taken into account, as required by the enabling statute, the commission made a number of independent decisions about which offenders ought to go to prison and for how long. One of the commission's earliest prescriptive choices was its decision to adopt just deserts as the "primary" sentencing goal under the guidelines (Minnesota Sentencing Guidelines Commission 1984 pp. v, 10–14), while giving limited scope to other sentencing purposes and considerations—the theory of "modified just deserts" (Minnesota Sentencing Guidelines Commission 1980, p. 9).

The theory needs further elaboration—*how much* is desert theory "modified," and *by what?* Clearly, one important nondesert goal was the incapacitation of high-risk offenders. The commission admitted that this goal influenced the precise placement and slope of the disposition line (Minnesota Sentencing Guidelines Commission 1980, p. 9), and it appears that scaling of presumptive prison durations was also influenced by considerations of incapacitation. The commission recognized that recidivists are more likely to reoffend,[13] and it adopted a grid in which presumptive durations increase substantially, with increases in the defendant's criminal history score. As a result, the impact of criminal history under the guidelines goes well beyond the modest role that von Hirsch would allow prior record to play.[14]

[12] The cited statute limits the duration of probationary jail sentences, defines the available "intermediate sanctions," and encourages courts to impose such sanctions "when practicable." The statute further provides that the duration of a stayed felony sentence (and thus the length of probation) may be any period up to the maximum prison term that could have been imposed, or four years, whichever is longer (Minn. Stat. Annot. § 609.135, subd. 2[a]).

[13] The commission noted that the use of criminal history to increase sentences "has an implicit incapacitative effect, since offenders with longer criminal histories tend to be somewhat greater risks than those with lesser criminal histories. It may also provide an implicit rehabilitative effect, since those with longer criminal histories often have more severe problems and a longer period of control is thought necessary to deal with the problems" (Minnesota Sentencing Guidelines Commission 1984, p. 14).

[14] See von Hirsch (1981*a*, pp. 619, 632) (defendants deserve full punishment after a "modest" number of convictions; the effect of prior record on prison duration, under the Minnesota guidelines, exceeds what can be justified on desert grounds alone); see

The commission's implicit pursuit of incapacitative goals may also be reflected in its decision to define "prior" convictions as of the date of *sentencing*, rather than as of the date that the current offense was committed. Some writers believe that crimes committed after the current offense have no bearing on "desert" (Parent 1988, p. 163); however, such crimes are quite relevant if the goal is to identify and incapacitate (or specifically deter) high-risk offenders. The inclusion, in the criminal history scale, of a point for "custody status" (being on parole, probation, in prison, etc., at the time of the current offense) may also reflect selective incapacitation goals or considerations of specific deterrence.

The commission did not specifically address the goal of general deterrence, except to suggest that it would require a sentencing structure very similar to a desert model (i.e., with more serious offenses assigned the more severe penalties; Minnesota Sentencing Guidelines Commission 1984, p. 12). Presumably, the greater uniformity of guidelines sentences also promotes the goal of general deterrence, by increasing the "certainty" of punishment and decreasing would-be offenders' hopes of leniency (Zimring and Hawkins 1973, pp. 160–72, 207).

Another very important prescriptive choice was the commission's decision to strictly interpret the statutory mandate to consider correctional resources. The commission went further than the statute required and established a goal that state prison populations should never exceed 95 percent of capacity; it then developed a detailed, computerized projection model to test the expected prison population that would result from each proposed version of the guidelines (Minnesota Sentencing Guidelines Commission 1980, pp. 2, 13–14). Resource limitations affected both dispositional and durational decisions, especially the latter (Minnesota Sentencing Guidelines Commission 1980, p. 11).

The commission's other major prescriptive choices included the rank ordering of offense severities; the construction of the criminal history scale;[15] and the decision to adopt a disposition line that was "flatter" (i.e., more "desert"-oriented) than would have been sug-

---

also von Hirsch (1995, pp. 154–55, 157) (impact of criminal history on presumptive duration, as well as the steep "slope" of the disposition line, give far too much weight to prior record).

[15] The commission's original criminal history scale included one point for each prior felony; up to one point for multiple prior misdemeanor convictions; up to one point for serious juvenile record; and one point for "custody status." The commission subsequently adopted a "weighting" system for prior felonies (see Sec. III*C*4 below).

gested by prior sentencing practices, thus sending more low-criminal history "person" offenders to prison (especially those at severity levels 7 and 8), and fewer low-severity, high-criminal-history property offenders (Minnesota Sentencing Guidelines Commission 1980, pp. 2–15; Minnesota Sentencing Guidelines Commission 1984, pp. 8–14). In addition, the commission adopted a broad goal of sentencing "neutrality" relative to race, gender, and social or economic status (including an explicit rejection of departures based on the offender's employment status at the time of sentencing) (Minnesota Sentencing Guidelines Commission 1995*b*, §§ I(1), II.D.1). Finally, the commission endorsed a principle similar to Morris's concept of "parsimony": to ensure that prison and jail space is available for the most serious cases, sanctions "should be the least restrictive necessary to achieve the purposes of the sentence" (Minnesota Sentencing Guidelines Commission 1995*b*, § I[3]).

Most of the prescriptive policies mentioned above either reflect, or are easily reconciled with, a just-deserts model. As noted in Section II above, mitigation of sentences in order to stay within available resources is consistent with von Hirsch's theory, provided that *all* sentences are mitigated, without changing the relative severity among different offenses ("ordinal" desert) and provided further that the looser, "cardinal" (absolute) limits of minimum desert are respected.

However, the "parsimony" principle is more problematic. Von Hirsch would only allow such considerations to be used to lower the entire punishment scale; selective, case-level reductions would violate his principle of strict ordinal proportionality. The guidelines' reference to "the purpose*s* of *the* sentence" suggests consideration of multiple punishment goals and the granting of case-level mitigation unrelated to ordinal desert. The endorsement of case-specific parsimony implies that the commission, like Morris, viewed desert as permitting a *range* of permissible sanctions; within that range, courts may also consider nonretributive purposes and should impose the lowest penalty which adequately serves all relevant purposes.

The "range" theory above finds further support in the structure and foreseeable application of the guidelines. The Minnesota commission knew that, in the great majority of cases under the new guidelines, judges would retain a wide variety of sentencing options and would continue to apply utilitarian goals and make offender-specific assessments. Under the guidelines, about three-quarters of defendants have presumptive stayed prison sentences (Frase 1993*a*, p. 299), and the commission projected that about 80 percent of defendants would actually receive a stayed sentence.[16] No minimum "deserved" sentence is specified for presumptive stayed prison cases. However, the guidelines do set upper (maximum) limits on sentence severity in these cases, by means of the presumptive disposition (no immediate prison commitment) and the presumptive duration which applies if an aggravated dispositional departure is ordered, or if the initial stay of prison is later revoked. But the guidelines recommend and assume that departures and revocations will be exceptional. In the absence of departure or revocation, the guidelines do not specify any particular sentence for these defendants. Under Minnesota sentencing laws, such defendants may receive a sentence as light as unsupervised probation or as heavy as a twelve-month jail term (which may also be combined with treatment requirements, strict probation, and other conditions).

Moreover, the guidelines explicitly state that the proper penal objectives to be considered in establishing the *conditions* of stayed sentences include "retribution, rehabilitation, public protection, restitution, deterrence, and public condemnation of criminal conduct" (Minnesota Sentencing Guidelines Commission 1980, p. 35; Minnesota Sentencing Guidelines Commission 1995*b*, § III.A.2). The guidelines further provide that "the relative importance of these objectives may vary with both offense and offender characteristics" and that "multiple objectives may be present in any given sentence."

Thus for at least three-quarters of defendants, the guidelines essentially retain the traditional, offender-based indeterminate sentencing system, with no minimum severity requirements, and with all sentencing purposes allowed. However, maximum prison severity is limited by the presumptive disposition and stayed prison term. The nature and severity of stay conditions was not specifically limited under the original guidelines, but the commission may have expected the principle of parsimony to encourage moderation and attention to the actual need for each additional proposed condition of probation.

Von Hirsch has objected to the "range" theory suggested above. He maintains that the commission was not trying to "systematically" regu-

[16] The projected prison commitment rate for male felons was 20.7 percent and for females, 9.2 percent (Minnesota Sentencing Guidelines Commission 1980, p. 15). Due to a variety of transitional effects, the actual prison rate (for both sexes combined) was only 15 percent in the first year of the guidelines, but the rate has hovered around 20 percent ever since (Frase 1993*a*, p. 331, table 14; Minnesota Sentencing Guidelines Commission 1995*a*, p. 17).

late the sentences in stayed prison cases but was merely "setting forth a maximum applicable to the worst cases," while trying to limit the impact such cases would have on prison populations (von Hirsch 1995, p. 161). It may well be that the commission originally intended its presumptive stay rules as a temporary stopgap and fully intended to later develop more precise, desert-based rules for stay conditions. But the commission's clear endorsement of utilitarian sentencing goals in stay cases strongly suggests that the commission viewed stayed sentences as serving *different* purposes than prison terms and that it was not planning to develop a strongly desert-centered model for stayed sentences. Nor did the commission subsequently attempt to impose any such model. In the absence of guidance from the commission, the Minnesota Supreme Court began to develop a utilitarian, offender-based theory of stayed sentences and dispositional departures; the court also interpreted the commission's stayed prison durations as limiting not just the prison terms for cases of dispositional departure or stay revocation but also the maximum ordinarily deserved severity of probation sanctions in each guidelines cell above the disposition line.

As for the minority of defendants with presumptive executed prison terms, the commission adopted very narrow presumptive sentence ranges, which suggests a much stronger emphasis on (modified) just deserts. But here, too, the commission's rules do not strictly control minimum sanction severity, and the commission must have expected that utilitarian sentencing purposes would continue to play an important role in mitigating sentences. The guidelines imposed no limits at all on charging and plea-bargaining concessions, which can easily be used to mitigate presumptive prison terms. The commission must have expected that prosecutors and judges would continue to consider offender-based, utilitarian sentencing goals in deciding to grant or deny such concession (and it appears that they have done so; see Sec. III*C*3 below). Nor did the commission explicitly forbid courts from basing departures on nonretributive grounds. Although the commission's lists of allowable departure factors are mostly desert-related, these lists are expressly *not* exclusive (Minnesota Sentencing Guidelines Commission 1995*b*, § II.D.2). Given the pervasive practice of plea bargaining related to offender as well as offense factors, and the open-ended lists of permissible factors, it could be expected that many departures—especially mitigations—would continue to be based on nonretributive grounds.

Perhaps the commission intended to take up these issues later and close the theoretical "loopholes" described above. But it never announced such an intention, nor did it ever even begin to consider these issues; in the absence of commission action or guidance, courts and attorneys quite reasonably assumed that the commission tacitly accepted the legitimacy of a more flexible, multipurpose model of sentencing.

C. The Evolution of Sentencing Theory since 1980

The rough outlines of a limiting retributive theory, suggested by the enabling statute and the original version of the guidelines, have become much clearer since 1980. Important contributions to this evolution were made by appellate case law, legislative enactments, the actual practices of judges and attorneys, and some of the commission's own proposed amendments.

1. *Major Theory-Related Guidelines Case Law.* The appeal rights granted to defendants and prosecutors under the guidelines have generated a rich body of appellate case law, fully realizing Morris's ideal of an evolving "common law of sentencing."

The Minnesota Supreme Court almost immediately established the principle that sentence enhancement must generally be based on aggravated circumstances of the conviction offense and may *not* be based on the details of offenses dismissed or never filed (Minnesota Sentencing Guidelines Commission 1984, pp. 111–13).[17] The court also established that durational departures may not be based on assessments of the individual defendant's dangerousness (*State v. Hagen*, 317 N.W.2d 701, 703 [Minn. 1982]) nor on special needs for deterrence (*State v. Schmit*, 329 N.W.2d 56, 58, n. 1 [Minn. 1983]) or for extended, in-prison treatment (*State v. Barnes*, 313 N.W.2d 1 [Minn. 1981]). In *State v. Evans* (311 N.W.2d 481 [Minn. 1981]), the court ruled that upward durational departures should normally not exceed twice the presumptive duration (although in "rare," exceptionally aggravated cases, the trial court may depart all the way up to the statutory maximum). Uniformity goals were further strengthened by the court's early announcement that trial court decisions *not* to depart will rarely warrant reversal on appeal (*State v. Kindem*, 313 N.W.2d 6 [Minn. 1981]).

[17] However, some presumptive sentences are determined by factors (e.g., dollar amount of loss) which need not be proven as an element of the conviction offense; moreover, most upward departures are based on nonelemental facts (e.g., unusual cruelty to the victim), and a few involve facts which are not even part of the same course of conduct (e.g., "major economic offense" by defendant involved in other similar conduct) (Frase 1993*a*, p. 288, n. 29; Minnesota Sentencing Guidelines Commission 1995*b*, § II.D.2.b).

In *State v. Randolph* (316 N.W.2d 508 [Minn. 1982]), the court held that the trial judge must grant a defendant's request for execution of the presumptive stayed prison term whenever the judge's proposed conditions of a stayed sentence are so onerous that they would, in the aggregate, be more severe than that prison term. This case, in effect, limits maximum sanction severity in stayed prison cases and thus reinforces and extends the commission's implicit policy of setting upper (but not lower) limits on sanction severity in these cases.

In *State v. Hernandez* (311 N.W.2d 478 [Minn. 1981]), the court held that criminal history points may accrue on a single day when defendants are sentenced concurrently for multiple offenses. Thus a defendant with no previous convictions who was sentenced concurrently on four separate felonies (one point each) would have a criminal history of three when he was sentenced on the fourth count. Prior to *Hernandez*, prosecutors could serialize prosecutions to achieve the same result, and all additional concurrent counts would increase the defendant's future criminal history if he committed further offenses, but *Hernandez* increases the immediate impact (and plea-bargaining leverage) of multiple counts. The *Hernandez* rule also helps prosecutors target "high-rate" offenders and thus further emphasizes the utilitarian (incapacitative) purposes which were already implicit in the commission's criminal history scale (in particular: the inclusion of convictions as of the date of sentencing, rather than as of the date of the current offense, and the substantial weight given to criminal history in determining the presumptive disposition and duration).

In another very significant line of cases, the court held that dispositional departures (but *not* durational departures) may be based on individualized assessments of the offender's "amenability" to probation or prison.[18] In *State v. Park* (305 N.W.2d 775 [Minn. 1981]), the Minnesota Supreme Court upheld an upward dispositional departure (i.e., commitment to prison, rather than the presumptive stayed term) because of the defendant's unamenability to probation. The latter finding was based on the defendant's serious chemical dependency problem, his refusal to accept that he had a problem or needed treatment, and his complete failure to cooperate during previous probation terms.

In later cases, the supreme court applied several other "amenability" concepts to uphold downward dispositional departures (i.e., granting

[18] These cases are discussed at length in Frase (1991*a*, pp. 740–48). A similar line of cases, under the federal sentencing guidelines, is discussed in Frase (1991*b*).

probation—usually accompanied by a short jail term and/or required residential treatment—in lieu of the presumptive executed prison term). In *State v. Wright* (310 N.W.2d 461 [Minn. 1981]), the departure was based on two independent grounds. First, the court found that the defendant was unusually vulnerable, and was therefore unamenable to prison, because his extreme immaturity would cause him to be victimized or led into criminal activity by other inmates. Second, the court found that the defendant was particularly amenable to treatment in a probationary setting; he needed psychiatric care unavailable in prison and would not endanger public safety provided he received appropriate outpatient treatment.

In *State v. Trog* (323 N.W.2d 28 [Minn. 1982]), the court upheld a downward dispositional departure based solely on the defendant's particular amenability to probation. The presentence report indicated that, prior to the current offense (burglary with assault) Trog had been an "outstanding citizen," with no police record of any kind, even as a juvenile; he had also done well in school and at work, was intoxicated at the time of the offense, had cooperated fully with the police, and was shaken and extremely contrite about the incident. The departure in this case appears to be based on the aberrational and uncharacteristic nature of the defendant's crime, rather than on any particular treatment needs. The supreme court also quoted with approval the testimony of a retired chief of the police juvenile division, that nothing would be served by sending Trog to prison. This case provides a clear example of the rejection of strict, desert-based lower limits on punishment; Trog's sentence was mitigated for reasons of utilitarian "parsimony"—greater severity would serve no social purpose and might even be harmful.

Of all the theory-related decisions described above, the "amenability" case law seems most out of character with the dominant "just-deserts" theory of the guidelines. The supreme court has never explained why it limited this doctrine to "dispositional" departures (stay or execution of prison) or how amenability departures relate to the structure and purposes of the guidelines. However, as I have argued at greater length elsewhere (Frase 1991*a*, pp. 740–48), a closer analysis of the amenability cases reveals that they are quite consistent with the guidelines and are supported by strong practical and policy considerations. The following is a summary of the main points of that argument.

First, as noted in Section III*B* above, the guidelines strongly imply that stayed sentences serve different and broader purposes than prison terms. The guidelines also state that dispositional and durational departures are separate decisions, requiring separate justification (Minnesota Sentencing Guidelines Commission 1995*b*, comment II.D.02), and the guidelines do not limit either type of departure to retributive grounds.[19] The supreme court's amenability cases reconcile these policies by treating dispositional presumptions and departures as primarily offender-based,[20] whereas durational presumptions and departures are entirely offense- and culpability-based (*State v. Heywood*, 338 N.W.2d 243, 244 [Minn. 1983]).

Second, the offender-based disposition theory above finds support in the manner in which the guidelines regulate stayed sentences. Judges are given broad discretion not only to base stay conditions and severity on nonretributive grounds but also to revoke stayed sentences based on technical violations and other indicia of "unamenability" to probation. Such revocations are difficult to reconcile with a theory that assumes that probation was all the defendant deserved, and will *ever* deserve, for the original offense (Parent 1988, p. 231; von Hirsch, Wasik, and Greene 1989, p. 609). The simplest answer to this retributive anomaly is that such a defendant *did* deserve the presumptive prison term provided for his original offense and prior record (for further discussion of this, see Sec. IV*A* below) but was initially given *less* in an attempt to achieve the utilitarian purposes of probation (rehabilitation, restitution or community service, and "parsimony"). Any subsequent revocation is justified not only by the need to deter probation violations but also by acts of the defendant that suggest that he is unamenable to probation and should now be given his full (modified) deserts. But why did we think that such a defendant was "amenable" in the first place? The answer must be: because he was *presumed* to be amenable, given his less serious offense and prior record. From this theory, it was a short step to conclude that, in exceptional cases, judges may decide at the outset that the presumption of amenability has been overcome, thus justifying an aggravated dispositional departure. Such departures, like stay revocations, reflect a theory of "limiting" retribu-

[19] The commission has expressed concern that amenability departures may permit race and class bias but has declined to forbid them (see Sec. IV*C*4 below).

[20] Although dispositional departures are generally offender-based, courts may, and occasionally do, depart dispositionally for reasons related solely to culpability. See, e.g., *State v. Olson*, 325 N.W.2d 13 (Minn. 1982) (mitigated departure) and *State v. Gartland*, 330 N.W.2d 881 (Minn. 1983) (aggravated departure).

tivism: retributive values determine the maximum deserved punishment (prison duration), while utilitarian goals (along with considerations of parsimony and uniformity) determine initial and subsequent disposition decisions.

Third, a similar theory explains mitigating amenability departures in presumptive commit cases: such offenders are normally presumed to be unamenable to probation, but this presumption, too, may be overcome in exceptional cases.

Fourth, since there are no guidelines or other legal controls over stay revocations, charging, and plea bargaining, judges and prosecutors could and probably did achieve similar results without the use of aggravating and mitigating "amenability" departures. Formal recognition of such departures merely encourages courts and prosecutors to make these decisions openly, stating reasons. Open decision making is consistent with the "truth-in-sentencing" theme of the guidelines (Frase 1993*a*, p. 281) and permits adversary argument, appellate review, and commission guidance, rather than subterfuge and evasion. The latter dangers would be particularly great in such a heavily treatment-oriented state (Frase 1993*a*, p. 334); Minnesota, "the land of 10,000 lakes," is also sometimes called "the land of 10,000 treatment centers."

Fifth, given the ease with which the same results can be achieved informally, formal recognition of amenability departures does not significantly *add* to sentencing disparity or undercut the deterrent value of presumptive prison terms. In practice, amenability departures are limited to exceptional cases and do not appear to be granted in a racially discriminatory manner.[21] It can also be argued that individualized amenability assessments are sufficiently reliable, provided they are limited to fairly clear-cut (i.e., exceptional) cases. Indeed, even von Hirsch seems to accept occasional dispositional departures for "amenable" or "responsive" individuals (von Hirsch, Wasik, and Greene 1989, pp. 606, 614).

Sixth, amenability departures help to conserve scarce correctional resources. Probation services are not wasted on clearly unamenable offenders (nor are the latter likely to be made much worse if sent to prison). Amenable offenders can be effectively treated in the community, often at lower cost, while avoiding harmful prison influences,

[21] See Frase 1993*a*, pp. 326–28 (mitigated amenability departures occur in about 15 percent of presumptive prison-commit cases; aggravated amenability departures occur in less than 1 percent of cases with presumptive stayed prison terms).

conserving prison beds for dangerous offenders and promoting parsimony.

Seventh, all three of the leading amenability decisions summarized previously (*Park*, *Wright*, and *Trog*) were joined by the two former members of the guidelines commission, Justices George Scott and Douglas Amdahl, and the *Trog* opinion was written by Amdahl (who also wrote many other leading guidelines opinions, including *Randolph* and *Hernandez*). Thus at least two of the original nine drafters of the guidelines saw no fundamental conflict between amenability concepts and the commission's "original intent."

2. *Legislative Developments Related to Sentencing Theory.* As noted earlier, the legislature which enacted the 1978 guidelines enabling statute wanted sentencing to become more uniform, with prison duration no longer based on individualized treatment or parole-risk assessments; at the same time, the legislature also remained committed to the pursuit of crime-control goals and sound fiscal and prison management.

Subsequent legislation has reinforced the importance of crime-control goals. Numerous laws have been enacted permitting judges to make individualized assessments of offender dangerousness[22] or amenability to treatment, for certain, narrowly defined groups of offenders (Frase 1993*b*, pp. 356–57, 360–63). The legislature has also enacted additional crime-control-motivated mandatory minimum statutes (Frase 1993*b*, pp. 356, 360, 363). In 1989, the legislature amended the guidelines enabling statute to specify that the commission's "primary" consideration in drafting guidelines should be "public safety." In 1993, the enabling statute was further amended to provide that violations of prison "disciplinary" rules (which form the basis for loss of good-time credits) may include "refusal to work" and "refusal to participate in treatment or other rehabilitative programs" (Minn. Stat. Annot. § 244.05, subd. 1b[b]).

3. *Sentencing Theories Implicit in Guidelines Practices.* Empirical analysis of charging and sentencing practices under the guidelines suggests that attorneys and trial courts remain firmly attached to offender-based, crime-control-oriented sentencing goals (Frase 1993*a*, pp. 295–

[22] In 1994, the legislature enacted a civil commitment statute for "sexually dangerous persons" (Minn. Stat. Annot. §§ 253B.02, subd. 18b and 253B.185). This new law, as well as an older statute covering "psychopathic personalities" (Minn. Stat. Annot. §§ 253B.02, subd. 18a and 253B.185), are being applied with increasing frequency to chronic sexual offenders who are nearing the end of their prison sentences.

328). Prosecutors have used their charging discretion to avoid presumptive and mandatory-minimum prison terms, especially for high-severity-level "person" offenders with very low criminal history scores and for low-severity-level weapons offenders (who are subject to presumptive prison sentences even if their cases fall above the disposition line). Prosecutors have also used their charging and plea negotiation powers to steadily increase the average criminal history scores of property offenders. By filing or retaining additional counts, prosecutors can push low-severity recidivists across the grid, thus increasing their presumptive prison duration and making more of them eligible for presumptive prison-commit sentences.

As for judicial decisions, departure rates have gradually increased, with mitigating departures far outweighing aggravated departures in all years (Frase 1993*a*, pp. 296–328; Minnesota Sentencing Guidelines Commission 1995*a*, pp. 35, 37, 42). Aggravated, "unamenable-to-probation" departures remain extremely rare, but mitigated, "amenable-to-probation" departures are granted in about 15 percent of presumptive prison cases (and account for about half of all mitigated dispositional departures). Multiple regression analysis of mitigated and aggravated dispositional departures and of the imposition of jail as a condition of probation reveals that criminal history factors—especially "custody status" (probation, parole, etc., at the time of the current offense)—are consistently among the strongest predictive factors, usually much stronger than offense severity or offense type. Method of disposition (guilty plea vs. trial) is also usually a strong predictor of sentence severity, among otherwise comparable cases, but race is generally not a significant independent explanatory factor. Analysis of the limited data available on demographic variables indicates that offender employment continues, as it was before the guidelines, to be a significant predictor of a noncustodial sentence (Minnesota Sentencing Guidelines Commission 1991, pp. 15–18; Dailey 1993, p. 774)—even though the guidelines have always listed this as an impermissible departure factor (Minnesota Sentencing Guidelines Commission 1995*b*, § II.D.1).

The high rates of sentence mitigation, via charge reduction or formal departure, suggest once again that the guidelines have been much less successful in setting lower limits on sanction severity than in setting upper limits. The strong influence of prior record (even *beyond* its formal role in determining the presumptive disposition and duration), together with the important role of the offender's employment status and "amenability" to probation, result in a system in which both the form and the severity of sanctions are often determined by utilitarian, offender-based assessments, rather than by considerations of desert. These findings are consistent with Morris's limiting retributivism theory, in which desert (as measured by conviction offense and prior record) sets strict upper limits on sanction severity, but where many offenders receive lesser penalties whose precise severity is determined primarily by nonretributive considerations (crime control, resource limits, and "parsimony").

4. *Important Commission-Initiated Amendments.* The commission has made many changes in the guidelines since 1980. Most are consistent with its original, modified deserts approach (e.g., the decision in 1989 to weight prior felony convictions according to their guidelines severity level ranking; Minnesota Sentencing Guidelines Commission 1995*b*, § II.B.1). However, the commission's occasional modifications of the presumptive prison durations in certain grid cells are harder to justify, since they violate the important concept of "ordinal" proportionality (relative severity of sanctions, among different offenses and offenders; see Sec. II*A* above). Reductions in certain durations at low severity with medium-to-high criminal history were motivated by a need to avoid expected prison overcrowding (Minnesota Sentencing Guidelines Commission 1984, p. 92), rather than by any decision that the prior durations exceeded ordinal desert. On several occasions (especially in 1989), presumptive durations for violent offenses were substantially increased. Although some commissioners may have felt that these durations had always been too low, the principle motivating factor behind these changes was political pressure to respond to increased rates of drug and violent crime (Frase 1993*b*, pp. 359–61).

The commission has never seriously addressed any of the guidelines ambiguities or omissions that have allowed courts and attorneys to continue to strongly pursue nondesert goals. Thus no attempt has been made to regulate charging and plea-bargaining mitigations, stay revocations, or stay conditions, nor has the commission made any major attempt to clarify what theories of punishment may be considered as grounds for departure.

The commission has on several occasions considered the possibility of enacting stay guidelines (most recently in 1988–89, pursuant to a legislative directive to consider the issue). Each time, the commission backed away from recommending any specific guidelines. This was partly for practical reasons, in particular, local resource limits and massive field resistance. But it was also because there was a lack of commission consensus on the primary sentencing goals to be served in stay cases (Minnesota Sentencing Guidelines Commission 1989, pp. 20, 35).

In 1989, the commission added two sentences to the guidelines commentary (Minnesota Sentencing Guidelines Commission 1995*b*, Comment II.D.101), requiring the trial court to demonstrate that an amenability departure is not based on impermissible social or economic factors. But the commission expressly declined to forbid all amenability departures and did not otherwise change or clarify the guidelines departure standards or lists of permissible and impermissible departure standards.

D. Summary

The Minnesota guidelines were, from the outset, a *very* "modified" version of just deserts and have become even more so over time. Although the original guidelines emphasized just deserts, they also retained a major role for nonretributive sentencing goals. First, the strong influence of criminal history, in determining presumptive dispositions and durations, tests the limits of even the broadest conceptions of "desert" and clearly exceeds the role which von Hirsch finds acceptable. Second, although presumptive disposition and duration rules set fairly strict "modified desert" limits on maximum sanction severity, they impose no limits on minimum severity in presumptive stay cases and (because charging discretion is not controlled) set rather weak lower limits in presumptive commit cases. Third, utilitarian sentencing purposes are explicitly endorsed in the determination of stay conditions and are not precluded as factors in charging, plea bargaining, or decisions to revoke a stayed sentence; utilitarian purposes are also implicit in the guidelines' endorsement of case-specific "parsimony."

Postimplementation legislation and appellate case law have each reinforced the importance of nonretributive goals. Case law has increased the importance of criminal history and has given formal recognition to dispositional departures based on the offender-based, nonretributive concept of "amenability" to prison or probation. Statutes have also endorsed the concept of amenability, while encouraging courts and the commission to promote public safety (especially by increasing sentence severity for dangerous offenders).

Analysis of sentencing practices under the guidelines confirms the strong continuing influence of utilitarian sentencing goals, especially rehabilitation, incapacitation, and the need to make efficient use of limited correctional resources. Minnesota has been especially successful in avoiding prison overcrowding and promoting the parsimonious use of prison sentences (Frase 1993*a*, pp. 329–33). Minnesota's per-capita prison population remains lower than any other state with a major metropolitan area—only North Dakota has a lower rate (Bureau of Justice Statistics 1995, p. 3, table 2). Moreover, the increases in Minnesota's prison population since 1980 have primarily been due to increased felony caseloads (Frase 1995*a*, p. 194, fig. 7.6). During the same time period, of course, other states and the federal system experienced dramatic increases in sentencing severity and inmate populations, and these increases do not appear to be explained by rising crime rates (Frase 1995*a*, p. 194, fig. 7.7 and accompanying text).[23]

Nor has Minnesota's parsimonious use of prison sentences resulted in escalating crime rates. The major increases in rates of reported crimes, arrests, and felony caseloads in Minnesota, since the guidelines became effective, have involved violent and drug offenses; index property crime rates have actually fallen by about 11 percent (Federal Bureau of Investigation 1981, p. 52; Federal Bureau of Investigation 1994, p. 72; Minnesota Sentencing Guidelines Commission 1995*a*, p. 49). But, compared with other states, Minnesota sentences are relatively severe for drug and violent crimes (Minnesota Sentencing Guidelines Commission 1992, p. 1; Frase 1993*c*, pp. 28–32); "parsimony" has been achieved through community-based sentencing of property offenders.

Minnesota's experience thus lends support to Morris's view that the severity of criminal penalties has very little effect on overall crime rates (Morris 1977*b*, pp. 267–69; Morris 1993, p. 309). In line with Morris's strong endorsement of the principle of parsimony, Minnesota's experience further suggests that other states could substantially reduce their overall rates of incarceration, with no loss in crime-control effectiveness, and at great savings in public expense and private hardship.

IV. Limiting Retributivism and Minnesota Sentencing Policies

There are numerous similarities between the theory of punishment that has evolved under the Minnesota guidelines and Morris's theory

[23] In the absence of comparable data on criminal caseloads, the best available base for cross-jurisdictional comparisons of prison populations is adult arrests, weighted according to the seriousness of the offense. In the cited study, arrests for violent crimes were weighted (multiplied) by a factor of ten. Total inmate populations (prison plus jail)

of limiting retributivism. The similarities are particularly strong when sentencing practices in Minnesota are examined.

"But"—as Morris likes to say—there are a number of differences. And yet on closer inspection, many of these differences are either minor shifts in emphasis or degree or else reflect practical considerations of the kind that Morris has often noted and to which he would certainly be sympathetic.

In the following discussion of major similarities and differences, I often refer for convenience simply to "Morris" and "Minnesota." But as shown in Section III above, Minnesotans do not always speak with a single voice on these matters; thus I occasionally note the differing views or emphasis that appear in the guidelines commission's theoretical pronouncements and aspirations, in the guidelines themselves, in occasionally discordant state statutes, in guidelines case law, and in actual practices.

A. Desert Limits

Both Morris and Minnesota recognize fairly strict, desert-based limits on maximum sanction severity, with relatively weak limits on minimum severity (or none at all). Both base their assessments of desert on the offender's current conviction offense and prior record, and both give substantial weight to prior record.

1. *Upper Limits on Sanction Severity.* For Morris, the upper limits of desert may not be exceeded for any reason. Minnesota comes close to, but does not quite achieve, this humane and principled constraint.

Durational Rules. The guidelines presumptive prison durations define the ordinary maximum of desert. Guidelines departure rules, together with appellate case law, further provide that these upper durational limits may only be exceeded for reasons of case-specific desert, on a showing of "substantial and compelling circumstances" demonstrating aggravated culpability or harm. Only in rare, exceptionally aggravated cases may an upward durational departure exceed twice the presumptive duration (in which case, the statutory maximum becomes the upper limit).

"But"—various "dangerous offender" statutes enacted in 1989 and 1992 permit or even require aggravated durational departure, imposi-

---

at year end were analyzed as a percent of weighted adult arrests for that calendar year. The arrest-based incarceration rates for Minnesota and for the United States as a whole were very similar, from 1975 through 1980. But from 1981 through 1991, Minnesota incarceration rates remained constant, while the U.S. rate increased by 80 percent.

tion of the maximum statutory term, or use of extended maximum terms for certain offenders (Frase 1993*b*, pp. 356–57, 360–63). Such statutes appear to permit sentences in excess of maximum desert (as measured by guidelines on presumptive durations and departure rules). However, these statutes are narrowly drafted and thus infrequently used. Furthermore, it appears likely that adoption of such statutes in 1989 was the political "price" for not enacting a death penalty or broader increases in sentencing severity (Frase 1993*b*, pp. 359–60). In light of the extreme political pressure to respond to increased rates of violent and drug crime, adherence to von Hirsch's more rigid model of "ordinal" desert might very well have resulted in elevation of the *entire* sentencing scale, thus increasing overall severity (and probably also increasing formal and informal [charge-induced] departure rates, thereby decreasing uniformity and race and class neutrality). Nevertheless, such selective, seemingly undeserved sentence enhancements are very troubling to Morris, who questions whether it is proper to "deal unjustly with a few so that we can persuade the legislature to deal more effectively and fairly with the many" (Morris 1974, p. 65).

Moreover, adoption of these special, sentence-enhancement statutes did not prevent the legislature and the commission, in 1989, from also substantially raising presumptive durations for offenders at severity levels 7–10. For example, the presumptive durations for defendants at these four levels, with zero criminal history, were raised from 24, 43, 105, and 216 months,[24] respectively, to 48, 86, 150, and 306 months. (Curiously, the greatest proportionate increases were for offenders with the lowest criminal history scores.) These increases were primarily motivated by rising crime rates and public fear, rather than any reevaluation of ordinal desert.

If they were not so large, the durational increases described above might be consistent with Morris's theory, since he viewed crime rates and the public's fear of crime as relevant factors in the determination of maximum desert. Even if Morris would reject such substantial increases on desert grounds, he might—despite his concerns about injustice to the "few"—concede that political realities sometimes create hard choices for policy makers, with no clear "right" answer. And he would certainly appreciate Minnesota's continued success, even after 1989, in limiting the use of prison sentences. The overall pattern of

[24] Presumptive sentences at levels 9 and 10 had already been raised once; prior to 1983, the durations at these severity levels (for defendants with zero criminal history) were 97 and 116 months, respectively.

Minnesota sentencing remains closer to Morris's model of custodial "parsimony" and community-based corrections than any other American jurisdiction.

The sentencing guidelines commission has also *lowered* some of its presumptive durations, to avoid prison overcrowding. Thus in 1983, the commission lowered the durations at severity levels 1–3, for offenders with criminal history scores of 2 or greater. Such reductions are quite easy to justify under Morris's flexible theory of desert (especially regarding lower or minimum desert requirements) but are inconsistent with von Hirsch's strict requirements for ordinal spacing of penalties. Under von Hirsch's theory, Minnesota's choices would have been to lower all penalties, build more prisons (if that could be done in time), or do as most states have done: operate overcrowded prisons.

Dispositional Rules. Under the guidelines, presumptive stayed prison terms may be revoked if the defendant violates probation and, very exceptionally, may be executed *ab initio* if the offender is found unamenable to probation. Such probation revocations and "upward" dispositional departures do *not* require a case-specific finding of increased desert. However, these practices are still consistent with a recognition of strict upper desert limits—provided that one views a prison term, equal in length to the presumptive stayed term, as the offender's maximum desert (Frase 1991*a*, pp. 742–47).

Support for the latter view is found in the commission's own work, as well as in guidelines case law. The commission views its guidelines as strongly desert-based, yet it has never required stay revocations and upward dispositional departures to be based on findings of increased desert. This implies that the presumptive durations of prison specified for stay cases are already presumed to be "deserved" but that most offenders are recommended to initially receive less than their full deserts. The apparent reasons for this leniency are to achieve parsimony and to permit judges to consider a variety of nondesert purposes (the guidelines explicitly authorize courts to consider such purposes, in determining the conditions of stayed sentences). The Minnesota Supreme Court implicitly accepted this "already deserved" theory when it held that dispositional departures may be based on defendant "unamenability to probation," with no showing of increased culpability (*State v. Park*, 305 N.W.2d 775 [Minn. 1981]). In contrast, all upward durational departures require a showing of increased culpability and may not be based on "unamenability" (*State v. Jackson*, 329 N.W.2d 66 [Minn. 1983]).

Furthermore, the structure of presumptive sentence durations on the guidelines grid strongly suggests a direct link between stay durations and desert. As shown in the current grid in figure 1, these durations increase smoothly and proportionately across each row within each severity level, with no noticeable "break" at the disposition line. Durations also increase fairly steadily within each column of the grid, and this was even more true in the commission's original, 1980 grid.[25] The largest cell-to-cell jumps in presumptive duration correspond to severity level and criminal history increases, rather than to the location of the disposition line. The supreme court evidently agreed that stay durations measure maximum desert, when it decided that defendants may demand execution of the presumptive stayed term if proposed stay conditions are, in the aggregate, more onerous than such a term would be (*State v. Randolph*, 316 N.W.2d 508 [Minn. 1982]).

As noted in Section III above, von Hirsch has objected to the above theory, arguing that the commission was not trying to "systematically" regulate sentences in stayed prison cases but was merely setting forth a maximum applicable to the worst (i.e., most culpable) cases. But von Hirsch's "worst offenders" theory does not fit the pattern of presumptive durations on the Minnesota guidelines grid. His theory implies that these durational numbers mean very different things on either side of the disposition line—"aggravated culpability" durations above the line and "ordinary culpability" durations below. Yet, the durational numbers generally increase smoothly across and down the grid and show no systematic shifts across the disposition line. If anything, the increases in presumptive durations *accelerate*, rather than pause or slow down, as one crosses the disposition line from the supposed zone of "aggravated" culpability durations to the zone of "ordinary" culpability durations.

Von Hirsch has also objected that the "already deserved" theory above would permit courts routinely to sentence minor offenders to prison (von Hirsch 1994, p. 45). However, this should not occur frequently under Minnesota's theory, nor has it occurred in practice; Minnesota's emphasis on uniformity, combined with the goal of parsimony, yields a very *strong* presumption in favor of the recommended stayed sentence and discourages probation revocation. In practice, upward dispositional departures are very rare (Frase 1993*a*, p. 326), and

[25] In 1980, the presumptive durations in the first three columns at severity level 6 were (and remain today) twenty-one, twenty-six, and thirty months. At level 7 the durations were twenty-four, thirty-two, and forty-one months.

probation revocation rates have also been modest in most years (Frase 1993*d*, p. 10).

2. *Lower Limits on Sanction Severity.* In Minnesota, as under Morris's theory, lower desert limits are often not present and, when present, are much more flexible than the upper limits described above. In presumptive stay cases (over 75 percent of the caseload), the guidelines impose no requirements of minimum sanction severity.[26]

As for presumptive prison-commit cases, the guidelines do prescribe minimum severity limits (i.e., the low end of the range of presumptive prison terms in each grid cell). However, these formal limits are often avoided by means of departures and charging mitigations. The mitigated dispositional departure rate for these cases has varied between 19 and 34 percent (Minnesota Sentencing Guidelines Commission 1995*a*, p. 37). If de facto departures achieved by charging leniency are included, the mitigated dispositional departure rate is over 40 percent (Frase 1993*a*, p. 302, table 1).

Finally, consistent with Morris's views, Minnesota statutes impose relatively few mandatory-minimum prison terms or probation exclusions. Moreover, the two most frequently applicable "mandatory" minimum statutes actually contain provisions allowing for the grant of probation under certain circumstances (Minn. Stat. Annot. § 609.11, subd. 8 [certain offenses committed with a firearm or other dangerous weapon]; Minn. Stat. Annot. § 609.342, subd. 2 [sex-offense recidivists]). In practice, probation is very frequently granted in these two groups of cases, especially for defendants whose cases fall above the disposition line (Frase 1993*a*, p. 309).

3. *Width of Ranges, between Maximum and Minimum Desert.* Morris would probably view the allowable ranges in Minnesota's guidelines cells as either too narrow or too broad. For presumptive commit defendants, the range of presumptive prison terms is very narrow, especially in the upper right corner of the grid (e.g., eighteen to twenty months). It would be quite difficult to apply much "fine-tuning" within such a narrow range. However, in practice, this may not be a serious problem given the frequently used power to mitigate sentence durations via departures and charge reductions.

In the case of presumptive stay defendants, the "desert range" (from zero to twelve to zero to thirty months, depending on the cell) may be

[26] There are, however, a few statutory provisions imposing minimum jail terms; see, e.g., Minn. Stat. Annot. § 609.583 (presumptive sentence for first-offense residential burglary is a ninety-day jail term, restitution, or community service).

broader than Morris would prefer. For example, he suggests that a range of probation (zero custody) to six months would be appropriate for second-offense purse-snatchers (Morris 1982, pp. 194–95). However, to say that a range is appropriate does not necessarily mean that a broader range would be inappropriate, and Morris has always given greater emphasis to upper (maximum) severity limits than to lower limits or the goal of equality per se. Thus his principal objection here would probably not be that the range is too broad but rather that there are no guidelines at all for the selection of intermediate punishments within that range.

4. *Case-Specific Desert.* Morris and Minnesota agree that case-specific desert considerations are part of the "fine-tuning" of the sentence, within the normally applicable limits of maximum and minimum desert. Morris primarily addressed mitigation based on mental illness (Morris 1982, pp. 168–69), but in doing so he appeared willing to accept other desert-based, case-specific reasons for adjusting the severity of the penalty.

5. *The Meaning of "Modified" Desert in Minnesota.* The Minnesota commission stated that its original guidelines were based on a theory of "modified just deserts" (Minnesota Sentencing Guidelines Commission 1980, p. 9). Von Hirsch also discusses this concept, but his usage differs from the meaning of "modified" deserts in Minnesota—especially as the guidelines have evolved over time. Morris does not mention this term, but his more flexible conception of desert permits a wide variety of sentencing practices to be viewed as falling within the range of "deserved" punishment for the offense of conviction. Minnesota's version of "modified" desert appears to be much closer to Morris's "range" theory than to von Hirsch's conception.

In von Hirsch's view, "modified" desert means a "desert-based hybrid" which permits restricted *departures* from desert, in order to achieve nondesert sentencing purposes. Such departures are said to be of two types: "substantial" departures, limited to "extraordinary situations; or more "routine" departures, "with fairly narrow limits on their permissible extent" (von Hirsch 1994, p. 48, n. 3; see also von Hirsch 1993, chap. 6). Minnesota's recent "dangerous offender" legislation, appears to fall within von Hirsch's first category.

However, Minnesota also permits at least two types of "routine" departure from von Hirsch's conception of strict, ordinal desert. These would have to fit within von Hirsch's second category, but neither appears to respect his requirement of "fairly narrow limits" on the extent to departure. The very broad range of sanction severity in presumptive stay cases, accompanied by explicit acceptance of nondesert goals, would seem to permit routine and *major* departures from strict ordinal desert. Alternatively (and more plausibly, given the Minnesota commission's strong emphasis on desert), the treatment of presumptive stay cases suggests a more flexible, Morris-style "range" conception of the meaning of "desert" itself.

Similarly, the strong effect of prior record on presumptive dispositions and durations in Minnesota not only exceeds the role that von Hirsch would allow this factor to play in a purely desert-based system (von Hirsch 1985, pp. 77–91; von Hirsch 1994, pp. 39–40), it may also exceed the "narrow limits" of his second category of "modified" desert, described above.[27] Again: did the Minnesota commission really intend to authorize routine and *major* "departures" from desert? Or did it simply have a more flexible conception of "desert" than von Hirsch would accept?

The Minnesota Supreme Court apparently does not view the strong role of prior record as a "departure" from desert. The steep upward "slope" of the disposition line, for offenders with three or more criminal history points, involves no "departure" from desert because the court views all disposition decisions as primarily raising issues, not of what is deserved, but rather of the form of punishment (and whether the defendant should receive his full deserts); under the court's amenability case law, duration decisions are the measure of what is deserved.

The supreme court does not seem to view the long presumptive durations assigned to offenders with high criminal history scores as exceeding "deserved" punishment. The court has repeatedly stated that durational departures must be justified by atypical, case-specific culpability. But if the presumptive durations for high-criminal-history offenders were viewed by the court as exceeding desert—presumably for utilitarian reasons—then the court should have been willing to permit such nondesert reasons to be used to depart up or down from the presumptive duration. This would be especially appropriate in the case of *mitigating* durational departures; if the presumptive sentence were seen

[27] However, Minnesota did adopt von Hirsch's view that the criminal history scale, and its effect on the presumptive sentence, should be "closed-ended": at some point (in Minnesota: when the defendant has six or more criminal history points), the defendant has reached the full "deserts" applicable to the offense of conviction and cannot receive any further enhancement for additional prior convictions (von Hirsch 1981*a*, pp. 618–20).

as exceeding desert, for utilitarian reasons, then such reasons should quite readily permit downward departure (bringing the sentence back to "pure" desert, or closer to it).

Thus except for the "dangerous offender" statutes, "modified just deserts" in Minnesota does not seem to mean "departure" from desert but rather a broader conception of what "desert" means. Like Morris's theory, Minnesota's broader conception of desert permits a wide range of deserved penalties, and a strong role for criminal history.

B. Other Guiding Factors (Fine-Tuning) within Desert Limits

This subsection, which examines Minnesota's approach to incorporation of various punishment rationales in sentencing policy, generally follows the examination of Morris's views on these subjects set out in Section I*C* above.

1. *Rehabilitation.* Minnesota, like Morris, agrees that rehabilitation should primarily be pursued *out* of prison. Thus the defendant's need for treatment in prison is not a sufficient reason to impose a prison term (i.e., it is not a basis for an upward dispositional departure), and prison release does not depend on an assessment of the inmate's progress in treatment. Under the original guidelines, prison programs were entirely voluntary, as Morris argued they should be, and good-time credits could not be denied for refusal to participate in treatment programs. Starting in 1993, the Minnesota legislature permitted the commissioner of corrections to define "disciplinary" rules to include not only violation of general "institution rules" but also refusals to work and "refusal to participate in treatment or other rehabilitative programs" (Minn. Stat. Annot. § 244.05, subd. 1b[b]). Thus to a limited extent, the inmate's willingness to participate in treatment programs can now affect the length of his or her prison term. It should be recalled, however, that Morris would allow inmates to be forced to participate in prison programs long enough to "know what it is about" (Morris 1974, pp. 18–19). In practice, this may be all that Minnesota requires. It is not clear how often Minnesota inmates are "ordered" into prison treatment or education programs (as opposed to being ordered to do *something*, including the option of accepting various institutional work assignments), nor is it known whether unamenable offenders expelled from prison programs continue to forfeit good-time credits.

Both Morris and Minnesota also permit rehabilitative assessments to determine conditions of stayed sentences and of postprison supervised release.

"But"—Morris might be critical of the rehabilitation-related concepts of "amenability" and "unamenability" to probation, which Minnesota cases recognize as a basis for aggravated and mitigated dispositional departures. Morris generally opposes all individualized assessments of treatment needs and receptivity, progress toward cure, and dangerousness.

However, in discussing unamenable-to-probation departures (imposition of prison, instead of the presumptive stayed term), Morris did suggest that upward departures might be appropriate in "a few such cases" (Morris 1982, p. 176). Morris was specifically addressing departures based on mental illness, but he might be willing to consider other offender characteristics which require enhanced severity (within desert limits). As noted previously, unamenability departures are entered in less than one percent of presumptive stay cases; thus at least in terms of frequency, Minnesota practice is consistent with Morris's theory. Morris has also argued that greater severity is appropriate when "other less restrictive sanctions have been frequently or recently applied to this offender" (Morris 1974, pp. 60, 79–80). Many "unamenable-to-probation" departures (including the leading *Park* case) are based on prior failures to complete probation.

Morris did not specifically discuss mitigating "amenability" departures (i.e., granting of probation, instead of the presumptive prison term), but he did address two factors which sometimes underlie a finding of amenability to probation: the offender's support of his wife and children and his employment at the time of sentencing. At one point, Morris seems to completely rule out consideration of either factor (Morris 1982, p. 186); at another point, he admits that as a judge he would grant mitigation based on family support, but would not say why (Morris 1982, p. 196). As for employment at sentencing, Morris later appeared to agree that this factor sometimes permits a different form of punishment, and perhaps also somewhat lower severity: "To insist on equal suffering for Criminal B [the more fortunate, employed defendant] because of the adverse social conditions of Criminal A is to purchase an illusory equality at too high a price. It is a levelling down and benefits neither Criminal A nor the community. The criminal law cannot rectify social inequalities; those inequalities will inexorably infect rational punishment policies. But this hypothetical situation leaves an uneasy sense of moral imbalance and forces us to the consideration of how deserved punishments can operate fairly in a world of social inequality" (Morris and Tonry 1990, pp. 102–3). It should also be noted that amenability mitigations are consistent with Morris's more flexible approach to minimum sanction severity and help to achieve several of his goals: preservation of the offender's social and community ties, parsimony, and "mercy."

Like Morris, Minnesotans are conflicted and ambivalent about allowing social and economic factors to influence sentencing. The guidelines formally rule out any consideration of family or employment status, but these factors find considerable acceptance in practice and are indirectly sanctioned by the amenable-to-probation case law.

Finally, as to both types of amenability departure, Morris would certainly be sympathetic to the practical realities of implementing sentencing reforms: Minnesota trial judges, attorneys, and probation officers believe strongly in the appropriateness of amenability departures. Morris is a realist. Thus he might very well conclude that, in a heavily treatment-oriented state like Minnesota, it is wiser to permit (and then seek to regulate) amenability departures, rather than attempt to prohibit them; total prohibition in this context, as in many others, only invites subterfuge and evasion (Morris and Hawkins 1977, p. 21; Morris 1982, p. 158; Morris 1992, p. 139).

2. *Incapacitation.* Minnesota and Morris both sharply limit the extent to which individualized predictions of offender "dangerousness" may affect sentencing severity. Morris would never allow sentences to be increased on this basis above maximum desert and would very rarely permit enhancement within the desert range; however, he would permit some "anamnestic" predictions of risk (based on the offender's past behavior) to affect conditions of probation or parole.

Similarly, Minnesota permits dangerousness considerations to affect probation conditions, as well as the selection of the precise prison duration within the range of presumptive executed prison terms. The Minnesota guidelines prohibit aggravated durational departures based on offender dangerousness. However, recent "dangerous offender" statutes appear to permit enhancement of duration without regard to guidelines measures of desert, for certain narrowly defined groups of offenders.

Although upward dispositional departures cannot be based solely on a finding of offender dangerousness, such departures (as well as probation revocations) are sometimes based on a finding of "unamenability" to probation. Such a finding, in turn, is often supported in part by concerns that the offender is too dangerous to remain on probation. Morris would only support such enhancements if the prison term imposed does not exceed the upper limits of desert and if dangerousness assessments are limited to rare cases. These conditions appear to be met, in Minnesota; "unamenability" departures are very rare and do not appear to exceed the maximum deserts of presumptive stay defendants (as measured by the duration of the prison term for that grid cell).

3. *Failure of Prior, Lesser Penalties; Categoric Recidivist Enhancements.* Morris supports increased punishment (within desert limits) when "other less restrictive sanctions have been frequently or recently applied to this offender" (Morris 1974, pp. 60, 79–80). He also accepts enhanced punishment for recidivists as a group, seeing such enhancement as justified on both incapacitative and desert grounds (Morris 1982, pp. 162–63).

Minnesota occasionally permits aggravated dispositional departure based on defendant "unamenability" (which, in turn, is often based on prior failures to successfully complete probation). Minnesota also strongly links punishment severity to criminal history.

4. *General Deterrence.* Morris would permit enhancement for deterrent purposes (exemplary punishment) within the range of deserved penalties. Minnesota permits consideration of special needs for deterrence, within the range of presumptive executed prison terms, and in deciding on conditions of probation. Consistent with Morris's views, special needs for deterrence are not a proper basis for aggravated durational departure; such departures must be desert-based.

5. *Equality (Uniformity).* Minnesota and Morris agree that equality is an important goal but appear—at least on first inspection—to differ as to just how important it is. Morris states that equality is only a "guiding" principle, which will often be "trumped" by other considerations—especially "parsimony." The Minnesota Guidelines Commission identified uniformity as a major goal (Minnesota Sentencing Guidelines Commission 1984, pp. v, 33–53).

However, the Minnesota commission also recognized the goal of case-level parsimony which, because it allows sentences to depend on case-specific utilitarian needs, is often in conflict with equality (Tonry 1994, p. 62). Moreover, the commission has provided very little guidance as to the specific type or severity of nonimprisonment sanctions and has not tried to regulate prosecutorial charging and plea bargaining, which permit considerable "adjustment" of the commission's seemingly strict prison commitment and duration presumptions. Minnesota case law has added additional flexibility to the commission's rules. Thus in practice, Minnesota's system seems to be much closer to Morris's theory than to von Hirsch's in terms of the importance of equality.

6. *Parsimony and Community-Based Sentencing.* Both Morris and Minnesota accept the principle of parsimony: a preference for the least restrictive alternative consistent with the purposes of the particular sentence. Morris and Minnesota both prefer nonprison sanctions and strongly support community-based sentencing. As noted in Section III above, nonprison sentences constitute about 80 percent of felony sentences in Minnesota. Furthermore, mitigating departures far outnumber aggravated departures, under the guidelines, and the difference is even greater when de facto mitigating departures (achieved by charging discretion) are included (Frase 1993*a*, pp. 299–303, 317–18).

"But"—Morris's concept of parsimony appears to apply to *all* issues of sentencing, including conditions of probation, whereas the Minnesota commission's statement of this principle only seems to apply to the use of custodial sentences (Minnesota Sentencing Guidelines Commission 1995*b*, § I[3]). Also, Morris implies a general preference in favor of sentencing toward the low end of the "desert" range, and he may further assume that judges will use the bottom of that range as a starting point. In Minnesota, the "starting point" for sentencing of cases falling below the disposition line is the *midpoint* of the range of presumptive prison terms; for cases falling above the disposition line, no specific guidance or starting point is provided.

However, in practice Minnesota judges prefer to use the lower half of the available range of custodial terms. Thus in over three-quarters of the grid cells below the disposition line, the average length of prison terms imposed is less than the presumptive midpoint for that cell (Minnesota Sentencing Guidelines Commission 1995*a*, pp. 31, 51). As for cases above the disposition line, prison terms are rarely imposed, and the duration of jail terms imposed is modest (Minnesota Sentencing Guidelines Commission 1995*a*, pp. 21, 32): in only two of these twenty-six cells is the average duration greater than half of the maximum (twelve-month) jail term allowed (and average jail durations are far lower than the presumptive stayed prison term, in all grid cells). All of these judicial preferences for "low end" sentencing would appear even stronger if custody durations were analyzed relative to the higher-severity grid cells in which many of these defendants would have been convicted had they not received charging leniency (Frase 1993*a*, pp. 301–3, 317–18).

"But"— Morris would still probably say that Minnesota relies too heavily on jail terms and should instead use fines and other intermediate sanctions (Morris and Hawkins 1970, pp. 142–43; Morris and Tonry 1990, p. 79). About two-thirds of convicted felons in Minnesota now receive a local jail sentence. Moreover, the frequency of such sentences has grown considerably since guidelines sentencing began—in 1978, only 35 percent of felons received a jail sentence (Minnesota Sentencing Guidelines Commission 1995*a*, p. 21). As discussed more fully below, Morris would also lament the lack of any limits or guidelines for the use of jail terms.

Morris would probably appreciate that Minnesota uses jail terms in many cases where other states impose prison (Frase 1993*a*, p. 332, n. 120); thus he might agree that, if a custody term is deemed necessary, it is better that it be shorter and served closer to the defendant's home community. It should also be recalled that, even when jail inmates are counted, Minnesota's arrest-based custodial sentencing rate (inmates per weighted adult arrest) remained constant throughout the 1980s (while the rate for the nation as a whole increased by 80 percent); Minnesota's jail population, as well as its prison population, increased only as much as would be expected, given increased arrests and felony caseloads. It thus appears that the increase in felony jail sentencing was balanced by decreased use of jails for pretrial detention and misdemeanor sentencing. Such a substitution effect is a very defensible allocation of limited resources.

7. *Rewarding Guilty Pleas and Other Forms of Cooperation.* Minnesota and Morris both permit good-time credits, in recognition of the need to maintain order in prison, once parole release discretion has been eliminated.

The Minnesota Guidelines Commission, like Morris, was concerned about disparity resulting from plea bargaining. The guidelines specify that "the exercise of constitutional rights by the defendant during the adjudication process" may not be a basis for departure (Minnesota Sentencing Guidelines Commission 1995*b*, § II.D.1.e). However, this carefully worded language does not prohibit the granting of leniency to defendants who *waive*, rather than "exercise," their rights. In practice, the defendant's plea remains a major factor in the granting of formal mitigating departures and is undoubtedly at least as strong a factor in charge reductions which produce de facto mitigating departures; plea bargaining is "alive and well" in Minnesota (Frase 1993*a*, pp. 310, 316–19).

Morris advocated stricter "regulation" of guilty-plea-based sentences, by means of judicially supervised "settlement" conferences. However, he appeared to assume that some degree of sentence mitigation would continue to be available in such conferences. He would also support the commission's implicit judgment that plea-rewarding mitigations are not as bad as trial-punishing aggravations (in part because, under both the Minnesota and Morris approaches, minimum-severity limits are more flexible), and he would appreciate that plea-bargained mitigations are one of the most common vehicles for achieving parsimony and "mercy" in sentencing.

The pervasive need to reward guilty pleas and other forms of defendant cooperation has important theoretical implications, in the Morris–von Hirsch debate. All modern adjudication and sentencing schemes depend to a great extent on the cooperation of defendants. Before and at trial, defendants must be promised leniency to induce and reward guilty pleas, jury trial waivers, testimony against other defendants, and so forth. At sentencing, the court must initially "underpunish" (give defendants *less* than they deserve)—not only to reward the defendant's cooperation up to that point but also to induce further cooperation (in holding employment, family support, restitution, treatment, supervision, etc.) and leave room for subsequent tightening of sanctions (e.g., by revocation of probation or loss of good-time credits) if the defendant fails to cooperate.

Although some forms of cooperation might be seen as reducing the defendant's "deserts" (at least under a broad definition of that term), many forms do not; society often needs, and must reward, cooperation whether or not mitigation is deserved. Thus in practice, modern systems of law enforcement and punishment always function according to a "limiting" retributive model—most defendants *do* cooperate, at least to some extent, and thus receive less than their full "just deserts." In the real world of sentencing, a system of strict "defining" desert is unworkable. Moreover, any attempt to impose such a strict system is very likely to result in the imposition of excessive and undeserved severity—on defendants who refuse to cooperate. The position of Morris and other limiting retributivists is clear: punishment in excess of desert is unacceptable; excessive leniency is a less serious moral and political problem. The approach is both practical and principled; it is deliberately "biased" in favor of defendants, for reasons similar to those underlying the requirement of proof beyond a reasonable doubt.

C. *Other Important Sentencing Issues*

At least in stayed prison cases (over three-quarters of presumptive terms, and about 80 percent of actual sentences), Minnesota follows Morris's proposal that the judge should first decide the sentencing purpose or purposes to be served and should then select a package of intermediate sanctions designed to parsimoniously achieve those purposes.

In presumptive prison cases Minnesota judges have much less choice, at least formally. The judge must ordinarily sentence within a very narrow range of prison terms and may consider only whether exceptional factors of desert justify an aggravated or mitigated durational departure; or whether the defendant's "amenability to probation" (or, rarely, exceptionally mitigated culpability) justifies a mitigated dispositional departure. However, Morris did agree that presumptive prison, with few case-level options, is appropriate for the most serious cases. He would draw the line at cases presumptively punished with at least twenty-four months of actual incarceration (i.e., after subtraction of good-time credits). In Minnesota, most of the presumptive prison cases falling below the disposition line have presumptive minimum prison terms (after deduction of maximum good-time credit) at least this long: thirty-five of the forty-four grid cells below the line have presumptive minimum durations of at least twenty-four months.[28]

1. *Nature and Scope of Guidelines.* Morris felt that additional guidance could be provided to trial courts by the use of multiple presumptions or "bands" on the sentencing grid; for example, he expressed approval of a four-band grid: never prison; presume no prison, absent departure; permit either prison or community-based sanctions; and always prison (Morris and Tonry 1990, pp. 60, 77).

Minnesota's grid only has two formal "bands": presume no prison and presume prison. However, in practice, four bands are clearly discernible, year after year. In the upper left corner of the grid, there are

[28] Minimum prison terms for presumptive commit cases falling *above* the disposition line (mainly weapons and recidivist sex offenders) are shorter. However, departure rates are extremely high in these cases (Frase 1993*a*, p. 309), so judges in practice exercise broad discretion in the selection of sentencing purposes and alternatives.

several cells in which prison is almost completely absent; in the bottom two rows (murder cases), prison is almost always imposed; in the center of the grid, on either side of the disposition line, are two bands of cells with very high departure rates (aggravated departures, in cells just above the line; mitigated departures, just below) (Frase 1993*a*, p. 323 [1989 data]; Minnesota Sentencing Guidelines Commission 1995*a*, p. 21 [1993 data]).

"But"—there remains one very important departure from Morris's theory: Minnesota has declined to enact any guidelines, or even any "equivalency" or "exchange" rates, for nonprison sanctions. The Minnesota commission has considered the possibility of such guidelines on several occasions but has declined to adopt them—primarily because of massive resistance of attorneys, judges, and probation officers, but also due to a lack of commission consensus on specific stay guidelines. Experience under the guidelines has clearly shown that, where field resistance is high and consensus is lacking, guidelines rules have been widely evaded (Frase 1993*a*, p. 337). Morris thus would appreciate the commission's dilemma and might hesitate to impose highly unpopular rules.

However, Morris would still probably insist that *some* form of guidance is feasible and desirable here. He would be particularly interested in guidelines that limit the *maximum* aggregate severity of stay conditions (using a point system and equivalency scales), and he might also want to set upper limits on jail sentences, in each guidelines cell. As I have argued elsewhere at greater length (Frase 1993*c*, pp. 19–23), stay guidelines would prevent unjustly severe sentences, would encourage substitution of noncustodial sanctions, and would give courts more concrete guidance in assessing the overall "onerousness" of stay conditions, for purposes of deciding when defendants may demand execution of the stayed prison term (*State v. Randolph*, 316 N.W.2d 508 [Minn. 1982]).

At the same time, I have argued that there are some very serious hurdles to overcome in enacting stay condition guidelines—especially those that impose *minimum* sanction severity. Such guidelines might prove undesirable for one or more of the following reasons (most of which Morris would probably accept):

a. Stay limitations would make the guidelines much more complex, whereas a major goal of the Minnesota commission has always been simplicity of application (Frase 1993*a*, pp. 281–82). Simplicity serves to promote broader understanding and acceptance of the rules and to reduce errors of application. Indeed, the unpopularity of the federal sentencing guidelines may be due, at least in part, to their complexity. Morris has recognized that, in general, "simpler is better" (Morris and Tonry 1990, p. 78); at some point, the cost of further complexity outweighs any added benefits.

b. What are the benefits here? Given the upper limits already imposed by the *Randolph* case, the frequency and degree of disparity in the imposition of stay conditions may not be very great and may seem less troubling than disparity in the imposition and duration of prison terms. Morris himself has argued that equality is only one consideration and may be outweighed by other factors. Minnesotans appear to agree and have been content with the current system for over fifteen years. Like Morris, and unlike von Hirsch, Minnesotans do not seem to feel that occasional, or even frequent, imposition of more severe stay conditions on less culpable offenders is "too unfair." If desert and equality goals do not require closer regulation in this context, then trial courts should retain discretion to tailor stay conditions to the particular purposes at sentencing and should remain free to mitigate punishment for reasons of parsimony—to avoid imposing greater severity when it would not serve any practical purpose.

c. Minimum requirements for stay condition severity are designed to increase the onerousness of stay conditions. But stricter or more numerous stay conditions inevitably mean an increase in the frequency of probation violations and thus at least some increase in prison commitment rates (Tonry 1994, p. 61). Minimum stay condition requirements also tend to reduce the court's reserved sentencing power, on revocation of the stay. If (as seems only fair) defendants are credited with the equivalent, in prison days, of the stay conditions already completed (von Hirsch, Wasik, and Greene 1989, p. 610)—just as they are now credited with any days spent in local jail—then more onerous stay conditions mean that there is less deserved punishment "left over" to use as a sanction for violation of such conditions. Conversely, less severe stay conditions reduce the risk of noncompliance and increase the incentive to fulfill all conditions (because the defendant faces swift execution of most of the stayed prison term).

d. Minimum stay conditions—especially jail terms—risk overloading the available corrections resources in many counties, especially those which are locally funded. Moreover, periodic overload is a greater risk at the local than at the state level; given the smaller scale of local operations, criminal caseloads and available capacities are probably subject to wider day-to-day fluctuations than occur in larger, statewide systems.

e. Flexibility in the imposition of stay conditions permits a desirable degree of "local control," so that sentencing policy and the use of local resources may reflect important variations in local values and traditions.

f. Experiments with stay guidelines in other states suggest some difficulty in achieving consensus as to specific equivalency or exchange rates for widely differing sanction types.

g. Stay guidelines—especially minimum severity requirements—would be very difficult to enforce consistently. Prosecutors are already very unlikely to appeal leniency in the application of the existing prison guidelines (Frase 1991*a*, pp. 752–73; Frase 1993*a*, pp. 316–19). Prosecutors would be even less likely to appeal departures from stay guidelines, given the lesser degree of severity and disparity involved. Defendant appeals (of sentences exceeding stay condition maxima) are more likely, but extremely onerous stay conditions are already substantially limited by the *Randolph* rule.

h. If lower limits on stay condition severity are unenforceable, and perhaps undesirable, could upper limits alone be adopted? Or would such a proposal fail to gain sufficient bipartisan support within the commission, and elsewhere, thus forcing the adoption of minimum severity limits?

In sum, it will be quite difficult to implement and enforce any comprehensive system regulating conditions of stayed sentences, especially a system imposing minimum requirements of sanction severity. Morris would probably agree with many of the reasons why Minnesota has thus far declined to adopt any such system. Nevertheless, he might still argue for a more limited version of stay guidelines.

2. *Sentencing Appeals.* To maximize guidance to trial judges in sentencing, Morris and Minnesota both support the development of a substantial body of appellate case law—a "common law of sentencing." Minnesota case law extensively defines the desert and nondesert factors which may appropriately be considered as a basis for departure, although it has done little to address fine-tuning within the range permitted by presumptive disposition and duration rules. In the case of presumptive commit cases, this may be because the ranges are already quite narrow. The ranges are much broader in presumptive stay cases; the problems of providing detailed guidance for these cases are discussed above.

To make appellate review of sentences more effective, Morris proposed that the trial court should state reasons for its sentence, if an appeal is filed. Minnesota requires the trial court to state reasons whenever the sentence is a departure from the guidelines (which, as a practical matter, is the only time a sentence is likely to be appealed, given the Minnesota Supreme Court's reluctance to reverse nondeparture sentences; *State v. Kindem*, 313 N.W.2d 6 [Minn. 1981]).

3. *Parole and Prison Population Control.* Given Minnesota's and Morris's rejection of the "rehabilitative ideal" of coerced, in-prison treatment, and their further rejection of most forms of selective incapacitation via imprisonment, it was natural that both would eventually favor abolition of discretionary parole release. Both also recognized the need for additional mechanisms to control prison population size, if parole is abolished.

"But"—Minnesota approached the problem of prison population control in a manner different than Morris anticipated. Morris had initially proposed to retain parole, as a prison population "safety valve" (but with parole guidelines and the setting of target release dates soon after the offender's arrival in prison). Like almost all other early proponents of sentencing reform, Morris did not foresee the use of sentencing guidelines as a means of "front-end" resource management, via sophisticated computer-based projections of the prison population impact of proposed guidelines. Minnesota pioneered this approach, and it has been a central feature of state guidelines systems since the mid-1980s (Frase 1995*b*, pp. 173–74, 175–76). However, Morris did foresee and appreciate the value of having prison commitment and duration decisions made by a body insulated from direct electoral political pressures.

V. Conclusion

Although the Minnesota guidelines give greater emphasis to retributive values than did the previous, indeterminate sentencing regime, Minnesota guidelines sentencing is, and has always been, much closer to Morris's "limiting retributive" approach than to the more "defining" desert theory advocated by von Hirsch. Retributive values set firm upper limits on sanction severity in Minnesota but rather weak lower limits (or none at all). Judges and attorneys retain substantial discretion to consider utilitarian sentencing goals and to vary the form and severity of the sentence. Uniformity and proportionality of sentencing have increased under the guidelines. But Minnesotans appear to agree with

Morris that these are only two of the many important goals of, and at, sentencing. All in all, Minnesota's hybrid sentencing system has achieved an appropriate and stable compromise, balancing the values of uniformity versus case-level flexibility, retributive versus utilitarian goals, and public protection versus parsimony and fiscal limitations (Frase 1993*c*, pp. 13–33). Such balance is the essence of Morris's approach.

How was it that Minnesota policy makers came to adopt so much of Morris's theory without, as far as this writer can tell, ever specifically citing his writings? It is possible that Morris's theory indirectly affected policy developments in Minnesota through his strong influence on the thinking of other scholars and reformers in the late 1970s—especially the drafters of the second edition of the American Bar Association Standards on Sentencing (American Bar Association 1979; von Hirsch 1981*b*, pp. 783–84). Of course, the currents of influence have also flowed in the other direction: Morris continued to develop his theory *after* the Minnesota guidelines were implemented. Although his later writings clearly built on themes which he had begun to develop many years before, they were also strongly influenced by the new concepts and procedures being pioneered in Minnesota (and later, in many other states, and in the federal courts).

In seeking to understand the remarkable correspondence between Morris's theory and the theory that has evolved in Minnesota, it is important to recognize that Minnesota's current sentencing system is not the product of any single person, group, or agency. Rather, the Minnesota approach was the combined result of decisions made, over a period of several years, by the legislature, the guidelines commission, the supreme court, trial courts, prosecuting and defense attorneys, correctional officers, and perhaps even victims and defendants. These key actors not only did not consult Morris, they generally did not consult each other in any systematic way. Yet they settled on a theory of punishment which is coherent, balanced, and workable. Perhaps the best explanation, then, for the many similarities between Minnesota's and Morris's theory is to be found in Morris's empirically based, consensus-seeking, "from-the-ground-up" approach. Morris has always sought guidance in the actual practices of system actors and has tried to craft an approach which will gain broad acceptance (Morris and Tonry 1990, pp. 87–88, 108). (If only the drafters of the much-criticized federal guidelines had followed this approach.) Morris's theory became reality in Minnesota because Morris was articulating fundamental and widely held values that will, and must, be accommodated in any progressive sentencing reform which is likely to be adopted and to survive. Whether such a sentencing theory could be adopted and survive in a less politically progressive state, or in a more punitive age, is another matter.

What will the future hold, in Minnesota? Will Morris's humane and efficient model continue to survive? No American state—Minnesota included—is immune from periods of "crime wave" hysteria, "law and order" political posturing, and strong public pressure to increase criminal penalties. In the late 1980s, Minnesota began to experience alarming increases in rates of violent crime—despite the fact that violent crime penalties were already quite severe. Drug crime rates also increased, as the epidemic of crack cocaine, the "War on Drugs," and the problems of deteriorating inner cities finally "arrived" in Minnesota. In 1986, the Minnesota legislature began a steady increase in the severity of drug penalties (Minnesota Sentencing Guidelines Commission 1992, pp. 3–5); further major increases in sentencing severity for violent crimes were enacted by the sentencing guidelines commission in 1989 and by the legislature in 1989 and 1992 (Frase 1993*b*, pp. 359–63).

Von Hirsch has suggested that these increases in severity could be the result of Minnesota's more flexible, Morris-style "limiting retributive" model—or, at least, that such a model provides a weaker basis for criticism than von Hirsch's more restrictive concept of desert (von Hirsch 1994, pp. 39–45). It is certainly true that von Hirsch's strict requirements of ordinal desert, if accepted in Minnesota, would have made it more difficult to selectively increase penalties for drug and violent crimes. Readers will have to decide for themselves whether von Hirsch's one-dimensional theory could ever have been implemented in Minnesota, and even if it could have, whether such a theory would have better helped Minnesota to resist very strong political pressures to increase penalties. The danger under von Hirsch's theory is that such pressures will lead to an escalation of the *entire* penalty scale, resulting in unwanted (and very expensive) increased severity for lesser offenders or massive increases in departure rates and disparity for such offenders.

It should also be kept in mind that, notwithstanding recent increases in sentencing severity and inmate populations, Minnesota sentencing remains—by any American standard of comparison—a model of the "parsimonious" use of custodial sanctions. Von Hirsch would only permit parsimony to be considered by the legislature and the sentencing commission, and only in the determination of "cardinal" sentencing policy issues. But parsimony is too important a concept to be so limited in its application. It encourages moderation in sentencing and serves as an essential counterweight to the strong, ever-present political pressure to escalate penalties beyond what is necessary (and often, beyond what the public is actually willing to fund). For this reason, Minnesota and Morris recognize the value of parsimony in *all* sentencing policy and application decisions.

It must be recognized, however, that much of Minnesota's success in holding the line in sentencing severity during the 1980s was due to another factor: the high priority which the Minnesota sentencing guidelines commission placed on avoiding prison overcrowding. Minnesota's "capacity constraint" (the goal of never exceeding 95 percent of current or planned capacity) was a very wise strategy, reflecting two fundamental truths about American sentencing in the late twentieth century. First, expansion of prison capacity is a slow process, and legislators often fail to provide sufficient funds in time to avoid significant overcrowding; the best way to avoid such overcrowding is to adopt the conservative assumption that *no* further prison expansion will be provided. Second, all American jurisdictions (state *and* federal) already have substantial capacity to incarcerate; by any rational standard (and certainly, by any international standard; Frase 1995*c*, p. 275; Frase and Weigend 1995, pp. 346–48), American jurisdictions are already making excessive use of custodial sanctions. The question is, thus, not whether more capacity is needed but rather whether better use could be made of the existing capacity. The assumption of no further growth in capacity encourages the sentencing commission and other policy makers to explore alternatives to incarceration that may be just as effective and are almost always cheaper and more humane (Morris and Tonry 1990). Such an assumption, coupled with sophisticated, computer-generated inmate population projections, also forces advocates of greater severity, both within the commission and outside it, to take responsibility for the fiscal impact of their proposals, in terms of increased taxes or reduced penalties for other offenders (Parent 1988, pp. 43–44).

Thus it may very well be that Morris's principle of parsimony would not have been effective in Minnesota, if it had not been combined with "capacity-based" sentencing policy. But at the same time, capacity-based sentencing policy may not work without case-level parsimony.

Prison population projections are still an inexact science, and the Minnesota commission has often seriously underestimated the impact of rising caseloads, changing prosecutorial charging practices, legislative changes, and other factors which increase prison populations (Minnesota Sentencing Guidelines Commission 1984, pp. 90–91). Fortunately, the commission also underestimated various mitigating factors (especially rates of downward dispositional departure and charge reductions; Frase 1991*a*, p. 735). If the guidelines had not included so many possibilities for case-level mitigation, it is very likely that sentencing severity, inmate populations, and prison overcrowding would have increased substantially.

Minnesota's pioneering sentencing reform has now been emulated in almost twenty states and has also recently been endorsed by the American Bar Association (American Bar Association 1993; Frase 1995*a*, pp. 169, 197; Frase 1995*b*, p. 174). Increasingly, states are turning to guidelines as a means of gaining better predictions of, and control over, rapidly escalating prison populations and correctional costs (Frase 1995*b*, p. 175). But reformers should not lose sight of the original goal of sentencing guidelines: to promote more rational and fair sentencing. They should look to Minnesota not only for guidance in controlling prison populations but also for an example of a balanced, humane, and effective sentencing system. And they should look to Morris's writings for an original and often eloquent statement of the key features of, and rationale behind, the Minnesota "model."

REFERENCES

Allen, Francis A. 1964. *The Borderland of Criminal Justice: Essays in Law and Criminology*. Chicago: University of Chicago Press.

———. 1981. *The Decline of the Rehabilitative Ideal: Penal Policy and Social Purpose*. New Haven, Conn.: Yale University Press.

American Bar Association. 1968. *Standards Relating to the Administration of Criminal Justice: Sentencing Alternatives and Procedures*. Chicago: American Bar Association.

———. 1979. *Standards Relating to the Administration of Criminal Justice: Sentencing Alternatives and Procedures*. 2d ed. Washington, D.C.: American Bar Association.

———. 1993. *ABA Standards for Criminal Justice: Sentencing*. 3d ed. Washington, D.C.: American Bar Association.

American Law Institute. 1962. *Model Penal Code, Proposed Official Draft.* Philadelphia: American Law Institute.

Ashworth, Andrew J. 1992. *Sentencing and Criminal Justice.* London: Weidenfeld & Nicolson.

Bottoms, Anthony. 1995. "The Philosophy and Politics of Punishment and Sentencing." In *The Politics of Sentencing Reform,* edited by Rod Morgan and Chris Clarkson. Oxford: Oxford University Press.

Bureau of Justice Statistics. 1995. *Prisoners in 1994.* Washington, D.C.: U.S. Department of Justice, Bureau of Justice Statistics.

Cragg, Wesley. 1992. *The Practice of Punishment: Towards a Theory of Restorative Justice.* London: Routledge.

Dailey, Debra L. 1993. "Prison and Race in Minnesota." *University of Colorado Law Review* 64:761–80.

Federal Bureau of Investigation. 1981. *Crime in the United States: Uniform Crime Reports, 1980.* Washington, D.C.: U.S. Government Printing Office.

———. 1994. *Crime in the United States: Uniform Crime Reports, 1993.* Washington, D.C.: U.S. Government Printing Office.

Frase, Richard S. 1991*a*. "Sentencing Reform in Minnesota, Ten Years After: Reflections on Dale G. Parent's *Structuring Criminal Sentences: The Evolution of Minnesota's Sentencing Guidelines.*" *Minnesota Law Review* 75:727–54.

———. 1991*b*. "Defendant Amenability to Treatment or Probation as a Basis for Departure under the Minnesota and Federal Sentencing Guidelines." *Federal Sentencing Reporter* 3:328–33.

———. 1993*a*. "Implementing Commission-Based Sentencing Guidelines: The Lessons of the First Ten Years in Minnesota." *Cornell Journal of Law and Public Policy* 2:279–337.

———. 1993*b*. "The Role of the Legislature, the Sentencing Commission, and Other Officials under the Minnesota Sentencing Guidelines." *Wake Forest Law Review* 28:345–79.

———. 1993*c*. "The Uncertain Future of Sentencing Guidelines." *Law and Inequality* 12:1–42.

———. 1993*d*. "Prison Population Growing under Minnesota Sentencing Guidelines." *Overcrowded Times* 4(1):1, 10–12.

———. 1994. "Purposes of Punishment under the Minnesota Sentencing Guidelines." *Criminal Justice Ethics* 13:11–20.

———. 1995*a*. "Sentencing Guidelines in Minnesota and Other American States: A Progress Report." In *The Politics of Sentencing Reform,* edited by Rod Morgan and Chris Clarkson. Oxford: Oxford University Press.

———. 1995*b*. "State Sentencing Guidelines: Still Going Strong." *Judicature* 78:173–79.

———. 1995*c*. "Sentencing Laws and Practices in France." *Federal Sentencing Reporter* 7:275–80.

Frase, Richard S., and Thomas Weigend. 1995. "German Criminal Justice as a Guide to American Law Reform: Similar Problems, Better Solutions?" *Boston College International and Common Law Review* 18:317–60.

Goodstein, Lynne. 1983. "Sentencing Reform and the Correctional System." *Law and Policy Quarterly* 5:478–501.

Heinz, Anne M., and Wayne A. Kerstetter. 1979. "Pretrial Settlement Conference: Evaluation of a Reform in Plea Bargaining." *Law and Society Review* 13:349–66.

Miller, Marc, and Norval Morris. 1986. "Predictions of Dangerousness: Ethical Concerns and Proposed Limits." *Notre Dame Journal of Law, Ethics, and Public Policy* 2:393–444.

Minnesota Sentencing Guidelines Commission. 1980. *Report to the Legislature.* St. Paul: Minnesota Sentencing Guidelines Commission.

———. 1984. *The Impact of the Minnesota Sentencing Guidelines: Three-Year Evaluation.* St. Paul: Minnesota Sentencing Guidelines Commission.

———. 1989. *Report to the Legislature on Three Special Issues (Feb. 1989).* St. Paul: Minnesota Sentencing Guidelines Commission.

———. 1991. *Report to the Legislature on Intermediate Sanctions.* St. Paul: Minnesota Sentencing Guidelines Commission.

———. 1992. *Report to the Legislature on Controlled Substance Offenses.* St. Paul: Minnesota Sentencing Guidelines Commission.

———. 1995*a*. *Sentencing Practices: Highlights and Statistical Tables; Felony Offenders Sentenced in 1993.* St. Paul: Minnesota Sentencing Guidelines Commission.

———. 1995*b*. "Sentencing Guidelines and Commentary." In *Minnesota Statutes Annotated*, chap. 244 (Appendix). St. Paul, Minn.: West.

Morris, Norval. 1951. *The Habitual Criminal.* New York: Longmans, Green.

———. 1953. "Sentencing Convicted Criminals." *Australian Law Journal* 27: 186–200.

———. 1964. "Penal Sanctions and Human Rights." In *Studies in Criminal Law*, edited by Norval Morris and Colin Howard. Oxford: Clarendon.

———. 1974. *The Future of Imprisonment.* Chicago: University of Chicago Press.

———. 1977*a*. "Punishment, Desert, and Rehabilitation." In *Equal Justice under Law.* U.S. Dept. of Justice, Bicentennial Lecture Series, pp. 137–67. Washington, D.C.: U.S. Government Printing Office.

———. 1977*b*. "Towards Principled Sentencing." *Maryland Law Review* 37: 267–85.

———. 1982. *Madness and the Criminal Law.* Chicago: University of Chicago Press.

———. 1992. "Incapacitation within Limits." In *Principled Sentencing*, edited by Andrew von Hirsch and Andrew Ashworth. Boston: Northeastern University Press.

———. 1993. "The Honest Politician's Guide to Sentencing Reform." In *The Socio-economics of Crime and Justice*, edited by Brian Forst. Armonk, N.Y.: M. E. Sharpe.

Morris, Norval, and Gordon Hawkins. 1970. *The Honest Politician's Guide to Crime Control.* Chicago: University of Chicago Press.

———. 1977. *Letter to the President on Crime Control.* Chicago: University of Chicago Press.

Morris, Norval, and Colin Howard, eds. 1964. *Studies in Criminal Law.* Oxford: Clarendon.

Morris, Norval, and Marc Miller. 1985. "Predictions of Dangerousness." In *Crime and Justice: A Review of Research*, vol. 6, edited by Michael Tonry and Norval Morris. Chicago: University of Chicago Press.

Morris, Norval, and Michael Tonry. 1990. *Between Prison and Probation: Intermediate Punishments in a Rational Sentencing System.* New York: Oxford University Press.

Parent, Dale G. 1988. *Structuring Criminal Sentences: The Evolution of Minnesota's Sentencing Guidelines.* Stoneham, Mass.: Butterworth Legal Publishers.

Tonry, Michael. 1994. "Proportionality, Parsimony, and Interchangeability of Punishments." In *Penal Theory and Penal Practice*, edited by Antony Duff and Sandra Marshall. Manchester: Manchester University Press.

von Hirsch, Andrew. 1976. *Doing Justice: The Choice of Punishments; Report of the Committee for the Study of Incarceration.* New York: Hill & Wang.

———. 1981*a*. "Desert and Previous Convictions in Sentencing." *Minnesota Law Review* 65:591–634.

———. 1981*b*. "Utilitarian Sentencing Resuscitated: The American Bar Association's Second Report on Criminal Sentencing." *Rutgers Law Review* 33: 772–89.

———. 1984. "Equality, 'Anisonomy,' and Justice: A Review of *Madness and the Criminal Law.*" *Michigan Law Review* 82:1093–1112.

———. 1985. *Past or Future Crimes: Deservedness and Dangerousness in the Sentencing of Criminals.* New Brunswick, N.J.: Rutgers University Press.

———. 1987*a*. "The Enabling Legislation." In *The Sentencing Commission and Its Guidelines*, edited by Andrew von Hirsch, Kay Knapp, and Michael Tonry. Boston: Northeastern University Press.

———. 1987*b*. "Structure and Rationale: Minnesota's Critical Choices." In *The Sentencing Commission and Its Guidelines*, edited by Andrew von Hirsch, Kay Knapp, and Michael Tonry. Boston: Northeastern University Press.

———. 1992. "Proportionality in the Philosophy of Punishment." In *Crime and Justice: A Review of Research*, vol. 16, edited by Michael Tonry. Chicago: University of Chicago Press.

———. 1993. *Censure and Sanctions.* Oxford: Clarendon.

———. 1994. "Sentencing Guidelines and Penal Aims in Minnesota." *Criminal Justice Ethics* 13:39–49.

———. 1995. "Proportionality and Parsimony in American Sentencing Guidelines: The Minnesota and Oregon Standards." In *The Politics of Sentencing Reform*, edited by Rod Morgan and Chris Clarkson. Oxford: Oxford University Press.

von Hirsch, Andrew, Martin Wasik, and Judith Greene. 1989. "Punishments in the Community and the Principles of Desert." *Rutgers Law Journal* 20: 595–618.

Zimring, Franklin, and Gordon Hawkins. 1973. *Deterrence: The Legal Threat in Crime Control.* Chicago: University of Chicago Press.